ACCOUNTING INFORMATION SYSTEMS

Concepts and Practice for Effective Decision Making

ACCOUNTING INFORMATION SYSTEMS
Concepts and Practice for Effective Decision Making

STEPHEN A. MOSCOVE, Ph.D.

Chairman, Department of Accounting and Information Systems
University of Nevada, Reno

MARK G. SIMKIN, Ph.D.

Department of Decision Sciences
University of Hawaii

JOHN WILEY & SONS

New York • Chichester • Brisbane • Toronto

Library of Congress Cataloging in Publication Data:

Moscove, Stephen A
  Accounting information systems.

  (Wiley series in accounting and information systems)
  Includes index.
  1. Accounting—Data processing. I. Simkin,
Mark G., joint author. II. Title. III. Series.
HF5679.M62   657'.028'54   80-15445
ISBN 0-471-03369-3

Printed in the United States of America

10 9 8 7 6 5 4 3 2

Material from the Certificate in Management Accounting
Examinations, Copyright © 1972, 1973, 1974, 1975, 1976,
1977, 1978, 1979 by the National Association of Accountants,
is reprinted (or adapted) with permission.

Material from the Uniform CPA Examinations, Copyright ©
1962, 1963, 1964, 1965, 1967, 1969, 1970, 1971, 1972, 1973,
1974, 1975, 1976, 1977, 1978, 1979 by the American Institute
of Certified Public Accountants, Inc., is reprinted (or
adapted) with permission.

To our Parents, and
Linda, Justin, and Jodi

ABOUT THE AUTHORS

Stephen A. Moscove earned his B.S. degree in accounting (June 1965) and his M.S. degree in accounting (June 1966) from the University of Illinois. He received his Ph.D. degree in business administration (majoring in accounting) from Oklahoma State University (July 1971).

Dr. Moscove worked as an auditor for Price Waterhouse & Company during 1966 and 1967. From 1970 to 1980 he was a member of the faculty of the Department of Accounting at the University of Hawaii. During this period Dr. Moscove was a visiting professor at the University of Miami (Coral Gables, Florida) in 1973, and a visiting professor at the University of New Orleans, in 1974. In September 1980, Dr. Moscove became chairman of the Department of Accounting and Information Systems at the University of Nevada, Reno.

Dr. Moscove has published numerous articles in professional journals. One of his articles ("Accountants' Legal Liability," *Management Accounting,* May 1977) won a national award from the National Association of Accountants. Dr. Moscove is the author of *Accounting Fundamentals: A Self-Instructional Approach* (Reston Publishing Company, 1977), the second edition of which was published in January 1981.

Mark G. Simkin received his A.B. degree (1965) from Brandeis University and his MBA degree (1968) and Ph.D. degree (1972) from the Graduate School of Business at the University of California, Berkeley. In 1967 he was installed as a member of Beta Gamma Sigma, the honorary business administration society. Prior to assuming his present post in the Department of Decision Sciences at the University of Hawaii, Professor Simkin worked as a programmer for IBM's Data Processing Division, taught business courses at California State University, Hayward, worked as a research analyst at the Institute of Business and Economic Research (Berkeley), and served as a consultant to various California businesses.

Since coming to Hawaii in 1971, Professor Simkin has taught statistics, computer science, economics, and operations research courses at the University of Hawaii and also at the Japan-America Institute of Management Science in Hawaii Kai. He has been the recipient of numerous grants and awards, including a National Science Foundation grant, and became a full professor in 1980. Professor Simkin is the founder and current president of the Hawaii Chapter of The Institute of Management Science (TIMS) and a member of the American Institute of Decision Sciences (AIDS).

Professor Simkin is the coauthor of two other textbooks, *Managerial Economics* (Irwin, 1975) and *Electronic Data Processing* (HEIM International, 1981). In addition, he has written many articles for *Decision Sciences, JASA,* and *Interfaces.* He regularly presents papers at the national meetings of AIDS, ORSA/TIMS, and the Hawaii International Conference of System Sciences.

PREFACE

The introduction of a computer into a company's business system greatly alters the accountant's organizational duties. Automating the accounting information system means the accountant no longer has to perform time-consuming functions such as recording journal entries, posting these entries to ledger accounts, and preparing trial balances. Instead, the computer is able to handle these data-processing activities on a routine basis. As a result, accountants are becoming involved in the more dynamic functions of their organizations, such as aiding management decision making and designing more effective business information systems.

The purpose of this book is to analyze the role of accounting information systems within companies' operating environments. In our current era of technology, it is difficult to discuss modern accounting information systems without emphasizing the computer. Therefore, the computer's effects on these systems will be stressed throughout. Our intent is not to make accounting students computer programmers or electronics experts. However, today's accounting graduate must be able to understand the capabilities, as well as the limitations, of computers in order to interact effectively with a company's computerized data-processing system.

Especially for the student, a reasonable question to ask of any book is: "What's in it for me?" A brief overview of the book's contents is provided shortly. First, however, we describe several of the book's important features.

The book concentrates on modern computer equipment and modern procedures for processing accounting data. Thus, throughout the various chapters we provide extensive discussions of minicomputers, integrated accounting packages, and real-time processing systems.

The writing style is simple and clear. There are many figures and photographs to aid the learning of the subject matter.

Each chapter begins with a chapter outline and a list of important questions that aid studying and alert students to the important concepts of the chapters.

The arrangement of the text enables flexible coverage of basic computer topics. A special three-chapter supplement in the last section of the book can be included or omitted depending on whether students have taken a prior computer course.

A wide variety of end-of-chapter exercises include discussion questions, problems, and cases. This variety enables students to examine many different aspects of each chapter's subject matter, and also enables instructors to vary the exercises assigned each semester. A number of exercises are adapted from the Certified Public Accountant (CPA) and the Certificate in Management Accounting (CMA) examinations and will thus help students prepare for these professional examinations.

With respect to the last point, this book is not intended to serve as a review for the CPA or CMA professional examinations. However, we have taken great pains to draw upon the questions from prior CPA and CMA examinations as helpful study aids for students.

The arrangement of the chapters permits *flexibility* in the instructor's subject matter coverage. As is discussed below, certain chapters may be omitted if students have covered specific topics in prior courses. The *only* assumption we have made in writing the text is that all students will have completed a basic financial accounting course and a basic managerial accounting course. The text is designed principally for a one-semester course covering accounting information systems.

Our book is divided into seven parts plus the Appendixes. Part One (Chapters 1–3) introduces the vital role that accounting information systems play in today's business world. Because managers are major users of accounting information, Part One examines various management concepts of importance to accountants and discusses how these concepts affect the design and operation of accounting information systems. Budgets are important managerial planning and controlling tools. Because accountants play an active role in their organizations' budgetary activities, Chapter 3 stresses the *informational* aspects of budget systems and also examines the computer's functions in the budgetary process. Most students will have been exposed to the detailed procedural aspects of budget preparation in their prior accounting courses. Therefore, the detailed procedural work in preparing budgets is minimized in Chapter 3. The subject of budgeting is approached from the standpoint of its importance to an organization's *planning* and *controlling* activities. For those schools having a separate budgeting course, however, it is possible to exclude the Chapter 3 material or just cover the section that analyzes the computer's use within a budgetary system.

Part Two's chapters (Chapters 4–6) emphasize the accounting information system's functions of collecting, recording, and storing business data. Most of the discussion in these chapters assumes that the accounting information system operates within a computerized data-processing environment. Chapter 4 studies the collection and recording of accounting data. Chapter 5 emphasizes the types of data processing that can be achieved when performing accounting functions if a company implements a computerized *data base* system. Chapter 6 brings together many of the concepts discussed in Part Two by providing an extensive illustration of both a manual and a computerized data-processing system (emphasizing the computerized system) for handling a company's "accounts receivable" transactions.

The three chapters in Part Two and many of the remaining chapters assume that the student has prior knowledge of electronic data processing. Because of differing prerequisites at colleges and universities for enrolling in an accounting information systems course, however, the students at certain schools may not have been previously exposed to the computer area. At those schools, our "Part Seven Supplement" (Chapters 17–19) should be covered prior to beginning Part Two. In the supplement, we examine many *hardware* and *software* concepts of electronic data processing that are important to accounting students. For the schools that require a computer course as a prerequisite to the accounting information systems course, this supplement can be omitted from coverage if desired.

An important function of accountants working within organizations' accounting information systems is to develop efficient and effective internal control systems. The subject of internal control (both in manual and in computerized systems, emphasizing the latter types of systems) is examined in Part Three (Chapters 7–10). A unique chapter in Part Three is that on computer crime (Chapter 9). This chapter discusses and analyzes the more important real-world computer crimes that have been committed to date. We provide some suggestions concerning how specific computer crimes might have been prevented through the existence of more effective internal control systems. To conclude Part Three, Chapter 10 covers the important topic of *auditing* computerized accounting information systems.

Accountants often participate in systems studies of companies' data processing problems, leading to the development of more efficient and effective accounting information systems. Part Four (Chapters 11–14) examines systems studies through an in-depth coverage of all the activities involved in performing a systems study for an organization. The topics in Part Four are illustrated by a prototype example—the conversion of a company's manual accounting information system to a computerized accounting information system and the accountant's role in this conversion process. Many of the computer and accounting information system concepts developed in previous chapters are integrated in Part Four's discussion of systems study.

Three important types of organizations (the

small business organization, the service organization, and the not-for-profit organization) not covered previously in the text are directly examined in Part Five (Chapters 15 and 16). Accounting information systems for the small business firm are explored in Chapter 15, whereas accounting information systems for service and not-for-profit organizations are examined in Chapter 16. Because all three of these special-types of organizations play important roles within our business environment, we suggest that these two chapters be covered as part of the accounting information systems course. However, depending on the course goals of individual instructors, one or both of these chapters can be omitted.

Part Six contains five comprehensive, real-world cases for analysis. The cases present decision-oriented situations described in real-life settings. In most of these cases, the questions asked are demanding and there is no one right set of answers. Although case analyses have the potential to be a frustrating type of exercise for the student, they offer the most realism in terms of making business decisions. We have observed that most students find such cases challenging and enjoyable. The five cases included in Part Six cover many of the concepts discussed throughout the book and tie together the various topics previously analyzed within individual chapters. These cases have been classroom tested prior to publication, and all of them have the potential of contributing to vigorous debate and a rewarding educational experience.

This accounting text provides a wide variety of exercises at the end of each chapter. In most chapters there are three types of exercises: discussion questions, problems, and cases. The discussion questions rely heavily on the material presented in the chapters, although some of them require that students use their prerequisite accounting knowledge for complete answers. Problems are largely computational in nature, and provide alternate illustrations of the analyses discussed in the various chapters. The end-of-chapter cases are shorter than the cases provided in Part Six. However, these cases still require considerable thought in arriving at logical answers.

Throughout the text, the amount of discussion on any particular topic is allocated in proportion to its importance to accounting information systems concepts and practice. Thus, for example, there is little material on noncomputerized, punched-card data processing, since this type of data processing is becoming obsolete, but quite substantial coverage of internal control systems and systems study work. Within the chapters on systems study (as well as in other chapters), we have integrated the analyses of the important roles that a company's individual subsystems (such as production, personnel, and marketing) play in a total information system. Whereas some other texts have separate chapters on the individual subsystems, we believe that the examination of organizational subsystems as an integral part of various chapters analyses is a more effective means of covering the essential features of these subsystems.

An issue frequently raised is the extent to which topics involving quantitative methods should be covered. As previously mentioned, our book assumes only an introductory background in financial and managerial accounting. But at a few points within the discussion, quantitative techniques such as linear programming become relevant. Because quantitative topics are covered extensively in other business courses, we have chosen to minimize quantitative-methodology, relegating essential mechanics to Appendix A. Individual chapters are thus written in such a way that the quantitative methods may be omitted without detracting from an understanding of the chapter material. At the discretion of the instructor or the interest of the student, however, the quantitative examples in Appendix A may be included as part of the reading materials to expand the scope of a particular chapter.

To emphasize the coverage flexibility within the 19 text chapters and the Part Six comprehensive cases, a textbook flowchart is shown on page xiii. The *numbers* in parentheses refer to the specific chapter numbers. (The letters "AIS" stand for accounting information systems.)

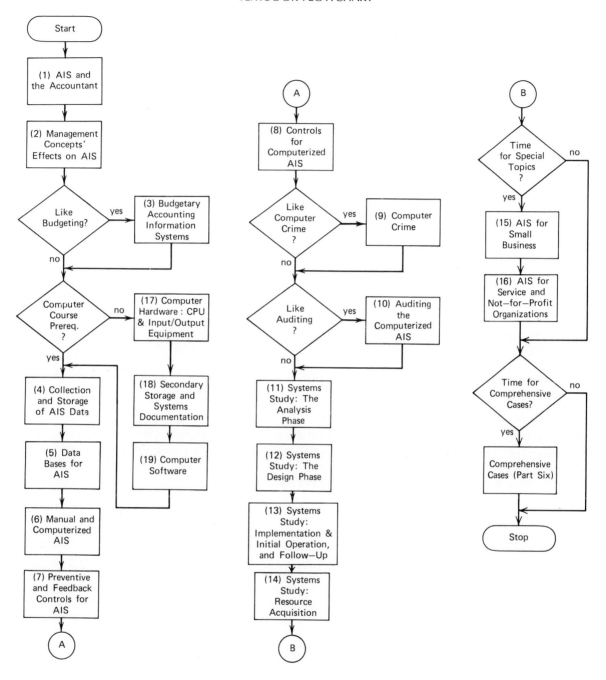

ACKNOWLEDGMENTS

We thank the many people who struggled with us during the writing, editing, and production of this book, and without whose help this endeavor would not have been possible. First on our list of acknowledgments are the loved ones who stuck by us, sacrificed for us, and supported us while the midnight oil burned dimmer and dimmer. Few but these people know the trials and tribulations of textbook writing. For their patience and understanding, we are deeply indebted.

A large number of our colleagues and professional acquaintances were also extremely helpful. In this regard, we owe a special tribute to the memory of the late John Crain, our initial Wiley editor. John inspired, encouraged, and supported us, and gave this effort the head start that enabled us to push to completion. We also gratefully acknowledge the work of our present editor, Donald Ford, our executive editor, Serje Seminoff, and our production supervisor, Mary Halloran. In addition, we wish to thank the various reviewers who spent many hours of their valuable time reading and evaluating the earlier drafts of our work. They include Jerome V. Bennett, John W. Buckley, Deane M. Carter, Owen Cherrington, Thomas Gibbs, Leonard W. Hein, Richard W. Lott, Robert L. Paretta, Martin B. Roberts, E. Burton Swanson, and John H. Wragge.

Our colleagues at the College of Business, University of Hawaii, were especially supportive of our efforts. For this support, we thank David A. Heenan, Dean, David H. Bess, Associate Dean, Howard D. Lowe, Chairman—Department of Accounting, and Ralph H. Sprague, Chairman—Department of Decision Sciences. We also thank N. Lane Kelley and Reginald G. Worthley from the College of Business for their roles in our project. Other individuals from outside the College of Business who contributed insightful comments or suggestions include Ronald Copeland, Chuck Deliot, Patricia Edge, Linda Golding, Richard Hughs, Frank Logan, Terry Nunley, Avi Rushinek, Peter Shannon, and Hugh Watson.

A special vote of thanks is due to our typists, Joan Karimoto, Gail Masaki, and Emi Troeger. All worked hard in pursuit of that elusive goal—a clean manuscript.

Two professional accounting groups we especially thank are the American Institute of Certified Public Accountants and the Institute of Management Accounting of the National Association of Accountants. The AICPA permitted us to use problem materials from past CPA examinations, and the Institute of Management Accounting permitted us to use problem materials from past CMA examinations.

The last group of people we wish to thank are also the foundation of our work—our students. Many semesters' worth of accounting information systems classes, plus several summer school classes, struggled with us through earlier drafts of our manuscript and served as "guinea pigs" for ambiguous test questions, unclear exercises, and overdemanding cases. We collectively thank these students for their patience and understanding. In addition, several students were particularly helpful to us in the development of this textbook. They are Carla Chock, Chi-Duk Choi, Kathryn Chung, Kevin Dooley, Sandra Iwamoto, Kalfred Kam, Lo-sai Rose Kwan, Gary Nakayama, Richard Zon Owen, William Pape, Norma Jean Puerner, Donna Rhodes, Harry Spiegelberg, and Terry E. Trout.

July, 1980
Stephen A. Moscove
Mark G. Simkin

CONTENTS

Contents

Contents

PART ONE

An Introduction to Accounting Information Systems and Their Role in Management Decision Making

Chapter 1
Accounting Information Systems and the Accountant

Chapter 2
Management Concepts and Their Effects on Accounting Information Systems

Chapter 3
Budgetary Accounting Information Systems

Part One will examine the accounting function in today's complex business world. Since accounting's principal goal is to communicate relevant decision-making information to individuals and organizations, Chapter 1 will look at the process by which accounting achieves this goal within the environment of business systems.

A major user of the information provided by accounting is the *management* of business organizations. Accounting information is often essential to managers when performing their decision-making endeavors. Consequently, for accountants to achieve efficient and effective information communications which contribute toward managerial decision-making activities, they must have a good understanding of management concepts (such as *planning* and *controlling*) and how these concepts affect the design

and operation of accounting information systems. Chapters 2 and 3 will therefore examine those management concepts relevant to accountants working within an accounting information system. Chapter 2 will provide definitions and analyses of various managerial concepts, stressing their relationship to accounting information systems. Budgets are important managerial planning and controlling tools. Since accountants in most companies have a major role in the budgetary processes, Chapter 3 will emphasize the important contributions that accountants, working within organizational accounting information systems, make to budgetary planning and controlling activities. This chapter will stress the informational aspects of budget systems and devote minimal attention to budget preparation.

1

Accounting Information Systems and the Accountant

Among the important questions that you should be able to answer after reading this chapter are:

1 **What is an accounting information system and how does it differ from a management information system?**
2 **In what ways should accounting and elec-tronic data-processing employees interact within a business system?**
3 **Why is an accounting "audit trail" important to an efficiently-operated business system?**
4 **What contribution does the accountant make to an organization's planning and controlling activities?**
5 **Why should today's modern accountant have an understanding of behavioral analysis, quan-titative methods, and computerized systems?**

INTRODUCTION

The accounting function has an important role in the successful operation of today's business world. This function centers on providing rele-vant decision-making information to individuals and groups both within and outside of a com-pany's system. The current chapter will first analyze the systems concept to give the reader a basic understanding of business information systems. Then, the various contributions of an accounting information system to modern busi-ness systems will be examined.

Accounting information systems within many companies consist of two major components, financial accounting and managerial accounting. Both of these components will be discussed from the viewpoint of their information-providing functions. An important objective of financial ac-counting is to process efficiently a company's business transactions so that informative finan-cial statements (e.g., the income statement and the balance sheet) can be prepared. Therefore, within our discussion of financial accounting, we will review the *accounting cycle* activities that enable organizations to process their business transactions. The field of managerial accounting typically encompasses three major areas: (1) cost accounting, (2) budgeting, and (3) systems study. Each one of these managerial accounting components will in turn be discussed.

The computer's current popularity in handling firms' data-processing activities has significantly affected accountants' organizational functions. This chapter will briefly analyze some of the important ways that the accounting function and the computer function should interact with each other in a computerized data-processing environment. Later chapters will stress the operational aspects of computerized accounting information systems. In addition to computers, two areas that have influenced accounting are behavioral analysis and quantitative methods. Each one of these two areas will be briefly discussed in terms of their effects on the accounting function.

SYSTEMS CONCEPT

A *system* is an entity consisting of interacting parts (called subsystems) which attempt to achieve a multiplicity of goals. We will now examine this definition in detail. An "entity" is a separate unit of accountability. In our book, the *business entity* will be emphasized. For a system to function efficiently and effectively, its subsystems must interact with each other. This interaction is achieved principally through the communication of relevant information among the subsystems. Figure 1-1 reflects the business entity called the Alan Company and its interacting parts. The Alan Company manufactures and sells sporting goods equipment such as baseballs, basketballs, and footballs.

The large circle in Figure 1-1 is the total business organization system. The company's top management will establish broad goals for the entire system to achieve in the future. Included within the Alan Company's multiplicity of goals could be such objectives as a satisfactory level of income, a high quality production product, and a program of minimum environmental pollution.

As will be emphasized in later chapters, this book assumes that most business organizations attempt to achieve a long-run satisfactory profit performance rather than a long-run maximizing profit performance (which economists often discuss). The former represents income-earning performance at a lower level than the latter. The Alan Company's internal environment includes all its subsystems (also called "departments") that will attempt to contribute to achieving the system's broad goals. Each subsystem establishes its own specific operational goals based upon the broad goals of the total system. An effectively functioning system exists when each subsystem achieves its operational goals, which in turn contributes to satisfying the company's broad goals. To accomplish this, the subsystems must continually interact with one another so that every subsystem is aware of its internal and external environment. In fact, the external environment represents a large element which affects the internal operations of a system.

The interaction of subsystems with the internal and external environment occurs through the communication of relevant decision-making information within the system. Toward this end, the Alan Company has a subsystem called electronic data processing. This subsystem acquires a large quantity of data from the system's internal and external environment. The data must then be sorted, processed, and communicated through meaningful reports to the other subsystems. Data that are communicated so that they have meaning to the recipient (e.g., a production manager) are called *information*. In this text, the word *data* will refer to facts or figures with little if any meaning to recipients and therefore not useful to aid their business decision-making activities. On the other hand, the word *information* will refer to facts or figures that are meaningful to recipients and can thereby be utilized to help them make business decisions. An important function of any modern business system is to efficiently convert the massive amount of available internal and external data into relevant decision-making information. Based upon the types of decision-making information needed by subsystem managers to achieve their operational

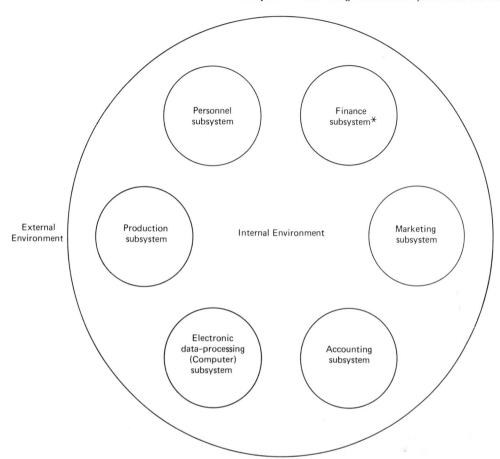

Figure 1-1. The Alan Company system. [*This subsystem's major responsibility is to obtain asset resources for the company at a reasonable cost (e.g., borrowing money from a bank and having to pay 10 percent interest on this borrowed money) and then monitor the efficient use of those resources by the other subsystems.]

goals, a communication network of information that flows to the subsystems is thereby established.

To illustrate the inefficiencies that can occur in a system from a lack of information communication among subsystems, assume that the Alan Company's production subsystem has as one of its 1983 goals the monthly production of 10,000 cartons of golf balls. However, based upon demand forecasts by the marketing subsystem, it appears that 1983 sales will be only about 6000 golf ball cartons a month. In each of the first six

months of 1983, the production subsystem achieves its goal of producing 10,000 cartons of golf balls. Also, actual monthly sales are between 5500 and 6500 cartons from January through June.

This example illustrates system *suboptimization* and is commonly caused by poor communication among subsystems. Suboptimization results from an individual subsystem achieving its own goal (or goals) but not contributing in a positive manner toward the total system's goal (or goals). The production subsystem actually manufactured 10,000 cartons of golf balls each month. Therefore, its production goal was achieved. However, because the original projected demand as well as the actual monthly sales was far short of 10,000 cartons, a large stockpile of golf ball inventory items occurred during January through June. The extra dollars tied up in this inventory asset are nonproductive to the total system (i.e., the Alan Company). These excessive dollars invested in inventory could possibly have been invested in some other endeavor of the Alan Company, thereby earning a positive rate of return. Thus, the high monthly activity level of the production subsystem contributed *negatively* to the total system operation.

The Alan Company's suboptimization problem could have been avoided through the effective communication of information between the production and marketing subsystems. The information obtained by the marketing subsystem from the external environment regarding sales demand for the Alan Company's golf balls should have been communicated to the production subsystem. This, in turn, would have caused the production subsystem to reduce its manufacturing level of golf balls during January through June. The result would have been a smaller dollar investment in the golf ball inventory. Following the decision to curtail the monthly production level of golf balls, perhaps a portion of the unused plant facilities could have been utilized for the increased monthly production of another product line (based upon demand forecasts by the marketing subsystem). In addition, the Alan Company's management may have decided to invest some of the extra inventory dollars (from the reduced golf ball production) in marketing research for the eventual development of a new product line.

The above example emphasizes the extreme importance of communicative interaction among an organization's subsystems. When one subsystem is aware of activities and decisions occurring in other subsystems of the organization, it is better able to make efficient and effective decisions within its own subsystem that contribute positively to the organization's goals.

THE ACCOUNTING INFORMATION SYSTEM DEFINED AND ANALYZED

Each subsystem within the Alan Company's system (see Figure 1-1) could be analyzed in considerable depth to understand its contribution to the company's operating performance. Because this text is accounting-oriented, however, we will now direct our attention to the accounting subsystem's role in a business information system. The accounting subsystem performs a *service function* for an organization. The service that accounting provides is to transform financial-oriented data into useful *information* that aids management, creditors, current and potential investors, and so on, in their decision-making activities. Because accounting's function is to convert data into information for others, the accounting subsystem will often be referred to in this book as the "accounting information system." We specifically define an accounting information system as:

an organizational component which accumulates, classifies, processes, analyzes, and communicates relevant financial-oriented, decision-making information to a company's external parties (such as federal and state tax agencies, current and potential investors, and creditors) and internal parties (principally management).

The accounting information system is actually one major component of a management information system. The difference between the former and the latter is in the scope of coverage. Whereas an accounting information system performs the functions of accumulating, classifying, processing, analyzing, and communicating relevant *financial information*, a management information system performs the above functions for *all* types of information (financial as well as nonfinancial) affecting a company's operating activities. Thus, the management information system is concerned with providing relevant decision-making information whether or not this information is accounting-oriented.

For example, the Alan Company's electronic data-processing subsystem may perform an analysis of customer product preferences based upon input data accumulated by the marketing subsystem. The resultant information from this analysis should aid the marketing subsystem in planning its future sales promotion efforts. This market report represents processed information from the Alan Company's management information system, but is beyond the scope of the accounting information system.

The following illustrations emphasize the types of data provided by a company's accounting information system:

1. The Stanley Schmidt Swimming Suit Manufacturing Company (which produces and sells beach apparel) has experienced significant increases in demand for its products. The limited manufacturing capacity of its current production plant has resulted in the company losing considerable sales because of its inability to maintain adequate merchandise inventory in stock. Stanley Schmidt, president of the swimming suit company since its inception 10 years ago, wants to expand current operations but is unsure which of two directions should be pursued: (a) expand the present manufacturing capacity of his company's 10-year-old plant facility, or (b) construct an additional plant facility 20 miles from town where Stanley owns 15 acres of land. To help him reach the best decision among these two alternatives, Stanley should request his company accountants to estimate the expected costs and the expected benefits from each alternative. Based upon this information from accounting, Stanley will be in a better position to plan his swimming suit company's best course of action.

2. Archibald Archer, a recent college graduate with a degree in architecture, has been operating his own construction design business for the past few months. Business has been proceeding quite well, except for one problem: Archy (as his friends call him) has found it difficult to maintain an adequate cash balance to meet day-to-day operating expenditures.

Most of Archy's creditors sell supplies to his company with cash discount terms of 2/10, n/30. However, the company's inadequate cash balance has often resulted in Archy being unable to pay an invoice within the 10-day discount period, thereby losing the 2 percent cash discount. Archy says that it's impossible for him to know what level of cash the company should maintain since he is never sure what expenditures are necessary each business day. To help solve this problem, the company's accounting system for accounts payable disbursements needs some modifications. Perhaps the accounts payable invoices should be filed according to specific payment dates (i.e., for each invoice, the final date on which it can be paid in order to receive the allowed cash discount). Also, Archy's accountant should perform some cash budgeting of the company's weekly projected cash inflows and projected cash outflows. These weekly cash planning projections from the accounting information system will enable Archy to control his company's cash flow activities more efficiently.

3. The Brown Bagel Company has just purchased a $50,000 piece of equipment to use in its bagel manufacturing operations. The company's top management is uncertain regarding which depreciation method (straight-line, declining-balance, or sum-of-the-years'-digits) should be used on this equipment for income tax purposes. Top management realizes that accelerated depreciation methods (compared with the straight-line method) such as the declining-balance method and the sum-of-the-years'-digits method will result in a company having smaller tax payments to the government during the early years of an asset's depreciable life. If an accelerated depreciation method is utilized, however, these managers are not sure what the negative tax effects will be in the later years of the equipment's estimated useful

life. The accountants within the Brown Bagel Company's accounting information system should be able to provide top management an analysis comparing the estimated income tax effects from using accelerated versus straight-line depreciation during the equipment's depreciable life.

4. The Brian Burger Bargain Basement Bonanza is a retail clothing store which sells low-quality apparel at discount prices. The store has its own credit card system whereby customers, once approved, can charge their clothing purchases. Due to the large volume of credit sales, the company's management has decided to computerize the previous manual system for processing accounts receivable. Computer specialists within the store's electronic data-processing subsystem are uncertain regarding what data should be maintained in the computer file of customer receivables. The computer specialists are also uncertain about the data content of weekly and monthly printout reports to management reflecting accounts receivable transactions. The clothing store's accountants should be able to enlighten the computer specialists about the collection and processing of accounts receivable data. Information concerning each credit customer (such as name and address, account number, credit terms, and credit limit) should be stored within the computer system. A weekly printout of an accounts receivable aging analysis should be provided to management along with a report disclosing the names and balances owed from those customers whose account balances are over 90 days past-due. The individual accounts which are over 90 days past-due can be immediately turned over to the store's credit and collection department for investigation, and these customers should be denied any further credit until their accounts are cleared up. A monthly printout of each customer's statement should also be provided by the computer. The accounts receivable transactions statements will serve as bills for mailing to the individual customers.

These examples have demonstrated some of the informational needs of companies that can be satisfied by their accounting information systems. Example (4) illustrates an important relationship that will be stressed throughout this text—the interaction between the accounting information system and the electronic data-processing subsystem. Under a manual data-processing system (i.e., a system in which the majority of data-processing work is performed without the aid of machines), the clothing store's accountants would accumulate credit card sales transaction data on a sales invoice source document, classify the transaction data on the sales invoice according to type of product sold and customer account number, and process the sales transaction through the company's sales journal and ledgers (both general and subsidiary ledgers). Finally, the accountants would communicate the relevant credit sales information needed by a department manager (e.g., the credit and collection department manager) through manually prepared reports such as an accounts receivable aging analysis and customer billing statements. The analysis of the communicated accounting report information would then be performed by the manager (or managers) within the specific department receiving the report.

When a company acquires a computer and establishes an electronic data-processing subsystem, this subsystem takes over the detailed and time-consuming processing activities formerly performed by accountants. Before a company's computer can process financial-oriented data, however, the accounting information system must still accumulate and classify the transaction data (in our example, credit sales transactions) so that these data can subsequently be processed by the computer. To achieve this requires close coordination among accounting subsystem employees and electronic data-processing subsystem employees. The accountants must understand the capabilities and limitations of their company's computer in order to accumulate and classify the accounting data in a suitable form for subsequent computer processing. On the other hand, electronic data-processing employees must understand the processing needs of the accountants so that they can design adequate computer files for storing the accounting data and to enable them to write suitable computer programs which prepare information reports containing the relevant accounting data for decision making.

Upon completion of the computerized processing of an accounts receivable aging analysis report, for example, the accountants obtain this report and deliver it to credit and collection department managers for their analysis. Under a manual data-processing system (as discussed above), the accountants normally spend so much of their time in processing accounting data that they often do not participate in the analysis of their communicated report data. With a computerized data-processing system, however, the accountants are relieved of many time-consuming processing activities (such as recording and posting journal entries, determining general ledger account balances, and preparing trial balances) and typically become directly involved in the analysis of accounting report data. Thus, in our example, the accountants would likely contribute to the analysis of the computerized accounts receivable aging schedule by discussing its contents with credit and collection department managers. If credit and collection department managers were, for example, dissatisfied with the number and dollar amounts of credit customers having balances over 90 days past due, they might want to consider tightening the company's credit-granting policies. Before adopting stricter credit policies, however, the accountants should analyze what effects these changed policies would likely have on the company's future earnings and future cash flows. Upon receiving these projections from the accounting information system, credit and collection department managers should have an improved basis for deciding whether or not to change current credit granting policies. Of course, in providing the managers with accounting information regarding future earnings and future cash flows, the accountants would ac-

cumulate the relevant report input data which would then be processed by their company's computer.

The establishment of an electronic data-processing subsystem within an organization normally results in the accounting information system being the central focal point of data communications. Often, a report request comes into the accounting subsystem from another subsystem. The accountants then accumulate the necessary data for this report and send the data to the electronic data-processing subsystem for report preparation. The processed report is transmitted to the accountants who, in turn, deliver the report to the specific subsystem that requested it. Figure 1-2 illustrates the communication network of possible report requests by some of the Alan Company's subsystems and the subsequent preparation and distribution of these reports to the subsystems.

The Alan Company's marketing subsystem, for example, is considering the introduction of several new product lines into the company's sales mix. As reflected in Figure 1-2, marketing subsystem managers request the company's accounting subsystem to perform an analysis of expected profit margins from the proposed new product lines. The accountants then begin their work of projecting the expected cost and revenue data associated with each proposed product line. These data are subsequently submitted to the electronic data-processing subsystem where an informational report is prepared based upon the input provided from the accounting information system. The finished report goes first to the accounting subsystem, which in turn passes it on to the marketing subsystem managers. Of course, the accountants will likely meet with marketing managers to discuss the report's contents.

It should also be noted that additional communications beyond those indicated in Figure 1-2 will be required. Before the accountants can perform their analysis of expected costs and revenues from the introduction of the new product lines, both marketing and accounting subsystem employees must talk with production subsystem managers regarding available capacity within the plant to handle the manufacture of the new prod-

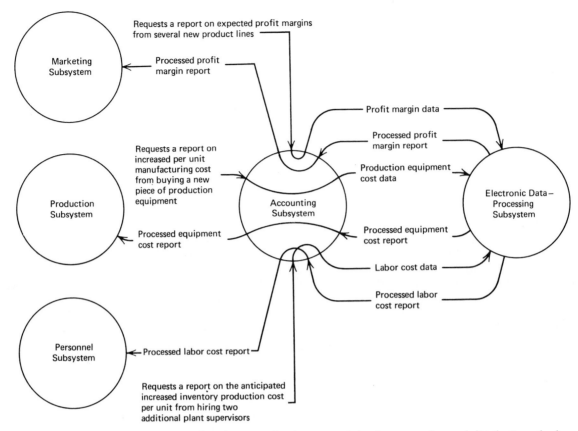

Figure 1-2. The Alan Company examples of communication network for the processing and distribution of subsystem report requests.

uct lines. Furthermore, if the present factory labor force is not sufficient to handle the increased manufacturing activities, production subsystem managers and the accountants will have to communicate with personnel subsystem managers concerning the hiring of additional factory labor. The data relating to increased labor costs will be used by the accountants in their analysis of the proposed new product lines' profit margins.

The above discussion has emphasized two relevant aspects of modern business systems: (1) the importance of communicative interaction among a company's subsystems prior to reaching a specific decision, and (2) the vital role played by the accounting subsystem in generating information to aid other subsystems in their decision-making endeavors.

Within the accounting subsystems of many organizations there are two major informational components, financial accounting and managerial accounting. Figure 1-3 illustrates these two accounting subsystem components for the Alan Company. The financial and managerial accounting areas are each *sub-subsystems* of the accounting subsystem. These two accounting information system components are now analyzed further.

Financial Accounting

The major objective of financial accounting is to provide relevant decision-making information to individuals and groups outside the organization's boundaries. (Of course, individuals within a company such as the managerial employees also

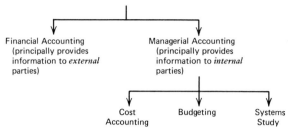

Figure 1-3. An accounting subsystem. (The financial and managerial accounting components are not mutually exclusive; that is, information from the financial accounting component is used within the managerial accounting component, and vice versa.)

utilize financial accounting information in their decision-making endeavors.) As previously mentioned, these external parties include federal and state tax agencies, current and potential investors, and creditors. Financial accounting's objective is achieved principally through the preparation of periodic financial statements (income statement, balance sheet, retained earnings statement, statement of changes in financial position, etc.).

The basic inputs to the financial accounting structure are transactions measured in monetary terms. An *audit trail* of accounting transactions is maintained within a company's system which enables one to follow the flow of data that moves through the system. The Alan Company's financial accounting audit trail is reflected in Figure 1-4. Upon inputting the relevant data from source documents into the financial accounting structure, these documents are filed for possible later

reference and use in preparing financial reports. The processing-of-transactions function encompasses *recording* journal entries from the source documents, *posting* these entries to general and subsidiary ledger accounts, and *preparing* a trial balance from the general ledger account balances. Since the Alan Company has an electronic data-processing subsystem, this subsystem handles the processing function. Thus, the journal entries and the ledger account balances information are maintained on computer storage devices (punched cards, magnetic tape, magnetic disk, or some other media). Through computer programs, the company's financial statements are printed out periodically as are any other desired output reports. A good audit trail within the Alan Company's financial accounting information system permits a manager to follow any source document data from the initial input stage to the data's location on an output report. This following of data through a system is possible because an effectively developed audit trail means that people within the system thoroughly understand the methods and procedures for accumulating and processing data. As a result, an individual (if so desired) is able to reconstruct how data were handled by the system.

Later text chapters will analyze various audit trail problems that can occur when a company utilizes a computerized data-processing system. For example, before the Alan Company acquired a computer, its accounting transactions were recorded manually and posted to the general ledger. If, at some later date following a specific trans-

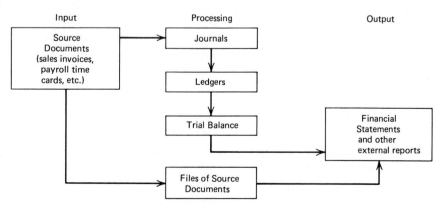

Figure 1-4. A financial accounting audit trail.

action's processing, an Alan Company manager wanted to verify the recording accuracy of the transaction, this manager could obtain the manually prepared journal. The manager would locate the journal page where the transaction was recorded, compare the transaction with the original source document (e.g., compare the dollar amount of a recorded sales transaction with the filed copy of the transaction sales invoice), check for correct posting of the transaction to the general ledger, and also check the mathematical accuracy of those general ledger account balances affected by the transaction. Thus, because all of the accounting work was performed with pencil and paper and could easily be seen by the human eye, the manager would have no difficulties following a transaction's audit trail through the accounting information system. When the Alan Company obtained a computer to handle its accounting transaction processing work, however, the processing activities (described above) associated with a business transaction would no longer be visible to the human eye. The work of recording a journal entry, posting the entry, and determining updated general ledger account balances would all be performed internally within the company's *computer*. Because the internal processing work performed by a computer cannot be observed visually by an individual, the Alan Company's manager would have a more difficult job tracing the audit trail of a specific accounting transaction. As future chapter discussions will emphasize, many fraudulent acts have been successfully committed as a result of difficulties within organizations' audit trails. We will spend considerable time in later chapters analyzing how companies utilizing computers for data-processing work attempt to solve their audit-trail problems.

Through the "processing of transactions," a financial accounting information system generates a large amount of decision-making information for both external and internal parties. Transaction processing is a major part of an organization's *accounting cycle*. We will now examine the information-generating attributes of

the accounting cycle and the role of transaction processing within this cycle.

The accounting cycle and transaction processing. Figure 1-5 illustrates the typical accounting cycle steps utilized by most organizations for processing their business transactions.

Financial statements provide useful decision-making information to current and potential investors, creditors, management, and so on, regarding the periodic operating success of a company (reflected by the *income statement*), the financial condition of a company as of a specific date (reflected by the *balance sheet*), and the periodic sources as well as uses of working capital (reflected by the *statement of changes in financial position*). In order to obtain the monetary amounts for their financial statements, organizations must maintain a record-keeping system on a day-to-day basis. This record-keeping system, in effect, transforms *data* that are generated by a company's day-to-day business transactions (e.g., selling merchandise, purchasing inventory, and paying liabilities) into meaningful *information* for communication to external parties (as well as the company's management). This record-keeping or data-transformation process is called the *accounting cycle*.

Each one of the nine accounting cycle steps illustrated in Figure 1-5 is now examined. The discussions will stress the information-providing aspects of these accounting cycle steps.

Step 1: Preparing Transaction Source Documents. An accounting "business transaction" results from any monetary event which causes a change in an asset, liability, owners' equity, revenue, or expense account. Remember, separate accounts are maintained in an organization for every monetary item so that information is available regarding the dollar balances of these individual financial items—the dollar balance of *cash*, the dollar balance of *accounts receivable*, the dollar balance of *notes payable*, and so on. Transactions can occur from business activities between a company and either some external party to the company (e.g., when the Alan Company sells sporting goods to a customer) or an

Figure 1-5

ACCOUNTING CYCLE STEPS

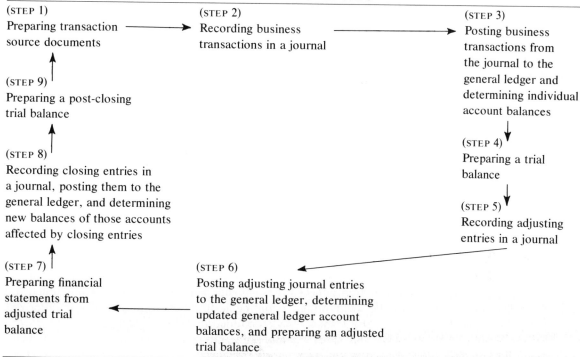

internal party within the company (e.g., when the Alan Company pays its employees their salaries). For a business transaction to enter an organization's accounting information system, the transaction must be of a quantitative nature and also be measurable in monetary terms.

Business transactions result in *source documents* being created. To illustrate, assume that Joe Namouth (a customer) walks into the Alan Company and purchases a football for $14. At the time of Namouth's purchase, a sales invoice would be prepared by the Alan Company's clerk who made the sale. This sales invoice represents a transaction *source document* (also called an *original record*), which is the basis for entering the football sales transaction into the Alan Company's accounting information system. As shown in Figure 1-4, a sales invoice source document is used as "input" for the financial accounting audit trail.

Source documents represent visual evidence

regarding the occurrence of business transactions. A common policy existing in many companies today is that a financial transaction is not subject to entry into their accounting information systems until proper source documents are first prepared and approved. The types of source documents utilized by business firms will vary depending upon each firm's special operating characteristics. A few of the more common source documents used by business organizations, in addition to the previously discussed *sales invoice,* are:

Purchase invoices	reflect the bills received from another company for the quantity and cost of inventory items or other assets purchased from that company.
Receiving reports	reflect the actual quantity of inventory items or

	other assets delivered to a company from another company.
Bills of lading	reflect the freight charges on physical goods shipped to a company.
Employee time cards	reflect the number of hours worked by a company's employees during a specific pay period (the time card is the basis for computing an employee's salary).
Voucher checks	reflect the payees (i.e., individuals to whom cash is paid) and amounts paid for various goods and services.

By utilizing source documents, a company is able to collect (or accumulate) its transaction data for subsequent entry into the accounting information system. Furthermore, the transaction source documents represent the starting point in a company's *audit trail* flow of data through its information system's accounting cycle. The collection of accounting data in an efficient format so that the data can be properly reflected within a firm's accounting information system is a major topic which will be analyzed in Chapter 4. At that time, various types of source documents and various mechanized approaches for collecting accounting data will be discussed and illustrated.

Step 2: Recording Business Transactions in a Journal. Upon collecting accounting data on a source document, the data are then recorded in a company's journal. The purpose of maintaining a journal within an accounting information system is to enable an organization to keep a chronological record of the economic activities (measured in monetary terms) that occur throughout its life. If, for example, a managerial executive of the Alan Company needs information regarding specific economic activities that took place on June 12, 1983, the executive can turn to the page (or pages) of the company's journal utilized

on June 12 and obtain this financial information. It should be noted that if a company processes accounting data with the aid of a computer, the journal might be maintained on a storage medium such as magnetic tape. In this case, to provide an executive with information concerning a specific day's journal entries, a computer printout of that day's journal entries would have to be prepared.

Even though many organizations have a large volume of monetary transactions occurring during their accounting periods, normally these transactions can be classified within a few broad categories (discussed below). The classification of transactions by categories permits the firms' accounting information systems to process efficiently the hundreds or thousands of monetary events that take place during various accounting periods. Furthermore, the enormous volume of transactions that occur in many organizations today has been one of the major factors causing these organizations to replace their manual accounting information systems with computerized accounting information systems. Some of the more common categories of business transactions are: (1) the purchase of economic resources (i.e., assets), (2) the incurrence of operating expenses, (3) the sale of products and/or services, and (4) the receipt and payment of cash. A very important category of business transactions (not listed above) commonly found in a manufacturing firm would relate to the accumulation of production costs (i.e., the direct raw materials, the direct labor, and the production overhead) associated with the firm's "work in process inventory" and "finished goods inventory" accounts. This business transaction category will be discussed further in Chapter 4. In order to review the processing of business transactions and to emphasize the relevant information that is generated from business transaction processing, each one of the four broad categories of transactions described above is now discussed.

1. *Purchase of Economic Resources.* In a merchandising firm, two major types of asset resources acquired are: (1) inventory (a current asset), and (2) equipment such as cash registers and display racks (long-term assets). The basic

journal entries to reflect the acquisitions of these two types of asset resources are:

(1) *Acquisition of Inventory*
Merchandise inventory*   X
    Accounts payable   X

(2) *Acquisition of Equipment*
Equipment   X
    Due to equipment
    suppliers†   X

*This *debit* assumes the use of a perpetual inventory system. If a periodic inventory system were employed, the "purchases" account rather than the "merchandise inventory" account would be *debited*.
†Because many companies use their "accounts payable" liability account only to reflect credit purchases of inventory, a special liability account "due to equipment suppliers" is therefore *credited* here.

If cash is immediately paid for the acquisition of inventory or equipment, the transaction would be classified under category 4—the receipt and payment of cash. Examining journal entry (1), the "merchandise inventory" account is a general ledger asset account that accumulates the total costs of all inventory items acquired for eventual sale to customers. In those companies that sell several different product items, a subsidiary inventory ledger would likely be maintained. This subsidiary ledger would contain a separate account for each inventory item. The use of individual inventory accounts within the subsidiary ledger enables a company's managers to know the quantity and cost balance of every product item. This information, which is not provided by the general ledger inventory account, is essential to management in planning the acquisitions of additional inventory product items (for those products whose subsidiary ledger balances have reached their economic reorder points) and in analyzing slow-moving inventory product items (products whose subsidiary ledger balances have little or no reductions from sales transactions). If a company has a large number of suppliers from whom it purchases inventory on credit, detailed managerial information is essential regarding the dollar amounts owed to each creditor so that future cash disbursements can be planned. In addition, for those creditors offering cash discount terms such as 2/10, n/30, the company needs informa-

tion about the specific cash discount terms of each creditor so that the various creditors can be paid within the allowed discount periods. The accounting information system can provide the above types of data to management concerning accounts payable liabilities through the utilization of an accounts payable subsidiary ledger. (Note that the *credit* part of journal entry 1 is to the "accounts payable" general ledger account.) Within this subsidiary ledger, a separate account is maintained for each creditor, indicating such things as the dollar balance due and the cash discount terms available.

In journal entry (2) above, the general ledger "equipment" account is *debited* for long-term asset acquisitions. To provide management with detailed information about each piece of equipment (such as the equipment's cost, estimated useful life, and estimated salvage value for computing the annual depreciation), an equipment subsidiary ledger containing a separate account for each equipment item can be utilized.

2. *Incurrence of Operating Expenses.* The basic journal entry to recognize a company's operating expenses is:

OPERATING EXPENSES

Wages expense	X	
Payroll taxes expense	X	
Rent expense	X	
Advertising expense	X	
Utilities expense	X	
Wages payable		X
Taxes payable on wages		
(separate accounts		
would be used for		
F.I.C.A. taxes,		
withholding taxes,		
etc.)		X
Rent payable		X
Advertising payable		X
Utilities payable		X

Note that this journal entry is illustrative only of some of the more common business operating expenses. Individual companies are likely to have many other operating expenses besides the ones indicated here. Also, for an expense transaction in which cash is immediately paid, the transaction would be classified under category 4—the receipt and payment of cash.

In order to determine the operating expenses for "wages expense" and "payroll taxes expense" as well as the liabilities for "wages payable" and "taxes payable on wages," detailed payroll data would have to be maintained within a company's accounting information system. A payroll subsidiary ledger containing a separate account for each employee would likely be used. The accounting information system must accumulate within this subsidiary ledger specific payroll data about every employee (such as social security number, exemptions claimed, gross earnings, deductions for F.I.C.A. and withholding taxes, and net pay) both for tax purposes and financial statement reporting purposes. In a manufacturing firm, the accounting information system must be designed to distinguish between production wages and nonproduction wages. Regarding production wages, a further distinction is necessary between the wages of direct laborers (which are *debited* to the inventory manufacturing accounts) and the wages of indirect laborers (which are *debited* to the production overhead accounts). The wages earned by nonproduction employees (salespersons, administrative employees, etc.), on the other hand, are recognized as operating expenses of the period in which they are incurred. Because of the large volume of computations often required within the payroll area, computerized payroll processing is a tremendous time saver to many organizations.

The expenses recorded for rent, advertising, and utilities are reflective of typical operating efforts put forth by a company in carrying out its business activities. Concerning the "advertising expense" account, its dollar balance at any point in time would likely be of interest to a company's marketing manager. By relating the balance of this account to the company's "sales" account balance, the marketing manager has a basis for evaluating the effectiveness of various advertising endeavors (e.g., commercials on radio and television, display ads in newspapers, etc.).

3. *Sale of Products and/or Services.* A merchandising firm (such as a hardware store or a clothing store) sells a *tangible* product to its customers, whereas a service organization (such as a law firm or a medical clinic) sells an *intangible* product to its customers. Presented below are the basic journal entries to reflect the revenue-earning functions of: (1) a merchandising firm, and (2) a service organization (in our example, a law firm):

(1) *Merchandising Firm*
Accounts receivable	X	
Product sales revenue		X
Cost of merchandise sold	X	
Merchandise inventory		X

(2) *Service Organization*
Accounts receivable	X	
Legal services revenue		X

If cash is received immediately at the time merchandising firms or service organizations perform their revenue-earning functions, the revenue recognition transactions would be classified under category 4—the receipt and payment of cash. In a merchandising firm's journal entries which reflect its product sales, several detailed records that support these entries are maintained within the accounting information system. To provide credit and collection department managers with information regarding the dollar balance owed to the firm by each credit customer, an accounts receivable subsidiary ledger could be utilized. The total of the individual customer account balances within the subsidiary ledger should equal the total of the general ledger "accounts receivable" account. Many companies that have a large volume of credit sales transactions use a computer for maintaining their accounts receivable subsidiary ledger. Once a week, for example, credit sales transactions together with customer payments can be recorded by the electronic data-processing subsystem's computer in order to update a firm's accounts receivable subsidiary ledger. In addition, the computer can be programmed to prepare a weekly accounts receivable aging analysis (which provides valuable information to credit and collection department managers concerning the effectiveness of their firm's credit-granting policies) and to prepare customers' monthly billing statements.

The merchandising firm can also maintain a

product sales subsidiary ledger to support the various *credits* to its general ledger "product sales revenue" account. This subsidiary ledger might include such detailed information as sales by product lines, sales by individual salespersons, and sales by regions of the country. The above types of sales information would be extremely vital to the firm's marketing subsystem managers in evaluating prior periods' sales activities and in forecasting future periods' sales activities.

The second journal entry illustrated for the merchandising firm assumes the use of a *perpetual* inventory system, whereby the "cost of merchandise sold" expense account and the "merchandise inventory" asset account are both updated each time a sales transaction occurs. Separate detailed subsidiary ledgers can be maintained within the accounting information system to support the "cost of merchandise sold" general ledger account and to support the "merchandise inventory" general ledger account. The cost of merchandise sold subsidiary ledger would include detailed cost information about each product item sold. This information as well as information from the product sales subsidiary ledger enables accounting subsystem employees to analyze the profit margins of their firm's various product lines. With product line profit margin information available, the firm's marketing subsystem managers are able to do a better job of planning their company's future sales mix of specific products (whereby the managers attempt to emphasize within the sales mix those product lines having the largest profit margins). As discussed previously, a subsidiary inventory ledger provides important information for planning the acquisitions of additional inventory product items and for analyzing slow-moving inventory product items.

Since a law firm service organization does not sell a tangible product, its journal entry to reflect earned revenue would include only a *debit* to the "accounts receivable" account (or if cash is immediately received, a *debit* to the "cash" account) and a *credit* to the "legal services revenue" account. For those service organizations that bill customers for work performed, the use of accounts receivable subsidiary ledgers would provide them with important information regarding the dollar balance owed by each customer. In a service organization that provides a variety of different services to its customers, a subsidiary ledger to support the organization's general ledger revenue account can provide useful managerial information. For example, the law firm's subsidiary ledger relating to its "legal services revenue" general ledger account would contain specific information about the firm's earned revenues from each of its many legal services provided to clients (such as revenues from divorce cases, revenues from felony cases, and revenues from estate and trust cases). By examining this subsidiary ledger, the law firm's partners are able to analyze the types of legal services that are earning the greatest revenues for the firm.

4. *Receipt and Payment of Cash.* Many business organizations (both merchandising and service organizations) have cash receipts from two major types of transactions: (1) cash sales, and (2) collections of accounts receivable from previous credit sales. The basic journal entry to reflect cash receipts from these two types of business transactions is:

CASH RECEIPTS

Cash	X	
Product sales revenue*		X
Accounts receivable		X

*For a service organization, the account name "service sales revenue" could be used.

As discussed previously, subsidiary ledgers can be maintained for each of the general ledger accounts (i.e., "product sales revenue" and "accounts receivable") *credited* in the above journal entry.

It is quite common for most companies to make cash payments based upon previously incurred liabilities. Therefore, the journal entry below is representative of an organization's cash payment activities:

CASH PAYMENTS

Accounts payable	X
Due to equipment suppliers	X

Taxes payable on wages (separate accounts would be used for F.I.C.A. taxes paid, withholding taxes paid, etc.)	X	
Rent payable	X	
Advertising payable	X	
Utilities payable	X	
Cash		X

Each one of the *debits* is to a liability account, indicating a reduction in the liability as a result of making a cash payment. For any of the liability accounts in which there is a large volume of transactions (such as "accounts payable"), a subsidiary ledger providing detailed information about the individual transactions affecting the account can be maintained.

Current information regarding a company's "cash" account balance is very important to management (especially to the financial executives within the finance subsystem). In those organizations having a separate finance subsystem apart from the accounting subsystem, the finance managers are responsible for their company's cash-planning activities. Cash planning involves a projection of the future *sources* of cash (e.g., cash sales, collections of accounts receivable, and sales of stocks and bonds) and the future *uses* of cash (e.g., operating expense payments, interest payments to bondholders and short-term creditors, and dividend payments to stockholders). Following a company's cash planning activities, the cash account should be monitored quite closely by the finance managers. This monitoring of cash enables the finance managers to ascertain whether the actual cash activities (reflected by the "cash" account) are in line with the original cash planning projections.

If, for example, the cash account balance is becoming too large, the finance subsystem managers should examine possible investment opportunities for this excessive cash. Because the buildup of cash within an organization's checking account does not contribute to a positive rate of return on assets, the finance managers may want to consider investing excessive cash in more productive assets such as marketable securities.

On the other hand, should the cash account balance become too small, a company may find it difficult to meet some of its liabilities that are coming due. Consequently, the finance managers will have to investigate possible sources of cash (such as borrowing money from the bank) so that the company can avoid being delinquent in paying any liabilities. If an unanticipated capital acquisition becomes necessary (e.g., a major piece of manufacturing equipment requires replacement), this situation can result in a heavy drain on a company's cash balance. To obtain the needed cash for the purchase of an expensive piece of equipment or other long-term asset, the finance managers may want to consider the issuance of bonds and/or stocks.

Step 3: Posting Business Transactions from the Journal to the General Ledger and Determining Individual Account Balances. Within an accounting system, a *general ledger* is a "book" containing detailed monetary information about an organization's various assets, liabilities, owners' equity, revenues, and expenses. A separate account (often called a "T" account) is established for each type of monetary item in a business firm. Without information available to both external and internal parties regarding the dollar balances of the firm's many assets, liabilities, and so on, successful business performance would be difficult to achieve because effective organizational decisions by external parties (e.g., potential investors and creditors) as well as internal parties (e.g., management) are often based on specific account-balance information. If the Alan Company's personnel manager, for example, wants accounting information concerning the total wages paid to employees after the first quarter of the year, this manager can refer to the page within the general ledger where the "T" account for wages expense is located.

Step 2 of our accounting cycle discussed the recording of business transactions in a journal. As was emphasized during the accounting cycle step 2 discussion, the journal provides a chronological record of all monetary events occurring in a company and indicates the accounts and amounts of the *debits* and *credits* for every business transaction. However, this journal fails to provide information regarding the individual dollar balances of the various financial items in a company. For example, if an organization's management wished to know the monetary balance of its company's "accounts receivable" asset, the specific "T" account maintained for accounts receivable within the company's general ledger would contain this information. The journal, on the other hand, would *not* provide information regarding the actual dollar balance of accounts receivable. Rather, the journal would include only the various *debits* and *credits* that were recorded to the accounts receivable account during a specific time period (e.g., one month). Therefore, to permit the company's management to have its desired information concerning the accounts receivable dollar balance at any particular time, the specific debits and credits recorded in the journal for accounts receivable must be transferred to the "T" account for accounts receivable in the general ledger. This process of transferring individual debits and credits from journal entries to their proper accounts within the general ledger is called *posting*. After completing the posting process, the dollar balance of each general ledger account is then determined.

For a company to have an effective accounting information system, both a journal and a general ledger are necessary. The major benefit from having a journal is that it provides a complete chronological listing of an organization's monetary transactions. The journal tells the "complete story" of each business transaction, because the debit and credit parts of the transaction are shown together with a short explanation. However, if a company elected to use a journal without a general ledger, it would be rather difficult to determine the monetary balances of the individual accounts. The general ledger takes over where the journal leaves off by providing information regarding the dollar balances of an organization's accounts. If, on the other hand, a company utilizes only a general ledger without a

journal, the company thereby sacrifices valuable information, because the general ledger does not disclose in one location the complete picture of an economic transaction. For example, the *debit* part of a transaction may be recorded in account number 200 of the general ledger, whereas the *credit* part of this same transaction may be recorded in account number 380 of the general ledger. As a result, the components making up a specific business transaction become separated. Functioning together in a company's accounting system, the journal and the general ledger provide relevant information about the monetary transactions that have occurred. Through the posting process, a cross-reference between the journal entries and the general ledger accounts is accomplished.

Step 4: Preparing a Trial Balance. The time period over which companies prepare financial statements (e.g., monthly, quarterly, semiannually, yearly, etc.) is determined by individual company policy. Because income taxes, both federal and state, must be paid to the government each year, a firm must prepare financial statements at least once a year as a basis for computing its tax liability.

When a company wants to prepare an income statement and a balance sheet (i.e., the financial statements), all of the posting work must be finished so that the dollar balances of the various general ledger accounts, which are used in preparing the financial statements, can be determined. Assume that the Alan Company prepares monthly financial statements. Therefore, by the end of every month, all of the company's posting from its journal to the specific general ledger accounts should be completed. Upon completion of this posting work, each general ledger account balance is then determined so that the company will know the dollar amounts of its individual accounts.

After these account balances are computed, a financial schedule called a *trial balance* is prepared. A trial balance lists all the general ledger accounts together with their end-of-period dollar balances. The trial balance facilitates (1) the determination of whether the *total debit* and *total credit* account balances *equal* one another, and (2) the preparation of a company's financial statements. The trial balance is just what the title implies; that is, it represents, in essence, a "trial run" to ascertain the monetary equality of an organization's accounts with *debit* and *credit* balances before the organization's financial statements are formally prepared.

Step 5: Recording Adjusting Entries in a Journal. After finishing the step 4 "trial balance" of the accounting cycle, a company's general ledger accounts have dollar balances within them which represent the account balances at the end of a specific time period (e.g., a month, a year, etc.). Before preparing the company's financial statements, however, certain *adjustments* (called "adjusting journal entries") may be necessary in the accounts. The need for adjusting journal entries within an accounting information system is based upon two accounting principles: (1) the *periodicity* principle, and (2) the *matching* principle.

The *periodicity* principle is derived from the word *periodic*, which means "occurring at regular intervals." In accounting, we assume that after a specific time period (a month, six months, a year, etc.), a company can accurately determine the dollar balances of its general ledger accounts and then prepare its financial statements. This process is commonly called "adjusting and closing the books." (The *books* are an organization's accounting records: the journal, the general ledger, etc.) At the end of a month, for example, when a business firm wants to prepare its income statement and balance sheet, the *periodicity* principle assumes that the firm is at a specific "cutoff point" in its operating activities and can therefore provide relevant financial information to interested parties such as potential investors, creditors, and management. These parties do not want to wait until the end of a business firm's life to acquire financial information about the firm. They want financial information at specific times throughout the organization's operating life. The periodicity principle enables a company to provide interested parties

with financial statements at specific time intervals prior to the company's termination. Furthermore, an organization *should* attempt to present to its financial statement users the most accurate income statement and balance sheet possible at periodic intervals. This will enable the users to have reliable information for financial decision-making activities surrounding the organization.

The *matching* principle has as its objective the accurate computation of a company's net income (or net loss) as well as the accurate determination of dollar amounts for balance sheet accounts each time the company's financial statements are prepared. An organization should recognize "revenues" when they have been *earned,* either by selling products or providing services to customers (even though "cash" has not yet been received), and "expenses" should be recognized upon receiving a *service* from someone or something (even though "cash" has not yet been paid). The matching principle attempts to accurately relate a company's *revenues earned* (i.e., the *accomplishments*) to its *expenses incurred* (i.e., the *efforts put forth*) in earning those revenues prior to the preparation of the financial statements.

Basically, there are four major types of adjusting entries possible at the end of a company's accounting period, as described and illustrated below:

1. Adjusting entries for *accrued liabilities* (commonly referred to as *unrecorded expenses*)—EXAMPLE:

Wages expense	X	
Accrued wages payable		X

2. Adjusting entries for *accrued assets* (commonly referred to as *unrecorded revenues*)—EXAMPLE:

Accrued rent receivable	X	
Rent revenue		X

3. Adjusting entries for *prepaid assets* (commonly referred to as *deferred expenses* or *prepaid expenses*)—EXAMPLE:

Insurance expense	X	
Prepaid insurance		X

4. Adjusting entries for *advanced payments*

by customers (commonly referred to as *deferred revenues*)—EXAMPLE:

Advanced payment for services*   X

Services revenue   X

*This account is a liability account which would be initially *credited* when the advanced payment was received by a company. Having provided the customer with some product or service, the company records the above adjusting entry at period-end.

The above four examples of adjusting entries do not represent all the types of adjustments necessary by a business firm at the end of its accounting period. However, these examples do illustrate the adjusting entry concept. At the end of an accounting period when a company wants to prepare financial statements, it should strive for accuracy within the financial data. To achieve this accuracy, all the monetary activities during the accounting period should be examined and a determination made if anything has happened that is not presently recognized in the accounting records. If unrecorded economic events exist, adjusting entries are required. After all adjusting entries are recorded, an organization's financial data have been updated. The resulting financial statements reflect a more accurate picture of the organization's business activities for the accounting period, thereby providing better decision-making information to the statements' users.

Step 6: Posting Adjusting Journal Entries to the General Ledger, Determining Updated General Ledger Account Balances, and Preparing an Adjusted Trial Balance. After a firm's adjusting entries are recorded in the journal, the debits and credits of these entries are then *posted* to the correct general ledger accounts in the same manner as the regular business transactions recorded during the accounting period. Upon completion of the posting work, the new updated monetary balances of those accounts affected by the adjusting journal entries are determined. Once the updated general ledger account balances are determined, a company's financial data are then current for the preparation of its financial statements. Preceding the preparation of the company's income statement and balance sheet, however, is an *adjusted trial balance*. Because a

trial balance is prepared after all business transactions during an accounting period are recorded and posted and each general ledger account balance is determined, the equality of total debits and total credits within the accounts is ascertained prior to recording and posting the adjusting journal entries. The purpose of preparing this second trial balance (called the "adjusted trial balance") is to determine if the equality of debit and credit account balances still exists upon the completion of the adjusting entry process.

Step 7: Preparing Financial Statements from Adjusted Trial Balance. When the adjusted trial balance (prepared in accounting cycle step 6) is finished and thus reflects the updated financial data of a company, its financial statements (principally the income statement and the balance sheet) can then be prepared. The adjusted trial balance contains all the information needed for the preparation of the financial statements. Figure 1-6 illustrates a computerized printout of the Alan Company's income statement and balance sheet.

Step 8: Recording Closing Entries in a Journal, Posting Them to the General Ledger, and Determining New Balances of Those Accounts Affected by Closing Entries. An organization's revenue and expense accounts are *subdivisions* of the owners' equity accounts. The major reason for utilizing separate revenue and expense accounts is to provide better information about a company's operating activities to management and other interested parties. Remember, however, that a business firm's net income or net loss belongs to its owner (or owners). Therefore, at the end of an accounting period, a company records and posts *closing entries* to eliminate its individual revenue and expense account balances and transfer the net income (or net loss) into the owner's (or owners') equity account (or accounts). Because revenue and expense accounts are subdivisions of the owners' equity accounts, whose balances are closed at the end of an accounting period, revenue and expense accounts are often called *temporary accounts* or *nominal accounts* (since they are "temporarily" established each accounting period in order to accumulate the monetary information regarding the period's operating activities). On the other hand, balance sheet accounts (the asset, liability, and owners' equity accounts) are not subdivisions of any other business accounts whose balances are closed at period-end, and are thus often called *permanent accounts* or *real accounts*.

It is important for a company to prepare financial statements as soon as possible after the close of its accounting period so that the information contained in the financial statements is available for analysis by such interested parties as management, potential and current investors, and creditors. The owners' equity accounts on the company's balance sheet include the net income (or net loss) for the particular period. Before the recording and posting of the closing journal entries, the owners' general ledger accounts do not include the net income (or net loss) for the accounting period. To update the owners' capital

accounts and thereby have them agree with the owners' equity shown on the balance sheet, closing journal entries are thus recorded and posted upon completion of the financial statements.

Step 9: Preparing a Post-Closing Trial Balance. After a company's closing entries are journalized and posted, all the revenue and expense accounts have *zero* dollar balances and the new monetary balances of the owners' equity capital accounts include the current period's net income (or net loss). A *post-closing trial balance* is then prepared to ascertain if the accounts with debit balances equal the accounts with credit balances. (Remember, the last time that we prepared a trial balance in our accounting cycle was in step 6, the *adjusted trial balance*.) The preparation of the post-closing trial balance is the final accounting cycle step. The "equality" of debit and credit

Figure 1-6

```
              ALAN COMPANY
             Income Statement
       For the Month Ended May 31, 1983

Sporting goods sales                                          $50,000
Less:   Sales returns and allowances        $ 1,000
        Sales discounts                         800            1,800
Net sales                                                    $48,200

Less:   Cost of sporting goods merchandise sold              18,000
Gross profit on sales                                        $30,200


Operating expenses
    Administrative expenses                 $15,000
    Selling expenses                         10,000
Total operating expenses                                      25,000

Income from operations                                      $ 5,200

Less:   Nonoperating items
            Interest expense                                    500

Net income                                                  $ 4,700
```

Figure 1-6 (continued)

```
ALAN COMPANY
Balance Sheet
May 31, 1983


        Assets

Current assets:
  Cash                                        $   5,000
  Accounts receivable (net)                       8,000
  Raw materials inventory       $  1,500
  Production in process inventory  5,000
  Finished goods inventory        15,000       21,500

  Office supplies                                  650
  Prepaid expenses                                 500
Total current assets                                      $ 35,650

Long-term assets:
  Machinery and equipment               $200,000
  Less: Accumulated depreciation          50,000       150,000

Total assets                                             $185,650
                                                         ========


        Equities

Current liabilities:
  Accounts payable              $18,000
  Wages payable                   2,000
Total current liabilities                   $ 20,000

Long-term liabilities:
  Notes payable (due in 3 years)            30,000
Total liabilities                                        $ 50,000

Stockholders' equity:
  Common stock, $20 par value (6,000 shares
    authorized, 5,000 shares issued)       $100,000
  Retained earnings                          35,650
Total stockholders' equity                                135,650

Total equities                                           $185,650
                                                         ========
```

account balances provides a company some assurance that no errors were made in its accounting records during the period. The company is then ready to repeat the accounting cycle steps for the next accounting period.

Summarizing comments on the accounting cycle. Since the major objective in performing the nine accounting cycle steps is to enable a business firm to prepare its financial statements as well as update the dollar balances of its general ledger accounts, the length of the cycle is determined by how often these statements are prepared during the year. If monthly financial statements are desired, the accounting cycle is repeated every month. On the other hand, if a firm prepares only quarterly financial statements, the accounting cycle is performed every three months. There are, however, exceptions to this rule which specific firms incorporate into their accounting information systems. For example, certain organizations may prepare monthly financial statements without going through the formal process of recording and posting their closing journal entries each month. Rather, the organizations wait until year-end to journalize and post the closing entries. The monthly performance of the accounting cycle would thus involve only steps 1 through 7 (step 7 being the preparation of the financial statements from the adjusted trial balance). Then, at the end of the year, accounting cycle steps 8 and 9 (involving the closing entry process and the post-closing trial balance) would also be performed along with steps 1 through 7.

Managerial Accounting

The managerial accounting sub-subsystem has as its principle objective providing relevant decision-making information to a company's management (the internal parties). The three components within the Alan Company's managerial accounting sub-subsystem are cost accounting, budgeting, and systems study (see Figure 1-3).

The two major managerial functions in a modern organization are *planning* and *controlling*. Each of these important functions will be analyzed thoroughly in later chapters. At this point, it should be emphasized that *planning* in-

volves establishing goals and objectives for the future performance of a company, whereas *controlling* is a monitoring procedure to enable the company's management to ascertain whether the planned goals and objectives are being achieved. When actual performance deviates significantly from the plan, management attempts to determine the causes for this deviation and then institutes corrective action.

For example, the Alan Company estimates that 5000 basketballs will be sold during January 1983. This estimation reflects the company's *planned* basketball sales for January. At month-end, a comparison of actual basketball sales with the planned sales is made. This comparison represents the *control* mechanism. Assume that actual January sales are only 2400 basketballs. Management will then investigate the causes for the actual sales being 2600 basketballs below the planned estimate (5000 estimate − 2400 actual) and attempt to institute corrective action so that future months' actual basketball sales will increase. (It should be noted, however, that a possible cause of this unfavorable variation could be due to inaccuracies in the January sales estimate.)

The managerial accountant makes an important contribution to the planning and controlling functions of a company's management through the utilization of cost accounting, budgeting, and systems study. These three components of managerial accounting are now briefly discussed.

Cost accounting. A cost accounting system aids management in planning and controlling its various acquisitions, processing, distribution, and selling activities. In its broadest sense, the focus is on the *value-added* by the organization to its goods or services, and this focus remains the same whether the organization is a manufacturing firm, a bank, a hospital, or a police department. For example, a plumber who repairs a customer's water pipe leak performs a value-added function because the repair increases the operating efficiency of the customer's plumbing system.

For an organization producing a physical product, there are typically three major cost elements incurred in manufacturing the product: direct raw materials, direct labor, and production overhead (the indirect production costs). A valuable planning and controlling technique used by many production companies within their cost accounting systems is *standard costs*. These costs are determined before the production process begins and represent estimates of what the manufacturing costs should be under conditions of efficient production. The accountant helps management determine the standard costs for direct raw materials, direct labor, and production overhead. Because the standard costs are determined in advance of production, they are an important managerial planning tool. The control aspect of standard costs comes into play when actual production occurs. By receiving timely reports which compare actual with standard production costs, management is able to ascertain areas of production inefficiency which require corrective action.

For the control aspect of a standard cost accounting system to function effectively, the timely production performance reports to management must also disclose who was responsible for any unfavorable performance. A timely report means that the information is received by management within a relatively short period following the actual performance. This enables management to institute corrective action before too many inefficiencies occur. If, for example, Alan Company's management receives monthly performance reports comparing actual with standard production costs, any inefficiencies within the system will continue throughout a particular month. Management is unable to investigate immediately any ineffective performance because it is not aware of the inefficiencies until month-end. If weekly production reports are provided to management, however, more timely corrective action can then be taken before too many inefficiencies occur in the production process. The *speed* of computerized data-processing systems utilized by many companies today has contributed to the timely reporting of production information to management.

Upon receiving a timely production report, the Alan Company's management is in a position to take corrective action on unfavorable performance only if the company's information system enables a manager to determine who specifically within the organization is responsible for the inadequate performance. Many organizations utilize a *responsibility accounting system* to help their managements trace unfavorable performance to the individual (or individuals) in a specific subsystem that caused the inefficiencies. Under a responsibility accounting structure, each subsystem within an organization is held accountable only for those financial items over which the subsystem's employees have control. A subsystem's controllable items are the ones that the subsystem's employees can cause to increase or decrease. Thus, when a particular cost expenditure exceeds its standard cost, management is able to then trace this inefficiency to the responsible subsystem employee (or employees) and institute immediate corrective action.

For example, the Alan Company's purchasing department (a component of the company's production subsystem) is responsible for acquiring the necessary raw materials to manufacture basketballs. From an analysis of the quality of raw materials desired in the basketballs and the suppliers' market prices for these materials, the standard raw materials costs are established. Weekly reports from the electronic data-processing subsystem are then provided to management, disclosing any significant variations between the actual and standard raw materials purchase costs as well as any significant variations between the actual and standard raw materials used in production. Management can immediately investigate these variances to determine their causes and decide on necessary corrective action. An unfavorable raw materials purchase cost variance, for example, may be caused by the purchasing department ordering better quality materials (which cost more) than the production standards specify.

The relevancy of the above brief illustration is that it demonstrates a responsibility accounting system with timely performance reports. Because the purchasing department is responsible for raw materials acquisitions, any purchase cost variation from standard can be traced to this department. (Similarly, a raw materials usage variance can be traced to the specific production department which actually used the raw materials in its manufacturing activities.) Also, the weekly computerized reports to management of significant variances from standard allows management to analyze the variances and initiate corrective action within a relatively short time period after their occurrence.

The preceding discussion in this section of the chapter has emphasized that an effectively developed cost accounting system is a valuable aid to management's planning and controlling functions. And, the managerial accountant is an important contributor to the development of a company's cost accounting system.

Budgeting. A budget is a financial projection for the future and thus is a valuable managerial *planning* aid. (Whereas *standards* within a standard cost accounting system reflect future conditions of efficiency, *budgets* represent what a company expects its operations to be in the future, regardless of whether or not these operations reflect efficient performance.) The Alan Company develops both short- and long-range budget projections. The former represent detailed financial plans for the coming 12-month period, whereas the latter reflect less-detailed financial projections for 5 to 10 years into the future.

A good budgetary system is also a useful managerial *control* mechanism. Because budgets indicate future financial expectations, the Alan Company's management is concerned about the causes of any significant variations that occur during the budget year between *actual* and *budget* results. Through timely performance reports comparing actual operating results with the pre-established budgets, the company's management can then investigate the reasons for significant budget variations. Management should initiate corrective action on unfavorable variations and reward favorable variations (e.g., a salary increase). A favorable budget variation may direct management to specific activities that can benefit the company's future operating performance. For example, assume that the Alan Company's actual sales of footballs in January

1983 significantly exceed the original budget projection. This favorable performance may be the result of the company's footballs having wider public appeal than the marketing subsystem anticipated. To take advantage of the situation, the Alan Company's marketing managers may increase their future advertising expenditures for promoting football sales and thereby obtain an even larger share of the market.

A budgetary system affects all subsystems within an organization. Budget preparation therefore requires good communication among all the organization's subsystems. The strong financial emphasis found in budgets leads to the Alan Company's managerial accounting component having major responsibility for the organization's budget program. The managerial accounting component coordinates the preparation of the other subsystems' budgets and then monitors each subsystem's actual performance under the budget program. The computerized processing of the Alan Company's budgetary and actual operating data by its electronic data-processing subsystem enables the company's management to obtain timely feedback reports comparing actual with budget results. This allows the Alan Company's management to then take corrective action on unfavorable budget performance within a shorter time span following the inefficient performance.

The budgeting area of managerial accounting will be analyzed further in later chapters.

Systems study. An organization having a problem with its current information system (e.g., production performance reports may be taking too long to prepare following actual manufacturing activities) may hire outside consultants (also called systems analysts) to recommend changes or, as in the Alan Company, utilize company employees to help solve information systems problems. The managerial accountants' abilities to understand internal financial systems have qualified them to perform systems studies for organizations. Many CPA firms (such as Price Waterhouse and Company, Ernst and Whinney, and Arthur Andersen and Company) have separate management advisory services departments which perform systems studies as well as other consultation activities for their clients. Of course, accountants are not the only professional group doing systems work. Because all the subsystems (marketing, electronic data processing, production, personnel, accounting, etc.) within a business system must interact effectively, a systems study of an organization's problems requires expertise in business areas beyond just accounting. In fact, many business consulting firms utilize a *team approach* when performing a systems study. This team of consultants might include accountants, marketing specialists, computer experts, production management people, engineers, and industrial psychologists.

The essential steps in performing a systems study are:

1. *Analysis.* The consultant becomes thoroughly familiar with the company and its current system so that the system's strengths and weaknesses can be ascertained.
2. *Design.* Based upon his or her analysis of the company and its system, the consultant suggests changes that will eliminate the weaknesses and maintain the strengths of the system. By eliminating the weaknesses, hopefully the company's systems problems will be solved.
3. *Implementation and Initial Operation.* Based upon the design recommendations, the consultant incorporates the necessary changes into the company's system. The revised system will then replace the old system in handling the company's daily operating activities.
4. *Follow-up.* After the revised system has been operating for a certain time period (four months, for example), the consultant evaluates the new system to determine if it has solved management's problems and is thereby contributing toward the company's objectives and goals. If areas of weakness are still found in the newly installed system, further change recommendations can then be made and implemented.

The preceding discussion of the systems study steps was very broad in order to briefly introduce the subject. Later chapters will intensively cover the systems study area by analyzing each of the four essential steps in greater detail.

MAJOR INFLUENCES ON ACCOUNTING INFORMATION SYSTEMS

The growth and sophistication of modern organizational systems have caused accountants' information-providing functions to become more difficult. To meet the challenges of complex systems, accountants have expanded their knowledge beyond traditional accounting subject matter. Three areas that have greatly affected accounting information systems are behavioral analysis, quantitative methods, and computers. Each of these areas is now briefly discussed.

Behavioral Analysis

Whether involved with a cost accounting system, a budgetary system, or a systems study change, the accountant must recognize that *people* work in the system. The best system "on paper" will not be effective upon implementation unless the needs of an organization's people are considered when designing the system. Accountants do not have to be psychologists. But they should understand how people are motivated toward positive organizational performance.

When, for example, accountants are designing some changes in the Alan Company's current information system, they should recognize that some employees might resent the suggested changes even if these modifications contribute positively to the company's goals. A systems change ordinarily will require certain individuals to perform their jobs differently from the way they have in the past. A change from the normal routine can be frustrating. To reduce this frustration and thereby foster positive employee attitudes toward a systems change, the accountants should encourage the employees to *participate* in the systems study activities. This participation includes not only keeping the employees well informed regarding the reasons for change, but also encourages the employees to make suggestions in areas where they feel changes are needed. The employees should be motivated to operate under a new system if they contributed to its development.

Since the job of accountants is to communicate relevant decision-making information to people (both inside and outside an organization), they must have an understanding of how people *perceive* information and then reach decisions from this information. Basically, perception is the specific meaning that an individual attaches to a communicated message. Identical information may be perceived differently by two people partly because of each person's dissimilar environmental background. Thus, accountants should be familiar with the basic psychological characteristics of the decision-making persons to whom they will communicate so that their information messages can be designed and communicated in a manner that will allow the best possible organizational decisions.

A production supervisor, for example, typically thinks in terms of physical manufactured units rather than dollar production costs. Thus, if the actual raw materials used in manufacturing the Alan Company's basketballs exceed the standard quantity during a specific week, the accountant should communicate this unfavorable variance information to the supervisor in terms of the excess number of physical raw materials used, rather than merely reporting the excess dollar cost of the raw materials entering production. The supervisor's environmental background should allow this individual to better understand the production inefficiency if the information report emphasizes physical units rather than dollars. As a result, the supervisor will likely be motivated toward corrective action on the production inefficiency.

Quantitative Methods

The *operations research* field includes various quantitative techniques to aid management decision making. Some of these quantitative techniques are statistical analysis, linear programming, PERT (program evaluation review technique) analysis, waiting-line theory, simulation, and regression analysis.

Modern accountants use quantitative tools to increase the effectiveness of the decision-making information they provide to management. For example, due to increased sales of sporting goods equipment and the resultant need for additional productive capacity to meet these sales, the Alan Company's accountants could be asked by management to help it reach a decision regarding whether a new production plant should be built across town or whether the current plant should be expanded. The accountants would attempt to project the future costs and the future benefits associated with both alternatives and then make a recommendation to management. Because the future involves *uncertainty* and the accountants are trying to forecast the future operating results from two alternative managerial actions, their analysis might be made more meaningful by utilizing statistical probability theory in these projections.

As another example of accountants' use of quantitative techniques, assume that the Alan Company's management is attempting to determine the optimal sales mix of its sporting goods products that will maximize the company's total contribution margin (sales revenue *minus* controllable expenses, which are normally the variable expenses). The company's accountants can aid management's decision by preparing a linear programming analysis of the various sales mix combinations.

Let us assume that the analysis and design steps of a systems study have just been completed for the Alan Company and the recommended changes are ready for implementation. To aid the implementation process, the accountant who participated in the systems study can develop a quantitative PERT network of the specific activities required (and their expected time estimates) for implementing the new system.

A few of the quantitative techniques that accountants can employ to perform their organizational functions more effectively have been briefly described in this section of the chapter. A couple of specific quantitative examples will be presented in Appendix A to illustrate the accountant's use of quantitative techniques in business situations involving decisions which affect the future.

Computers

Electronic data processing has significantly changed accountants' functions in an organization. Prior to computerized business information systems, accountants often spent a large amount of their work day manually processing data (e.g., recording journal entries, posting these entries to ledger accounts, preparing trial balances, and preparing the financial statements). In many firms, the computer has taken over the bulk of these accounting data-processing tasks and thereby allowed accountants to become more involved in decision-making activities in their organizations. The computer's ability to handle an organization's routine bookkeeping functions has been a major cause for the growth of managerial accounting. Accountants are now concentrating on the design of systems, the development of budgets, and the recommendation of future managerial actions in a wide variety of operational areas.

The accounting subsystem must continually interact with the electronic data-processing subsystem. A large quantity of the input data to the computer must be provided by the accounting subsystem. Accountants should understand the capabilities as well as the limitations of a computer so that they can perform their jobs effectively in those companies utilizing computers. In fact, the computer's ability to perform complex mathematical calculations in a short time period has been one of the important stimuli for accountants' increased use of operations research quantitative techniques when providing decision-making information to management.

OVERVIEW OF REMAINING TEXT MATERIALS

The current chapter has examined the role of accounting information systems in today's business world. In order that accountants can contribute to the development of efficient and effective business systems, they must have a good understanding of management concepts (principally *planning* and *controlling*) and how these concepts affect the design and operation of accounting information systems. Continuing Part One of our text, Chapters 2 and 3 will therefore emphasize those management concepts of importance to accountants working within an accounting information system. Chapter 2 will define and analyze various managerial concepts, stressing their relationship to accounting information systems. Budgets are quite useful as planning and controlling tools for management. Because most students have been previously exposed to the computational aspects of preparing budgets, Chapter 3 on budgetary accounting information systems will stress the important contributions of budget systems to managerial planning and controlling activities.

A vital role played by an accounting information system within an efficient and effective organizational system is to aid the collecting, recording, and storing of financially oriented data as well as converting these data into useful managerial decision-making information. Thus, Part Two (Chapters 4–6) will examine several data-processing approaches used by companies to enable relevant decision-making information to be provided to their managements. The emphasis throughout these three chapters will be on data collecting, recording, and storing within a computerized accounting information systems environment. To complete Part Two of the text, a detailed illustration will be provided in Chapter 6 of both a manual and a computerized accounting information system for processing an organization's "accounts receivable" business transactions.

Part Two's chapters (beginning with Chapter 4) and many of the remaining chapters assume that the student has prior knowledge of the hardware and software concepts associated with electronic data processing. For those students lacking a basic knowledge of electronic data processing (EDP), the "Part Seven Supplement" should be covered before beginning Chapter 4. This supplement includes three chapters (Chapters 17 and 18 emphasize computer hardware, whereas Chapter 19 emphasizes computer software) designed to provide the student with an understanding of computer fundamentals, terminology, and so on. Because modern business systems are often characterized by computerized processing of accounting data, accounting subsystem employees must be familiar with the capabilities and limitations of computers and be able to communicate with EDP subsystem employees. The materials on computers presented in Part Seven will expose the students to essential computer concepts that should enable them to function effectively within an electronic data-processing environment.

To reduce the risk of errors and irregularities in the accounting information system's functions of collecting, recording, and storing business data, a system of *internal controls* is essential. Part Three (Chapters 7–10) will analyze in-depth the topic of internal control within both manual and computerized data-processing systems. Chapter 7 will introduce the reader to the internal control concept, whereas Chapter 8 will examine the development of good internal controls in companies using computers for processing their accounting data. Because fraudulent acts of significant dollar magnitude have sometimes been committed in those business firms that utilize computers for processing accounting data, Chapter 9 will analyze the important and interesting subject of computer crime and its effects on the design and operation of accounting internal control systems. As a means of both preventing and detecting fraudulent acts within companies' computerized data-processing systems, the performance of good *audit* procedures is extremely important. Therefore, to complete Part Three, Chapter 10 will look at accountants' audit control procedures in those organizations with computerized accounting information systems.

The discussion of the accounting information system's role in managerial planning and controlling activities (Part One), the accounting information system's role in collecting, recording, and storing accounting data which are subsequently converted into useful decision-making information for management (Part Two), and the accounting information system's role in estab-

lishing, operating, and evaluating internal control systems (Part Three), is followed by Part Four. Part Four will "tie together" many of the previous chapter materials by examining the activities involved in developing efficient and effective business information systems (Chapters 11–14). Accountants often participate in the performance of a systems study to help a company solve its problems associated with a lack of good information flows for managerial decision making. Part Four will thus examine the activities that are essential when performing a study of a company's information systems problems, emphasizing accountants' functions in systems study work. A large part of the discussion in these four chapters will assume that accountants are employed by a consulting firm and that they are participating in systems studies of organizations' operating problems. The major emphasis throughout Part Four will be on a systems study to convert an organization's manual accounting information system to a computerized accounting information system.

The next two chapters of the book (Part Five—Chapters 15 and 16) will cover some special topics important for accounting information systems. Chapter 15 will examine the information needs and problems facing a small company in today's competitive business world, stressing the accounting information system's functions within small companies. Chapter 16 will analyze the unique aspects of accounting information systems in service organizations (such as a restaurant or a law firm) and not-for-profit organizations (such as a state university or a city police department).

In addition to the text's 19 chapters, two additional features are provided. Following Chapter 16, we have included in Part Six several comprehensive real-life cases for analysis. These cases will require the student to apply many of the concepts presented within the textbook chapters. Finally, the Appendixes will cover some specific quantitative analysis problems that were referred to in previous chapters as well as several other topics of peripheral importance to the text.

SUMMARY

The subsystems included in an organization's management information system must communicate with one another so that each subsystem contributes positively to the total system's goals. The accounting subsystem of most organizations includes two major components: financial accounting and managerial accounting. The former's major function is to provide relevant decision-making information to external parties, whereas the latter's major function is to provide relevant decision-making information to internal parties (i.e., management).

The accounting information system is a major component of an organization's management information system. A company's external and internal parties rely heavily upon the financially-oriented information that accounting provides for their decision-making endeavors. Because a large amount of accounting information is generated through the periodic performance of the accounting cycle, this chapter analyzed each of the nine cycle steps typically performed within an organization's financial accounting information system. The "heart" of the accounting cycle revolves around the processing of business transactions. Therefore, in discussing the accounting cycle steps, *transaction processing* was emphasized.

The significant areas where managerial accountants perform an important role in an organization's information system include the design and operation of cost accounting systems, the planning and controlling of budgetary systems, and the performance of systems studies to improve the organization's information system.

Today's accountants must be familiar with computerized information systems and be able to interact with an organization's electronic data-processing subsystem. When working in a business system's environment, the accountants must understand the motivations of people and their decision-making processes. Furthermore, the accountants can be more positive contributors to a business system's effectiveness by utilizing operations research techniques in many

of their decision-making analyses for management.

DISCUSSION QUESTIONS

1-1. Discuss the relationships, if any, between an organization's operational goals and its broad goals.

1-2. This chapter illustrated suboptimization within the Alan Company's production subsystem. Try to think of additional suboptimization situations that could occur in an organization's system.

1-3. Discuss some of the possible behavioral problems which managerial accountants may face when they attempt to communicate relevant decision-making information about an organization's system to internal parties.

1-4. Many people have a stereotyped image of an accountant as a person with icewater veins, who sits at a desk all day recording debits and credits, and who has as a number one priority the balancing of the books to the penny. If a high school senior (trying to decide what major to study in college) asked you what accounting is and what types of functions the accountant performs in an organization, what would you tell this student?

1-5. Because financial accounting and managerial accounting perform different functions for an organization, do you see any possible conflicts between these two accounting components?

1-6. Two major functions of an organization's management are planning and controlling. Discuss some of the ways that an accountant contributes to these managerial functions.

1-7. Discuss some of the important characteristics of a good organizational system.

1-8. Assume that you are the chief accountant of the Bogle Bright Corporation, a household furniture manufacturer and retailer. Your company is having some problems with its information system. For example, the marketing subsystem manager claims that the production subsystem supervisor often ignores (for several months) the requests for increased production of specific types of furniture. These production requests are the result of actual furniture orders by customers. The excessive delays within the production subsystem to manufacture the furniture have often caused dissatisfied customers to take their future business to competitors. The Bogle Bright Corporation's president has assigned you the job of hiring an accountant systems analyst to come into the company and help solve its current problems.

Questions: A. What major characteristics would you look for in the accountant to be hired as your company's consultant?

B. Assume for a moment that you are the outside consultant hired by the Bogle Bright Corporation. What approach might you use to solve the company's current problem between its marketing and production subsystems?

1-9. This chapter has briefly discussed the impact of computers on organizational information systems. Just for fun, project yourself 10 years into the future. Describe what you think the computer's functions in a modern organization will be at that time.

1-10. What purpose is served by an organization's periodic performance of the accounting cycle steps?

1-11. Differentiate between an accounting information system and a management information system.

1-12. Why do many organizations bother to classify their business transactions into a few broad categories? Discuss some of the categories of business transactions that would likely exist for a professional baseball team.

1-13. Discuss the following statement:

With the availability in many companies today of computers for performing data-processing activities, the accountant's organizational role has declined significantly.

1-14. Discuss some of the communicative interactions that should take place between a com-

pany's accounting subsystem employees and its electronic data-processing subsystem employees.

1-15. What is meant by the phrase "financial accounting audit trail"? In which type of accounting information system, manual or computerized, would you expect to find a "clearer" audit trail? Explain your answer by providing an audit trail example under both a manual data-processing system and a computerized data-processing system.

CASE ANALYSES

1-16.   *The Parable of the Spindle**

Once upon a time the president of a large chain of short-order restaurants attended a lecture on "Human Relations in Business and Industry." He attended the lecture in the hope he would learn something useful. His years of experience had led him to believe that if human relations problems ever plagued any business, then they certainly plagued the restaurant business.

The speaker discussed the many pressures which create human relations problems. He spoke of psychological pressures, sociological pressures, conflicts in values, conflicts in power structure, and so on. The president did not understand all that was said, but he did go home with one idea. If there were so many different sources of pressure, maybe it was expecting too much of his managers to think they would see them all, let alone cope with them all. The thought occurred to him that maybe he should bring in a team of consultants from several different academic disciplines and have each contribute his part to the solution of the human relations problems.

And so it came to pass that the president of the restaurant chain and his top-management staff

*Reprinted by permission of the *Harvard Business Review*. Excerpt from "The Parable of the Spindle" by Elias H. Porter (May–June 1962). Copyright © 1962 by the President and Fellows of Harvard College. All rights reserved.

met one morning with a sociologist, a psychologist, and an anthropologist. The president outlined the problem to the men of science and spoke of his hope that they might come up with an interdisciplinary answer to the human relations problems. The personnel manager presented exit-interview findings which he interpreted as indicating that most people quit their restaurant jobs because of too much sense of pressure caused by the inefficiencies and ill tempers of co-workers.

This was the mission which the scientists were assigned: find out why the waitresses break down in tears; find out why the cooks walk off the job; find out why the managers get so upset that they summarily fire employees on the spot. Find out the cause of the problems, and find out what to do about them.

Later, in one of the plush conference rooms, the scientists sat down to plan their attack. It soon became clear that they might just as well be three blind men, and the problem might as well be the proverbial elephant. Their training and experience had taught them to look at events in different ways. They decided that inasmuch as they couldn't speak each other's languages, they might as well pursue their tasks separately. Each went to a different city and began his observations in his own way.

First to return was the sociologist. In his report to top management he said:

"I think I have discovered something that is pretty fundamental. In one sense it is so obvious that it has probably been completely overlooked before. It is during the rush hours that your human relations problems arise. That is when the waitresses break out in tears. That is when the cooks grow temperamental and walk off the job. That is when your managers lose their tempers and dismiss employees summarily."

After elaborating on this theme and showing several charts with sloping lines and bar graphs to back up his assertions, he came to his diagnosis of the situation. "In brief, gentlemen," he stated, "you have a sociological problem on your hands." He walked to the blackboard and began to write. As he wrote, he spoke:

"You have a stress pattern during the rush hours. There is stress between the customer and the waitress. . . .

"There is stress between the waitress and the cook. . . .

"And up here is the manager. There is stress between the waitress and the manager. . . .

"And between the manager and the cook. . . .

"And the manager is buffeted by complaints from the customer.

"We can see one thing which, sociologically speaking, doesn't seem right. The manager has the highest status in the restaurant. The cook has the next highest status. The waitresses, however, are always 'local hire' and have the lowest status. Of course, they have higher status than bus boys and dish washers but certainly lower status than the cook, and yet they give orders to the cook.

"It doesn't seem right for a lower status person to give orders to a higher status person. We've got to find a way to break up the face-to-face relationship between the waitresses and the cook. We've got to fix it so that they don't have to talk with one another. Now my idea is to put a 'spindle' on the order counter. The 'spindle,' as I choose to call it, is a wheel on a shaft. The wheel has clips on it so the girls can simply put their orders on the wheel rather than calling out orders to the cook."

When the sociologist left the meeting, the president and his staff talked of what had been said. It made some sense. However, they decided to wait to hear from the other scientists before taking any action.

Next to return from his studies was the psychologist. He reported to top management:

"I think I have discovered something that is pretty fundamental. In one sense it is so obvious that it has probably been completely overlooked before. It is during the rush hours that your human relations problems arise. That is when the waitresses break out in tears. That is when the cooks grow temperamental and walk off the job. That is when your managers lose their tempers and dismiss employees summarily."

Then the psychologist sketched on the

blackboard the identical pattern of stress between customer, waitress, cook, and management. But his interpretation was somewhat different:

"Psychologically speaking," he said, "we can see that the manager is the father figure, the cook is the son, and the waitress is the daughter. Now we know that in our culture you can't have daughters giving orders to the sons. It louses up their ego structure.

"What we've got to do is to find a way to break up the face-to-face relationship between them. Now one idea I've thought up is to put what I call a 'spindle' on the order counter. It's kind of a wheel on a shaft with little clips on it so that the waitresses can put their orders on it rather than calling out orders to the cook."

What the psychologist said made sense, too, in a way. Some of the staff favored the status-conflict interpretation while others thought the sex-conflict interpretation to be the right one; the president kept his own counsel.

The next scientist to report was the anthropologist. He reported:

"I think I have discovered something that is pretty fundamental. In one sense it is so obvious that it has probably been completely overlooked before. It is during the rush hours that your human relations problems arise. That is when the waitresses break out in tears. That is when the cooks grow temperamental and walk off the job. That is when the managers lose their tempers and dismiss employees summarily."

After elaborating for a few moments he came to his diagnosis of the situation. "In brief, gentlemen," he stated, "you have an anthropological problem on your hands." He walked to the blackboard and began to sketch. Once again there appeared the stress pattern between customer, waitress, cook, and management.

"We anthropologists know that man behaves according to his value systems. Now, the manager holds as a central value the continued growth and development of the restaurant organization. The cooks tend to share this central value system, for as the organization prospers,

so do they. But the waitresses are a different story. The only reason most of them are working is to help supplement the family income. They couldn't care less whether the organization thrives or not as long as it's a decent place to work. Now, you can't have a noncentral value system giving orders to a central value system.

"What we've got to do is to find some way of breaking up the face-to-face contact between the waitresses and the cook. One way that has occurred to me is to place on the order counter an adaptation of the old-fashioned spindle. By having a wheel at the top of the shaft and putting clips every few inches apart, the waitresses can put their orders on the wheel and not have to call out orders to the cook. Here is a model of what I mean."

When the anthropologist had left, there was much discussion of which scientist was right. The president finally spoke. "Gentlemen, it's clear that these men don't agree on the reason for conflict, but all have come up with the same basic idea about the spindle. Let's take a chance and try it out."

And it came to pass that the spindle was introduced throughout the chain of restaurants. It did more to reduce the human relations problems in the restaurant industry than any other innovation of which the restaurant people knew. Soon it was copied. Like wildfire the spindle spread from coast to coast and from border to border.

Questions

1. In your opinion, which of the three scientists offered the most plausible explanation of the restaurant's problems? Explain.

2. In recommending the spindle, the scientists are tacitly admitting that the restaurant is a form of system. Name the kind of system they are thinking of and show how the restaurant meets the requirements of a system.

3. All the three scientists have recommended the use of a spindle to solve the restaurant's problems. Can you think of any new problems the spindle system might cause?

1-17.   *A Need for Control**

Standard Building Service Company of St. Louis is a 15-year-old company that provides janitorial services for office buildings and industrial plants. Standard was purchased five years ago by Leslie Waller and, at the time of the purchase, annual sales were approximately $500,000. In three years he was able to double the sales volume to the present level of $1,000,000, but for the past two years sales volume has remained relatively constant. Waller attributes the lack of growth for the past two years to his being unable to call on new accounts because the business has grown to such an extent that his full energies and time are required in solving the myriad of problems that arise each day. He recognizes that the few new accounts he does obtain do no more than offset the normal turnover of accounts lost each month.

Janitorial services are usually performed after the tenants have left the building for the day; consequently, very few of Standard's employees start work before 6 P.M. Waller has found from experience that in order to keep employees, he must offer them at least 20 hours of work a week. On the other hand, very few people seem willing to work more than 25 hours a week. As a result, the work force of approximately 275 men and women are part-time employees. Waller also found that by hiring persons presently employed he is assured of stable, motivated employees. However, since his employees are working full-time elsewhere, there is considerable resistance when supervisors expect an above-average amount of work from them.

A recent analysis of the 121 accounts serviced by the company shows that 40 customers require the services of only one person working a maximum of 25 hours a week. Thirty-five accounts require two people with total man-hours ranging from 35 to 50 hours a week. Fifteen accounts require an average of 100 man-hours a week, thus utilizing the services of up to four employees. There is one large industrial plant

*Used with the permission of Henry L. Sisk, *Management and Organization* (Cincinnati: Southwestern Publishing Company, 1977).

that requires 500 hours of service each week and approximately 20 workers. The remaining 30 accounts range between 100 and 400 man-hours each week, and require between four and sixteen employees.

Mr. Waller is not sure which size job yields the most profit. Jobs are priced on a rule-of-thumb basis and depend upon the type of floor surfaces, the amount of building traffic, number and types of offices, and other similar factors. Mr. Waller and one of his two full-time supervisors estimate the man-power requirements for each new job. An analysis of company records shows that for the past five years, variable costs—direct labor and materials (waxes, detergents, etc.)—average about 80 to 85 percent of total revenue.

The full-time organization consists of Mr. Waller, two supervisors, a secretary, an accountant, and a supply man who also maintains some of the larger pieces of cleaning equipment such as the floor polishers. In addition, there are five part-time supervisors, each of whom supervises 40 to 50 workers in a given geographic area of the city. Most of their time and energy is spent in delivering supplies and materials to the various buildings within a given geographic area of the city. They also reassign personnel as the need arises and collect the weekly time cards. The two full-time supervisors have no specific duties assigned to them nor is either one responsible for the work of any particular part-time supervisor.

At the present time Mr. Waller has only two sources of information to guide him in the operation of his business. One of these is customer complaints, which serve as a check on the quality of the work. The other source is the weekly payroll, which is prepared by a local bank. Each week time cards are submitted to the bank and from these records payroll checks are prepared. The bank also maintains the necessary social security and income tax records. In addition, a summary is prepared showing the total man-hours per week for each job. At present, no consistent use is made of this information. However, on the occasions when he has examined these weekly reports, Mr. Waller has found that the total hours per week run as much as 400 hours in excess of the number of hours used in computing the price of the services. There is no record of the use of supplies for each job.

Questions

1. Is there a need for control in this company? Why?

2. If controls are needed, which areas of the business are most in need of control?

3. What type of standards are now being used? What kind would you recommend?

4. How can the organization be modified to improve the control function?

2

Management Concepts and Their Effects on Accounting Information Systems

Among the important questions that you should be able to answer after reading this chapter are:

1 Why don't most organizations attempt to maximize their long-run profits?

2 How can an organization's accounting information system contribute toward environmental pollution control?
3 How do the accounting and electronic data-processing subsystems interact in developing and implementing a responsibility accounting system with a management-by-exception reporting structure?
4 How can an organization integrate centralization and decentralization into its structural design?
5 Is it preferable to locate an organization's computer facility within the accounting subsystem or as a separate subsystem?

INTRODUCTION

Today's accountant is an important contributor to management decision making. To operate a business efficiently, management requires information for both short-range decisions (affecting the current 12-month period) and long-range decisions (affecting several years into the future). For accountants to provide management this short-range and long-range decision-making information, they must understand the organization's structural design. Knowledge of the organizational structure will enable accountants to be aware of the specific types of decision-making information required at the various managerial levels (top management, operating management, etc.). The accountants can then communicate the relevant information to management so they can make effective organizational decisions.

This chapter discusses some important management concepts that underlie an organization's structural design. Those management concepts which are essential for accountants to understand so that they can perform their information communication function effectively are emphasized in the current chapter. Additional management concepts of importance to accountants when performing systems studies will be analyzed in later chapters. As discussed in Chapter 1, a company's accounting subsystem performs a service function of converting financially-oriented data into useful decision-making information. Consequently, the accounting subsystem can be referred to as the accounting information system. In this chapter as well as later chapters, the phrase "accounting information system" will therefore be used as a synonym for a firm's accounting subsystem.

ESTABLISHING ORGANIZATIONAL GOALS (A PLANNING FUNCTION)

Accountants must thoroughly understand their organization's goals in order to make a positive contribution toward the goals' accomplishment. A *goal* basically represents what one is attempting to achieve. Most people, as well as organizations, have several goals. Ideally, the multiplicity of goals that employees and their organizations have should be in harmony with each other. The harmony among employees' goals and organizational goals is called *goal congruence*. This means that in the process of achieving personal goals, the individual employee also contributes toward accomplishing organizational goals. On the other hand, frustration can result when the positive achievement of one goal conflicts with other goals, which is called *goal incongruence*. This type of frustration occurs both in individuals and organizations.

Organization theory suggests that an individual usually joins a company for personal gain, but that he or she, in the course of time, gradually learns to accept, and work toward, the company's goals. Both large and small businesses

encourage such learning and acceptance of organizational goals by permitting employees to participate in developing these goals, by creating profit-sharing and employee professional-improvement programs, by organizing social activities such as bowling leagues, picnics, and the like, which create the feeling of a working "family," and in general, by making employees feel that it is their company. Nevertheless, discord between personal goals and organizational goals still can occur. One example would be the individual's desire for promotion to an area for which he or she is not fully qualified. You might also recognize this problem as the "Peter Principle"—a person is promoted to his or her highest level of incompetency. In such situations, the individual's goal of personal achievement conflicts with the organization's goal of increased operating efficiency. Other examples of conflict would include personal locational preferences versus organizational geographic needs, and personal desires for more subordinates versus organizational policy on maximal supervision (called "span of control").

For an organization's multiplicity of goals to harmonize, the organization should consider its employees' needs when establishing these goals. The accounting information system plays a major role in providing relevant information to an organization's management regarding the establishment and eventual achievement of its specific goals. An important way to resolve conflict is through the generation of information about organizational operating activities. The accounting information system attempts to provide this relevant decision-making information to each organizational subsystem (as well as to top management) so that each subsystem can contribute positively to its company's goals, thereby avoiding goal conflict. This topic will be examined more thoroughly in later chapters.

The two major organizational goal categories are: (1) nonoperational goals (which are normally long-range, broadly stated goals of top management), and (2) operational goals (which are normally short-range goals established by each subsystem for the purpose of contributing positively toward the accomplishment of the nonoperational goals). Each of these categories is now discussed.

Determining Nonoperational Goals (Typically a Long-Range Planning Function)

As discussed in Chapter 1, two important managerial functions are planning and controlling. Most organizations perform both long-range and short-range planning. The former is normally the function of an organization's top management people and is sometimes also called *strategic planning*. Through its long-range strategic planning, the organization develops a "plan of attack" for the future. The strategics established by top management are usually expressed in a broad, nonoperational manner. For example, the long-range nonoperational goals developed by the Alan Company's top management are the attainment of:

1. A satisfactory level of net income.
2. A high quality of manufactured sporting goods.
3. A responsive and motivated group of employees.
4. A contribution toward a clean environment through pollution control.

These goals are nonoperational because they are stated very broadly and reflect the long-range accomplishments desired by the Alan Company's top management.

Chapter 1 pointed out that most organizations do not attempt to maximize their long-run income (or profit). Rather, it is more common for an organization to have a satisfactory profit performance as one of its goals. It is difficult to attach a quantitative number to this satisfactory level of income. Basically, a satisfactory income is below a maximizing income which *satisfies* the various persons (the stockholders, the board of directors, etc.) associated with the specific organization. If management's profit performance fails to satisfy its stockholders, for example, many of the top management people may find themselves looking for other jobs.

Arguments against long-run profit maximization goal. There are three major reasons why most or-

ganizations strive for a satisfactory, rather than a maximizing, level of long-run net income. First, and probably most important, is the fact that a nonoperational goal of profit maximization would probably conflict with an organization's other nonoperational goals. To maximize profits would require each of the specific nonoperational goals to also be directed toward profit. In many organizations, this is not true. Often, one or more of an organization's nonoperational goals are actually counter to increased profit performance. For example, some of the employee benefit programs that the Alan Company institutes (which will be reflected as additional operating expenses on the company's income statement) to achieve its nonoperational goal of a responsive and motivated work force will actually decrease the company's annual net income. Or, the additional expenditures incurred by the Alan Company to contribute toward a clean environment will also cause reduced profits. Thus, when an organization has a multiplicity of goals that are not all directed at increased profitability, considerable goal conflict would result if one of these goals was profit maximization. A satisfactory profit performance goal, on the other hand, should be in harmony with the other organizational goals.

A second argument against profit maximization relates to an organization's difficulty in ascertaining its profit maximizing performance level. Economists tell us that profit maximization occurs when an organization operates at the point where marginal revenue equals marginal cost. This theory sounds nice, but actually deriving the marginal revenue and marginal cost data for a specific company can be quite difficult, if not impossible.

Third, if an organization attempted to develop a current year budget that incorporated a profit maximization goal, certain decisions may be made that actually harm long-run organizational performance. For example, within the Alan Company's marketing subsystem is a research and development component. Its function is to develop new and innovative products as well as improve the quality of current product lines. Because research and development costs represent operating expenses in the year of their incurrence, Alan Company's management could increase its 1984 income performance by reducing the current year's expenditures for research and development. However, this decision could lead to reduced profits in future years if the Alan Company's competitors continue to develop new and improved products in their research departments. The long-run effects of the Alan Company's attempt at maximizing its short-run profits in 1984 might cause the company to obtain a smaller share of the future sporting goods sales market because of its competitors' superior products. This would obviously lead to a reduction of profits for the Alan Company in the long run.

Determining Operational Goals (Typically a Short-Range Planning Function)

Employees within the Alan Company's individual subsystems (accounting, production, marketing, finance, personnel, and electronic data processing) must thoroughly understand their company's long-range goals and attempt to contribute positively toward these goals. Each subsystem is responsible for developing operational goals that will aid the accomplishment of the company's nonoperational goals. To achieve these nonoperational goals, employees from the various subsystems should communicate with one another so that each subsystem's goals are in harmony, rather than in conflict, with the other subsystems' goals. We will now examine the role played by the Alan Company's accounting information system in achieving the company's operational goals.

Accounting information system's role in achieving operational goals. The accounting information system's major contribution toward the Alan Company's top management nonoperational goals is in the development of long-range as well as short-range operational budgets for its organization. Because budgets affect all organizational subsystems, the acountants must communicate with each subsystem's employees and seek their participation in planning, implementing, and controlling the budgetary system. The budgeting area (both long-range and short-range budgets)

will be covered extensively in Chapter 3. The purpose of briefly analyzing budgeting at this point is to show the accounting information system's major contribution to its organization's planning and controlling functions, which lead to the accomplishment of the organization's multiplicity of goals.

In its short-range planning, assume that the Alan Company wishes to prepare the 1984 operating budget. A budget committee, including representatives from top management and each of the company's subsystems, meets in September of 1983. Due to the accountants' training as financial experts and because the budget is a financial projection, the Alan Company's managerial accountants on the budget committee are appointed as coordinators of this committee. In the process of developing the 1984 budget, the committee's job is to make operational the previously stated nonoperational goals of top management. Each subsystem's operational budget should contribute positively toward these strategic, nonoperational goals.

The accounting information system's specific role in aiding the accomplishment of the Alan Company's four nonoperational goals (mentioned earlier in the chapter) is now discussed.

Accounting information system's contribution to nonoperational goal of satisfactory net income performance. The previously discussed arguments against profit maximization should be understood by the accountants when they perform their functions as budget coordinators. Accountants on the budget committee must develop projected financial statements for 1984 that will guide the Alan Company toward satisfactory income performance.

For example, in accumulating the data for the Alan Company's 1984 projected income statement budget, the accountants must develop the revenue and expense estimations with an understanding of top management's goal to achieve satisfactory rather than maximizing profits. One of the major expenses on a manufacturing firm's income statement is its "cost of goods sold" resulting from sales of manufactured inventory items. When the accountants aid the production subsystem in developing its standard manufacturing costs for raw materials, direct labor, and production overhead, they should be aware of the Alan Company's goal of achieving satisfactory operating performance. Therefore, these standard manufacturing costs (determined in advance of production activity) should be based upon a reasonably efficient level of performance rather than a maximizing performance output. Once determined, the company's standard manufacturing costs for its various types of sporting goods inventory items would represent useful information to aid the development of the production subsystem's 1984 operating budget.

In attempting to develop a satisfactory level of sales revenue for the 1984 income statement budget, the Alan Company's marketing subsystem must estimate the expected sales of the many sporting goods equipment product lines. Some techniques of forecasting sales demand will be discussed in Chapter 3. It should be emphasized here, however, that an important marketing subsystem function is to determine a satisfactory sales mix of product lines for the company's projected sales budget. A sales mix represents the quantity combination of an organization's many products that it hopes to sell. As an aid to the marketing subsystem in determining this sales mix, the Alan Company's accounting information system can provide the marketing people with relevant information regarding the manufacturing costs associated with the various sporting goods product items.

Accounting information system's contribution to nonoperational goal of high quality manufactured goods. The production subsystem has the primary responsibility for achieving this top management goal. The production managers may hire quality control experts who inspect the manufactured sporting goods to make sure they meet the designated quality standards.

The accounting information system's major role concerning quality production would be to financially justify the level of quality sporting goods desired by top management. To execute this function, the accountants would perform a cost/benefit analysis for the Alan Company's in-dividual sporting goods products. Ideally, the benefits expected from each product line (i.e., the revenues that eventually will result from selling the specific product) should exceed the company's costs associated with manufacturing each product line. At a minimum, each product line should make a positive *contribution margin* (excess of selling price over variable manufacturing, selling, and administrative expenses) toward covering those fixed costs associated with the product.

One of the important variable costs that affects the quality level of a company's manufactured product is the purchase price of the raw materials used in production. The accountant's analysis of the raw materials costs that would be necessary to achieve top management's desired production quality level may indicate that these high quality raw materials are too costly, resulting in a negative product line contribution margin (total variable costs exceed selling price). As a result of this information, the accountant may then recommend that top management decrease the quality level for the specific product line. This would enable the production subsystem to purchase a lower cost raw material for manufacturing the product line. By slightly altering the finished product's quality level, the company may be able to convert a negative product line contribution margin to a positive contribution margin.

Once an agreement is reached regarding the quality level of raw materials for each manufactured product line, the accountant can further contribute to top management's quality product goal through timely performance reports disclosing any significant variations between the actual quality of raw materials purchased and the quality level of raw materials that should have been purchased (based upon the established quality standard). The subject of timely performance reports will be emphasized later in this chapter.

Accounting information system's contribution to nonoperational goal of responsive and motivated employees. The personnel subsystem has the primary responsibility for achieving this top management goal. Through effective personnel selection procedures, adequate compensation, efficently operating training programs, and the involvement of the employees in challenging activities, the Alan Company's labor force should have positive attitudes toward their work environment.

As discussed in Chapter 1, the accountants, in performing their cost accounting functions, budgetary functions, and systems study functions, must consider the human element within a company. Rather than just informing the employees of the various subsystems what their budget allowances will be or unilaterally introducing a systems change, the accountants should seek the employees' participation in making these decisions (called *participative* management). Employees should be more responsive and positively motivated toward achieving their company's goals if they participate in various decisions affecting their work environment.

Consider, for example, the process involved in developing the standard number of labor hours for manufacturing the Alan Company's many sporting goods product lines by the production subsystem. The accountants within the accounting information system would have a major role in developing these labor standards and subsequently reporting to management any significant variations between actual and standard labor hours. If the standards for employee performance are set too high (often called *strict* standards), most production employees will be unable to attain them, causing management to evaluate the employees unfavorably. Obviously, this situation can lead to employee frustration. If the accountants allow the production employees to participate in the development of the standards with the objective of setting the labor standards at a level that the "average" employee can achieve (often called *attainable* standards), however, the employees should feel that the standards are fairer. As a result, the employees should be more responsive, and thus motivated to operate effectively under the standard cost system. Timely performance reports from the accounting information system which compare actual with standard labor hours should motivate

employees to perform favorably in relation to these "average" established standards. Further motivation can result from monetary and promotional benefits to those employees who perform favorably compared to these standards.

Another behavioral aspect of the accountants' organizational duties concerns the design of subsystem managers' performance reports that fairly reflect each manager's contribution to top management's nonoperational goals. If a subsystem manager is evaluated on the basis of operating items over which he or she has no control, the individual may become frustrated. As will be emphasized later in this chapter, the accountants can contribute toward employee motivation by designing subsystem performance reports which evaluate each subsystem manager on only those controllable operating activities of the manager. This is called a *responsibility accounting system.*

Accounting information system's contribution to nonoperational goal of a clean environment through pollution control. The Alan Company's production subsystem makes an important contribution to this goal by utilizing efficient machinery and equipment in its manufacturing process, thereby minimizing environmental pollution.

The accounting information system's role in achieving adequate pollution control within a company would be directed toward helping management decide which of the many possible pollution reducing approaches is economically more efficient. For example, assume that the Alan Company's present manufacturing equipment is causing a level of environmental pollution in excess of minimum government pollution standards. The accountants could perform an analysis of the expected costs versus the expected benefits to the Alan Company of either making its current manufacturing equipment more efficient (possibly by adding pollution control devices to the equipment and replacing some of the motors, etc., on the older equipment) or completely modernizing the production plant (by disposing of this current equipment and purchasing new equipment). The benefits that the accountants would attempt to measure from each alternative include such things as reduced pollution, improved quality of manufactured products (from using more efficient production equipment), which would likely lead to increased sales of the company's sporting goods, and the estimated increase in sporting goods sales resulting from the favorable public image created by the Alan Company's environmental pollution program. The accountants would recommend that pollution control alternative offering the greatest benefits in relation to its costs.

Once management has reached a decision on which pollution program to undertake (this decision would result from discussions between manufacturing department managers and top management) and has established its standard level of acceptable pollution, the accounting information system would further contribute by providing pollution control *variance* (i.e., the difference between an *actual* and a *standard* level of performance) reports. These reports would compare the actual levels of pollution from the new program with the predetermined standard pollution levels, thereby informing manufacturing department managers and top management whether or not their pollution control program is operating effectively. The accounting information system's role in environmental control is only part of a recent movement in the accounting profession called *social reporting*. Under this type of reporting, accountants attempt to measure within their financial reports the impact on society of various organizational activities such as conserving energy and fair employment practices (e.g., hiring a sufficient number of women and minorities).

EVALUATING THE ACHIEVEMENT OF ORGANIZATIONAL GOALS (A CONTROLLING FUNCTION)

Upon establishing each subsystem's operational goals (a planning function) which will contribute to top management's nonoperational goals, a reporting structure is needed to ascertain whether or not the subsystems' planned operational goals are being achieved. Through timely reports comparing each subsystem's actual performance with

its budgeted performance, those organizational areas that are operating inefficiently can be determined and necessary corrective action taken. This controlling function is extremely crucial because without timely performance evaluation reports, top management as well as operating management (i.e., the subsystem managers) would be unaware of a specific subsystem's positive or negative contribution to the nonoperational goals. Figure 2-1 reflects the important relationship between organizational planning and controlling.

After an organization's future plans are established, the controlling function takes over and monitors the success or failure of these plans. Timely performance feedback reports (the control function) can isolate any specific organizational inefficiencies that require an operating manager's attention and subsequent correction. As Figure 2-1 illustrates, the controlling function can lead back to further planning where revisions are made to correct specific inefficient operating performance. Obviously, if actual performance is progressing according to original plans, revised planning will be unnecessary.

The Accounting Information System's Role in Performance Reporting

Chapter 1 emphasized that the principal function of managerial accounting is to communicate relevant decision-making information to internal parties. These internal parties include an organization's top management as well as the operational managers within each subsystem. Even though many organizational communications are

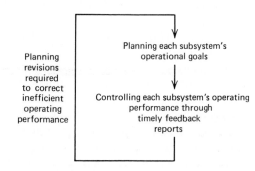

Figure 2-1. The planning and controlling relationship.

oral, a large amount of a company's communications also take place through written reports. An extremely important type of written report is the *performance report*, which evaluates a subsystem's success or failure in accomplishing its operational goals. One of the major criteria for assessing a subsystem's achievement of its operational goals is the subsystem's actual performance compared with its predetermined budget. Because accountants within the accounting information system are usually the coordinators of their organization's budgetary system, they have the important function of designing and communicating the organization's performance reports.

For these reports to fulfill their control objectives, they must satisfy two conditions. First, the reports should be *timely* so that a minimum period elapses between an activity's occurrence and the feedback reflecting the actual performance of this activity. Second, the reports must provide *relevant information* to their recipients so that the recipients can take the necessary action to accomplish the organization's goals.

To achieve the above two characteristics in performance reports, the accountants work closely with electronic data-processing subsystem employees. The speed capability of a computer to process data has enabled faster feedback of performance information to individual subsystems and top management. This allows a subsystem's managers to institute corrective action on inefficiencies in a shorter time span following the occurrence of these inefficiencies. However, the computer's ability to quickly process data is unproductive to a company's decision-making activities unless the data provided the computer are relevant.

The data input stage is the principal link between the accounting information system and the electronic data-processing subsystem. The accountants must understand the information needs of each manager (subsystem managers and top management) in their organization. Only by knowing the types of information required by management to adequately perform its organizational functions can the accountants accumulate for computer processing the relevant data needed by the various managers for effective decision making.

An important organization concept is the delegation of authority by top management to the managers within each subsystem. In small organizations, this delegation of authority is often minimal because the owner (or owners) can be aware of everything that occurs in the organization and is able to make all the necessary decisions. However, in large organizations, it is impossible for one or a few top management people to keep abreast of all organizational activities and make timely decisions within the various subsystems. The size and complexity of many organizations has been the major factor causing top management to delegate decision-making authority to lower-level managers in order that these organizations will be able to function more efficiently. Good organizational theory emphasizes that when a subsystem manager is given the authority to perform certain activities, this manager should also be held responsible for his or her actions. It should be emphasized, however, that in the final analysis, top management remains responsible for the actions of its subsystem managers in achieving the organization's goals. In other words, responsibility cannot be delegated from one individual to another. For example, if a specific subsystem fails to accomplish its operational goals, the organization's stockholders will hold top management responsible for this inefficient operating performance.

The accountants should be aware of the authority and responsibility relationships within their organization so that they can design relevant reports that measure fairly the subsystems' operating performances. Each subsystem's performance report must be "tailor-made" to measure the success or failure of the subsystem to execute those functions over which it has authority and responsibility.

Responsibility Accounting System for Performance Reporting

In designing performance reports which attempt to provide relevant decision-making information regarding the positive or negative contribution of each subsystem toward achieving the organization's nonoperational goals, the accountants should utilize a responsibility accounting system. Under this type of reporting system, the accountants must first analyze the authority and responsibility structure of their organization. Then, a reporting system is developed whereby each subsystem is evaluated only on those activities over which the subsystem has *control*. As discussed in Chapter 1, a controllable item is one that the subsystem can cause to change. By evaluating a subsystem's performance on the basis of activities that it can control, a fairer and truer picture of the subsystem's efficient or inefficient operating performance is obtained. In developing each subsystem's budget, only those operating items over which the subsystem has control and for which it is therefore responsible should be included in its budget. When subsequently evaluating a particular subsystem's performance, the report would include a comparison of the subsystem's actual controllable items with its budgeted controllable items. Because the subsystem is being evaluated only on its controllable operating activities, any significant variations between actual results and budget projections would be the responsibility of that subsystem.

A control system is normally not effective unless one can trace who is responsible for an inefficiency. That is, how can one correct something without first knowing the cause of this irregularity? Through a responsibility accounting system, inefficiencies within an organization can be traced to the specific subsystem (or subsystems) that caused these inefficiencies, and corrective action can then be planned.

Another important advantage of a responsibility accounting system is from a *behavioral* point of view. If a responsibility accounting system is not used in evaluating subsystem performance, a subsystem will often be evaluated on the basis of activities outside of its control. This can cause frustration to the subsystem management. In many organizations, the accountants' performance report concerning a particular subsystem is the major criterion used by top management when evaluating the subsystem managers' effec-

tiveness. Think of yourself for a minute as Alan Company's manager of the basketball manufacturing department. Figure 2-2 illustrates two possible performance reports that could be prepared by the managerial accountant to evaluate your department during January 1984. Version 1 of the report is based upon a responsibility accounting system, whereas Version 2 includes cost items over which you have no control (i.e., a nonresponsibility accounting system). Which of these two performance reports would you consider to be a truer picture of your effectiveness as basketball manufacturing department manager?

Figure 2-2 assumes that the basketball manufacturing department has authority and responsibility for the dollar expenditures on raw materials, direct labor, and variable overhead utilized in production (which may not be true in all organizations). Therefore, the first report evaluates this department's performance on the basis of the monetary items it can control. Because the department's actual controllable costs were $500 below the January budget, you as the manager would likely receive a favorable evaluation from top management.

The second performance report in Figure 2-2 could make you somewhat frustrated. Here, monetary items over which you have no control (the fixed overhead, the allocated selling and administrative expenses, and the allocated research and development expenses) are being charged to your budget and used to evaluate your subsequent performance. The end result is that your department's actual costs are $900 over the January budget, causing top management to look unfavorably at your department. This negative evaluation would probably be frustrating to you because the major factors causing the unfavorable performance were due to the three monetary items for which you had no authority and responsibility. For example, the $800 excess of allocated selling and administrative expenses over the budget may have been the result of overtime wages paid to administrative personnel. This overtime pay may have been necessary because of careless and inefficient performances by some administrative employees, causing them to work extra hours.

Figure 2-2

Version 1:

THE ALAN COMPANY

Basketball Manufacturing Department Performance Report for the Month of January 1984

Costs	Budget	Actual	Variation—Favorable (Unfavorable)
Raw materials for production	$ 6,000	$ 5,800	$200
Direct labor for production	10,000	10,100	(100)
Variable overhead	8,000	7,600	400
Totals	$24,000	$23,500	$500

Version 2:

THE ALAN COMPANY

Basketball Manufacturing Department Performance Report for the Month of January 1984

Costs	Budget	Actual	Variation—Favorable (Unfavorable)
Raw materials for production	$ 6,000	$ 5,800	$200
Direct labor for production	10,000	10,100	(100)
Variable overhead	8,000	7,600	400
Fixed overhead	7,000	7,200	(200)
Allocated selling and administrative expenses	3,000	3,800	(800)
Allocated research and development expenses	2,000	2,400	(400)
Totals	$36,000	$36,900	($900)

Naturally, if the Alan Company's top management executives receive the second report in Figure 2-2 and examine each line closely, they would see that your department performed successfully on its controllable financial items. But, as is often true, top management may look only at a performance report's bottom line, indicating a $900 net unfavorable operating performance. Because top management now considers your department inefficient during January, your morale and motivation level may drop considerably because of the unfair basis utilized in evaluating your department's performance.

Management-by-Exception for Performance Reporting

A common problem faced by many organizations having computerized information systems is the massive quantity of data printed out by their computers. A company may intentionally create additional unnecessary reports just so the company will feel it is obtaining full value from its expensive computer equipment. Another factor causing this "excessive data reporting" problem is the belief of many business managers that receiving internally generated reports is a status symbol. Thus, the more reports a specific manager receives (even though this manager may never read many of these reports), the greater status and importance the manager attaches to his or her role in the organization.

Whatever the specific factors causing these excessive reports in an organization's system, the result can often lead to inefficient decision making. If a subsystem manager is faced with a situation where a quick decision is needed, the relevant information for this decision may be "buried" in the mass of reports on the manager's desk. Consequently, being unable to find the relevant information immediately, the manager may reach a decision based on some irrelevant criteria. Assuming the needed information had been readily available, perhaps the manager's final decision would have made a more positive contribution to achieving the company's goals.

Along with designing a responsibility accounting system, the accountants can help reduce the massive number of reports flowing through a company's system by incorporating a "management-by-exception" reporting structure into their company. The underlying assumption of "management-by-exception" is that if a specific operating activity is progressing according to plan, there is no reason to report this information to management. Only when a particular activity deviates significantly from the original plan (which represents an *exception*) should the information be immediately reported to the responsible manager (or managers) so that necessary action can be initiated.

A management-by-exception reporting structure offers several advantages to a company. First, it reduces the length and number of reports generated by the company's information system because reports are prepared only when significant operating deviations exist and the reports include only information about these significant deviations. This advantage results in important cost savings to a company because the time required to process a report and then communicate it through the system can be a costly endeavor. Second, management-by-exception reporting reduces the amount of time that highly paid managers must spend reading reports. They will therefore have additional time available to perform more productive organizational functions. Third, and perhaps the most important advantage of a management-by-exception system, the managers will receive reports only when it is essential for them to take action on some aspect of their specific subsystem's performance activities. A subsystem exception report will thus direct a manager to actual operating functions that require immediate attention rather than the

manager receiving a report about each one of the subsystem's many activities, and thereby possibly losing sight of which activities, if any, need corrective adjustments.

What constitutes a significant variation from plan and should therefore be reported to management often involves subjective judgment. Accountants, with their understanding of an organization's financial operating activities, should have a valuable input to the decisions regarding what represents exceptions from the original operational plans.

To demonstrate the advantages of a management-by-exception reporting system, assume that a weekly computerized report goes to the Alan Company's marketing subsystem managers comparing this subsystem's actual sales with its budgeted sales. The input for the report comes from each salesperson's actual orders as well as from the budget projections that the accounting information system helped develop. The format of this weekly report was designed by the company's accountants. Figure 2-3 illustrates the Alan Company's sales report for the third week of January 1984.

Imagine yourself as a manager within the Alan Company's marketing subsystem having to read this detailed sales report each week (together with many other market reports). You may become frustrated and begin skimming the large volume of reports that cross your desk. This could cause you to overlook some relevant information that requires your immediate attention. If a management-by-exception reporting structure had been designed by the accountants, the weekly computer printout would not include all the data in Figure 2-3. Rather, only those budget variations that were considered significant would be reported to the marketing subsystem managers for their investigation. For example, examining the total budget and total actual sales of golf balls, the 70 cartons under budget may not be considered significant. After a closer look at the individual causes of this variation, however, two significant facts are revealed. Mr. Baker's golf ball sales in region F were 250 cartons under budget, whereas Ms. Worthley's sales in region S were 100 cartons over budget.

Figure 2-3

THE ALAN COMPANY
Report of Budget to Actual Sales Quantities
Third Week of January 1984

Product Description	Baker — Sales Regions[a]						Barnes — Sales Regions[a]						Myers — Sales Regions[a]		
	A			F			C			R			B		
	B[b]	A	V	B	A	V	B[b]	A	V	B	A	V	B[b]	A	V
Baseball bats	75	80	5	40	70	30	70	35	(35)	90	92	2	80	77	(3)
Baseball gloves	48	50	2	38	37	(1)	50	47	(3)	35	38	3	60	65	5
Baseball shoes	25	28	3	32	31	(1)	30	31	1	31	21	(10)	40	38	(2)
Baseballs	110	100	(10)	90	94	4	80	85	5	100	95	(5)	85	87	2
Basketball shoes	40	38	(2)	40	57	17	35	32	(3)	25	24	(1)	50	53	3
Basketballs	100	98	(2)	90	93	3	110	108	(2)	100	98	(2)	80	84	4
Bowling balls	60	63	3	50	51	1	70	67	(3)	40	42	2	50	52	2
Bowling shoes	10	11	1	8	10	2	15	13	(2)	18	19	1	8	9	1
Footballs	80	84	4	90	91	1	100	104	4	60	62	2	90	87	(3)
Golf bags	30	31	1	18	16	(2)	10	11	1	23	15	(8)	20	19	(1)
Golf balls	80	90	10	300	50	(250)	70	95	25	100	105	5	160	175	15
Golf carts	5	6	1	10	6	(4)	10	12	2	9	7	(2)	15	18	3
Tennis balls	100	110	10	90	91	1	100	98	(2)	80	83	3	110	114	4
Tennis rackets	50	51	1	80	83	3	70	69	(1)	90	92	2	40	44	4
Tennis shoes	35	38	3	30	31	1	40	37	(3)	20	23	3	15	14	(1)

[a]These letters (A, F, C, R, etc.) represent codes for the different geographical areas that each salesperson is assigned.

[b]B represents budget projection of sales quantity, A represents actual sales quantity, and V represents variation from budget (parentheses indicate below budget).

Under management-by-exception reporting, this information about Baker and Worthley's golf ball sales would be provided to the marketing subsystem's management. Information regarding any one of the Alan Company's other product-line regional sales whose budget variations were considered significant would also be included in the exception report.

Assume that accounting and marketing subsystem managers have agreed as to what constitutes a significant budget variation for each product line in the various sales regions. Figure 2-4 reflects the Alan Company's sales *exception report* for the third week of January 1984.

By comparing Figure 2-4 with Figure 2-3, it is obvious that the exception report of Figure 2-4 will permit more efficient and effective decision making by the marketing subsystem's managers. This exception report can be read faster than the complete sales data in Figure 2-3, and more im-

portantly, it immediately discloses those budget variations that are significant.

It is important to note from Figure 2-4 that management-by-exception reports include both favorable and unfavorable budget variations. This reporting method can thus be a useful motivational device for recognizing superior employee performance. For example, Ms. Worthley's 100 golf ball sales cartons over budget in region S would be fully recognized by her superiors. On the other hand, Mr. Baker's 250 golf ball sales cartons below budget in region F would be discussed with him and plans made for trying to increase this region's future golf ball sales.

The computer's role in management-by-exception reporting. Through communications among managers of the accounting information system, the marketing subsystem, and the electronic data-

Figure 2-3 (continued)

	Sales Personnel																
	Myers (cont.)			Williams						Worthley								
	Sales Regions[a]			Sales Regions[a]						Sales Regions[a]						Totals		
	T			G			I			S			C					
	B[b]	A	V	B[b]	A	V	B	A	V	B[b]	A	V	B	A	V	B[b]	A	V
	50	54	4	80	83	3	70	68	(2)	20	35	15	40	41	1	615	635	20
	70	64	(6)	45	49	4	50	48	(2)	40	43	3	25	21	(4)	461	462	1
	44	47	3	30	34	4	28	30	2	30	32	2	40	37	(3)	330	329	(1)
	110	115	5	90	88	(2)	85	88	3	90	92	2	100	104	4	940	948	8
	40	42	2	40	25	(15)	40	42	2	35	33	(2)	40	42	2	385	388	3
	90	86	(4)	80	76	(4)	90	88	(2)	75	78	3	85	84	(1)	900	893	(7)
	60	58	(2)	30	33	3	25	28	3	40	39	(1)	55	53	(2)	480	486	6
	10	13	3	11	14	3	5	4	(1)	10	11	1	20	22	2	115	126	11
	60	61	1	100	101	1	95	97	2	80	78	(2)	90	94	4	845	859	14
	8	10	2	20	23	3	30	29	(1)	11	14	3	15	17	2	185	185	0
	100	90	(10)	500	525	25	160	175	15	300	400	100	100	95	(5)	1870	1800	(70)
	15	17	2	10	9	(1)	3	7	4	20	18	(2)	24	26	2	121	126	5
	90	92	2	100	98	(2)	80	83	3	90	92	2	110	114	4	950	975	25
	70	73	3	60	61	1	20	18	(2)	10	11	1	30	27	(3)	520	529	9
	20	22	2	10	8	(2)	40	41	1	30	28	(2)	40	42	2	280	284	4

Figure 2-4

THE ALAN COMPANY
Exception Report of Budget to Actual Sales Quantities
Third Week of January 1984

	Sales Personnel																				
	Baker			Barnes						Myers			Williams						Worthley		
	Sales Region[a]			Sales Region[a]						Sales Region[a]			Sales Region[a]						Sales Region[a]		
	F			C			R			T			G			I			S		
Product Description	B[b]	A	V	B[b]	A	V	B	A	V	B[b]	A	V	B[b]	A	V	B	A	V	B[b]	A	V
Baseball bats	40	70	30	70	35	(35)													20	35	15
Baseball shoes							31	21	(10)												
Basketball shoes	40	57	17										40	25	(15)						
Bowling shoes										10	13	3	11	14	3						
Golf bags							23	15	(8)												
Golf balls	300	50	(250)	70	95	25													300	400	100
Golf carts	10	6	(4)													3	7	4			

[a] These letters (F, C, R, T, etc.) represent codes for the different geographical areas that each salesperson is assigned.

[b] B represents budget projection of sales quantity, A represents actual sales quantity, and V represents variation from budget (parentheses indicate below budget).

processing subsystem, decisions can be reached for each product line as to what constitutes a significant budget variation and therefore represents a reportable exception. Because budgets reflect future projections, in most cases it is quite unlikely that actual operating results will be identical with the various budget projections. Some budget variation should be expected solely because of random chance.

Let's assume that the Alan Company's marketing managers and its accountants believe that a budget variation of ±12 cartons of golf balls per week is acceptable in sales region A. Because the budget during the third week of January was 80 cartons in region A (see Figure 2-3), this particular week's acceptable range of sales for the region would have been from 68 cartons to 92 cartons (80 ± 12). The Alan Company's electronic data-processing subsystem employees would have programmed their computer for this acceptable range of golf ball sales in region A. The budget data for each week's regional golf ball sales (as well as the sales of the other sporting goods product items) would be contained on computer storage media. We will assume that the Alan Company uses magnetic tape for storing its budget data. Then, every week when the transaction tape of actual sporting goods sales is processed with the master tape containing the budget data, the computer program will check whether the actual sales of each product item fall within the acceptable limits. For golf balls, this would mean that as long as the actual third week's sales are within 68 to 92 cartons in region A, no exception report on golf balls is generated. Only for those sporting goods items of specific regions where the actual sales are outside the acceptable limits would an exception report (similar to that illustrated in Figure 2-4) be printed out for management's attention.

The type of reporting structure discussed here increases the computer's usefulness to a company's information system. The speed capability of the computer in processing the Alan Company's sales data permits a timely analysis of budget versus actual sales for the individual sales personnel in their assigned regions. And, by incorporating a management-by-exception reporting structure into the company's system, the computer will print out on a timely basis only those significant budget variations that require management's immediate attention. Naturally, this reporting method can be utilized for analyzing operational performance in areas other than just sales (e.g., comparing actual with standard manufacturing costs within the Alan Company's production subsystem).

CENTRALIZED AND DECENTRALIZED ORGANIZATIONAL STRUCTURE

The role of the accounting subsystem (as well as the other subsystems) within an organization's operating environment is greatly influenced by top management's philosophy of organizational structure. The two major structural types are centralized and decentralized systems. When comparing a centralized and decentralized organizational structure, two relevant functions should be considered: *information processing* and *decision making*.

Before computers became popular in business, many organizations were decentralized for both information processing and decision making. Under a decentralized structure, top management delegates decision-making authority and the responsibility for decisions to lower-level operating managers. Thus, prior to the utilization of computerized data-processing systems, each subsystem was often responsible for accumulating and processing its operational data (decentralized information processing), and then having the subsystem managers make decisions from this processed information (decentralized decision making). From a behavioral viewpoint, decentralized decision making usually causes positive motivational responses by an organization's employees. People will ordinarily have a higher level of morale and loyalty toward achieving their subsystem's goals if they have participated in making organizational decisions. Furthermore, people will often become more dedicated to their jobs if they are attempting to achieve goals that they helped to establish.

The implementation of a computer into an organization's system ordinarily causes its information processing functions to be *centralized* within the electronic data-processing subsystem. This may result in the organization also converting its previous decentralized decision-making functions to a *centralized* structure. This conversion from decentralized to centralized decision making may cause negative reactions from subsystem managers. Under decentralization, these managers were directly involved in making decisions affecting their specific subsystem's operating performance. Then, upon implementing a computerized information system, each subsystem manager's previous decision-making authority is removed and taken over centrally by top management.

For those organizations having computerized data-processing systems, the "ideal" organizational structure may be to integrate both centralization and decentralization. The information processing functions would be centralized within the electronic data-processing subsystem. The advantages of this are to vastly increase the speed of the organization's data-processing activities and to permit more challenging work opportunities for the other subsystems' employees. The computer, in effect, takes over the often time-consuming and noncreative "busy work" of processing organizational data. For example, before a computerized data-processing system existed in the Alan Company, its accountants spent large amounts of time performing bookkeeping-type functions. With the computer taking over many of these bookkeeping activities, the accountants were able to get involved in more dynamic functions such as advising top management on financial decisions, designing more efficient and effective operating systems, and so forth.

The major point is that centralization of information processing does not automatically require centralization of decision making. On the contrary, centralized information processing by the computer will allow subsystem employees more opportunities for creative activities because much of the previous data-processing "busy work" is eliminated from their jobs. Therefore, through computer processing of timely reports which are communicated to the specific subsystem (or subsystems) managers requiring the report information, decentralized decision making can continue within an organization. The behavioral advantages resulting from participation by subsystem managers in decision making will also continue.

It should be emphasized, however, that even in a decentralized decision-making structure, certain organizational decisions are still typically centralized. For example, the Alan Company's top management maintains decision-making authority concerning which subsystem managers are to receive periodic salary increases as well as the specific dollar amounts of these salary increments.

ORGANIZATIONAL LOCATION OF ELECTRONIC DATA-PROCESSING FACILITY

The computer's placement within an organization is very important from a structural point of view because its location will tend to dictate the type of data processing performed. In discussing the Alan Company's system, the computer facility has been treated as a separate subsystem. However, because many organizations utilize their computers primarily for processing financial-type data, the electronic data-processing activity is often located within the accounting subsystem. A possible negative consequence of locating the computer within a company's accounting subsystem is that the accountants will then exercise too much control over data-processing functions and incorporate their personal biases into the company's information system (e.g., overemphasis on monetary compared with nonmonetary quantitative data).

When computers first became popular for business data processing, they were used principally for processing financial data. This factor justified the location of the computer facility within the accounting subsystem. However, the computer's increased popularity in business, together with the better understanding of its capabilities, has caused many organizations to use their computers for nonfinancial processing activities. People in the marketing subsystem, for example, may utilize the company computer to aid their forecasting of future market demand for specific product lines. Production subsystem managers can use the computer to help plan optimal inventory manufacturing schedules as well as to determine economic reorder points and reorder quantities for the efficient purchase of raw materials needed in the manufacturing process. Because of these varying specialized demands for computer-processed data by each subsystem within an organization, many organizations favor the establishment of their computer facility as a separate subsystem apart from accounting.

SUMMARY

This chapter has discussed some of the important management concepts that affect an organization's accounting information system.

After top management plans its long-range, nonoperational goals, each organizational subsystem must then develop operational goals that contribute positively to these nonoperational goals. The accounting information system's major contribution toward accomplishing top management's nonoperational goals is in the development of operational budgets that will achieve a satisfactory long-run net income for its organization. Several arguments were presented in the chapter as to why most organizations do not attempt to maximize their long-run profits. Because of the strong financial emphasis in budgets, the managerial accountants working within the accounting information system are normally the coordinators of their organization's budgetary system. An organization's accounting information system also makes important contributions to top management's other nonoperational goals, such as a high quality of manufactured inventory, a responsive and motivated group of employees, and a program of environmental pollution control.

Following an organization's budget planning process, the accounting information system has a major role in monitoring the success or failure of these plans. The accountants, being familiar with each subsystem's delegated decision-making authority and its responsibility for decisions,

must interact with the electronic data-processing subsystem in order to prepare timely performance reports which analyze each subsystem's contribution to the organization's nonoperational goals. To fairly evaluate each subsystem's performance, the accountants should design a responsibility accounting system. Under this system, a subsystem's operational performance evaluation is based upon a comparison of the subsystem's actual results with its pre-established budget on only those activities that are controllable by employees of the subsystem.

To emphasize the variations from budget that require management's immediate attention, the accountants will often incorporate a management-by-exception system into their responsibility performance reports. The computer programs for processing the organization's operating data can be written to recognize significant budget variations. Upon identifying these variations, the computer can immediately print out the managerial exception reports.

The use of a computer ordinarily causes centralization of an organization's information processing functions within the electronic data-processing subsystem. Through timely computerized performance reports being communicated to the responsible subsystem managers, however, decentralized decision making can be maintained within each subsystem. As a result of top management continuing to delegate decision-making authority to subsystem managers, these managers should be positively motivated toward achieving their organization's nonoperational goals.

An organization's computer facility is typically located either within the accounting subsystem or is established as a separate subsystem. Locating the computer within the accounting subsystem may result in the accountants exerting too much control over the types of data-processing functions performed. Because each organizational subsystem often needs different types of computer-processed data, the computer facility may perform a more valuable information-providing service to the organization's entire system if it is established as a separate subsystem.

DISCUSSION QUESTIONS

2-1. Why is it important for today's accountant to have an understanding of management concepts?

2-2. Discuss how frustration can enter into an organization's multiplicity of goals.

2-3. What do you think is the rationale in most organizations for having strategic planning performed by top management rather than subsystem managers?

2-4. Why is it essential for an organization's planning and controlling functions to be highly interrelated?

2-5. Because budgets represent future financial projections and an organization's accountants are considered the financial experts, wouldn't the most expedient and efficient budgetary development approach be to have the accounting information system take complete charge for determining each subsystem's future budget? Explain.

2-6. Do you agree or disagree with the arguments given in this chapter that most organizations do not attempt to maximize their long-run profits? Discuss.

2-7. You have learned in a prior accounting course that many organizations incorporate standards for raw materials, direct labor, and production overhead into their cost accounting systems. Then, for each of these three manufacturing costs, variances are computed by comparing the actual costs with the predetermined standard costs. Let's look closer at only the raw materials manufacturing cost. Rather than computing just one total raw materials variance by comparing the actual costs with the standard costs, normally the accountant will analyze two components of the total raw materials variance: the price variance and the usage variance. What do you feel are the advantages, if any, of determining a separate price and usage variance for raw materials as compared with computing just one total raw materials variance?

2-8. You are an accountant within the accounting information system of the Dumbo and Dang Land Development Company. Through computerized processing methods, the company's electronic data-processing subsystem handles all the financial data affecting each subsystem's operating performance. Most of the subsystems' financial data are processed weekly. Assume that you are given the job of implementing either a responsibility accounting system or a management-by-exception system into the company (you definitely cannot implement both systems). Which of these two systems would you choose to implement? Explain.

2-9. A major function of a management-by-exception reporting system is to disclose inefficient operating performance so that management can initiate corrective action. Why is it therefore common for management-by-exception reporting to also reflect favorable operating performance for which no corrective action would be necessary?

2-10. What are some of the important ways that employees from the accounting information system and from the electronic data-processing subsystem interact in designing, implementing, and controlling a management-by-exception reporting system?

2-11. What are the major differences between a centralized and a decentralized organizational structure? How does each of these two structures affect the role of the accounting information system in an organization?

2-12. For an organization's controlling function to be effective, why is it essential to prepare performance evaluation reports on a timely basis?

2-13. Comment on the following statement: "Because an organization's computer facility will handle the processing of timely performance reports about each subsystem's operating activities, the accounting information system need no longer concern itself with the organization's performance reporting system."

2-14. Why is it important for accountants to understand the decision-making authority and responsibility of each subsystem manager in their organization?

2-15. Because top management can delegate decision-making authority to subsystem managers, doesn't it seem logical that top management should also delegate to these subsystem managers the responsibility for efficient or inefficient decisions? Discuss.

2-16. What are the advantages, if any, to an organization of utilizing a responsibility accounting system?

2-17. The Palmer Company has a manual data-processing system and the Pocket Company has a computerized data-processing system. Both companies are approximately the same size in terms of business volume and number of employees. For which of these two companies do you think a management-by-exception performance reporting system would be more beneficial? Explain.

2-18. As a subsystem manager, which type of organizational structure (centralized or decentralized) would you prefer to work under? Why?

2-19. For an organization having a computerized data-processing system, it was pointed out in this chapter that the best organizational structure would probably be *centralized* information processing and *decentralized* decision making. Do you agree or disagree with this recommendation? Explain.

2-20. Think of some specific organizational situations where centralized decision making would likely be preferable to decentralized decision making.

2-21. Because accountants are not trained to be either environmental experts or psychologists, is it therefore fair to expect them to contribute toward achieving top management's nonoperational goals of pollution control and highly motivated employees? Explain.

2-22. The Big Bright Bagel Company began business February 15, 1984 and has established the following subsystems: accounting, electronic data processing, production of bagels, marketing and sales of bagels, and personnel. The company's top management is currently analyzing several of the important decision-making activities within its system, and attempting to decide which of these decision

functions should be centralized and which should be decentralized. The activities being considered for either centralized or decentralized decision making are:

1. Capital expenditures for production equipment.
2. Capital expenditures for the pollution control program.
3. Establishing selling prices for the different types of bagels that are manufactured.
4. Scheduling the production of bagels.
5. Granting credit to bagel customers.
6. Allowing sales discounts to bagel customers.
7. Salary increases and promotions for subsystem managers.

Requirement

Assume that you are hired as a consultant to help the Big Bright Bagel Company decide which of the seven decision-making functions should be centralized and which decentralized. With the limited information provided in this question, make a recommendation to the company's top management regarding centralized or decentralized decision making for each of these functions. Give good arguments for every recommendation.

2-23. You are a member of the Bribe Bargain Basement Company's top management. Your company currently has the following subsystems: accounting, production, marketing, and personnel. Due to the rapid growth in the past few years, the company's present manual data-processing system (under the accounting subsystem's coordination) has been unable to keep up with the increased information demands by the various subsystems. Therefore, your company has decided to replace its manual data-processing system with a computerized data-processing system. As a top management executive, you are given the responsibility for deciding whether to establish the new computer facility as a separate subsystem or to integrate it within the accounting subsystem. What are some of the key factors that you should consider in reaching your decision regarding the organizational location of the computer facility?

PROBLEMS

2-24. The Big Juicy Hamburger Corporation operates a chain of restaurants throughout the United States. The top management at corporate headquarters exercises control over each restaurant's following functions: the construction of each restaurant's building facility and the depreciation method selected for the building, the number of managers hired at each restaurant as well as their annual salaries, and all expenditures associated with promotional efforts and advertising at each restaurant.

The managers of the individual restaurants have decision-making authority and responsibility for all the many other operating activities associated with their specific restaurant. Presented below is the monthly budget performance cost report for the Big Juicy

Cost Item	Budget	Actual
Salaries of clerical workers at the Springfield restaurant	$ 5,000	$ 5,200
Salaries of cooks, waitresses, and dishwashers at the Springfield restaurant	7,000	7,400
Salaries of supervisory managers at the Springfield restaurant	12,000	12,500
Depreciation of Springfield restaurant's cooking equipment, dishes and silverware, tables and chairs, and cash registers	4,500	4,300
Depreciation of Springfield restaurant's building	3,000	3,400
Electricity, water, and telephone expense	300	375
Cost of food used in cooking meals	25,000	24,500
Cost of cooks' and waitresses' uniforms	400	420
Cost of napkins, dish towels, and cleaning soap	175	190
Advertising and promotional expense	1,000	1,400
Totals	$58,375	$59,685

Hamburger Corporation's restaurant located in Springfield, Illinois, for June 1984.

Problem Requirement

The Big Juicy Hamburger Corporation's top management has decided that a responsibility accounting system would be an effective means for evaluating each restaurant's monthly operating cost performance. Prepare the June 1984 performance report for the Springfield, Illinois restaurant under the corporation's responsibility accounting system.

2-25. The Best Sellers Book Company is a publisher of college textbooks. The company's operating data are centrally processed by its electronic data-processing subsystem. Each subsystem (production, marketing, accounting, finance, and personnel) receives computerized performance reports and has decision-making authority delegated from top management.

In the past few months, the managers of most subsystems have been complaining about the criteria used by top management for evaluating their operating performances. The major complaint has been the number of noncontrollable items included within an individual subsystem's performance report.

You are one of the accountants working in the company's accounting information system and have been asked by top management to design and implement a responsibility accounting system for evaluating each subsystem's monthly operating performance. You suggest to top management that a further improvement could be made in the company's performance reporting system if a management-by-exception structure were also incorporated into the new system. The top management executives agree with the suggestion, and you are therefore given the approval to design and implement the new reporting system.

You are currently analyzing the marketing subsystem's budget projection compared with actual cost performance during March 1984 under the company's old reporting system. The March 1984 performance report computer printout appeared as follows:

Cost Item	Budget	Actual	Variation—favorable (unfavorable)
Allocated depreciation of company building	$ 1,000	$ 1,100	($ 100)
Salaries of salespeople	8,000	9,000	(1,000)
Promotional textbook materials sent to college professors	2,000	2,600	(600)
Allocated portion of administrative expenses	1,000	1,600	(600)
Textbook advertising in professional journals	800	825	(25)
Utilities expense	300	375	(75)
Salaries of clerical employees in marketing subsystem	5,000	4,900	100
Totals	$18,100	$20,400	($2,300)

After familiarizing yourself with the delegated authority given the marketing subsystem managers by top management, you accumulate the following information:

1. The marketing subsystem managers make their own decisions regarding the number of salespeople and clerical people to hire as well as how much to pay these employees.
2. The marketing subsystem occupies the entire second floor of the company's building and has a separate electric utilities meter on this floor.
3. The marketing subsystem managers have complete decision-making authority for all advertising expenditures associated with promoting textbook sales.

Your next major task was to determine the variations from budget that should be considered significant. Through discussions with marketing subsystem personnel and top management, the following budget variability schedule was developed:

Budgeted Dollar Cost Range	Acceptable Budget Variation
$ 1–$ 500	±$ 50
$ 501–$1000	±$ 100
$1001–$3000	±$ 300
$3001–$5000	±$ 500
$5001–$7000	±$ 700
$7001–$9000	±$ 900
Over $9000	±$1200

You then talked to computer specialists within the company's electronic data-processing subsystem about the required revisions in the marketing subsystem's monthly performance report. Based upon the information you provided these computer specialists, they made the necessary computer program changes to accomplish your new responsibility accounting system with a management-by-exception reporting structure.

Problem Requirement

Prepare the computer printout of the marketing subsystem's March 1984 performance report as it would actually appear under your newly designed system.

CASE ANALYSES

2-26. *Decentralization–Fact or Fiction?**

Dynamic Industries, a diversified manufacturer of automotive replacement parts, is a company that is growing rapidly as the result of an aggressive policy of acquisition. Board chairman John Rafferty believes that the growth of his company is sound and that the main reason for the extremely rapid growth is due to the operation of the company on a highly decentralized basis. Since growth is the result of acquiring companies

*Used with the permission of Henry L. Sisk, *Management and Organization* (Cincinnati: Southwestern Publishing Company, 1977).

that are going concerns, Rafferty encourages the managements of the subsidiary companies to carry on as they had prior to joining Dynamic Industries. At present, discussions regarding merger are being held with Central Electronics, a company that manufactures a broad line of electronic components, many of which have applications in the defense and space industries. Central Electronics is interested in Dynamic Industries because Dynamic could supply the much-needed capital to complete the final stages of the development of a high-performance transformer and the building of a plant in which to manufacture the new product. However, George Owens, the founder and president of Central, realizes the potential dangers of merging with another company in that he might lose control of his own firm and be placed in the position of being an employee for a larger corporation.

But Rafferty continually assures Owens that Dynamic Industries operates on a highly decentralized basis and describes their concept of decentralization as follows:

> We expect you, as the president of a subsidiary company, to manage as you have in the past. You are successful with your own company and there is no reason why you shouldn't continue to be a success operating as a part of Dynamic. The major functions of sales, manufacturing, engineering, and product development are all yours to do with as you see fit. In a sense we are sort of the banker; that is, we supply the money that you need for capital improvements and expansion. Even though the profits of each subsidiary company go into the corporate till, it is still like having your own company because your pay for the year is a combination of a guaranteed salary and a percentage of the net profits of your company.

Thus assured, Owens decided to merge with Dynamic Industries.

During the first six months all went well and Owens saw very little of anyone from corporate headquarters. At the beginning of the seventh month, the corporate controller paid Owens a visit and explained to him in detail the company's requirements for profit planning and requested that Owens develop a profit plan, a detailed forecast of Central's revenues and operating expenses, for the coming year. Though very pleasant, the controller made it quite plain that should the performance of the company deviate significantly from the forecast, a team of cost accountants and industrial engineers would arrive from headquarters to determine the cause of the deviation and to recommend necessary changes.

Shortly after this experience with the controller, the industrial relations vice-president of Dynamic Industries called on Owens and informed him that a member of the corporate industrial relations staff would be on hand to conduct the coming negotiations with the union representing Central's employees. Owens protested, saying that he had been negotiating his own labor contracts for years; however, it was explained to him that because of company-wide employee benefit plans, such as pensions and insurance, and to prevent the unions from pitting one subsidiary company against another in the area of wages, centralized control over negotiations was very necessary. At the time of this visit, the provisions of the company's salary plan were outlined to Owens and arrangements were made for the installation of the corporate clerical and supervisory salary plans by a member of the headquarters industrial relations staff.

The following month Owens called Rafferty and asked what steps should be taken to secure capital for the new building intended for the manufacture of the high-performance transformer. Rafferty answered by saying, "I'll have someone from the treasurer's office call on you and show you how to fill out the forms used in requesting funds for capital expansion. It's quite a process, but remember you are only one of 15 subsidiaries and they all seem to want money at the same time. Whether or not you get it this year depends not only upon your needs but also upon the needs of the other 14 companies."

Questions

1. Has Dynamic Industries decentralized its operations as much as possible? Explain.
2. As George Owens, president of Central Electronics, would you regard the management policies

of the parent corporation as primarily centralized or primarily decentralized? Explain.
3. Is Dynamic Industries exerting too much control over Central Electronics? Why or why not?
4. Recommend the optimum degree of decentralization for the situation described in this case.

2-27.   Dual Standards at Harden

Harden Company has experienced increased production costs. The primary area of concern identified by management is direct labor. The company is considering adopting a standard cost system to help control labor and other costs. Useful historical data are not available because detailed production records have not been maintained.

Harden Company has retained Finch & Associates, an engineering consulting firm, to establish labor standards. After a complete study of the work process, the engineers recommended a labor standard of one unit of production every 30 minutes or 16 units per day for each worker.

cost comparisons. After much discussion, management decided to use a dual standard. The labor standard recommended by the engineering firm of one unit every 30 minutes would be employed in the plant as a motivation device, and a cost standard of 40 minutes per unit would be used in reporting. Management also concluded that the workers would not be informed of the cost standard used for reporting purposes. The production vice-president conducted several sessions prior to implementation in the plant, informing the workers of the new standard cost system and answering questions. The new standards were not related to incentive pay but were introduced at the time wages were increased to $3 per hour.

The new standard cost system was implemented on January 1, 1984. At the end of six months of operation, the following statistics on labor performance were presented to top management (U designates an unfavorable variance; F, a favorable variance):

	January	February	March	April	May	June
Production (units)	5100	5000	4700	4500	4300	4400
Direct labor hours	3000	2900	2900	3000	3000	3100
Variance from labor standard	$1350 U	$1200 U	$1650 U	$2250 U	$2550 U	$2700 U
Variance from cost standard	$1200 F	$1300 F	$ 700 F	$ 0	$ 400 U	$ 500 U

Finch further advised that Harden's wage rates were below the prevailing rate of $3 per hour.

Harden's production vice-president thought this labor standard was too tight and the employees would be unable to attain it. From his experience with the labor force, he believed a labor standard of 40 minutes per unit or 12 units per day for each worker would be more reasonable.

The president of Harden Company believed the standard should be set at a high level to motivate the workers, but he also recognized that the standard should be set at a level to provide adequate information for control and reasonable

Raw material quality, labor mix, and plant facilities and conditions have not changed to any great extent during the six-month period.

Questions

1. Discuss the impact of different types of standards on motivation, and specifically discuss the effect on motivation in Harden Company's plant of adopting the labor standard recommended by the engineering firm.

2. Evaluate Harden Company's decision to employ dual standards in its standard cost system.

(CMA Adapted)

3

Budgetary Accounting Information Systems

Among the important questions that you should
be able to answer after reading this chapter are:
1 What are the three major principles for effective budgeting?
2 What are the essential items that should be
included in a subsystem's long-range budgetary program proposal?
3 What is a cost/benefit analysis and some of the
difficulties involved in preparing one?
4 Does "zero-based budgeting" mean that a
company is so unsure about its future that no
budgetary planning exists?
5 What are responsibility centers and how do
they contribute to an efficient and effective
budgetary information system?
6 What role does the electronic data-processing
subsystem play in the planning and controlling functions associated with an organization's budgetary system?

INTRODUCTION

Today's business world is characterized by rapid
technological change, strong competition among
companies in many industries, and large organizations with sophisticated computerized information systems. Under these conditions, it is essential for organizations to operate efficiently
and effectively so they can obtain the most value
from their limited financial resources (monetary
items) and their limited nonfinancial resources
(people, scarce commodities such as electricity
and gasoline, etc.). To survive and prosper, an

organization should attempt to plan and control its future course of action. Without formal planning, the organization would function on a day-to-day basis with little or no thought about future challenges and opportunities. Consequently, the organization's management may find itself at an operating disadvantage to those competitors who are planning their short-range and long-range future.

As discussed in Chapter 2, both long- and short-range budgets are important to an organization's planning and controlling functions. Through a formal budgetary system, the organization attempts to quantify its long- and short-range plans so that each subsystem contributes positively to top management's goals (such as satisfactory long-run profit performance and high quality inventory items for sale to the consuming public). Periodic performance reports comparing budget allowances with actual results communicate information to management regarding whether or not its goals are being achieved.

Chapter 2 emphasized that accountants working within a company's accounting information system are the coordinators of their organization's budgetary system. Because no extensive discussion of budgetary systems was provided in Chapter 2, and due to the important role played by accountants in planning and controlling a budgetary information system, this topic will be examined in the current chapter. Most students should have been exposed to the procedural aspects of budgeting in prior courses. Therefore, our discussion of budgetary systems will place less emphasis on specific budget procedures and concentrate more on the valuable contribution that the budget process makes to an organization's information system.

A complete budgetary information system includes long-range budgets (which project operating activities beyond one year; for example, 5, 10, or 15 years into the future) and short-range budgets (which project operating activities for the upcoming 1-year period). This chapter's objectives are threefold: (1) to examine the essential principles of a good budgetary information system, (2) to analyze the accounting information system's role in long- and short-range

budgetary activities, and (3) to discuss computerized budgetary information systems.

IMPORTANT PRINCIPLES FOR EFFECTIVE BUDGETING

Whether discussing long- or short-range budgeting, there are three major principles that should be followed when planning and operating a budgetary system: communication, participation, and flexibility. Each one of these three principles will now be briefly analyzed.

Communication Within Budgetary System

To develop realistic budgets for the future, an organization must have information concerning its internal and its external environment. The internal environment encompasses all the subsystems within the organization. Because budgetary planning covers the entire organization, each internal subsystem (accounting, marketing, production, electronic data processing, etc.) will be affected by the budgetary process. As discussed in Chapter 1, the external environment is a major element that affects the organization's current and future operating activities. This external environment includes the state of the economy (inflation, war, unemployment, etc.), the degree of competition from other companies in the same industry, and the like.

The development of an effective budgetary system requires that complete information be available about each organizational subsystem. After all, how can you plan for the future without information about those subsystems that will play a role in your future? In order to acquire this information so that meaningful budgets can be developed, a communication network among the organizational subsystems must be instituted by those individuals performing the budget planning function.

This communication network cuts across all subsystem boundaries and permits the accumulation of relevant information needed in the budget process. For example, when the Alan Company's marketing subsystem is developing the detailed product line sales budget for 1984, it must obtain information about total market demand for sporting goods equipment, about competitors' share of this market, and so on. After developing its tentative sales plan, the marketing subsystem must communicate with the production subsystem to ascertain whether the latter's manufacturing capacity is adequate to produce the quantity of sporting goods expected to be sold.

Participation Within Budgetary System

An organization's employees often have a negative attitude toward budgets. This is caused by the confining or restrictive nature of a budget. For example, once the budgets are established, employees are expected to operate within their budget allotments. Thus, for many people, budgets represent limitations that are imposed upon them and are also a means by which others "watch over" and control their performance. Consequently, there are two major reasons for having an organization's employees participate in the development of the budgetary system: (1) to motivate employees to have a positive outlook toward their company's budgets, and (2) to achieve more realistic budgets, thereby contributing to the company's operating performance.

Motivation of employees. If, for example, only accountants from the accounting information system are involved in preparing the budgets, many employees working within the other subsystems may be unresponsive to their organization's budgetary system. One of the most effective means of motivating these people to react favorably to budgets is through employee participation in the budgetary process. Because all employees (regardless of which organizational subsystem they are part of) will be affected in some manner by the budgets, the organization should, within reasonable limitations, attempt to involve as many employees as possible in the budgetary planning process. As Chapter 2 discussed, a company often forms a budget committee which is responsible for planning and controlling the company's budgets. Representatives from top management and each subsystem are included on this committee, and man-

agerial accountants serve as budget committee coordinators. The committee may also include members from the company's union to represent employee interests in such matters as equitable budget allocations for salaries and for fringe benefits.

Each subsystem's employees will participate in developing their departmental budget. The resulting budget then goes to the budgetary committee, which reviews the departmental proposals, and either accepts or rejects these proposals. A rejection should be accompanied with an explanation of the reasons for not approving the subsystem's budget. The subsystem's employees can then go back and make the necessary changes in their original proposal that will lead to eventual acceptance. The budget committee can also make specific suggestions concerning a subsystem's dollar allotment. Once the subsystem's budget is approved by this committee and actual operating performance under the budget begins, the subsystem employees should be more positively motivated to achieving the budget because they have had a voice in determining their future course of action. Behaviorally, most people have a strong desire to accomplish something they have initially participated in developing. Thus, through budget participation by all organizational subsystems, the resultant budgets can be a positive, rather than a negative, planning tool. Each subsystem's budget will reflect operational goals that its employees are motivated to accomplish. As a result, the nonoperational goals of top management will likely be achieved.

Realistic budgets. When developing an organization's budgets, two dangers should be avoided: (1) making the budgets *too strict*, and (2) making the budgets *too loose*.

Budgets which are "too strict" mean that an organization's budgets are established at such a high level of performance that very few subsystem employees are able to meet them. Because employees' operating performance will be evaluated by their subsystem managers (and, in turn, the subsystem managers will be evaluated by top management) on the basis of actual results against budget projections (the control function of a budgeting system), unduly strict budgets will likely give the "appearance" of unfavorable subsystem performance. Many of the subsystems may actually be operating quite efficiently; however, with strict budgets being based upon the expectation of unrealistically high performance, the subsystems appear inefficient. This situation can cause negative employee attitudes toward the budgetary process because the employees will feel they are being evaluated on the basis of inequitable criteria.

Budgets that are "too loose" can also be harmful to an efficiently operated organizational system. Loose budgets mean that the various organizational budgets are set at such a low level of performance that most employees can function inefficiently and still meet the operating targets. The inefficiencies in operating performance will not be disclosed, however, because each subsystem will have the appearance of successful performance when actual results are compared with the performance levels established in the extremely loose budget. These easily attainable budgets can cause employee laziness due to the ease with which they can be met. Loose budgets can even be counterproductive because they do not challenge the participants and thus have the potential to make an employee feel that his or her work "does not matter."

The "ideal" budgetary system falls somewhere in between the budgets that are too strict and the budgets that are too loose. These budgets are often called realistic (or attainable) budgets because they reflect a reasonable level of performance that is neither too difficult nor too easy to achieve. In actual practice, realistic budgets are quite difficult to develop. On the one hand, operating employees (and even subsystem managers) will be pushing for loose budgets. At the same time, top management may be arguing for strict budgets. Consequently, for an efficient and effective budgetary system to emerge, some compromise is necessary.

One of the best techniques for achieving this compromise and the resultant realistic budgets is through subsystem employees' participation in developing the budgetary plans. For example, a subsystem may initially prepare a budget projec-

tion which is too loose. When this budget is subsequently reviewed by the budget committee, however, the committee should spot the budget's looseness and make this fact known to the subsystem. The subsystem's employees will then have to revise their budget projection to make it acceptable to the committee. The revised budget should reflect a higher level of performance, thereby eliminating the operational looseness. Thus, the participation between the subsystem's employees and the budget committee in developing the subsystem's budget should eventually lead to a departmental budget that closely reflects realistic performance within the organization's system.

Although it cannot solve the budgetary dilemma of subsystem employees and top management, the accounting information system *can* provide a basis for compromise. This compromise is achieved largely through periodic performance reports identifying the causes of significant budget variations. For example, it is very difficult for a union to argue that the budgets are too strict and should therefore be loosened if the record shows that unfavorable budget performance was caused by high worker absenteeism and turnover. (Of course, the union's counter argument may be that this employee absenteeism and turnover was the result of the employees' frustrations from being unable to work within the strict budgets.) Similarly, it is very difficult for top management to argue that the prior budgets were either attainable or too loose if performance reports show that a considerable amount of overtime work from experienced employees was required to meet the budgets. Clearly, all this is just common sense. Yet, it is equally obvious that the relevant information *must be available* if objective decisions are to be made regarding fair and attainable performance levels within the operating budgets. The accounting information system should be able to provide this valuable budgetary decision-making information.

The participation leading to the establishment of each subsystem's budget should be a positive motivator for budget acceptance by all the subsystems. The resultant motivation should cause the subsystems' employees to have favorable attitudes about achieving their realistic budgets. If this occurs, each subsystem will then be making a positive contribution to its organization's operating performance.

Flexibility Within Budgetary System

When budgets are prepared, they should reflect the best expectations of an organization's future operating activities. As the future unfolds, however, conditions may change from what was originally projected in the budgetary system. For example, a new sporting goods manufacturer may appear on the market during 1984 and greatly affect the Alan Company's original expectations of 1984 sales demand for sporting goods. When the Alan Company's budget committee was coordinating the 1984 budgets back in September 1983, it may not have been aware of this new competitor.

Flexibility within a budgetary system means that once an organization's budgets have been prepared and actual operations commence, the budgets should be monitored continually to ascertain whether the many assumptions upon which these budgets were based are still valid. If internal and/or external environmental factors change and make the original budget projections invalid, the flexibility principle would lead to a revision of the budgets. This revision would take into consideration the new information now available about the organization's operating environment. A flexible budgetary system should provide improved information to guide an organization's operating activities because of the most current information (affecting present and future operations) being incorporated into the budgets.

The opposite of flexible budgets is known as static (or fixed) budgets. Once developed, static budgets are never revised regardless of the subsequent knowledge obtained about the internal and external environment. Static budgets can result in an organization's budgetary system contributing *negatively* to its operations. Because additional knowledge about the organization's operating environment would not be included in its budgets under a static budgetary system, comparisons of actual operating results (which are based upon the current operations) with budget projections (which are based upon inaccurate expectations about the current operations) could lead to improper management decision making. For example, when the Alan Company's monthly budget of baseball sales for 1984 was originally developed back in September 1983, young people's interest in playing baseball was just beginning. This factor caused the Alan Company's budget committee to underestimate the 1984 demand for baseball purchases. With static sales budgets, the Alan Company's managerial reports comparing 1984 actual baseball sales with 1984 budgeted baseball sales would continue to be based upon the now outdated sales projections made in September 1983. Assuming that the actual week-by-week baseball sales during 1984 are continually in line with the original sales budget, the Alan Company's management would probably consider the sales program for baseballs to be successful. This could therefore cause the company to lose the opportunity to increase its 1984 baseball sales. If flexible budgets had been utilized, the Alan Company should have revised its production and sales budgets of baseballs for the remaining months in 1984 as soon as the information about the increased market demand was known. These production and sales revisions would have caused the company to increase its selling efforts in the baseball market. If the subsequent week-by-week actual sales did not increase, an unfavorable budget variation would occur (actual sales being less than the revised sales budget), causing management to investigate and institute corrective action.

The point of the above example is that an actual operating activity may appear favorable when compared with an outdated, static budget. However, by comparing actual results with an updated, flexible budget, managerial conclusions about the success of an operating function may be completely different.

Flexible budgets are an important part of an organization's *control* system because internal and external environmental changes are immediately recognized through revised budgets. For example, a weekly computerized report comparing an organization's actual sales with budget sales for a newly introduced product line can provide marketing managers with timely informational feedback regarding consumers' positive or negative reactions to this new product line. If actual weekly sales are continually below budgetary expectations, this unfavorable situation may be due, for instance, to quality deficiencies in the product line. This information will permit production managers to initiate immediate action to modify the product line's manufacturing specifications with the hope that consumer demand will subsequently increase. Based upon new expectations for the revised product line, adjustments to the original sales budget will then be necessary. Due to the manufacturing specification changes, the accountants will have to provide revised cost data for the production budgets associated with this product line.

LONG-RANGE BUDGETARY SYSTEMS

Chapter 2 defined strategic planning as a long-range planning approach whereby top management establishes its organization's broad, nonoperational goals. These goals reflect the organization's "plan of attack" (or strategies) for long-run success. Nonoperational goals are the framework within which each organizational subsystem develops operational goals that contribute positively toward achieving these long-range goals.

In addition to an organization's subsystems' short-range operational goals for the coming year, many of these subsystems will be involved in long-range projects that extend beyond a one-year period. The long-range projects that are either currently in progress or are being considered for future implementation form the framework of an organization's long-range budgetary system. Because an organization's long-range budgeting consists of various projects (or programs) that cover a time period longer than one year, another term commonly used for this type of budgeting is *programming*.

Some of the more important characteristics of long-range budgeting will now be analyzed. In-

cluded within this discussion will be an example of long-range budget programs for the Alan Company.

Characteristics of Long-Range Budgeting

The essential features that should be included in an organization's long-range budgetary system are:

1. a systematic method for generating program proposals by each subsystem.
2. a systematic method for evaluating program proposals, and objective criteria by which to select programs for implementation.
3. a systematic method for periodic zero-based review of ongoing programs and new program proposals.

Each of these characteristics of a long-range budgetary system is now analyzed further.

Program proposals. Most long-range budget programs involve a major monetary expenditure that will commit the organization to a specific course of action for several years into the future. Therefore, each organizational subsystem that wishes to undertake a long-range project should be required to prepare a formal proposal for the budget committee describing the project's goal (or goals), the project's estimated costs, and the project's estimated benefits. The process involved when performing a cost/benefit analysis of a project proposal will be illustrated later in the chapter. It should be emphasized at this point, however, that normally a project will not be approved by the budget committee unless its expected benefits exceed its expected costs.

The fact that a significant long-term asset investment is associated with most program proposals makes it imperative for an organization's top management to be directly involved in reviewing the proposals, and either accepting or rejecting them. Because an important top management function is to contribute toward the survival of its organization by performing long-range planning, top management's direct involvement in program proposal review is essential. The degree of top management involvement in reviewing program proposals depends upon the individual company. This chapter assumes that the type of budget committee previously discussed (i.e., a committee with representatives from top management as well as each organizational subsystem and the union) will also be responsible for reviewing long-range program proposals and deciding whether or not to implement these proposals.

Even though qualitative factors can influence the acceptance or rejection of a program proposal, each proposal prepared by a subsystem should contain as much quantifiable data as possible. The quantifiable data included within every proposal should be expressed in terms of the dollar cash costs compared with the dollar cash benefits expected from the proposal's implementation. This provides the budget committee with a common denominator (i.e., *dollars*) for comparing one project proposal with another. The individual projects that are proposed may be quite dissimilar; however, the monetary quantification of each project proposal permits comparative evaluation. Regardless of which subsystem is submitting a program proposal, the requirement for monetary quantification within the proposal normally results in the accountants from the accounting information system aiding the subsystem in gathering the monetary data for its program proposal. Figure 3-1 illustrates the program proposals submitted to the budget committee by the Alan Company's subsystems

Figure 3-1

ALAN COMPANY PROGRAM PROPOSALS
September 1983

Subsystems	Program Proposal	Estimated Years of Value from Program	Program Goals
Production	Replace some of the current sporting goods manufacturing equipment with new equipment.	5 years	To increase the efficiency of the sporting goods manufacturing process and also to increase the quality of manufactured sporting goods.
Marketing	Advertising promotion campaign on the national television networks.	6 years	To broaden the market for sporting goods equipment and thereby increase current and future years' sales.
Personnel	Educational program to allow managerial employees the opportunity of returning to college for their master's degrees.	20 years	To increase the supervisory skills of managers so that they can be more efficient and effective employees.
Accounting and Electronic Data Processing	Convert the inventory record-keeping system for sporting goods from batch processing to online, real-time processing.[a]	5 years	To provide more timely reports to management on sporting goods inventory activities and thereby increase the effectiveness of management's decision-making functions relating to the inventory system.

[a]Under the Alan Company's present batch-processing system, day-to-day inventory transactions are accumulated (i.e., batched) at week's-end and then processed by the computer in order to update the various inventory accounts. With an online, real-time processing system, however, each inventory transaction would be immediately processed through the accounts at the time the transaction occurs, thus providing management with continuous updated inventory account balance information.

during September 1983 for possible implementation as of January 1, 1984.

When the four program proposals in Figure 3-1 are submitted to the Alan Company's budget committee for review, it will be better able to compare one program with another if, as discussed above, each program's expected monetary costs and monetary benefits are available. The systematic approach for evaluating program proposals is now examined.

Evaluating program proposals and selecting programs for implementation. Because most organizations have only so much money annually that can be allocated to long-range programs, and because the total dollar cost of program proposals may exceed the maximum allocated budget expenditures, the evaluation of program proposals often results in the acceptance of certain projects and the rejection of others.

The cost/benefit analysis for each program proposal submitted to the budget committee for review should contain a comparison of the expected cash outflows (costs) with the expected cash inflows (benefits) during the estimated number of future years that the program will be of value to the organization. The benefits from a program will also include any cash outflow reductions (called cash savings) that are anticipated. For example, computerizing a company's bookkeeping procedures may cause a reduced cash outlay for clerical salaries. This expected cash savings would be one of the benefits from the proposed computer system.

The various program proposals submitted by an organization's subsystems involve *future* cash outflows and *future* cash inflows. In addition, each program's future cash flows often cover an expected time period that is of a different length than the other program proposals (see the estimated years of value from the Alan Company's four program proposals in Figure 3-1). To facilitate comparison of the costs and benefits of the program proposals having different years of future value, each proposal's annual net cash flow (a *positive* net cash flow occurs when cash inflows exceed cash outflows) should be converted to its *present value*. Because the budget committee is *presently* attempting to compare one project proposal with another, all project proposals should be based upon the present values of their net cash flows. Having each project proposal converted to its present value will provide the committee an objective basis for selecting and rejecting projects.

Present value analysis for ranking program proposals. Present value analysis is founded upon the "time value of money." For example, $1 received today has more value than $1 to be received a year from today. In the former case, you have the opportunity of immediately using the dollar acquired today for some productive purpose, or, at worst, put it in a bank and collect interest. However, if you must wait a full year to receive this dollar, you thereby lose the opportunity to use the dollar in the following 12 months.

Basically, the greater the time interval until you receive the dollar, the less valuable that dollar is today. The largest rate of return that could be earned on a dollar by having it in your possession today is called the "opportunity cost." For example, if you could earn 12 percent annually on a $1 investment, but had to wait a year to acquire this dollar, you therefore sacrifice the *opportunity* to obtain the 12 percent return this year. Assuming you can always earn a positive return on your available cash, then waiting to receive dollars in the future makes these dollars less valuable today.

The present value tables (Figures B-1 and B-2) shown in Appendix B have been mathematically derived based upon the compounding of interest. (Those readers not previously exposed to present value analysis and the mathematical logic of Figures B-1 and B-2 should read the section of Appendix B entitled "Present Value Computational Examples.") It should be noted, however, that both tables are based upon the present value of $1. Once you know the present value of $1 for some future number of years at some opportunity cost (the various interest percentages in the present value tables' columns), you can then convert this $1 present value result to any other present value dollar quantity desired.

Assume, for example, that your grandfather's will specifies that you shall receive a lump-sum payment of $5000 two years from today. If you currently had this $5000 in your possession, you estimate that an 8 percent return could be earned. Using the present value table in Figure B-1 of Appendix B (which determines the present value of a future lump-sum payment based upon your opportunity cost), this $5000 has a present value of $4285 [the present value of $1 to be received in two years at an 8 percent interest rate (the opportunity cost) = 0.857; 0.857 × $5000 = $4285]. Since the present value of $1 two years hence at an opportunity cost of 8 percent is $0.857, multiplying this $1 present value amount by $5000 gives you the desired answer. The present value table for a future lump-sum payment *assumes* that this payment does not occur until year's end (rather than during some month prior to the end of the year). If a lump-sum payment is actually to be received at a specific time other than the end of a year, the present value mathematical difference (from continuing to use the assumption of the present value table in Figure B-1) would normally be minimal.

To illustrate the use of the present value table in Figure B-2 of Appendix B, assume now that you own a small apartment building. You estimate that the net cash flow from this apartment building will be $7000 per year for the next ten years, computed as follows:

Cash receipts per year from		
rental leases		$25,000
Less: Cash disbursements per year		
for building expenses . . .		
Maintenance	$12,000	
Utilities, taxes,		
and insurance	4,000	
Repairs on building	2,000	18,000
Net cash flow per year		$ 7,000

Whenever a series of equal cash flows is anticipated for several years into the future (called an annuity) and you wish to determine the present value of these future cash flows, Figure B-2's present value table is used. This present value table *assumes* that each year's cash flow does not occur until the end of the year (which obviously is not always the case; however, the mathematical difference from this assumption compared with the assumption of uniform cash flows throughout the year is normally minimal). If your opportunity cost is estimated to be 12 percent, the ten-year, $7,000 annual net cash flow from your apartment building has a present value of $39,550 (the present value of $1 to be received annually for the next ten years at a 12 percent opportunity cost = 5.650; 5.650 × $7,000 = $39,550). Because the present value of $1 annually for the next ten years at an opportunity cost of 12 percent is $5.65, multiplying this $1 present value amount by a $7,000 annual net cash flow gives you the desired answer.

The above discussion of present value analysis has been covered in this section of the chapter because it is essential for the budget committee to know the present value of each program proposal's anticipated costs and benefits in order to review and compare adequately all the subsystem proposals. It should be kept in mind, however, that the actual computation of a program's present value is performed at the time the proposal is being prepared by an organizational subsystem. The accountants' knowledge of financial data will usually lead to their participation in a subsystem's cost/benefit analysis as well as the conversion of the results to present value. Thus, when a subsystem (with the aid of the accountant) submits its program proposal for budget committee review and eventual acceptance or rejection, the proposal's present value has already been determined.

After reviewing all the program proposals, the budget committee will then rank each proposal based upon the proposal's *excess present value index* (the ratio of the program's total anticipated net cash flow present value to the present value of the total expected cash investment required for the program). For example, the Alan Company's four program proposals in September 1983 (see Figure 3.1) would be ranked from one through four by the budget committee. The proposal with the largest excess present value index would be ranked first, the one with the next largest excess present value index would be ranked second, and so on. It should be pointed out, however, that there are other methods besides the excess present value index method for ranking program proposals (e.g., the internal rate of return method, the payback method, etc.). Because these methods are emphasized in other managerial accounting courses, they will not be discussed here.

To illustrate the ranking procedure for project proposals under the excess present value index method and the resultant decision-making process by the budget committee for accepting and rejecting current proposals, Figure 3-2 presents the rank hierarchy of the Alan Company's four subsystem program proposals in September 1983 (the dollar figures are assumed).

As Figure 3-2 discloses, the key factor that determines a program proposal's ranking is the program's excess present value index. The numerator of this index reflects the present value of the program proposal's cash benefits over its cash costs. The denominator, being the present value of the total cash asset investment, reflects the fact that for most long-range programs, dollar investments in assets are required. If a program's total cash asset investment is to be paid over a period of several years, this investment must also be converted to its present value by using present value tables. The cash asset investments for the program proposals in Figure 3-2 are already reflected at their present values because it is assumed that the cash outlays necessary for those programs selected would be made immediately. Determining each program proposal's index provides information to the budget committee regarding how much greater the present value of a program's expected future net cash flow will be compared with the present value of the program's required cash asset investment.

If the budget committee only used each proposal's net cash flow present value as the criterion for approving or rejecting programs, and thereby ignored a program's present value asset investment, misleading program rankings could result. For example, Figure 3-2 indicates that the Alan Company's program for converting its inventory system to online, real-time processing has the number one ranking. Even though the new manufacturing equipment program proposal has a greater present value for its projected annual net cash flows ($44,800) than the online, real-time inventory system proposal ($36,680), the former is less attractive than the latter because the present value of the asset investment required for the equipment ($35,000) is larger than the present value of the asset investment necessary to convert the company's inventory system to online, real-time processing (only $28,000).

The use of an excess present value index for ranking program proposals results in the highest rankings for those proposals expected to contribute most productively to the efficient use of an organization's limited asset resources. By comparing the number one and the number two ranking program proposals in Figure 3-2, it can be seen that the present value annual net cash flow of the inventory system proposal is 1.31 times greater than this proposal's present value asset investment, whereas the present value annual net cash flow of the manufacturing equipment proposal is only 1.28 times greater than the program's present value asset investment. Therefore, more efficient asset utilization is expected from the inventory system program proposal.

Assuming that the Alan Company is able to allocate a maximum of $65,000 in 1984 for implementing long-range programs, those proposals that are ranked 1 and 2 in Figure 3-2 (a total asset investment of $63,000) would be approved. The program proposals that are ranked 3 and 4 would have to be rejected based upon the $65,000 maximum budget allocation for long-range projects. For example, implementing the national television promotional campaign program (which was ranked number 3) would cause the 1984 cost of programs (totaling $69,000) to exceed the $65,000 maximum.

It should be emphasized here that the process of estimating the annual cash costs and the annual cash benefits from programs can be ex-

Figure 3-2

ALAN COMPANY'S RANKING OF PROGRAM PROPOSALS
September 1983

Ranking	Subsystem's Program Description	Total Cash Asset Investment Required	Total Present Value of Program's Projected Annual Net Cash Flow During its Estimated Years of Value (Alan Company's Opportunity Cost is assumed to be 10%)	Excess Present Value Index
1	Converting the sporting goods inventory record-keeping system from batch processing to online, real-time processing.	$28,000[a]	$36,680	1.31, or 131% $\left(\dfrac{\$36,680}{\$28,000}\right)$
2	Acquiring new sporting goods manufacturing equipment (this equipment's expected salvage value at the end of five years will be zero) to replace some of the old equipment.	$35,000	$44,800	1.28, or 128% $\left(\dfrac{\$44,800}{\$35,000}\right)$
3	Increasing the sporting goods sales market through a national television promotional campaign.	$ 6,000[b]	$ 7,500	1.25, or 125% $\left(\dfrac{\$7,500}{\$6,000}\right)$
4	Allowing managerial employees to increase their educational levels by returning to college for master's degrees.	$ 2,000[c]	$ 2,300	1.15, or 115% $\left(\dfrac{\$2,300}{\$2,000}\right)$

[a]Included within this $28,000 investment would be the costs of computer equipment (the specific equipment required for this conversion will be leased rather than purchased from the computer manufacturer) and computer programming changes, the costs of transferring the inventory data from a batch processing storage medium (for example, magnetic tape) to a storage medium better suited to online, real-time processing (e.g., magnetic disk), etc.

[b]Included within this $6,000 investment would be the costs of market research that determine the best advertising strategy to use, the costs of negotiating a marketing contract with an advertising agency, etc.

[c]Included within this $2,000 investment would be the costs of personnel subsystem managers' travel, food, and lodging to enable them to visit several college campuses and then determine which one offered the best graduate program to meet the company's needs, the costs of administering aptitude tests to the company's managerial employees as a basis for selecting those managers who will initially enter the Master's degree program, etc.

tremely difficult. The present values of the annual cash flows for the Alan Company's four programs were assumed so that the important concepts of a long-range budgetary system could be emphasized, rather than stressing the detailed procedural computations required to determine each program's annual cost/benefit relationship. In Chapter 12, which covers systems design, we will present an analysis of how a program's annual cash costs and annual cash benefits are estimated. This example will illustrate the various financial analyses that must be performed on a program proposal as a basis for the decision regarding the acceptance or rejection of the program. The specific program proposal to be examined will involve converting an organization's current manual data-processing system to a computerized data-processing system.

Two further comments are warranted here regarding the data in Figure 3-2 and the budget committee's acceptance or rejection of specific program proposals. First, the *risk* factor associated with each program proposal was ignored. Risk refers to the possibility of the expected outcome from a proposed program not occurring. The greater the uncertainty associated with an expected outcome, the greater the risk factor. Some companies attempt to compensate for this risk factor by increasing their opportunity cost percentage (thereby giving a lower present value result) on those program proposals with higher uncertainty of expected outcomes. For program proposals with less uncertainty of expected outcomes, the opportunity cost percentage can be decreased (thereby giving a higher present value result). Thus, incorporating risk factors into program proposal analyses can have a major effect on program rankings. It should be pointed out, however, that it is quite difficult to determine how much to increase or decrease a company's opportunity cost (and thereby include risk factors in long-range budgeting).

Second, the Alan Company accepted for implementation only those program proposals ranked 1 and 2 in Figure 3-2. Due to the $65,000 maximum budget allotment in 1984 for long-range programs, the proposals ranked 3 and 4 were rejected. Assume that the $65,000 maximum was established because this dollar amount represents the maximum cash the Alan Company can generate internally in 1984 for long-range programs. Rather than immediately rejecting the programs ranked 3 and 4, however, the Alan Company may investigate outside sources of cash (e.g., selling additional shares of stock, issuing bonds, etc.) to enable otherwise rejected programs to be accepted. As long as the anticipated rate of return from programs exceeds the *cost of capital* (e.g., the after-tax interest expense on bonds and the dividend payments on stock) associated with this external financing, raising additional cash from outside sources can be good financial strategy. The subject of outside cash sources for financing long-range programs can become quite complex; therefore, it was ignored in our analysis of the Alan Company's four program proposals.

The point should also be mentioned here that when the estimated years of value from program proposals differ widely, it may be necessary (for purposes of computing each program proposal's net cash flow total present value) to establish a life span that is common to all the investments being considered for implementation. To illustrate, one possible approach is to use as the time period for analysis that program proposal having the *shortest* estimated years of value. Program proposals with longer estimated years of value would be treated as if they were terminated early (i.e., at the time when the program proposal with the shortest estimated years of value is terminated). For these proposals, their expected salvage values on the early termination date are used to measure the proposals' *values* as of this termination date. In the analysis of program proposals in our text, however, we will not concern ourselves with making adjustments to individual program proposals because of differing estimated years of value for various long-range project proposals.

Periodic zero-based program review. A company's budget committee approves specific program proposals for implementation in the coming budget year because it feels that these programs will make the greatest contributions to the organization's strategic plans. By attempting to monetarily quantify program proposals' annual cash costs and annual cash benefits, converting these costs and benefits to present values, and then comparing each program proposal's total net cash flow present value with the present value of the proposal's total asset investment, the budget committee has a reasonable basis for approving or rejecting specific programs.

Periodic program review should be part of an organization's budgetary planning and controlling system. Before beginning a new budget year, all of the currently operating long-range programs should be reviewed by the budget committee to ascertain whether or not the original contemplated goal (or goals) of each program is actually being achieved. The committee may find that certain programs are deficient in accomplishing their anticipated goals. Consideration should then be given to dropping these programs and replacing them with other more productive long-range projects.

The process of periodically reviewing both new program proposals and ongoing programs before they are approved for the subsequent year is called *zero-based budgeting*. The objective of zero-based budgeting is to eliminate waste and inefficiency in an organization's budgetary system. In a nutshell, zero-based budgeting prevents a company from "wasting more dollars in the future." For illustrative purposes, assume that in 1984 the Alan Company purchased only $8,000 worth of the total $35,000 of new manufacturing equipment approved in the production subsystem's program. When the budget committee is evaluating this program's achievements during the latter months of 1984 to decide whether to continue the program into 1985 (and thereby acquire additional new manufacturing equipment), the committee may believe that the increased quality level of manufactured sporting goods (one of the program's goals shown in Figure 3-1) is not being accomplished. Rather than continuing this program into 1985 and thereby spending more dollars for new equipment, the budget

committee may decide to drop the program and not replace the present manufacturing equipment with additional new equipment. The new equipment already acquired during 1984 would continue to be used in the manufacturing process. Because of this equipment's failure to achieve its original program goals, however, no further dollar investment in additional new equipment will be made.

Zero-based budgeting means that each year when the budget committee is considering the continuation of existing programs as well as the approval of new program proposals for the subsequent year, the existing programs have no priority over new program proposals. Thus, the previously approved programs and the newly proposed programs must compete on an equal footing (in other words, at a *zero-base*) for the following year's asset resources devoted to long-range programs. A cost/benefit analysis must again be performed on every existing program to ascertain whether each one's continuation is justified. By also performing cost/benefit analyses on all the new program proposals, priorities are re-established through a ranking hierarchy of both the existing programs and the new program proposals based upon their excess present value indexes, as previously discussed. The result may be that certain newly proposed programs will emerge with higher excess present value indexes than some existing programs, causing the budget committee to phase out certain old programs and replace them with the new, more efficient ones.

A zero-based budget review is quite expensive because each ongoing program has to be re-evaluated in depth. Also, the evaluation process can have adverse behavioral effects on the particular subsystem managers whose programs are being re-evaluated because no manager typically likes to have an ongoing program dropped by the company. For these reasons, the zero-based review is often performed once every few years rather than annually. The hope of the budget committee is that no specific ongoing program will have a significant negative effect on the organization's strategic goals during the intervening years (perhaps three or four) between zero-based reviews.

SHORT-RANGE BUDGETARY SYSTEMS

In addition to program budgets which reflect long-range plans, an organization must also include within its budgetary information system short-range operational budgets for the coming year. Each organizational subsystem's short-range budget should reflect that subsystem's operational goals. Successful performance (favorable actual results compared with the budget projections) by the subsystems will result in their positive contributions to accomplishing the goals of the total system.

Both short-range and long-range budgets are important planning and controlling devices within many organizations' information systems. Because long-range program budgets reflect an organization's "plan of attack" for current and future success, these budgets normally are prepared prior to the 12-month, short-term budgets. However, when planning the detailed short-term budgets, the monetary consequences of long-range approved programs must be considered.

For example, the operation of the Alan Company's long-range program which converts its inventory system from batch processing to online, real-time processing will begin in January 1984, and is expected to have a five-year life (see Figure 3-1). During each of these five years from 1984 through 1988, when the Alan Company's short-range budgets are planned, the costs of operating the new inventory system must be incorporated into each year's annual budgets. In effect, the short-range budgetary process takes the organization's long-range programs as given and attempts to ascertain annu-

ally the monetary costs and the monetary benefits of the approved programs.

Short-range budgets are often prepared according to the functional areas of an organization. Thus, the Alan Company's annual budgetary planning system would include budgets for the sales function (by product line), the inventory and manufacturing functions (also by product line), the marketing function, the personnel function, the electronic data-processing function, and so on. Rather than emphasizing the functional approach to short-range budgeting, this book will stress a more modern technique in developing an organization's short-range budgets: the *responsibility center* approach. A responsibility center approach to budgeting is based upon the concept of a *responsibility accounting system*, which has been discussed in both Chapters 1 and 2. Under this budgetary method, each subsystem's annual budget includes only those cost and/or revenue items over which the subsystem has control (and therefore has responsibility for the monetary amounts of these items).

The concept of a responsibility center is illustrated in Figure 3-3. This schematic diagram of a responsibility center is a broad representation and can be applied to most types of organizations (manufacturing, service, or not-for-profit organizations). In a manufacturing firm, various quantities of direct raw materials, direct labor, and production overhead (indirect manufacturing items such as insurance on the factory, depreciation on the factory building and equipment, taxes associated with the factory, salaries of the factory supervisors, etc.) reflect the efforts (or inputs) put forth to create a salable product (the accomplishment or output). The specific manufacturing process represents the conversion work performed to achieve the desired outputs.

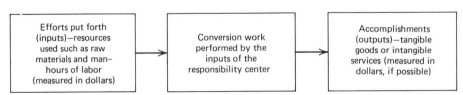

Figure 3-3. A schematic diagram of a responsibility center.

A service organization (such as a medical clinic) also uses combinations of inputs to obtain one or more outputs. For example, the principal input of a medical clinic is the *hours* of professional skill exercised by its doctors in treating patients. These hours put forth by doctors (the conversion work) should accomplish an intangible service product, the improvement of patients' health services. Both service organizations' and not-for-profit organizations' (such as a university) information systems will be discussed intensively in Chapter 16.

When utilizing a responsibility center approach in developing an organization's short-range budgetary system, the various inputs (quantities of raw materials, labor-hours, etc.) must be combined somehow to arrive at a total budget allowance for the specific responsibility center involved. It is not possible, for example, to add directly 1000 units of raw materials to 400 labor hours and arrive at any sort of common denominator to reflect the responsibility center's total short-run budgeted inputs. To arrive at a common measuring unit of a center's short-range budgeted inputs, the accounting information system will convert all of the responsibility center's dissimilar inputs to dollars of cost. The resultant total costs become a reflection of the center's resources used to achieve its specific goal (or goals).

Ideally, the outputs of a responsibility center can also be measured in dollars. For a profit-oriented organization such as a manufacturing firm or a medical clinic, the output measurement is dollars of revenue earned from providing a product or service to its clientele. The revenue function may not always represent a complete measure of output, especially in the short run. It may be quite difficult, for example, to measure the output from an organization's promotional expenditures. The additional dollars of sales revenue resulting from an advertising promotional campaign may be impossible to quantify.

The preceding discussion of responsibility centers has been of a general nature to familiarize the reader with this topic. It should be kept in mind that the major reason for using a responsibility center approach within an organization's budgetary system is to provide better managerial information regarding the planning and controlling of the annual budgets. Through a responsibility budgetary approach, each organizational responsibility center is held accountable for only those inputs and outputs it can actually cause to increase or decrease. Therefore, when actual performance varies significantly from the budget, management is able to trace this budgetary variation to the specific responsibility center accountable for the variation, and planning revisions can then begin.

Since the operating characteristics of organizations (as well as the individual subsystems within the same organization) often vary widely, there are several different types of responsibility centers that may be established. The four major types of responsibility centers are cost (or expense) centers, revenue centers, profit centers, and investment centers. Based upon a company's organizational design and the types of budgetary information desired, more than one of these responsibility center formats may be incorporated into the company's system.

Each one of these four approaches to establishing responsibility centers is now briefly discussed. In addition, we will examine the use of *divisionalized* structures within profit and investment responsibility centers.

Cost (or Expense) Centers

Cost centers are responsibility centers in which only *inputs* are measured monetarily. No attempt is made to measure a cost center's output in monetary terms. The two major types of cost centers are the *engineered cost center* and the *discretionary cost center.*

In an engineered cost center, budgetary planning and controlling are normally based upon a standard cost accounting system. Utilizing financial data accumulated by the accounting information system, standard costs are determined in advance of the cost center's business performance activities. These standards represent what the center's costs should be under conditions of operating efficiency. For example, each of the Alan Company's manufacturing components (such as basketball manufacturing, baseball manufacturing, and football manufacturing) within its production subsystem would likely be established as a separate engineered cost center for budgetary purposes. Following the budgetary planning of each center's standard costs, the accounting information system then performs budgetary control by accumulating the individual center's actual incurred costs and preparing management-by-exception reports covering significant budget variations. In the case of the Alan Company, which has an EDP subsystem, the accountants will provide actual and standard cost data for each cost center to the computer facility. The company's computer then prepares these management-by-exception reports.

However, predetermined standards of efficiency cannot be developed for a discretionary cost center. By definition, discretionary costs involve the *subjective judgment* of management. It is extremely difficult, if not impossible, to determine an "efficient" amount of these costs for a responsibility center. Therefore, from a comparison of actual costs with budget costs within the accounting information system's report covering a discretionary cost center, no measure of efficiency can be ascertained. A good example of a discretionary cost center is the research and development component found in many organizations. This operating component is often part of a company's marketing subsystem. When, for instance, the Alan Company's budget committee is attempting to determine the dollar budgetary allowance for the research and development function, there is no way to establish a standard, efficient number of dollars for research projects. Most research projects are of a long-term nature, thereby making a determination of their success or failure in any 12-month, short-term time frame very difficult. Also, even though a specific research project may appear unsuccessful, some of its findings may eventually lead to other fruitful research endeavors.

The major managerial control in a research and development discretionary cost center budget is the decisions by the budget committee regarding which research projects to undertake. Once this decision is reached (through a cost/benefit analysis of various alternative research proposals), the specific number of dollars allocated annually by the budget committee to the research and development responsibility center involves a high degree of subjectivity. Subsequent accounting information system reports comparing the actual costs with the budget costs of specific research projects are not designed to measure operating efficiency of the research and development function. Rather, these reports merely serve to inform management whether or not the actual research costs are exceeding the budget. Any requests by research personnel for additional dollar expenditures in excess of their annual budgets should require justification (based upon a cost/benefit analysis) by these employees and formal approval by the budget committee.

Revenue Centers

The use of revenue centers for budgetary planning and controlling is often found within the sales component of an organization's marketing subsystem. Revenue centers are responsibility centers in which *outputs* are measured monetarily; however, no formal procedure is established for relating revenue centers' monetary outputs to their monetary inputs (costs).

Revenue center budgets are designed to measure the performance of a company's sales component in selling products to customers. Normally, this component is part of the company's marketing subsystem. Thus, a separate revenue responsibility center should be maintained for each one of the Alan Company's product lines sold by the marketing subsystem. The revenue responsibility centers' budgets for the individual product lines are based upon each product's forecasted sales (sales forecasting will be discussed later in this chapter) during the coming 12-month period. As the budget year unfolds, the Alan Company's accounting information system will accumulate the sales data for management-by-exception computer reports of actual product line sales to budget product line sales for every revenue center. These reports will reveal favorable and/or unfavorable performances by the individual revenue responsibility centers.

Even though specific managers of each revenue center are held "responsible" for meeting their budgets, the revenue budget does have limited usefulness as a tool for evaluating a center's operating efficiency. For example, the revenue center budget of the basketball sales component within the Alan Company's marketing subsystem is derived by multiplying expected sales quantities of basketballs by the expected unit selling price of basketballs. However, many of the relevant variables (such as marketing efforts by competitors and unemployment in the economy) that affect the product line's actual sales quantity and actual selling price are beyond the control of this revenue responsibility center's sales managers. It is therefore difficult to hold these basketball sales managers completely responsible for significant variations between actual and budgeted sales of their product line. If the company's budget committee uses the responsibility budgets for the revenue centers as its basis for evaluating specific sales managers' operating performances, the committee should be aware of the many uncontrollable variables that affect the revenue centers' activities. Otherwise, the budgetary information reporting system can lead to unfair evaluations of these centers' positive or negative contributions to the Alan Company's goals.

Profit Centers

Under a profit center organizational structure, a specific responsibility center is accountable for "both sides of the ledger," which are inputs (costs or expenses) and outputs (revenues). Where feasible and practical within an organization, the use of profit centers for budgetary planning and controlling has several important advantages over the use of cost centers and revenue centers. Neither cost centers nor revenue centers by themselves measure the totality of an organizational component's performance. Cost centers are responsible only for monetary inputs with no attempt to relate these inputs to monetary outputs. At the other extreme, revenue centers are responsible for monetary outputs, but no attempt

is made to relate these outputs to monetary inputs.

For a specific organization to earn a satisfactory level of net income, the efforts put forth (inputs or expenses) must result in a greater amount of accomplishments (outputs or revenues). You should recognize this basic relationship between revenues and expenses as the accountant's income statement. When an organization's revenues exceed its expenses, we call the resultant difference *net income*. Thus, the profit center approach makes each organizational center responsible for a specified level of income performance that will contribute positively to the company's goals.

Another important advantage of profit centers is that the centers' managers are typically delegated more authority and responsibility for decision making. This causes an increased emphasis on decentralization within the organization. Because the measure of performance in a profit center is broadened to include both inputs and outputs, the profit center's managers should have decision-making authority and responsibility for their *controllable* inputs and their *controllable* outputs. To emphasize only the controllable monetary activities of a profit center when evaluating its performance, many organizations utilize a *contribution margin profit measure* (profit center's revenues minus profit center's controllable expenses, which are typically the variable expenses) for planning each center's budget. A positive contribution margin (excess of revenues over controllable expenses) indicates that the profit center is "contributing" toward covering its noncontrollable expenses (which are typically the fixed expenses). Any excess of the contribution margin over the noncontrollable expenses reflects a profit for the center. The profit center's operating efficiency is determined by comparing its actual contribution margin with its budgeted contribution margin.

Investment Centers

In those organizations for which a significant asset investment is necessary to generate income, the investment center approach may be favored over the profit center approach. Both of these organizational configurations commonly use the actual contribution margin compared with the budgeted contribution margin of each responsibility center as the key criterion in evaluating operating performance. With the profit center arrangement, however, no direct consideration is given to the dollar investment of assets that were necessary to earn a certain level of contribution margin. Under the investment center structure, a specific responsibility center's contribution margin is directly related to the assets utilized while earning this contribution margin income. Because the efficient use of assets is important to all organizations, failure to relate a responsibility center's income to its assets can cause misleading evaluations of the center's operating performance.

For example, assume that the home appliances department of a major manufacturer had contribution margin income of $20,000 in 1983 and contribution margin income of $30,000 in 1984. At first glance, it may appear that the department had a significant improvement in operating performance during this two-year period. By treating the department as a profit center, top management would be evaluating the home appliances department's two-year operating performance on the basis of these two earnings figures, resulting in a favorable evaluation of this department. On the other hand, if the home appliances department had been established as an investment center, the department's annual contribution margin during each of these two years would be directly related to its asset investment that was necessary to generate each year's contribution margin income. On further investigation, it was determined that an $80,000 asset investment existed in the home appliances department during 1983. At the beginning of 1984, however, this department acquired $70,000 worth of additional manufacturing equipment, causing its total asset investment to be $150,000. As a result of this increased asset investment, the home appliances department's return-on-capital (contribution margin income/asset investment) actually decreased from 25 percent in 1983 ($20,000 contribution margin income/$80,000 asset investment) to 20 percent in 1984 ($30,000 contribution margin income/$150,000 asset investment). The use of the investment center approach in evaluating the home appliances department's performance thus reveals a decline in the efficient use of assets in 1984 as compared with 1983.

The above illustration was oversimplified (e.g., no consideration was given to the depreciation factor relating to the home appliances department's capital assets), but it serves to demonstrate the more accurate information that can be provided to the budget committee about a department's performance when the investment center approach rather than the profit center approach is used. Increased contribution margin income by a department from one year to the next does not automatically reflect improved operating performance if this income growth is the result of a more than proportional increased asset investment.

When developing an investment center's annual budget, the projected contribution margin earnings of the center should be related to its budgeted asset investment. In most cases, this would result in a budgeted asset investment increase being accompanied by a budgeted contribution margin income increase. By then relating this budgeted income to the budgeted asset investment, a projected return-on-capital criterion can be pre-established for the investment center. The budget committee's evaluation of the investment center's operating performance would thus be based upon accounting information system reports comparing the center's actual return-on-capital with its budgeted return-on-capital.

Divisionalization of Profit and Investment Centers

Profit centers as well as investment centers are commonly used in large organizations having a structural configuration called "divisionalization." Under this structural arrangement, each center is entirely responsible for the manufacturing and marketing functions relating to its product line (or lines). General Motors Corporation is a good example of a divisionalized organizational structure. Each of its five major divisions (Chevrolet, Pontiac, Buick, Oldsmobile, and Cadillac) is treated as a separate investment center, individually responsible for the manufacturing and marketing functions relating to the division's specific automobile models.

Divisionalization has both advantages and disadvantages. On the advantage side, the large degree of decision-making authority and responsibility held by the division managers should cause these managers to have stronger motivation toward achieving their organization's goals. Also, with top management personnel at company headquarters delegating this decision-making authority and responsibility to the division, these higher-level managers will be relieved of the time-consuming, day-to-day operational decisions necessary at each division. Top management will thus be able to spend additional time on such important activities as strategic planning for the company's long-range future.

A disadvantage that can result from divisionalization is too much competition and friction among division managers. Because each division is, in effect, a separate organizational unit, it is possible for the divisions to lose sight of the fact that they are all part of one big organizational entity. Because top management at company headquarters places strong emphasis on each division's profit performance as a measure of divisional efficiency, a division's managers may become so involved in their own profitability that some of their activities actually harm other divisions' performances. This can cause overall lower accomplishments for the total organization, resulting in *suboptimization* (discussed in Chapter 1). For example, Division A of a company may have the opportunity to obtain a major manufacturing order from a customer. However, the division does not currently have machine time available within its plant to manufacture this order within the specified deadline date. Another division (Division B) of the same company may be aware of this manufacturing capacity shortage, but still might not allow Division A the temporary use of some of its idle machinery. Division A therefore loses the order, causing this division's profitability and the entire

company's profitability to be less than it could have been.

To avoid a problem of this nature, the company's top management personnel must encourage cooperation among its division managers. One possible approach to achieving cooperation among divisions is for top management to give verbal praise to a specific division that aids another division's operating performance. Also, top management should encourage a "team spirit" among all its division managers and emphasize to these managers that even though certain of their activities may not directly benefit their own divisions, the performance of the activities does contribute positively to the organization's total goals.

COMPUTERIZED BUDGET SYSTEMS

This section looks at the role played by a company's electronic data-processing subsystem in the budget process. In doing so, we will discuss some ways that the computer can be used within a budgetary information system, analyze the role of quantitative methods and the computer in budget planning, and also examine possible responsibility center designs for the electronic data-processing subsystem.

Computer's Use Within a Budgetary Information System

Up to this point in the text, we have discussed only briefly the computer's role in the budget process. For example, in the execution of budgetary control, the computer's data-processing speed capability enables it to process on a timely basis management-by-exception performance reports reflecting significant budget variations. With timely computer reports in hand, management can immediately investigate significant budget variations and initiate corrective action.

A common reaction from people with no practical experience in budgetary planning is: "Big deal! Estimating a company's future sales, planning its inventory levels to satisfy sales demands, hiring sufficient employees to handle the company's expected operating requirements, and so on, all appear to be rather straightforward.'' Actually, quite the contrary is true. Whether performing long- or short-range budgetary planning, the process tends to become very complex. This complexity is caused by the many variables that must be considered when planning an organization's budgets. To illustrate, presented below are descriptions of some of the variables that the Alan Company's budget committee must consider in performing its budgetary functions:

1. *Historical company performance*—Past historical results cannot be ignored when planning the company's future course of action because historical data often provide good insights into probable future outcomes.

2. *Internal and external variables affecting sales*—When forecasting future sales demand for the Alan Company's many sporting goods product lines, several key questions must be answered. For example, if an additional $20,000 is budgeted this year for advertising efforts associated with the company's product lines (an *internal* variable), what will be the expected increase in the current year's sporting goods sales? Or, what are the adverse effects, if any, on this year's sporting goods sales as a result of increased unemployment and inflation in the economy (*external* variables)?

3. *Asset resources of company and their allocation*—The Alan Company has only so many dollars worth of asset resources such as cash and production equipment. Budget decisions must be made regarding the most efficient use of these asset resources. For example, the manufacturing capacity of the company's present production equipment may be insufficient to produce the various quantities of sporting goods that the sales forecasts reveal can be sold in the coming year. A long-range decision must then be made by the budget committee either to purchase additional equipment that will enable increased sporting goods production or to maintain the present level of manufacturing equipment, with the result that production output to meet the projected sales forecasts will be impossible. If the latter decision is made, the budget committee must determine the optimal production mix feasible based upon the plant's available manufacturing capacity. This will likely result in the reduced production and the resultant lost sales of those product lines having the smallest *contribution margins*.

The above examples demonstrate some types of variables that must be considered in a company's budgetary planning activities. Proper consideration of these variables will normally require the analysis of large volumes of data, with many of the analyses becoming quite complex. Because of the processing slowness of a manual system, its use for analyzing budget variables would require considerable time and would likely slow down the entire budget planning process. However, the availability of a computer within a company's system could greatly facilitate the analysis of the many complex variables that are expected to affect a company's future financial projections.

For example, in planning the Alan Company's short-range budgets for 1984, historical financial data (such as cash and credit sales by product lines, cost of merchandise sold by product lines, current and acid-test ratios, etc.) for the past three years would be available on computer storage media such as magnetic tape. Assume that the accountants on the budget committee are currently preparing projected cash flow budgets (i.e., budgets showing estimated cash inflows *minus* estimated cash outflows) for each month in 1984. Important projections required for the monthly cash budgets are estimations of the average time interval to collect the accounts receivable from credit sales. To help the accountants in projecting these cash collections, they could request a computer report reflecting the company's collectibility experience during the past three years. This report may reveal that on the average, for each month's credit sales of the last three years, approximately 30 percent of the month's credit sales is collected in the actual month of sale, another 50 percent is collected in the subsequent month, 17 percent is collected in the second month following the actual sales, and the remaining 3 percent of receivables are written off as uncollectible.

The above information regarding the Alan Company's accounts receivable collectibility experience would likely be quite time-consuming to obtain under a manual data-processing system. With the use of the company's computer, however, this information can be acquired rather quickly by the accountants. The credit and collection department's managers and the accountants will then discuss the historical collectibility percentages and determine whether these percentages are reflective of the future and should thus be used in preparing the 1984 monthly cash budgets. Assuming that the decision is made to use the average collectibility percentages of the prior three years in the 1984 cash flow budgets, monthly estimations of credit sale cash collections could then be determined from multiplying the monthly projections of product line sales (based upon sales forecasts) by the collectibility percentages. These calculations would, of course, be performed by the computer and the resultant computerized cash collections schedule would be available for subsequent use in the cash budgets. Figure 3-4 reflects the Alan Company's computer printout budget projections of monthly cash collections from credit sales. (Because this projection schedule is only for illustrative purposes, the dollar amounts are assumed.)

One of the major advantages of using computers in budget planning and controlling is to answer "what if" questions. For example, assume that the cash collections from credit sales data in Figure 3-4 are incorporated into the Alan Company's monthly cash flow budgets for 1984. Following three months of operations (the end of March 1984), a management-by-exception performance report covering the sales of baseballs reveals that actual quantity sales are far in excess of budget. As a result, unless the baseball production level is increased, adequate inventories of this product line will not be available to meet newly revised estimates of future baseball sales for the remaining months of 1984. The extra demand over budget for baseballs is analyzed by the marketing managers as a short-range condition; therefore, action to acquire additional manufacturing equipment (a long-range budget decision) that will increase the plant's manufacturing capacity is rejected by the budget committee. Because the plant is currently operating at near full-capacity, an increase in baseball production will necessitate a reduction in the manufacture of one or more of the company's other sporting goods product lines. In reaching a budget revision decision, the budget committee will want answers to "what if" questions such as the following:

1. WHAT IF, for the remaining months in 1984, we increased the production of baseballs by 4000 units each month, decreased the monthly production of footballs by 1000 units and basketballs by 2000

Figure 3-4

ALAN COMPANY
Budget Projections of Monthly Cash Collections in 1984 from Credit Sales

Cash From Credit Sales	Jan.	Feb.	Mar.	Apr.	May	June	July	Aug.	Sep.	Oct.	Nov.	Dec.
30% of total credit sales for the month	$ 6,000	$ 4,500	$ 5,400	$ 4,800	$ 5,100	$ 5,700	$12,000	$11,500	$10,000	$10,500	$ 8,000	$11,000
50% of previous month's credit sales	12,000	10,000	7,500	9,000	8,000	8,500	9,500	12,000	11,500	10,000	10,500	8,000
17% of second previous month's credit sales	4,000	4,080	13,600	2,550	3,060	2,720	2,890	3,230	4,080	3,910	3,400	3,570
Total Monthly Cash Collections	$22,000	$18,580	$26,500	$16,350	$16,160	$16,920	$24,390	$26,730	$25,580	$24,410	$21,900	$22,570

units, WHAT effect would this change have on future months' cash flows?

2. WHAT IF we initiated the same budget revisions as in (1), WHAT effect would this change have on future months' operating incomes?

To answer "what if" questions such as the above will require considerable data-processing work. For example, in answering question (2) regarding future months' operating incomes, revised sales budgets and revised cost of merchandise sold budgets during each of the remaining months in 1984 will have to be prepared. Furthermore, to prepare the revised budgets for cost of merchandise sold will necessitate revised production budgets (which reflect the monthly quantities of each product line to be manufactured) and revised cost budgets for raw materials, direct labor, and production overhead.

Through the budget committee's use of the company's computer, however, those revised budgets which reveal the operating income performance changes from production-mix changes can be quickly prepared by the electronic data-processing subsystem. With the revised budget data in hand, the budget committee can then determine whether or not to institute the inventory production revisions.

Thus, to answer "what if" questions (which occur frequently within many organizations' budget systems), the speed capability of computers makes them a valuable tool for providing the budget committee with timely financial information for decisions concerning budget changes. If the financial effects from anticipated budget revisions have to be determined manually, the time interval required to provide the financial information to the budget committee will likely be so long that the committee will be unable to take immediate action on the proposed revisions. The resultant consequences will often be less operating efficiency by the company due to the time delays in initiating budget revisions.

To further explore the computer's role in a budgetary information system, we will now look briefly at a few quantitative methods and their use within a computerized system for budget planning.

Quantitative Methods and the Computer: Aids to Budget Planning

In analyzing here the role of quantitative methods and the computer in budgeting, we will examine two major phases of the budgetary planning process: (1) the sales forecasting phase, and (2) the allocation-of-resources phase. An important analytical trait common to both of these budgetary planning phases is the ability to abstract their important characteristics in a mathematical model. Such models attempt to represent "real-world" behavior through the construction of mathematical relationships. When it is possible to construct such relationships, recognized quantitative methods may then be applied to generate solutions to the forecasting and the allocation-of-resources problems at hand. At the outset, however, the temptation to oversimplify real-world complexities as a means of "fitting" known mathematical techniques to difficult problems must be avoided. The use of a sophisticated model does not necessarily guarantee "good" answers if the model has been misapplied in the first place.

The sales forecasting phase. The major difficulty in forecasting short-range as well as long-range sales demand lies in the potentially large number of *variables* (such as the unemployment rate and the level of inflation in our economy, the actions of competitors, etc.) and their degree of influence on future demand. Inaccurate judgment regarding any of the variables' influence on sales demand can lead to inaccurate forecasts.

Ideally, all the relevant variables influencing a company's sales demand should be quantified. Then, it is desirable to measure the *separate* effects of each variable on sales demand in order to forecast future demand levels (both short- and long-range) for the company. One of the most widely recognized analytical tools utilized for this purpose is the *multivariate forecasting model*, in which the "dependent" variable, sales, is presumed to be a linear function of a set of "independent" (causal) variables.

In the past, many organizations have hesitated to use mathematical models for sales forecasting because of the tedious and time-consuming nature of the calculation process. For example, performing a multivariate regression analysis "by hand" would take many hours. Furthermore, the calculation time required increases geometrically with the number of variables included in the initial, causal equation. The computer can perform such calculations in fractions of a second, making this drawback negligible.

The multivariate model, as well as other types of forecasting models, tend to provide "point" estimates of future demand (i.e., a single value of future demand) based upon "point" estimates of each of the model's independent variables. Because expectations concerning the future are uncertain (especially for such causal variables as the unemployment rate or competitors' selling prices), however, the levels of the independent variables are more likely to be predictable within some potential range of future operating activity.

Fortunately, the computer can play a major role in the sales forecasting process even when only imprecise estimates of the independent variables are known. This involves the use of simulation. By programming the computer with the sales forecasting model (regardless of the model's degree of complexity) and then inputting (by a repetitive process) various assumptions about the magnitude and causality of key variables, a company's computer can provide as many different sales forecast outcomes (based upon the differing assumptions about the independent variables) as the company desires. These various outcomes can then be reviewed by the budget committee and a determination made of which sales forecast estimate appears most realistic.

The allocation-of-resources phase. Following the sales forecasting process, any *constraints* (limitations) relating to production must then be considered in finalizing a company's sales budgets. It is a reality of business life that most organiza-

tions have asset resource constraints of some type (e.g., a limited amount of "cash"). To find a specific company with unlimited asset resources for current and future operating activities would be quite rare. Thus, another major phase of the budget planning process is the allocation of an organization's scarce resources in the most optimal manner possible. Allocating a company's limited asset resources to various activities as part of budgetary planning can be very difficult if there are several possible resource allocation alternatives.

A quantitative modeling method that is available to solve business optimizing problems is called *linear programming*. This mathematical approach to solving problems can be used when the following conditions exist:

1. the optimizing objective desired is subject to mathematical quantification of a linear form.
2. the optimizing objective desired is subject to limited resource constraints that can also be mathematically quantified.
3. the quantified limited resource constraints must all have linear relationships.

Quantitative analysis example 1 (see Appendix A) provides a simple illustration of the graphic method of linear programming in solving a company's optimal resource allocation problem. Normally, the accountants' major role in helping to solve a linear programming problem is to provide the relevant cost data that is incorporated into the mathematical relationships. For example, in deciding upon the Alan Company's optimal production mix based upon the limited manufacturing capacity of its plant, the company should attempt to emphasize the production of those product lines having the largest contribution margins. (Of course, a possible constraint on the volume manufactured of a specific product line is the market demand estimated for this product from the sales forecast. Ignoring the sales demand for a product line when planning production volume can result in stockpiles of inventory that no one will buy.) The accountants, through their company's cost accounting system, will be able to provide the budget committee with information concerning the estimated per-unit manufacturing costs of each of the company's product lines. This information can then be used to analyze the product lines' individual contribution margins. Additional information, such as the estimated time it takes to manufacture each product line, must also be provided to the budget planners in establishing their linear programming model. These time estimates will come from the production subsystem.

The linear programming example discussed in Appendix A does not involve a large number of variables and can thus be solved with "pencil and paper." However, in many budgetary planning situations where linear programming is used, the number of variables to be considered is much greater, making a manual calculation impossible. In these complex problem situations where an optimizing solution is desired, it is possible to use a "canned" computer program (a prewritten set of computer program steps) to solve the problem. The computer can be programmed with the many mathematical relationships, thereby building a linear programming mathematical model. The quantifiable decision-making data can than be inputted into the computerized linear programming model and the optimal solution to the problem can be printed out by the computer.

Responsibility Center Designs for the EDP Subsystem

The electronic data-processing facility is a service subsystem within an organization. Among its responsibilities is the provision of relevant and timely performance reports requested by the organization's other subsystems as well as top management. In designing its budgetary information system, the Alan Company must decide whether to treat the electronic data-processing subsystem as either a cost center, a profit center, or an investment center.

Under the cost center approach, the EDP subsystem would be given a dollar operating budget. The performance efficiency or inefficiency of this subsystem would then be based upon a comparison of its actual costs to provide computer services with its operating cost budget.

On the other hand, establishing the EDP subsystem as a profit center or an investment center would require that the subsystem actually generate an income from its internal service providing activities. In addition to including estimated operating costs within its budget, an estimated dollar amount of revenues would be budgeted for the computer facility. The revenues earned by the EDP subsystem would result from this subsystem charging its users (the other subsystems and top management) for the computer time required to process report data. This internal billing rate of the EDP subsystem is called a *transfer price*. Since the computer services are being requested internally by managerial employees within the same organization, no actual dollars change hands when using the transfer price mechanism. Charging for services according to a specific transfer price is solely a budgeting procedure.

For example, if the Alan Company's marketing subsystem requests a computerized report of the week's sales by product lines and sales personnel, the transfer price charged for this report would be reflected as earned revenue for the EDP subsystem and would be shown as an operating cost of the marketing subsystem. This "revenue" of the EDP subsystem and this "cost" of the marketing subsystem would be included within these subsystems' other actual operating activities when performance reports comparing actual with budget results are prepared to analyze each subsystem's operational efficiency or inefficiency.

A major advantage of both the profit center and the investment center approaches to budgetary design is that either one can lead to increased organizational efficiency by eliminating unnecessary and irrelevant report processing requests by other subsystems. For example, if the Alan Company elected to establish its EDP subsystem as a cost center, the company's production subsystem may be continually requesting computerized reports, many of which have little or no value to the subsystem's efficient and effective manufacturing performance. Since the user (in this case, the production subsystem) receives these reports "free of charge" when the EDP subsystem is treated as a cost center, it may ask for many more reports than are necessary. (If you can get something for nothing, why not?) However, by organizing the EDP subsystem as a profit or investment center, the production subsystem would now be charged for a processed report, causing it to think twice about, and thus be more selective in, requesting reports. In actual practice, many companies have found that converting their EDP subsystems from cost centers to profit or investment centers has drastically reduced the flow of reports through their systems. The end result has been the elimination of many reports that were unnecessary in the first place.

Organizing the EDP subsystem as a profit or investment center should *cause* the company's managers to thoroughly assess their *needs* for decision-making information before they request a processed report from the computer facility. Of course, there is always the risk that if a subsystem's actual costs are already approaching its pre-established budget, the subsystem manager, fearful of exceeding the budget, may not request a specific computer processed report which is actually needed for a decision. This situation could obviously lead to poor managerial decisions and thereby cause organizational inefficiency.

A possible way to solve this problem is through *flexibility* within a company's budgetary system. For example, assume that the Alan Company's basketball manufacturing component of its production subsystem has already incurred, by the third week of June 1984, actual operating costs that are approaching the entire month's budget allocation. Therefore, to enable the basketball component to avoid a significant unfavorable budget variation by month-end, its manager may stop requesting necessary reports from the computer facility. Rather than doing this, however, the manager of the basketball component should attempt to justify to the budget committee the necessity for an increase in the June operating budget. Assuming the budget committee approves this budget increase, the manager can

then request the needed reports from the computer facility without worrying about exceeding his or her budget.

Another serious problem that can occur from treating the EDP subsystem as a profit or investment center rather than a cost center is friction between the EDP manager and the specific user regarding a *fair* and *equitable* transfer price. For example, based upon the anticipated computer time to process a personnel subsystem report, the Alan Company's EDP manager may believe that a $300 transfer price is a fair and equitable charge for this report. However, the personnel subsystem manager views the $300 as unreasonable and is willing to be charged only $200 on his or her budget for the processed report. This difference of opinion between the EDP and personnel managers regarding a fair and equitable transfer price for computer services can thus cause serious friction between these two managers. Disputes of this nature between subsystem managers can reduce the operating effectiveness of the entire organization.

An approach for solving the dispute among the EDP and personnel managers as to a fair and equitable transfer price is to use a *market-based* transfer price for the computerized report requested by the subsystem manager. This market-based transfer price could be determined by obtaining an estimate of how much it would cost to have the report processed outside of the Alan Company (i.e., in the "marketplace") by a *service bureau* (an organization that sells computer time for report processing to other companies; service bureaus will be analyzed in later chapters). The price estimate obtained from the service bureau for processing the personnel subsystem's report would be used as the transfer price charged by the Alan Company's EDP subsystem for internally processing this report. Both the EDP manager and the personnel manager should consider this market-based transfer price as fair and equitable.

CONCLUDING COMMENTS ON BUDGETARY INFORMATION SYSTEMS

This chapter has emphasized the role of budget systems in an organization's information system.

The accountant's valuable contribution to budgetary information systems has been stressed throughout the discussion.

The topic of budget systems has been given this intensive coverage because of its extreme importance in successful organizational information systems. In fact, budgetary systems are the focal point of many organizations' entire information systems. Through an efficient and effective budget system which includes both long-range and short-range budgets, an organization is able to obtain a fairly accurate picture of what it can expect to take place in the future. Budgets provide a "road map" of the future which guides the organization's long-run survival. Any significant deviations from the "planned route" will be reported to the organization's management for investigation and subsequent action.

Budgeting systems allow "management by logical planning and controlling." Without budgetary information systems, the consequences may be "management by crises." Lack of budgets may mean that a company's management does not know if operations are heading in the right direction until it is possibly too late for corrective action. Imagine yourself beginning a cross-country trip with no formal plans regarding your ultimate destination. You may end up in the right place, but on the other hand, you may not!

SUMMARY

The strong financial emphasis within budgets means that accountants have an important role in the development, implementation, and control of their organization's budgetary system. An efficient and effective budget system requires good communication among all the organizational subsystems, that employees from all the organizational subsystems participate in the budgetary planning process, and that flexibility be built into the budgetary system so that environmental changes during the budget year can be reflected through revised budgets.

An organization's long-range and short-range budgets enable management to plan and control its future operations. The focal point of long-range budgets is individual financial programs

which extend several years into the future, whereas short-range budgets are financial projections for the coming 12-month period, and the focal point of these budgets is often based upon an organization's responsibility centers.

A firm's long-range budgetary system includes various subsystem programs that extend for several years into the future. Each subsystem program proposal for budget committee review should include the anticipated goal (or goals) of the program and the estimated life of the program. To enable the budget committee's comparison and subsequent ranking of all subsystem proposals, every program proposal should include a cost/benefit analysis of the proposal's anticipated cash costs and anticipated cash benefits. The costs and benefits relating to programs concern long-range future financial events. Therefore, to provide the budget committee with better information when evaluating the proposals, all anticipated costs and anticipated benefits of each program should be converted to their present values (based upon the company's opportunity cost). By then relating each program proposal's total projected net cash flow present value to the present value of the total expected cash investment required for the program, an excess present value index can be determined for every program proposal. Ranking all the program proposals based upon these indexes will provide the budget committee with a reasonable criterion for approving or rejecting specific programs.

The four principal responsibility center configurations for short-range budgetary purposes are cost or expense centers (only *inputs* are measured monetarily), revenue centers (*outputs* are measured monetarily with no attempt to relate the monetary inputs to the monetary outputs), profit centers (both *inputs* and *outputs* are measured monetarily and related to one another to enable a measurement of these centers' income performances), and investment centers (same as profit centers except that a center's income performance is related to its required asset investment to generate earned income). Large organizations having a divisionalized structure often use either a profit center or an investment center responsibility arrangement for budget planning and controlling purposes. In those divisionalized organizations where major asset investments are necessary for the individual centers to earn an income (as in an automobile manufacturing firm), the investment responsibility center approach will typically provide a better measure of the centers' operating performances than the profit responsibility center approach.

The computer's speed capability in processing data makes it an important tool to aid a company's budgetary planning and controlling activities. For example, when contemplating budget revisions, a considerable amount of computational work is normally required to analyze the effects of the proposed revisions on the company's future operating performance. Under a manual data-processing system, a lengthy period of time will likely be necessary to perform this computational work. With a computerized data-processing system, however, proposed budget revisions and their resultant effects on future company financial performance can be processed quickly. The computer's processing speed thus enables timely budget revision reports to be available to the budget committee as a basis for its decision regarding whether or not to implement proposed budget changes.

Because of the many variables that affect an organization's budgetary planning, this aspect of budgeting is often quite complex. Budget planning includes two major phases: the forecasting phase and the allocation-of-resources phase. In both these budgetary activities, mathematical models can be developed to aid the budget committee's planning functions. The degree of sophistication that characterizes many mathematical planning models makes the computer an indispensable tool of the budgetary planners. Using sales forecasting models and linear programming models for budget planning offers the potential for significantly increasing the efficiency and effectiveness of an organization's budgetary planning process.

In companies having an EDP subsystem, a managerial budget decision must be made to establish this subsystem as either a cost center, a profit center, or an investment center. The profit or investment center designs are often favored because either one can contribute to increased organizational efficiency. Under the profit or investment center responsibility design, the EDP subsystem has the opportunity to generate an income because it charges users a transfer price for processing report data. Because this transfer price mechanism results in users being charged for data-processing services, they will likely assess their needs for information prior to requesting computerized reports.

DISCUSSION QUESTIONS

3-1. Discuss the advantages, if any, of having a computerized information system for processing budget performance reports.

3-2. Discuss some of the important items that should be included in a subsystem program proposal. For each of these named items, indicate *why* you think it is important.

3-3. The Novelty Toy Company has a manual data-processing system. Increased sales volume in the past few years has led to a significant increase in its accounts receivable transactions from credit sales, a significant increase in its inventory of various toys to meet sales demand, and a significant increase in new employees. The toy company's top management is currently reviewing an accounting subsystem program proposal that recommends the conversion of the accounts receivable, sales, inventory, and payroll processing functions from the present manual system to a computerized data-processing system (using batch processing).

In the cost/benefit analysis accompanying this program proposal, what do you think would be some of the quantitative monetary benefits?

3-4. This chapter discussed three important principles of good budgeting: communication, participation, and flexibility. If you were limited to including only one of these principles in your organization's budgetary system, which of the three would you choose? Why?

3-5. In developing the long-range and short-range budgets for a retail store which sells stereo equipment, records, television sets, and radios, what types of information would you need about the store's internal and external environment? Be specific in describing this information.

3-6. Give some specific examples of *constraints* that may prevent a company that manufactures automobile tires from selling a specified number of tires during the year.

3-7. Why should an organization attempt to analyze its long-range future outlook before making a major capital expenditure?

3-8. This chapter emphasized that one effective way of motivating people to have a positive attitude toward their organization's budgetary system is through participation. Can you think of additional ways that might motivate people to respond favorably to a budgetary system? Discuss.

3-9. Why is it important to have realistic budgets within an organization's budgetary system?

3-10. Give arguments for either agreeing or disagreeing with the following statement: "Flexibility of budgets allows an organizational subsystem to change its original budget projection whenever actual operating results vary significantly from the subsystem's predetermined budget. As a result, the subsystem's actual performance will always appear fairly close to its budget."

3-11. One of your best friends (who possesses very little knowledge of accounting) has recently been promoted to a top management position at an advertising agency. An important function that this person will now perform is reviewing program proposals for various promotional campaigns to benefit the agency's clients. How would you (as a knowledgeable accountant) explain in simple terms to your friend the importance of using "excess present value indexes" when evaluating various program proposals?

3-12. Periodic program review should be part of an organization's long-range budgetary system. Would you consider this review process a

planning function or a *controlling* function? Explain.

3-13. What do you feel are some of the inefficiencies, if any, that could occur within an organization's long-range budgetary system if "zero-based budgeting" did not exist?

3-14. The Gutter Ball Bowling Company manufactures all types of bowling equipment (balls, shoes, etc.). For the first time in the company's ten-year operating history, its management has decided to incorporate a budgetary system for planning and controlling. The company's treasurer believes that the detailed short-range budgets for the coming year should be prepared prior to the five-year, long-range budget projections because the former are easier to plan than the latter. Do you agree with the treasurer? Why?

3-15. Discuss some of the important similarities and differences between short-range and long-range budgeting.

3-16. What is the *responsibility center* approach to short-range budgeting? Discuss the similarities and differences among the four major types of budgetary responsibility centers analyzed in this chapter.

3-17. Steve Miller, marketing manager of the Priced Right Pill Company, recently made the following comments to the company treasurer: "With our company's recent policy of cost efficiency, it seems to me that we could save a great deal of money by eliminating the budget committee. The subsystem managers on this committee spend hours working on the budgets and they never seem to agree on anything! Meanwhile, these managers are continuing to receive their large salaries while they waste time sitting around talking about the coming year's budgets. I feel that our company's budgetary planning for each year would be much more effective as well as less costly if every subsystem submitted its own budget directly to you for approval."

What are your reactions to Steve Miller's comments?

3-18. Traditional short-range budgeting is based upon functional areas of a company, whereas a more modern approach to short-range budgeting is to structure the annual budgets according to responsibility centers. If you were the coordinator of your company's budget system, which of these structural configurations for the company's short-range budgetary system would you favor? Why?

3-19. Because earned revenues are one of the key variables that affect the annual profit of an organization, is there any difference between the revenue center budgetary approach and the profit center budgetary approach to establishing an organization's responsibility centers? Explain.

3-20. Discuss some of the advantages and disadvantages of a *divisionalized* organizational structure. Try to think of some real-life organizations (other than the one discussed in this chapter) that probably would have a divisionalized structure.

3-21. What are the differences, if any, between an engineered cost center and a discretionary cost center? Is it possible to have both of these cost center structures within the same organizational subsystem? If your answer to the previous question was "yes," try to think of an example where both engineered and discretionary cost centers might exist within a specific subsystem.

3-22. The Portwood Brain Power Company is a management consulting firm with offices in several major cities. The managers of each office have been complaining continually to top management about their limited decision-making authority and responsibility under the company's present revenue center budgetary organizational structure. After considerable thought, top management has finally agreed to change the responsibility center arrangement of the individual offices so that each one will have decision-making authority and responsibility for both its controllable inputs and its controllable outputs.

Assuming that you are a member of the Portwood Brain Power Company's top management staff, what type of responsibility center structure would you recommend for the consulting firm's individual offices? Justify your recommendation.

3-23. The Sink-Free Ship Building Corporation manufactures and sells recreational boats as well as all types of boating supplies (maps, compasses, CB radios, etc.). In the past few years, the corporation's boat sales have increased at a higher percentage than those of its competitors.

The corporation's planners are currently accumulating the relevant data for the long- and short-range budgets. Discuss some of the key variables that should be considered in developing the Sink-Free Ship Building Corporation's long- and short-range budgetary systems. Also, include in your discussion the complexities that would affect your analysis of each of these key variables.

3-24. What advantages might the investment center approach offer over the profit center approach in establishing an organization's responsibility center budgetary system?

3-25. The Kurtiss Kandy Kompany (more popularly known as the 3 K's) recently installed a computer facility to process timely reports needed by its accounting, marketing, and production subsystems. The company's management has elected to establish its computer facility as a cost center for budgetary planning and controlling purposes. Each month the computer facility is allocated a fixed number of dollars with which to operate. At month-end, a performance report is prepared which analyzes the actual costs compared with the budgeted costs of the computer facility.

The Kurtiss Kandy Kompany's budget committee is confused regarding the causes of a recurring problem that arises during the latter part of every month. Beginning in either the third or fourth week of the month, complaints start coming in from the company's subsystem managers about the refusal of the computer facility to process certain reports. Typically, these complaints do not occur in either the first or second week of the month.

As a member of the company's budget committee, what do you think is the cause (or causes) of this problem among the computer facility and the other subsystems? What recommendations would you make to solve the problem?

3-26. Which type of budgetary responsibility center (a cost center, a revenue center, a profit center, or an investment center) do you feel should be used for a company's EDP subsystem? Why?

3-27. During its consideration of budget revisions, a company's budget committee will often want answers to "what if" questions. Describe (with some specific examples) what is meant by "what if" questions and discuss how an organization's computer can help to answer these questions.

3-28. The Modern Clothing Store manufactures and sells evening apparel for women. Its management recently installed a batch processing computerized data-processing system. This mechanized system enables the company to acquire more current information about clothing inventory balances, and to increase the timeliness of the billing function (a majority of the company's clothing sales result from customers using their credit cards), thereby speeding up the cash collection process from credit sales.

The clothing store's computer facility was established as a profit center, whereby a transfer price was charged to each subsystem which requested a computerized report. Linda Moss, president of the Modern Clothing Store, felt that one of the major advantages of establishing the company's computer facility as a profit center would be the increased monthly income that the store would earn as a result of the computer facility earning an income on its data-processing services to other subsystems. By adding the computer subsystem's monthly income to the income from clothing sales, she logically concluded that the company's profits would be higher.

As a knowledgeable accountant, how would you explain to Linda the fallacy in her thinking?

3-29. What is meant by "the allocation-of-resources phase" of budgetary planning? Are there any similarities between "the sales forecasting phase" and "the allocation-of-resources phase" of budgetary planning? Discuss.

3-30. Discuss some of the possible ways that an organization's computer facility can aid the budgetary planning process.

3-31. The Big Bun Hamburger is a fast-food restaurant chain located throughout the East. The company's budget committee is currently attempting to put together the 1984 sales budget for the entire chain of restaurants.

Each of the individual restaurants is established as a profit center. The only cost responsibility that is excluded from each restaurant's profit budget is the marketing function. Marketing activities for all the restaurants are centralized at the Big Bun Hamburger's main office in Chicago.

Assume that you are an employee of the company's marketing subsystem and are responsible for developing a forecast of 1984 anticipated sales for the total chain. Your forecast will then be turned over to the budget committee for review and either acceptance or rejection. Discuss some of the variables that you would consider when developing the 1984 sales forecast. Indicate how a change in each of these variables could have either a positive or a negative effect on sales. (*Note:* Make any reasonable assumptions that you think necessary regarding the external and the internal environmental factors which affect the Big Bun Hamburger restaurant chain.)

PROBLEMS

3-32. The Buffalo Blades (a professional baseball team) has experienced a serious reduction in ticket sales during the past few seasons. As a result of this decline in attendance, top management is currently considering several long-range program proposals that hopefully would lead to increased future ticket sales.

Presented below are the program proposals that have been submitted for top management review. Any approved programs will be implemented January 1, 1984. Assume that the present time period during which these proposals are being reviewed is September 1983.

Proposal 1. Acquire Harvey Goldman (last year's top home run hitter in professional baseball) from the Detroit Devils. An $80,000 cash payment would have to be made immediately to Detroit for Goldman's contract. Goldman would then be signed to a five-year contract with the Buffalo Blades at an annual salary of $150,000. By having a top star of Goldman's caliber playing baseball with Buffalo, management estimates that ticket sales will be approximately $175,000 greater next year, and will decrease by $10,000 a year over the following four years. Harvey is expected to retire at the close of the 1988 baseball season.

Proposal 2. Institute a three-year marketing campaign in Buffalo and surrounding cities within 100 miles of Buffalo. This promotional campaign will include advertising announcements on television, radio, and newspapers with the intent of stimulating public interest in attending Buffalo baseball games. The initial cash investment necessary to begin this promotional campaign will be $30,000. The annual cash operating costs of the advertising program are estimated to be $40,000 for each of the program's three years (1984, 1985, and 1986). Also, the increase in ticket sales resulting from this promotional program is anticipated to be as follows during the next three years:

1984	$50,000
1985	$60,000
1986	$64,000

Proposal 3. Construct a modern restaurant within the baseball stadium grounds. This restaurant would be situated so that people could enjoy a meal while watching the action on the baseball field. A $100,000 initial cash investment would be required to purchase the necessary equipment associated with the restaurant. As a public gesture to help the baseball franchise survive, a local Buffalo construction company has offered to build the restaurant structure at no cost to the Blades. It is anticipated that the restaurant's equipment will have a six-year useful life and a $10,000 salvage value at the end of this time period. Annual depreciation on this equipment will be $15,000. Also, the annual net cash flow (excess of annual cash receipts over annual cash disbursements) expected from the restaurant's operations during the six years from 1984 through 1989 is $16,000. Management believes that the added attraction of having a modern restaurant at the baseball stadium will result in approximately $9,000 additional ticket sales in each of the next six years.

Problem Requirements

Assume that a maximum of $135,000 is allocated for long-range project expenditures during 1984 and that the Buffalo Blades' opportunity cost is 10 percent. Ignoring income tax considerations, perform the necessary analyses on the three program proposals to enable top management's determination of which projects to approve and which to reject in 1984. Based upon your analyses, which program proposal (or proposals), if any, should be implemented by top management?

3-33. The Gercken Corporation sells computer services to its clients. The company completed a feasibility study and decided to obtain an additional computer on January 1, 1984. Information regarding the new computer follows.

1. The purchase price of the computer is $230,000. Maintenance, property taxes, and insurance will be $20,000 per year. If the computer is rented, the annual rent will be $85,000 plus 5 percent of annual billings. The rental price includes maintenance.

2. Due to competitive conditions, the company feels it will be necessary to replace the computer at the end of three years with one that is larger and more advanced. It is estimated that the computer will have a resale value of $110,000 at the end of the three years. The computer will be depreciated on a straight-line basis for both financial reporting and income tax purposes.

3. The income tax rate is 50 percent.

4. The estimated annual billing for the services of the new computer will be $220,000 during the first

year and $260,000 during each of the second and third years. The estimated annual expense of operating the computer is $80,000, in addition to the expenses mentioned above. An additional $10,000 of start-up expenses will be incurred during the first year.

5. If it decides to purchase the computer, the company will pay cash. If the computer is rented, the $230,000 can be otherwise invested at a 15 percent rate of return.

6. If the computer is purchased, the amount of the investment recovered during each of the three years can be reinvested immediately at a 15 percent rate of return. Each year's recovery of investment in the computer will have been reinvested for an average of six months by the end of the year.

7. The present value of $1 due at a constant rate during each year at a 15 percent opportunity cost is:

Year	Present Value
0–1	$.93
1–2	$.80
2–3	$.69

The present value of $1 due at the end of each year at a 15 percent opportunity cost is:

End of Year	Present Value
1	$.87
2	$.76
3	$.66

Problem Requirements

A. Prepare a schedule comparing the estimated annual income from the new computer under the purchase plan and under the rental plan. The comparison should include a provision for the opportunity cost of the average investment in the computer during each year.

B. Prepare a schedule showing the estimated annual cash flows under the purchase plan and under the rental plan.

C. Prepare a schedule comparing the net present values of the cash flows under the purchase plan and under the rental plan.

D. Comment on the results obtained in parts A and C. How should the computer be financed? Why?

(AICPA Adapted)

3-34. The electronic data-processing subsystem of the Williams Mattress Corporation was initially established January 1, 1983 as a profit center for budgetary planning and controlling purposes. The total asset investment necessary to begin operations within the corporation's computer center was $400,000. Presented below is this subsystem's summarized budget and actual results for the calendar year 1983.

	Budget	Actual
Transfer price revenues earned	$300,000	$315,000
Expenses:		
Controllable fixed and variable expenses	180,000	175,000
Noncontrollable fixed and variable expenses	70,000	73,000

At the beginning of 1984, the Williams Mattress Corporation purchased $100,000 worth of additional hardware equipment for its computer center. As of December 31, 1984, the corporation's summarized budget and actual operating data appear as follows:

	Budget	Actual
Transfer price revenues earned	$370,000	$415,000
Expenses:		
Controllable fixed and variable expenses	240,000	250,000
Noncontrollable fixed and variable expenses	80,000	82,000

In evaluating the operating performance of the computer center during 1983 and 1984, management used a contribution margin profit measure. Discussions are currently taking place within the corporation's budget committee to change the responsibility structure of the electronic data-processing subsystem from a profit center to an investment center. Should this change be approved, the income measure used to evaluate the performance of the computer center will continue to be the subsystem's contribution margin.

Problem Requirements (see Note below)

A. Under the present responsibility center structure of the computer center, evaluate quantitatively the subsystem's operating performance during 1983 and during 1984. Do you feel that the electronic data processing subsystem's operating performance improved in 1984 compared with 1983? Explain quantitatively.

B. Assuming that the computer center had originally been established as an investment center rather than a profit center on January 1, 1983, repeat the same quantitative analysis as in (A). In performing your analysis here, further assume that the $400,000 capital expenditure in 1983 and the $100,000 capital expenditure in 1984 were the actual amounts budgeted for these expenditures in each of the two years.

C. If you were a member of the Williams Mattress Corporation's budget committee, would you recommend the continuance of the profit center structure for the computer center or the conversion of this subsystem's organizational structure to an investment center? Explain.

NOTE: When analyzing each problem requirement, ignore the depreciation associated with the assets of the computer center.

3-35. NOTE TO INSTRUCTOR: This problem should be assigned only if quantitative analysis example 1 on linear programming (see Appendix A) is covered in the course.

The Spotless Carpet Company manufactures and sells two types of vacuum cleaners, upright and cannister. The company's budget committee is currently involved in evaluating the marketing and production subsystems' short-range budget projections for the calendar year beginning January 1, 1984.

The sales forecasts from the marketing subsystem show that the maximum number of upright vacuum cleaners and cannister vacuum cleaners that can be sold during 1984 is approximately 100,000 and 200,000, respectively. These demand estimates are based upon a $150 selling price for each upright vacuum cleaner and a $100 selling price for each cannister vacuum cleaner.

The production subsystem manager reports that the capacity level of the plant for manufacturing vacuum cleaners during 1984 is 120,000 hours. The manager of this subsystem also indicates that the standard production time for an upright vacuum cleaner is 1 hour and the standard production time for a cannister vacuum cleaner is 30 minutes.

The company's managerial accountant, after studying the production process for vacuum cleaners, estimates the standard variable manufacturing costs to be $120 for each upright and $75 for each cannister. The total standard fixed costs for operating the production plant during 1984 are estimated to be $150,000.

Problem Requirement

Using linear programming (the graphic approach), determine the optimal mix of upright and cannister vacuum cleaners that should be manufactured by the Spotless Carpet Company's production subsystem during the 1984 budget year.

3-36. NOTE TO INSTRUCTOR: This problem should be assigned only if quantitative analysis example 1 on linear programming (see Appendix A) is covered in the course.

Excelsion Corporation manufactures and sells two kinds of containers—paperboard and plastic. The company produced and sold 100,000 paperboard containers and 75,000 plastic containers during the month of April. A total of 4,000 and 6,000 direct labor hours were used in producing the paperboard and plastic containers respectively.

The company has not been able to maintain an inventory of either product, due to the high demand. This situation is expected to continue in the future. Workers can be shifted from the production of paperboard to plastic containers and vice versa, but additional labor is not available in the community. In addition, there will be a shortage of plastic material used in the manufacture of the plastic container in the coming months due to a labor strike at the facilities of a key supplier. Management has estimated there will be only enough raw material to produce 60,000 plastic containers during June.

The income statement for Excelsion Corporation for the month of April is shown below. The costs presented in the statement are representative of prior periods and are expected to continue at the same rates or levels in the future.

Excelsion Corporation
Income Statement
For the month ended April 30, 1984

	Paperboard Containers	Plastic Containers
Sales	$220,800	$222,900
Less: Returns and allowances	$ 6,360	$ 7,200
Discounts	2,440	3,450
	$ 8,800	$ 10,650
Net sales	$212,000	$212,250
Cost of sales		
Raw material cost	$123,000	$120,750
Direct labor	26,000	28,500
Indirect labor (variable with direct labor hours)	4,000	4,500
Depreciation— machinery	14,000	12,250
Depreciation— building	10,000	10,000
Cost of sales	$177,000	$176,000
Gross profit	$ 35,000	$ 36,250
Selling and general expenses		
General expenses—variable	$ 8,000	$ 7,500
General expenses—fixed	1,000	1,000
Commissions	11,000	15,750
Total operating expenses	$ 20,000	$ 24,250

	Paperboard	Plastic
Income before tax	$ 15,000	$ 12,000
Income taxes (40%)	6,000	4,800
Net income	$ 9,000	$ 7,200

Problem Requirements

A. The management of Excelsion Corporation plans to use linear programming to determine the optimal mix of paperboard and plastic containers for the month of June to achieve maximum profits. Using data presented in the April income statement, formulate and label the
   1. objective function.
   2. constraint functions.
B. Identify the underlying assumptions of linear programming.
C. What contribution would the management accountant normally make to a team established to develop the linear programming model and apply it to a decision problem?

(CMA Adapted)

CASE ANALYSES

3-37. *Prinse and Frogg**

As Harry Hudson, president of the Hudson Company, started the drive from his suburban home to the plant, he was particularly pleased with the beautiful day and his golf score the day before. He thought happily that things were going smoothly at the plant, especially since they had hired a new budget director, L. P. Frogg, who had a degree from a graduate school of business and several years of heavy experience with a major CPA firm.

As he entered his office, his secretary was obviously trying to answer an emotional voice on the telephone, "But Mr. Hudson has not come in yet—no, here he is now." When Mr. Hudson picked up the telephone on his desk, the voice, although somewhat subdued now, stated, "Mr. Hudson, this is Prinse. That darn young budget director has stirred up a hornet's nest. Bolen just

*Contributed by Dr. Doris Cook, Professor of Accounting, University of Arkansas.

left my office and has threatened to quit if Frogg doesn't get off his back!''

"But Frogg has done an excellent job in the short time he has been here. He has that department well organized, the budget was ready on schedule for the first time, and the recent performance reports indicate that our costs are closer to budget than they have ever been. What is the problem?'' replied Mr. Hudson.

Mr. Prinse, by now becoming more calm, answered: "He's always putting the pressure on the managers to cut costs, and to increase production efficiency. No wonder our costs are closer to the budget than they have ever been before. Yesterday he went down to Bolen's division and reminded him again of his recent unfavorable cost variances and productive efficiency index. That's when Bolen blew his top.

"Last week when Bolen received his monthly performance report with all the red figures showing his costs had exceeded the budget, he came to see me and asked why he didn't get a chance to explain the variances before they were sent all the way to the president in the performance reports. He feels the reports should show the reasons. Last month was a particularly bad month for him because two of his key men had quit and he had to replace them with inexperienced men. In the preceding three months his division had an excellent record, but he said nobody seemed to remember that.

"Another complaint Bolen made was that his production quota was too high. He said that if Frogg knows so much about production efficiency, then let him run the division. In my opinion, if you ever want to discourage a man, just give him a budget he can't meet.''

Mr. Hudson was finally able to assure Mr. Prinse that he would call a meeting of the budget committee after he had talked to the controller, Mr. Campbell, and Frogg. The meeting would be devoted to budget procedures, policies, and responsibilities.

After listening to Mr. Hudson, Campbell remarked that he had complete confidence in Frogg and that it was his understanding that Frogg had gone to Bolen's office to discuss improvements in budget procedures with a view to making them more responsive to the needs of each department. "We all know (even Frogg knows now) that Bolen has a low flash point!''

Mr. Hudson answered, "I hope that you can talk to Frogg and find out what the problem is. He appears to me to be one of the most capable men that we have employed recently and I certainly want to keep him. The two of you come in to see me in the morning and we'll try to solve this problem and also discuss the meeting I mentioned to Prinse.''

The principal characters in this situation are shown on the organization chart below.

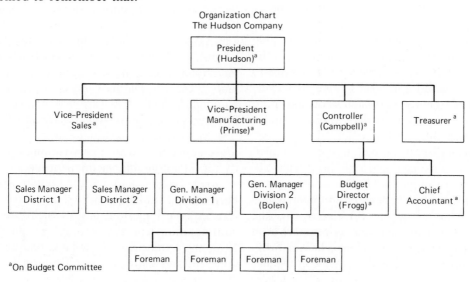

Organization Chart
The Hudson Company

President (Hudson)[a]

Vice-President Sales[a]

Vice-President Manufacturing (Prinse)[a]

Controller (Campbell)[a]

Treasurer[a]

Sales Manager District 1

Sales Manager District 2

Gen. Manager Division 1

Gen. Manager Division 2 (Bolen)

Budget Director (Frogg)[a]

Chief Accountant[a]

Foreman   Foreman   Foreman   Foreman

[a]On Budget Committee

Questions

1. What are the fundamental issues involved in this situation?
2. If you were Mr. Campbell, what would be (a) your response to Mr. Hudson the next morning concerning the Bolen-Frogg incident, and (b) your suggestions concerning the upcoming meeting?

3-38. *Forecasting Automobile Demand*

Mr. Ted Salsberg is a marketing vice-president with the National Vehicles Corporation. He has served with the company for 17 years, beginning his career as an assembly line supervisor, and then gradually working his way up through the company ranks in marketing, production, and corporate finance. For the last three years, Mr. Salsberg had been assigned the task of forecasting future private automobile sales for the purpose of making detailed marketing and production decisions. No task had ever given him more headaches. Projections of the future were inevitably risky and consumers had been especially erratic of late in the purchase of what was becoming a very expensive durable good.

The history of automotive production in the last few years had been very unusual. More and more safety items such as seat belts and shock-absorbing bumper equipment were required by law, and emission control standards also required the production of increasingly sophisticated smog-control devices. These requirements also resulted in raising the production cost of the average automobile, and had been responsible for National's three biggest price increases in the last five years. Because consumers' reactions to higher prices varied from year to year, however, the effects of tighter safety standards and more stringent emission controls upon future automotive sales were difficult to predict.

Other factors besides production costs tended to affect the consumer price of the typical automobile. For example, of late, the company had experimented with a rebate program in which new owners were given certificates by the dealers. These certificates were redeemable from the manufacturer for $250, $300, $400, or $500, depending upon the particular car the consumer

had purchased. Results of the program were mixed. In some areas of the country, the rebate program had spurred large increases in automotive purchases; in others, the increases had been negligible.

Because automobiles were "big ticket" items, Mr. Salsberg knew that consumer income also played an important role in the decision to purchase a new vehicle. At the present time, the national economy was in a moderate upswing and consumer personal disposable income had been climbing slightly over the last year. Last week, the President of the United States appeared on television to report an optimistic view of the nation's economic future. However, Mr. Salsberg didn't trust politicians very much, especially in a year just prior to election, as was the present situation. He did take note of the President's promise for a tax cut for the current calendar year. Mr. Salsberg especially pondered the effect of such a tax cut upon personal disposable income, the likelihood of such a tax proposal passing the Congress in the face of the nation's current budget deficit, and the influence such a tax cut would be likely to have upon consumer durable-goods spending, should it pass the legislature.

Credit was also an important consideration. Interest rates had fluctuated widely in the last few years, and this was also known to have an important bearing upon automobile purchases. Sometimes, for example, an extra 2 percent, 1 percent, or even ½ of 1 percent in installment loan interest rates, made the difference between a family qualifying for a car loan or being rejected for a loan. Financing was considered so important in the car purchase decision, in fact, that National Vehicles was seriously considering the formation of a new subsidiary, tentatively called "N. V. Finance," to provide stable financing to those consumers who otherwise might not qualify for an automobile installment loan.

Other factors also weighed upon Mr. Salsberg's mind, although he did not have a clear idea of how important any of them were. One consideration was the price of gasoline. Since 1973, the retail price of gasoline had more than doubled, and there was good reason to believe that even higher prices could be expected in the near future. What effect this would have on automobile purchases was speculative. It appeared that some families bought compact cars expressly to save on gasoline expenditures. Other purchasers seemed to consider the automobile a status symbol and bought luxury cars despite their relatively poorer fuel economies and greater maintenance costs.

A second consideration was depreciation on cars purchased for business use. In many instances, depreciation was the most important "expense" that the typical business car owner incurred, although no out-of-pocket money was spent for this expense. How fast the newer cars could be depreciated was an interesting point for Mr. Salsberg, especially because he knew that the new car market broke down into two major groups: first-time purchasers and replacement purchasers.

As he pondered this point, Mr. Salsberg also realized that he had neglected to consider the fleet owners. Included in such businesses were rent-a-car companies, leasing companies, and taxicab companies, all of which acquired new vehicles yearly. How important was their business, Mr. Salsberg wondered.

Questions

1. Evaluate the factors Mr. Salsberg has considered in his analysis of the purchase of a new automobile. Which factors would you consider important, and which would you consider unimportant?

2. What additional factors would you consider if you were asked to construct a three-month forecast of automobile sales demand for Mr. Salsberg?

3. What variables would you wish to *quantify* in your automobile sales demand analysis and where would you get this information?

4. What qualitative factors would influence your automobile sales forecast? How would you incorporate such factors into a quantitative prediction of future automobile sales?

year ... taken to ... implement ...
trails ... the ... long-range
budgetary system. Because an organization's
long-range budgeting consists of various projects
(or programs) that cover a time period longer than
one year, another term commonly used for
this type of budgeting is *programming*.

Some of the more important characteristics of
long-range budgeting will now be analyzed. In-

... makes it imperative
... management to be th...
... the proposals, and e...
them. Because an ...
function is to contribu...
organization by perfo...
top management's dir...
proposal review is es...

PART TWO

Accounting Information Systems for Collecting, Recording, and Storing Business Data

Chapter 4
The Collection and Storage of Accounting Data

Chapter 5
Data Bases for Accounting Information Systems

Chapter 6
A Manual and a Computerized Accounting Information System

Beginning with Part Two's chapters and continuing throughout the text, our assumption is that the student has an understanding of computer concepts. For those students lacking a basic knowledge of *hardware* and *software* concepts associated with electronic data-processing, however, the "Part Seven Supplement" (Chapters 17, 18, and 19) should be covered prior to beginning Part Two.

A major role of an accounting information system within an organization is to aid the collecting, recording, and storing of financially-oriented data as well as converting these data into meaningful decision-making information for management. Thus, the three chapters in Part Two will stress various data-processing approaches used by companies to enable relevant decision-making information to be provided to their managements. The emphasis throughout these chapters will be on collecting, recording, and storing accounting data within a computerized accounting information system environment.

Chapter 4 will discuss some of the techniques for collecting as well as storing accounting data in those organizations having automated systems. This chapter also will examine the collecting and recording of accounting journal entry data by a manufacturing firm which utilizes a manual data-processing system.

To achieve integration of accounting functions when the accounting information system is involved with collecting, recording, and storing financially oriented data for managerial decision making, many modern companies employ a computerized *data base*. Therefore, Chapter 5 will discuss the various concepts associated with a data-base system and also illustrate how many accounting functions can be performed more efficiently and effectively under a computerized data-base system. To emphasize the value of data bases to accounting information systems, several common accounting processes (such as preparing financial statements, planning and controlling budgets, and purchasing inventory on credit) will be examined using traditional manual data-processing systems as well as computerized data-base systems.

97

Finally, to conclude Part Two, Chapter 6 will provide an in-depth illustration of both a manual and a computerized accounting information system for processing one of the most important areas of accounting transactions, *accounts re-* *ceivable*. Through this chapter's extensive illustration, many of the concepts surrounding data collecting, recording, and storing will be integrated.

4

The Collection and Storage of Accounting Data

Among the important questions that you should be able to answer after reading this chapter are:

1 What is the difference between *data* and *information?*
2 What are the meanings of the terms POS, MICR, and OCR and how are they used in accounting information systems?
3 How do you design, encode, and interpret a punched card?
4 What are *key-entry systems?*

INTRODUCTION

Modern technology has irreversibly changed the functions, and to some extent even the role, of the managerial and financial accountants. Thus, today, it is quite difficult to get a good accounting job without an extensive understanding of *automation* and its uses in data processing systems. In our text, the term *automation* refers principally to electronic devices (such as computers) used within a firm's data-processing system. However, mechanical devices such as adding machines and bookkeeping machines also are part of the broad term *automation*. Because great strides have been made in automating many phases of the accounting process, a complete review of all aspects of this automation is impossible in a single textbook chapter. Therefore, the present chapter focuses only upon a company's data-collection and data-storage functions within an automated data-processing environment. (An example will also be provided of the data-collection process utilized by a manufacturing firm having a manual accounting information system.) We shall begin with a general discussion of data collection, and then examine in some detail a selected group of data-collection and storage devices available for use by a firm having an automated accounting information system.

While reading this chapter, you should pay particular attention to the advantages and disadvantages of each type of data-collection and data-storage device discussed. This is because accountants are often asked to assist management in choosing among various data-collection and storage devices once the decision to automate the accounting information system has been reached. Careful attention should also be given to those data media that are machine-readable because these media will appear again in later chapters which discuss examples of computerized accounting information systems.

This chapter, as well as many of the remaining textbook chapters, assumes that the reader is familiar with the computer terminology and concepts as might be taught in a first course in data processing. Thus, familiarity with the central processing unit as it resides within the general framework of the computer system, the uses of such secondary storage devices as magnetic tape and disk media, the role of computer software in the data-processing cycle, and the meaning of system and program flowcharts are critical to an understanding of what follows. Those readers who presently have such background may proceed directly to the remainder of the chapter. Those readers who lack such background, however, as well as those readers whose backgrounds are weak in the computer area, should first read Chapters 17, 18, and 19, which may be found in the "Part Seven Supplement" of this text.

DATA COLLECTION

As the name implies, data processing involves the transformation of data—raw facts, figures, sales magnitudes, and the like—into the type of information useful for decision making. A good decision is dependent upon good information which in turn is dependent upon good data. It stands to reason, therefore, that the better the data-collection process, the better the decision which can potentially be made from it.

Good data must be timely, accurate, and have potential meaning. The less these properties are found in the data, the less the chances of turning these data into useful information. For the data to be timely, they must be collected (and processed) fast enough so that action may be taken. Thus, it is of little value for management to learn of a leak in the gas main after the plant has already burst into flames. In 1880, the data gathering and processing of the census took so long that it was predicted the 1890 census would not be completed before the next one was to be undertaken. The necessity of finding a faster way to collect and interpret the data led to the invention of punched-card data processing.

It should be self-evident that data must be accurate if they are to serve the needs of an organization. Thus, a buyer for a retail store cannot make good purchase decisions unless accurate data on past and present sales are available, a manufacturer cannot construct a production schedule unless accurate data on raw materials stocks are available, and the state controller cannot construct the annual budget unless accurate data on tax revenues are available.

Inaccuracy in the data-collection process is a "double-edged" sword. Not making the right decision may be costly in the sense of a lost opportunity, but attempting to recover from the wrong decision may be *very* costly. Moreover, it is a personal embarrassment for an individual to admit that a decision was in error principally because of a failure to check the accuracy of the data on which the decision was based. In short, therefore, an organization has only one choice with regard to the accuracy of its data: make the data accurate. Otherwise, it's GIGO: garbage in, garbage out!

The last characteristic of good data mentioned above is that they have potential meaning. This, in fact, is the technical distinction between data on the one hand, and information on the other. Data are figures that are not meaningful; information is data that has meaning and therefore serves some useful purpose. In effect, therefore, information is interpreted, or processed, data. A good example of data that have potential meaning is the relatively long series of numbers on your credit card. Most credit-card issuers have standardized their number format in a system approved in 1974 by the International Organization of Standardization. Thus, the first four digits of your credit card identify your correspondent bank, a few of the middle digits indicate the period of each month when your bill is sent, and the last three digits (on some cards) serve as a credit rating assigned to you by the issuing credit-card company. To the casual observer, the numbers on your credit card are meaningless. To an informed individual, however, a credit card, once properly interpreted, is loaded with information.

As suggested by our credit-card example above, computerized accounting information systems often make use of codes and assigned numbers rather than names or English descriptions of things because the former require less space while uniquely identifying an individual or account. For example, two people might be named Peter Tompson, but each one could be assigned a separate account number if they both opened checking accounts at the same bank. The problem with such number assignments is that they tend to obscure meaning. For example, even Peter-Tompson-Number-One might not recognize a particular sequence of digits as his own bank account number if it were typed on a plain piece of paper. Thus, accounting information systems must take great pains to make sure that the meaning inherent in assigned numbers and codes is not lost. We shall return to this point in our discussion on internal controls in Part III. Also, because the distinction between data and information can be dependent upon who observes the data, this text will sometimes use these two terms interchangeably when referring to the contents of computer files, computer input, and computer output. This convenience, however, should not detract from the technical distinction between the two terms as described here.

Report Design: A Prerequisite to Effective Data Collection

The majority of accounting data collected by an organization ultimately appears on some type of internal and/or external report. Therefore, as a prerequisite to establishing its data-collection processes, the organization must first determine the types and contents of reports that should be provided by its accounting information system. Once decisions are reached regarding the types and contents of both internal and external reports, a data-collection process can be established which will accumulate the necessary data for these reports.

For example, one of the major financial reports prepared by the Alan Company for its management, stockholders, and creditors is a *Statement of Changes in Financial Position*. Accountants within the Alan Company's accounting subsystem determined the basic design of this report as follows:

Alan Company
Statement of Changes in Financial Position

RESOURCES PROVIDED

Working capital from operations—		
net income	X	
Add: Depreciation expense	X	
Add (or Deduct): Loss (or Gain) on disposal of long-term assets	X	
Total resources from operations		X
Working capital from the sale of long-term assets		X
Working capital from the sale of common and/or preferred stock		X
Working capital from other sources (sale of bonds, etc.)		X
Total resources provided		X

RESOURCES APPLIED

Working capital used to purchase long-term assets	X
Working capital used for the declaration of a cash dividend to preferred and common stockholders	X

101

Working capital used for other purposes
(development of a patent, etc.)   X

    Total resources applied   X

    Total increase (or decrease) in net
    working capital   X

Upon establishing the design of the above report and thereby determining the types of information that must be included in this report, the accounting information system can implement data-collection procedures to accumulate the necessary data for the statement of changes in financial position.

For instance, if the Alan Company sells a piece of its production equipment on September 18, 1984 at a price of $5000 cash (assume that this equipment had originally cost $8000 when purchased, and as of September 18 the accumulated depreciation on the equipment was $4000), the data collected surrounding this September 18 transaction would result in the following journal entries:

Depreciation expense	100	
Accumulated depreciation—		
production equipment		100
(To update the depreciation on the sold		
equipment)—See *Note* below		
Cash	5000	
Accumulated depreciation—production		
equipment	4000	
Production equipment		8000
Gain on disposal of long-term assets		1000
(To recognize the sale of the equipment)		

NOTE: This adjusting entry updates the depreciation on the production equipment since the last time (which was September 1) depreciation was recorded on the equipment.

The data collected regarding the $100 depreciation expense, the $1000 gain, and the $5000 cash proceeds from the sale would appear within the Alan Company's general ledger accounts after the above entries are posted. Because the design format of the company's statement of changes in financial position necessitates the inclusion of the $100 depreciation expense (it is added to the working capital from operations), the $1000 gain (it is deducted from the working

capital from operations), and the $5000 cash proceeds (it is added to the resources provided), the accountants must make sure they have properly collected (in journal entries and then posted to correct general ledger accounts) the $100, $1000, and $5000 amounts for ultimate inclusion in the statement of changes in financial position. It should further be noted that both the $100 depreciation expense and the $1000 gain will appear in the Alan Company's income statement, and the $5000 cash proceeds will appear in the company's balance sheet as part of its "cash" asset.

The preceding example has been somewhat oversimplified. This example, however, does serve to emphasize the point that for data collection to be performed effectively by a company, the types and contents of reports must first be known. Otherwise, either the data required for certain reports may not be properly collected or data that are unnecessary may actually be collected. Both of these situations will cause inefficiencies in a company's data-collection process.

Collecting Accounting Data: Source Documents

Record-keeping lies at the foundation of business and governmental activity. A great deal of such data collection is required by law, and is therefore mandatory. In 1978, for example, the cost of governmental compliance to American business was estimated at $62 billion. One large, private organization noted that it alone was required to file 8800 reports to 18 federal agencies in a single year!

From the standpoint of the accounting information system, the chief concerns in the data-collection process are accuracy, timeliness, and cost-effectiveness. (From an accounting viewpoint, an activity or process is considered to be *cost-effective* if the anticipated benefits from the activity or process are expected to exceed the anticipated costs associated with the activity or process.) The purchase order in Figure 4-1 is a case in point. The document represents a purchase order by Sneaks and Cleats, a retail sporting-goods shop, for 15 sets of golf clubs and 20 basketballs from the Alan Company. Although

```
                    PURCHASE ORDER                      ORDER NO.
                                                         36551

      SNEAKS AND CLEATS                       DATE: OCT. 5, 1984
      Route 59
      Nanuet, New York, 10955
                                              SHIPPING INSTRUCTIONS:

      To:  ALAN COMPANY                       DO  ( DO NOT ) INSURE

           125 KING STREET
                                              SHIP VIA:
           HONOLULU, HAWAII 96822
                                                   ALPHA TRUCKING
```

We wish to order the following:

CATALOG NO.	QNTY	DESCRIPTION	PRICE	TOTAL
A356024	15	"SWEATY PALMS" GOLF CLUBS	$60.00	$900.00
A135757	20	MITEEDUNK BASKETBALLS	3.50	70.00
		TOTAL		$ 970.00

Signed: F. Winnett

SNEAKS AND CLEATS

Figure 4-1. A serially numbered purchase order.

the purchase order must be completed manually, the fact that the order blank has been preprinted assures legibility of the name and address of the purchasing company and completeness in the ordering data. If Sneaks and Cleats (the purchasing company) were a large organization, additional copies of the purchase order, each on a different colored paper, would be prepared for internal use. For example, one copy would be retained by the purchasing department to document the order and to serve as a reference for future inquiries. Copies would also be sent to the accounting department and the receiving department. The use of carbon sheets for the preparation of these duplicate copies would be cost-effective inasmuch as the preparation of the original copy would automatically create the additional, departmental sheets. We also note that the purchase order bears a serial number, 36551. When purchase or-

ders are numbered sequentially, each such form is uniquely identified. This both enhances later referencing and serves as an important means of internal control.

To accommodate the purchase order of the Sneaks and Cleats Company, the Alan Company will ship the desired merchandise and send, under separate cover, a sales invoice with shipment. The sales invoice document is illustrated in Figure 4-2. Note that much of the information on the original purchase order is duplicated on the invoice. New information includes the terms of the sale, "2/10, n/30" (2 percent discount allowed if bill paid within 10 days, full amount due within 30 days otherwise), the date of the purchase order (reference date), the date the order was shipped, and the (preprinted) sales invoice number. The Alan Company would prepare at least six copies of the invoice. Two (or more)

103

SALES INVOICE

INVOICE NO.
18977

ALAN COMPANY
125 King Street
Honolulu, Hawaii 96822

To: Sneaks and Cleats ....

Route 59 ....

Nanuet, N.Y., 10955 ....

Terms: 2/10, n/30 ....

Purchase Order No.: 36551 ....

Reference Date: Oct. 5, 1984 ....

Date Shipped: Oct. 14, 1984 ....

Shipped Via: Alpha Trucking ....

CATALOG NO.	QNTY	DESCRIPTION	PRICE	TOTAL
A356024	15	"Sweaty Palms" Golf Clubs	$60.00	$900.00
T34566B	20	Miteedunk Basketballs	3.50	70.00
				$970.00
			Sales Tax at 5%	48.50
			Total Due	$1,018.50

Figure 4-2. The sales invoice used for the accounting entry.

copies would serve as a bill to the customer. A third copy would be retained by the shipping department as a record that the order had been filled. A fourth copy would be sent to the accounting department to be used in the processing of accounts receivable. A fifth copy would be kept by the sales department for future reference. Finally, a sixth copy would be sent to the inventory department for updating its records regarding the specific inventory items sold.

Both the purchase order of the Sneaks and Cleats Company and the sales invoice of the Alan Company are good examples of the "source document"—the fundamental reference of the accounting information system and almost always the starting point in the recording of business transactions. Examples of such source documents are everywhere. Time cards, job-application forms, packing slips, survey results, production logs, interoffice memos, sales summary forms, cash disbursement vouchers, and so forth, all can serve as potential source documents for collecting data by the business firm if

need arises. If some of this data is to be maintained on magnetic tape or disk files, the original source documents become important reference documents which serve both as back-up copies in the event of computer failure and, in certain instances, the final proof of the existence and accuracy of the computer file itself. As discussed in Chapter 1, the accountant is very much concerned about the maintenance of a traceable audit trail as data flows through a system. Because data is processed electronically when a computer is utilized by an organization, and because the individual cannot visually observe this data-processing function (as in a manual system), an effective audit trail which allows reconstruction of systems data is essential. The source document is thus the starting point of this audit trail.

Manually Collecting and Recording Data: An Example for a Manufacturing Firm

To examine the collection of accounting data in greater depth, let us consider the journal entries for recording the business transactions of a typical manufacturing company. For simplicity, we will assume that the data is collected manually, although the sections that follow will suggest several automated techniques for accomplishing this data-collection function.

The Alan Company sells its sporting goods on both a wholesale and retail basis to buyers around the country. Let us assume that the company uses a *process cost system* to collect the accounting data associated with the manufacture of baseball bats. This is a system in which production costs are accumulated in a separate account as manufacturing processes are performed. The journal entries, in summary form, which would reflect the production and sale of these baseball bats would be as follows:

(1) Direct raw materials inventory	X	
Indirect raw materials inventory	X	
Accounts payable		X
(2) Production in process inventory—		
baseball bats	X	
Baseball bat production overhead	X	
Direct raw materials inventory		X
Indirect raw materials inventory		X
(3) Baseball bat production payroll	X	
Cash		X
(4) Production in process inventory—		
baseball bats	X	
Baseball bat production overhead	X	
Baseball bat production payroll		X
(5) Baseball bat production overhead*	X	
Cash		X
Accumulated depreciation—		
production equipment		X
(6) Production in process inventory—		
baseball bats	X	
Baseball bat production overhead		X
(7) Finished sporting goods inventory—		
baseball bats	X	
Production in process inventory—		
baseball bats		X
(8) Cash	X	
Sporting goods sales		X

*This *debit* includes the allocated rent, utilities, and depreciation associated with baseball bat production activities.

(9) Cost of sporting goods sold	X	
Finished sporting goods inventory—		
baseball bats		X

For each one of the nine journal entries shown above, some type of source document (or documents) would be needed to collect the required data for the accounting entry. To study this problem in more detail, let us examine each of these entries in order.

(1) Direct raw materials inventory	X	
Indirect raw materials inventory	X	
Accounts payable		X

This entry reflects the purchase on credit of both direct and indirect raw materials needed for baseball-bat production. Separate subsidiary ledgers would be maintained for each of these two categories of raw materials (also, an "accounts payable" subsidiary ledger would likely be used) so that production subsystem managers will have information available regarding the physical quantity and cost balance of every raw material item. The detailed data within the subsidiary ledgers for direct and indirect raw materials inventory and accounts payable would be maintained both for reference and later use. For example, a listing of each inventory item's balance within the direct raw materials inventory subsidiary ledger would assist management in identifying low inventory levels, enabling the company to replenish its raw materials stocks in a timely fashion. Journal entry (1) is recorded based upon the following two source documents: the *purchase invoice* (i.e., the *bill*) mailed to the Alan Company by its supplier, and the *receiving report* prepared at the time the raw materials arrive at the Alan Company.

(2) Production in process inventory—		
baseball bats	X	
Baseball bat production overhead	X	
Direct raw materials inventory		X
Indirect raw materials inventory		X

This entry reflects the requisition of both direct raw materials (the cost of which is *debited* to the "production in process inventory—baseball bats" account) and indirect raw materials (the cost of which is *debited* to the "baseball bat production overhead" account). A source document called a *raw materials requisition* would be prepared by the baseball bat production supervisor at the time additional raw materials were needed for manufacturing activities. This source document is delivered to the production materials storeroom where a clerk would then issue the quantity and type of raw materials listed on the requisition form. The raw materials requisition source document would then be used by the accounting department for recording the journal entry.

(3) Baseball bat production payroll   X
    Cash   X

This entry reflects the total wages earned by those employees involved in baseball bat production activities. To simplify, payroll taxes and withholdings have been ignored. For accounting purposes, a payroll subsidiary ledger with information about each employee's earnings would be maintained. Entries to this subsidiary ledger would be initiated by the individual employee time cards, reflecting the number of hours worked during the specific pay period.

(4) Production in process inventory—
    baseball bats   X
  Baseball bat production overhead   X
    Baseball bat production payroll   X

This entry allocates the period's total wages between direct labor and indirect labor. The cost of direct labor is debited to the "production in process inventory—baseball bats" account, and the cost of indirect labor is debited to the "baseball bat production overhead" account. To make this labor allocation, each production employee would be classified as either direct labor or indirect labor. For hourly employees, information recorded directly on their time cards would serve to make the distinction between direct and indirect labor. Almost all supervisory employees would be classified as indirect labor.

(5) Baseball bat production overhead   X
    Cash   X
    Accumulated depreciation—
      production equipment   X

This entry reflects additional overhead costs associated with baseball bat production activities. The Alan Company's total period costs for rent, utilities, and depreciation on manufacturing equipment would be ascertained from the following source documents: the *lease agreement* for the period's rent, the *utilities bill* (or *bills*) received through the mail for the period's electricity, water, and so on, and the *fixed asset ledger* (which contains detailed information about each long-term asset such as original cost, estimated salvage value, estimated useful life, and depreciation method used) for the period's depreciation. Concerning the fixed asset ledger, the *actual* source documents are the *purchase invoices* which disclose the original costs of each long-term asset. Because all of the long-term, asset cost data would be recorded within the fixed asset ledger, however, we treat this ledger itself as the source document. By using conventional allocation methods, a portion of these rent, utilities, and depreciation costs incurred by the Alan Company would be charged to the manufacturing activities associated with baseball bat production. For example, depreciation could be allocated to baseball bat production based upon the percentage of machine-hours utilized in baseball bat manufacturing activities in relationship to the total machine-hours that the specific production equipment was utilized in the factory for all inventory-manufacturing activities.

(6) Production in process inventory—
    baseball bats   X
    Baseball bat production overhead   X

This entry reflects the application of production overhead costs to the period's manufacturing work performed on baseball bats. Following conventional procedure, overhead costs are applied to production work on the basis of a "predetermined overhead rate." For example, let us assume that the Alan Company uses a predetermined overhead rate based upon direct labor hours. Therefore, the source document serving as a basis for this journal entry would be time cards of "direct-labor" employees. By adding all the actual labor hours reported on these time cards, the total number of direct labor hours would be computed. This figure would then be multiplied by the predetermined overhead rate, and the resultant dollar amount recorded in the above journal entry.

(7) Finished sporting goods inventory—
   baseball bats   X
   Production in process inventory—
   baseball bats   X

This entry reflects the completion of some baseball bat inventory and the transfer of the inventory from the production department to the finished goods storeroom. Throughout our illustration, we have assumed that individual general ledger accounts were maintained specifically for baseball bat production overhead, baseball bat production in process inventory, and baseball bat finished sporting goods inventory. If, however, the Alan Company utilized a single production overhead account, a single production in-process inventory account, and a single finished sporting goods inventory account to accumulate the various costs of manufacturing *all* of its sporting goods items (basketballs, footballs, etc., as well as baseball bats), then separate subsidiary ledgers would be necessary to support each of these three general ledger accounts.

In a process cost accounting system, the focal point for collecting the costs associated with each type of manufactured product is the *departmental cost report*. This report (a separate one is prepared, for example, each week for every manufactured product) discloses the direct raw materials, direct labor, and applied overhead costs of both finished inventory work and in-process inventory work. Thus, the data within the departmental cost report relating to baseball bat production would, in effect, be the source document utilized in determining the dollar cost of finished baseball bat production.

(8) Cash   X
   Sporting goods sales   X

This entry reflects the actual sale of finished baseball bats to a customer for cash. To provide information to company management regarding the sales of each one of the many sporting goods products, a "sporting goods sales" subsidiary

ledger would likely be maintained. Included within the subsidiary ledger would be a separate account, indicating both physical quantities and dollars of sales, for every sporting goods product sold by the Alan Company. A sales invoice source document would be the basis for recording journal entry (8).

(9) Cost of sporting goods sold   X
   Finished sporting goods inventory—
   baseball bats   X

This final entry, which is recorded only under a perpetual inventory system, reflects the expense and inventory reduction to the Alan Company for specific quantities of merchandise sold. In terms of reference, the sales invoice mentioned above for journal entry (8) would also be the source document generating journal entry (9). However, the dollar amount of the debit and the credit for entry (9) would be determined by using the company's inventory records and applying an inventory costing method (such as FIFO or LIFO) to the physical quantity of baseball bats sold.

The assumption throughout the above example was that the Alan Company's data collection and recording activities were performed under a manual data-processing system. In a firm having a large volume of accounting transactions, the major drawback of a manual system for data collection and recording is the slowness of the system in handling various accounting data-processing functions. As a consequence, output reports reflecting the company's accounting transactions are not provided to management on a timely basis.

For example, under the Alan Company's manual data-processing system, considerable time delays may occur until the company's accountants are able to provide a departmental cost report to the baseball bat production supervisor. The unavailability of a timely departmental cost report could result in the supervisor not being aware of inefficiencies that exist in the production activities associated with baseball bats. As will be discussed in Chapter 5, the use of a computerized cost accounting system would enable a production supervisor to receive timely cost reports regarding manufacturing activities. With these reports available, the supervisor would be able to take action sooner "after the fact" to correct inefficient production performance.

Problems in Data Collection

In effect, the data fed *into* the accounting information system controls the information read *out*. We have already used the acronym "GIGO"— "garbage in, garbage out"—which means that you can't turn straw into gold. The accounting information system can output meaningful reports only if it is fed meaningful data at the beginning of the data-processing cycle.

In its broadest sense, mechanizing the data gathering process is intended to speed the flow of information through an organization. One important hindrance is the presence of clerical errors, copying mistakes, "typos," and so forth, which degrade the accounting information system and prevent it from operating at peak efficiency. However, these mechanical transcription problems are not the only reason that a strict control of the data-collection process is important. In the discussions that follow, we shall concentrate on some typical difficulties in the data-collection area, deferring our discussion of controls until Part Three of the text.

Definitions. Consider the following story. Students in a graduate marketing class were assigned the task of designing an automobile-purchasing questionnaire to be answered by middle-income families in a certain metropolitan area of the United States. One particular student asked the question, "How many cars do you own at present?" The choices he gave were: (a) none, (b) 1, (c) 2, and (d) 2 or more. The marketing professor noted there was a problem with this and asked, "What category do I choose if I own exactly two cars?" "Oh I see what you mean," replied the student, and took the questionnaire back for revision. The next week, he handed it in to the professor. To the question "How many cars do you own at present?" he had provided the choices (a) none, (b) 1, (c) 2, and (d) more than 3.

It is hard to believe that this story is true, but it is. Among other things, it points out the importance of clearly specifying definitions for things *before* the data are collected. A failure to do so is one *sure* way to start with "garbage in." Admittedly, it is easier to point out a problem such as this than to find solutions. In taking surveys, for example, problems arise in deciding what qualifies as income, who is a student, and even what is a car. Similar difficulties are found in such common accounting tasks as making the distinction between capital and revenue expenditures on plant and equipment assets, the classification of security investments as either long- or short-term assets, and the identification of what should, or should not, constitute a sale.

In sampling theory, it is permissible to discard certain observations if their classification is difficult *and* if such items constitute a small proportion of the sampling population. Accountants rarely, if ever, enjoy this privilege, thus making clear definitions imperative.

The human element. When it comes to performing simple and repetitive tasks with accuracy, humans are very poor processors. This fact, coupled with the observations that (a) no two people are likely to see the same event in exactly the same way, and (b) people do not like to admit they are wrong, conspire to make the human element one of the most pervasive, as well as one of the most interesting, aspects of the data-collection function. With the possibility of errors as well as irregularities (e.g., embezzlement) occurring in the data-collection process, accountants attempt to establish effective internal control systems for organizations. An internal control system is designed to safeguard an organization's assets from inefficient use and misappropriation. Also, a good internal control system aids organizational operating efficiency so that the organization's goals can be achieved. The topic of internal control within both manual and computerized data processing systems will be analyzed extensively in Chapters 7, 8, 9, and 10.

Another aspect of the human element in data collection deals with the relationship between the data collector on the one hand, and his or her supervisor on the other. The Greeks and Romans had one idea about this. The bearer of good news was given food, wine, and his choice of concubines for the evening. The bearer of bad tidings was beheaded. Today (presumably) things aren't as bad (or as good!) as this, yet the tendency to *distort* data in order to tell the supervisor what the reporter thinks the supervisor wishes to hear is still very much with us.

Organizational communications. The requirement that different organizational subsystems coordinate their activities within the total organization necessitates a flow of data among the subsystems. Often, the data required by one subsystem are collected by another. For example, sporting goods sales data might be collected by the Alan Company's marketing subsystem but also used by its production subsystem for planning current and future levels of inventory. In such situations, the potential for a very real and grievous problem is at hand. At the very minimum, a time lag is introduced between the actual collection of the data and its reporting since, at least in theory, the report is communicated via the subsystem managers and thus passes through multiple organizational levels on its way to the ultimate users. Another problem is that the user subsystem (i.e., the recipient of the data) is forced to base decisions upon data over which it has no control, and therefore perhaps little confidence. For example, based upon the sales forecast data from the Alan Company's marketing subsystem, the production subsystem would then make decisions regarding the quantities of raw materials, labor, and so on, needed to manufacture the sporting goods inventory. If it subsequently turns out that too much sporting goods inventory is manufactured by the production subsystem (causing excessive, unproductive dollars to be invested in this inventory), the question arises as to which subsystem is at fault—the marketing subsystem that provided the sales-forecast data or the production subsystem that made a bad decision based upon these data.

AUTOMATED DATA COLLECTION

Today most commercial enterprises must process data in large volume. For example, the Alan Company might fill thousands of orders each year, and therefore have thousands of invoices similar to the one illustrated in Figure 4-2. Processing these invoices is the responsibility of the accounts receivable section of the accounting subsystem, and includes (1) matching customer payments with specific invoice documents, (2) checking for correct payment amounts, (3) issuing credit memos for returned merchandise, and (4) pursuing buyers who are delinquent with their payments. All this work takes time, energy, and valuable resources.

The need to collect increasing amounts of data and the potential error in human collection methods has motivated a continuing search for greater speed, accuracy, and economy in the data-gathering functions of business and governmental organizations. Historical developments furthering these ends would include the invention of the telegraph, the telephone, the punched card (discussed below), the dry copier, the portable tape recorder, microfilm, and the portable video camera. Technological innovation has also been matched with a little common sense in the business world. For example, it would be a simple matter for the Alan Company to provide Sneaks and Cleats with a special set of Alan Company invoices, and let the Sneaks and Cleats purchasing agents complete these invoices themselves as the need to place an order arises. When the invoice prepared by Sneaks and Cleats is received, Alan Company personnel would review the form and make whatever minor changes were necessary to assure prompt delivery. Generally speaking, this would save the Alan Company time and money because it is much easier to check data which has already been prepared than it is to generate the data initially.

Today, machines can process information millions of times faster than humans. Thus, the real cost savings to the accounting information system in terms of data collection occurs when the data is prepared in machine-readable form at the beginning of the data-processing cycle. For this reason, a great deal of effort has been expended to develop ways of generating data that starts out in computer-processable format. A few of the more successful achievements in this area are discussed below.

POS (Point-Of-Sale) Data Collection

Since an estimated 75 percent of the information required by retailers can be captured at the point of sale, business attention has focused upon the development of automated terminals—in effect, "smart cash registers"—to record pertinent data electronically at the time a sale is made. The breakthrough has been not so much in the recording of the information as the customer might see it, but in the fact that the cash register has direct access to a computer and the computer files. Figures 4-3 and 4-4 illustrate POS terminals manufactured by IBM and NCR corporations.

With a POS recording system, the sales data obtained at the checkout-station cash register is transmitted directly to a computer. Here, the data can be stored for later use, for example, in the preparation of sales reports. One obvious advantage of the POS data-gathering system is that it thereby eliminates the preparation of an "intermediary" data medium, for example, the listing of a day's worth of sales, which would have to be transcribed into a machine-readable form before it could be processed by a computer. Other advantages of POS data-collection systems are:

1. Clerical errors, such as a salesperson's incorrect reading of a price tag, are detectable, and even potentially correctable, automatically.
2. Such standard procedures as the computation of a sales tax, the multiplication of prices times quantities sold, or the calculation of a discount, can be performed by using the register-terminal as a calculator.
3. A reduction in processing errors caused by illegible sales slips.
4. Credit checks and answers to questions about customers' account balances are

Figure 4-3. A Point-Of-Sale (POS) terminal. (Photo Courtesy of IBM.)

Figure 4-4. A Point-Of-Sale (POS) terminal. (Photo Courtesy of NCR Corporation.)

routinely handled by using the cash register as an inquiry terminal.

5. The inventory-disbursements data required for inventory control are collected as a natural part of the sales transaction.

6. A breakdown listing by the computer of sales by type of inventory item, dollar volume, sales clerk, or even store location is possible because the data required for such reports are collected automatically with the sales transaction and may be stored for such use.

7. A reduction in sales and inventory personnel is possible because the manual data-processing functions required of such personnel has largely been eliminated.

A POS recording system achieves an efficient integration of accounting transactions. Without this type of system, the accountant would have to record a separate journal entry for a sale (and the resulting accounts receivable or cash collection) and for the cost of merchandise sold expense relating to the sale (under a perpetual inventory system). The POS recording system performs these accounting functions simultaneously at the time a sale is made to a customer.

The advantages of the POS recording system have been of great value to the large-scale merchandiser. Montgomery Ward, for example, recently implemented a centralized POS system utilizing 30,000 terminals in its retail outlets around the country. Sears, Roebuck, and Com-

111

pany has also introduced a system of its own which presently includes terminals in its catalog and retail-distribution chain. With growing acceptance of the POS system at both the merchant and customer levels, a larger, more intensive use of such systems in the near future is practically a certainty.

Automatic Tag Readers

The introduction of the POS terminal at the retail sales station means, in effect, that the sales clerk need only input such information as inventory stock number, price, and quantity into the register and the system will do the rest. The one remaining potential for error therefore lies in the transmittal of information from the sales tag to the terminal. An automatic tag reader eliminates this potential error by performing the reading function automatically. In effect, the tag for this particular system is a type of punched card with circular holes punched through stiff paper. By in-

serting the tag between the "jaws" of the reader and momentarily shutting them, the tag is read and the information pertinent to the sale is automatically entered into the register/terminal at the sales counter.

Other systems using such variations as magnetized price tags are also being developed. Of particular interest among these systems are "optical bar codes," which are often used to identify merchandise inventory items. There are various types of these codes, and most can be interpreted by passing a hand-held wand over the retail price tag or label to record the coded information. An example of such a wand is illustrated in Figure 4-5. Although optical bar codes were first used by railroads in 1967 to help identify railroad cars, the most popular use of optical bar codes has been in supermarkets. Here, over 85 percent of the products sold use the *Universal Product Code* (UPC) in which ten pairs of vertical bars bear the manufacturer's identity as well as the identity of the item itself.

Figure 4-5. An example of an optical wand.

At one point, retail managers had high hopes for optical bar codes because their use would enable retailers to store price information directly in a computer memory accessible to the cash register rather than on each item in stock. This would eliminate the need to price each item separately, and additionally would facilitate price changing since only the price information stored in the computer would have to be altered. Finally, it was hoped that optical bar codes would facilitate the collection of customer charges at the check-out counter itself. Such hopes have been thwarted, however, by consumer resistance (it appears that customers like to see prices on each item rather than trust stores) and, in certain instances, by state and local ordinances.

MICR (Magnetic Ink Character Recognition)

As an outstanding example of automated data collection, the banking industry has pioneered the development of magnetically-encoded paper which is machine readable. If you have your own checking account, you are probably already familiar with this system if you tried to read the odd-looking numbers printed at the bottom of your check. Actually, there is a method to this madness because the "font," that is, the set of machine-readable letters and numbers used in the code, has been standardized for the entire country. Thus, you are now able to write a check

anywhere in the United States or Canada, and your check is machine-processable by any bank.

Check processing begins with the individual bank which is assigned a "check routing symbol" and a unique American Banking Association (ABA) transit number. (See Figure 4-6.) When a customer opens an account at the bank, a unique account number is added to this information and encoded in special magnetic ink at the bottom of the customer's check. When a check is eventually used, the dollar amount is manually imprinted (using special encoding machines) in the lower right-hand portion of the check by the bank initially receiving it. The check is then forwarded to the customer's bank, perhaps through a clearing house, for payment.

Use of a standard MICR system in the banking industry has been of considerable advantage. For one thing, the check serves as a direct input mechanism; it need not be transcribed to another data medium before being machine-readable. The check can therefore be immediately sorted or used as input for computer processing. MICR coding is also quite flexible. In particular, checks of varying sizes, thicknesses, or widths may be used without hampering the processing capability of the reading/sorting equipment (see Figure 4-7). Another advantage would be that the standard MICR code (see Figure 4-8) is readable by humans (although perhaps just barely!). This is a rare exception to the general rule that an item is

Figure 4-6. The MICR code of the American Banking Association.

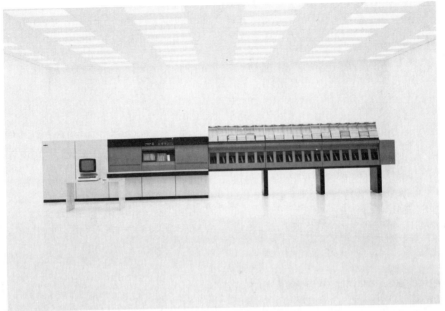

Figure 4-7. An IBM 1419 magnetic-ink character reader-sorter. (Courtesy, IBM.)

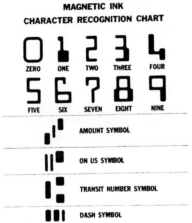

Figure 4-8. The American Banking Association MICR chart.

either machine-readable or human-readable, but not both. The fact that both a bank teller and an MICR reader are able to interpret the numbers and symbols in the code means that errors are more easily detectable and corrective action is thus facilitated. A final advantage of the MICR process is that it eliminates the checking account customers' responsibility to encode the checks themselves—the important account number and routing information are already inked on the check paper. This simultaneously reduces our work as check writers, assures uniformity in the coding process, and expedites check clearing through the mechanized system discussed above.

The chief disadvantage of the MICR process is that the magnetic strength (called the magnetic flux) of the inked characters diminishes over time, thus making the check unreliable as an input mechanism when it must be used in several different applications. This problem is compounded by the fact that, by law, the checks themselves must be returned to the individuals who initially wrote them. But even if this law were ignored, a single check is a rather bulky storage medium compared with alternative media presently available (see below), and it is doubtful that a bank with several hundred thousand accounts would ever consider saving its customers' individual checks in their original form. For this reason, most banks save check information on microfilm (described later) rather than saving the checks.

OCR (Optical Character Recognition)

As the name implies, optical character recognition involves the use of optical, rather than magnetic, reading devices to interpret the data found on the common source document. Typical OCR devices therefore make use of light-sensing mechanisms and laser technology to perform the character-recognition function required in the interpretation of recorded data.

The essence of OCR is *pattern recognition*: the ability of a machine to identify a recorded symbol as a familiar form. For this reason, the simpler the character "font" (set), the cheaper and more efficient the OCR system. Mark-sense media (see below), in which the "characters" are simple rectangles or ovals blackened with a pencil, are perhaps the most elementary data form using optical scanning techniques for data interpretation. One common use of OCR data collection may be found in the billing operations of a public utility company. For example, a meter reader may use an ordinary pencil to record the water or gas usage at your home simply by marking the appropriate columns of a special meter form. Such forms are then collected later at the utility company's processing office where your bill can then be prepared (see Figure 4-9).

More sophisticated versions of OCR involve the use of a complete character set of numbers and letters, and therefore achieve a more versatile recording system. Machine-printed characters, such as the type font of the American National Standards Institute illustrated in Figure 4-9, may be used to encode bills, invoices,

tickets, and other source documents which are ultimately interpreted with optical scanning devices when processing is required. For example, the attendant at the gasoline service station often makes use of an inexpensive OCR imprinting device (Figure 4-10) in processing a credit-card sale. As you already know if you have such a credit card, the customer gets the top, "throw-away" receipt and the station forwards the heavier card invoice to the company data-processing center. There, an optical character reader is used to interpret the card and prepare your bill.

Like magnetic ink character recognition, the chief advantage of OCR is the ability to use the source document as a direct input medium to the reader/sorter of the computer, thereby avoiding the necessity of transcribing the data into punched cards or magnetic tape. (These two data storage media are discussed later in this chapter.) The Social Security Administration in Baltimore, Maryland, for example, reported that the use of an OCR system to process the quarterly earnings of over 70 million wage earners has saved the bureau over $1,250,000. Thus, in general, an organization may look to high potential savings in clerical services with the utilization of an OCR system.

The most critical problem in the use of OCR processing is one of economy. Optical character readers tend to be expensive in comparison with other "reading machines." Thus, unless the volume of activity is quite high, alternate processing systems (such as magnetic-ink or card-processing systems) tend to be more cost-effective. Some authors also suggest that OCR requires a more rigid format than other systems. Although this is true for human-generated formats using handwritten input, the standardized format of the American National Standards Institute, as illustrated in Figure 4-9, does enable the use of preprinted forms for data-processing functions.

Mark-Sense Media

If you've ever taken a computerized examination, you are already familiar with mark-sense

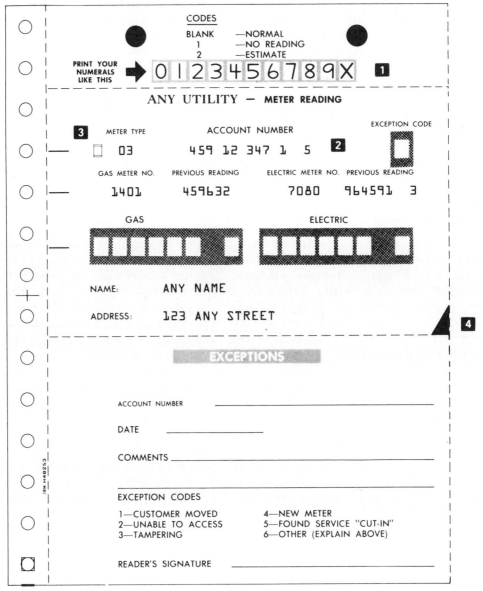

Figure 4-9. A form to collect utility-meter data using OCR. (Form Courtesy of IBM.)

media. Special cards as well as coding sheets are available, although the coding sheets are probably the more popular form today (see Figures 4-11 and 4-12). Mark-sense media are especially efficient in encoding pure numerical data, although any type of information may be recorded on the card or coding sheet if there are only a few possible choices and a coding process (e.g., red = 1, green = 2, etc.) is used to record the necessary data.

Mark-sense media are encoded by blackening a small square, circle, or oval on the coding sheet or card. Electromagnetic sensing devices were used in earlier versions of this data-recording process, which necessitated the use of special, magnetized, graphite pencils. Today, a common

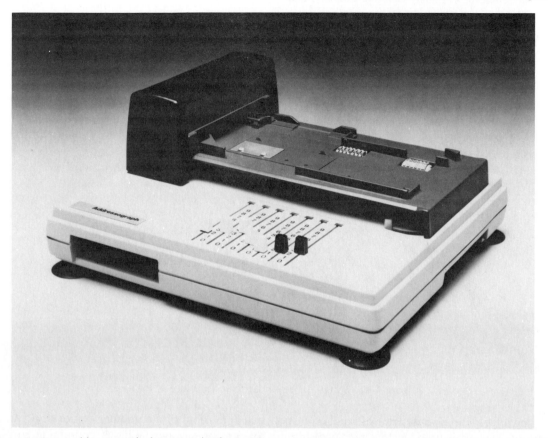

Figure 4-10. An addressograph data recorder for imprinting an OCR credit card sales slip. (Photo Courtesy of AM International.)

lead pencil is usually sufficient to encode the media because the scanners which interpret the cards or sheets currently perform this function optically rather than magnetically.

Mark-sense cards enjoy a distinct advantage over many other recording media in that mark-sense cards can be recorded on-site (e.g., on the loading platform of the shipping/receiving department) whereas, for example, the punched card (discussed below), is almost always prepared from a source document at a keypunching room. On the other side of the coin, however, the mark-sense form cannot be verified mechanically (i.e., checked for accuracy via machine) and, in addition, is slower and less accurately ''read'' by the scanner than is a card reader. Moreover, it should be noted that the mark-sense form uses a forced-answer format which leaves no opportu-

nity to supply data not covered by any of the choices on the coding form. A final drawback of mark-sense media is that they can be smudged, changed, erased, or double-coded (i.e., more than one box filled in), the results of which imply a high likelihood of ambiguous, and therefore potentially unusable, data.

Plastic Cards with Magnetic Stripes

These cards have a magnetic stripe affixed to one side of them much like a piece of magnetic recording tape. Credit cards are good examples. Other uses for such cards include magnetically encoded badges, which are used for identification purposes, and microcomputer cards, which are used to store computer-programming instructions.

117

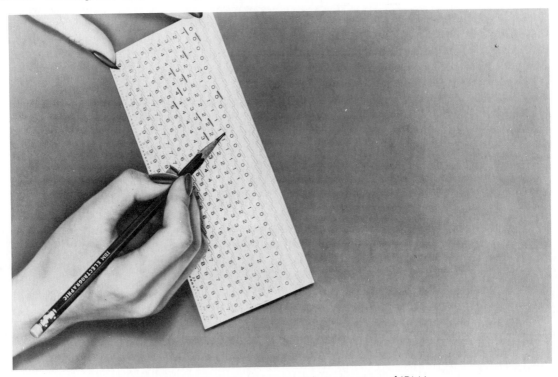

Figure 4-11. A mark-sense card. (Photo Courtesy of IBM.)

Typically, the magnetic stripe affixed to plastic cards of this sort is used to store pertinent information about the user. Thus, for example, a credit card stripe can be used by a bank to encode the user's checking account number, savings account number, credit card number, as well as the last date the card was used, the total number of times the card has been used to date, the credit card's expiration date, and so forth. Some of this information on the card (such as the individual's bank account numbers) is encoded on the card at the time of issuance, whereas other information (such as the date of last transaction) is updated every time the customer uses the card.

An additional function of these cards is for security purposes. Because the stripes are unreadable to the naked eye, only the individual who knows the secret codes or passwords encoded on the magnetic stripe can use the card itself. Thus, the cards' stripes are efficient control devices for cash withdrawals made at automated bank-teller windows, for limited-access facilities such as the machine room of a computer center or a parking lot, or for storage facilities containing rows of locker bins activated by card access.

In the United States, the magnetic stripe of the plastic card has been divided into distinct physical areas, and by agreement, each major industry using these cards has been assigned its own space. Thus, for example, the International Airline Transport Association (IATA), the American Banking Association (ABA), and the Savings-and-Loan or "Thrift" Industry each use a separate portion of the card's magnetic stripe. This enables each industry to code information pertinent to its own needs on the card without fear that, by accident, the card will be used mistakenly in another application.

The importance of magnetic cards to accounting information systems rests in the fact that important accounting data can be acquired at the same time that the cards are being used. For example, credit cards can be encoded with credit limits directly on the card and this information

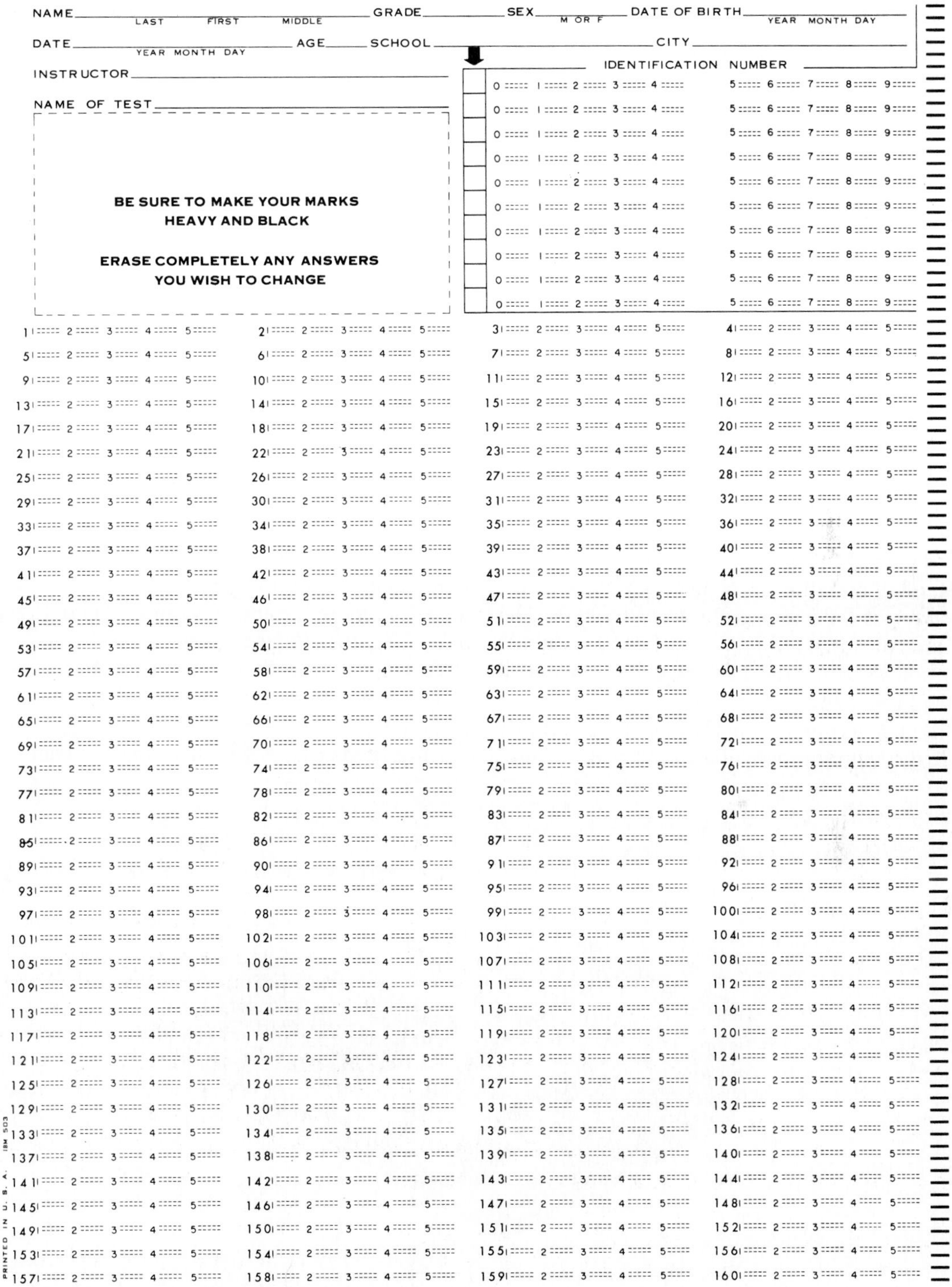

NAME ______ LAST FIRST MIDDLE GRADE ______ SEX ______ M OR F DATE OF BIRTH ______ YEAR MONTH DAY

DATE ______ YEAR MONTH DAY AGE ______ SCHOOL ______ CITY ______

INSTRUCTOR ______

NAME OF TEST ______

IDENTIFICATION NUMBER ______

BE SURE TO MAKE YOUR MARKS HEAVY AND BLACK

ERASE COMPLETELY ANY ANSWERS YOU WISH TO CHANGE

0 1 2 3 4 5 6 7 8 9
0 1 2 3 4 5 6 7 8 9
0 1 2 3 4 5 6 7 8 9
0 1 2 3 4 5 6 7 8 9
0 1 2 3 4 5 6 7 8 9
0 1 2 3 4 5 6 7 8 9
0 1 2 3 4 5 6 7 8 9
0 1 2 3 4 5 6 7 8 9
0 1 2 3 4 5 6 7 8 9
0 1 2 3 4 5 6 7 8 9

1 1 2 3 4 5	2 1 2 3 4 5	3 1 2 3 4 5	4 1 2 3 4 5
5 1 2 3 4 5	6 1 2 3 4 5	7 1 2 3 4 5	8 1 2 3 4 5
9 1 2 3 4 5	10 1 2 3 4 5	11 1 2 3 4 5	12 1 2 3 4 5
13 1 2 3 4 5	14 1 2 3 4 5	15 1 2 3 4 5	16 1 2 3 4 5
17 1 2 3 4 5	18 1 2 3 4 5	19 1 2 3 4 5	20 1 2 3 4 5
21 1 2 3 4 5	22 1 2 3 4 5	23 1 2 3 4 5	24 1 2 3 4 5
25 1 2 3 4 5	26 1 2 3 4 5	27 1 2 3 4 5	28 1 2 3 4 5
29 1 2 3 4 5	30 1 2 3 4 5	31 1 2 3 4 5	32 1 2 3 4 5
33 1 2 3 4 5	34 1 2 3 4 5	35 1 2 3 4 5	36 1 2 3 4 5
37 1 2 3 4 5	38 1 2 3 4 5	39 1 2 3 4 5	40 1 2 3 4 5
41 1 2 3 4 5	42 1 2 3 4 5	43 1 2 3 4 5	44 1 2 3 4 5
45 1 2 3 4 5	46 1 2 3 4 5	47 1 2 3 4 5	48 1 2 3 4 5
49 1 2 3 4 5	50 1 2 3 4 5	51 1 2 3 4 5	52 1 2 3 4 5
53 1 2 3 4 5	54 1 2 3 4 5	55 1 2 3 4 5	56 1 2 3 4 5
57 1 2 3 4 5	58 1 2 3 4 5	59 1 2 3 4 5	60 1 2 3 4 5
61 1 2 3 4 5	62 1 2 3 4 5	63 1 2 3 4 5	64 1 2 3 4 5
65 1 2 3 4 5	66 1 2 3 4 5	67 1 2 3 4 5	68 1 2 3 4 5
69 1 2 3 4 5	70 1 2 3 4 5	71 1 2 3 4 5	72 1 2 3 4 5
73 1 2 3 4 5	74 1 2 3 4 5	75 1 2 3 4 5	76 1 2 3 4 5
77 1 2 3 4 5	78 1 2 3 4 5	79 1 2 3 4 5	80 1 2 3 4 5
81 1 2 3 4 5	82 1 2 3 4 5	83 1 2 3 4 5	84 1 2 3 4 5
85 1 2 3 4 5	86 1 2 3 4 5	87 1 2 3 4 5	88 1 2 3 4 5
89 1 2 3 4 5	90 1 2 3 4 5	91 1 2 3 4 5	92 1 2 3 4 5
93 1 2 3 4 5	94 1 2 3 4 5	95 1 2 3 4 5	96 1 2 3 4 5
97 1 2 3 4 5	98 1 2 3 4 5	99 1 2 3 4 5	100 1 2 3 4 5
101 1 2 3 4 5	102 1 2 3 4 5	103 1 2 3 4 5	104 1 2 3 4 5
105 1 2 3 4 5	106 1 2 3 4 5	107 1 2 3 4 5	108 1 2 3 4 5
109 1 2 3 4 5	110 1 2 3 4 5	111 1 2 3 4 5	112 1 2 3 4 5
113 1 2 3 4 5	114 1 2 3 4 5	115 1 2 3 4 5	116 1 2 3 4 5
117 1 2 3 4 5	118 1 2 3 4 5	119 1 2 3 4 5	120 1 2 3 4 5
121 1 2 3 4 5	122 1 2 3 4 5	123 1 2 3 4 5	124 1 2 3 4 5
125 1 2 3 4 5	126 1 2 3 4 5	127 1 2 3 4 5	128 1 2 3 4 5
129 1 2 3 4 5	130 1 2 3 4 5	131 1 2 3 4 5	132 1 2 3 4 5
133 1 2 3 4 5	134 1 2 3 4 5	135 1 2 3 4 5	136 1 2 3 4 5
137 1 2 3 4 5	138 1 2 3 4 5	139 1 2 3 4 5	140 1 2 3 4 5
141 1 2 3 4 5	142 1 2 3 4 5	143 1 2 3 4 5	144 1 2 3 4 5
145 1 2 3 4 5	146 1 2 3 4 5	147 1 2 3 4 5	148 1 2 3 4 5
149 1 2 3 4 5	150 1 2 3 4 5	151 1 2 3 4 5	152 1 2 3 4 5
153 1 2 3 4 5	154 1 2 3 4 5	155 1 2 3 4 5	156 1 2 3 4 5
157 1 2 3 4 5	158 1 2 3 4 5	159 1 2 3 4 5	160 1 2 3 4 5

PRINTED IN U. S. A. IBM 503

Figure 4-12. A mark-sense coding sheet. (Form Courtesy of IBM.)

can be acquired immediately every time the card is used. Similarly, data gathering is facilitated in general because the information is obtained by highly sensitive, but reliable, electronic equipment which is not prone to human transcription error. Thus, a 13-digit credit card number which is time consuming to communicate vocally is accurately transmitted in much less time via electronic methods.

Terminals

Terminals are probably the fastest growing segment of the computer-device market because of their use in conjunction with small-scale computers and minicomputers. A common example of a terminal, the Teletype 43, is illustrated in Figure 4-13. This terminal utilizes a typewriter-like keyboard which the user strikes to provide data to the CPU. Usually, the terminal assembles a line of information at a time, which is transmitted to the CPU as a group of characters. The user indicates that a full line has been assembled by hitting a special transmission key, often called the RETURN key.

Although terminals might be placed directly beside the central processing unit, it is more common for them to be situated in locations convenient to the user. For this reason, we refer to such terminals as *remote terminals*. Remote terminals may be connected directly to the CPU via a cable, but it is more common to utilize a telephone line when they are sufficiently distant from the computer center. In effect, therefore, a POS cash register is just a specialized kind of remote terminal.

In recent years, terminals have become faster in data transmission, more reliable in operation, and cheaper in cost. For example, the older type machines, which "chugged" along at ten characters per second, are now being replaced with terminals capable of transmission speeds of more than 1200 characters per second. Similarly, in terms of cost, even pushbutton telephones can be used by particular computers as inquiry terminals and/or data-input devices. From the standpoint of the accounting information system, therefore, terminals are becoming more and more attractive as an alternate to manual data-gathering processes.

To help the user verify what has been assembled in the way of input for the CPU, terminals usually have a typewriter or video screen which illustrates the assembled data line, character for

Figure 4-13. A computer terminal with a papertape reader/punch. (Photo Courtesy of Teletype Corporation.)

character. Because these typewriters or video screens (in most cases) are also used for receiving data, it is tempting to call the terminal a combination input/output device. However, some terminals do not have a receiving capability.

The speed with which terminals have been able to transmit data to the CPU in the past has been quite slow in comparison with other input methods. Since most of this lack of speed is attributable to the fact that the user is keying in the information directly (e.g., from a source document such as sales invoice), the likelihood of a large improvement in the overall transmission rate is not great. As a means of improving this situation, however, some computer manufacturers have invented *smart terminals;* that is, terminals that include a limited processing capability. Because such terminals may act as either data transmitters or as stand-alone minicomputers, they have the flexibility of answering certain questions directly without using the valuable processing time of the central computer. For this reason, it is highly likely that we shall see the continued development of terminals such as these in the next few years.

From the standpoint of an accounting information system, perhaps the single greatest advantage of terminals is that they can be placed at several different data-collection sources and can be set up to feed data directly into a common computer for aggregated data processing. Thus, for example, an airlines reservation system permits agents to reserve seats on a specific flight from a large number of different offices scattered throughout a geographical region or even the entire country. This direct-linkage feature of terminals allows users to avoid the problems of physical collection of accounting data on paper forms, and in some cases, also the transcription of such data from initial source documents to computer-readable media. Thus, terminals have the potential to play an important role in a "paperless office."

Terminals which are capable of both sending and receiving messages also permit the distribution of data from the central computer location to regional offices. This capability has given rise to the name *distributed data processing system,* which means a data processing system using smart terminals for both local and central data processing. Thus, for example, an airline can notify its agents immediately via terminals that a particular flight has been cancelled. Where a high volume of data is to be communicated over the course of time, this feature of terminals is very *cost-effective.* This capability has also prompted a serious consideration of "electronic mail," in which letters are transmitted directly from the terminal of the sender to the terminal of the receiver. At present, of course, almost any company using terminals and a common central processor already has this electronic-mail capability. To make this concept work on a broad scale, however, it would be necessary to link the computers of many users together. Because there are both technical and philosophical barriers to this idea, electronic mail was still more a concept than a reality at the time our book went to press.

Key-Entry Systems

It is possible to transcribe accounting data directly to magnetic tapes or magnetic disks through the use of specialized key-to-tape recording devices or key-to-disk recording devices. Figure 4-14, for example, illustrates a key-to-tape device and Figure 4-15 illustrates a key-to-disk system. Key-to-cassette-tape systems and key-to-floppy-disk systems are also available. Key entry systems would normally be classified as off-line devices as opposed to terminals, which are normally online to a computer. In reality, however, these systems commonly use minicomputer processors which may be programmed to edit input data and guard against certain types of data-transcription errors.

To use a key-entry recording device, the user sits down at a typewriter-like console and keystrokes data directly from the console onto the tape or disk recording medium. To assist the user, many key-entry systems also have video screens which output the information as it is keyed into the console. When transcription errors or other problems arise during the course of the system's use, these screens are also used to indi-

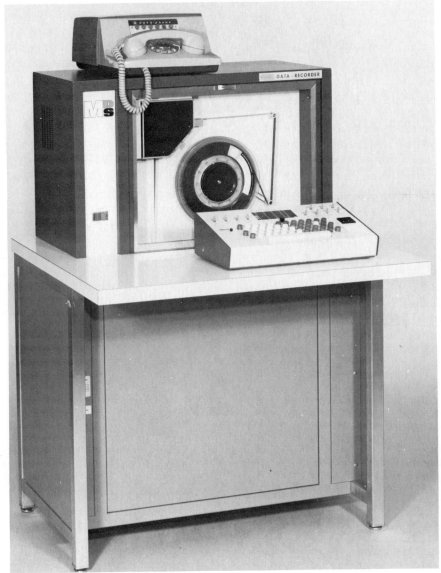

Figure 4-14. A key-to-tape system. (Photo Courtesy of Mohawk Data Sciences.)

cate the type of problem encountered. Thus, for example, when an operator attempts to key in alphabetic data in a place where only numeric data are permitted, an error message will be flashed on the video screen indicating this difficulty.

The combination of typewriter-like input console and video screen (or other output device) is conventionally termed a *work station* in a key-entry system. Key-entry systems can have as few as one work station or as many as 64 in a

single system. In many key-entry systems, the exact number can vary with the needs and budget of the user, and work stations can be added or subtracted as desired.

Using key-entry systems to encode source-document information directly to disks or tapes is helpful to the accounting information system because their use avoids the "intermediate" transcription of accounting data onto punched cards or punched paper tape (discussed below)

Figure 4-15. A key-to-disk system. (Photo Courtesy of Mohawk Data Sciences.)

before ultimately transferring the data to these magnetic tape or disk media. Also, because of the editing and error-detection features of key-entry systems discussed above, greater accuracy is usually possible in the final magnetic-tape information or magnetic-disk information than with card-oriented systems.

Because much of the data-processing equipment in key-entry systems is electronic as opposed to mechanical, key-entry systems are often faster, quieter, and more reliable than card-processing equipment which might handle the same data. This results in less down-time for work stations and, of course, greater productivity for the company that uses them. In fact, it is claimed that as much as a 30 percent increase in *throughput* (i.e., amount of useful work performed within a specific time period) is possible.

The principal drawback of key-entry systems is that they are relatively expensive. Thus, where data-processing volume is low, they are not especially cost-effective. An additional drawback would be that, whereas each card keypunching machine stands alone, key-entry systems

configure as many as 32 or even 64 stations around the same miniprocessor for data transcription. The dependency of this many work stations upon the same piece of electronic gear is troublesome when the miniprocessor malfunctions.

DATA STORAGE

Although the source document is adequate for recording business transaction data initially, it is often inefficient for subsequent storage and computerized data processing. This is because source documents are large and cumbersome compared with other storage media, and also because many source documents are not machine-readable. Thus, the data recorded on source documents at the start of the data-collection process is usually transcribed into a more convenient media form for computer access, storage, and use. Among these media forms are: punched cards, punched paper tape, microfilm, magnetic tapes, and magnetic disks. With the exception of microfilm, all of these media have the advantage

123

of being machine readable in addition to the capability of storing data in compact format. In the pages that follow, we shall look at each of these storage media forms in greater detail.

The Punched Card

A standard, 80-column punched card is illustrated in Figure 4-16. This card was developed in 1887 by Dr. Herman Hollerith to assist in the tabulation of the census by the U.S. government. Both the size of the card (which was based upon the size of a dollar bill at that time) and the encoding of the card have remained intact to this day—a remarkable achievement in an industry changing as rapidly as the computer field.

Not only is the punched card the oldest computer-readable storage medium, it is also one of the most popular. For example, a great deal of the data processed by the average computer today begins as a punched card. Of course, much of this data is ultimately transferred to other types of storage, as described below. However, some companies still use punched cards as a type of data storage medium.

As illustrated in Figure 4-16, the encoding of the standard punched card is performed column-wise on the card, with one column used for one number, one letter, or one special character (such as a decimal point). Each column has 12 potential punch positions, or rows, for this purpose, and a unique combination of punches in some of these rows is used to represent a single character. These rows are *not* numbered in a natural order, so care must be exercised in identifying any particular row of the card. As may be observed in Figure 4-16, the top row is designated by the number 12, the next, 11, then 0, 1, 2, 3, and so forth. The bottom row is therefore row 9—a strange end-row for a 12-row card. The top edge of the punched card is called the *12-edge*, whereas the bottom edge of the card is called the *9-edge*. Since computer card readers must have cards input in a certain way, the phrases "9-edge, face down," or "12-edge, face up," more than "top" or "bottom," are used at the computer center to describe the way cards are input.

All 80-column cards are keypunched in a standard "Hollerith" code, named after the card's inventor. As illustrated in Figure 4-16, the ten numeric symbols, "0," "1," "2," . . . , "9," are coded with a single punch in the corresponding "numeric" row of the card. All letters of the alphabet are coded with two punches, one in a "zone" row of the card and one in a "numeric"

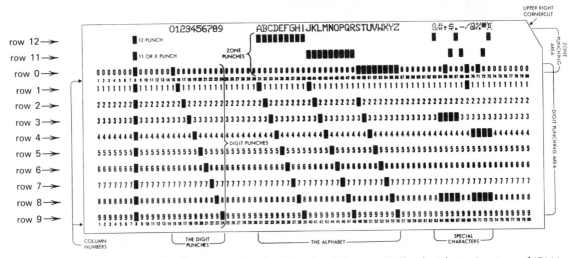

Figure 4-16. The standard IBM punched card and card code of Herman Hollerith. (Photo Courtesy of IBM.)

row of the card. Thus, for example, the letter "j" is coded with a punch in row 11 (a zone row) and a punch in row 1 (a numeric row), the letter "w" is coded with a punch in row 0 (viewed as a zone row) and a punch in row 6 (a numeric row), and so on. The special characters of the English language—for example, commas, periods, dollar signs, etc.—may also be coded in a punched card, although their punch representations are rather unsystematic.

Because an accounting information system utilizing card input depends upon accurate keypunching if it is to avoid data errors, the card-encoding process is of special importance in computerized accounting applications. To assure accuracy and also to increase encoding productivity, all cards containing important accounting data such as payroll hours or sales receipts are keypunched on special-purpose keypunch machines, never by hand. In addition, these cards are usually checked for accuracy and completeness with the use of a card verifier (see Chapter 8).

To help keep punched cards in their proper order, one corner—either the left or right top one—is cut. A card turned around in a card deck is easy to spot because its whole (uncut) corner juts out. For a person to read what has been punched in a card, it is usually possible to observe the printing above each of the 80 columns. However, special machines presently exist which can take a punched but unprinted card and print selected information on the card anywhere desired. Your electric bill or telephone bill is likely to be an example of such a card. Thus, it is not always safe to interpret a computer card by assuming that the writing on the top of the card corresponds to the punches underneath. A more accurate analysis would require a column-by-column interpretation either manually or with the aid of mechanical, card-reading devices.

IBM's announcement of its System/3 computer series in July 1969 included the introduction of a new type of punched card: the 96-column card (see Figure 4-17). This new card is about one-third the size of the "standard" 80-column card, yet holds 20 percent more data through the use of a more compact coding format. The card is punched with relatively smaller round holes instead of rectangular ones, and a

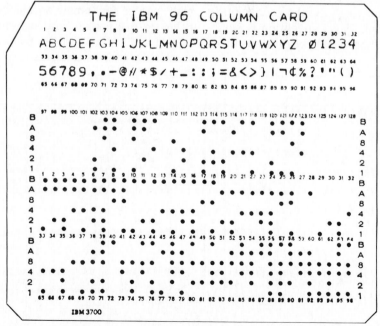

Figure 4-17. The IBM (System/3) 96-column punched card. (Courtesy, IBM.)

compact 6-row column, instead of the standard 12-row column, is used to encode a single character. As illustrated in the figure, the space savings is obtained by "stacking" the characters on top of each other in the 96-column card, so that three characters are encoded in the space formerly used for a single character on the "old" card. Understandably, IBM's system/3 has proven especially popular with those firms which rely heavily upon card processing.

Card formats. The information to be punched on a card is logically assigned columns on a space-needed basis. Thus, to record sales-transaction data, for example, perhaps 6 columns of the card would be set aside for a customer account number, 30 columns of the card would be set aside for the customer name, and so on, as illustrated in Figure 4-18. A group of card columns reserved for a common purpose, such as the retention of a customer's account number, is called a "field," and the contents of a punched card are more easily considered a set of fields rather than individual columns of data. It might also be noted that, because all the information about the sales transaction has been recorded on a single card in Figure 4-18, the card may also be called a *unit record*, a term that has come to be used synonymously with a punched card. This convention is somewhat misleading, however, because at times more than one card is devoted to the information of the same employee, account, or whatever, in commercial applications. Yet the term remains.

Because there are just 80 columns on the standard punched card, it is desirable to conserve as much space as possible when designing card layouts. Towards this end, the designer disposes of unessential punctuation, redundant or repetitive characters, and other kinds of noninformational elements when composing the card layout. Thus, the dashes in a social security number, the slashes in a date, the commas in large numbers, the dollar sign, and even the decimal point are usually eliminated in the process. Although this tends to give the punched card a confusing, cluttered look, the practice obviously conserves space. No real information is lost, however, because the computer can be instructed to properly interpret the card data on a column-by-column basis through the computer program. (Programming is discussed more thoroughly in Chapter 19.)

One final "trick" that might be discussed involving card formatting is the use of codes to represent certain characteristics of a customer's account, an employee, and so on. For example, using a one-column code with the letters M for male and F for female would be preferable to using as many as 6 card columns to spell out "FEMALE." Similarly, a pay code of a single

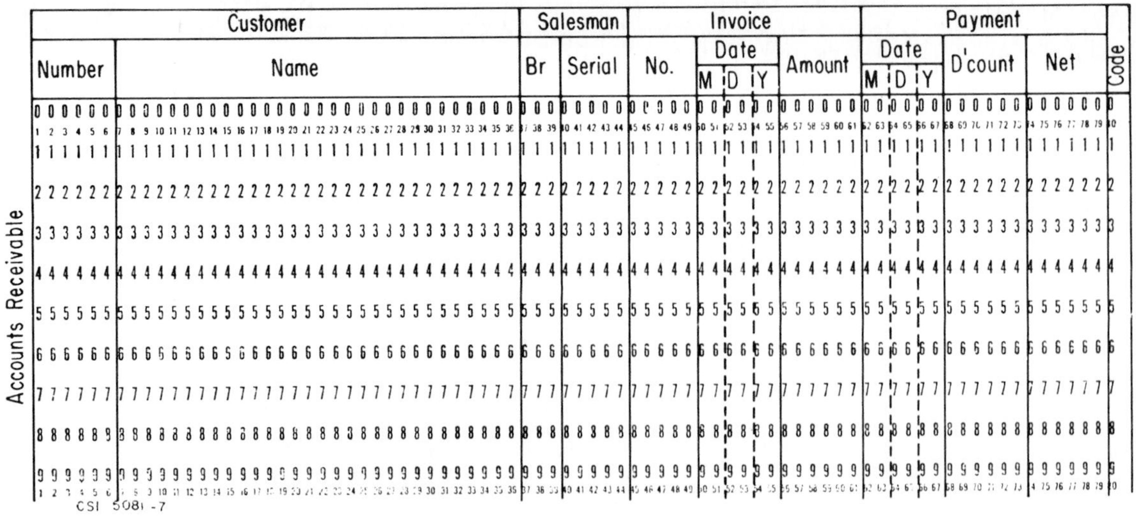

Figure 4-18. The punched card layout for a sales transaction.

character might be used to represent an employee's monthly salary instead of a six-digit, dollar-and-cents format. As discussed above, the computer program is designed to decipher the code and substitute the correct money figure at the time of data processing.

Punched-card data processing. Historically, the punched card has served as a vital link between the manual accounting methods prior to 1950 and the earliest computer generations of the 1950s and 1960s. Because computers were once much more expensive to acquire and use than they are today, many of the earliest accounting applications relied solely on punched-card equipment to perform the necessary data processing. An illustration of such punched-card data processing, as might be used to perform the accounting tasks involved in accounts receivable credit sales transactions, is provided in Appendix E.

Although punched-card data processing might have been cost-effective in the past, today in the 1980s, computer power and reliability have improved to the point where punched-card data processing is obsolete. Thus, for example, computer systems have been developed which perform most of the card-processing tasks electronically, thereby enabling the user to avoid the varied card-processing machines involved in punched-card data processing, and to realize processing economies as well.

Another reason for the trend away from card processing might have already occurred to you from the topics discussed earlier in the chapter. In particular, the development of more efficient data-collection techniques permits the accounting information system to bypass completely the punched-card preparation stage when processing data. Point-of-sale terminals, for example, allow the information pertinent to a sales transaction to flow directly to a computer: no sales cards need be punched because none are necessary. Thus, there is a clear trend away from the use of the punched card, both as the principal data-storage medium in punched-card data-processing systems and as the intermediate, machine-readable medium for data on its way to computerized processing.

The facts stated above should not detract from the observation that, at present, the punched card still serves as an important data-recording, data-transmission, and in certain instances, even data-storage medium within computerized data-processing accounting information systems. Over 100 billion punched cards are used each year for various data-processing functions. Thus, a continued reliance upon the punched card, at least in the near term, seems likely.

Advantages and disadvantages of punched cards. Using punched cards to encode information within the accounting information system has both advantages and disadvantages. The fact that such cards are unit records is an advantage in that the card-deck sequence can be reordered either manually, or by special mechanical card sorters, when necessary. Thus, for example, we could take a set of sales transaction cards (one such card is illustrated in Figure 4-18), first sort them by sales-transaction date to get a chronological listing of sales, and then sort them by salesperson number to get a new list by sales personnel. This flexibility in reordering is not possible on punched paper tape, as described below.

The fact that interpreted cards—that is, cards that have writing on them—are human readable is another advantage. This means that a file of punched cards—for example, containing information about company office suppliers—can be maintained manually, and that a clerk could insert or remove cards from the deck as need arises.

An additional advantage of computer cards is their use as *turn-around documents*. A turn-around document is a document that is sent to a company's customer or non-EDP subsystem, and that eventually returns to the EDP subsystem for data-processing. Thus, for example, when a company automates its payroll function, it is convenient to use a punched card for the check itself. When a check is cashed and subsequently returned to the company with other cancelled checks, the company can use these turn-around documents to reconcile its payroll bank balance electronically. Other familiar examples of punched-card turn-around documents used in accounting applications include utility-billings, dividend payments, common-stock proxy inquiries, and audit confirmations. Space does not permit a detailed explanation of each of these applications. However, it is obvious that the punched card plays a vital role to the accounting information system in its use as a turn-around document.

Punched cards also have drawbacks. The fact that their order is flexible—a fact that was mentioned as an advantage above—is also a disadvantage in circumstances where *accidental* reordering is undesirable. Computer programs written on punched cards are an obvious example.

Although punched cards are computer-readable, they are not an especially efficient storage medium. Magnetic tapes and magnetic disks, for example, are able to store considerably more data at considerably less cost and space. Moreover, card-reading must depend upon mechanical processes that are relatively slow compared with the input or output rates of magnetic tapes and magnetic disks. Thus, where the speed of data transmission is important (e.g., in the processing of thousands of customer accounts), the use of punched cards actually slows down data-processing operations.

A final disadvantage of punched cards is that, today, their encoding is almost always an intermediate step between the initial recording of data on a source document and the processing of this data by a computer. In this sense, the encoding process is redundant, and serves no real productive purpose except that of converting accounting data to machine-readable format. For this reason, there has been a noticeable trend in recent years to bypass the card-encoding process, and to use wherever possible the more-

direct key-to-disk or key-to-tape systems previously discussed.

Punched Paper Tape

In design, paper tape closely resembles the punched card. Like the card, the tape is encoded by punching holes in one or more rows, or "channels," running along the length of the tape. A vertical column of the tape (across the tape width) is used to represent a single character of information. Figure 4-19 illustrates the coding of 8-channel tape. Five-channel tape (i.e., tape consisting of only 5 punch rows) is also available. The series of holes between channels labeled "4" and "8" on the tape in Figure 4-19 are sprocket holes used to move the tape through the punch or read stations of the paper tape machine.

Compared with punched cards, punched paper tape offers both advantages and drawbacks. Because punched paper tape is a continuous storage media, the paper-tape user is not limited to the 80 columns of data available on the punched card. In addition, punched paper tape is slightly cheaper to use. However, paper tape usually does not have a printed line, as does a punched card, so paper tape is virtually unreadable by the human eye. The paper in punched paper tape tends to be thinner than that used in cards and thus has the potential to tear more easily. Partially for this reason, paper tape readers tend to be slower than card readers in transferring data. Finally, the continuity of the paper tape is itself a disadvantage as well as an advantage because the order of the information on the tape is fixed; it cannot be "reshuffled" as can be done with punched cards.

The popularity of punched paper tape has both waned and revived during the last 20 years. At

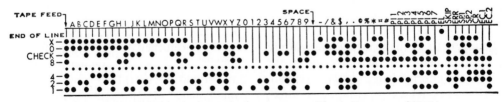

Figure 4-19. Eight-channel punched paper tape. (Photo Courtesy of IBM.)

first, the aforementioned disadvantages caused it to lose popularity in comparison with punched cards. However, its cost advantage has since been "rediscovered," and a revival of sorts has occurred in its use in the small, or "minicomputer" systems currently available. (Minicomputers are discussed in Chapter 15.)

Microfilm

Microfilm economizes on storage space by substituting a miniature picture or film slide for the bulky source document. Generally speaking, microfilm requires only 2 percent of the space required by the paper document. Thus, both a space savings as well as an increase in the useful life of the recorded information may be achieved with the use of microfilm data storage.

Microfilming can be accomplished in three different ways. The oldest technique uses a photographic process which develops a permanent microfilm slide negative. In this technique, therefore, the information on a source document is reduced in size much like a person's picture is reduced in size through the camera lens. Also, as with photographic slides, microfilm is interpreted by the human eye with the aid of a microfilm viewer.

Most microfilming is performed with high-speed cameras using rolls of microfilm, called *microfiche*. One common variation of this process flashes source-document images on a cathode ray tube (CRT) screen, where these images are photographed at high speed and developed with special chemicals. This microfilm process has found useful applications when recording the information generated by the computer (see below). Finally, newer microfilm techniques have been developed which enable the user to avoid the film-developing stage entirely. In one technique, a silver-plated film is exposed and the microfilm becomes encoded with the use of an electron-beam recorder.

Although microfilm has been popularized in television espionage serials and secret-agent movies, microfilm data recording plays a vital role in commercial data processing. Most banks, for example, use microfilm machines to photo-graph customer checks, enabling the banks to record check information quickly (up to 800 checks per minute) and return the actual paper to the check writer. Other commercial users have mounted microfilm on punched cards known as *aperture cards*. Identification information punched in a portion of the card enables the aperture-card user to create a microfilm storage and retrieval system using punched-card processing equipment. Such systems are used, for example, to maintain inventory files or production files. Retrieval information, such as a part number or supplier number, is maintained in the punched portion of the card, whereas descriptive information, such as technical specifications and/or diagrams, is recorded in the microfilm portion of the card.

Recent technological developments have permitted the direct coupling of a microfilm machine with a computer in order to record output information. This process uses the CRT microfilm approach described above and is called *computer output microfilm*, or COM. It is one of the fastest data-recording mechanisms commercially available, enabling the user to create permanent informational documents at the rate of 500,000 characters per second! The "print rate" translates to approximately 60,000 lines of output per minute. In addition, microfilm can also be used as a data medium for direct input to a computer. This is accomplished with the use of special optical character recognition equipment, but obviously is limited to interpreting only those microfilm rolls encoded with recognizable OCR-readable symbols.

Microfilm equipment is not cheap, and its chief drawback is the large volume of data processing required to make it cost-effective. Other drawbacks of microfilm would include: (1) the fact that it is human-readable only with the assistance of a viewer, (2) the fact that it is permanent and therefore nonreusable, and (3) the fact that the sequence of information encoded on microfilm cannot be changed as it can with cards. Against these drawbacks are some important advantages: (1) microfilming is easy and reliable, (2) microfilm completely avoids a human-transcription phase: the camera automatically captures the data and avoids the potential for clerical errors when manual copying is performed, (3) microfilm is human readable, yet can be interpreted automatically in special circumstances, and (4) it is extremely fast in capturing output data through a COM process.

Magnetic Tape and Magnetic Disk Storage for Processing Accounting Data

Much of the accounting data collected by the typical organization during the normal course of business operations is both voluminous in size and in constant need of update. To meet the simultaneous requirements of size, convenient storage, and speedy access in a computerized environment, the data-processing industry has developed such specialized storage media as magnetic tapes and magnetic disks for automated accounting information systems. Such storage media are indispensable to even the simplest automated accounting information system, and for this reason, are discussed extensively in Chapter 18. Because the discussions in that chapter also include the advantages and disadvantages of magnetic tape and magnetic disk, both with respect to other types of storage media and each other, these advantages and disadvantages will not be repeated here.

From the standpoint of accounting information systems, magnetic tapes and magnetic disks are important both for their cost-effectiveness in *storing* accounting data, and also for their flexibility when *processing* accounting data. In terms of cost-effectiveness, for example, a standard reel of magnetic tape can store the equivalent of 225,000 punched cards worth of data, or in excess of 18 million characters (if recorded at high densities), yet costs less than $25. In comparison, 225,000 punched cards would occupy much more physical space and cost more than $300. Because of the faster data transmission rates of magnetic tapes and magnetic disks, the data stored on these devices would also be cheaper to process.

Magnetic tapes and magnetic disks also enable the user to expand the number and types of re-ports which may be generated from the "raw" accounting data stored on them. This is possible partially because of the flexibility with which accounting data may be stored on magnetic tapes and (especially) magnetic disks, and partially because of the great speeds with which modern computers can process machine-readable data. The logical use of magnetic tapes and magnetic disks to store accounting data is explained more fully in the next chapter on accounting information system data bases.

An additional point regarding computerized accounting information systems should also be made here. Within many organizations' computerized accounting information systems, the only accounting cycle step (the accounting cycle steps were previously discussed in Chapter 1) requiring manual work is step 1, the preparation of transaction source documents. For the most part, all of the remaining accounting cycle steps (cycle steps 2 through 9) can then be handled by the EDP subsystem's computer. As a result of the computer's speed capability, an organization's accounting cycle steps can be performed quite rapidly when using electronic data-processing techniques. In fact, the entire accounting cycle of many companies (excluding the manual preparation of transaction source documents) could be performed by a computer in a matter of minutes. The organization is thus able to provide management, creditors, potential investors, and so on, timely financial reports at the end of its accounting period.

SUMMARY

This chapter has emphasized the collection and storage of accounting data within automated data-processing systems. An important distinction was made between *data* on the one hand, which has little meaning, and *information* on the other, which does have meaning and may therefore be helpful for decision making. Because data are the "raw ingredients" from which information is created, the first step toward good decision-making information is the accurate, timely, and cost-effective acquisition of good data. The point was made that as a prerequisite to the establishment of an efficient and effective data-collection process within a company's accounting information system, the company must first determine the types and contents of both internal and external reports that should be provided by its accounting information system.

A variety of automated devices assist in the collection of a firm's accounting data. Among those discussed were POS ("smart") cash registers, automatic tag readers, magnetic ink character recognition systems, optical character recognition systems, mark-sense media, plastic cards with magnetic stripes, terminals, and key-entry systems. It was stressed, however, that these automated devices are not perfect in terms of eliminating problems associated with a company's data-collection activities. The following circumstances can contribute to problems in an organization's data-collection activities: the potential for design errors, the ambiguity of data categories, the impact of the organization's structure on who gathers the data versus who actually uses the data, and the fact that the primary users of any information system are ultimately *humans* with "other things on their minds."

Various media forms for storing accounting data were examined next. The initial form of storage medium used to reflect accounting transactions is normally the *source document*. Within an automated data-processing system, however, source-document data are commonly transferred to machine-readable storage media such as punched cards, punched paper tape, magnetic tape, or magnetic disk. Microfilm, which is usually not machine readable, is also used for storage purposes. Particular emphasis was placed on the *format*, or layout, of a punched card. Many data-processing systems still rely upon the punched card as their *initial* storage media form for machine-readable data. Thus, an understanding of the design of the punched card is critical to an understanding of how human-collected data are provided to accounting information systems using card input.

DISCUSSION QUESTIONS

4-1. Explain why data collection is a potential problem to a business organization.

4-2. Discuss the importance of the "human element" in data collection.

4-3. Why are machines replacing humans in the data-collection function?

4-4. Describe the process by which a punched card layout is designed for computer processing.

4-5. Name as many advantages as you can that punched cards have over punched paper tape.

4-6. Enumerate as many advantages as you can that mark-sense has over *either* punched cards or punched paper tape.

4-7. Explain what is meant by the card reader stacking instruction "9-edge in, face down."

4-8. Explain the difference between an 80-column punched card and a 96-column punched card. Which is bigger? Which holds more data? Which is more popular? Which uses rectangular holes?

4-9. Why is it unsafe to assume that the letters printed over a particular set of columns on an 80-column punched card are necessarily the letters punched *in* the columns directly underneath them?

4-10. Explain the ordering of the rows on a standard 80-column card. Why is the last row in the card not the 12th row when there are in fact 12 rows in the card?

4-11. Explain the concept of "coding" when constructing a punched-card layout. Why is coding used when it requires people to look things up and tends to be confusing when interpreting a card?

4-12. Consider the dollar figure: $5,125,000.00. How many spaces would each of the following media *most likely* require to encode this number, assuming that each medium would try to economize space as much as possible.

   a. typewriter
   b. 80-column punched card
   c. 96-column punched card
   d. 8-channel punched paper tape
   e. 5-channel punched paper tape

4-13. What is the Hollerith Code? In this code, what is the difference between the code for a letter versus the code for a number? In designing card or tape layouts, explain why it is the largest-sized item, rather than the average-sized item, which dictates the number of spaces to set aside for a particular data figure.

4-14. What advantages does a POS system have over a manual, sales-tag system? Many of the largest, most sophisticated firms are adopting POS systems despite the fact that a POS cash register is much more expensive than a nonautomated cash register. What does this tell you about the analysis that went into the decision to purchase such systems?

4-15. Explain why you agree or disagree with the following statement.

> As a prerequisite to the establishment of an efficient and effective data-collection process by its accounting information system, a company must first determine the types and contents of both internal and external reports that should be provided by its accounting information system.

4-16. A common journal entry recorded by a business firm is:

Accounts receivable   X
Sales revenue   X

Assume that the firm recording the above journal entry utilized a computer for processing its accounting transactions. Describe on a step-by-step basis how both the *debit* part and the *credit* part of this journal entry would be processed through the firm's computerized data-processing system.

4-17. Indicate why you would agree or disagree with the following statement. "Mark-sense cards would be much more efficient than employee time cards for gathering data about employee working hours."

4-18. Why might a manufacturing firm, in collecting and storing accounting data associated with production activities, convert its present manual data-processing system to a computerized data-processing system?

PROBLEMS

4-19. Below are a set of terms that might be arranged to form a natural hierarchy. Rearrange them so that they read in ascending order (i.e., from smallest or least significant, to largest or most significant).

(a) card deck   (c) character
(b) field   (d) unit record

4-20. All the terms below may be found in everyday language, but have special meaning to the computer-oriented accountant. Provide both a common definition and a more technical definition for each of them.

a. card   f. punch
b. field   g. column
c. tape   h. character
d. information   i. smart
e. data   j. channel

4-21. Data-processing is replete with special terms, phrases, and other special language unique to the industry. Below is a set of *acronyms*— special words which are composed of the first letter, or first few letters, of a set of words. Some of these have already been discussed in this chapter, whereas others are explained in Chapters 17, 18, and 19. Identify as many as you can.

a. POS   e. OCR
b. I/O   f. MIS
c. MICR   g. CPU
d. EDP   h. FORTRAN

4-22. Below is an inventory report from the Perry Products Company. Suppose that the report were generated from a deck of issuance-and-receipt ("transaction") cards which were keypunched from slips filled out by the warehouse personnel. (a) What information would be required on the card to generate such a report? (b) Design an efficient card layout which would serve the company.

PERRY PRODUCTS WEEKLY INVENTORY TRANSACTIONS
Week of: January 3–10, 1984

Date of Transaction	Stock Number	Supplier Code	Unit Cost	Units Received	Units Issued	Net Value of Transaction
1-3-84	152349	51–978	$21.50	100		$2,150.00
	245637	52–888	.59		200	118.00–
1-4-84	567883	80–875	1.68	100		168.00
	23567	11–677	22.98	1		22.98
	876665	14–987	98.00		2	196.00–

4-23. The Nebrasco Oil Company operates its own charge card division, enabling holders of the company's credit card to charge all service station bills to their account as needed. Each time a charge is made, the pertinent information is recorded and ultimately encoded in a punched card. *Design* and *draw* an *efficient* card layout for the Nebrasco Company based on the information listed below:

a. Customer account number (10 digits)
b. Station number (5 digits)
c. Entry date
d. Date of transaction
e. Amount of gasoline purchased (always less than $100)
f. Amount of oil, fluids, etc. purchased (always less than $75)
g. Amount of parts and automotive supplies (always less than $4000)
h. Amount of labor charges (always less than $1000)
i. Amount of taxes charged on transaction (always less than $600)

4-24. Design and draw the *card layout* for the Gilbert Company's accounts receivable cash collections system, as dictated by the following informational needs. Remember that a compact format is important.

a. Date of entry
b. Invoice reference number (5 digits)
c. Amount paid (maximum is $999.99)

d. Discount (percent)
e. Name of company making payment (allow 25 characters)
f. Number of check (5 digits)
g. Date of check

4-25. Puerner Products manufactures a variety of machine tools and parts used primarily in industrial tasks. To control production, the company requires the information listed below. Design an *efficient* punched card format for Puerner Products.

a. Order number (4 digits)
b. Part number to be manufactured (5 digits)
c. Part description (10 characters)
d. Manufacturing department (3 digits)
e. Number of pieces started (always less than 10,000)
f. Number of pieces finished
g. Machine number (2 digits)
h. Date work started
i. Hour work started (use 24-hour system)
j. Date work completed
k. Hour work completed
l. Work standard per hour (3 digits)
m. Worker number (5 digits)
n. Foreman number (5 digits)

4-26. Below is a typical payroll check that might be issued to an employee of the Gary Company. Suppose the company used a payroll system that first used a computer to calculate the amount due each employee, *then* punched the information out on paper tape, and *then*, at a later time, transferred the information from the punched paper tape to the punched card shown below. Now admittedly this is a somewhat roundabout way of doing things. But if such a system were to exist:

a. What information would have to be stored on the tape in order to provide all of the information for the payroll check?

b. Design an efficient paper tape layout for this problem.

```
Gary Corporation                        Date:
55 Union Street
Maintown, USA 12345

Pay to the order of _____ $ _____
_____ Dollars
Check is not valid after ninety (90) days from date above.
                        Signed:
                        _____
                        Signature of Company Treasurer
```

CASE ANALYSES

4-27. *Town and Country Building Supply*

Town and Country Building Supply was founded in 1899 by Chung Ali Kai, who immigrated from China at the age of 15. Beginning with $60,000 in starting capital, the company thrived for almost a year before burning to the ground in an accidental fire. After the disaster, the young Chinese entrepreneur was faced with a $25,000 liability because the business had not been insured. Determined to rebuild, he began afresh, managing to survive a panic in 1907, a second catastrophic fire in 1919, the Great Depression of 1930–1933, and the ravages of World War II.

Town and Country had begun as a wholesale and retail supplier of home building materials, an interior decorator, and a wholesale supplier of rice. In 1920, the interior-decorating segment and rice-supply segment of the business were abandoned, and the firm began to devote its entire attention to hardware, plumbing, and building supplies. In 1950, a brand new $200,000 facility was constructed on 5 acres of land purchased on Highway 52—close enough to town to permit easy access for downtown shoppers but far enough away to permit the construction of a 50-car parking lot.

Today, after over 80 years in business, the firm continues to prosper: Town and Country is one of the busiest building supply companies in the area. In part, this success is due to the firm's popular chief executive and son of the founder, David Kai, who is well known for his many charitable activities, and also due to the company's purposeful response to the retail growth of the industry. The firm now operates four stores, some of which have as many as 20 merchandising departments. A special House-Planning Department has also been created to provide consultation and information services to the contracting trade and also to private homeowners. Other new programs include a full service garden center and (in the main store) a complete kitchen and bath improvement center.

The company has also concentrated on the wholesale side of its business. Almost all of the area's building contractors are personal acquaintances of David Kai, and the company does a substantial amount of wholesale business, most of which is conducted on credit. As in the retail side of the business, Town and Country's wholesale policy has been to develop a one-stop shopping center for all home-improvement needs.

One recent proposal placed on Mr. Kai's desk is to use point-of-sale terminals instead of the company's standard cash registers. These would be connected to a new computer system. It has been suggested that automating the company's sales activities would be of great value in both the retail and wholesale segments of the business. Mr. Kai is not familiar with computer equipment but is forward thinking and realizes that other businesses have been installing such equipment. Certainly he is anxious to do anything which would be cost effective for the business, to make things easier for his customers, and to increase the efficiency of his operations. Your task is to assist Mr. Kai by evaluating the proposal and making a recommendation.

4-28.   *Wingard National Bank*

Wingard National Bank's credit-card department issues a special credit card that permits credit-card holders to withdraw funds from the bank's automated teller windows at any time of the day or night. These windows are actually "smart" terminals connected to the bank's central computer. To use them, a bank customer inserts the magnetically-encoded card in the automated teller's slot and types in a unique passcode on the teller keyboard. If the passcode matches the authorized code, the customer goes on to indicate (1) whether a withdrawal from a savings account or a withdrawal from a checking account is desired, and (2) the amount of the withdrawal (in multiples of $10). The teller-terminal communicates this information to the bank's central computer and then gives the customer the desired cash. In addition, the automated terminal prints out a hard copy of the transaction and provides this information to the customer together with the cash.

To guard against irregularities in the automated cash transaction described, the credit-card department has imposed certain restrictions on the use of the credit cards when customers make cash withdrawals at automated teller windows. These restrictions include:

1. The correct passcode must be keyed into the teller keyboard before the cash withdrawal is processed.
2. The credit card must be one issued by Wingard National Bank. For this purpose a special bank code has been encoded as part of the magnetic-stripe information.
3. The credit card must be current. If the expiration date on the card has already passed at the time the card is used, the card is rejected.
4. The credit card must not be a stolen one. The bank keeps a computerized list of these stolen cards and requires that this list be checked electronically before the withdrawal transaction can proceed.
5. For the purposes of making withdrawals, each credit card can only be used twice on any given day. This restriction is intended to hold no matter what branch bank(s) are visited by the customer.
6. The amount of the withdrawal must not exceed the customer's account balance.

Questions

1. What information must be encoded on the magnetic card stripe on each Wingard National Bank credit card in order to permit the computerized testing of the policy restrictions enumerated above?
2. What tests of the restrictions indicated above could be performed at the teller window by a "smart terminal" and which tests would have to be performed by the bank's central processing unit and other equipment?
3. Prepare a program flowchart indicating the ordered processing logic that would have to be followed in order to enforce the credit-card limitations identified above.

5

Data Bases for Accounting Information Systems

Among the important questions you should be able to answer after reading this chapter are:

1 What is the difference between "batch" and "real-time" data processing?
2 What is meant by the term *accounting data base* and how does this data base differ from any other set of computer files?
3 What are the major differences between sequential computer files and direct-access computer files, and what data-processing operating characteristics make some accounting applications better suited to one of these file systems rather than the other?
4 What is meant by "chaining," and how is it used to speed the access of information in the computerized accounting information system data base?
5 How are accounting data bases used in practice? For example, how is the data required for their creation, maintenance, and use, organized, stored, and processed in order to provide meaningful decision-oriented information for management?
6 What are the advantages and disadvantages of accounting data bases?

INTRODUCTION

Chapter 4 discussed the data-collection process for the accounting information system, and suggested some ideas for automating the collection process in order to obtain a more efficient recording operation. In this chapter, we continue to trace the flow of information through the accounting information system by examining this data-storage process in detail. Here, we are not concerned with how the data are collected—our only concern is how to organize and store the data for efficient retrieval and use once the data have been obtained.

Conceptually, an accounting information system data base is a central collection of facts and figures that serves the accounting information needs of the various organizational subsystems. Although it is possible to provide such data bases manually, usually the data-processing volume of the typical business organization will be large enough to make a computerized data-base approach cost-effective. Thus, in this chapter we shall concentrate on computerized accounting data bases.

We begin by reviewing the concept of the computer file, and discussing how this computer file is updated in both batch and real-time processing environments. This background then sets the stage for our central chapter topic—the creation, maintenance, and use of accounting information system data bases. Finally, in the last section of the chapter, we examine some applications of the accounting data base through the study of some systems flowcharts and some brief descriptions of familiar accounting data-processing applications. For comparative purposes, these accounting applications will also be flowcharted and analyzed under a manual data-processing system.

COMPUTER FILES

The principal storage mechanism for computerized accounting data is the computer file, and the basic unit of information on the computer file is the computer record. The computer record stores all the information about one employee,

one customer, one inventory part, one checking account, one invoice, and so forth. Typically, the status information of the employee, the customer, the inventory part, and so forth is stored on a perpetual file called the *master file*. Thus, for example, the Alan Company would maintain a status file of inventory records (*inventory master file*), a status file of employees (*employee master file*), and so forth.

Figure 5-1 illustrates the Alan Company's computer record for an inventory application. Here, we recognize such basic information as the inventory item number, the unit price, and, of course, the quantity-on-hand balance. These data fields represent the basic, "status" data of the file record, and are critical to the decision-making efficiency of the Alan Company's managerial staff. In addition, we observe some less-familiar information such as vendor code and pointer addresses. These will be discussed at length in the later section on "Data Bases."

The data item in each computer record that distinguishes one record from another on the computer file is called the *record key*. This key identifies the record on the file and is used when information retrieval requires that a specific employee, inventory item, or credit account be accessed. Because of this identification function, the record key must also be unique. Thus, an employee file often uses the individual's social security number, an inventory file often uses a special part or raw-materials number, and an accounts receivable file often uses a special account number. In each case, the data item will be unique to the individual master file record and therefore useful for record-identification purposes.

In practice, it is sometimes convenient to combine two or more record fields to serve as the record key for a single computer record. For

Inventory item number	Assembly code	Vendor code	Assembly pointer address	Vendor pointer address	Balance on hand	Order quantity	Purchase price	Standard price	Standard quantity	Item description	Other information and codes
2120	38	100	C	D	260	2000	4.57	3.89	500	wood stock	. . .

Figure 5-1. The Alan Company's inventory master file record.

example, an inventory file might combine the part number with a warehouse or location code to uniquely identify a record, or a bank might combine its branch code with a customer account number to serve as the record key. This latter example was illustrated in Figure 4-6. The advantage of this approach is that the record key serves "double duty." On the one hand, the combined number serves to uniquely identify the computer record as discussed above. On the other hand, the separate numbers in the record key have informational content in their own right although individually, these items may not be unique to the record in which they are stored. Thus, for example, two checking accounts might have the same account number, but could be distinguished from each other if their separate branch codes were affixed to the numbers for identification purposes.

The status of the information on a computer file must be updated continuously to reflect business activity. People write checks, raw materials get requisitioned from inventory, and customers buy merchandise on credit. In each case, it is necessary to update the status information on the computer file. Customarily, the activity requiring master file updating is called *transaction activity*, and the information reflecting this activity is recorded on special computer records called *transaction records*. For control and audit purposes, moreover, transaction records are almost always recorded on a file of their own. Thus, the typical company is likely to have at least two principal files for each accounting application: a master file which maintains the account status, and a transactions file which maintains the activity information described above. The relationship between these two files and their role in accounting information systems is explored in detail below.

Batch Versus Real-Time Data Processing

To update an accounting master file, the transaction data are processed in one of two ways: either in *batch* or in *real-time* data processing. Each technique has both advantages and disadvantages, but both have the same fundamental purpose: to update the status information of the master file with the data of the transaction file in a cost-effective manner. Each of these approaches is examined more carefully below.

With batch processing, transaction items are collected, grouped, and processed together, that is, in a batch. Where transaction activity is low, the transaction data are collected over time and processed only when there are enough data to make a master file update efficient; for example, once a week or even on a demand (as desired) basis. However, banks which may process as many as 100,000 checks per day often choose to process check-cashing activity in batch because of certain financial control procedures available in batch-processing environments. (Controls are discussed in Part Three.)

Just because transaction data are processed in batch does not mean that these data must be collected entirely with manual methods. Figure 5-2, for example, illustrates a systems flowchart for our inventory example in which the data-collection process has been partially automated. In the figure we observe that computer terminals have been installed at the Alan Company's receiving dock, in the Alan Company's warehouse, and in the offices of the Alan Company's accounting subsystem. These terminals are online to the Alan Company's central computer, where the central processing unit can route incoming data directly to a waiting transactions file. In the flowchart, this file is stored on a magnetic disk. When a shipment of raw materials is received at the receiving dock, a warehouse clerk will enter the receipts data directly to the computer via the remote terminal. These data will be checked for accuracy (at least where input format is concerned), and then written directly on the special online transactions file where the data will await batch processing.

A similar description applies to the warehouse. As raw materials are disbursed from the warehouse, and also as finished goods flow back to the warehouse for temporary storage, the appropriate information is logged into the computer via the on-site computer terminal. Like the raw materials receipts data, the warehouse data may be checked for input accuracy and transferred to the transactions file to await batch processing.

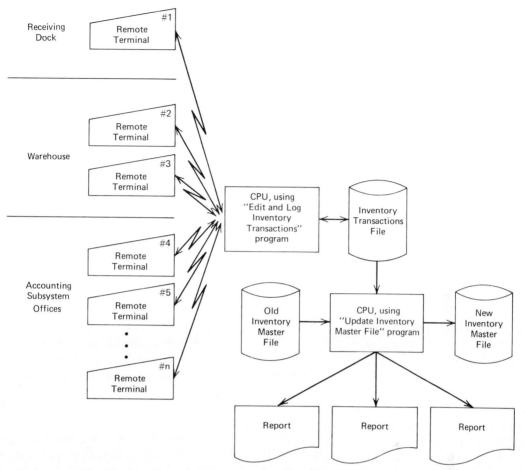

Figure 5-2. A systems flowchart for the collection, storage, and use of inventory transaction data for the Alan Company's batch-processing operations. This system is a remote job-entry system.

The terminals in the accounting subsystem are used primarily for inventory file maintenance. When authorization is obtained to buy raw materials from a new supplier, for example, it will be necessary to create new inventory records to reflect the new inventory items. Similarly, when suppliers go out of business, when business with an existing supplier is terminated, or when certain raw materials are no longer purchased by the company, it may be necessary to delete specific computer records from the inventory master file. Finally, with the passage of time, it will probably become necessary to update certain other data fields in the computer record, for example, the inventory item's purchase price. In all these instances, the accounting subsystem's staff will perform the required file-maintenance by inputting the transactions information into the computer via their terminals. As before, the data will be checked for accuracy and placed on the transactions file to await data processing.

In a batch-processing environment, the inventory transaction data described above would simply be stored on the transactions file until a master file update is executed. At that time, the status of the master file records would be changed to reflect the transaction activity, and the process of collecting transaction data would then begin anew. The transactions file containing the "old" transaction data would no longer be of immediate use to the Alan Company and could conceivably be erased or its disk storage used for some other purpose. More commonly, however, this information would be retained as a history of activity and for certain other functions not pertinent to our immediate discussion of batch processing. Thus, in all likelihood, the data would be transcribed from the disk medium to a magnetic tape reel (which is cheaper for storage purposes), and stored in the computer center library.

Were the inventory records of the Alan Company to be processed in real-time, the intermediate steps of maintaining the transaction data temporarily on a transactions file would not be required. In real-time processing, each transaction would cause an update of the appropriate master file at the time the transaction was entered at a particular terminal. Thus, inventory-receipts data would immediately increase the inventory balances of the affected items, inventory-requisition data would immediately decrease these inventory balances, and any file-maintenance data would immediately change the file as dictated by the type of change requested by the accounting staff. The inventory file would therefore consistently be updated at the time that the transaction data were input to the computer—hence the term, *real-time* data processing.

Real-time data processing is obviously much faster than batch data processing, and therefore has the potential to maintain a more current master file (i.e., a master file whose records more closely reflect the true status of the accounts). Moreover, because the master file record is accessed at the time that the input transaction is processed, the real-time data processing approach results in a much more thorough editing job. For example, when the Alan Company's warehouse clerk inputs an inventory account number in preparation for increasing the balance field, the computer system can find the record and output the item description on the terminal screen to help the clerk verify that the desired master file record has, in fact, been found. Similarly, if the clerk inputs a master file number for which no inventory record exists, this condition can also be determined immediately in real-time data processing and the clerk so notified. Corrections of inaccurate transactions data are thus greatly enhanced with real-time data processing

because faster feedback from the computer system is possible.

Real-time data processing systems also have drawbacks. For one thing, they are more expensive than batch processing systems because they must use direct-access devices such as disks or drums instead of cheaper magnetic tape. To guard against unwarranted access to the computer system and also to guard against costly human errors which might severely alter the computer master file, a much more elaborate set of controls and back-up procedures must be implemented. Typically, such controls are costly to develop, costly to maintain, and almost never 100 percent foolproof. Thus, a real-time computer system has the potential to be much more vulnerable than a batch-processing system to both intentional and unintentional input error. These problems are discussed more fully in the Part Three chapters on internal control.

A final difficulty with real-time computer systems is that they are harder to audit. This problem arises from the technicalities involved in updating direct-access files, a problem which is discussed more fully in the following section of this chapter. Suffice it to say here, therefore, that this difficulty also tends to add to the expense of developing, running, and documenting real-time computer systems, and makes such systems less desirable.

Despite their shortcomings, it should also be mentioned that real-time computer systems are gaining in popularity and are likely to replace many of the batch systems currently in commercial operation during the next few years. One reason for this is that computer hardware costs have been decreasing rapidly, and although disks and drums are still considerably more expensive than tapes, the price disparity has been decreasing steadily over the years. Thus, in relative terms, it is now easier for a company to afford a real-time data processing system. A more telling argument, however, is that companies now appear to be more willing to pay the price to obtain the real-time computer system. Thus, real-time systems are highly valued and more companies are implementing them.

The method by which accounting data is organized in the accounting files has an important bearing upon what can be done with the data in terms of our now-familiar chores of updating, record retrieval, and file maintenance. Although there are many file structures that might conceivably be used to maintain accounting data on a computer file, we shall concentrate on only two of these: sequential files and direct-access files. These are two of the most common forms of file organization and a knowledge of the way these structures work, their advantages, and their disadvantages, is important in understanding how the accounting files are used to support the various accounting activities of a business organization. In the following four sections of the chapter, therefore, we look at each of these methods of file organization in greater detail.

Sequential Files

As their name implies, sequential files are typically organized in ascending, record-key sequence. A good analogy would be a group of elementary school children who have been asked to line up in a single line according to height. The smallest child is analogous to the lead, or low-order record of the file; the largest child is analogous to the last, or high-order record of the file.

Magnetic tape is the most common computer storage medium for sequential files, although paper tape files and card files are also typically organized in ascending, record-key order. Such direct-access devices as magnetic disks and magnetic drums can also be used to store sequential files, and a surprising amount of accounting data is, in fact, stored on these devices in sequential format. Sometimes, for example, a disk will be used to store a sequential file on a temporary basis, as when two sequential files are being merged together (to form a single file of records organized in sequential order). At other times, it is more convenient to store a permanent sequential file on disk because disks have faster data transmission rates (i.e., input/output rates) than magnetic tapes, and thus, faster data processing can be obtained. Today, many computer systems are being installed without any magnet-

ic tape storage whatsoever. In these circumstances, of course, all sequential files required by the computer system's users will be stored on direct-access media by default.

Sequential files are easy to conceptualize and therefore have intuitive appeal. This appeal is strengthened by the fact that most manual accounting systems maintain accounting data in similar, ascending sequential order (e.g., according to invoice data, employee social security number, or bank-account number). Perhaps less obvious is that when sequential files are computerized, they also tend to make efficient use of computer storage. This results from the fact that, by definition, a sequential file is written on contiguous storage locations of a magnetic tape or disk, thus completely filling the computerized storage areas assigned to the file. This characteristic is not always true of direct-access storage files. (The reason is explained in greater detail shortly.)

There are many reasons why an accounting information system might choose to organize at least some of its files on a sequential basis. When chronological order is important (as would be necessary, for instance, in assessing the delinquency status of credit customer accounts), a sequential ordering of credit sales records by activity date would be useful in determining which accounts receivable customers' sales were overdue. This organization, by the way, would also serve as an internal control of data processing since the sequential order of the records on the file guarantees that all delinquent records will be identified because they would follow all the nondelinquent records on the file. A similar sequential ordering of purchase invoices, inventory receipts, or payment vouchers would make sense for those files that require processing in the chronological order in which their records are generated.

A sequentially-ordered file of accounting records may also be an efficient method of file organization when a large number of transaction records are involved in updating the master file at any one time. In such instances, a substantial proportion of the master file records will have to be accessed and changed no matter how the file is organized. A sequential file may be even faster than a direct-access file to perform this data processing if both the master file and the transactions file are already in sequential order. Thus, sequential files are particularly well suited to batch-processing accounting information systems in which the time between processing updates is of sufficient duration to guarantee the high volume of transactions required to make the sequential-update process cost-effective. In such situations, the direct-access file approach may not be as efficient.

In commercial accounting applications, there are many times in which every record on an accounting file must be processed. Sequential files are a convenient way of storing accounting records for such times, and in addition, assure that this data processing occurs completely. When the Alan Company prepares billing statements for its customers, for example, it will have to access every credit record on its accounts receivable file to make sure that all customers are sent billing statements. Similarly, a bank will want to send account-balance statements to every one of its active accounts, and an inventory-control manager may want the computer to scan the balance field of every inventory record on the company's inventory master file in order to identify stock items requiring replenishment.

A final argument in favor of the sequential file is found when the ''processing'' involved in a given computer processing task requires little more than printing selected information from each record on the file. For example, it may be necessary to print a listing of accounts payable invoices or employee payroll checks. In these circumstances, computer files organized sequentially by invoice number or employee social security number would probably be as effective as any method of file organization for maintaining the necessary file information.

Updating Sequential Files

The systems flowchart of Figure 5-2 has already illustrated the coordination of transaction records with an accounting information system master file for the purpose of updating the status

information on the latter file. Figure 5-3 illustrates the program, or logic, flowchart which would be followed in performing the update processing if the inventory master file in our example were organized in a sequential manner. Here, we shall be assuming that the inventory master file is being updated with transaction records that are processed in batch. Further, for purposes of illustration, we will assume that transaction records either change the data fields of the master file, or, alternately, create new master file records. To simplify the processing logic, we do not allow this processing to purge or drop master records from the files, and we also assume that it is not possible to reach the end of the master file before reaching the end of the transaction file. (In Figure 5-3, TX refers to transaction.)

The symbols in the program flowchart use the processing symbols adopted by the American National Standards Institute, as discussed in Chapter 19. However, many companies do not use these standard symbols and thus, it is advisable to concentrate on the logic *behind* the flowchart rather than memorizing the symbols themselves. We have also taken one liberty by numbering each symbol within the program flowchart. Again, this is for our own convenience in identifying the processing sequence rather than an adherence to convention.

It is easiest to follow the sequence of processing steps involved in the update of the sequential master file by looking at an example. The insert in the lower, left-hand corner of Figure 5-3, therefore, provides an abridged set of master file record keys, numbered 10, 20, 30, 40, 50, and 60, and a set of transaction records with numbers 20, 30A, 30B, 45, and 50. Transactions 20, 30A, 30B, and 50 reference existing master file records, and transaction 45 requires the creation of a new inventory record. There are two transactions for inventory record 30, which we have designated 30A and 30B. A ''double reference'' would occur, for example, if both an inventory reduction and a receipt for the same inventory item occurred within the same batch-processing period.

Although space does not permit a complete description of the processing involved in updating the inventory file as described in the example

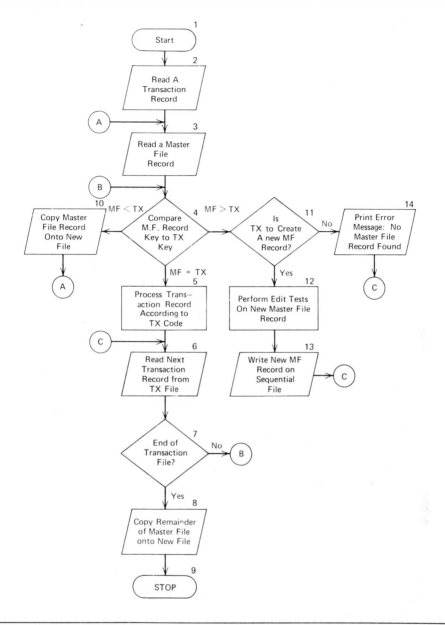

Figure 5-3. A program flowchart for updating a sequential computer file of inventory records.

Record Keys of Master File Records And Transaction Records to be Processed		Logical Order of Data Processing for These Master File and Transaction Records	
Master File	**Trans-actions**	**Master File**	**Sequence of Data Processing, by Symbol Number**
10	20	10	1 - 2 - 3 - 4 - 10
20	30A	20	3 - 4 - 5 - 6 - 7 - 4 - 10
30	30B	30	3 - 4 - 5 - 6 - 7 - 4 - 5 - 6 - 7 - 4 - 10
40	45	40	3 - 4 - 10
50	50	45	3 - 4 - 11 - 12 - 13
60		50	6 - 7 - 4 - 5 - 6 - 7 - 8
		60	8 - 9

above, we have included a symbol-by-symbol summary of the update logic in an insert in the lower right-hand corner of Figure 5-3. The sequence of numbers in this summary represents the sequence of computer steps that would be executed to accomplish the update routine. Thus, for example, we would start with symbol #1, read a transaction record in symbol #2, read a master file record (i.e., master file record number 10) in symbol #3, compare the master file and transaction record keys in symbol #4, and decide to copy the (low-order) master file record onto a new file in symbol #10. Since this sequence completes the processing of the first master file record, we have identified it on a single line of the lower right-hand corner insert summary. The processing continues on the next line with a reading of another master file record (symbol #3), a second comparison with the "old" transaction key already accessed (symbol #4), and so forth. Thus, each line of the process-description insert describes the processing logic for one computer record of the master file. When the processing is complete, the entire master file will have been recopied onto a new output medium—for example, a new tape reel—and, where appropriate, new master file records will have been inserted in their proper (ascending) sequence on the file.

In the above description of updating the master file records of a sequential file, it is important to note that the transaction records are being processed in a batch. Although this is the most common approach to processing sequential files, it is also possible to update sequential files on a real-time basis. With this alternative, each inventory transaction would trigger a search of the master file for the proper inventory record until either the matching master file record was obtained or a "not-found" master file condition was detected. Assuming a match occurs, the master file record would be updated and rewritten on the master file in the same physical place it occupied before. If a "not-found" condition occurs, of course, no master file updating can take place. In this latter case, therefore, the only thing that can be done is to signal the user—for example, through an error message on the user's remote

terminal video screen—that the not-found condition has been detected, and that it will be necessary for the user to recheck the input data before further processing is possible.

The reason a sequential master file is not normally used in real-time processing is because the master file must be searched from the beginning of the file, record by record, every time an update transaction is to be processed. On the average, therefore, half the master file will have to be passed (i.e., read) before the required master file record is encountered—if, in fact, it is encountered at all. With a sequential file of any reasonable length, this search time would be exorbitant. A further argument against the use of a sequential master file for real-time data processing is that such a system virtually precludes the insertion of new records or the deletion of old records on the master file. To accomplish these tasks, it would be necessary to recopy the entire file every time such a request for an addition or deletion were encountered. Clearly, unless the master file was tiny or these types of requests were very infrequent, this constant recopying of the master file would be impractical. Thus, for real-time processing it is necessary to use direct-access files, which are discussed in the paragraphs below.

Direct-Access Files

Direct-access files are commonly stored on magnetic disks or magnetic drums, where each record on the file can be located directly once its physical address on the storage medium is known. This addressability characteristic of direct-access files makes them ideal for inquiry applications in which a user wants to know the up-to-the-minute status of a particular accounting record. Thus, for example, airline reservation systems, perpetual inventory systems, and point-of-sale recording systems all make use of direct-access files. Normally, these files are constantly online, thus enabling the user to access the file around the clock.

Normally, only master files are maintained as direct-access files. This is because only master file records need be accessed repeatedly for updating and other file-maintenance purposes. Transaction files, which maintain activity data, can also be used more than once, but with these files, the accountant will rarely need to access a *specific* record. Thus, transaction files are usually maintained sequentially in either chronological or account-number order.

Direct-access files may be organized in any number of ways, but for purposes of illustration we shall concern ourselves with only two methods: (1) a dictionary approach and (2) a hashing approach. With a dictionary approach, direct-access file records are stored in random storage locations of the disk or drum, and a computer program creates a dictionary-like table of record keys and associated storage locations. The table is kept in CPU storage or maintained as a separate computer file. Figure 5-4 illustrates such a dictionary.

In Figure 5-4, the dictionary record-key entries are in ascending numeric sequence, and the letters in the figure represent physical addresses on the disk. In actual practice, of course, these letters would be numbers specifying the exact location on the disk at which the corresponding master file record can be found. The master file records identified in this portion of the dictionary are illustrated in Figure 5-7 and we shall be describing them in greater detail shortly.

Although the dictionary of record keys will list these keys in ascending sequence, the actual records themselves can be scattered throughout

Record Key	Disk Address[a]
⋮	⋮
2120	A
2121	B
2135	C
3436	D
4009	E
4668	F
⋮	⋮

Figure 5-4. A dictionary of disk addresses for the Alan Company's inventory file. ([a]Letters are used symbolically here. Each letter represents a different disk address consisting of cylinder number, track number, and record count.)

the file in any order. After all, as long as we have the address of a desired master record, its physical position on the disk should not matter. Sometimes, however, it is convenient to sequentially order these master records on a direct-access device but still maintain a dictionary for search and retrieval purposes. In these cases, the master file is said to be an *indexed sequential file*. An indexed sequential file is a direct-access file because the dictionary is still used to access records directly. Because the records themselves are ordered on the file, however, the master file is also sequential.

Accessing a master file record using a dictionary approach is much like finding a book in a library. At the library, the user first goes to the card catalog, finds the physical location of the book via the entry in the catalog card, and then proceeds to the shelf stacks to locate the book. In similar fashion, when a computer master file record is to be accessed, the user first has the computer program search the (sequentially-ordered) dictionary entries and, finding the appropriate record-key listing, proceeds to the physical address of the disk or drum dictated by the associated dictionary entry.

With a hashing approach, the record key is converted directly to a physical address on the direct-access file and the record subsequently stored in the location thus computed. Chapter 18 discusses files in detail. When the master file record is to be accessed using this approach, the computer program will perform the same algorithmic computations as when the master file record was first stored on the file. This should compute the same physical location address as before, and the computer system can then proceed directly to the computed address on the disk or drum in order to access the record desired.

An important characteristic of direct-access files using a hashing approach for record storage and retrieval is that the file records tend to be scattered randomly throughout the file. One implication of this characteristic is that not every physical location available for use on the file will necessarily have an actual record stored in it. Some areas of the file will in fact be "blank." Thus, a hashing approach to organizing a direct-access file has at least one important advantage and one important disadvantage. The advantage is that such an approach enables the user to avoid a sequential search through a dictionary before accessing a particular file record. The disadvantage is that even efficient hashing techniques cannot guarantee the complete utilization of file space on the computer-storage medium. Some areas of the file will not be used.

Updating Direct-Access Files

Direct-access files can be updated with either batched transactions or transactions taken one at a time on a real-time basis. In either case, the updating process is roughly the same. The process begins by taking a single transaction and determining which master file record requires updating. This will identify a unique record-key. The master file record desired can then be accessed directly using either the dictionary approach or the hashing approach discussed above.

Once the required master file record has been accessed, the actual data processing can take place. The master file record stored on the direct-access file is read and copied into the storage of the central processor. Here, the record's key may be verified again to make sure this is the master file record desired, and then the record may be updated as necessary—for example, by decreasing the balance field by the quantity of an inventory-reduction transaction. Once updating has been completed, the "new" master file record is written back on the direct-access file in exactly the same location at which it was found. This completes the update process for a single transaction. If transactions are processed in batch, subsequent operations repeatedly perform these steps in analogous fashion until all the transactions have been processed.

A common question asked when reviewing the update process of direct-access files is: "What happens to the information of the 'old' master file record after an updated master file record has been written in its place on the file?" The answer to this question is simple: the information is lost. From an accounting standpoint, therefore, direct-access files have a very undesirable

feature—updating in place has the potential to lose the audit trail. If the Alan Company were 100 percent certain that all of its transactions were recorded accurately, the audit trail problem might not be too serious. There is little likelihood, however, that all transactions are accurate. Consequently, the problem remains of how the system can recover when one or more incorrect transactions have "contaminated" the file. Furthermore, a similar problem is posed when the physical device itself fails (e.g., when the disk device suffers a "head crash" and the read/write head scars the writing surface of a disk), thus rendering the file unreadable. In both instances, the user must take precautionary measures.

The most common solution to these problems is a process called the *false update*. In effect, two copies of the master file are used at the start of each processing period—for example, at the beginning of each day. The first file is stored away as a backup copy, whereas the second file is placed online for processing purposes. Updating is "false" in the sense that all accounting transactions processed into the master file are considered temporary until the processing day is over. At this time, the transactions stored on yet a third file may be "proofed" or checked to make sure they are legitimate by using a variety of techniques (discussed in Part Three under "Internal Control"). Only when there appears to be assurance that the day's processing has in fact been executed properly will the updated master be accepted as current. At this point, the new file is copied and another day's "false-update" processing can commence.

DATA BASES

The proliferation of computerized accounting applications in recent years has been marked by a parallel growth in the number of computer files needed to support the various data-processing functions of a business organization. Typically, companies have computerized their operations "piecemeal," that is, by computerizing first one, then another, of its manual accounting tasks until all operations are automated. Under such circumstances, the computer files needed to support such applications are developed independently of each other, and the coordination of the information stored on these files is often minimal. The result is *data redundancy*, in which many of the computer files of an organization contain duplicate information. For example, in the top portion of Figure 5-5, three files of the Alan Company are depicted in which the computer record of each file is observed to contain at least one data field common to the other two files.

Although the maintenance of separate file information for each accounting application is not a bad solution, it does have several drawbacks. The maintenance of each file will require separate computer processing, for example, and the practice of preparing two back-up copies of each file for security purposes leads to the maintenance of nine files for our three-file illustration. Thus, where feasible, it often makes sense to pool the data from separate accounting applications into a common body of information called a *computer data base*. This leads us to the definition: a computer data base is a set of one or more

computer files which minimizes data redundancy and which is accessed by one or more application programs for the purposes of data processing.

An example of a data-base approach for our three-file illustration is provided in the bottom portion of Figure 5-5. In this case, all three files have been combined into one, and most, if not all, of the data redundancy has been eliminated. Now, all three application programs can utilize the same computer file, computer operations have been simplified, and less back-up files need be maintained for security purposes.

The data-base approach has several additional advantages. One obvious advantage is that the data base makes efficient use of computerized storage space while continuing to serve the informational needs of the heretofore separate file users. Moreover, when separate subsystems within an organization pool their data, a second advantage is that each subsystem has access to the other's information. For example, pooling of manufacturing and marketing data will have the added capability of providing distributional sales data which may be of assistance to the produc-

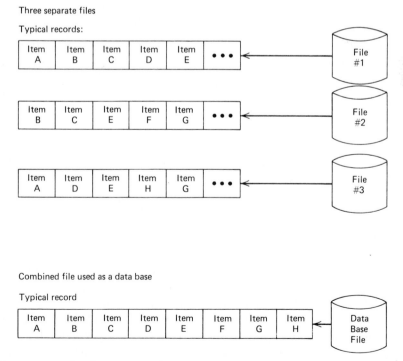

Figure 5-5. A data-base approach to accounting files eliminating data redundancy.

tion subsystem in planning manufacturing levels. Similarly, the marketing department staff may better fulfill its sales responsibilities if previously unknown information about manufacturing efforts are now made available.

Where subsystems are each gathering their own data, the data-base approach also has the important advantage of relieving some of the users from their data-gathering responsibilities. Of course, this is not always the case. Sometimes, the data required by one subsystem can be acquired only by that subsystem's users. However, even partial relief from the burdens of data collection and storage can sometimes save a company thousands of dollars yearly in terms of labor hours and computer data-processing time.

Sequential Files Are Rarely Used as Data Bases

Although sequential computer files can be used as accounting data bases, this use is not common. This is because, by definition, these files are accessed in sequential order. Usually, it is unlikely that any particular sequential ordering is ideal for more than one organizational subsystem sharing a common computer file. Multiple use of the same file therefore requires that the file be sorted into a different logical sequence with every different accounting application. This is both inefficient and time consuming. Thus, sequential files are rarely used as data bases in accounting information systems.

Direct-Access Files Used as Data Bases

The conceptual flexibility of the data base becomes clearest when it is implemented on direct-access files for multiple-user data processing. Consider again the Alan Company inventory example in which inventory balances are maintained as a direct-access file stored on one or more magnetic disks. The record format has already been presented in Figure 5-1. Two potential users of this file would be: (1) production managers, who might want a listing of the on-hand balances of various raw materials required in the manufacture of a certain type of sporting goods inventory, and (2) purchasing agents, who might want a listing of all raw materials supplied by the same vendor as a means of analyzing whether adequate trade discounts are being offered by certain vendors. Yet a third use of this file that would be applicable to both of these user groups would be an analysis of raw materials price and usage variances for each manufactured sporting goods product.

The information required to satisfy all three requirements is available in the same file, hence the term *data base*. To access the necessary inventory master file records, the production managers will concentrate upon the "assembly codes" of the inventory records which identify raw materials inventory items by assembly number. All raw materials required to produce a single finished product (e.g., catchers masks) will have the same assembly code. These codes therefore identify the inventory records of interest for the production process. An example of a report reflecting raw materials information for production managers is illustrated in Figure 5-6. Alternately, purchasing agents will concentrate on the vendor codes. All raw materials supplied by the same vendor will have the same vendor code. Thus, the purchasing agents will want to see all inventory master file records printed on a listing that have the same vendor code.

If the inventory file described above was maintained on a sequential basis, the listing processes required by the production managers and the purchasing agents would be quite tedious. For example, the raw materials records required by the production managers could be identified only by reading the entire master file and selecting those master file records with similar assembly codes. The necessary information from these records would then be printed on an output listing as the records were encountered sequentially on the file. The resulting listing would be a printout of raw materials, listed in ascending order of raw materials file number. Still further data processing would be required if the production manager wanted a printout in anything other than this sequential order.

Direct-access files permit their users to order accounting data "internally," or within the file structure itself. Figure 5-7, for example, illustrates the data base concept for inventory rec-

ALAN COMPANY INVENTORY STOCK REPORT
Subassembly: 40 "Catchers Masks"
Type: 1105   Date: 10-15-84

Inventory Code Number	Alphabetic Description	Balance on Hand	Vendor Number	Unit Cost
2121	Wire framing	310	228	$2.48
4009	Adjustable strap	225	402	0.37
4668	Rivets	9900	100	0.02

Figure 5-6. The Alan Company's raw materials inventory stock report for Assembly 1105.

FINISHED GOODS INVENTORY RECORDS

	Inventory Item Number (Record Key)	Assembly Code	Vendor Code	Assembly Pointer Address	Vendor Pointer Address	Balance on Hand	Order Quantity	Purchase Price	Standard Price	Standard Quantity	Other Information and Codes
Catchers masks	1105	40	—	B	—	525				100	. . .
Basketballs	1117	38	—	A	—	2090				500	. . .
Football Helmets	1125	25	—	H	—	6885				100	. . .

RAW MATERIALS INVENTORY RECORDS

Disk address

A	2120	38	100	C	D	260	2000	4.57	3.89	500	. . .
B	2121	40	228	E	C	310	1000	2.53	2.48	100	. . .
C	2135	38	228	D	XX	220	5000	9.77	8.75	500	. . .
D	3436	38	100	XX	F	180	1000	.58	.53	250	. . .
E	4009	40	402	F	H	225	2500	.35	.37	100	. . .
F	4668	40	100	XX	L	9900	10000	.02	.02	400	. . .

End-of-chain indicator

Figure 5-7. The Alan Company's direct-access file of inventory records.

ords that are stored on a magnetic disk. In the figure, finished goods inventory items have record keys beginning with a "1," whereas raw materials inventory items have record keys beginning with "2" or more. Each inventory master file record will have two special fields in them: a field containing an "assembly" pointer address and a field containing a "vendor" pointer address. These fields store disk addresses of additional inventory records which have something in common with the initial record. For this reason, these fields are said to store "pointer addresses." For example, the assembly pointer address field contains the disk address of the "first" raw materials record required for the listing of raw materials used in manufacturing a specific sporting goods product. Therefore, this is the physical location on the disk where the first master file record required for the raw materials production list of Figure 5-7 can be found. The term "first" is placed in quotes because this record is not likely to be the lead record stored on the file, except by chance. Rather, it is *logically* the first record we shall need to access in order to prepare the listing.

For illustration, let us trace the master file records required to print out the raw materials used in the assembly of catchers masks. The catchers mask inventory record is a finished-goods inventory record with record key 1105. Looking at the assembly pointer address field, we note that it has address "B" stored in it. This is the disk address of the first record (i.e., record 2121) to be printed on the raw materials assembly list. We note that record 2121 also has an address in its assembly pointer address field: address "E." This is the address of the next record (i.e., record 4009) to be printed on the raw materials assembly list. This record in turn has an address in its assembly pointer address field: address "F." This is the address of the third record (i.e., record 4668) to be printed on the raw materials assembly list. The process continues in succession, with each master file record in the internal list containing the address of the next record in the logical sequence, until the sequence is exhausted. A special code in the reference field (i.e., in this case the assembly pointer address field), or

perhaps simply a blank in the reference field, signals the end-of-list (or "chain") condition for the processing.

The vendor pointer address fields perform the same function as the assembly pointer address fields, except that the vendor pointer address fields link together raw materials inventory records whose inventory items are supplied by the same vendor. Thus, for example, should the Alan Company require a list of raw material inventory items supplied by vendor #38 in Figure 5-7, it can use these pointer addresses to access the necessary computer records directly. This type of internal list is useful when reordering is required because it is convenient to consolidate reorders for several different items on one purchase order if all such items are supplied by the same vendor.

Conventionally, the set of records which together make up an internal list on a computer file are said to form a *record chain* because they are linked together logically by their pointer addresses. If the address of the starting record (in our example, the catchers masks finished goods inventory record) is stored as the pointer address of the last record in the chain (i.e., instead of an end-of-chain symbol of some kind), the collection of data records in the chain is called a *ring*. The practice of storing the lead record's address in the ending record's pointer address field is useful when it is necessary to reprocess the starting record in some fashion after all other records have been accessed.

With a direct-access file, it is possible to create as many internal lists as are needed for data-processing purposes. In addition to our assembly list of the raw materials used in manufacturing a specific sporting goods product, therefore, we can construct a chain of records for each vendor on the file, for each type of raw material record stored on the file, for each purchasing agent, and so forth.

The advantages of chaining records on a direct-access file becomes immediately apparent if one envisions a master file of 10,000 inventory records and an assembly list or vendor list of less than 50 items. Clearly, it is more efficient to access 50 records directly using direct-access techniques than to examine each of 10,000 inventory records on a sequentially-ordered file in order to obtain the same list information. In actual practice, before sophisticated chaining techniques were developed and most data files were sequentially ordered, organizations often did without such information because it was too expensive to generate. Now, with computer hardware costs decreasing in relative terms, cost-effective data processing which exploits the direct-access data base concepts discussed above is more realistic.

Once the inventory file has been set up to print out a raw materials on hand report (as illustrated in Figure 5-6), it is a straightforward matter to extend the data processing to perform an analysis of raw materials price and usage variances for production-control purposes. To understand this extension, consider the necessary computations as outlined in Figure 5-8. The basic data required for the raw materials variance report are (1) actual quantity of raw materials used in production, (2) actual price paid for these raw materials, (3) standard quantity of raw materials that should be used in production, and (4) standard raw materials cost per unit. The actual quantity of raw materials used in production is obtained from the cost accounting transaction records associated with the manufacture of a particular finished good (e.g., the manufacture of catchers masks). The actual cost per unit for the raw materials, the standard quantity that should be used in production, and the standard cost per unit are all available directly from the inventory record.

To compute the actual cost of the raw materials used in the manufacture of a standard, 100-unit lot of catchers masks, for example, we would perform the following calculations:

Similar computations as outlined in Figure 5-8 can be used to compute the standard costs, the price variances, and the usage variances. A summary of such computations is provided in Figure 5-9, which illustrates the Alan Company's complete Raw Materials Variance Report for the 100-unit catchers mask production lot.

The importance of the Raw Materials Variance Report rests in the computational ease with which such a report can be generated once the data base has been properly organized. In effect, it is the file structure, not the agility of the central processor, which enables this report to be prepared quite easily. For one thing, the inventory file provides the basic data. More importantly, however, is the fact that these data are easily retrievable through the addressing capability of direct-access storage. Thus, the preparation of such reports becomes a straightforward task.

Data-Base Management Systems

Together with the development of the data base has been the development of *data-base management systems* (DBMS's). As the name implies, data-base management systems are special computer programs that maintain, manipulate, and retrieve the basic data within organizational files, and provide useful reports to organizational management. Thus, for example, a typical data-base management system would be capable of adding, deleting, or modifying accounting records on an accounting-information system file, sorting these records into a predetermined sequence according to any identifiable data field within the file records, modifying chains or rings, and/or printing specific file records according to some specified selection criterion.

Inventory Number	Description	Actual Cost Per Unit	Actual Quantity Used in this Production Lot[1]	Cost × Quantity Used
2121	Wire framing	$2.53	103	$260.59
4009	Adjustable straps	0.35	101	35.35
4668	Rivets	0.02	452	9.04
			Actual cost of 100 catchers masks	$304.98

[1]These figures would be obtained from transaction activity records not shown.

CALCULATION OF TOTAL RAW MATERIALS VARIANCE

Total Raw Materials Variance = Actual Cost − Standard Cost
where:

$$\text{Actual Cost} = \left(\begin{array}{c}\text{Actual Quantity}\\\text{Used in Production}\end{array}\right) \times \left(\begin{array}{c}\text{Actual Price}\\\text{Paid Per Unit}\end{array}\right)$$

$$\text{Standard Cost} = \left(\begin{array}{c}\text{Standard Quantity That}\\\text{Should be Used in Production}\end{array}\right) \times \left(\begin{array}{c}\text{Standard Cost}\\\text{Per Unit}\end{array}\right)$$

CAUSES OF RAW MATERIALS VARIANCE

Total Raw Materials Variance = Price Variance + Usage Variance
where:

Price Variance = (AP − SC) × (AQ) (Purchasing Agent's Responsibility)
Usage Variance = (AQ − SQ) × (SC) (Production Manager's Responsibility)
AP = Actual Price Paid Per Unit
AQ = Actual Quantity Used in Production
SC = Standard Cost Per Unit
SQ = Standard Quantity That Should be Used in Production

Figure 5-8. Analysis of Raw Materials Variance Within the Alan Company's Production Subsystem

ALAN COMPANY
ANALYSIS OF RAW MATERIALS VARIANCE
Product: Catchers Masks
Subassembly: 40   Type: 1105

Inventory Item Number	Description	(1) Actual Cost	− (2) Standard Cost	= (3) Price Variance	+ (4) Usage Variance
2121	Wire framing	$260.59	$248.00	($ 5.15)[a]	($ 7.44)[a]
3009	Adjustable straps	35.35	37.00	2.02[b]	(0.37)[a]
4668	Rivets	9.04	8.00	(0.60)[a]	(0.44)[a]
	Totals	$304.98	− $293.00	= ($ 3.73)[a]	+ ($ 8.25)[a]
	Raw materials Total variance:		($11.98)[a]	=	($11.98)[a]

[a] Unfavorable variance.   [b] Favorable variance.

Figure 5-9. The Alan Company's raw materials variance report.

Perhaps the most important aspect of the data-base management system is the formal recognition that many different types of accounting applications (or other information processing applications) can use the same type of data-base system, and that the development of a good, flexible, file-maintenance-and-retrieval system is not application-dependent. The result of this discovery is that software developers have been able to write very sophisticated data-base management systems which greatly expand the user's capacity to store accounting data, greatly accelerate the user's ability to retrieve data, and greatly improve the user's flexibility in changing, processing, or reporting accounting data. These advances have led accounting information systems specialists to think not in terms of specific accounting applications, but in terms of the general file structures and data-manipulating requirements of the applications.

ILLUSTRATIONS OF ACCOUNTING APPLICATIONS USING DATA BASES

To conclude this chapter, we will present here illustrations of how the computerized data-base concept can efficiently contribute to the processing of accounting transactions and the preparation of financial reports. Our illustrations will center around the following accounting processes:

1. The accounting cycle steps leading to the preparation of a company's income statement and balance sheet.
2. The preparation of budget projections, the comparison of actual operating results with these projections, and the completion of budget performance reports.
3. The processing of cash disbursements for credit purchases (emphasizing the credit purchase of inventory).

The above three accounting processes will first be discussed using manual data-processing methods. Then, to emphasize the data-processing effectiveness of computerized database systems, these accounting processes will again be examined with a data-base approach. It should be emphasized, however, that because every company's system is somewhat different, the specific data-processing procedures described below will vary from one company to another.

Manual Data-Processing Systems

Under a manual data-processing system, much of the work associated with each one of the three accounting processes described above would have to be performed independently. As business transactions occur, they would be processed through a company's accounting cycle steps (discussed in Chapter 1) for ultimate appearance

within financial reports—principally, the income statement and the balance sheet.

Subsequently (perhaps monthly), various transaction data recorded within the company's general and subsidiary ledgers (e.g., the total sales reflected in the general ledger account and the sales by product line reflected in the sales subsidiary ledger) would then be used to prepare budget performance reports. Under the supervision of the company's budget committee (discussed in Chapter 3), the long-range and short-range budgets would have been prepared prior to the beginning of the particular year's operating activities. At the close of each month the accountants would take the budget projection financial data, compare these data with the actual financial results contained within the ledgers, and prepare management-by-exception performance reports of significant budget variations. The system flowcharts in Figure 5-10 summarize the data-processing described above for the accounting-cycle activities and for budgetary analysis.

We will now turn our attention to the manual data-processing activities associated with inventory credit purchases and the issuance of cash disbursement checks for these inventory purchases. These activities are summarized in Figure 5-11. As various inventory items (such as raw materials needed for sporting-goods production) reach their reorder points, a company's inventory storeroom clerks would initiate purchase order requisitions for each inventory item's reorder quantity.

When the inventory items arrive at the receiving warehouse, the warehouse managers check their purchase-order files to ascertain that this inventory delivery was actually ordered by the company. The inventory items are then counted, and this count is recorded on a receiving report. When the receiving report arrives in the accounting subsystem, the accountants compare the receiving report data with their copies of the purchase order and the purchase invoice bill from the vendor. The accountants then record the inventory purchase transaction in the *purchases journal* (assuming a periodic inventory system, the journal entry would be: *debit* the

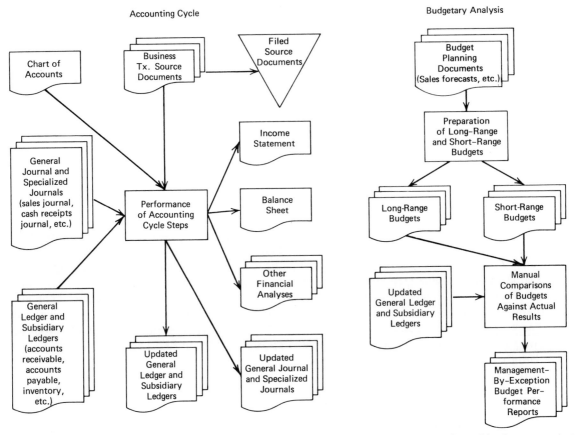

Figure 5-10. Systems flowcharts of the manual processes associated with accounting cycle and budgetary analysis work.

purchases account and *credit* the *accounts payable* account). This transaction is eventually posted to both the general ledger and the subsidiary ledgers for inventory and accounts payable. In order to take advantage of cash discounts offered (e.g., terms of 2/10, n/30), the purchase invoice would be filed (together with the receiving report copy) according to cash discount payment date so that it can be paid within the discount time period.

When the payment date of the invoice arrives, a cash disbursement check is authorized, prepared, and recorded in the cash disbursements journal, posted to the general ledger and the accounts payable subsidiary ledger, and mailed to the vendor together with one copy of the purchase invoice. (The journal entry recorded would be: *debit* the *accounts payable* account and

credit the *cash* account.) The second copy of the purchase invoice is kept on file within the accounting subsystem in a *paid invoices file*. The system flowcharts in Figure 5-11 summarize in broad terms the accounting processes described above for an inventory credit purchase and for the issuance of a cash disbursement check relating to this inventory purchase.

Computerized Data-Base Systems

As emphasized in the previous section's discussion of a manual data-processing system for executing various accounting processes (such as performing the accounting cycle steps, analyzing budget variations, and processing inventory purchase and cash disbursement transactions), each of these processes is performed independently.

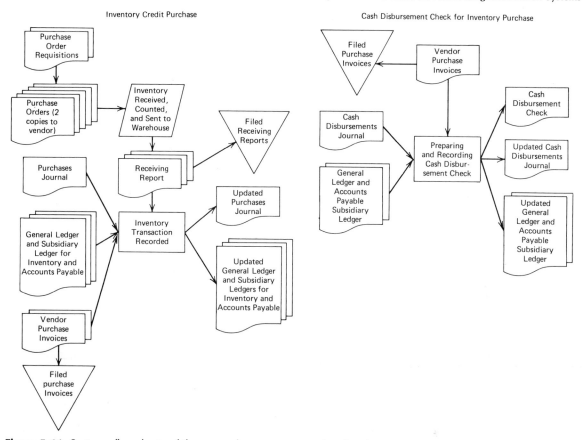

Figure 5-11. Systems flowcharts of the manual processes associated with an inventory credit purchase and a cash disbursement check for that purchase.

With the use of a computerized data-base system, however, a company's computer is able to integrate the performance of accounting processes, thereby contributing to data-processing efficiency.

To illustrate, Figure 5-12 reflects in broad terms a system flowchart integrating the accounting processes associated with financial statement preparation and budgetary planning and controlling activities. A company's journal entries during an accounting period and its period-end adjusting entries are accumulated on a magnetic disk file called the *journal transactions file*. Using this file together with the *chart of accounts file* and the *general ledger file*, and utilizing the *financial statements program*, the computer then performs the necessary accounting cycle steps for the preparation of the com-

pany's financial statements. (Additional computer runs would be necessary to update the accounts receivable subsidiary ledger, the accounts payable subsidiary ledger, the inventory subsidiary ledger, etc.) An income statement, a balance sheet, and other financial analyses (such as a retained earnings statement) are printed out by the computer and an updated file for the general ledger is created.

Figure 5-12 also discloses the budgetary planning and controlling activities within the company. The *budget file* in Figure 5-12 includes long- and short-range budget projection data. This file resulted from the execution of the *create budget file program*. By utilizing the *projections program*, the computer can print out the company's long- and short-range budgets as well as the projected financial statements. The "heart"

155

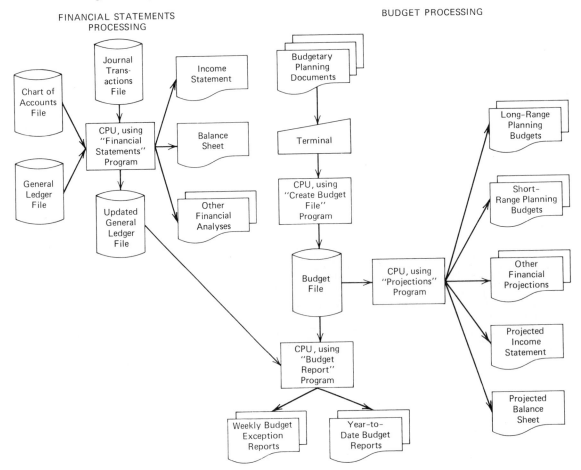

Figure 5-12. System flowchart of the computerized data-base processes associated with financial statement preparation and budgetary planning and controlling.

of the integration between the accounting cycle activities and the budget activities is in the *budget report program*. The data inputs to this program are the *budget file* and the actual operating results contained within the *updated general ledger file*. Through the execution of the *budget report program* using these files, weekly budget exception reports and year-to-date budget reports are printed out by the computer.

An examination of the system flowchart for the credit purchases of inventory and the authorization of accounts payable cash payments for these purchases (see Figure 5-13) reveals further integration of accounting processes. Using the *edit and purchase order log program* with purchase order requisitions as input,

an *unsorted purchase orders file* is prepared. Using a sort utility program, a *sorted file of purchase orders* by vendors is created. The *vendor master file* (which contains information about each inventory vendor such as name, address, etc.) and the *purchase orders sorted by vendors file* are then used as input to the *purchase order program*. This program creates five purchase order copies, a summary log by vendors of purchase orders processed, and a *pending purchase orders file* (i.e., purchase orders mailed to vendors for which the inventory items have not yet been received).

The heart of the integration of the accounting processes for inventory purchases and cash payment authorizations associated with these

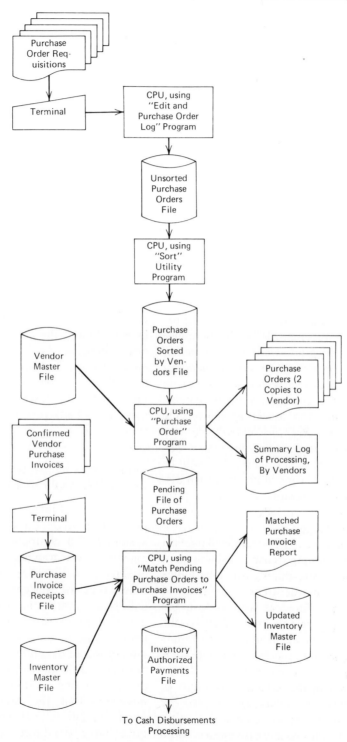

Figure 5-13. System flowchart of the computerized data-base processes associated with credit purchases of inventory and cash payment authorizations.

purchases centers around the *match pending purchase orders to purchase invoices program.* The set of input data for this program will be the file of pending purchase orders and the purchase invoice receipts file. The latter file is created as follows: when a vendor purchase invoice is mailed to the company, the invoice is manually compared to the receiving report relating to the particular inventory purchase. If the two source documents are in agreement (that is, the quantity of inventory items shown on the receiving report agrees with the quantity reflected on the purchase invoice), the data from the "confirmed vendor purchase invoice" such as inventory description, inventory quantity, and total cost, are keyed into the terminal to create the *purchase invoice receipts file.*

Regarding those pending purchase order file items for which a match is obtained between a purchase order and a purchase invoice (from the "purchase invoice receipts file"), the purchase invoice data will be printed out on a *matched purchase invoice report.* The *match pending purchase orders to purchase invoices program* will also update the company's inventory accounts (i.e., the updated inventory master file created from the old *inventory master file;* see Figure 5-13) and prepare the *inventory authorized payments file.* This latter file will be used in other computer runs to process cash disbursement checks for creditors (see Figure 5-14) and to update the general ledger and accounts payable subsidiary ledger.

Figure 5-14 illustrates the systems flowchart associated with issuing cash disbursement checks to creditors. Determining which liabilities are due for payment in order to take advantage of any cash discounts offered as well as to avoid delinquent vendor payments is handled by the *create authorized payments program.* The inputs to this program are the *accounts payable subsidiary ledger file,* the *inventory authorized payments file* (created in the systems flowchart of Figure 5-13), and the *payments request file.* The payments request file reflects liabilities other than for the credit purchase of inventory. Both this file and the *payments request register* are created by using the *payments request transac-*

tion log program, whose input consists of various payment request forms (such as requests for insurance premium payments, for monthly utility bill payments, and for monthly rent payments).

The *merged authorized payments file* and a *summary listing of authorized payments* are prepared using the *create authorized payments program.* Included on the *merged authorized payments file* are data (such as name, address, and amount owed) regarding each creditor that should be issued a cash disbursement check.

Through the execution of the *pay-em program,* which uses as input the *merged authorized payments file,* the *accounts payable subsidiary ledger file,* and the *cash disbursements file* (containing the date, check number, payee, amount, etc., for each cash disbursement check issued), individual cash disbursement checks for issuance to creditors are prepared. In addition, this program updates the accounts payable subsidiary ledger file and the cash disbursements file, and also creates a *check register of cash disbursements report.* The *updated cash disbursements file* will be used as input in a subsequent computer run (not described here) to prepare the company's bank reconciliation statement.

Concluding Comments on Accounting Applications Illustrated

The purpose of illustrating the above accounting applications under both a manual data-processing system and a computerized data-base processing system was to emphasize the data-processing effectiveness that can result from utilizing the latter type of system. With a computerized data-base system, the performance of many accounting processes can be integrated, thereby contributing to data-processing efficiency. This integration in executing accounting processes is normally difficult to achieve under a manual data-processing system. It should be noted, however, that the establishment of a computerized data-base system in a company will require an expenditure. Unless the anticipated benefits from the computerized data-base system are expected to exceed the system's costs, some

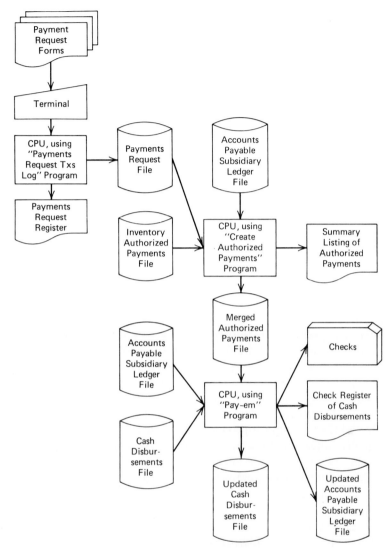

Figure 5-14. System flowchart of the computerized data-base processes associated with issuing cash disbursement checks to creditors.

alternative data-processing system should be considered.

SUMMARY

This chapter has discussed the concept of computerized data bases, and has illustrated how such data bases are used in accounting information systems. In such systems, the principal means by which accounting data are stored and referenced is through the use of individual records which are collectively organized into computer files.

Typically, the master file in an accounting application is maintained and updated by transactions which reflect business activity. These transactions may be used to update the master file in at least one of two ways: (1) in batch data processing, and (2) in real-time data processing. Using a batch approach, transaction records are collected on a separate computer file for a period of time and then used to update the master file in

159

chronological data-processing cycles. Using a real-time approach, the master file is updated as soon as the transaction record is input to the computer. Both magnetic tape files and magnetic disk files are suitable computer storage media for batch processing. However, only magnetic disk (or magnetic drum) files are normally used in real time data-processing situations because of the need for immediate access to the master file record.

There are two principal types of file organization: sequential and direct-access. Normally, sequential files store computer records in ascending record-key sequence, although the use of some other data field in addition to the record key is sometimes used for this purpose. Sequential files have a natural organizational logic, use file space efficiently, and are often as effective as any method of file organization when a large proportion of a master file must be accessed in a data-processing task. Direct-access files, on the other hand, exploit the addressability characteristic of their storage media, and permit their users to locate file records on a more immediate basis. This chapter has discussed two major techniques for accessing file records on direct-access files: (1) a dictionary approach, and (2) a hashing approach. Although fundamentally different in concept, both of these approaches permit the direct access of a computer record on a direct-access file without the need to search through a master file on a record-by-record basis.

Accounting information system data bases are typically implemented as direct-access files using magnetic disks. Data bases minimize the data redundancy which results when different accounting applications each maintain duplicate information in their files, and data bases are also an efficient means of integrating the accounting information which is collected, processed, and used by different subsystems within an organization. Thus, we have defined an accounting information system data base as a set of one or more computer files which minimizes data redundancy and which is accessed by one or more application programs for the purposes of data processing.

To produce reports from information stored in a data base, it is usually necessary to access specific master file records in a specific order. A common means of accomplishing this data access is through the use of record chains, in which each computer record in the logical sequence stores the disk address of the next record in one of its data fields. The use of chained records to produce managerial reports was illustrated with an inventory example, in which a data base of inventory records of the Alan Company was used to produce an Inventory Stock Report and also an Analysis of Raw Materials Variance Report.

The last section of this chapter illustrated three accounting applications which might be performed either manually or with a computerized data base: (1) the preparation of a company's financial statements, (2) the preparation of budget reports, and (3) the processing of cash disbursements for credit purchases, emphasizing the credit purchase of inventory. The manual processing involved in each of these accounting applications was reviewed, and both system flowcharts and brief descriptions were used to illustrate how these tasks might be computerized. Under manual processing, it was noted that each processing task is performed independently of the others. With a computerized, data-base approach, however, the execution of these accounting processes can lead to a high degree of integration. This integration, in turn, increases the effectiveness of the accounting information systems involved.

DISCUSSION QUESTIONS

5-1. Describe the function of the *record key* in the typical accounting file. Are such keys simple or complicated? Name four files that might commonly be found in an accounting information system environment and for each file, identify a data field which could conceivably be used as a record key.

5-2. Describe the relationship between an accounting master file and an accounting transactions file. Are both of these files created about the same number of times? Explain.

5-3. Provide some reasons why a company might want to keep a permanent copy of its transaction records. Why aren't these records thrown out after they have been used?

5-4. What is the difference between batch and real-time data-processing systems? Give some advantages of using each approach to data processing.

5-5. A common difficulty encountered in data-processing updating of a master file is the "no-master-file-record-found" condition. Explain this condition in detail. When would such a condition be likely to occur? What can be done about this condition in both batch and real-time data processing environments?

5-6. What problems do real-time data processing systems pose for auditing functions? How are these problems avoided with batch processing systems? What steps are commonly taken in accounting practice to overcome the real-time data-processing problems which you have described?

5-7. What is an *accounting data base*? What distinguishes an accounting data base from a typical, "garden-store-variety" accounting file of computer records?

5-8. This chapter has stressed several advantages of the accounting information system data base. Identify and explain in detail three such advantages. Identify some specific costs associated with implementing data-base methodology in practice.

5-9. Mr. John Langtree has been an auditor with an old, reliable CPA firm for many years. He had seen the first computers installed in his clients' offices, and had seen the computer's use expand rapidly over the past 30 years. When asked why he had never learned computer methodology, Mr. Langtree responded: "No need. The computer does nothing more than what it is told, and further, mostly does only what manual accounting systems have been doing for more years than I care to remember." Comment.

5-10. Describe the relationship, if any, between: (1) computer technology, and (2) the manner by which accounting records are logically ordered on a computer file. Consider in your discussion, for example, data-processing speeds, type of secondary-storage devices, remote-terminal access to the central processing unit, and so forth.

5-11. Name some advantages of sequential computer files. What are the disadvantages of this method of file organization?

5-12. Why are sequential files not normally used in real-time data processing applications? Is such an approach impossible or simply impractical? Explain.

5-13. Direct-access files, by definition, must have an "addressability" characteristic. What is this characteristic, and why is it important for direct-access files?

5-14. Direct-access files use either a "dictionary approach" or a "hashing approach" to organize and/or retrieve records stored on them. Describe each approach in detail. What are the advantages and disadvantages of each approach? Which of these two approaches do you prefer? Explain.

5-15. How is a direct-access file updated? How does this updating differ from updating sequential master files? How would you respond to the following common question regarding direct-access file updating: what happens to the old record?

5-16. What is meant by the term *false update*? What is "false" about it? If it is false, why is it used?

5-17. Discuss both the advantages and the disadvantages of using a computerized data-base system rather than a manual system for executing accounting processes. In this discussion, provide some specific accounting application examples which illustrate your previously-mentioned advantages and disadvantages.

5-18. Refer back to Figure 5-12. Discuss the advantages of a computerized data-base system compared with a manual system for executing the accounting functions associated with "financial statement preparation" and "budgetary planning and controlling."

5-19. Refer back to Figure 5-13. Discuss the advantages of a computerized data-base system compared with a manual system for executing the accounting functions associated with "credit purchases of inventory" and "cash payment authorizations."

5-20. Refer back to Figure 5-14. Discuss the advantages of a computerized data-base system compared with a manual system for executing the accounting function associated with issuing cash disbursement checks to creditors.

Item	Actual Quantity Used	Standard Quantity	Actual Cost Per Unit	Standard Cost Per Unit
7664	100	100	$ 3.98	$ 3.50
7990	240	200	4.50	4.75
8777	310	300	25.85	25.50
8832	290	300	8.77	8.77

PROBLEMS

5-21. Refer to Figure 5-1. For each data field in the inventory record of the figure, identify the individual(s) or department(s) most likely to be responsible for the initiation of changes when alterations to that particular field become warranted.

5-22. Refer to Figures 5-6 and 5-7. Prepare a Basketball Raw Materials Stock Report using the inventory data in Figure 5-7.

5-23. Refer to Figures 5-7, 5-8, and 5-9. Prepare a Raw Materials Variance Report for the Alan Company in the production of basketballs. Assume the following usages:

Item:	2120	2135	3436
Actual usage:	530	565	240

5-24. Will Grant is the head accountant for the John Wallace Construction Company. This company manufactures hardwood cabinets and counters used in the construction of single-family homes and multiple-family condominiums. The cabinets and counters are prefabricated in the factory and then shipped, ready-made, to the construction site for installation. One day, Will Grant was given the data listed below describing the prices and quantities of various raw materials which the company had just used in the manufacture of 200 kitchen counters, company catalog number 1098-E (Koa wood finish). Using the data provided Will Grant, prepare a Raw Materials Variance Report for the Wallace Company.

5-25. The Ekroth Company is currently involved in the conversion of its manual data-processing system to a computerized data-processing system for handling of its accounting functions. One of the major accounting processes that will be handled by the new computer system is the company payroll. As the company began to analyze its needs, it became clear that the payroll file would be utilized by several departments within the company. For example, the personnel department would need to access the file in order to prepare the initial employee record and make pay-rate changes. The accounting department would also need access to the file in order to disburse paychecks. Even the company credit bureau would need to access the file in order to credit employees with contributions.

Making any assumptions you consider reasonable, draw a set of system flowcharts indicating how the various users of payroll information might utilize a payroll file: (1) using manual methods, and (2) under a new, computerized, data-base approach.

5-26. Refer to Problem 5-25 above. Assume that the Ekroth Company will also be computerizing the information describing its plant and equipment. Again, making any reasonable assumptions you wish, draw system flowcharts of: (1) how the company's plant and equipment data might be processed under a manual system, and (2) how the company's new computerized system might handle this same accounting function using a data base.

5-27. Ann Sproul and Associates has just computerized its accounts receivable file and wishes to age its credit-sales transactions.

Each record on the file represents a separate sales transaction which is yet to be paid, and the file is organized as follows. All sales transactions for the same credit customer have been stored together on the file in ascending order of transaction date. Each set of all such transaction records is blocked as a variable-length physical record. The record blocks are arranged in ascending account-number order.

Required:

(a) Draw a diagram illustrating how the transaction records will be stored on the accounts receivable file.

(b) Develop a system flowchart for the com-

puter processing required for this aging task, assuming the accounts receivable transaction file is stored on magnetic disk. The output from this processing is the aging report.

5-28. Below is a system flowchart for processing the sales transactions and sales remittances of the Berger Corporation. The analyst who prepared the flowchart was able to draw the appropriate symbols, but was called away before she could finish putting labels in their proper places. Fill in the missing description for each symbol. Don't forget to identify the processing runs.

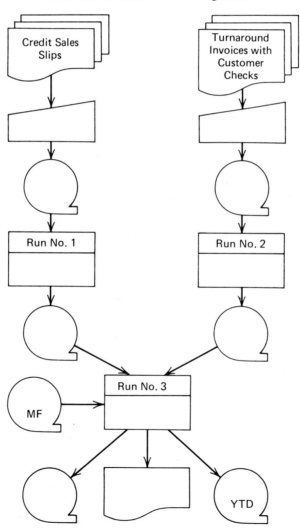

5-29. The City of Bettem is contemplating legalizing off-track betting on horse races, and has hired a systems analyst to design a real-time computer system which might perform the data gathering, recording, and data processing for it. The systems analyst drew the systems flowchart below just before mobsters from the syndicate "rubbed him out." In your own words, describe how the system would work based upon this flowchart. Assume that your description would be presented to the city council, so try not to be too technical.

CASE ANALYSES

5-30. *Paper, Inc.**

A systems-analysis study has been completed in a large company (called Paper, Inc.) which manufactures and markets various types of paper for the printing industry. This study initially was intended to identify the informational requirements related to the purchasing function, but was subsequently expanded to include the accounts payable function as well. The justification for expanding the study was based on the similarity of the data required in the data base to support each function.

The study identified the need for purchasing to maintain three files: (1) a customer master file containing name, address, purchasing terms, and

*Used with the permission of John G. Burch, Jr., and Felix R. Strater, Jr., *Information Systems: Theory and Practice* (New York: John Wiley and Sons, Inc., 1979).

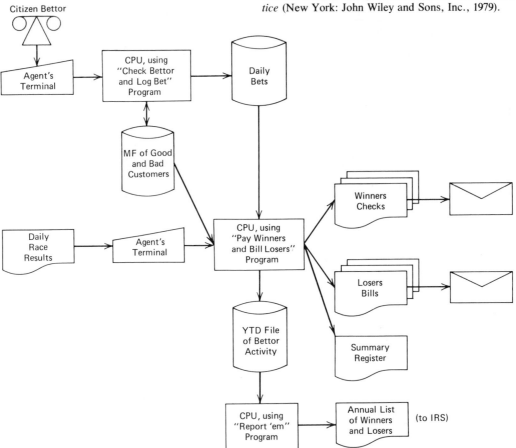

miscellaneous descriptive data, (2) an open purchase order file containing all of the data related to purchase orders placed but not yet completed, and (3) a history file of purchases made in a two year period, by product, within customer. At the time of the study, these files were maintained in a manual system.

The accounts payable department on the other hand required the following files: (1) a customer master file which contains the descriptive data necessary to produce and mail a check for purchases received, (2) a file of invoices from vendors received but not yet paid, and (3) a one year history file of paid vendor invoices. Currently, accounts payable maintains a manual customer master and open invoice file. A tab system was used to create checks to vendors and to maintain paid invoice history.

The company leases a medium-sized computer with both magnetic tape and disk storage available in a batch processing mode. Approximately 20% of all purchases are considered re-buys from an existing vendor. At any point in time there are 3000 active vendors; 5000 open purchase orders; 1500 open invoices; and annually, the company places 40,000 purchase orders.

From the above facts, your assignment is to determine the following:

1. How many data files are necessary in the required data base?
2. What data fields will be required in each data file? (Prepare a table or matrix which illustrates the relationship of data fields among files.)
3. What storage medium should be used for each data file?
4. How should each file be updated, and which department is responsible for keeping each file current?

5-31. *Santa's Toys**

A large manufacturer of children's toys (called Santa's Toys) is considering the implementation

*Used with the permission of John G. Burch, Jr., and Felix R. Strater, Jr., *Information Systems: Theory and Practice* (New York: John Wiley and Sons, Inc., 1979).

of a marketing information system to assist its sales force. There are approximately 300 salespeople working out of 15 branch offices throughout the continental U.S. and Canada. The goal of the system will be to have customer sales history files online at central headquarters which can be accessed by remote terminals at each branch office during normal business hours. New customer orders, and shipments which are received from each branch office nightly, will update the sales history file that same night.

There are approximately 30,000 customers on the file at any one time. Approximately 50 customers are added, and 20 customers deleted, daily. History will be maintained for 13 months by product for each customer. Each customer is expected to have a master record with descriptive data equal to 100 characters. The average number of product records per customer is expected to be 20, each with 70 characters of information. Finally, projections indicate that the volume of order and shipment records for updating the history file will be 3000 nightly.

Questions

1. How many files would you recommend for this data base?
2. Would you recommend that these files (this file) be placed on tape, disk, or some other medium? Explain.
3. Roughly, how much room would be required to store 30,000 customer records on your recommended file(s)? How much room would be required to store 13 months worth of product history records on your recommended file(s)?

5-32. *The Huron Company*

Huron Co. manufactures and sells eight major product lines with fifteen to twenty-five items in each product line. All sales are on credit, and orders are received by mail or telephone. Huron Co. has a computer-based system that employs magnetic tape as a file medium.

All sales orders received during regular working hours are typed on Huron's own sales order form immediately. This typed form is the source document for the keypunching of a shipment or backorder card for each item ordered. These cards are employed in the after-hours processing at night to complete all necessary record keeping for the current day and to facilitate the shipment of goods the following day. In summary, an order received one day is to be processed that day and night and shipped the next day.

The daily processing which has to be accomplished at night includes the following activities:

1. Preparing the invoice to be sent to the customer at the time of shipment.
2. Updating accounts receivable file.
3. Updating finished goods inventory.
4. Listing of all items backordered and short.

Each month the sales department would like to have a sales summary and analysis. At the end of each month, the monthly statements should be prepared and mailed to customers. Management also wants an aging of accounts receivable each month.

Required

A. Identify the master files which Huron Co. should maintain in this system to provide for the daily processing. Indicate the data content which should be included in each file and the order in which each file should be maintained.

B. Employing the system flowcharting symbols used in the chapter, prepare a system flowchart of the daily processing required to update the finished goods inventory records and to produce the necessary inventory reports (assume that the necessary magnetic tape devices are available). Use the annotation symbol illustrated below to describe or explain any facts which cannot be detailed in the other flowcharting symbols.

Annotation (Explain details within the symbol and attach by a dotted line to the pertinent point in the flowchart)

C. Describe (1) the items that should appear in the monthly sales analysis report(s) the sales

department should have and (2) the input data and master files that would have to be maintained to prepare these reports.

(CMA Adapted)

5-33. Car Consultants*

A car manufacturer has implemented a program whereby its customers can call a district representative toll-free to lodge any complaints, or dissatisfactions, which they feel were not adequately handled by their dealer. The district representative then attempts to aid the customer by coordination with the dealer, the manufacturer, or both. Phase I of this program was launched by a national advertising campaign. The major objectives of Phase I were to fortify the company's image in the area of customer service, and to increase customer confidence in the reliability of the company's product.

The objective of Phase II has been formulated, but the detailed modifications to the original program have not been firmed up. The basic goal of Phase II is to create feedback from the customers to the manufacturer. The data flowing through the feedback loop would be stored in a data base, where it would be available to various functional areas within the corporation. Two obvious users would be the design engineers and quality control people. It is apparent that information from the field would be valuable in quickly replacing defective parts and improving the design of parts and components. The corporation executives see the network of district representatives as a skeletal framework which could be expanded to handle the demands of Phase II.

Additional Background Information

In addition to handling customer complaints, the district representative also serves as a watchdog on the dealers in his zone. In this role, he must ascertain that the individual dealers, franchised by the company, are complying with the service standards imposed by the corporation. The office

*Used with the permission of John G. Burch, Jr. and Felix R. Strater, Jr., *Information Systems: Theory and Practice* (New York: John Wiley and Sons, Inc., © 1979).

staff and facilities of the representatives are presently limited to those needed in the performance of Phase I duties.

Two coding structures utilized by the corporation may be useful in this problem. The first is the serial number affixed to each auto. A sample serial number and its interpretation is given below.

2 G 2 9 R 4 G 1 0 6 1 1 3

2 G	Brand name (major manufacturers produce several brands)
2 9	Body style (station wagon, sedan, etc.)
R	Engine (code representing engine model)
4	Year (last digit of year)
G	Factory (factory where produced)
1 0 6 1 1 3	Car's serial number (unique code depicting one particular car)

A second code structure is used for identifying parts. Each individual part of an automobile is coded with a nonintelligent, 7-digit number. (A nonintelligent number is one · used only for identification and has no coded meaning.) To facilitate the retrieval of part numbers, all the part numbers are structured within a directory code. The directory code is composed of five digits. The first two run from 00 to 15 and identify the major subsystems; i.e., 01 represents Engine Cooling, Oiling, and Ventilating systems. The last three digits are a serial code representing the individual parts incorporated in the major subsystem. An example may provide clarity. Let us assume that we're trying to locate the part number for the oil pump cover gasket for a 1981 6-cylinder Bassethound. The Bassethound is one of the brands produced by the major manufacturer, Dogs, Inc. Searching the directory we find that 01.724 is the directory number for oil pump cover gaskets. This number is the general part number for all oil pump cover gaskets produced by Dogs, Inc. Looking in the parts manual under 01.724 we find the specific part numbers for this particular gasket for the individual years and models. Searching this list we find that the gasket for a 1981 Bassethound 6-cylinder has a part number of 3789970. This number identifies the exact part.

In concluding the background information, one point should be emphasized. Under the present system, the district representative only receives information concerned with customer complaints. The details and financial arrangements of warranty service, performed by the dealer in a satisfactory manner, are communicated directly between manufacturer and dealer, bypassing the district representative. You may desire to alter this information flow in your solution.

Questions

Bearing in mind the extensive resources available to a major automobile producer, present your ideas about the following aspects of the proposed Phase II system:

1. Specific description of the data which should be collected.
2. How the data should be collected, and by whom.
3. How the data should be transmitted to the manufacturer.
4. How the data should be stored at the corporation's main office in order to facilitate retrieval by numerous users.

6

A Manual and a Computerized Accounting Information System

Among the important questions you should be able to answer after reading this chapter are:

1 In what ways can the maintenance of a manual accounts receivable system be boring and error-prone?

2 In what ways can the maintenance of a computerized accounts receivable system be boring and error-prone?

3 What does the automated accounts receivable processing system use to replace the subsidiary ledger of the manual accounts receivable processing system?

4 Why does a computerized accounts receivable processing system break down the processing into a number of "runs"? In particular, why can't all the data processing be done at once?

5 A computerized accounts receivable processing system is accurate, reliable, and cost-effective when a large number of accounts are to be maintained. Why would anyone argue in favor of continuing a manual system?

INTRODUCTION

Up to this point, we have discussed the accounting information system piecemeal. This was necessitated by the large amount of computer concepts and systems background to be understood and which have now been discussed in prior chapters. Here, we illustrate a typical accounting information system which integrates these various concepts and systems ideas in a unified data-collecting, data-processing, and information-dissemination system. Thus, the purpose of this chapter is to tie together our preceding discussions of subsystem interaction, data collection, and so on, through the examination of a practical accounting application. To accomplish our purpose, we have chosen an accounts receivable system for illustration, although this choice is somewhat arbitrary—a payroll application, inventory application, or accounts payable application would be equally appropriate.

To set the stage, the following section discusses the accounts receivable function, and how such a function would be performed in a manual system. Next, we shall look at an automated accounts receivable system and examine what must be done to implement a computerized version of this system. Finally, in the last section of this chapter, we shall briefly compare the two systems and examine the advantages and disadvantages of each.

A MANUAL ACCOUNTS RECEIVABLE INFORMATION SYSTEM

The American commercial system thrives on credit. Wholesalers purchase items on credit in order to carry the inventories eventually required by their retailers. Retailers purchase on credit in order to carry the inventories eventually required by their customers. Consumers require credit in order to finance big-ticket items, in order to smooth out consumption payments, in order to avoid the problems resulting from erratic incomes, and in order to avoid carrying large sums of cash when shopping. The purpose of the accounts receivable system is to accommodate the individual or firm desiring to defer payment, and to provide orderly procedures for the recording, processing, and reporting of the acquisitions of, and payments for, goods purchased on credit.

For illustration, let us assume that the Alan Company sells sporting goods equipment to department stores, sporting goods shops, and other retail outlets on a credit basis. Salespeople write up the bulk of the company's business on sales invoices which are then forwarded to the accounting subsystem for processing. At the time a new customer wishes to make purchases on credit, pertinent credit information would be requested and sent to the credit manager for appraisal. If the credit application is approved, a credit limit would be imposed, representing a maximum dollar amount of purchases which could be made without cash payment. The new customer would then be informed of the credit decision and advised of company approval to buy sporting-goods equipment up to the limit of the credit allowance.

In a manual accounts receivable system, the dollar total of each credit sale would be recorded as a debit in a specialized sales journal, as illustrated in Figure 6-1. One copy of the sales invoice serves as the source document for each entry, and the invoice number as well as the transaction amount are recorded. Sales discount terms have been omitted from the entries in the figure under the assumption that all credit sales are 2/10, n/30 (2 percent discount if payment is made within 10 days of the invoice date, and full amount due within 30 days if discount not taken). If the Alan Company allowed for variable credit terms, an additional column of the journal would be required to record this information as well. The sales journal is used only for recording credit sales. Cash transactions would be recorded in a separate cash receipts journal. Periodically (e.g., weekly or monthly), the totals entered in the sales journal would be posted to the proper general ledger accounts: a debit to accounts receivable and a credit to sales.

The sales journal provides a running tally of the company's credit sales transactions but is insufficient to provide the information required to compute the account balances of individual customers—for example, to permit monthly customer billing or to check on an individual customer's current account balance prior to approving an additional credit sale. The detailed information required for these functions is maintained in the accounts receivable subsidiary ledger, which contains an account for each credit customer of the company. Each time a credit sale is made, the total invoice amount is recorded in the sales journal and posted to the customer's subsidiary ledger account, as illustrated in Figure 6-2. The check marks in the "Subsidiary Ledger Posting" column of Figure 6-1, as well as Figure 6-2, indicate that this posting has been performed. Figure 6-2 also illustrates the posting of

Alan Company Sales Journal				Page 1
Date	Account Debited	Invoice Number	Subsidiary Ledger Posting	Amount
1984				
Nov. 2	Cuff Links Golf Shop	152–325	✓	653.00
2	Laynor's Department Store[a]	152–326	✓	4,622.18
2	Laynor's Department Store[a]	152–327	✓	264.18
2	Blacky's Beer and Sports	152–328	✓	58.25
4	Roxanne's Resort	152–329	✓	612.00
30	Jump and Gyp	152–388	✓	752.15
				25,652.81

Figure 6-1. The recording of credit sales information in the Alan Company sales journal—posting reference numbers have been excluded. ([a]It is assumed that two separate credit sales were made to Laynor's Department Store on November 2; thus, two separate sales invoices were prepared.)

the totals from the sales journal to the two general ledger accounts: accounts receivable and sales.

Payments made by credit customers reduce their financial liability to the Alan Company and are recorded in the specialized cash receipts journal illustrated in Figure 6-3. When a payment is received, the date is carefully scrutinized to determine the customer's eligibility for a discount. For those payments that do not qualify for a discount, the payment is simply entered in the specialized cash receipts journal as a debit to the cash account and a credit to the accounts receivable account. For those payments that do qualify for a discount, a portion of the gross amount of the original sale is treated as a debit to the sales discount account. Naturally, a large number of different cash receipt items will be entered in the cash receipts journal, but we have principally illustrated the transactions affecting accounts receivable in order to focus upon this one aspect of the accounting process.

In addition to posting the credit payments in the specialized cash receipts journal, credit entries are also made to the individual customer ac-

counts within the subsidiary ledger. The posting of the cash receipts transactions to the general ledger as well as to the accounts receivable subsidiary ledger follows the same logic as was previously discussed for sales invoices, and thus has not been illustrated. When a payment is made by a customer, however, it is treated as a credit to the customer's account and entered in a straightforward manner in the accounts receivable subsidiary ledger.

In the area of accounts receivable, a problem arises in that customers' payments may not correspond to individual line-item entries within their subsidiary ledger accounts. This could happen, for example, when a partial payment is made by a customer. If the Alan Company were to use a *balance-forward system*, this would not cause any particular difficulty because under a balance-forward system, only the net total balance owed by the customer is important. If the Alan Company were to use an *open system*, in which customer payments were coordinated with particular invoices, however, this could pose some problems. For the sake of simplicity, it is easiest to assume that when a partial payment is

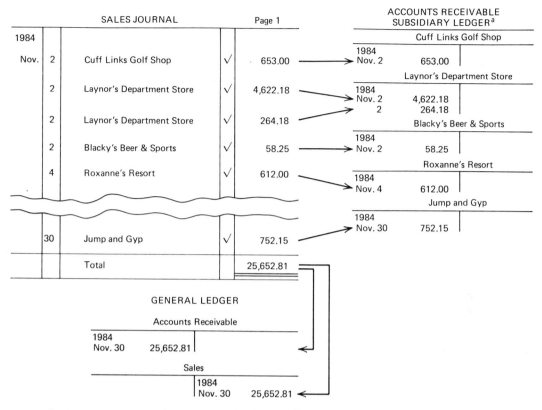

Figure 6-2. The posting of information from the sales journal to: (1) the subsidiary ledger, (2) the Accounts Receivable account of the general ledger, and (3) the Sales account of the general ledger—posting reference numbers have been excluded. ([a]The accounts within the subsidiary ledger are normally kept alphabetically by customer name. For illustrative purposes here, we have not maintained this alphabetical sequence.)

made, it reduces the balance(s) of the customer's oldest invoice(s) due in the accounts receivable subsidiary ledger. The distinction between an open accounts receivable system and a balance-forward accounts receivable system is especially important to the computerized version of this accounting system as we shall soon see.

Once a month, billing statements are prepared for those customers owing money to the Alan Company. To perform this function, the information from each accounts receivable subsidiary ledger account must be examined, and for those customers having outstanding balances, a billing statement must be prepared. Obviously, for those accounts with a large number of credit purchases and payments during the month, it is easiest to prepare a single-line statement indicating the total amount due. Yet, because of the potential for misunderstanding, it is highly desirable to prepare a detailed statement showing all transactions with accompanying sales invoice information as illustrated in Figure 6-4. Inasmuch as the customer who generates a large number of transactions is also likely to be considered a "good customer" (in terms of sales volume and therefore profitability), the need for detailed communication becomes very important. However, this itemization process also involves a lot of work. For example, detailed customer billing statements would require that sales invoice numbers be maintained in the subsidiary ledger, therefore requiring the recording of this additional information every time a credit sales transaction takes place. In addition, there would be

Alan Company Specialized Cash Receipts Journal							
Date	Payment Description	Subsidiary Ledger Posting	Sales Discounts Debits	Cash Debits	Accounts Receivable Credits	Misc. Credits	Acct. No.
1984							
Nov. 6	Blacky's Beer & Sports	✓	1 17	57 08	58 25		
6	Rental Income	✓		250 00		250 00	
9	Cuff Links Golf Shop	✓	13 60	639 40	653 00		
10	Jack's Jungle Shop	✓	6 44	315 56	322 00		
12	Blue Pearls	✓		48 00	48 00		
12	Roxanne's Resort	✓		84 32	84 32		
29	Don's Desert Digs	✓	1 93	94 55	96 48		
30	Haugerud's Hoops	✓		29 99	29 99		
			33 87	4,000 00	3,783 87	250 00	

Figure 6-3. The entry of payments to the Cash Receipts journal—posting reference numbers have been excluded.

the time and effort expended in the preparation of the detailed billing statements.

Beyond the preparation of monthly customer billing statements, it is highly desirable for the Alan Company's credit manager to review customer accounts on a periodic basis. One obvious reason for this review would be to make sure that individual accounts have not exceeded their credit limits. Another reason would be to determine which customer transactions, if any, to write off as bad debts. A third reason would be to assess credit policy—for example, to examine the possibility of extending additional credit if the Christmas season were near or to increase the credit limits of those accounts that appear to merit higher risks. Yet a fourth reason would be to use this credit information in the evaluation of related activities—for example, a policy to offer cash discounts to those customers ordering "slow-moving" merchandise or a policy to discontinue the acceptance of credit cards other than those of the company itself. A final reason

would be to utilize the credit-sales data as a means of evaluating the marketing staff.

Each of these uses of the company's credit information would necessitate the analysis of the accounts receivable data in a slightly different way. For example, in assessing bad debts, a common approach is to perform an aging analysis in which each customer's account balance is classified into categories of: (1) portion not past due, (2) portion from 1–30 days past due, (3) portion from 31–60 days past due, (4) portion from 61–90 days past due, and (5) portion over 90 days past due. Figure 6-5 provides an example of such an analysis. The greater the proportion of a customer's account balance that is past due, the more likely it is that the credit customer will default. Thus, as the majority of a customer's credit purchases fall further and further in arrears (i.e., become listed in the rightmost columns of the aging analysis report), the greater the potential that the customer's account balance will have to be written off as a bad debt.

DMAS CORP.

STATEMENT

1336 EL CAMINO REAL
MILPITAS, CALIFORNIA
94040

(408) 257-3286

DMAS CORP.

TO AVOID EXTRA CHARGES

11960099 G & S DISTRIBUTION COMPANY
CUSTOMER 9980 FIFTH AVE
          LOS, ALTOS, CA.   95230

8/31/7-
DATE

11960099   8/31/7-
CUSTOMER   DATE

*RETURN THIS PORTION
WITH YOUR PAYMENT*

LOCATION (IF OTHER THAN ABOVE)
11960001 WORLDWIDE *STORE 1*

11960001

DATE	TRANSACTION	INVOICE	AMOUNT	INVOICE	AMOUNT
6/16/7-	INVOICE	115151	273.06	115151	273.06
7/20/7-	INVOICE	116293	586.84	116293	586.84
7/23/7-	INVOICE	116784	363.33	116784	363.33
8/20/7-	PAYMENT	116784	363.33-	116784	363.33-
8/03/7-	INVOICE	117430	50.69	117430	50.69
8/10/7-	INVOICE	117945	720.80	117945	720.80
8/29/7-	ADJMENT	117945	108.44-	117945	108.44-
8/15/7-	INVOICE	118302	1,043.40	118302	1,043.40
11/01/7-	INVOICE	118303	256.59	118303	256.59
8/30/7-	INVOICE	119187	546.09	119187	546.09
7/31/7-	ADJMENT	999999	4.10	999999	4.10
8/31/7-	ADJMENT	999999	12.96	999999	12.96

ACCUMULATED PRIOR LATE CHARGES	4.10	PLC	4.10
CHARGE ON AMOUNT OVERDUE	12.96	LTC	12.96
DEFERRED CHARGES	256.59	DEF	256.59

.00	273.06			
90 & OVER	OVER 60			
590.94	2,265.50	PLEASE PAY ▶	3,129.50	TOTAL 3,129.50
OVER 30	CURRENT			

Figure 6-4. A customer billing statement. (Statement Courtesy of IBM Corporation.)

ALAN COMPANY
ANALYSIS OF ACCOUNTS RECEIVABLE BY AGE
December 31, 1984

Customer	Total	(1) Not Yet Due	(2) 1–30 Days Past Due	(3) 31–60 Days Past Due	(4) 61–90 Days Past Due	(5) Over 90 Days Past Due
G. M. Schley	$ 500					$ 500
D. Jenness, Inc.	500		$ 150	$ 350		
Peterson's	800		200	380	$ 220	
Kramer Corp.	2,000	$ 800	450	750		
Bogle Shop	550	500	50			
Others	38,650	18,150	11,650	3,770	2,780	2,300
Totals:	$43,000	$19,450	$12,500	$5,250	$3,000	$2,800
Percentage:	100	45	29	12	7	7

Figure 6-5. An aging analysis for the accounts receivable of the Alan Company.

The relative percentages at the bottom of the analysis are also useful to the manager. For example, large percentages in the intermediate ranges of the past-due categories (columns 3 and 4 of Figure 6-5) may signal a lack of adequate cash incentives for prompt payment or an indication of inadequate pursuit of delinquent accounts. Investigation of possible reasons for delinquent accounts may lead to appropriate managerial action. It should also be noted that a large dollar figure at the bottom of the last column, indicating a high possibility of nonpayment from the accounts past due over 90 days, is not necessarily a poor reflection on the credit manager. As in any business decision-making situation, there must be some allowance for acceptable risks. Thus, the absence of any accounts over 90 days past due may, in actuality, be signaling too stringent a credit policy rather than a desirable credit situation.

Further uses of the credit information as enumerated above would require alternate data analyses, very few of which could be performed easily using manual methods with a large volume of credit sales transactions. For example, if the Alan Company sold to 5000 retailers on credit, then a time-consuming customer-by-customer examination of all 5000 accounts would be necessary to determine those customers who had exceeded their credit limits. Similarly, information concerning credit sales by region, product line, or salesperson would be quite time-consuming to calculate. In the absence of this information, the preparation of many useful reports would not be possible.

A COMPUTERIZED ACCOUNTS RECEIVABLE INFORMATION SYSTEM

As an alternate to the manual accounts receivable system described above, a business might consider an automated version of this accounting process. The computerized accounts receivable system closely resembles the manual accounts receivable system in concept, although not in appearance or procedure. Computer files on magnetic tape or disk replace the sales journal, the cash receipts journal, the general ledger, and the accounts receivable subsidiary ledger of the manual system. In addition, the posting functions are automated. Ultimately, however, the computerized accounts receivable system performs the same principal functions that the manual system does: the collection, processing, and reporting of transactions involving credit sales.

Computer Files

The basis of the automated accounts receivable system is the accounts receivable computer file, which, for the purposes of illustration, will first be assumed to be a file of magnetic tape records. Not counting the header and trailer labels on this file (which contain file-control information), the tape will contain two basic types of records: master records, as illustrated in Figure 6-6, and transaction (tx) records, as illustrated in Figure 6-7. The master record contains the customer's account number, which serves as the file's record key, a special record code to distinguish master records from the transaction records, the customer's name and address, the customer's balance due (as of the beginning of the month), the customer's credit limit, and certain other information such as assigned salesperson's code, a flag (one-digit code) to indicate if the account is past due, a shipping code, a special code for sales discounts, and so forth. This master record is "permanent" on the file, and is removed only when business with the associated customer is terminated.

The transaction records, or "detail" records, represent customer activity on the file. There will be one such record for each credit sale or cash payment transaction by the customer in a given

time period. Like the master record, the detail record will contain the customer's account number to serve as a record key, a record-type code to identify the record as a transaction record, an additional transaction code to indicate a payment or credit sale, a reference sales invoice number, an "amount" field to indicate the dollar value of the transaction, a product-type code, a sales-terms (discount) field, a salesperson code in the event that more than one sales representative can make a sale to the same customer, a transaction date, and perhaps yet additional information not shown in Figure 6-7.

Records on the accounts receivable tape file are maintained in strict numerical sequence according to each record's account number. Master records are followed by transaction records, if any, as illustrated in Figure 6-8. For sorting purposes, the record-type code (1 = master record, 2 = transaction record) is combined with the account number to maintain this order. For example, a master record with account number 23465 would use the six-digit number, 234651, for sequencing purposes on the file. This same customer's transaction records would utilize the

Master Record

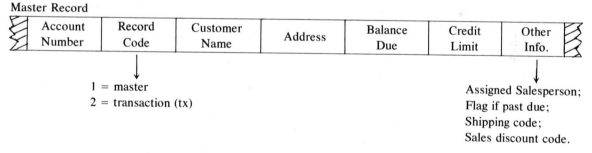

Figure 6-6. The master record for an accounts receivable file.

Transaction (Detail) Record

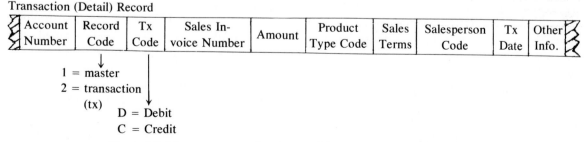

Figure 6-7. The transaction (detail) record for an accounts receivable file.

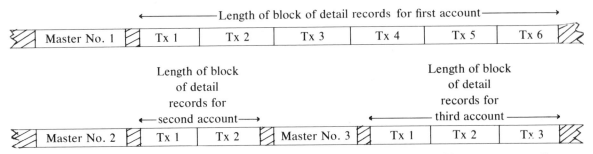

Figure 6-8. The sequence of master and detail records on the accounts receivable magnetic tape file.

six-digit number 234652. The addition of the record-type code to the account number for sequence-checking purposes automatically assures that the master records will precede the transaction records on the file.

If transaction records were first keypunched onto punched cards and then maintained in card-image format on the magnetic tape, it would be desirable that these records be blocked (see Chapter 18). The reason is that each detail record would require less than 80 characters of tape length and unblocked records of this type on the file would waste too much magnetic tape with interrecord gaps. Blocked records would eliminate this problem. Because each customer would probably have a different number of transaction records than other customers, it would also be desirable to permit those record blocks to be of variable length. Thus, although all detail records would be the same length, each *block* of detail records trailing the master record would be variable in length, as illustrated in Figure 6-8.

In effect, the accounts receivable file represents a merging of the sales journal, the cash-collections-from-credit-sales portion of the cash receipts journal, and the accounts receivable subsidiary ledger of the manual accounts receivable system. When the accounts receivable file is first created (e.g., in transition from a manual system), only the master records would be placed on the file in order to initialize it with customer account data. (Transaction records can be added later through normal processing once the file has become operational.) For example, the master-record information could first be keypunched on cards in tape-image format and

then transferred to the tape reel with a specially created computer program, or perhaps, a card-to-tape utility program. Alternatively, the information could be encoded directly on magnetic tape with a key-to-tape device.

After the accounts receivable file has become operational, new master records can still be added. As in the manual system, a new customer has presumably submitted a credit application which is reviewed by the credit manager. Upon approval, the new customer is assigned a unique account number which serves as the customer's reference number for all future transactions. New account numbers are likely to be higher in sequence than the numbers of existing accounts on the file because a higher number would enable the computer processing to simply *add* the new account record *to the end* of the file.

As an alternate to using a magnetic tape file to store accounts receivable master file records, it is also possible to maintain this file as a direct-access file stored on one or more magnetic disks. Using this approach, the sequential ordering of accounts receivable master records on the file would no longer be necessary: these records could be scattered throughout the file in random fashion. To find any particular record on the magnetic disk file, one or more of the direct-access techniques discussed in the previous chapter would enable the computer to find each master record directly as needed.

Like master records, accounts receivable transaction records could also be scattered throughout the file in random order. To link master records and transaction records together, however, the transaction records pertaining to each master record would be chained. With this approach, therefore, a specially created field in each record would be used to store the disk address of the next transaction record in the sequence. Thus, for each account, the entire sequence of master record "followed" by transaction records, which would have to be maintained in a strict *physical* sense if the file were stored on magnetic tape, would be maintained only in a *logical* sense if the accounts receivable file were stored on magnetic disk.

Daily Processing Runs

The daily processing for the accounts receivable system, as might be implemented using a random-access computer disk master file, is illustrated in Figure 6-9. Here, we are assuming that the Alan Company would use remote terminals located in regional offices to input credit-sales data on a daily basis. Thus, credit sales invoices, adjustment slips (e.g., an invoice for a sales return), and cash receipts slips would provide the source document data to be keyed into the terminals for computer processing. This type of input system is conventionally called *remote job entry* because the data necessary for the computer processing are collected and input to the computer from locations other than the immediate computer site.

For the illustration at hand, it is assumed that the Alan Company's marketing staff will be responsible for the input of credit sales data, that the Alan Company's accounting offices will be responsible for the input of cash receipts data, and that both offices can make adjustments. This assumption reflects the primary responsibilities of these respective subsystems (i.e., marketing and accounting) to generate source data for an accounts receivable accounting information system. When later processing takes place, each subsystem can check the resulting reports using their own source data and make corrections as needed. (The type of control information required for such checks is discussed in Chapter 8.) However, as long as the data were input to the computer on a remote basis, no material changes in our Figure 6-9 flowchart would be necessary if

different input responsibilities were assigned to these subsystems.

As the sales and cash receipts data are entered by the marketing and accounting subsystems through remote terminals, these data would be edited by the Alan Company's computer to check for accuracy and completeness using the company's "Edit and Transaction Log" program. Those transactions that pass the screening tests of this program would be logged onto a transactions file stored on magnetic disk to await further processing. Those transactions that fail one or more of these tests would be rejected. In this latter case, the computer would relay an error message to the sending remote terminal, indicating the reason(s) for the transaction's rejection. The program would then direct the computer to await new instructions from the user—for example, an indication that a corrected version of the rejected transaction data is to be input, or a request for information regarding the customer account in question. Thus, with the Alan Company's accounts receivable system, the user is able to interact with the computer system in a kind of question-and-answer format. In such instances, the user is said to *dialogue* with the computer because the user inputs data, the computer responds, the user goes again, and so forth, as though the user and the computer are having a conversation. This type of processing environment is quite efficient because errors may be corrected immediately at their input source, and because very little training is necessary for those who are assigned the task of inputting the data.

At the computer center, the daily use of the "Edit and Transaction Log" program will produce two principal types of output. The first of these is the disk transactions file which stores the transactions from the day's processing, as previously discussed. The second output is the Control Information Report, which contains descriptive information concerning the day's data processing. At a minimum, for example, this report would identify (1) each remote terminal accessing the system and using this accounts receivable processing routine, (2) how many transactions of each type (credit sales, credit adjustments, cash receipts, etc.) were logged onto the

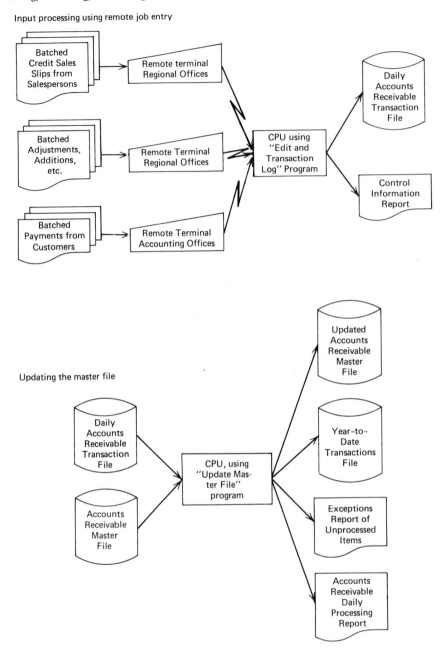

Figure 6-9. Accounts Receivable daily processing.

transactions file, and (3) the time(s) of day when this input took place. Normally, the report would also compute certain control totals, such as the dollar total of credit sales, the dollar total of cash receipts, and so forth. This Control Information Report would be reviewed by responsible employees to confirm the completion of the day's processing and would also serve as a control mechanism should the batch totals maintained by the regional offices fail to match the batch-control totals computed by the processing run itself.

Once the data have been logged onto the transactions file, it is possible to use this file to update the accounts receivable master file. Thus, in the accounts receivable "update" run, new transactions would be added to the file and the various informational fields of each master record would be modified as needed to reflect the current status of each account. This update run is shown in the bottom portion of Figure 6-9, reflecting the assumption that the master file would be updated daily. If the Alan Company so desired, however, it could also collect these transactions on its transactions file until, say, the end of the week and update the master file on a weekly basis. This decision would depend upon the volume of processing involved, how current the Alan Company wanted its accounts receivable file to be at any point in time, and the willingness of the company to incur the costs of running its master-file update processing five times per week instead of only once.

As illustrated in Figure 6-9, the outputs from the master-file update run include a year-to-date (YTD) transactions file, an updated accounts receivable master file, an "Exceptions Report of Unprocessed Items," and an "Accounts Receivable Daily Processing Report." The year-to-date transactions file contains all the transactions that have affected the accounts receivable master file since the beginning of the (calendar or fiscal) year. If necessary, the year-to-date transactions file can be used with a back-up copy of the accounts receivable master file (containing information about credit customers' accounts up to the end of the last calendar or fiscal year) to recreate the present accounts receivable file should

the present copy be lost, stolen, or vandalized. It should be pointed out, however, that it is more convenient to save an extra copy of yesterday's current master file, an extra copy of the day-before-yesterday's master file, and the corresponding days' transactions files for this type of security consideration. This is because less transaction records are involved in a single day's activity than in several months' worth of activities, and thus less data processing would have to be performed if error-recovery procedures were required to recreate a current copy of the accounts receivable master file from historical data.

The three sets of files discussed above constitute the so-called "grandfather-father-son" file-control relationship. With this file-control relationship, each succeeding (younger) generation of the file set can be obtained from the last (older) one should the recreation of a current master file prove necessary. Normally, the grandfather and father files in the set are physically removed from the computer center and stored in secure places elsewhere. We shall return to this control feature in Chapter 8.

The second output from the daily accounts receivable processing run is the updated master file. As a result of this processing, accounts receivable transactions for existing records, which reflect the day's receivables activities, will be added to the file, defunct master file records will be dropped from the file, and new accounts receivable master records, representing new customers to which the company has extended credit, will be added to the file. In addition, for selected master file records, certain field information such as the customer's address or credit limit will be changed to reflect the current informational status of customer accounts.

The third output from the daily processing run is the "Exceptions Report of Unprocessed Items." There are many reasons why transactions cannot be processed: the use of an account number in a transaction record for which no associated master record can be found, the presence of an unrecognizable transaction code (i.e., a code that does not represent a cash receipt, a credit sale, or other conventional transaction), the indication of a credit sale at discount terms for which the customer does not qualify, and so forth. All such unprocessable items are listed in this "Exceptions Report."

The items listed in the Exceptions Report must be handled by the computer center on an item-by-item basis. As in the case of edit rejections, the invoice or other source document supporting the transaction record is referenced and the appropriate corrections are made. In more extreme cases, the salesperson, customer, or both, must be contacted to correct the difficulty.

Perhaps the most immediately useful output from the daily processing run is the "Accounts Receivable Daily Processing Report." This "hard-copy" document contains all the transactions and other corrections which were accepted by the processing program and used to update the accounts receivable master file. A sample portion of this report may be found in Figure 6-10. For a company with thousands of credit customers, this document has the potential of being quite bulky. Yet, it is much less bulky than the corresponding storage required for the

			Additions		Deductions				Balance
Customer	Date	Invoice Number	Amount Billed	Misc.	Payment Received	Discount Allowed	Returns & Allowances	Misc.	
	Nov.								
63421									0 —
	2	152-325	653 00						
	2	152-325			639 40	13 60			0 —
63422									200 —
	2	152-328	58 25						
	2	152-328			57 08	1 17			200 —
63423									215 34
	2	152-326	4,622 18						
	2	152-327	264 37						5,101 89

Alan Company Accounts Receivable Daily Processing Report

Date: Nov. 2, 1984

Figure 6-10. A portion of the Accounts Receivable Daily Processing Report. (See Figures 6-1 and 6-3. The Cuff Links Golf Shop is account 63421, Blacky's Beer and Sports is account 63422, and Laynor's Department Store is account 63423. Also, for the purposes of illustration, customer payments have been accelerated to the date of the credit sales so that they might appear on the same daily report.)

subsidiary ledger accounts and journal entries of the manual accounts receivable system. The Daily Processing Report is printed on a customer-by-customer basis. Obviously, the Daily Processing Report is an important reference for employees helping customers who desire information about their accounts, for managers who desire information about the credit status of selected customers, and for data processors who wish to check on the completeness of the processing runs. In addition, the Daily Processing Report of customer activity contains important control information which may be used to assure the accuracy of the data processing. For example, the cash receipts total from this report *plus* the cash receipts total from the exceptions report should equal the total cash receipts accumulated by all of the regional accounting offices.

Weekly Processing Runs

Weekly, the Alan Company will want to produce summary reports describing credit sales and selected types of customer payment activity. Two such reports that might be produced weekly are a "Weekly Sales Report by Region" and a "Status Report of Delinquent Accounts." These reports would be produced using a current copy of the accounts receivable master file, as illustrated in Figure 6-11.

The "Weekly Sales Report by Region" summarizes the company's credit sales (we are ignoring cash sales) on a region-by-region basis. Individual customers would not be shown on the report, but within each region a breakdown by product type would be made showing credit sales on a product-by-product basis. Using this report,

key marketing and production managers would be able to adjust company policy to changed credit-sales conditions. To produce such a report, the "Weekly Processing" computer program would scan the accounts receivable master file on an account-by-account basis looking for those credit-sales transactions that have taken place during the past week. The information regarding these current-sales transactions would be used to prepare the report, whereas the information regarding other transaction records or master file records would simply be ignored.

Scanning the entire contents of the accounts receivable master file will take time even if the file were stored on a very fast magnetic disk. If sales volume were low, therefore, a company might choose to produce this type of report monthly instead of weekly. As an alternative, however, it would also be possible to store each week's transactions on a separate "Week-to-Date" transactions file. At the end of each week, the necessary transaction records—and only the necessary transaction records—required for the preparation of the Weekly Sales Report would be available on the "Week-to-Date" transactions file. The convenience of this approach, however, would have to be weighed against the inconvenience of maintaining a separate computer file for this purpose.

The second report to be produced each week is the "Status Report of Delinquent Accounts." This report would list the names, account numbers, and balances of those customers who were "seriously in arrears" in their payments. The question of "how far behind" a customer must be before the account would be considered "seriously in arrears" is not an easy question to answer. Interestingly enough, most retail stores who buy on credit do not suddenly stop making payments when their businesses turn sour. At first, only a few payments are missed, and thus some of the retail store's credit purchase transactions become past due, whereas others are current. With the passage of time, however, the store in trouble will begin to send payments for current transactions only, taking advantage of the cash discounts offered for speedy payments on these purchases, and allow its older credit

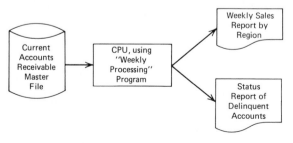

Figure 6-11. Accounts Receivable weekly processing.

purchase transactions to fall further and further in arrears. Thus, the question of "when is an account seriously delinquent" is actually a policy question which must be answered by the company credit manager, the financial vice-president of the company, or perhaps a policy committee.

The Status Report of Delinquent Accounts would (1) permit the credit manager to exercise managerial discretion in cutting off additional credit to problem accounts or (2) serve as an aid in declaring a particular account a bad debt. The delinquency report is a perfect example of the management-by-exception reporting principle discussed in Chapter 2, in which the attention of the decision-maker is focused only on those items that violate anticipated behavior.

Monthly Processing Runs

To study the delinquency of accounts receivable in greater detail, it is advisable to perform a complete aging analysis on a monthly basis. Because a complete aging analysis would require a search through the entire master file, it is not necessary, or even desirable, that this function be performed weekly; once a month is sufficient. Inasmuch as we have discussed the purpose of this analysis earlier, it should not be necessary to repeat that discussion here. It should be pointed out, however, that the computer run time for such processing, when several thousand accounts must be examined, would be considerably less than what would be required in staff time for the preparation of a complete aging analysis under a manual data-processing system.

Some accounts receivable systems maintain the aging status of the transactions of each customer account as an integral part of the customer's master file record. Thus, in addition to the fields of the master record as illustrated in Figure 6-6, balance fields for the total amount of credit purchases not yet due, the total amount of purchases 1–30 days past due, the total amount of purchases 31–60 days past due, and so forth, would be included in each master record of the file. Each day, these fields would be updated by the daily processing run, utilizing the date-field information of all transaction records on the ac-

counts receivable master file to help perform this function. The advantage of such a system would be that the information required for the status report of delinquent accounts would be immediately available at the time the report was to be generated. The chief disadvantage of the system would be that the above information would have to be stored in each of potentially thousands of master records, thus utilizing a considerable amount of file storage space.

At the same time that the master file is processed to produce the aging analysis (top half of Figure 6-12), it may also be possible to produce a salesperson report. Because there is a salesperson code in each sales transaction record of the file, and because at the end of a month there will be approximately four weeks of such sales records on the file, all the information required to produce such a report would be at hand. The report would indicate the credit sales of each sales-

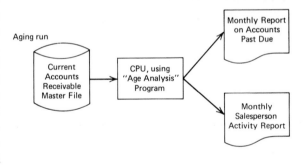

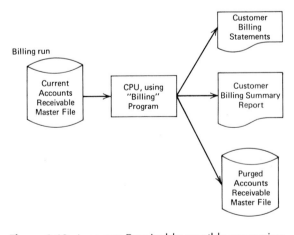

Figure 6-12. Accounts Receivable monthly processing.

person, possibly broken down into subcategories such as customer type, quantity, and dollar sales value of specific inventory items sold, or some other classification deemed important to the company and for which the required data are available on the file. Such information would be useful in setting sales quotas, for evaluating performance by comparing actual sales with budget projections, and perhaps, for making other related personnel decisions (e.g., promotion decisions).

The other processing run performed on a monthly basis would be the billing-statement routine (bottom half of Figure 6-12). Again, the accounts receivable master file would serve as the primary input. The output would include the billing statements to be sent to each customer and a summary report (for processing control). Note that all the information required for the customer statements (see Figure 6-4 for an example) is immediately available from the master records of the file, or from the associated transaction records. Of course, the billing-statement output would be printed on specially-prepared, preprinted forms so that only the information pertinent to each customer's account would be printed out. Heading information such as company logo, field-identification information, and the like, would be preprinted on the forms. (The less work required of the printer, the faster the entire operation.)

Once the billing process has been completed, there would be little reason to maintain the past month's transaction records on the file (under a balance-forward system). Thus, these records could be purged from the file by the monthly-processing program, and the processing run would probably output a "new" file of master records only. Each master file record would, however, contain an updated "balance" field to reflect the account's current amount owed.

If the company processed accounts receivable using an "open" system, a slightly different approach would be required. In particular, only those credit-sales transactions for which there was a matching customer payment could be dropped from the file. All credit-sales transactions for which there was no corresponding pay-

ment transaction would have to be maintained on the file until such time as a credit payment to the company was received or the customer account was written off as a bad debt. The open system approach would therefore result in the maintenance of a fairly large number of transaction records on the file for certain customer accounts, and in addition, would require extra processing effort to match customer payments with corresponding credit-sales transactions. However, the open system would also be more precise in maintaining customer account-activity information.

Further Data Processing Using the Accounts Receivable Files as a Data Base

Inasmuch as the year-to-date transactions file contains a year's credit sales and payment activity of the company's customers, it is a veritable gold mine of raw data awaiting evaluation. If, for example, the account numbers had been assigned to customers in such fashion that the first few digits represented a geographical location of customers, then the year-to-date transactions file could be used to prepare a marketing report of credit sales by region. Similarly, because each sales transaction contains the total amount billed the customer, a histogram of sales invoices (i.e., the number of sales invoices less than $100, the number of sales invoices between $100–$250, etc.) could be constructed from the data. Such a report might be useful in deciding the amount of trade discounts offered to customers doing business with the company, in evaluating changes to salespersons' commission rates, and so forth. As yet a third possibility, cross-tabulation reports could be generated in which salesperson versus regional credit sales, customer types versus credit sales terms, or credit sales terms versus dollar business categories, could be prepared. As you can probably tell from these suggestions, the possible combinations are endless.

It is unlikely that such reports would be prepared on a weekly, or even monthly, basis. At best, quarterly, semi-annual, or annual runs of these reports would be made inasmuch as the compilation of such information would take time even on the computer, and such things as seasonal fluctuations in sales and changes in company policies would likely make computations on less than a quarterly basis meaningless. Unlike the weekly or monthly operational reports discussed above, however, the usefulness of this type of data processing is not diminished by the fact that these reports are processed less often. The major point is that the year-to-date transactions file can serve as a valuable data base for many different management informational needs, and that these needs can be adequately met through the proper exploitation of the information contained on the file. Also, with a computerized accounts receivable processing system, it is now possible to generate these reports on a cost-effective basis.

The Computerized Accounts Receivable System Summarized

Figure 6-13 summarizes the entire information flow of the computerized accounts receivable accounting information system with a comprehensive system flowchart. Note that daily, weekly, and monthly accounting system processing runs have been included on the same flowchart in order to provide the necessary summary information. A chronological distinction between these runs may be made, however, by observing the titles of the programs within the CPU processing symbols, and observing the titles of the output reports.

It should also be noted that the summary flowchart does not fully reveal the additional accounting and computer processing tasks normally made to support this accounts receivable accounting function. For example, the computation and maintenance of control-total information at the Alan Company's regional offices, the preparation and physical movement of back-up computer files, and the actual distribution of copies of the various reports to the users have been omitted. These are vital activities in the normal, everyday functioning of such an accounting information system, and their importance should not be overlooked. We shall study document flowcharts in Chapter 11.

A final point which should be made concerning the accounts receivable accounting information system is that it does not exist in isolation. The same sales information captured by the Alan Company's regional sales offices, for example, might also be used in a computerized point-of-sale inventory system to update inventory account balances. In similar fashion, information about the cash received in the payments portion of the accounts receivable application would also be used when the Alan Company reconciles its bank statements. Finally, it should be clear that accounts receivable business activity has an important bearing upon the company's balance sheet and also on its income statement. Thus, in effect, the accounts receivable accounting information system is actually part of an even larger accounting information system and an application which we have studied in isolation primarily for illustrative purposes.

A COMPARISON OF THE TWO ACCOUNTS RECEIVABLE SYSTEMS

There are considerable differences between the manual and the automated versions of the accounts receivable application as these two systems have been described. Care must be taken to avoid saying one is better than the other—this conclusion is not obvious despite the heavy emphasis of our text on the advantages of computerized data processing. As the paragraphs below will (hopefully) make clear, this depends upon a number of factors.

One clear distinction between the two accounts receivable data-processing systems is the different amounts of machinery and other special equipment required for the two approaches. Under the manual system, only one or more bookkeepers and some accounting journals and ledgers would be required, whereas with the automated version of this accounting application, a complete computer system would need to be in place. If only an accounts receivable system were to be automated in a business organization, then there might be a processing cost advantage in utilizing the manual system. The decision would require a comparison of the expected costs

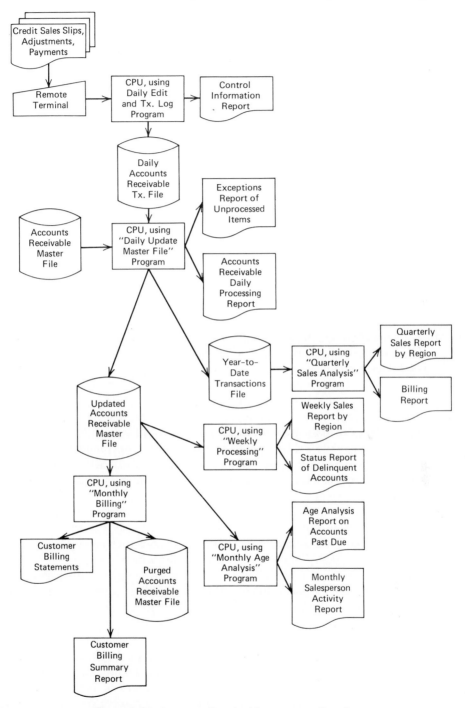

Figure 6-13. Accounts Receivable summary flowchart.

and the expected benefits of the manual system versus the computerized system. If the computer hardware required for the accounts receivable processing were also used for such other tasks as payroll preparation or inventory file maintenance, however, then only the incremental costs of utilizing the computer system for the accounts receivable processing function should be used in the evaluation. Whether or not this incremental cost would be less than the processing costs of the manual system is speculative.

Yet another consideration would be processing speed. In order for the accounts receivable function to be effective, the processing of the data and the preparation of the required reports must be made on a timely basis. Where the processing environment involves large volumes of data and limited staff, the automated accounts receivable system would appear to have an advantage. Many thousands of transaction records can be processed in an hour using computerized equipment, and high-speed printers can output reports at the rate of 20,000 lines a minute.

For all the speed of the automated accounts receivable system, however, surprising lags in the processing work still can occur. For example, where transactions are batched until the end of the week, any sale that is made late Friday might not be keyed into the computer until Friday of the following week—a lag of seven days! In addition, if a transcription error were made in this transaction but was not detected until the update routine of the weekly processing run, the transaction would not be recorded for another week, resulting in a lag of 14 days. Finally, if this processing lag extended just past the monthly billing run, the customer could potentially not be billed for nearly six weeks past the purchase date! This is one reason why batch systems are inferior to real-time processing systems for such accounting functions as accounts receivable, where timely processing and a current master file are important.

A manual system could be expected to be much more responsive. Even if errors were made in the recording, posting, or billing operations, it would be reasonable to expect the manual system to handle these problems on an exceptions basis, and prepare a special customer statement by hand, if necessary. In any event, there would be no compelling reason to wait an entire month. This is not to say that the automated version of the system would make no provision for "manual overrides" (i.e., processing customer accounts as an exception to normal processing) or other special ways of handling problems on an individual basis. In practice, however, the fact that the computer is "supposed to handle" the accounts receivable operation often compels employees to process as many transactions as possible through "normal channels."

There is also the question of processing errors. As far as the automated version of the accounts receivable system is concerned and barring hardware failures, the computer will never make a processing error. Moreover, both hardware and software controls usually are adequate to assure processing accuracy even in the presence of unrepresentative data situations. Because the manual system is dependent upon error-prone humans to perform the brunt of the processing, there is clearly a greater potential for *processing errors* in this system.

However, processing errors are not the only kind of errors that can be made. There are also transcription errors, and here, the manual system may have an advantage. This is because, as the two versions of the systems have been designed, the manual accounts receivable system works directly with the sales invoices and other source documents of the system, whereas the computerized accounts receivable operation works principally with a *transcribed* version of these documents on magnetic disk. Because the bookkeeper in the manual system avoids the computer-version task of transcribing the data from the invoice or other activity item to the disk, there is less chance for transcription errors. In addition, the bookkeeper is likely to have more direct contact with the marketing staff and steady customers of the firm, and is therefore better able to resolve data questions quickly.

The matter of individual judgment may also be considered in our comparative analysis. In general, for processing applications in which the overwhelming proportion of the work is algorithmic in nature (i.e., predefined and step-by-step) and in which large volumes of similar transaction items must be processed, the accounts receivable computer version is the better alternative. On the other hand, where transaction items are largely dissimilar and a high degree of individual judgment is required, the accounts receivable manual version may prove superior. Just how judgmental the accounts receivable system is for the particular firm would determine the desirability of utilizing the one version over the other.

Finally, there is the psychological aspect of the automation itself. By and large, customers do not like to be treated as impersonal numbers. But in the computerized version of the accounts receivable system, customers become just that—numbers. Furthermore, the computerized version of the accounts receivable application puts distance between the credit customer on the one hand and the creditor company on the other: the computer system comes between them. For example, the purchaser no longer actually pays his or her creditor. Rather, the purchaser pays a mechanical, robotlike intermediary which neither recognizes individuality nor appreciates the customer's business.

There is obviously a tradeoff between the mechanical efficiencies of the computer and the humanity of personal relationships. Some businesses want efficiency in their operations and little else. Others prefer the give and take of face-to-face contact with those involved in the credit aspect of business transactions. Thus, as in so many other aspects of accounting information systems, the ultimate decision of a company to utilize a manual versus a computerized version of the accounts receivable information system is dependent upon the company's operating characteristics.

SUMMARY

The purpose of an organization's accounts receivable accounting information system is to provide orderly procedures for the recording, processing, and reporting of credit activity. In this chapter, we have examined two systems

capable of performing this function: a manual accounts receivable system and a computerized accounts receivable system. Each attempts to satisfy certain basic informational needs associated with the accounts receivable processing operations, although the manner by which these needs are met differs considerably between the two systems.

In the manual accounts receivable system, the data surrounding credit sales are recorded in the sales journal, the cash receipts journal, the general ledger, and the accounts receivable subsidiary ledger. The mechanics of recording customer credit purchases and payments were reviewed, and it was noted that a large volume of credit customers would substantially limit the efficient generation of manually prepared customer billing statements as well as many of the specialized informational reports desired by management.

The basis of the computerized version of the accounts receivable system is the accounts receivable file, which for the purposes of illustration, was assumed to be a magnetic disk file. This file maintained two types of records: (1) master records, containing such information as customer account number, customer name and address, and balance due, and (2) transaction or detail records, containing such activity data as credit sales amount, cash receipts amount, or field changes (such as credit limits). In the automated accounts receivable information system, the master records are created initially from information obtained in the customer's credit application. Transaction records for the computerized system are created initially from such source documents as sales invoices and cash receipts slips. The information on these transaction source documents is keyed onto a temporary transactions file from remote company terminals. At the end of each day, these transactions are coordinated with the accounts receivable master file. The output from this daily processing includes an updated accounts receivable master file, a year-to-date transactions file, an "Exceptions Report of Unprocessed Items," and an "Accounts Receivable Daily Processing Report."

The processing needs of the Alan Company also included weekly, monthly, and quarterly reports. A weekly processing routine would provide, for example, a "Weekly Sales Report by Region" and a "Status Report of Delinquent Accounts." Monthly processing provides a "Monthly Aging Analysis Report," a "Monthly Salesperson Activity Report," customer billing statements, and a "Customer Billing Summary Report." Also, once a month, the Alan Company would purge all of the accounts receivable transaction records from its master file (if it used a balance-forward accounting system) or its payment-matched transaction records (if it used an open-file accounting system).

Comparing the manual accounts receivable system with the automated one, we observed that both systems gathered the same basic data, although the two systems differed in the way the data was recorded and stored for further data processing. In performing further data-processing tasks, however, it was noted that the automated system would probably be able to perform these tasks more quickly, would probably be able to perform these tasks more efficiently in greater volume, and would probably be able to perform these tasks with greater processing accuracy than would the manual system. In addition, it was noted that the transaction records of the computerized accounts receivable information system could be used as a data base for the generation of a large number of reports which might be of decision-making value to management.

The automated accounts receivable information system also has its drawbacks. Lags in the processing of transactions might develop despite the speed of the computer. Transcription errors would likely be higher than in a manual accounts receivable system, and the automated version of the system might not be as responsive to the needs of individual customers. Finally, it was emphasized that the use of the automated accounts receivable system might also introduce an undesirable "mechanical" or "inhuman" characteristic into the operation. For these reasons, we have concluded that, for all the advantages of the so-called modern computer version

of the accounts receivable processing system, the automated system is not necessarily the superior choice.

DISCUSSION QUESTIONS

6-1. Describe the procedure(s) by which a bookkeeper would enter a credit sales transaction and a cash receipts transaction into a manual accounts receivable system.

6-2. Describe the procedure(s) by which a credit sales transaction and a cash receipts transaction would be entered into a computerized accounts receivable system.

6-3. The Barry Render Sports Shop purchases sporting goods equipment from the Alan Company on a credit basis. On March 5, the shop made a purchase of $400 with cash discount terms of 2/10, n/30. When the shop received its monthly statement from the Alan Company on April 2, this $400 purchase was still shown as outstanding even though the shop was sure that the bill had been paid on March 12. How would an accountant go about checking this discrepancy:

    a. under a manual accounts receivable system?
    b. under an automated accounts receivable system of the type described in this chapter?

6-4. An automated accounts receivable operation often uses a preprinted billing statement form, as illustrated in Figure 6-4. How would a large-scale purchase of equipment by a company, making more purchases than could be listed on this form, be handled with the automated billing system?

6-5. Discuss the meaning of the following terms as they are used in the chapter: (a) dialogue, (b) remote job entry, (c) year-to-date, (d) manual override.

6-6. In what sense does the computerized accounts receivable system "put distance" between a company and its credit customers?

6-7. What types of decision-making information are provided to a company's management in an aging analysis of accounts receivable? If a company has no credit customers whose account balances are over 90 days past due, is this situation always a good sign of operating efficiency? Explain.

6-8. What advantages does the automated accounts receivable processing system have over the manual system?

6-9. What advantages does the manual accounts receivable processing system have over the automated system?

6-10. The William Remus Mattress Company manufactures and distributes mattresses, box springs, and headboards to companies throughout the Southwest. It sells to about 300 companies in total, and extends credit to approximately 150 of its customers. Most of these credit sales are to small retail outlets owned by personal friends of William Remus Mattress Company president, John Downs. Up until this point in time, Mr. Downs has used a manual accounts receivable system to maintain the credit information about his customers. Recently, a Mr. Kirkland Fasttrack has approached Mr. Downs to suggest that he automate his system, using a new small computer system sold by Mr. Fasttrack's company. Mr. Fasttrack has pointed out the many advantages of his computerized system, including the automated billing operation.

    a. Superficially, would you recommend that Mr. Downs "upgrade" his accounts receivable operation to an automated one? Why or why not?

    b. What information would you need to evaluate the proposal more thoroughly?

6-11. Mr. Paul Berry is the treasurer of a small aerospace manufacturing company in southern California. His company buys much of its equipment on credit from parts manufacturers throughout the country including the Tippy Wing Rivet Company. Mr. Berry is of the belief that his company should pay its bills promptly—within ten days of purchase (typical cash discount terms offered are 2/10, n/30) in order to maintain good credit relations with its creditors and also to take advantage of the 2 percent cash discount made available to the company for prompt payment. The Tippy Wing Rivet Company uses an automated accounts receivable system. On August 15,

Berry's company purchased $2,150 worth of equipment from Tippy Wing. However, on the company's billing statement received at the end of the month neither the purchase nor the payment (which was made August 24) appeared. What could have happened? If the transaction does eventually show up on the September bill, do you believe that Berry's company is still entitled to the 2 percent cash discount? Explain.

6-12. This chapter began discussing an automated accounts receivable system as it might be implemented with a sequential tape file of master records. Later in the chapter, the analysis assumed a random access disk file. What differences are there in the use of the tape file versus the disk file? (For example, could both of these files be updated the same way?) Do both types of files require the same kinds of processing runs? Be as specific as possible.

6-13. At the end of the chapter, it was suggested that the accounts receivable year-to-date transaction file was a very rich source of information and could be used as a data base for the generation of further decision-oriented reports. What reports might these be? What decisions might be based on these reports? Are these decisions limited to the accounting aspects of accounts receivable? Discuss.

6-14. How far in arrears must a delinquent account be before it should be written off as a bad debt? As a general credit manager, what policy would you install at the Alan Company for a situation in which a good customer has paid its bills regularly, but claims payment for a bill which, according to company records, is six months past due?

6-15. What is the difference between a "balance-forward" accounts receivable system and an "open" accounts receivable system? What are the implications of these differences to computerized accounts receivable systems?

PROBLEMS

6-16. In the text, it was suggested that some accounts receivable applications use a computerized master file record which includes an aging analysis for each account. Redesign the master file record of Figure 6-6 to include aging information. When would this information be updated?

6-17. One of the weekly reports suggested by the chapter for the accounts receivable processing system was a "Weekly Sales Report by Region." This report was described in the chapter, but not illustrated. Design such a report, indicating precisely what information would be contained in it.

6-18. Refer to problem 6-17. Prepare a detailed program flowchart that would enable a programmer to write a computer program for the preparation of the "Weekly Sales Report by Region." In this problem, note that regional sales information is not explicitly found in any transaction records. Yet, this information might be extractable from other data fields of the transaction records. Explicitly state what assumptions you have made regarding regional sales information.

6-19. Refer to Figure 6-9, which illustrates the updating of an "Accounts Receivable Master File" with a "Daily Accounts Receivable Transaction File." For this update run, design a detailed program flowchart which would illustrate the computer processing logic for this data-processing task.

6-20. Figure 6-12 illustrates the "Aging Run" for the Alan Company's Accounts Receivable Monthly Processing. Design a detailed program flowchart that illustrates the computer processing logic for this data-processing task.

6-21. Figure 6-12 illustrates the "Billing Run" for the Alan Company's Accounts Receivable Monthly Processing. Design a detailed program flowchart that illustrates the computer processing for this data-processing task.

CASE ANALYSES

6-22. *Jacobs Manufacturing Company*

Jacobs Manufacturing Company maintains an accounts payable system using magnetic tape files. The master file contains information about the major vendors supplying materials and other

supplies to the company. The transactions file contains expense detail records, which contain pertinent information about company purchases, and payment detail records, which contain pertinent information about supplier reimbursements. The formats of the master file record, the expense detail record, and the payment detail record are shown on the next page.

A purchase is initiated with the manual preparation of a purchase order, a signed copy of which is forwarded to the supplier. Upon receipt of the merchandise, this voucher information is coordinated with the invoice information of the shipment itself, and the complete set of data is forwarded to the EDP center for keypunching. Cards punched from this information create the expense detail record as illustrated.

Once a month, the following processing is performed:

A. cash disbursements by check number;

B. preparation of purchase journal reports arranged by (1) account charged and (2) vendor;

C. listing of outstanding payables.

Required

1. Explain when and how the expense detail transaction record and the payment detail transaction record would be created on the file.

2. Draw a set of system flowcharts which documents the data-processing runs outlined above.

3. What information would likely be found on the reports listed in the run(s) listed above? What information on the files would be required to generate these reports?

(AICPA Adapted)

6-23. *Wekender Corporation*

Wekender Corporation owns and operates 15 large departmentalized retail hardware stores in major metropolitan areas of the southwest United States. The stores carry a wide variety of merchandise but the major thrust is toward the

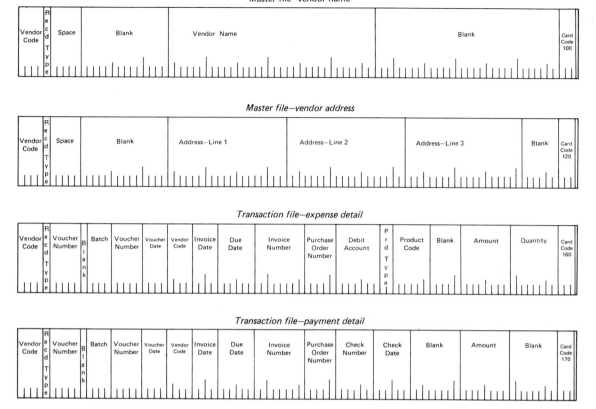

weekend "do-it-yourselfer." The company has been successful in this field, and the number of stores in the chain has almost doubled since 1978.

Each retail store acquires its merchandise from the company's centrally-located warehouse. Consequently, the warehouse must maintain an up-to-date and well-stocked inventory ready to meet the demands of the individual stores.

The company wishes to hold its competitive position with similar type stores of other companies in its marketing area. Therefore, Wekender Corporation must improve its purchasing and inventory procedures. The company's stores must have the proper goods to meet customer demand, and the warehouse in turn must have the goods available. The number of company stores, the number of inventory items carried, and the volume of business all are providing pressures to change from basically manual data

processing routines to mechanized data processing procedures. Recently, the company has been investigating three different approaches to mechanization—punched card system, computer with batch processing, and computer with real-time processing. No decision has been reached on the approach to be followed.

Top management has determined that the following items should have high priority in the new system procedures:

1. Rapid ordering to replenish warehouse inventory stocks with as little delay as possible.
2. Quick filling of orders and shipping of merchandise to the stores (this involves determining if sufficient stock exists).
3. Some indication of inventory activity.
4. Perpetual records in order to determine inventory level by item number quickly.

191

A description of the current warehousing and purchasing procedures is given below.

Warehouse Procedures

Stock is stored in bins and is located by inventory numbers. The numbers generally are listed sequentially on the bins to facilitate locating items for shipment; frequently this system is not followed, and as a result, some items are difficult to locate.

Whenever a retail store needs merchandise, a three-part merchandise request form is completed—one copy is kept by the store and two copies are mailed to the warehouse the next day. If the merchandise requested is on hand, the goods are delivered to the store accompanied by the third copy of the request. The second copy is filed at the warehouse.

If quantity of goods on hand is not sufficient to fill the order, the warehouse sends the quantity available and notes the quantity shipped on the request form. Then a purchase memorandum for the shortage is prepared by the warehouse. At the end of each day all the memos are sent to the Purchasing Department.

When ordered goods are received, they are checked at the receiving area, and a receiving report is prepared. One copy of the receiving report is retained at the receiving area, one is forwarded to Accounts Payable, and one is filed at the warehouse with the purchase memorandum.

Purchasing Department Procedures

When the purchase memoranda are received from the warehouse, purchase orders are prepared. Vendor catalogs are used to select the best source for the requested goods, and the purchase order is prepared and mailed. Copies of the order are sent to Accounts Payable and the receiving area; one copy is retained in the Purchasing Department.

When the receiving report arrives in the Purchasing Department, it is compared with the purchase order on file. The receiving report is also checked against the purchase invoice before forwarding the invoice to Accounts Payable for payment.

The Purchasing Department strives periodically to evaluate the vendors for financial soundness, reliability, and trade relationships. However, because the volume of requests received from the warehouse is so great, this activity currently does not have a high priority.

Each week a report of the open purchase orders is prepared to determine if any action should be taken on overdue deliveries. This report is prepared manually from scanning the file of outstanding purchase orders.

Required

A. Wekender Corporation is considering three possible automated data processing systems: punched card system, batch processing system, real-time computer system.

1. Which of these three systems would best meet the needs of Wekender Corporation? Explain your answer.
2. Briefly describe the basic equipment components which Wekender would need for the system recommended.

B. Regardless of the type of system selected by Wekender Corporation, data files will have to be established.

1. Identify the data files that would be necessary, and
2. Briefly indicate the type of information that would be contained in each file.

(CMA Adapted)

6-24. *Consolidated Electricity Company*

Until recently, Consolidated Electricity Company employed a batch processing system for recording the receipt of customer payments. The following narrative and the flowchart on page 194 describe this system.

The customer's payment and the remittance advice (a punched card) are received in the treasurer's office. An accounts receivable clerk in the treasurer's office keypunches the cash receipt into the remittance advice and forwards the card to the EDP department. The cash receipt is added to a control tape listing and then filed for deposit later in the day. When the deposit slips are received from EDP later in the day (approximately 2:30 p.m. each day), the cash receipts are removed from the file and deposited with the original deposit slip. The second copy of the deposit slip and the control tape are compared for accuracy before the deposit is made and then filed together.

In the EDP department, the remittance advices received from the treasurer's office are held until 2:00 p.m. daily. At that time the customer payments are processed to update the records on magnetic tape and to prepare a deposit slip in triplicate. During the update process, data are read, nondestructively, from the master accounts receivable tape, processed, and then recorded on a new master tape. The original and second copy of the deposit slip are forwarded to the treasurer's office. The old master tape (former accounts receivable file), the remittance advices (in customer number order), and the third copy of the deposit slip are stored and filed in a secure place. The updated accounts receivable master tape is maintained in the system for processing the next day.

Consolidated Electricity Company has revised and redesigned its computer system so that it has on-line capabilities. The new cash receipts procedures, described below, are designed to take advantage of the new system.

The customer's payment and remittance advice are received in the treasurer's office as before. A cathode ray tube terminal is located in the treasurer's office to enter the cash receipts. An operator keys in the customer's number and payment from the remittance advice and checks. The cash receipt is entered into the system once the operator has confirmed that the proper account and amount are displayed on the screen. The payment is then processed on-line against the accounts receivable file maintained on magnetic disc. The cash receipts are filed for deposit later in the day. The remittance advices are filed in the order they are processed; these cards will be kept until the next working day and then destroyed. The computer prints out a deposit slip in duplicate at 2:00 p.m. for all cash receipts since

the last deposit. The deposit slips are forwarded to the treasurer's office. The cash receipts are removed from the file and deposited with the original deposit slip; the duplicate deposit slip is filed for further reference. At the close of business hours (5:00 p.m.) each day, the EDP department prepares a record of the current day's cash receipts activity on a magnetic tape. This tape is then stored in a secure place in the event of a systems malfunction; after ten working days the tape is released for further use.

Required

A. Using conventional flowcharting symbols, prepare a system flowchart of Consolidated Electricity Company's new on-line cash receipts procedures.

B. Have the new cash receipts procedures as designed and implemented by Consolidated Electricity Company created any internal and systems control problems for the company? Explain your answer.

(CMA Adapted)

6-25. *Deake Corporation*

Deake Corporation is a medium-size, diversified manufacturing company. Fred Richards has been promoted recently to Manager, Property Accounting Section. Richards has had difficulty in responding to some of the requests from individuals in other departments of Deake for information about the company's fixed assets. Some of the requests and problems Richards has had to cope with are as follows:

1.   The controller has requested schedules of individual fixed assets to support the balances in the general ledger. Richards has furnished the necessary information, but he has always been late. The manner in which the records are organized makes it difficult to obtain information easily.

2.   The maintenance manager wished to verify the existence of a punch press which he thinks was repaired twice. He has asked Richards to confirm the asset number and location of the press.

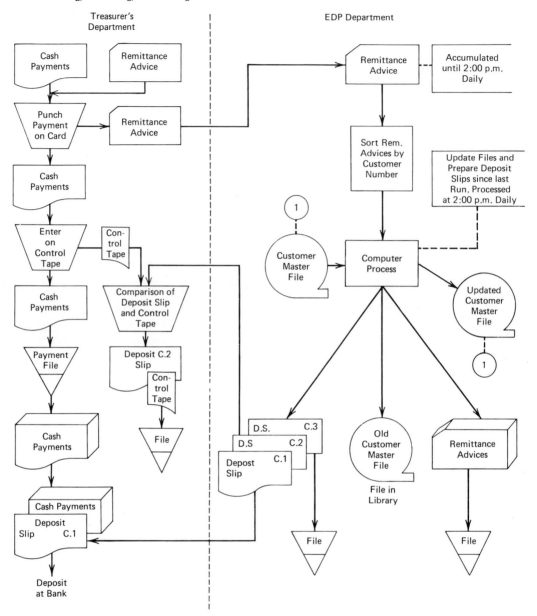

3. The Insurance Department wants data on the cost and book values of assets to include in its review of current insurance coverage.

4. The Tax Department has requested data that can be used to determine when Deake should switch depreciation methods for tax purposes.

5. The company's internal auditors have spent a significant amount of time in the Property Accounting Section recently, attempting to confirm the annual depreciation expense.

The property account records that are at Richards' disposal consist of a set of manual books. These records show the date the asset was acquired, the account number to which the asset applies, the dollar amount capitalized, and the estimated useful life of the asset for depreciation purposes.

After many frustrations Richards has realized that his records are inadequate and he cannot supply the data easily when they are requested. He has decided that he should discuss his problems with the controller, Jim Castle.

RICHARDS: "Jim, something has got to give. My people are working overtime and can't keep up. You worked in Property Accounting before you became controller. You know I can't tell the tax, insurance, and maintenance people everything they need to know from my records. Also, that internal auditing team is living in my area and that slows down the work pace. The requests of these people are reasonable, and we should be able to answer these questions and provide the needed data. I think we need an automated property accounting system. I would like to talk to the information systems people to see if they can help me."

CASTLE: "Fred, I think you have a good idea, but be sure you are personally involved in the design of any system so that you get all the information you need."

Required

A. Identify and justify four major objectives Deake Corporation's automated property accounting system should possess in order to provide the data that are necessary to respond to requests for information from company personnel.

B. Identify the data that should be included in the computer record for each asset included in the property account.

(CMA Adapted)

PART THREE

Internal Controls Within Accounting Information Systems

Chapter 7
Preventive and Feedback Controls for Accounting Information Systems

Chapter 8
Controls for Computerized Accounting Information Systems

Chapter 9
Computer Crime

Chapter 10
Auditing the Computerized Accounting Information System

Part Three will intensively analyze the topic of *internal control* within both manual and computerized data-processing systems, emphasizing the latter types of systems. Internal control structures are stressed in our text because in most organizations, the managerial accountants have the major responsibility for developing, implementing, and monitoring effective internal control systems. These systems of internal controls can reduce the risk of errors and irregularities going undetected in the accounting information system's functions of collecting, recording, and storing business data.

Chapter 7 will provide an introduction to the basic concept of internal control by analyzing the various characteristics of an effective internal control system. Many organizations have encountered difficulties with their internal control systems upon acquiring a computer to handle their accounting data-processing functions. Chapter 8 will therefore examine the types of internal controls that are commonly used within a computerized accounting information system.

Over the past several years, there have been a number of fraudulent acts (such as the embezzlement of assets) performed by organizational employees working in a computerized accounting information system. Often, the opportunities for employees to perform these fraudulent acts have been attributable to failures in the accountants' internal control systems. Chapter 9 will examine the important as well as interesting topic of computer crime (several *actual* computer crimes will be discussed and analyzed) and will look at its effects on the design and operation of accounting internal control systems. One useful way of both preventing and detecting fraudulent acts within companies' computerized data-processing systems is through the performance of good *audit* procedures. Therefore, to conclude Part Three on internal controls, Chapter 10 will analyze the audit control procedures of accountants in those business firms utilizing computerized accounting information systems.

7

Preventive and Feedback Controls for Accounting Information Systems

Among the important questions that you should be able to answer after reading this chapter are:

1 Why would a retail department store be willing to let customers shoplift some of its merchandise inventory?

2 Does a "hash total" represent your food bill at a student cafeteria?

3 Why has the introduction of an electronic data-processing subsystem into an organization sometimes led to employee embezzlement of asset resources?

4 If your company gave you the responsibility for handling cash receipts as well as recording the receipts, how might you commit a successful embezzlement of this cash?

5 Is the only purpose of an internal control system to enable management to detect employee fraudulent activities?

INTRODUCTION

The increasingly large number of employee fraudulent crimes attempted (some unsuccessful, some successful; the completely successful crimes go undetected, of course, and thus we are not aware of them) typically involve some aspect of an organization's financial resources. Because one of the principal functions of an accounting information system is to maintain accountability over a company's financial resources, the managerial accountants working in the accounting subsystem play a major role in designing, implementing, and monitoring a system of controls that reduces the risk of undetected errors and irregularities surrounding the company's financial resources.

This chapter is the first of four chapters that cover the important topic of "internal control" (i.e., controls established *within* an organization's system). The current chapter will examine the essential characteristics of a good internal control system and give some real-life examples of the types of irregularities than can occur without good controls.

THE INTERNAL CONTROL CONCEPT

A system of internal control has two major functions: (1) to safeguard an organization's asset resources from being misused, and (2) to encourage organizational operating efficiency so that management's prescribed policies and goals are achieved. These two internal control functions are highly interrelated because operational efficiency within an organization would be difficult, if not impossible, to achieve without adequate safeguards to prevent improper use of the organization's asset resources.

Controls that attempt to safeguard asset resources from misuse are often called *preventive* or *accounting controls* (or "before the fact" controls). In other words, these controls are established with the objective of attempting to *prevent* some inefficiency from occurring. For example, one of the Alan Company's preventive controls is its establishment of a *standard cost* accounting system within its production subsystem. The purpose for predetermining the standard costs of raw materials, direct labor, and production overhead for each sporting goods product line is to provide the production employees information "before the fact" regarding what the manufacturing costs should be, and thereby encourage them to *prevent* actual production costs from exceeding the standard production costs. As a result, the company's asset resources (e.g., cash disbursements for the acquisition of production raw materials, cash paid for production employees' wages, utilization of the manufacturing equipment in producing the finished sporting goods products, etc.) will likely be used more efficiently.

The controls which specifically encourage operating efficiency (and thereby enable management's prescribed policies and goals to be achieved) take over where the preventive controls end. This group of controls is often called *feedback* or *administrative controls* (or "after the fact" controls). For example, the Alan Company's EDP subsystem processes timely responsibility accounting performance reports for man-

agement (discussed in Chapter 2) which disclose significant variations of actual production costs from standard production costs. As a result, the company's management is provided "after the fact" *feedback* regarding inefficient manufacturing performance. Corrective action can then be initiated to eliminate these inefficiencies.

The American Institute of Certified Public Accountants (AICPA), a major accounting professional body which has as one of its functions the clarification of accounting terminology, provides thorough definitions of *administrative control* and *accounting control* which emphasize the importance of business transactions to an efficient and effective internal control system. In *Statement on Auditing Standards No. 1* (the Codification of Auditing Standards and Procedures), the definition of internal control by the AICPA encompasses both administrative control and accounting control as follows:

Administrative control includes, but is not limited to, the plan of organization and the procedures and records that are concerned with the decision processes leading to management's authorization of transactions. Such authorization is a management function directly associated with the responsibility for achieving the objectives of the organization and is the starting point for establishing accounting control of transactions.

Accounting control comprises the plan of organization and the procedures and records that are concerned with the safeguarding of assets and the reliability of financial records and consequently are designed to provide reasonable assurance that:

a. Transactions are executed in accordance with management's general or specific authorization.
b. Transactions are recorded as necessary (1) to permit preparation of financial statements in conformity with generally accepted accounting principles or any other criteria applicable to such statements and (2) to maintain accountability for assets.
c. Access to assets is permitted only in accordance with management's authorization.
d. The recorded accountability for assets is compared with the existing assets at reasonable intervals and appropriate action is taken with respect to any differences.*

*Auditing Standards Executive Committee, American Institute of Certified Public Accountants, *Statement on Auditing Standards No. 1*—Codification of Auditing Standards and Procedures (New York: American Institute of Certified Public Accountants, 1973), p. 20.

A major function of an accounting information system is to process business transactions. Since the above definitions of both administrative and accounting controls emphasize the important role of business transaction execution and processing within an internal control system, the internal control area is thus an integral part of an accounting information system. The point is further made in *Statement on Auditing Standards No. 1* that for an effective internal control system to exist in a company, the administrative controls and the accounting controls cannot be treated as mutually exclusive. Rather, these two components of internal control should be interrelated.

To illustrate the important interrelationship of accounting and administrative controls, assume that every Friday afternoon the Alan Company's sales departments (baseball sales department, football sales department, etc.) of its marketing subsystem send their week's batch of sales invoices to the EDP subsystem for processing. A "preventive or accounting control" that may be established within the sales departments is the *addition* of the sales invoice numbers before these invoices are sent to the EDP subsystem. This "control total" of invoice numbers is called a *hash total*—that is, a number that is meaningless to the information system, and is used only for control purposes. The computer is also programmed to *add* the sales invoice numbers and print out the result after all the week's invoices have been batch processed. The hash total of invoice numbers reported in the computer printout (the "feedback or administrative control") is then compared with the sales department's hash total. Ideally, the two numbers should agree, thereby providing reliable information that all the sales invoices sent to the EDP subsystem were actually processed. If the two hash numbers disagree, management is informed that something went wrong; for example, one or more sales invoices may have been lost "in transit" to the EDP subsystem. (This would result in the company never billing a customer for a credit sale.) The hash total control will also reveal any sales invoices that may have been accidentally processed twice.

The preceding internal control example illustrates two important characteristics of an internal control system: (1) both the preventive (accounting) and the feedback (administrative) aspect of an internal control must exist and be interrelated for the control to be effective, and (2) preventive and feedback controls are not designed solely to discourage fraud and embezzlement by company employees.

In the example of the Alan Company's hash total control, the feedback control (a computer printout showing the hash total summation of the sales invoice numbers) would not be effective without the initial preventive control (the sales departments' accumulation of a hash total of sales invoice numbers before the invoices are sent to the EDP subsystem). A printout disclosing the total of the sales invoice numbers is meaningless unless there is a previously determined number for comparison. On the other hand, the preventive control established by the sales departments would be useless without the feedback control from the company's EDP subsystem. What good is a hash total if there is no subsequent control number to compare it with? Figure 7-1 illustrates this important interrelationship between the Alan Company's preventive control and feedback control for the movement of sales invoices into the EDP subsystem. (It should be noted that throughout the remainder of this text, because of the authors' personal preference, the terms *preventive* and *feedback* controls will typically be used rather than the terms *accounting* and *administrative* controls.)

When the Alan Company's weekly sales report is received by the marketing manager, the manager should immediately compare the sales invoice number hash total printed on the computer report with the sales invoice number hash total accumulated by the sales departments before the invoices were delivered to the EDP subsystem. EDP's sales invoice hash total of 2377 shown in Figure 7-1 provides good evidence to the marketing manager that all the week's sales invoices were actually processed by the computer. Should the hash total numbers of the EDP subsystem and the sales departments disagree, the marketing manager (or some other designated

Figure 7-1

ALAN COMPANY'S INTERNAL CONTROL FOR
SENDING SALES INVOICES TO THE EDP SUBSYSTEM

Preventive Control (established by the sales departments of the marketing subsystem)—hash total of week's sales invoice numbers:

Feedback Control (established by the EDP subsystem as part of processing the week's batch of sales invoices)—hash total printout on sales report of total invoice numbers processed:

Invoice Numbers[a]
472
473
476
477
479

Total 2377 (hash total)   2377 (hash total)

HASH TOTAL NUMBERS AGREE

[a]In actual practice, the number of sales invoices transferred to the EDP subsystem would be much greater than the number assumed in this illustration. Also, the illustration further assumes that invoice numbers 474, 475, and 478 were *voided* during the week.

employee) must then attempt to determine the cause of this discrepancy.

The Alan Company's control structure for sales invoices sent to the EDP subsystem also demonstrates that a system of internal control is established for reasons other than just discouraging employee fraud and embezzlement. A major purpose for establishing good internal control within an organization's system is to detect errors caused by the fact that people are "human." For example, a discrepancy between the hash total maintained by the Alan Company's sales departments and the hash total printed by the computer would more likely be caused by human error rather than an outright attempt by some employee to falsify the week's sales data. A hash total discrepancy could have been caused by the keypunch operator accidentally misplacing one of the sales invoice source documents

before its contents were input on a punched card. This human error should be detected as a result of the Alan Company's internal controls for sales invoice processing. Even though incidents of fraud and embezzlement by employees against their companies get more publicity from the mass media, the majority of errors and other inefficiencies in an organization are the result of human mistakes. (After all, what newspaper would print a story about a company's keypunch operator accidentally failing to process a sales invoice?)

Ideal Controls Are Normally Too Costly

In deciding what types of internal controls to incorporate in its system, a company should attempt to estimate the operating costs of a proposed control and then relate these costs to anticipated benefits. Only those controls whose expected benefits exceed their expected costs should be implemented into the company's system.

For example, the Justin & Jodi Self-Service Company is a large discount store selling home appliances, clothing, and many other merchandise items. The company's management is currently worried about the large amount of shoplifting that has taken place in the past several months. As a result, management is considering some possible controls that would reduce this shoplifting problem. If no controls are implemented into the store, management estimates that the total annual loss to the company from shoplifting would be approximately $100,000. Two alternative preventive controls are being considered as a means of solving this shoplifting problem:

1. Hire 12 plain-clothed security guards to patrol each of the store's 12 aisles. At an approximate annual salary of $10,000 for each security guard, this control would cost the company $120,000 per year.
2. Hire two plain-clothed security guards to patrol the aisles and also install several cameras and mirrors throughout the store

to enable management to observe any shoplifters. The estimated annual cost of this control would be $35,000.

With the objective of reducing shoplifting, alternative 1 (hiring 12 security guards) would appear to be the *ideal* control. Assuming the guards are properly trained and perform their jobs efficiently, the discount store's shoplifting should be reduced to almost zero. Even if this were true and shoplifting were completely eliminated, alternative 1 should not be implemented. The reason is that the control's anticipated costs ($120,000 per year) exceed the control's anticipated benefits ($100,000 per year—the approximate annual shoplifting loss that would now be eliminated).

With alternative 2 (hiring two security guards plus installing cameras and mirrors), the store's management estimates that the annual loss from shoplifting can be reduced from $100,000 to $30,000, the net benefit therefore being $70,000. Since the second alternative's expected benefits ($70,000 per year reduction of shoplifting) exceed its expected costs ($35,000 per year), management should select this control for implementation into its system rather than the alternative 1 control proposal.

The point of the preceding example is that in many cases, the introduction of ideal controls (which would reduce the risk to practically zero for any undetected errors and irregularities) into an organization's system is impractical. If the control's expected operating costs exceed its expected benefits, the effect of implementing the control will be to decrease operating efficiency for the entire organizational system. From a cost/benefit viewpoint, therefore, a company's management is often forced to settle on controls that are less than ideal for detecting errors and irregularities. Management must learn to "live with" the fact that a certain degree of risk (caused by undetected errors and irregularities) is inherent within its preventive control system.

To emphasize the important role of a company's management in developing and maintaining an internal control system, the following statement was issued by the United States Senate Committee on Banking, Housing, and Urban Affairs:

The establishment and maintenance of a system of internal control and accurate books and records are fundamental responsibilities of management. The expected benefits to be derived from the conscientious discharge of these responsibilities are of basic importance to investors and the maintenance of the integrity of our capital market system. The committee recognizes, however, that management must exercise judgment in determining the steps to be taken, and the cost incurred, in giving assurance that the objectives expressed will be achieved. Here, standards of reasonableness must apply. In this regard, the term "accurately" does not mean exact precision as measured by some abstract principle. Rather, it means that a company's records should reflect transactions in conformity with generally accepted accounting principles or other applicable criteria. While management should observe every reasonable prudence in satisfying these objectives, the committee recognizes that management must necessarily estimate and evaluate the cost/benefit relationships of the steps to be taken in fulfillment of its responsibilities under this paragraph. The accounting profession will be expected to use their professional judgment in evaluating the systems maintained by companies. The size of the business, diversity of operations, degree of centralization of financial and operating management, amount of contact by top management with day-to-day operations, and numerous other circumstances are factors which management must consider in establishing and maintaining an internal control system.*

The ideas expressed in the above statement of the Senate Committee eventually were incorporated into the *Foreign Corrupt Practices Act of 1977*. This act was passed by Congress and signed into law by the President of the United States in December 1977. Besides prohibiting foreign bribes by publicly-held companies, the Foreign Corrupt Practices Act requires publicly-held companies to maintain accurate accounting records and to design and maintain effective internal control systems. The act's passage illustrates the extreme importance of good internal controls within business information systems. The need for the Foreign Corrupt Practices Act

---

*Report of the Senate Committee on Banking, Housing, and Urban Affairs, May 2, 1977 (Report No. 95-114).

grew out of the many questionable or illegal foreign payments made by publicly-held companies in the United States. The Foreign Corrupt Practices Act's requirement that these companies implement effective internal control systems is intended to reduce the risk of such questionable or illegal payments.

Internal Audit Subsystem's Control Function

Many organizations (especially the larger ones) have within their systems a separate subsystem called *internal auditing*. (The audit function will be discussed thoroughly in Chapter 10.) The internal audit area is a service subsystem whose major function is to help design and implement preventive controls within the other organizational subsystems and through the use of feedback controls, to periodically monitor the performance of each subsystem. The important role played by an organization's internal auditors is indicated by the American Institute of Certified Public Accountants' Committee on Auditing Procedure in *Statement on Auditing Standards No. 9*, as follows:

When internal auditors study and evaluate internal control or perform substantive tests of the details of transactions and account balances, they serve a special function. They are not part of internal accounting control in the same manner as would be an individual who verifies the mathematical accuracy of all invoices; instead, they act as a separate, higher level of control to determine that the system is functioning effectively.*

The internal audit staff usually consists of accountants who, because of their education and training, have the ability to design effective controls to safeguard an organization's assets and to evaluate the operating performance of individual subsystems. In those companies with no separate internal audit staff, the managerial accountants within the accounting subsystem normally play a major role in establishing the preventive controls and overseeing the performance of the feedback controls.

*Auditing Standards Executive Committee, American Institute of Certified Public Accountants, *Statement on Auditing Standards No. 9* (New York: American Institute of Certified Public Accountants, 1975), p. 2.

The principal advantage of having a separate internal audit function is that this subsystem is completely independent of all the other subsystems within an organization and can therefore be objective when reviewing the operating performances of each subsystem (which also encompasses a review of the accounting subsystem's operational activities). If the internal audit function were assigned to the accounting subsystem, complete objectivity would be more difficult, if not impossible, to achieve because the accountants working in this subsystem would be evaluating their own subsystem's activities. Due to the importance of objectivity, good organizational design would require the internal audit subsystem to report directly to top management. This enables the internal audit staff to be completely independent of the other subsystems whose work is evaluated.

The valuable service function performed by internal auditors in establishing and monitoring an organization's control system is also recognized by the external auditors working for public accounting firms (e.g., Ernst and Whinney, Price Waterhouse & Company, and Touche Ross & Company). When the external auditors come into a company to evaluate the fairness of its financial statements, these auditors rely upon much of the internal audit subsystem's previous work in establishing and monitoring controls within the company. The existence of an effectively-operated internal audit subsystem will normally cause the external auditors to perform less testing of an organization's financial transactions.

To thoroughly understand the importance of good internal control within an organization's information system, the major components necessary for an effective preventive control system and an effective feedback control system to exist will now be discussed in the following two sections of this chapter. All the examples used to illustrate many of these controls will be based upon the Alan Company's system. The discussion will also assume the existence of an independent internal audit function within the company's system (even though prior analyses of the Alan Company have ignored the establishment of an internal audit subsystem).

EFFECTIVE PREVENTIVE CONTROLS

The important components which are essential to an organization's preventive control system are: (1) a good audit trail, (2) competent employees, (3) separation of related organizational functions, and (4) physical protection of assets. Each of these preventive control components will now be analyzed.

Good Audit Trail

As discussed in Chapter 1, a good audit trail means that a manager (or any other employee) is able to follow the path of its organization's accounting transactions from the initial source documents to their final disposition on a report. The audit trail is probably the most important preventive control because it enables management "to know what is happening" throughout the phases of accounting data processing. As a result, management should be able to detect and correct any errors and irregularities occurring within the accounting information system. Without a good audit trail, it would be quite easy for errors and irregularities in the processing of accounting data to go undetected.

When establishing its audit trail, an organization should prepare policy and procedure manuals which include such things as: (1) a chart of accounts describing the purpose of each general ledger account (as well as subsidiary ledgers) so that the debits and credits from accounting transactions are recorded in the correct accounts, (2) a complete description of the types of documents (e.g., sales invoices, shipping reports, payroll time cards, and purchase orders) that will be used as the basis for recording financial activities, and the correct procedures for preparing and approving the data included on these documents, and (3) a complete description of the authority and responsibility that is delegated to individual employees for such functions as recording specific types of accounting transactions (e.g., inventory transactions, cash receipts and disbursements transactions, and payroll transactions) and making specific organizational decisions (e.g., when to disapprove further credit sales to a customer, when to write-off a customer's account as uncollectible, and when to purchase additional raw materials inventory required for production).

By defining the chart of accounts, describing the documents to be used, and indicating which employees have been delegated authority and responsibility for specific activities, an organization's audit trail is greatly enhanced. If, for example, one of the Alan Company's sales managers desires information about last week's sale of 100 basketballs to a specific customer, this manager can examine the policy and procedure manuals and immediately ascertain in which accounts the transaction should have been recorded, what source document (or documents) should have been prepared for the transaction, and which employee (or employees) was supposed to have the authority and responsibility for handling the transaction (e.g., approving the customer's credit and establishing cash discount terms). After acquiring the above information from the company's policy and procedure manuals, the sales manager should be able to follow easily the audit trail for this sale of basketballs. Any error or irregularity in handling the sales transaction (e.g., the shipping report disclosing that 110 basketballs were actually sent to the customer, whereas the sales invoice indicates that the customer was billed for exactly 100 basketballs) should be detected by the manager when tracing this transaction along the audit trail.

Computer's effect on audit trail. The introduction of a computer into an organization's data-processing system can create problems regarding the audit trail. In a manual data-processing system, following the audit trail of an accounting transaction is normally not a difficult task. In a computerized data-processing system, however, the transaction processing is performed within the computer. As a result, the audit trail becomes more difficult to follow. Figure 7-2 reflects the data-processing sequence for the Alan Company's financial transactions in a manual accounting information system compared to a computerized accounting information system.

Under a manual data-processing system, all four stages through the audit trail involve people

Figure 7-2

MANUAL COMPARED WITH COMPUTERIZED DATA
PROCESSING OF THE ALAN COMPANY'S FINANCIAL TRANSACTIONS

Manual System:

Transactions' Source ———→ Transactions Recorded in → Transactions Posted and → Transactions' Effects
  Documents Prepared   Journal   Account Balances   Included in Finan-
    (Stage 1)   (Stage 2)   Determined in   cial Reports
                                              General Ledger and   (Stage 4)
                                              possibly the sub-
                                              sidiary ledger or
                                              ledgers as well
                                                (Stage 3)

Computer System:

THROUGH CENTRAL PROCESSING UNIT

Transactions' Source ———→ 1. Log transactions on transactions file through batch processing (Stage 2)
  Documents Prepared[a]   2. Process the transactions file and update the general ledger file and possibly the
    (Stage 1)   subsidiary ledger (or ledgers) file (or files) (Stage 3)
                          3. Execute financial-reports program (or programs) using the updated general
                             ledger file and possibly the subsidiary ledger (or ledgers) file (or files) (Stage 4)

[a]In a batch-processing computerized system, data from source documents would first have to be converted to storage media such as punched cards or magnetic tape. In an online computerized system, data from source documents would typically be input directly into the computer system (and stored on media such as a magnetic disk or a magnetic drum) through an online device such as a terminal. This illustration of a computer system assumes the use of batch-processing techniques.

working with "pencil and paper." The procedural activities as well as the output from each data-processing stage are visible to the human eye, which makes it quite easy for a manager to trace the audit trail of specific accounting transactions. With a computerized system, however, the only stage of data processing clearly observable to the human eye is the preparation of transactions' source documents. (In fact, with some highly sophisticated online computer systems, hard copy source documents for transactions are not prepared.) Stages 2, 3, and 4 of the manual system are performed internally within the central processing unit of the computer equipment. This computerized handling of accounting activities and computerized preparation of financial reports cannot be seen by people, thereby obscuring the audit trail. Furthermore, some financial data processed internally by the computer may never be seen by an organization's management. For example, performance reports of the Alan Company's sporting goods manufacturing activities are based upon the "management-by-

exception" principle. Thus, only significant variations of actual production costs from standard production costs are printed out by the company's computer for analysis. This means that the large quantity of actual production cost data which does not deviate significantly from the standard costs never appears in hard copy management-by-exception performance reports.

When computers first became popular in business, internal auditors (as well as external auditors working for public accounting firms) tended to ignore the computer's existence within their company's information system. When an internal auditor wanted to trace the audit trail of specific accounting transactions, he or she would audit "around the computer." Under this approach, the auditor acquires computer printouts of financial data and then traces specific items from these printouts back to the various source documents. Basically, the auditor ignores the entire processing function within the computer itself.

The number of computer frauds that have been

committed in the last several years by employees has caused most internal auditors (and external auditors) to audit "through the computer." Using this approach, the internal auditor becomes familiar with the company's hardware and software, helps establish the preventive control system for the computer center, and also periodically reviews this control system to make sure it is functioning properly. Thus, a through-the-computer audit allows a company's internal auditor to better understand what is happening inside the computer, thereby making the data-processing audit trail easier to follow. Both "auditing around the computer" and "auditing through the computer" will be discussed in greater detail in Chapter 10.

Competent Employees

Another important preventive control that should exist in an organization is competent employees. Because company personnel will be working continually with organizational assets (e.g., handling cash, acquiring and disbursing inventory, and operating production equipment), incompetent employees can cause inefficient use of the organization's asset resources, thereby thwarting management's prescribed policies and goals.

Personnel subsystem's function in obtaining competent employees. The personnel subsystem has a major role in the successful implementation of this preventive control. Personnel managers are responsible for the initial interview of applicants for their organization's jobs. When interviewing potential employees for job vacancies, it is important that these managers thoroughly understand the level of human qualifications necessary for specific jobs. Otherwise, an individual hired for a job may be either overqualified or underqualified. Both of these situations are undesirable from the operational efficiency viewpoint.

Having employees assigned to jobs for which they are overqualified may mean that their salaries are too high (based upon the type of organizational functions performed), and also mean that employees may be bored with their work. Wages that are excessive in relation to the level of work being performed typically leads to operational inefficiency. (In effect, the company is paying too much for the employees' service benefits received.) Also, if we think of employees as being human-resource type assets, the placement of individuals in job functions for which they are overqualified leads to inefficient use of vital asset resources. Employees' boredom resulting from their job activities is also a cause of operational inefficiency. In fact, some bored employees, in an attempt to make their jobs more challenging and exciting, have initiated techniques for embezzling assets from their company (some of these embezzlement schemes will be illustrated in Chapter 9).

Employees hired for jobs for which they are underqualified can cause them to become frustrated and possibly cause them to resent their company. Inability of the employees to fulfill their job responsibilities will adversely affect operational efficiency. Furthermore, if the employees also display negative feelings toward their employer, this can lead to additional inefficiency within the company. To "get back" at the company for the frustrating nature of their jobs, the employees may intentionally violate company policies and procedures.

To avoid the negative aspects of hiring either overqualified or underqualified employees, a major function of personnel managers is to obtain the best possible *matching* of job qualifications to people qualifications. Even though a job applicant's educational background and prior work experience may not qualify him or her for a specific job, this problem can be alleviated in part through adequately planned training programs supervised by the personnel subsystem. Effectively-operated training programs should increase the skills of employees and thus make them more productive human resource assets to their organization. Through training programs, employees should become thoroughly familiar with their future job responsibilities and understand their important role in the organization's system.

The personnel subsystem should also establish equitable policy guidelines for employees' salary increases and promotions. Ideally, the criteria for these two reward mechanisms should be fairly uniform within all the organization's subsystems so that each employee, regardless of job assignment, feels that he or she is being treated fairly in relation to the other workers. Equitable, company-wide policies established by the personnel subsystem for salary and promotion rewards should contribute toward company loyalty and operational efficiency by the employees.

Bonding of employees. People working within an organization's accounting subsystem are often given responsibilities for handling assets susceptible to theft (e.g., liquid assets such as cash and marketable securities). These employees should not only be competent, but also honest. One approach used by many organizations to reduce the risk of loss from employee theft is to acquire *fidelity bond coverage* on those employees having direct access to assets subject to misappropriation. The fidelity bond can be obtained from an insurance company. The insurance company will investigate the backgrounds of all employees that the organization desires to have bonded. In issuing this fidelity bond, the insurance company assumes liability (up to a specified limit) for the individual employees who are named in the bond. Should some of these employees later embezzle assets from their organization, the insurance company is then responsible.

Separation of Related Organizational Functions

This preventive control measure means that those employees who are given responsibility for the physical custody of specific organizational assets should not also be given responsibility for the record-keeping functions relating to the assets. Otherwise, an employee could misappropriate company assets and then attempt to conceal this fraud by falsifying the accounting records.

Separation of functions example. Assume that one of the Alan Company's accountants (Jerome Stein) is responsible for preparing the daily bank deposit from accounts receivable check payments mailed in by credit sales customers. Jerome accumulates the day's cash receipts checks (the physical-custody function), endorses the checks, fills out the bank deposit, and prepares a listing of each customer's payment (these last three functions are the record-keeping functions). This list of customer payments is then sent to the computer center for the end-of-the-week update of the accounts receivable subsidiary ledger. Since separation of duties among employees does not exist for the cash receipts functions, it is conceivable that Jerome could steal some of the customer payment checks and then exclude them from the daily bank deposit and from the listing that goes to the computer center.

Let us further assume that one check today for $300 from Mary Kelley is "pocketed" by the Alan Company's accountant. Thus, Mary's cash payment is not recorded anywhere within the company's accounting information system (and Jerome Stein is $300 richer!). For Jerome to successfully commit this fraud, however, he must eventually reflect on his cash receipts list sent to the computer center a $300 credit to Miss Kelley's account. Otherwise, when she is mailed her monthly statement, we would expect her to complain about not receiving credit for the $300 payment. Therefore, to cover his tracks, Stein must make sure that before Mary Kelley's monthly bill is sent, the $300 fraud has been transferred from her account to some other customer's account.

For this example, assume that the Alan Company bills its customers monthly under a *cycle method*. (On the first of each month, all customers whose last names begin with A–F are billed; on the tenth of each month, all customers whose last names begin with G–O are billed; and on the twentieth of each month, all customers whose last names begin with P–Z are billed.) Thus, by the tenth of the month, when Mary Kelley's bill is mailed, Jerome Stein must eliminate the $300 fraud from her account. He easily solves this problem by using a $400 cash payment check received on the seventh of the month from another credit customer, Jack Taussig. Since Taussig's statement will not be mailed until the twentieth of this month, Jerome endorses the $400 check, includes the $400 within the daily bank deposit, and on the cash receipts list sent to the computer center, shows a $300 credit to Mary Kelley's account and only a $100 credit to Jack Taussig's account. Jerome has thus shifted his $300 embezzlement from Kelley's account to Taussig's account, and Mary Kelley's balance owed the company will be correct when her monthly statement is mailed. Before the twentieth of the month, when Jack Taussig's bill is sent, his account balance will also have to be "corrected" in this same manner (i.e., by using other customers' cash payment checks as the basis for crediting his account a total of $300). In actual practice, the Alan Company's accountant would probably be embezzling many cash receipts checks each month and attempting to cover his "tracks" for all these embezzled checks.

The preceding example illustrates the type of fraudulent activity that employees can execute on their company's cash asset. The technical term used for embezzling cash payments from credit sales in the manner described above is called the *lapping of accounts receivable*. This example emphasizes what can happen when a "separation of related duties" preventive control does not exist. One possible preventive control measure that the Alan Company could use to avoid this type of cash fraud is to make one employee (Harvey Hunt) responsible for taking the day's cash receipts checks and preparing an adding machine tape of the total dollar amount of checks (let's assume that Wednesday's cash receipts checks total $5000). Then, the checks are turned over to a second employee (the accountant, Jerome Stein), who endorses the checks, makes out the bank deposit, and prepares the detailed listing which is sent to the computer center. The computer center, when processing these checks at week's end, can obtain a separate printout total of each day's customer cash receipts checks. For Wednesday of this week, the total dollar checks processed by the computer should be $5000. The actual dollar figure printed out by the computer should then be compared with the adding machine's tape control total accumulated by Harvey Hunt. These two monetary totals should agree. Any discrepancy would be immediately investigated by management, and the irregularity causing the difference hopefully

detected. This control would thus prevent the employee (Jerome Stein) who is responsible for all the detailed record-keeping activities (endorsing checks, preparing the bank deposit, and listing each customer's cash payment) from embezzling any specific checks. Theft of any checks would cause the computer printout of a specific day's total cash receipts checks to be less than the control total accumulated by Harvey Hunt on the adding machine tape.

Further examples of the separation of related functions preventive control for accounting-oriented activities will be given later in this chapter and in subsequent chapters. When accountants participate in designing a company's information system (discussed in Part Four of the text), they have a major responsibility to design the system in such a way that no single employee has too many similar functions, thereby reducing the risk of asset embezzlement.

It should be emphasized here, however, that no separation of related functional duties preventive control completely eliminates the possibility of employee embezzlement. Through *collusive* efforts (in which two or more employees work together to commit a fraudulent act), the separation of related functions preventive control for safeguarding a company's assets can be circumvented. Good separation of duties merely reduces the risk of fraudulent acts because two or more people must now join forces to execute a fraud successfully. For example, the Alan Company's two employees (Hunt and Stein) involved in the accounts receivable cash collection process could steal check payments by working together. Harvey Hunt could omit specific checks from the daily adding machine tape control total. These same checks would also be excluded from Jerome Stein's daily bank deposit and his daily cash receipts listing sent to the computer center. Stein would then falsify the endorsements on the embezzled checks and split the proceeds with Hunt. Under this collusive procedure, the computer printout of a specific day's total cash receipts checks would still agree with Hunt's adding machine tape total. Thus, the embezzlement would not be detected. The lapping process for future accounts receivable cash payments could then proceed as described earlier. A control method for detecting this fraudulent activity is discussed below.

Role of internal audit subsystem. A company's internal audit staff would have a major role in *designing* good separation of duties among organizational employees (which is the *preventive* part of the control), and also in *monitoring* the efficient performance of this control (which is the *feedback* part of the control). For example, on a surprise basis, one of Alan Company's internal auditors can take possession of the day's endorsed cash receipts checks, the day's bank deposit, and the day's detailed cash receipts listing for the computer center as soon as the accountant, Jerome Stein, has finished these three record-keeping activities.

The auditor first ascertains whether the total bank deposit dollar amount agrees with the total dollar amount on the listing prepared for the computer center. Next, the auditor traces each customer's check to the cash receipts list prepared by Stein. If any discrepancies arise between specific customer checks and what is actually shown on Jerome Stein's cash receipts list, the possibility exists of accounts receivable lapping. The key to the internal auditor's verification work is the element of surprise. If, for example, Jerome Stein and Harvey Hunt knew in advance about the performance of this internal audit procedure, the two employees would obviously refrain from any fraudulent activities on the specific day the internal auditor planned to do the verification work.

Physical Protection of Assets

This last preventive control component has as its purpose maintaining a company's assets in a safe physical location, thereby reducing the risk of employee misappropriation. For example, an organization's inventory of merchandise should be kept in a storage area which is accessible only to those employees given the custodial responsibility for this asset, thus preventing an unauthorized employee from walking in and stealing some merchandise. Inventory items coming into the storage area (possibly a separate warehouse

in those organizations having large quantities of inventory) should be counted by the inventory clerk (or clerks). The clerk should then sign a receiving document, which formally establishes this employee's responsibility for the delivered inventory items. After the inventory is moved into the storage area, any authorized employees requesting some of the inventory should sign the inventory clerk's issuance report, thereby relieving the clerk of further responsibility for these requisitioned inventory items. Periodically, the organization's internal audit staff should supervise a physical count of the actual inventory items on hand in the storage area. The quantities of specific inventory items counted should then be compared with the quantities of these items shown in the detailed inventory records. (To achieve good separation of related organizational functions, these detailed inventory records should be maintained by employees of the accounting subsystem, rather than by the inventory clerk.) Any discrepancies between the physical count and the inventory records should be investigated by the internal auditors in order to determine the cause (or causes) of these discrepancies.

An organization's important documents, such as the corporate charter, all major contracts with other companies, registration statements required by the Securities and Exchange Commission, and so forth, should be accessible only to authorized management personnel. Many organizations keep these documents in a fireproof safe on their own premises or in a rented storage vault at a bank.

Physical protection of cash asset. The susceptibility of cash to employee theft as well as the risk of human error in handling cash (due to the large volume of cash receipts and disbursements transactions that many organizations have) makes it essential for an organization to institute physical protection safeguards for its cash asset. In addition to acquiring fidelity bond coverage (discussed previously) on those employees handling cash, the following physical protection controls for cash should also exist: (1) the majority of cash disbursements for authorized expenditures should be made by check, and (2) the daily cash receipts (either received in the mail from credit customers or received through over-the-counter sales) should be deposited intact at the bank. Each of these two physical protection control areas are now briefly discussed.

Cash disbursements by check. A good audit trail of cash disbursements is essential to avoid undetected errors and irregularities in the handling of cash. To this end, most organizations use prenumbered checks (so that they can maintain accountability over both issued and unissued checks) for making authorized cash disbursements.

An additional preventive control that may be incorporated into a company's cash payments system is a *voucher system* for its disbursements. As you may remember from a prior accounting course, a voucher is a document which thoroughly describes an accounting transaction requiring an eventual cash outlay (e.g., the purchase of office equipment on credit). A voucher can be approved for payment by a properly authorized employee (or employées) only after all the supporting documents relating to the payment have been attached to the voucher and reviewed by this employee.

For example, assume that the voucher in Figure 7-3 was prepared by one of the Alan Company's accountants (Harry Price) on June 15, 1984 for the purchase of an office typewriter from Swann Machine Company. Before this voucher is approved for payment by the Alan Company's treasurer, George Bone, the following supporting documents would be attached to the voucher and reviewed by Bone:

1. A copy of the *purchase order* prepared at the time the typewriter acquisition was approved. The purchase order indicates the Alan Company's intent to buy the electric typewriter from the Swann Machine Company at a specified cost ($900).
2. A copy of the *receiving report* prepared by the Alan Company's receiving department when the typewriter was delivered. The

receiving report indicates that the Alan Company actually received the typewriter asset that will eventually be paid for by a cash disbursement check.
3. A copy of the *purchase invoice* from the Swann Machine Company indicating the dollar amount owed. The purchase invoice should be compared with the purchase order and the receiving report before George Bone signs the $900 check. (At that time, the Date Voucher Paid and Check Number part of the Figure 7-3 voucher would be completed.)

Upon issuance of a cash disbursement check to pay a voucher, the specific supporting documents should all be stamped "PAID" to prevent their being presented at some future time for a second payment. Many organizations, as a further preventive control precaution, require two separate authorized employees to approve vouchers and sign cash disbursement checks for all expenditures over a specified dollar amount (e.g., over $500).

Thus, by using a voucher system and prenumbered checks for cash disbursement transactions, the audit trail of cash outlays can easily be traced. The prenumbered voucher document and the prenumbered check document (rather than using coins and currency for cash disbursements) are both physical items which reduce the risk of employee misappropriation of cash. Once a month, a company's bank reconciliation statement (analyzing the causes of discrepancies between the company's checking account records and what the bank's records indicate) should be prepared by an employee who has no cash-related responsibilities (perhaps the internal auditor).

As discussed above, making cash disbursements by *check* is an effective preventive control. However, a company may have various *small* cash expenditures to make during an accounting period. It is more efficient to pay cash for these expenditures rather than to follow the formal company procedure of using checks. For example, an executive of the Alan Company may want the company pickup truck washed. This

Alan Company

VOUCHER

Cash disbursement
to be made to: Swann Machine Company

8913 Southwest Avenue

New Orleans, Louisiana 70122

Voucher
No.   185

Date   June 15, 1984

Accounts	Debit	Credit	
Office equipment	900		
Vouchers payable		900	

Explanation: Purchase of an electric typewriter from Swann Machine Company

on purchase order number 74.

Voucher Prepared by:	Voucher Approved by:	Date Voucher Paid:	Check Number:
Harry Price	*George Bone*		
(Accountant)	(Treasurer)		

Figure 7-3. Alan Company voucher for the purchase of an office typewriter.

expenditure is so small (perhaps $2.50) that the time required to have a voucher and a disbursement check prepared and signed would not be justified. For good operating efficiency, the Alan Company should use a *petty cash fund* for its small, miscellaneous expenditures. To exercise control over this fund, one employee, called the petty cash custodian, should be given the responsibility for handling petty cash transactions. If the Alan Company establishes its petty cash fund at $100, this money should be kept under the custodian's control in a locked box, and the custodian should be the only individual with access to the fund.

Cash receipts deposited intact. The importance of having physical protection devices to safeguard an organization's cash expenditure ac-

tivities also holds true for cash receipts activities. Each day's accumulation of cash receipts should be "deposited intact" at the bank. In the typical retail organization, the total cash receipts for any specific working day will come from two major sources: checks arriving by mail from credit sales customers, and currency and checks received from over-the-counter cash sales. Daily intact deposits of cash receipts means that none of this cash inflow should be used by company employees to make cash disbursements. Rather, every penny collected should go directly to the bank and a separate checking account used for cash disbursements. The intact deposit of cash receipts enables the audit trail of cash inflows to be easily traced to the bank deposit slip and the monthly bank statement. On the other hand, if company employees were permitted to use some of the day's receipts for cash disbursements, the audit trail for cash could become quite confusing, thereby increasing the risk of irregularities.

Regarding the cash receipts from over-the-counter sales, a physical protective device that should be utilized here is a cash register. The specific type of cash register used (from a simple machine that merely "rings-up" a sale to the more sophisticated point-of-sale recorders that are connected to a company's computer) will be determined by the company's needs. For a small grocery store, the cash register that simply rings-up a sale would probably be adequate. For a major retailer with large daily volumes of over-the-counter sales, however, the point-of-sale recorder (which can integrate the company's credit function, sales function, inventory function, and billing function—discussed in Chapter 4) would probably be more beneficial to the organization's information system.

Good internal control for the cash register's efficient use is to give each employee operator a specific amount of currency (in order to make change) for which the operator is accountable at the beginning of his or her shift. The internal tape within the cash register that records the amount of each sale should not be accessible to the operator. (The employee's supervisor should have the key which unlocks that section of the cash register where the internal tape is stored.) This prevents the operator from manipulating the tape contents to cover up a fraudulent act. At the end of the employee's shift, the supervisor should examine the internally stored tape to ascertain the total cash sales that were recorded. The supervisor then counts the cash within the register (subtracting the specific quantity of money provided the operator at the beginning of his or her shift), and this amount should be equal to the total of the internal tape. The cash register operator is responsible for any discrepancy between the internal tape amount of cash sales and the actual cash in the register.

A further physical safeguard that should exist when using a cash register is that the register's display window (showing the actual amount rung-up by the operator each time a sale is made) should be visible to the customer. This preventive control, in effect, brings the customer into the control system. The fact that the display window can be observed by the customer enables this person to detect either an accidental error or an intentional error by the register operator in recording a sale. An obvious intentional error would occur when the operator rings-up an actual $10 sale for only $5 and pockets the difference. Some companies have signs located in their stores asking customers to tell the manager about any purchases which are recorded incorrectly on the cash register. As proof of the discrepancies, the customers can take their ejected cash register tape receipts directly to the store manager. The manager may even reward these customers with free gifts!

EFFECTIVE FEEDBACK CONTROLS

As discussed at the beginning of this chapter, feedback controls are established within an organization to encourage operating efficiency. The components that are essential to a company's feedback control system are:

1. Efficient preventive controls.
2. A responsibility accounting system.
3. Timely performance reports.

Since component (1) was thoroughly analyzed in the previous section of this chapter, and components (2) and (3) were discussed in Chapter 2 on management concepts, the discussion here of each of these three components will be directed toward their roles in a feedback control system.

Efficient Preventive Controls

For a feedback control system to achieve its objective of encouraging operating efficiency, some type of standards or criteria for the various organizational functions must already exist. This allows the feedback control system to then measure whether actual operating performance is efficient or inefficient based upon the pre-established standards or criteria.

These predetermined standards or criteria are an organization's *preventive controls*. A standard cost accounting system, a budgetary system, or criteria such as competent employees and physical protection of assets, are all preventive controls designed to safeguard an organization's asset resources from inefficient use. The preventive controls represent guidelines for efficient operating performance. Without these efficiency guidelines existing in the organization, it is very difficult for management to evaluate positive or negative performance activities (the feedback controls) within specific subsystems. For example, if the Alan Company did not have predetermined standard costs for the sporting goods manufacturing process, it would be difficult, if not impossible, for management to evaluate whether the actual production costs were too high or too low.

A Responsibility Accounting System

As discussed in Chapter 2, a responsibility accounting system means that each organizational subsystem's performance is evaluated on the basis of only those operating items or activities over which it has control. For feedback controls to achieve their objective of encouraging operating efficiency, these systems controls must be designed to differentiate between each subsystem's controllable and noncontrollable items (or activities). The production subsystem managers' noncontrollable items (such as the dollar amount of building depreciation allocated to the production subsystem), for example, should not be included within the feedback control criteria used to evaluate their operating efficiency because the managers are unable to influence changes in these noncontrollable items. On the other hand, the production managers should be held accountable for those activities that are controllable by them, such as excessive direct labor costs incurred in manufacturing inventory.

Because a responsibility accounting system makes a distinction between a subsystem's controllable and noncontrollable activities and then evaluates the subsystem's operating efficiency only on its controllable activities, the establishment of an effective responsibility accounting

structure is essential to an organization's feedback control system.

As discussed above, the predetermined standard costs for the Alan Company's sporting goods manufacturing process represent a *preventive control*. Included within the process of establishing this preventive control is the development of the *responsibility accounting system*. The responsibility structure is determined by ascertaining which of the standard costs are controllable by each manufacturing component (such as the basketball manufacturing component, the football manufacturing component, etc.) and which are noncontrollable by each manufacturing component. If the Alan Company's production subsystem managers were permitted to make the determination of their controllable and noncontrollable costs, they might tend to categorize certain controllable items as being noncontrollable, thereby eliminating their responsibilities for these cost items. Management's subsequent feedback control evaluation of operating efficiency would give misleading results because certain controllable costs that should have been included in the evaluation were excluded.

To prevent this type of situation from occurring, the Alan Company's internal auditors (who should have an objective, unbiased attitude toward the production subsystem) could participate in the decision-making function of determining each production subsystem manager's controllable and noncontrollable cost items. This effectively established responsibility accounting system should lead to an effective feedback control system.

Timely Performance Reports

Once an organization has implemented various preventive controls and a responsibility accounting structure, the "heart" of its feedback control system, which is timely performance reports, can become operative. The purpose of timely performance reports is to provide a company's management relevant information about how efficiently the implemented preventive controls are functioning. The use of a "management-by-exception" principle in preparing these performance reports (see Chapter 2) will enable management to have feedback information regarding those preventive control areas that deviate significantly from their pre-established standards or criteria. However, for management to specifically determine which employee (or employees) caused a deviation so that corrective action can be implemented, the timely performance reports should include only those functional activities that individual employees can control. Thus, performance reports which provide information to management about the operating efficiency of preventive controls should be based upon the organization's responsibility accounting structure. For example, having implemented the Alan Company's preventive control standard cost accounting system for each manufacturing component of the production subsystem, and having determined which manufacturing costs are controllable and noncontrollable by the individual manufacturing component managers, timely performance reports can then be prepared for each manufacturing area disclosing the significant deviations of actual controllable costs from standard controllable costs.

As emphasized in previous chapters, an organization's electronic data-processing subsystem can play a major role in increasing the timeliness of performance reports. The computer's speed in processing data has enabled management to receive feedback performance reports of exceptions in a much shorter time interval after the exceptions have occurred than would be possible with a manual data-processing system. Quicker "after the fact" performance reports should lead to increased operating efficiency because management's attention is directed to significant preventive control deviations requiring corrective action before these deviations get too far "out of hand."

Some accountants consider performance reports as reflecting only analyses of monetary events (e.g., comparing actual production costs with standard production costs). However, if an organization's performance reports are to function as true feedback controls which signal the need for corrective action, the term *performance reports* should be used in a broad sense to also include nonmonetary evaluations of preventive controls.

For example, one of the Alan Company's important preventive controls is that the functions of cash handling and cash record-keeping should be performed by different employees (the "separation of related organizational functions" preventive control). On paper, this preventive control sounds great. When the Alan Company's internal audit staff periodically observes the cash handling and cash record-keeping functions, however, they may find that this preventive control is being ignored. (The employee responsible for handling cash receipts checks is also participating in the record-keeping functions relating to these checks.) Upon discovering this deviation from the predetermined preventive control, the internal auditors should issue a performance report memo to top management and/or the accounting subsystem's management (depending upon the company's report communication structure) describing what is actually happening in the cash receipts function. Corrective action can then be initiated.

Whenever a company's internal audit staff (or some other organizational employees) evaluates the operational efficiency of preventive controls (whether a quantitative evaluation of a preventive control such as the standard cost system or a qualitative evaluation of a preventive control such as the separation of related organizational functions), the feedback control system is operational. Thus, all the major preventive control components discussed earlier in this chapter (a good audit trail, competent employees, separation of related organizational functions, and physical protection of assets) should be evaluated periodically by a company's feedback control system to ascertain whether these preventive controls are functioning properly. For any significant deviations reported, management should initiate immediate corrective action to enable its business system to function effectively.

SUMMARY

This chapter has analyzed the importance of good internal controls to an efficiently operated accounting information system. Before an organization introduces a specific control procedure into its system, the control's estimated annual operating costs should be compared with the control's estimated annual benefits. This cost/benefit analysis typically causes the organization to implement a ''less than ideal'' control because the perfect control's (one that reduces the risk to almost zero of any undetected errors and irregularities) costs would be likely to exceed its benefits.

An effective internal control system includes both preventive controls (also called ''before the fact'' or accounting controls) and feedback controls (also called ''after the fact'' or administrative controls). The preventive controls are designed to safeguard an organization's asset resources from misuse, either through accidental human error or intentional fraudulent acts by employees. The important components of a preventive control system include a good audit trail, competent employees, separation of related organizational functions, and physical protection of assets. Using the computer for processing accounting transactions has often caused a company's audit trail to be difficult to follow, thereby increasing the risk of employee misappropriation of assets.

Upon implementing the preventive controls into a company's system, the feedback controls begin functioning by evaluating the operational efficiency of these preventive controls. This evaluation is accomplished through timely performance reports which disclose any significant variations of actual operating performance from the standards or criteria established for the preventive controls. To enable management to determine which subsystem employee (or employees) caused these variations, the performance reports should be based upon the organization's responsibility accounting structure. If management knows which specific organizational area (or areas) caused the operating inefficiencies, it can then initiate corrective action on these inefficiencies. The computer's use in processing and printing out performance report data has enabled management to receive feedback reports about inefficient preventive controls requiring corrective action much sooner ''after the fact'' than in a manual data-processing system.

The employees of the internal audit subsystem (in those organizations having this service subsystem) play a major role in a company's internal control system. Because of the internal auditors' independence from the other organizational subsystems (and their resultant objective, unbiased attitude towards these subsystems), they should participate in designing and implementing each subsystem's preventive controls, and also participate in evaluating the efficiency or inefficiency of these implemented preventive controls. Periodic internal audit reviews of the preventive control system to ascertain whether the implemented controls are achieving their original intended goals enable the audit staff to make an important contribution to organizational operating efficiency. Through internal audit feedback reports, management can initiate necessary corrective adjustments to those preventive controls that are not functioning effectively.

DISCUSSION QUESTIONS

7-1.   Why are accountants so concerned about their organization having an efficient and effective internal control system?

7-2.   Discuss any similarities and differences among preventive controls and feedback controls. Which of these two categories of controls do you feel is more important to an organization's effectively operated accounting information system? Explain.

7-3.   An example was provided in this chapter of a hash total control for processing sales invoices. Try to think of some other examples where a hash total could be an effective control within an organization's accounting information system.

7-4.   Judy Williams recently earned her Masters' degree in accounting from a major university.

Her first job after college was as a managerial accountant for the Pretzel Pastry Company. The company is currently in the process of converting its manual data-processing system to a computerized data-processing system. Judy was asked by the chief systems consultant (Harvey Hyatt) to make some suggestions regarding the types of preventive controls that should be implemented into the company's new computerized information system.

After thinking about possible preventive controls for several days, Judy returned to Harvey with the following comments: "Harv, in my opinion, our new computer is the only preventive control we need. Since the computer is not capable of committing an embezzlement or making a computational error, my feeling is that all the types of preventive controls that I have studied in textbooks are unimportant to our company."

If you were Harvey Hyatt, would you agree or disagree with Judy Williams' observations? Explain.

7-5. What role does cost/benefit analysis play in an organization's internal control system?

7-6. Besides the separation of related functions approach illustrated in this chapter, can you think of any other procedures that an organization could use to help prevent lapping of its accounts receivable? Discuss.

7-7. The Mary Popkin Umbrella Manufacturing Company maintains an inventory of miscellaneous supplies (e.g., pens, pencils, typing paper, typewriter ribbons, and envelopes) for use by its clerical workers. These supplies are stored on shelves at the back of the office facility, easily accessible to all company employees.

The company's accountant, Percey Malcumson, is very much concerned about the poor internal control over the company's office supplies. He has estimated that the monthly loss due to theft of supplies by company employees averages about $150. To reduce this monthly loss, Percey has recommended to management that a separate room be set aside to store these supplies, and that a company employee be given full-time job re-

sponsibility for supervising the issuance of the supplies to those employees having a properly approved requisition. By implementing these controls, Percey believes that the loss of supplies from employee misappropriation can be reduced to practically zero.

If you were a member of the Mary Popkin Umbrella Manufacturing Company's management responsible for either accepting or rejecting Percey Malcumson's preventive control recommendations, what would your decision be? Explain. Try to think of some additional preventive control measures that the company might implement to reduce the monthly loss from employee theft of office supplies.

7-8. Evaluate the following statement: "Because an internal audit subsystem does not directly contribute to an organization's revenue-earning functions, and, in fact, often interferes with the other subsystems' operating activities (e.g., by entering a subsystem's work area and taking the time to evaluate the operating efficiency of its specific preventive controls), the organization would probably increase its overall profitability by completely eliminating the internal audit staff."

7-9. The following are descriptions of systems of internal control for companies engaged in the manufacturing business:

1. When Mr. Clark orders materials for his machine-rebuilding plant, he sends a duplicate purchase order to the receiving department. During a delivery of materials, Mr. Smith, the receiving clerk, records the receipt of shipment on this purchase order. After recording, Mr. Smith sends the purchase order to the accounting department, where it is used to record materials purchased and accounts payable. The materials are transported to the storage area by forklifts. The additional purchased quantities are recorded on storage records.

2. Every day hundreds of employees clock in using time cards at Generous Motors Corporation. The timekeepers collect these cards once a week and deliver them to the tabulating machine department. There the data on these time cards are transferred to punched cards. The punched cards are used in the preparation of the labor cost distribution records, the payroll journal, and the payroll checks. The treasurer, Mrs.

Webber, compares the payroll journal with the payroll checks, signs the checks, and returns the payroll checks to Mr. Strode, the supervisor of the tabulating department. The payroll checks are distributed to the employees by Mr. Strode.

3. The smallest branch of Connor Cosmetics in South Bend employs Mary Cooper, the branch manager, and her sales assistant, Janet Hendrix. The branch uses a bank account in South Bend to pay expenses. The account is kept in the name of "Connor Cosmetics—Special Account." To pay expenses, checks must be signed by Mary Cooper or by the treasurer of Connor Cosmetics, John Winters. Ms. Cooper receives the cancelled checks and bank statements. She reconciles the branch account herself and files cancelled checks and bank statements in her records. She also periodically prepares reports of disbursements and sends them to the home office.

Required:

a. List the weaknesses in internal control for each of the above.

b. For each weakness, state the type of error(s) that is (are) likely to result. Be as specific as possible.

c. How would you improve each of the three systems?

(AICPA Adapted)

7-10. Since an organization's internal audit staff is manned by accountants, shouldn't the internal auditors therefore be a component of the organization's accounting subsystem? Explain.

7-11. Why is an organization's accountant so concerned about a good audit trail through the accounting information system? Discuss some of the specific items that should be included in an organization's audit trail.

7-12. Lane Nelson, the recently-hired managerial accountant of The Wintergreen Sugar Company, made these following comments to his supervisor: "Our internal auditors waste a great deal of time and money auditing through the computer system. I strongly believe that the internal auditors could adequately perform their organizational functions by obtaining computer printout reports and tracing the report data back to the original source doc-

uments. There is no reason for the internal auditors to concern themselves with the sophisticated hardware and software of the computer system which created the output reports." Do you agree or disagree with Lane Nelson's comments? Explain.

7-13. Why are *competent employees* an important component of an organization's preventive control system? Discuss some of the personnel subsystem's important responsibilities in obtaining competent employees for its organization.

7-14. Clyde Pocket is currently working his first day as a ticket seller and cashier at the First Run Movie Theater. When a customer walks up to the ticket booth, Clyde collects the required admission charge and issues the movie patron a ticket. To be admitted into the theater, the customer then presents his or her ticket to the theater manager, who is stationed at the entrance door. The manager tears the ticket in half, keeping one half for himself and giving the other half to the customer.

While Clyde was sitting in the ticket booth waiting for additional customers, he had a "brilliant" idea for stealing some of the cash from ticket sales. He reasoned that if he merely pocketed some of the cash collections from the sale of tickets, no one would ever know. Because approximately 300 customers attend each performance, Clyde believed that it would be difficult for the theater manager to keep a running count of the actual customers entering the theater. To further support Clyde's reasoning, he noticed that the manager often has lengthy conversations with patrons at the theater door and appears to make no attempt to count the actual number of people going into the movie house.

Do you think that Clyde Pocket's method for stealing cash receipts from the First Run Movie Theater will be accomplished without his being caught? Explain why you think his theft will not be detected or, if you believe that he will be caught, explain how his fraudulent act will be discovered.

7-15. How can the separation of related organizational functions among employees hopefully prevent undetected errors and irregularities regarding a company's asset resources?

7-16. Why is a company's internal control system strengthened by having daily, intact deposits of cash receipts at the bank rather than using some of these cash receipts for making cash disbursements?

7-17. As a recently-hired internal auditor for the Dagwood Discount Department Store (which has approximately 500 employees on its payroll), you are currently reviewing the store's procedures for preparing and distributing the weekly payroll. These procedures are as follows:

Each Monday morning, the managers of the various departments (e.g., the women's clothing department, the toy department, and the home appliances department) turn in their employees' time cards for the previous week to the accountant (Morris Manning). Morris then accumulates the total hours worked by each employee and submits this information to the store's computer center to enable it to process the weekly payroll. The computer center prepares a transaction tape of employee hours worked and then processes this tape with the employee payroll master tape file (containing such things as each employee's social security number, exemptions claimed, hourly wage rate, year-to-date gross wages, FICA taxes withheld, and union dues deduction). The computer prints out a payroll register indicating each employee's gross wages, deductions, and net pay for the payroll period.

The payroll register is then turned over to Morris Manning, who, with help from the secretaries, places the correct amount of currency in each employee's pay envelope. The pay envelopes are provided to the department managers for distribution to their employees on Monday afternoon.

To date, you have been unsuccessful in convincing the store's management to use checks rather than currency for paying the employees. Most managers that you have talked with argue that the employees prefer to receive currency in their weekly pay envelopes so that they do not have to bother going to the bank to cash their checks.

Assuming the Dagwood Discount Department Store's management refuses to change its present system of paying the employees with cash, suggest some internal control procedures that could strengthen the store's present payroll preparation and distribution system.

7-18. You have been engaged by the management of Alden, Inc. to review its internal control over the purchase, receipt, storage, and issuance of raw materials. You have prepared the following comments which describe Alden's procedures.

- Raw materials, which consist mainly of high-cost electronic components, are kept in a locked storeroom. Storeroom personnel include a supervisor and four clerks. All are well trained, competent, and adequately bonded. Raw materials are removed from the storeroom only upon written or oral authorization of one of the production foremen.
- There are no perpetual-inventory records; hence, the storeroom clerks do not keep records of goods received or issued. To compensate for the lack of perpetual records, a physical-inventory count is taken monthly by the storeroom clerks, who are well supervised. Appropriate procedures are followed in making the inventory count.
- After the physical count, the storeroom supervisor matches quantities counted against a predetermined reorder level. If the count for a given part is below the reorder level, the supervisor enters the part number on a materials-requisition list and sends this list to the accounts payable clerk. The accounts payable clerk prepares a purchase order for a predetermined reorder quantity for each part and mails the purchase order to the vendor from whom the part was last purchased.
- When ordered materials arrive at Alden, they are received by the storeroom clerks. The clerks count the merchandise and agree the counts with the shipper's bill of lading. All vendors' bills of lading are initialed, dated, and filed in the storeroom to serve as receiving reports.

Required

Describe the weaknesses in internal control and recommend improvements of Alden's procedures for the purchase, receipt, storage, and issuance of raw materials. Organize your answers as follows:

Weaknesses	Recommended Improvements

(AICPA Adapted)

7-19. Discuss some of the internal control advantages to an organization by using a voucher system and prenumbered checks for its cash disbursement transactions. Are there any circumstances under which a voucher system with prenumbered cash disbursement checks would not be efficient for an organization to use? Explain.

7-20. The customer billing and collection functions of the Robinson Company, a small paint manufacturer, are attended to by a receptionist, an accounts receivable clerk, and a cashier who also serves as a secretary. The company's paint products are sold to wholesalers and retail stores.

The following describes *all* of the procedures performed by the employees of the Robinson Company pertaining to customer billings and collections:

1. The mail is opened by the receptionist who gives the customers' purchase orders to the accounts receivable clerk. Fifteen to twenty orders are received each day. Under instructions to expedite the shipment of orders, the accounts receivable clerk at once prepares a five-copy sales invoice form which is distributed as follows:

    a. Copy #1 is the customer billing copy and is held by the accounts receivable clerk until notice of shipment is received.
    b. Copy #2 is the accounts receivable department copy and is held for ultimate posting of the accounts receivable records.
    c. Copies #3 and #4 are sent to the shipping department.
    d. Copy #5 is sent to the storeroom as authority for release of the goods to the shipping department.

2. After the paint ordered has been moved from the storeroom to the shipping department, the shipping department prepares the bills of lading and labels the cartons. Sales invoice copy #4 is inserted in a carton as a packing slip. After the trucker has picked up the shipment, the customer's copy of the bill of lading and copy #3, on which are noted any undershipments, are returned to the accounts receivable clerk. The

company does not "back order" in the event of undershipments; customers are expected to reorder the merchandise. The Robinson Company's copy of the bill of lading is filed by the shipping department.

3. When copy #3 and the customer's copy of the bill of lading are received by the accounts receivable clerk, copies #1 and #2 are completed by numbering them and inserting quantities shipped, unit prices, extensions, discounts, and totals. The accounts receivable clerk then mails copy #1 and the copy of the bill of lading to the customer. Copies #2 and #3 are stapled together.

4. The individual accounts receivable ledger cards are posted by the accounts receivable clerk by a bookkeeping machine procedure whereby the sales register is prepared as a carbon copy of the postings. Postings are made from copy #2 which is then filed, along with staple-attached copy #3, in numerical order. Monthly, the general ledger clerk summarizes the sales register for posting to the general ledger accounts.

5. Since the Robinson Company is short of cash, the deposit of receipts is also expedited. The receptionist turns over all mail receipts and related correspondence to the accounts receivable clerk who examines the checks and determines that the accompanying vouchers or correspondence contains enough detail to permit posting of the accounts. The accounts receivable clerk then endorses the checks and gives them to the cashier who prepares the daily deposit. No currency is received in the mail and no paint is sold over the counter at the factory.

6. The accounts receivable clerk uses the vouchers or correspondence that accompanied the checks to post the accounts receivable ledger cards. The bookkeeping machine prepares a cash receipts register as a carbon copy of the postings. Monthly, the general ledger clerk summarizes the cash receipts register for posting to the general ledger accounts. The accounts receivable clerk also corresponds with customers about unauthorized deductions for discounts, freight or advertising allowances, returns, etc., and prepares the appropriate credit memos. Disputed items of large amount are turned over to the sales manager for settlement. Each month the accounts receivable clerk prepares a trial balance of the open accounts receivable and compares the resultant total with the general ledger control account for accounts receivable.

Required

Discuss the internal control weaknesses in the Robinson Company's procedures related to customer billings and remittances and the accounting for these transactions. In your discussion, in addition to identifying the weaknesses, explain what could happen as a result of each weakness.

(AICPA Adapted)

7-21. The Kowal Manufacturing Company employs approximately 50 production workers and has the following payroll procedures.

The factory foreman interviews applicants and on the basis of the interview either hires or rejects the applicants. When an applicant is hired, he or she prepares a W-4 form (Employee's Withholding Exemption Certificate) and gives it to the foreman. The foreman writes the hourly rate of pay for the new employee in the corner of the W-4 form and then gives the form to a payroll clerk as notice that the worker has been employed. The foreman verbally advises the payroll department of rate adjustments.

A supply of blank time cards is kept in a box near the entrance to the factory. Each worker takes a time card on Monday morning, fills in his name, and notes in pencil on the time card his daily arrival and departure times. At the end of the week the workers drop the time cards in a box near the door to the factory.

The completed time cards are taken from the box on Monday morning by a payroll clerk. Two payroll clerks divide the cards alphabetically between them, one taking the A to L section of the payroll and the other taking the M to Z section. Each clerk is fully responsible for her section of the payroll. She computes the gross pay, deductions, and net pay, posts the details to the employees' earnings records, and prepares and numbers the payroll checks. Employees are automatically removed from the payroll when they fail to turn in a time card.

The payroll checks are manually signed by the chief accountant and given to the foreman. The foreman distributes the checks to the workers in the factory and arranges for the delivery of the checks to the workers who are absent. The payroll bank account is reconciled by the chief accountant who also prepares the various quarterly and annual payroll tax reports.

Required

List your suggestions for improving the Kowal Manufacturing Company's system of internal control for the factory hiring practices and payroll procedures.

(AICPA Adapted)

7-22. Jane Dough is a cash register operator at the Fresh Food Grocery Store. She has been working at this job for the past five years. Recently, Jane has been buying many luxury items for her own personal use (e.g., last week she purchased a brand new 25-inch color television set as well as a new stereo system). Some of Jane's fellow workers have been curious about how she can afford these expensive items on the small salary paid to a cash register operator.

This gossip regarding Jane's expensive buying habits was accidentally overheard in the lunchroom by the store's accountant, Carl Bogle. After lunch, Carl walked over to the grocery store location where Jane worked. Without Jane being aware of Carl's presence, he observed her operating functions on the cash register. During this 15-minute observation period, Carl noticed several instances when Jane rang-up a smaller monetary amount on her cash register than the actual selling price of an item. For example, a 2-pound carton of cottage cheese sells for $1.45; however, Jane recorded this item on her cash register at only $.50.

Assume that the only internal control currently existing in the Fresh Food Grocery Store for its cash register operators is that the store manager provides each operator a specific amount of currency with which to make change at the beginning of his or her shift. Suggest some good internal controls (both preventive controls and feedback controls) that would have made it difficult, if not impossible, for Jane Dough to execute successfully her fraudulent activity.

7-23. Why are efficiently operated preventive controls essential to an organization's feedback control system?

7-24. Is it possible for a company to have an effectively operated feedback control system without also having a responsibility accounting system? Discuss.

7-25. Within an organization's budgetary system, what aspect of this system would represent *preventive controls* and what aspect of this system would represent *feedback controls*?

7-26. In recent years distribution expenses of the Avey Company have increased more than other expenditures. For more effective control, the company plans to provide each local manager with an income statement for his or her territory showing monthly and year-to-date amounts for the current and the previous year. Each sales office is supervised by a local manager; sales orders are forwarded to the main office and filled from a central warehouse; billing and collections are also centrally processed. Expenses are first classified by function and then allocated to each territory in the following ways.

Function	Basis
Sales salaries	Actual
Other selling expenses	Relative sales dollars
Warehousing	Relative sales dollars
Packing and shipping	Weight of package
Billing and collections	Number of billings
General administration	Equally

Required

a. Explain responsibility accounting and the classification of revenues and expenses under this concept.

b. What are the objectives of profit analysis by sales territories in income statements?

c. Discuss the effectiveness of Avey Company's comparative income statements by sales territories as a tool for planning and control. Include in your answer additional factors that should be considered and changes that might be desirable for effective planning by management and evaluation of the local sales managers.

d. Compare the degree of control that can be achieved over production costs and distribution costs and explain why the degree of control differs.

e. Criticize Avey Company's allocation pro-

cess for each of the following expense items: (1) other selling expenses, (2) warehousing expense, and (3) general administration expense.

(AICPA Adapted)

7-27. Why are timely performance reports considered to be the "heart" of an organization's feedback control system?

7-28. Each week, the inventory manager of the Easy Make Hardware Store receives a 10-page computer printout containing each merchandise inventory item's current quantity on hand. The manager, after analyzing this inventory listing, decides which inventory items have reached a sufficiently low quantity level to require reordering. The manager then sends the descriptions of these inventory items to the purchasing agent, who places the orders for additional inventory from the designated suppliers.

Try to think of a more efficient inventory reporting system that could be used in the Easy Make Hardware Store.

7-29. The Mass Media Company, which publishes a weekly news magazine, prides itself on having highly competent employees performing the various organizational functions. The company's personnel subsystem supervises training programs for all new employees hired by the company. These training sessions are designed to make the employees more productive once they begin executing their assigned company duties.

As an internal auditor working for the Mass Media Company, how would you go about evaluating the actual competency of the employees? *Note:* In answering this question, feel free to relate your discussion to specific types of jobs you would expect to find in a publishing company (e.g., typists, editors, sports writers, and accountants).

7-30. The cashier of the Easy Company intercepted Customer A's check payable to the company in the amount of $500 and deposited it in a bank account which was part of the company petty cash fund, of which he was custodian. He then drew a $500 check on the petty cash fund bank account payable to himself, signed it, and cashed it. At the end of the month while processing the monthly statements to customers, he was able to change the statement to Customer A so as to show that A had received credit for the $500 check that had been intercepted. Ten days later he made an entry in the cash received book which purported to record receipt of a remittance of $500 from Customer A, thus restoring A's account to its proper balance, but overstating the cash in bank. He covered the overstatement by omitting from the list of outstanding checks in the bank reconcilement two checks, the aggregate amount of which was $500.

List what you regard as five important deficiencies in the system of internal control in the above situation, and state the proper remedy for each deficiency.

(AICPA Adapted)

CASE ANALYSES

7-31.   TuneFork, Inc.

TuneFork, Inc. is a large wholesaler of sheet music, music books, musical instruments and other music related supplies. The company acquired a medium-sized, tape oriented computer system last year, and an inventory control system has been implemented already. Now the systems department is developing a new accounts receivable system.

The flow chart on page 224 is a diagram of the proposed accounts receivable system as designed by the systems department. The objectives of the new system are to produce current and timely information that can be used to control bad debts, to provide information to the sales department regarding customers whose accounts are delinquent, to produce monthly statements for customers, and to produce notices to custom-

ers regarding a change in the status of their charge privileges.

Input data for the system are taken from four source documents—approved credit applications, sales invoices, cash payment remittances, and credit memoranda. The accounts receivable (A/R) file is maintained on magnetic tape by customer account number. The record for each customer contains identification information, last month's balance, current month's transactions (detailed), and current balance. Some of the output items generated from the system are identified below and described briefly.

- Accounts receivable register (weekly)—a listing of all customers and account balances included on the accounts receivable file.
- Aging schedule (monthly)—a schedule of all customers with outstanding balances detailing the amount owed by age classifications—0–30 days, 31–60 days, 61–90 days, over 90 days old.
- Delinquency and write-off registers (monthly)—(1) a listing of those accounts which are delinquent, and (2) a listing of customers' accounts which have been closed and written off; related notices are prepared and sent to these customers.

Required

A.   TuneFork, Inc.'s systems department must develop the systems controls for the new accounts receivable system. Identify and explain the systems controls which should be instituted with the new system. When appropriate describe the location in the flow chart where the control should be introduced.

B.   The credit manager has indicated that the department receives frequent telephone inquiries from customers regarding their accounts. The manager has asked if the department could have a cathode ray tube (CRT) terminal connected to the main computer. Can a CRT terminal be used with the new accounts receivable system as pro-

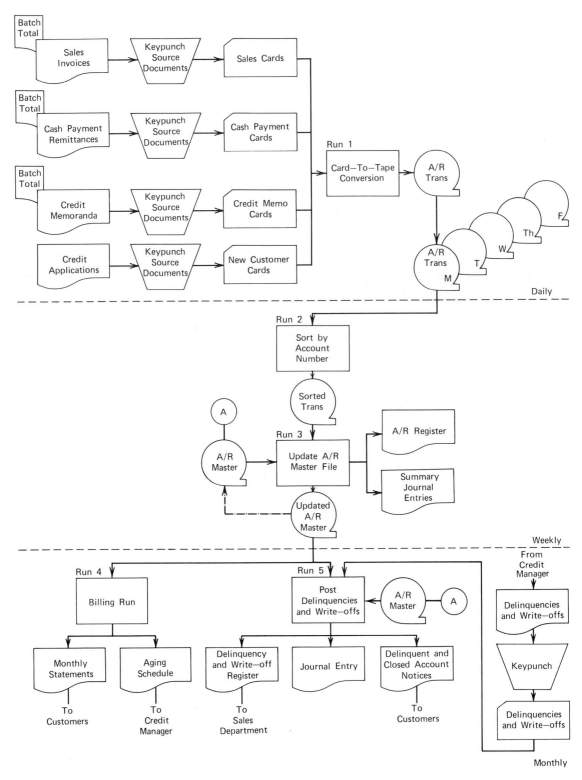

posed to satisfy the needs of the credit manager? Explain your answer.

(CMA Adapted)

7-32. Noble Company*

Several years ago, the Noble Company installed electronic data-processing equipment. Applications include inventory processing, accounts receivable and payable processing, production scheduling, and payroll preparation. Problems have occurred with the accounts payable system and the internal audit staff has been called in to evaluate proposed changes.

Current Procedures

The accounts payable section of the accounting department prepares punched paper tape for all vendors' invoices, which includes information about each vendor's name and address, invoice number, amount due, and either an expense account identification or inventory updating data including stock number, units received, units back-ordered, and so forth. On a weekly basis, the data is used to prepare an invoice register with appropriate distributions of dollar amounts to either inventory or various expense classifications.

Twice a month the data-processing subsystem also prepares checks and a check register for the accumulated invoices. The common discount terms for Noble are 10 days after the end of the month. In order to take advantage of the discounts on the second monthly processing run, check preparation is usually scheduled for either the 8th or 9th of the month, with the result that a large batch of checks is delivered to the accounting department on the 9th or 10th.

When the checks are received, the accounting department matches them with supporting data and forwards both checks and supporting data to two authorized check signers. The supporting documents are reviewed, initialed, and the

*Used with the permission of Roy E. Baker, *Cases in Auditing with Supplemental Readings*, Prentice-Hall, Inc., © 1969.

checks signed manually. Each check is countersigned by the treasurer. Under this system, checks are often not mailed until the 12th or 13th and some discounts are disallowed as a result.

Proposed Changes

To alleviate the problem, the company proposes to have all checks for amounts of $250 or less reviewed by two other clerks who will be authorized to sign with facsimile plates. No further review would be required. The company presents the following points to support its belief that there are adequate controls:

1. Typical check distributions by amounts are:

Amount	Percent of Checks	Percent of Total Disbursements
Under $50	36	2
$50–$250	44	5
Over $250	20	93

2. The clerks will review supporting documents. If there seems to be any irregularity, the checks will not be signed by facsimile, but will be forwarded to the regular check signing channels.
3. The signing devices will have counters. The number of checks signed will be reconciled to the number of checks prepared by the data-processing center.
4. Bank accounts are reconciled independently of the accounts payable division.
5. The clerks will have no duties involving data preparation or matching of checks to supporting documents.
6. Checks signed with the facsimile plate will be imprinted "VOID FOR AMOUNTS GREATER THAN $250."

Questions

1. Do the proposed changes include adequate controls?
2. If not, what further suggestions would you make?

225

7-33.   *Old New England Leather**

Old New England Leather is a large manufacturer and marketer of quality leather goods. The product line ranges from wallets to saddles. Because of the prevailing management philosophy at Old New England Leather, the company will accept orders for almost any leather product to be custom made on demand. This is possible since the leather craftsmen employed by the company perform a job in its entirety (i.e., the company does not utilize production-line techniques). Each leather craftsman is responsible for the complete manufacturing of a given product. Currently, the company employs about 150 leather craftsmen and has been growing at the rate of 20% the last three years. However, management does not anticipate this growth rate in the future, but instead sees a steady growth rate of 5% over the next ten years.

Old New England Leather markets a proprietary line of leather goods worldwide. However, these stock products compose only 50% of the output from the craftsmen. The remaining products are produced to special order. When a custom order is received, the specifications for the order are posted along with an expected shipping date. Each craftsman is then eligible to bid on the order or a part of it. Once the bids are evaluated, the company determines which individual has agreed upon the date, and accepts the lowest bid for production. It is this custom part of the business which has shown the greatest growth in recent years. During the last 12 months, there has been an average of 600 orders in process at any one time.

Along with growth, Old New England Leather management has incurred many problems related to providing consistent, on-time delivery. It appears that the skilled craftsmen often fail to report on a timely basis when a job is complete. In addition, management has never had a satisfactory control for ensuring that orders are worked on in a priority sequence. Other problems, such as a craftsman overcommitting himself in a given time period or simply losing an order, are also becoming serious.

The company leases a medium size computer for processing payroll, inventory, accounts receivable, accounts payable, and so forth. This computer has capabilities for online processing with as many as 20 terminals. Currently, there are ten terminals in operation throughout the plant.

*Used with the permission of John G. Burch, Jr., and Felix R. Strater, Jr., *Information Systems: Theory and Practice*, John Wiley & Sons, Inc., © 1979.

Question

Propose a system for controlling the production of orders which will benefit the craftsmen, management, and the company's customers.

8

Controls for Computerized Accounting Information Systems

Among the important questions that you should be able to answer after reading this chapter are:

1 Why bother with controls for an efficient computerized accounting information system since a computer never makes a mistake?

2 Youth Corps workers in New York programmed their computer to issue over $2,750,000 in bogus paychecks before they were caught. How could a fraud of this order have been avoided?

3 A smart janitor at a bank read computer manuals in his spare time, and eventually figured out a way to log on a terminal and credit his account with $2500. How can you guard the computer against your own employees?

4 Is there such a thing as a foolproof coding system that will eliminate unwarranted access to the CPU from "alien" terminals?

5 The computer of a western business refused to acknowledge a woman's credit until she paid her previous bill of $0.00. When she finally gave up writing letters and wrote out a check for $0.00, the computer accepted her "payment" but charged her extra for making it late. What might have gone wrong?

INTRODUCTION

In many ways, controls for the computerized accounting information system are even more important than they are for a manual one. One

227

reason for this is that the automated accounting information system is likely to process more data than the manual one, thereby making the number of potential errors that much greater. Another reason is that the automated accounting information system tends to gather, process, and store activity data in forms which are not human-readable. Hence, although human observation once served as a supervisor of data accuracy and integrity, this is no longer possible with computerized systems. Finally, it has been stressed in earlier chapters that the automated accounting system has blurred the audit trail, making the trail that much more difficult for accountants to follow, and enabling unscrupulous employees to embezzle hundreds, thousands, and in a few isolated cases, even millions of dollars from their employers.

The purpose of this chapter is to discuss the objectives and functions of controls for the automated accounting information system and to indicate how both automated and manual controls are integrated in the overall system configuration. Understanding these controls is essential to the accountant's ability to audit "through" the company's computer system, and also the auditor's ability to test these controls to see if they are operating correctly. Obviously, a thorough grasp of automated controls is crucial in the prevention of computer crime, fraud, and embezzlement.

At the outset, it should be made clear that detecting computer frauds is not the only function of computerized controls—a large number of these controls are in fact preventive (rather than feedback) in nature, and many of them are designed merely to detect processing errors that would otherwise go unnoticed. A few examples make clear the wide scope of problems that have plagued automated systems in the past:

- A man from Milwaukee, Wisconsin, received a letter from the Social Security Administration informing him of his death and notifying him that they were cutting off his monthly benefits. It took him three weeks to convince the local office that he was alive but that his wife had died.

- A business located in Palo Alto, California, found that it was losing sales because it did not have a particular computer program to use in conjunction with its engineering work. One of the company's programmers was able to plug into the computer memory of a rival firm and print out a copy of the program, which was valued at $300,000.

- A hotel in Chicago had a policy of sending thank-you letters to all its paid-up guests, thanking them for their patronage. A mix-up in mailing lists caused the letters to go out to the wrong people. As a result, hundreds of Chicago women received letters thanking their husbands for their business.

This chapter will discuss controls that help avoid some of the problems mentioned above, and, in some instances, will also describe circumstances in which such controls are most advantageous. It should be kept in mind, however, that not all the controls discussed in this chapter would be likely to exist in any one accounting information system. Each organizational system is somewhat different and a specific control that might be useful for one system may be of little or no value for another. Furthermore, if a specific company actually implemented all the computerized controls discussed in the pages which follow, there is a strong likelihood that the annual operating costs of maintaining this control system would greatly exceed the annual benefits obtained from it. Thus, when a company is setting up its accounting information system, it is important for management to conscientiously select only those controls which appear to serve its needs—that is, those controls that promise benefits in excess of their costs.

In the pages that follow, we shall attempt to outline a number of such controls which are of special use for computerized accounting information systems. For the sake of organization, it is convenient to follow the audit trail. Thus, we shall trace the data-flow through the computerized system, first discussing controls for input, then discussing controls for processing, and finally discussing controls for output. Input controls, processing controls, and output controls are all part of what *Statement on Auditing Standards No. 3* refers to as *application controls.* This statement reads, in part:

Application controls relate to specific tasks performed by EDP. Their function is to provide reasonable assurance that the recording, processing, and reporting of data are properly performed. There is considerable choice in the particular procedures and records used to effect application controls. Application controls often are categorized as "input controls," "processing controls," and "output controls."

a. *Input controls* are designed to provide reasonable assurance that data received for processing by EDP have been properly authorized, converted into machine sensible form and identified, and that data (including data transmitted over communication lines) have not been lost, suppressed, added, duplicated, or otherwise improperly changed. Input controls include controls that relate to rejection, correction, and resubmission of data that were initially incorrect.

b. *Processing controls* are designed to provide reasonable assurance that electronic data processing has been performed as intended for the particular application; i.e., that all transactions are processed as authorized, that no authorized transactions are omitted, and that no unauthorized transactions are added.

c. *Output controls* are designed to assure the accuracy of the processing result (such as account listings or displays, reports, magnetic tape files, invoices, or disbursement checks) and to assure that only authorized personnel receive the output.*

Two special sections at the end of this chapter have also been included. One section outlines a set of controls for a payroll accounting information system, and is intended to tie the control discussions in this chapter and the previous chapter together through the use of a comprehensive example. The last section of this chapter stresses the importance of physical security to accounting information systems, and indicates some means by which such security may be achieved at the computer center facility.

*Auditing Standards Executive Committee, American Institute of Certified Public Accountants, *Statement on Auditing Standards No. 3* (New York: American Institute of Certified Public Accountants, © 1974), pp. 3 and 4.

INPUT CONTROLS

As the name implies, input controls attempt to assure the accuracy and completeness of the data fed into the CPU for processing. Because the accounting information system cannot provide "good" information if it does not start with "good" data ("garbage in—garbage out"), input controls serve a vital function in the processing system. For the purposes of discussion, it is convenient to divide the classification of input controls into four subcategories: data observation, data recording, data transcription, and computer access. We shall look at each of these in greater detail below.

Data Observation

Recording the activities of individuals, groups, businesses, and institutions forms the bulk of the data entering the accounting information system. Thus, the deposits and withdrawals of savings account customers at the bank, the purchases and sales of shares of stock by stockholders at the stock exchange, and the course-activity of students at the university all generate data that require processing to be useful. Remarkably enough, humans make very poor observers of their own activity. For example, people notoriously overestimate the number of individuals in a crowd. Similarly, they are rarely able to relate the outcome of an exciting sporting event without prejudice. Finally, in the game of "telephone," in which the participants sit in a circle and "pass on" a whispered sentence from one player to another, the final "data" rarely resemble the original.

The examples above show the difficulties of gathering accurate data, and point out the importance of implementing safeguards to assure objectivity, accuracy, and completeness in the data-collection function. For these reasons, an organization often finds it useful to install one or more observational controls to assist in the data-collection process. As in all other kinds of controls, these are many and varied, and their usefulness or advisability is a question of weighing the benefits against the costs of their use.

As noted in Chapter 7, one such control is the

introduction of a feedback mechanism. A primary example in the data-collection process would be the use of confirmation slips in the preparation of sales orders. With such a mechanism, a salesperson might write up a sales order and present the completed document to the customer for approval. The customer confirms the order with a signature, thereby attesting to the accuracy and completeness of the data contained therein. Other examples of confirmation controls include (1) the use of turn-around documents, in which errors may be corrected directly on the data medium, and (2) the use of any other communication device—for example, a telephone —in which one party may validate the data gathered by another. In each of these cases, the probability of accuracy in the initial observation of the data is increased because a validating procedure is at hand.

In some cases, such as those involving long-distance transactions, inexpensive feedback may not be possible. As an alternate to feedback control (or perhaps in addition to such controls), the recording process can also make use of dual observation. Here, the accuracy of the data-recording function is enhanced because more than one person performs it. In the medical profession, the examination of X-rays by more than one physician provides an illustration. In commercial applications, the dual-observation control is often supervisory in nature. Here, the observer's supervisor is required to confirm the accuracy of the data gathered by the subordinate. Such a procedure would also serve to control fraud because it is difficult to record inaccurate data intentionally when the observation process itself is under supervision.

Data Recording

Once observed, the data must be recorded. When recording is performed manually, the recording sheet becomes the source document which then serves as the primary input to the manual, as well as to the computerized, accounting information system. As noted in Chapter 4, data collection has been an area in which a great deal of automation has taken place. For example, the use of magnetic-striped credit cards or point-of-sale recording devices to encode data has been found to lessen substantially the error rate in the recording process as well as to eliminate the expense involved in the translation of the data to machine-readable formats.

In some instances, automated data recording is not feasible and an initial source document must be prepared manually. To encourage recording accuracy, several controls are possible. One is to use preprinted recording forms such as the inventory receipts slip illustrated in Figure 8-1. Such forms ensure that *all* the information required for processing has been recorded and also enhances accuracy in the recording process. For example, the exact number of spaces required for such field items as the inventory part number or date is clear because a box has been provided for each numerical digit, thus guarding against a loss, or an addition, of any other digits in these fields.

Recording forms have other advantages. For example, the preprinted numbers at the top of each form serve as a transaction identification for reference purposes, and the fact that these numbers are preprinted also guarantees that this reference is unique. In terms of recording accuracy, the preprinted form is useful in that it imposes uniformity in the data-recording process. Referencing and cross-checking are thereby enhanced.

The dual observation or supervisory control described above can also be used in conjunction with the preprinted data-collection form to improve data-recording accuracy. In some instances, the signature of the approving officer for each document is warranted and a space on the form, as illustrated in Figure 8-1, may be designed in the format. Alternatively, if only special situations require approval—for example, the approval of a credit sale in excess of $500— the special situations triggering such action may be preprinted on the document, thus making such circumstances clear.

Data Transcription

Here, transcription refers to the preparation of data for computerized processing. If the data in

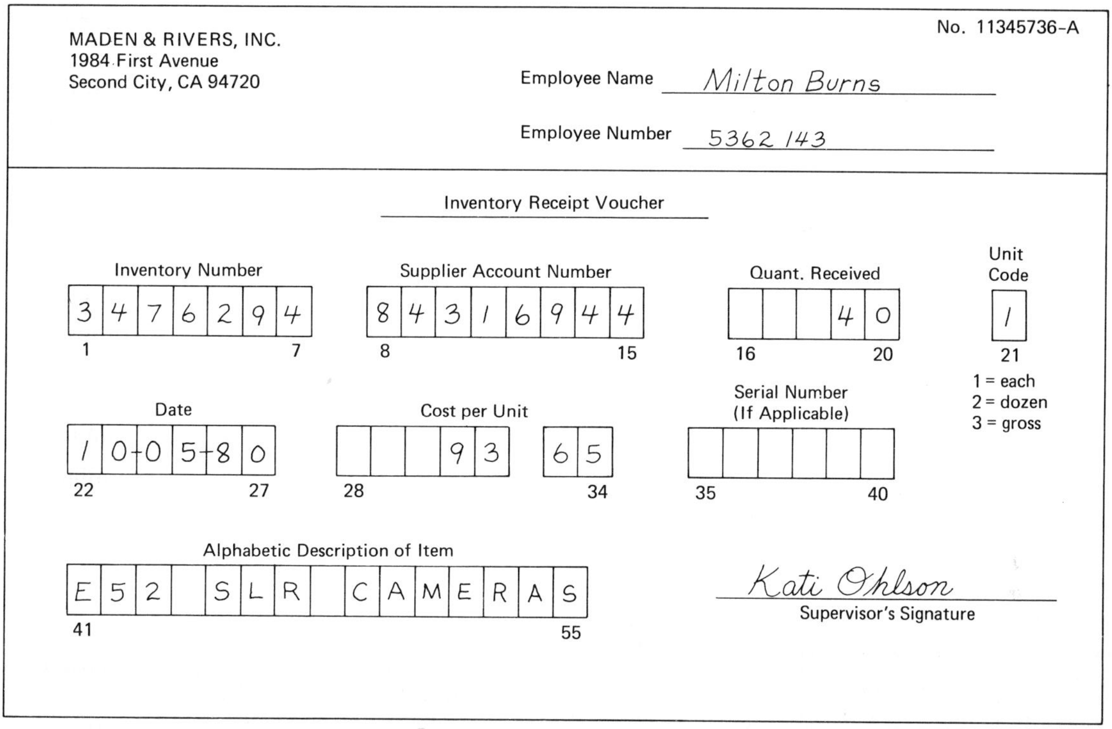

MADEN & RIVERS, INC.
1984 First Avenue
Second City, CA 94720

No. 11345736-A

Employee Name Milton Burns

Employee Number 5362 143

Inventory Receipt Voucher

Inventory Number: 3 4 7 6 2 9 4 (1–7)

Supplier Account Number: 8 4 3 1 6 9 4 4 (8–15)

Quant. Received: 4 0 (16–20)

Unit Code: 1 (21)

1 = each
2 = dozen
3 = gross

Date: 1 0-0 5-8 0 (22–27)

Cost per Unit: 9 3 6 5 (28–34)

Serial Number (If Applicable) (35–40)

Alphabetic Description of Item: E 5 2 S L R C A M E R A S (41–55)

Kati Ohlson
Supervisor's Signature

Figure 8-1. A preprinted recording form for inventory receipts.

the accounting information system were to be processed manually, the "transcription step" would not be necessary because no computer would be used. The avoidance of a transcription step is one obvious advantage of the manual system over the automated one. As we have seen, however, computerized accounting information systems using key-entry devices or terminals enable the user to transfer data directly to computer files, thereby also eliminating any intermediary processing tasks.

In computerized accounting information systems, it is important that the information gathered in the source document satisfy the input requirements of the particular accounting application. Moreover, wherever possible, this information should be organized on the source document in such a way as to facilitate the transcription process. Thus, well-designed, preprinted forms as discussed above are an important control for accounting information systems because they encourage adherence to this general principle of source-document/computer-input compatibility. Where source-document data is to be transferred to punched cards, for example, the boxes drawn for each potential character in Figure 8-1 ensure accuracy and completeness in the recording of this data. The small numbers below these boxes are card-column reference numbers which enable a keypunch operator to transfer accurately the source-document data to a punched card. Thus, in Figure 8-1, it is easy to understand that the inventory code number is to be punched in columns 1–7 of the punched card, that the date is to be punched in columns 22–27 of the card, and so forth.

In many instances, some of the data to be punched in the computer card is repetitive—for example, the discount terms of a sales invoice, the date (for a given batch of transactions), or the regional office code specifying the area in which a sale was made. Requiring keypunch operators to repunch such "redundant" information in each card increases the likelihood of keypunching errors and wastes time. For this reason, it is often useful to prepare a *program drum card*, which enables the keypunch operator to direct the keypunch machine to *automatically* punch predetermined information into preselected fields of the computer data card. The drum card that controls such punching sits in a window of the card punch and can be prepared in less than a minute by an experienced operator.

An alternate to the ''programming'' of the drum card is to use cards which have been pre-punched by the computer's card-punching machines. In certain inventory applications, for example, it was discovered that the entire computer card could be prepunched and held in stock by the inventory control manager. At the same time that an issue was made from inventory, the appropriate prepunched card was forwarded to the computer center for use in updating the balance records on the inventory file. Thus, the keypunching phase was avoided entirely! An additional advantage of the ''prepunched card'' alternative to the program drum card is that the prepunched cards may also be color coded and preprinted, making them more easily understood and more accurate.

For punched cards that require at least some variable information, it is common practice to check transcription accuracy with a card verifier. A card verifier looks very much like a card key punch. The verifier cannot punch cards, however, it can only test what has been punched in a card already. Thus, in a card-verification process, the cards are rekeyed through the verifier, which means that the operator keys in the same information on the verifier from the initial source document. If the information keyed on the verifier is the same as that punched on the card, the card passes through the reading station of the verifier without incident. (Some verifiers will clip a little half-circle notch at the end of the card to indicate a successful verification.) Where discrepancies are discovered, the verifier machine ''jams,'' and usually rings a bell or turns on a light. Typically, the operator is given two or three chances to key in the same information in order to avoid the possibility that the punched-card data is correct but that the verification in-

formation has been keyed wrong. When it becomes clear that a transcription error has been made in the original punched card, the card is removed from the verifier and returned to the keypunch station for corrections.

Where terminals, key-entry devices, and such direct-coding methods as key-to-tape or key-to-disk recording approaches are involved in the process of data transcription, alternate methods of input control are possible. When online terminals are used, for example, it is possible to program the computer to automatically edit computer input and interact with the user when data discrepancies are detected. Thus, for example, if an employee of the Alan Company were to input a seven-digit inventory code number when only six digits were allowed, the computer could be programmed to detect this mistake and output the error message:

```
TOO MANY DIGITS ENTERED.
DATA RECEIVED WAS: 1234567
PLEASE REENTER INVENTORY CODE NUMBER:
```

Virtually any input test that can be programmed on a computer can be used in conjunction with an online computer terminal. Therefore, we shall return to the subject of data access and computerized processing controls in the following section of this chapter.

Where CRT terminals are used for computer input, *preformatted screens* also make good data-transcription controls. A preformatted screen is much the same as the preprinted source document discussed earlier, except that the preformatted screen is flashed on the cathode ray tube of the terminal instead of printed on paper. When the format of the information is outlined on the CRT, the user follows this format to input the required data. Thus, for example, to input a six-digit inventory code number, the Alan Company might utilize the screen format:

```
INPUT DIGITS:      123456
INVENTORY CODE: ------
```

As the user inputs the inventory account number, the spaces over the underlines would fill with data. At the completion of the input cycle, therefore, the full six-digit inventory number will be clear.

A special type of preformatted screen makes use of a *mask* to accomplish the same purpose as the underlines mentioned above. For input purposes, a mask is nothing more than a set of blinking boxes on the screen with each box the size of a single input character. As the user inputs data, the boxes on the screen are replaced with the input characters. Upon completing the input for a particular data field, the user should find that the mask has been replaced with the completed input. If the data input is incomplete, however, a portion of the mask will still remain and the user is alerted to this fact because the unfilled boxes of the mask continue to blink.

Access to the Computer

An important type of input control not related to data accuracy involves access to the computer itself. Here, we are not referring to physical access, which is discussed in greater detail in a later section of this chapter, but rather to "logical access" or usage—for example, via a remote terminal. Such logical access would permit the user to call for printouts of sensitive corporate data (e.g., sales projections or executive salaries), or permit access to expensive programs acquired by the company's EDP subsystem. Thus, regulating who is permitted logical access to the computer is an important control in terms of safeguarding the physical assets (software) or sensitive information of the organization.

Since remote terminals may be placed anywhere in the country and hooked up to the computer via ordinary telephone lines (some facilities have a normal telephone number for this purpose), it is difficult to safeguard logical computer access with direct physical surveillance of terminals. Therefore, most computer centers have resorted to using *password codes* to restrict access. Such codes vary in length and type of password information required, but all have the same intent: to limit logical access to the computer only to those authorized to have it.

The construction of efficient, password codes has assumed a somewhat gamelike challenge to

the computer industry, and several years ago, the government sponsored an industry-wide competition to see who could construct the most foolproof system. Although IBM eventually won the contest, many experts doubt that it was much of a victory because passwords are like house keys: they can be lost, given away, or stolen. Thus, even the most elaborate security system can be broken easily if the computer thief has obtained the important information necessary for computer access via other means. Not long ago, for example, a security expert working as a management consultant bet an EDP manager $100 that he could gain access to the company's new million-dollar processing system in one hour. The manager quickly took the bet thinking that here was an easy $100. The company had just installed a new, elaborate, password-control system to safeguard computer access and new passwords were utilized daily. The bet was on!

The security expert calmly made two ordinary phone calls. The first was to the machine-room supervisor's home to inquire which machine operators were on duty that night. The expert was informed that "Steve" was one of them. The other phone call was to the machine room itself. The consultant asked for Steve. When Steve came on the line, the consultant told Steve that they knew each other, that he had misplaced his password, that he had an important computer program to run, that he had just talked to Steve's supervisor, and that the supervisor told him it would be all right for Steve to give him the code over the phone. Steve was hesitant but the security analyst persisted. Finally, Steve looked up the password in the security control log and gave it to the consultant. The consultant now had all the information needed to "rip-off" the computer at leisure. The whole process took less than 15 minutes!

This "horror story" is unusual only in that it involved a wager between two friends, and ultimately did not result in any loss to the company. In most other instances, the thefts are real, and therefore so are the losses. Thus, most computer experts point out that the security system of the computer facility is only as good as the people who run it. Statistics reveal, in fact, that a surprisingly high percentage of computer fraud is performed by the very people who are supposed to be guarding the computer system. We shall return to this point in Chapter 9.

PROCESSING CONTROLS

Processing controls are concerned with the manipulation of accounting data once such data is available to the CPU. As you know, once the data enters the computer, it disappears from human observation. However, good computer processing controls can "go underground" together with the data.

An interesting development in the use of computerized data-processing systems is that much of the data "screening" once performed manually by clerks and related personnel can now be performed automatically as part of the processing routines of the information system programs. Thus, it is convenient to divide our discussion of processing controls into two parts: (1) those controls related to processing at the time of data access, and (2) those controls that primarily involve data manipulation at a latter phase in the processing cycle. Each of these topics is discussed in greater detail below.

Data Access

Suppose you were the data-processing manager at a bank. The transactions each day consist of a large number of checks written by the bank's 100,000 customers. As you may remember from Chapter 4, these checks are magnetically encoded pieces of paper of varying length and width. The account number and bank number are precoded magnetically on the checks, and the amount of each check itself is later encoded by one of the bank's clerical staff after the check has been presented to the bank for payment. The problem: how to make sure that all these checks are correctly processed by the computer.

Control totals. One common processing control is to batch the checks in bundles of 100, 150, or 200 checks each, and prepare a special batch control "check" (Figure 8-2) to serve as a control on the contents of the bundle. The information on the control check might include the bundle number, today's date, and the total dollar amount for the checks themselves. When computer processing commences, the special information on the lead, control check is accessed first and the control total is stored in computer memory. As the checks are accessed individually, their amounts are also accumulated in computer

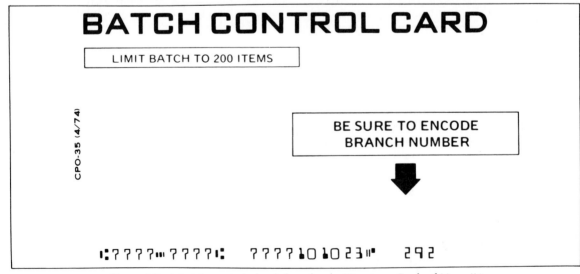

Figure 8-2. A batch control check for a bank. (Courtesy, Bank of Hawaii.)

memory. Once all the checks in the batch have been read, the accumulated total is compared with the figure in the control total. A match signals acceptable processing. A nonmatch signals an error, which may then be traced either to an error in the batch total or to some difficulty in the processing itself (e.g., the inability of the MICR reader to understand the information on one or more checks). When data problems such as this arise, it becomes clear why more than 200 checks are rarely used in the batching process. How would you like to find the input error in a batch of, say, 500 checks?

A control total such as the one illustrated in the example above involves a dollar amount and is therefore called a *financial control total*. Other examples of financial control totals would include the sum of credit sales in an accounts receivable application, the sum of cash disbursements in an accounts payable application, or the sum of net pay in a payroll application. Accounting information systems also make use of *nonfinancial control totals,* which compute non-dollar sums, to determine such things as total number of hours worked, total number of boxes shipped, or total number of discount coupons processed. Financial control totals and nonfinancial control totals are easy to compute and have obvious meaning. For these reasons, such controls are widely used in business and are an extremely important type of control in accounting information systems.

As we have observed already in Chapter 7, control totals do not have to make sense in order to be useful. For example, when processing bank checks, the sum of the account numbers in a batch of transactions might be computed to form a *hash total*. The actual figure is meaningless, but the fact that it has been computed is useful as a check against an "internal" tally of this same hash total by the computer at the time of data access.

Another type of data-access control often used by data-processing facilities because of its simplicity is the *record count*. Using this control, the number of transaction items are counted twice: once when preparing transactions in a batch, and again when actually performing the data processing. For example, if magnetic tape is used as an input medium, record counts of both the number of logical records on the file and the number of physical records on the file may be made. This information is stored in the trailer record (i.e., the last, control record) of the file, or, if the file is very large, on special control records placed at strategic "segment" portions of the file. Thus, for example, every time a computer program uses a magnetic tape file, the number of logical records and the number of physical records are counted and compared with the existing counts in the trailer records, or control records, to assure completeness in the processing function.

Record counts are not as popular as other types of control totals in batch operations because the record count serves only as a check on the *number* of items accessed, whereas the batch-control total (e.g., dollar sums) provides a test on the information contained *within* the batched transactions as well. However, there is nothing to prevent data-processing personnel from using both types of controls.

Edit tests. Whereas financial totals, hash totals, and record counts permit the data processor to check on the overall validity of the input, these controls do not test the accuracy or completeness of all the information that might be input, say, for a single accounts receivable transaction. One type of control to perform this data-testing function would be *editing tests* on selected fields of the input data. Any number of such editing tests are possible. Among them would be:

1. *Tests of numeric field content*, which make sure that such data fields as social security number, invoice number, or date contained only numeric information.

2. *Tests of alphabetic field content*, which make sure such fields as customer name contained only alphabetic information.

3. *Tests of alphanumeric field content*, which make sure that fields such as inventory parts descriptions contain letters or numbers, but no special characteristics.

4. *Tests for valid codes* (e.g., M = male, F = female).

5. *Tests of reasonableness* (e.g., regular

235

hours worked by an employee less than or equal to 40).

6. *Tests of algebraic sign* (e.g., account numbers always positive.

7. *Tests of completeness* (no blanks in fields requiring entries).

Editing tests can also be coordinated in what is called a *redundant data check* to ensure data accuracy. Basically, the idea is to encode repetitious data on a file or transaction record, thereby enabling a later processing test to compare the two data items for compatibility. For example, a candy company could use both an inventory code number and an alphabetic code designator to represent the same inventory item. A master list of numeric and alphabetic designators would be maintained by the computer program performing the inventory processing. Thus, if the inventory number 75642 (representing chocolate caramels) was encoded incorrectly in a punched card with the alphabetic designator "VC" (standing for vanilla caramels), the transaction would be rejected because the two designators for supposedly the same item failed to match.

In the early years of computer data processing, EDP personnel were hesitant to perform too much editing of data in processing applications because editing takes computer time and is something that can be done by hand. Today, with the internal cycle speeds of even minicomputers measured in nanoseconds (i.e., billionths of a second), this reservation is no longer valid, and editing routines can be constructed with as much detail and minute error-testing as desired without fear of "burning up" too much computer time.

Check digits. It is possible for a data field to pass all of the editing tests described above and still be invalid. For example, a bank might use the incorrect account number 537627 when preparing a transaction instead of the proper account number 537621. When the incorrect number is keyed into a remote terminal and submitted to the logical tests described above, it would (1) pass a test of content assuring that all digits were numeric; (2) pass a test of reasonableness assuring that the account number itself fell in a valid range of values (e.g., account number greater than

100,000 and less than 800,000); (3) pass a test of sign (account number positive); and (4) pass a test of completeness (no blanks). Thus, it is apparent that yet additional processing controls must be imposed on the above input data if the error in our example were to be detected.

There are at least two methods by which to accomplish this end. One would be to incorporate an *unfound record test* in the data-processing routine used to update the master file of bank records. With this approach, any transaction for which there was no corresponding master file record would be recognized as invalid and "kicked out" of the transaction sequence (i.e., rejected and printed as an error message) and returned for correction. But what if a master file record did exist for account 537627—the incorrect account number? This would indeed be grievous because our "unfound-record" control would not work, and, what is even worse, the legitimate master file record with account number 537627 would be updated with the data generated by another customer.

To guard against this possibility, a more subtle approach is necessary. An alternate technique is to expand the six-digit data field of the account number to seven digits in order to accommodate a *check digit*. Normally, the check digit is computed as a mathematical function of the other digits in a numeric field, and its sole purpose is to serve as a check on the validity of the associated data. To illustrate, consider the original correct account number 537621. The sum of these six digits is $5 + 3 + 7 + 6 + 2 + 1 = 24$. One type of check digit would use the low-order digit of this sum, or 4, for the account number. This check digit would be attached to the end of the account number and thus, the seven-digit value 5376214 would be used instead of the six-digit series 537621 to represent the account. The computer program accessing the transactions used to update master-file account records would duplicate this computational procedure at the time of data access, and therefore would be able to validate the propriety of the data before the transaction was used to update a master-file record. Thus, had we attempted to input the incorrect account number 5376274 for processing, this number would be detected immediately as erroneous data: the check digit computed from the first six digits (which is 0 for this account number since $5 + 3 + 7 + 6 + 2 + 7 = 30$) would not correspond to the attached check digit ($=4$).

It should be observed that the use of a check digit is not an automatic guarantee of data validity. For example, the check digit described above would be unable to distinguish between the correct account number, 5376214, and the transposed number 5736214, because the transposition of digits does not affect their sum. (See problems 28, 29, and 30 at the end of the chapter for check-digit techniques that do include order in the construction of check-digit values.) Moreover, check digits cannot detect fraudulent data. If an embezzler is clever enough to create a fictitious account number, the embezzler will certainly also be clever enough to code the correct check digit for the account number as well. Finally, most check-digit systems, no matter how complicated, cannot guard against the rare event in which two mistakes are made in the encoding of the same account number which "cancel each other out" in terms of the check-digit calcula-

tion. Thus, for example, the check-digit control *alone* would not catch the mistaken coding of account number 5826214 for the (correct) account number 5736214—the check digits are both correct at 4.

One final drawback of check digits is that they require the encoding, processing, and storage of a number that is redundant information—that is, a number easily computed from the other values of an account number which therefore serves no informational purpose. In this sense, the check digit is a waste of time and space. Thus, for all these reasons, check digits are not always recommended for use in an accounting information system application.

Special controls for tapes and disks. When computer files are stored on magnetic tapes and disks, yet additional processing controls are possible. To make sure that a magnetic tape input file is not used as an output file or accidentally written on, for example, the magnetic tape reel's *file-protect ring* can be removed, thus placing the reel in a "read-only" processing mode (see Figure 8-3). For minicomputers which use cassettes, lit-

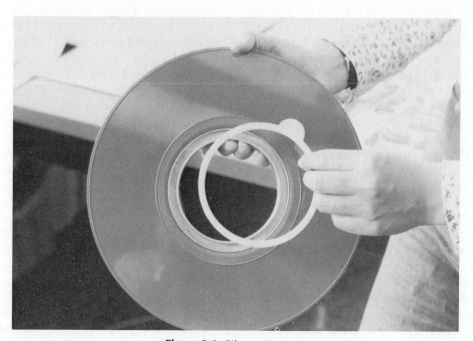

Figure 8-3. File protect ring.

tle plastic flanges on the back of the cassette casing can be broken off to obtain the same result.

For both magnetic tapes and disks, standard file label processing routines may be used which first access the file's header label and then validate the file name, file number, and so forth, of the tape or disk file. This type of control ensures that the computer program is processing the correct files, and that the files themselves are in proper order. If desired, special secret passwords can also be required of file users to make sure that only authorized computer programs or users access sensitive file information.

When the data stored on magnetic tapes or disks is accessed, still further controls can be used. For example, selected fields of each tape or disk record can be edited upon input to the CPU using methods discussed earlier to assure data accuracy. Check digits can be computed where necessary to validate codes. Internal consistency in the file can also be examined using specialized programming routines. For example, it is a simple matter to check a magnetic tape file of accounts receivable records for account-number sequence, or a magnetic disk file of payroll records for duplicate entries. Such routines are sometimes called *imbedded auditing routines* because, in effect, such routines audit the data stored on computer files in much the same fashion as an internal or external auditor might do if such files were maintained manually.

Processing controls invisible to the accountant (and even the computer operator or programmer) often run in parallel to the logical tests discussed above at the time data access and processing occurs from magnetic tape and disk files. Hardware parity tests, for example, are performed during data transmission to make sure that no communication errors occur during the data-access process. Similarly, standard file-processing routines programmed into the operating system of the computer center may be used to advantage. For example, as noted earlier, these routines will automatically count the number of logical and physical records on a particular accounting file, and compare these control totals with information stored in the file's trailer label in order to check for processing completeness. Error recovery procedures are also built into such operating systems so that, for example, tape-cleaning activity for a particular tape drive (which is a mechanical activity performed by the tape drive itself) can be initiated automatically in the event that a portion of a magnetic tape cannot be deciphered. Such procedures can be programmed into the computer software if desired, so that a computer operator is notified only when such recovery procedures fail.

Finally, processing controls for tapes and disks would also include the preparation of duplicate copies of current files for security purposes, and the manual storage of such file copies in secure locations away from the computer center. This control is important, for example, in the event of fire, theft, or vandalism, and should be part of the standard operating procedure of the company. The most common file control is the so-called *grandfather-father-son method of file protection*, in which three generations of a master file, together with the transactions files used to update them, are secured for this purpose.

Figure 8-4 illustrates the general idea for a master file which is updated at the end of each day. Monday's master file and Monday's transactions file are used to prepare the master file for Tuesday morning. Similarly, Tuesday's master file plus Tuesday's transactions file are used to prepare the current master file for Wednesday. Thus, at Wednesday noon, Monday's master file would be the grandfather file, Tuesday's master file would be the father file, and Wednesday's master file would be the current, or son, file. Thus, the Monday files and the Tuesday files would be stored at secure locations away from the computer center. In the event that Wednesday's master file is rendered inoperative, the company can recover simply by preparing another copy of it from the Tuesday (father) files. Even if both the Wednesday master file and the Tuesday master file are no good, there is still the Monday file.

On Wednesday night, the process moves forward. As soon as the master file for Thursday is prepared, there is a shift of file ranking. In particular, Tuesday's master file becomes the

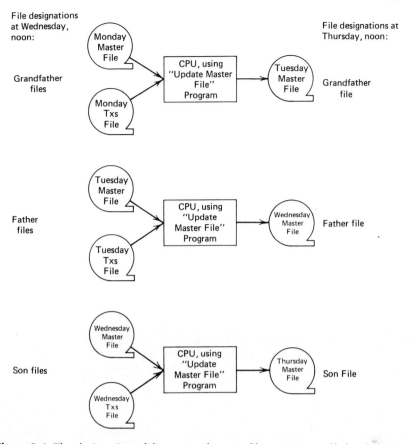

Figure 8-4. The designation of three sets of master files, using grandfather-father-son file security.

grandfather file, Wednesday's master file becomes the father file, and the now-current Thursday file becomes the son file. Monday's file is no longer needed and can therefore be erased. Thus the process continues in chronological sequence. Of course, all this need not occur on a daily or even weekly basis. Many master files are not updated every day. Thus, in alternate accounting applications, the periodicity of the work will differ, although the steps necessary to maintain the computer file's security will not.

When disk files are used, the problem of maintaining back-up copies of the disk pack is compounded by the fact that disk files are usually updated "in place." This means that the disk file is modified by accessing an old record, changing certain information, and then writing over the old record on the disk pack, thereby erasing what was there before. Thus, whereas it is a simple matter to relabel an "old" tape reel as a father or grandfather file, a concerted effort must be expended to physically copy the entire disk file if it is to be maintained as a back-up copy. Because disk packs are both bulky and expensive, this copying is normally done onto a tape reel. Occasionally, even card decks and printed output have been used for back-up purposes. Punching cards is a slow and tedious process compared with tape recording, however, and, of course, the printed page is not machine-readable. Thus, the tape or disk copy of the disk file has a distinct advantage over either card decks or printed output.

239

Data Manipulation

Once the data has been validated by earlier portions of the processing, it is used to generate useful information. As in other phases of the accounting information system, several types of controls may be used to guard against improper data handling. Inasmuch as some types of errors are likely to be accidental, whereas others are fraudulent and therefore intentional, we have chosen to discuss the controls pertinent to data manipulation under the headings of "accidental error" and "intentional error."

Accidental error. One of the most obvious protections against accidental processing error is to ensure the proper functioning of the central processing unit. This is clearly a hardware consideration, and is normally performed through the careful testing and maintenance of the CPU machinery. Usually, testing is performed on a periodic, scheduled basis—for example, once a week—and is accomplished with special, hardware-checking, machine-language programs. At busy computer centers, such testing takes time —time that might otherwise be used for processing files, testing programs, and so forth. Thus, testing and maintenance are not without cost to the user company, even if they are provided free of charge by the hardware manufacturer with the lease or purchase of the equipment. Usually, however, this work must be done.

Several data-manipulation controls are available to ensure processing accuracy in between hardware servicings. One is *dual computation,* in which the arithmetic-logic unit of the central processing unit is required to perform the same calculation twice, using different registers each time. The results are then compared to see if the answer is the same in each case. Another control is *CPU parity-testing,* in which the parity bit of each data value is checked whenever a data movement is initiated within the memory of the central processing unit. A third processing control tests for *overflow* (which happens when you attempt to store too large a number in CPU memory) and *underflow* (which happens when you attempt to store too small a number in CPU

memory). A fourth control involves the specialized use of "read-only memory," or ROM, in which portions of the CPU's internal storage are set aside for instructions or special data values related to program processing (e.g., the maintenance of record counts or hash totals), and which cannot be erased by the application programs in the CPU. A fifth control often used in multiprogramming (i.e., in time-sharing computer systems when more than one computer program uses the CPU at the same time) divides the memory portion of the central processing unit into user *workspaces*. The control involves the limitation of each user to his or her designated workspace, and, in some circumstances, making sure that one user cannot copy the data of another into the original user's work area.

Although most of the above hardware controls are performed automatically, many of them can be exploited to advantage by the computer programmer. In particular, it is possible for the programmer to code special processing routines which enable a computer program to recover from such "emergencies" as overflow or parity checks without halting data processing. Sometimes, for example, it may be possible for a particular calculation to be ignored without losing the overall effectiveness of the processing program. At other times, it may be more desirable for the program to output an error message than to "abort" the entire program because of one technical error. Thus, through programmed error routines, the user can maintain control of the data processing when processing irregularities arise. Since it is usually inconvenient, and sometimes even very costly, to rerun an entire file-processing program, error routines have the potential to be very effective as a processing control.

Another, somewhat obvious, processing control is to make sure that the processing program is complete and thorough in its data manipulation. Ordinarily, this is accomplished by logically examining the program flowchart, by translating the program into machine language with an error-testing computer to make sure there are no grammatical errors, and by testing the completed program with specially-designed test data that expose the program to all exception conditions likely to occur during actual program use. Because most computer programs go through many minor modifications after they have been used for a time at the computer center, it is also wise to perform periodic data-testing in order to assure continuing processing accuracy. This latter precaution is often overlooked. One data analyst stated, "Over the course of the last few years, we've made so many alterations to our programs that we're no longer sure of what we have in them. We can't keep up with the program change requests, much less the documentation changes. Any resemblance these programs have to the original flowcharts is purely coincidental." Here is a situation in which another "round" of tests using test data would be highly desirable.

A failure to observe such a simple control as coordinated data-testing has the potential for financial disaster. In September of 1975, for example, Social Security headquarters estimated that overpayments totaling $400 million had been made under its Supplemental Security Income Plan since the program had become operational on January 1, 1974. A study of the problem revealed that a large number of programmers and systems analysts from different bureaus within the Social Security Administration had been working without a common plan and each department had been designing its own changes into the system. In addition to the overpayments, a backlog of "lost" cases developed when the system became overloaded. Chaos developed. The confusion was sufficient to permit a number of employees to write fraudulent checks to themselves in large amounts. To top it all, the attempt to recover the overpayments proved so expensive that the entire amount was written off as a loss!

Once processing controls become operative in the accounting information system, they serve as the principal means of security against machine failures, calculation errors, and other such irregularities that might occur during normal processing activity. Occasionally, these controls are insufficient to avoid a processing error attributable to an unforeseen combination of data values, and sometimes, alterations to one computer program of the accounting information system may cause processing errors in another program.

Intentional error. A more serious difficulty occurs when employees take advantage of the existing accounting information system for personal gain. Here, there is intentional processing irregularity, a certainty of company loss, and a persistent avoidance of whatever processing controls have been constructed to detect these irregularities. Inasmuch as these latter processing errors are systematic, costs to the company are usually high.

Although it is difficult to guard against computer fraud, several courses of action are possible. One preventive control is to make sure that no individual programmer or systems analyst is responsible for the development of a complete processing segment of the accounting information system at the time the system is first designed. When individuals do not have complete control over the design of processing routines, they are less capable of building unwarranted subroutines into the computer coding. Furthermore, they must work harder to keep any of their own self-created processing routines from being discovered by others. Thus, if the computerized software package of an accounting information system is developed internally by the user's own EDP personnel, separation of duties during the development and testing of the computer program helps assure processing security. Similarly, when design changes are incorporated into the system at a later stage of the system's life cycle, close scrutiny of these modifications, and perhaps retesting the entire system with a heavy dose of "live" (i.e., real) data is essential.

An alternative to developing software internally is to contract out some, if not all, of the important processing portions of the accounting information system. This approach shifts accountability from the shoulders of the company's internal EDP staff and onto the shoulders of the contractor. Because there is usually less incentive for an "arms-length" contractor to create fraudulent processing programs, a company may anticipate a high likelihood of "honest work." If it so desires, the purchasing company can insist

241

that the contractor company be bonded so that there is provision for recovery of damages in the event of problems. (Of course, it is also possible for a company to bond its own EDP employees.)

In addition to planned testing, the data-processing organization can implement at least two controls to guard against the possibility of unapproved changes being ''sneaked'' into the processing routines after the processing system is in operation. One is the now-familiar *separation-of-duties* control in which the program planning, design, and modification tasks on the one hand, and the daily operation functions of the EDP subsystem on the other hand, are performed by different individuals. Thus, programmers and systems analysts form one segment of the data-processing personnel, whereas machine operators, keypunchers, EDP clerks, and the like form another segment.

Regarding the separation-of-duties control, the American Institute of Certified Public Accountants uses the term *incompatible functions* when referring to separation-of-duties weaknesses in a computerized accounting information system. For example, *Statement on Auditing Standards No. 3* suggests:

. . . incompatible functions for accounting control purposes are those that place any person in a position both to perpetrate and to conceal errors or irregularities in the normal course of his duties. Many EDP systems not only process accounting data but also include procedures for detecting errors and irregularities and for providing specific authorization for certain kinds of transactions. Since the procedures may be combined, incompatible functions may be more likely to be combined in an EDP activity than in a manual activity.*

Furthermore, *Statement on Auditing Standards No. 3* describes some irregularities that may occur in a company's electronic data-processing subsystem if incompatible functions are performed by individuals.

Frequently, functions that would be considered incompatible if performed by a single individual in a manual activity are performed through the use of an EDP pro-

gram or series of programs. A person having the opportunity to make unapproved changes to any such programs performs incompatible functions in relation to the EDP activity. For example, a program for an accounts-payable application may have been designed to process for payment a vendor's invoice only if accompanied by a purchase-order record agreeing with the invoice as to prices and quantities and a receiving record indicating receipt of the goods or services. In the absence of adequate control over program changes, an unapproved revision might change the application so that unsubstantiated payments could be made to vendors.

EDP data files frequently are basic records of an accounting system. They cannot be read or changed without the use of EDP, but they can be changed through the use of EDP without visible evidence that a change has occurred. A person in a position to make unapproved changes in EDP data files performs incompatible functions. In the example above of the accounts-payable application, an individual who could make unapproved changes in the files containing purchase orders and receiving reports might be able to add spurious records purporting to represent purchase orders and receiving reports to the files, thereby causing the program to process for payment unapproved vendor invoices.†

A second control associated with intentional processing errors is the *surprise audit*. As its name implies, the surprise audit is planned without the knowledge of the target work group and is used effectively by both internal and external auditors. We shall look at the surprise audit more closely in Chapter 10. It might be mentioned here, however, that the surprise audit is not necessarily executed solely for the purpose of detecting crime. Such an audit also permits the examiners to observe: (1) adherence to specific corporate operating policies and procedures, (2) employee attendance, (3) the accounting information system operating with real data and/or real accounts, and (4) the strengths and weaknesses of an accounting information system as the system is presently being implemented in a real-life setting. In fact, these latter considerations are almost always much more important goals to surprise audits than the intent to identify fraudulent activity. The fact that a surprise audit can be expected by

---

*Auditing Standards Executive Committee, American Institute of Certified Public Accountants, *Statement on Auditing Standards No. 3* (New York: American Institute of Certified Public Accountants, © 1974), pp. 4 and 5.

†Ibid., p. 5.

personnel within a work group, however, may also serve as a deterrent to dishonesty. In this sense, the surprise audit may be considered both a preventive control and a feedback control.

OUTPUT CONTROLS

Once the data has been processed internally by the CPU, it is usually transferred to some form of output medium for storage or, in the case of printed output, prepared as a report for distribution and managerial use. Output controls involve this aspect of the data-processing function. The two output controls we shall examine here are: (1) tape and disk output controls, and (2) printed output controls.

Tape and Disk Output Controls

Since computer output to tapes and disks is not normally verified by direct human observation as is the case with manually printed output, special care must be taken to ensure accuracy in the encoding of information on these output media. As suggested here and also in Chapter 18, hardware controls such as parity-bit checking, and software controls such as check digits, can be carried along with the informational output during output transmission to make sure that no digits are lost in the communication process. Because we have discussed these controls earlier, there is no need to discuss them again here.

One interesting feature of output controls for disk drives and tape drives that does not have an input counterpart is the presence of a built-in *dual recording mode* to enable these machines to check on recording accuracy. It works as follows. First, the tape or disk is encoded with the desired information, such as an accounts receivable record or a bank savings account record. Next, this information is read again using the reading mechanism of the tape or disk drive. Finally, a comparison is made to verify the original output. In most instances, the comparison of the initial output data with the newly recorded data will result in a confirmation of identical information, and the tape or disk system is then able to signal the CPU that the required writing opera-

tion has been successful. This is called an *echo check*. An unfavorable comparison implies that a hardware failure has occurred. In such instances, either a second write attempt can be initiated, or the computer operator notified for alternative action.

When tape and disk files are involved in the output function, file-label processing assumes an important role in output control. Among other things, this file-label processing requires the updating of information in the trailer-record to reflect the new status of the file. Thus, for example, the number of logical and physical records residing in an updated file must be recorded in the trailer record since this information will be used as a processing control when the file is later used for input. Similarly, the file expiration date should be carefully checked by the computer program and updated, if necessary, to indicate a longer retention cycle if one is deemed necessary.

The recording of output control totals other than the aforementioned record counts also serves a useful purpose in data processing. Examples would include the recording of dollar balances in an accounts payable file, the recording of hash totals for an inventory-parts file, and the recording of item summaries in a transactions file of credit-customer activity.

Printed Output Controls

Because the machine-printed document is the primary means by which the computer communicates with its users, it is important that the information contained on the printed output form be accurate. Like the computer, however, the printer is robot-like in activity and prints only what it is told to print, as indicated by the central processing unit. Since hardware controls such as parity checks detect transmission inaccuracies, the engineering aspects of print control are straightforward. Thus, any mistakes on the output page are almost assuredly attributable either to errors in the raw input data or processing errors that result in the misdirection of what output is to appear on the printed page. This problem is therefore a matter of input control or programming logic rather than one of output control or transmission failures.

One of the more compelling aspects of output control deals with the matter of forms control. Perhaps the most interesting situations involve computerized check-writing applications, in which punched cards or perforated printer forms become the encoding media for the preparation of company checks. Usually, these punched cards or printer forms are preprinted with the company's name, address, bank account number, and sometimes even the authorized signature of the company treasurer. (For obvious reasons, it is preferable that the authorized signature be put on later.) Thus, unless careful control is exercised over the disposition of these forms, such output documents have the potential to become ''found money'' to unscrupulous employees.

The most common type of control utilized with computer-generated check-writing procedures is the coordination of a preprinted check number on the printer form with a computer-generated number which is inked on the same form at run time. The preprinted numbers advance consecutively and are prepared by the form's supplier according to the specifications of the data-processing manager. The computer-generated numbers also run sequentially, and are initialized by adding 1 to the check sequence number stored from the last processing run. Both of these numbers should match during normal processing. Discrepancies should be examined carefully and the causes fully resolved.

Cash-disbursement checks are not the only type of printer form utilizing preprinted numbering as a control mechanism. Obviously, almost any type of perforated printer form that can be ''burst'' (i.e., separated) into pages has the potential to be prenumbered and therefore controlled. In fact, even common computer paper (the kind measuring 11 by 16 inches) is usually prenumbered as a matter of convenience to users. Other types of forms that enjoy a special control advantage when prenumbered would include (1) reports containing sensitive corporate information, (2) computer-generated lottery tickets, athletic event tickets, or cultural event tickets, and (3) utility and telephone bills. For example, by recording the numbers of the athletic events tickets assigned to district sales outlets, the central box office's accountant can make a complete analysis of which tickets were sold and which were returned.

Another dimension of output control concerns the distribution of reports. Computer reports often contain sensitive information and it is important that such information be restricted. Thus, for example, the payroll register indicating *who* was paid during a given pay period, and how much they were paid, would be the type of report whose distribution should be restricted.

Commonly, the potential users of a given report are classified into three categories: (1) individuals who *need to know* the information in order to perform their jobs efficiently, (2) individuals who would *like to know* the information but whose jobs are not dependent on it, and (3) individuals who, at least from an organizational standpoint, have *no interest* in the report. In general, an accounting report must always be given to the first category of users, and should never be given to the third category of users. The only difficulty is ''what to do about the second group''?

Because the generation of extra copies of a computer report is a relatively simple task, there was a tendency in the past to provide reports to ''interested parties,'' that is, to the second category of users. This resulted in a proliferation of paper in the office. Recent studies have indicated that a great deal of the reports are, in fact, never used by their recipients. Thus, a modern trend has been to limit reports to only ''need-to-know'' users, but to provide brief summary reports on a monthly basis to others concerned with, but not vitally dependent upon, the information found in accounting reports.

There is an interesting story along these lines about a company that prepared a certain report for over 100 operating departments within its organization. When a management consulting team asked ''who likes to get this report?'', almost all the departments answered affirmatively. When each department was asked individually whether it *needed* the report for its own functioning, however, not one department responded positively. As it turned out, each department thought that others needed it, and many department heads candidly admitted later that they had asked for the report because they were afraid it would be discontinued. The report was in fact discontinued, and no one missed it!

The most common form of distributional control is through an *authorization list*. Thus, for each output report, the computer facility keeps a list of authorized users and prepares just enough copies of the report to satisfy the number of users on this list. Where data-processing activities are centralized, it is sometimes possible to have representatives from each user group physically visit the computer center to pick up their copy of a sensitive report. In these instances, a notebook or other log of pickups can be maintained, and the pick-up employee asked to sign the book and provide an employee identification number for security purposes at the time the report is taken. Where this is not possible, bonded employees can be authorized to deliver reports to users, and random checks on the distribution of these reports can be made by their supervisors to verify distributional security.

AN EXAMPLE OF CONTROLS:
THE ALAN COMPANY PAYROLL

Chapter 7 has emphasized manual controls for the accounting information system, whereas this chapter has stressed automated controls for accounting information systems. This distinction between manual and automated controls was made largely for organizational convenience, and was not meant to suggest that a company should use only one type or another. Rather, both manual and automated controls should be implemented wherever the benefits of either type are expected to outweigh their costs.

One common accounting application in which both manual and automated controls are integrated in a single processing system is in the preparation of a company's payroll. Therefore, to illustrate the implementation of the many different types of controls into one operational system, we have chosen to illustrate an example of a computerized payroll for the Alan Company. This particular accounting application is discussed in Chapter 18. The system flowchart for the data processing (Figure 18-15) is illustrated again as Figure 8-5, and is described briefly below.

At a certain production facility of the Alan Company, employees are paid weekly. Overall responsibility for the payroll has been given to the director of personnel, whose office is in charge of maintaining the payroll file information for the production facility. The payroll file itself is a master file stored on magnetic disk. Each record contains basic information about one employee, and includes employee name, address, social security number, department code, deduction codes, pay rate, and so forth. Changes to this file are initiated by employees in the personnel department, using remote terminals located within the personnel office.

At the end of each week, employee time cards are collected. The information on the time card includes employee name, social security number, department code, number of regular hours worked, and number of overtime hours worked. The time cards are batched by production department and then forwarded to the EDP center for input to the payroll processing routines. The output from these routines includes: (1) payroll checks, (2) a summary report of payroll checks, listed by check number, (3) a summary report of payroll checks, listed by department, and (4) an updated master file (containing new year-to-date information).

One of the chief concerns in the processing of the payroll is the accuracy of the payroll master file. Special preprinted job-application forms are used by the production facility to assure completeness in the information used to create employee records, for example. When an individual applies for a job, this application form is filled out first, and is left with the subsystem manager conducting the job interview. Both the signature of the subsystem manager and the signature of the director of personnel are required on the form before a payroll master file record can be made for a new hire. This controls the potential creation of a fictitious employee on the master file.

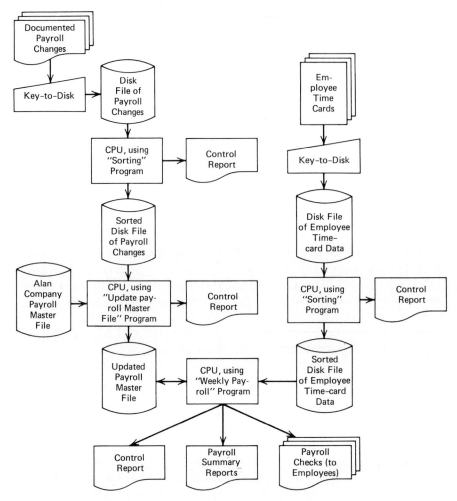

Figure 8-5. System flowchart for computerized processing of the Alan Company payroll.

Similarly, when changes to the master file involve pay rate increases or changes in certain categories of deductions, the signatures of both a personnel department employee and the director of personnel are required.

To control the payroll processing still further, the personnel director will maintain a manual control total of the number of company employees eligible to receive paychecks, and the total dollar amount of approved pay raises. Each time the company payroll is prepared, the computer will print out these control totals on a separate line of the summary reports. The personnel director can then compare the control-total figures maintained in the personnel office with those on the output report. Any discrepancies should be investigated immediately by the director. Thus, if the personnel director's control total of employees eligible to receive paychecks was 2504, and the computer printout indicated that 2505 paychecks were actually processed, it would appear that one paycheck too many had been prepared!

The managers of each operating department within the Alan Company facility also play an important role in payroll control. To guard against unauthorized overtime work, for example, the company requires the personal signature of the managers on all time cards indicating overtime hours. Also, when employees in a specific department turn in their time cards, the total hours of regular work and the total hours of all overtime work are computed. These figures are double checked for accuracy and then handwritten on a special slip of paper which is affixed to the set of time cards sent to the computer center for data processing.

At the computer center, the time-card data is keyed into the computer for eventual processing and the control slips are forwarded to the personnel office. Using these slips, the personnel director prepares a master list of control totals for each department at the production facility. When the computer processes the time-card data, these figures will be recomputed and printed on the output report listing employee payroll checks by department. The personnel director is given a copy of this report as soon as it is prepared, and can then compare the control totals of the report with the control totals manually prepared by each of the work departments. Discrepancies attributable, for example, to unauthorized overtime hours can then be investigated on an exceptions basis.

For good internal control, it should be obvious that the Alan Company employees responsible for accumulating and processing the payroll data should not be involved in distributing employee paychecks. Depending upon company preference, the company employees delegated this responsibility should be from the accounting subsystem, the internal audit staff, or perhaps some other organizational area. If these individuals are in charge of payroll distribution and physically maintain possession of all paychecks until they are handed to *individual employees*, it is very difficult for any other employee of the company to cash an unauthorized paycheck. Those employees that should be excluded from the payroll distribution or "output" function, therefore, would include the subsystem managers who accumulate the hours worked by their employees and the EDP personnel, such as programmers

and machine operators, involved in processing the payroll data.

A common deception practiced by dishonest managers working with uncontrolled payroll systems is to submit earnings data for a fictitious employee ostensibly working in that manager's department. Thus, when an extra paycheck is subsequently processed for this employee and returned in a batch of paychecks to the manager for the *manager* to distribute, the paycheck could simply be pocketed and later cashed. With the payroll system described above, such a deception would not be possible. As long as paychecks were distributed to *individuals* instead of simply left on the manager's desk, it would be difficult for a fictitious employee to be paid a paycheck. Further, as long as the payroll master file was accurate, it would be impossible to process a paycheck for an "extra" employee. This is because there would be no record for the employee and therefore no authorization for payment. Thus, with good computer controls, the no-master-record-found condition, which would result for the fictitious employee when the payroll program was run, would be indicated on a separate page of each of the output reports from the payroll processing run. Such a condition would then trigger an investigation. (However, since other circumstances might conceivably cause a no-master-record-found condition—e.g., a data-entry mistake of the social security number by which the payroll master file is organized—such a condition is not necessarily evidence of malfeasance.)

Another effective payroll control for those companies having a large number of employees is to maintain a separate checking account for payroll disbursements. If paychecks were issued from the Alan Company's general checking account (i.e., the account used to pay such items as credit purchases of equipment and supplies), any errors or irregularities in the payroll area would be more difficult to resolve. This is because payroll disbursements become mixed in with other disbursements, making it more difficult to focus on the company's payroll-payment function. Thus, the Alan Company uses an *imprest payroll system,* in which dollars required for the payroll are transferred to a separate payroll account on a cash-needed basis. For the present example, therefore, the cash required for the payroll would be transferred to the payroll checking account shortly before the Alan Company's production employees are due to receive their paychecks. Clearly, such a system limits the amount of cash involved at any one time within the payroll function, and thereby reduces the opportunity for anyone to embezzle funds from the payroll checking account. In addition, it might be added, the imprest system frees up monetary funds which might otherwise stand idle and unproductive if left in the payroll account from month to month.

Another aspect of the Alan Company payroll system involves the control of the payroll output reports. To make sure that each report is complete, the pages of each report would be prenumbered sequentially and also computer-numbered as part of the report processing. Copies of each payroll report would be maintained at the computer center until each authorized user visited the center to receive his or her copy. At the time a report is taken, the user would sign a report-distribution log book maintained by the computer center. In this log, the name of the report, the preprinted page numbers of the report, the name of the employee picking up the report, and the employee's identification number would be recorded. Should problems arise at a later point of time regarding the distribution, and/or whereabouts of a given copy of a report, this log can serve a useful purpose.

A final consideration involving the Alan Company payroll processing is control over the physical check forms themselves. These forms are kept in a locked storage room of the computer facility, and a special forms log is maintained by the EDP manager. When a computer operator is about to run the payroll programs, the numbers preprinted on the check forms are recorded in this log by the manager. The total number of forms used is then compared with the personnel director's control total of eligible payroll employees to verify the proper number. Should forms be destroyed during the actual course of data processing, a careful accounting of these forms is made, and the EDP manager's verification signature on a special EDP form is filed for accounting purposes.

As checks are processed, the computer prints a number on each check. Thus, a further forms control is the fact that preprinted check numbers and computer-printed check numbers should coincide. Preprinted check numbers and computer-generated check numbers which do not match would therefore be cause for investigation.

Once the checks are prepared, they are forwarded to the facility's treasurer's office for signature. Here, the checks can be further scrutinized for accuracy and completeness. Again for accountability, the check-number sequence is recorded at this point so that the numbers can be compared with the control information of the EDP manager's forms log. Finally, with the payroll checks duly signed and completed, they may be distributed to the Alan Company employees.

COMPUTER FACILITY CONTROLS

In 1969, a group of antiwar demonstrators vandalized the research center of a well-known munitions company, causing $100,000 in damages to computer equipment and data files. That year, there were numerous bombings in computer centers in the United States, and California alone averaged four per week.*

Like any other investment in capital resources, the physical assets of the computer center—the CPU, the peripheral devices, the tape and disk files of the computer library, and so forth—represent a large dollar investment which is deserving of protection. Destruction of, or damage to, these assets represents both a real danger and an important area of computer-systems control. Physical loss can happen in only one of two ways: through accident or through intent. The present-day reality is that very little effort is needed to protect the EDP subsystem's assets from accidents. Modern computers are quite rugged pieces of equipment

*Paula Selkow, "Great Computer Rip-Offs," *Capitalist Reporter,* 1972, pp. 49–52.

and can survive a surprising amount of punishment. Thus, most of the current effort in the area of physical security is devoted to controls that prevent intentional destruction. Therefore, we shall focus our discussion in this section on controls that guard against willful physical damage.

Locate the Computer Center in a Safe Place

In 1968, a disgruntled taxpayer decided to teach the Internal Revenue Service a lesson. First, the taxpayer walked to the outside of the IRS building where his tax forms had been processed. The unhappy man then proceeded to shoot at the agency's central processing unit through an open window with his 12-gauge shotgun! Although some might argue that the major lesson to be learned from this story is that taxes are too high, there is also the suggestion that the computer center of the typical organization should not be placed in locations that have easy public access. Thus, for most business data processors, the ground-floor showroom—once the desired location for many computer operations (see Chapter 17)—has given way to basements, separate buildings, and other sites away from passageways which are easily accessible to the public. Locations guarded by armed personnel are obviously the most preferred, but any placement which has a limited number of secured entrances and good fire protection is desirable.

Limit Employee Access

Very few people have reason to be *inside* the computer machine room. Once the computer software has been fully developed, implementation can proceed smoothly through the computer operator's use of the software run manuals. Therefore, executives, keypunch operators, and even company programmers have very little reason to enter the computer facility.

To discourage potential mischief makers, several facility safeguards are possible. One is to require all company personnel in the vicinity to wear color-coded identification badges with full-face pictures. Only people authorized to enter the machine room would be assigned an

identification badge of a particular color. A second precaution is to place a guard (sometimes even a secretary will do) at the entrance to the machine room; the door to the room is self-locking and can be "buzzed" open only by the control person, who would permit only authorized personnel to enter. Finally, there is the strict control of access to the center through the issuance of keys, dial-lock combinations, or other door-controls which would be accessible only to authorized employees. With regard to this last safeguard, it is also a good idea to change locks or lock combinations often and to use keys that cannot easily be duplicated.

Having listed all these safeguards, it must now be stated that the record of intentional vandalism as documented in the next chapter indicates that the overwhelming majority of vandalism has been performed by embittered former employees, corporate executives, and other vindictive personnel working for the company. These employees are likely to have a thorough understanding of the computer center's security systems and thus are likely to know how to get around them. If there is any lesson to be learned from the historical record, however, it is that an unhappy employee, or former employee, who has (or had) access to the computer center is a potential walking time bomb. Thus, there is special reason to make sure that there are no personnel problems in this area of corporate operations.

Outline Fall-Back Procedures

Several years ago, an angry employee programmed his company's computer to erase a few tape records from an accounts receivable file every time the accounts receivable program was run. It was not until several runs later that the mischief was discovered and the company found itself in a real bind. It contacted customers to request the information that would enable it to reconstruct records, and in desperation, even took out full-page advertisements in newspapers begging customers to come forward with their billing information. Few did, and the company eventually went bankrupt.

A horror story such as this points out that the preparation and maintenance of back-up copies of important tape and disk files is imperative if a firm is to recover from such disasters. Normally, the important tape reels and disk packs containing current information about the firm's activities are maintained by an EDP librarian in a secured file library. Access to such files is usually limited to authorized personnel. It is also clear, however, that such a control is insufficient to guard against the type of problem described above.

We have already discussed the grandfather-father-son control feature used to safeguard computer files. No matter how back-up copies of the files are obtained, it is conventional practice to store the grandfather and father files in areas away from the current, or son, file. This avoids the possibility of losing both the current file and both back-up copies should physical disaster strike a common storage location. Some companies rent bank vaults for this purpose, whereas others use their own fireproof safes. One small company we know stored back-up copies of its most current files in the garage of its EDP manager (which is fine provided you can trust the EDP manager!).

In addition to physical problems with its processing files, a company can also experience operational difficulty with its central processor. Just as with any other piece of hardware that is in constant use, there is a normal amount of wear and tear on the machine. Occasionally, something happens and the CPU "goes down." At such times, it is obvious that a fall-back plan for emergency processing is required. What is needed is processing time on another computer.

Not just any computer will do, however. Most computer programs are geared to the operating system and processing characteristics of the specific company's installation and thus, another computer configuration exactly like the inoperative one is required. Several possibilities exist. One alternative is to arrange for the rental of computer time from a service bureau organization or a time-sharing organization. (Both of these types of organizations are discussed in later chapters.) A second approach would be to reach a reciprocal agreement with another nearby

company which has the same computer model. Common to both of the above-mentioned possibilities is the forward planning necessary to reach such agreements, and the forethought for contingencies.

Buy Insurance

Although the purchase of insurance is the first activity that occurs to many persons when computer safeguards are discussed, it is actually the protection of last resort. The reason is that insurance does not actually protect the purchaser from loss—it merely compensates for such losses when they occur. Thus, it is not a preventive control but serves only "after the fact."

Insurance policies for computer damages are limited in coverage and often will not reimburse policy holders for such occurrences as civil disorder, earthquakes, "acts of God," or employee larceny. Furthermore, compensation usually is restricted to the actual damages suffered by the firm. As you may imagine, a "fair" estimate of what these losses entail is not an easy matter. Of special difficulty is placing dollar values for second- or third-generation computer equipment which has long since lost any real market value, yet performs vital data-processing services for the computer center. Partially-damaged equipment is yet another problem. The list goes on and on, but you get the idea: there is little advantage to relying solely upon insurance for the protection of the computer facility.

SUMMARY

This chapter has focused upon controls for computerized versions of the accounting information system. It was noted that controls for automated accounting systems were important for a number of reasons, including (1) the fact that computerized systems tend to involve large volumes of data which are more efficiently processed, and therefore controlled, by automated (as opposed to manual) methods, (2) the fact that much of the processing involves data media which are not in human-readable form and hence must be controlled through mechanized methods, (3) the fact that the audit trail has become more difficult to follow (especially in online computerized systems) and therefore must be traced with automated methodology, and (4) the fact that computer crime has become an important consideration which requires that computerized systems have stringent supervision and sophisticated controls for adequate protection and detection. It was noted, however, that computer controls are not necessarily oriented toward catching, or frustrating, computer crooks. Any number of "honest" mistakes in data observation, collection, transcription, processing, or output can occur. Computerized controls are as much involved in catching these types of errors as they are in catching criminals.

For purposes of organization, we divided our discussion of computer controls into three main categories: input controls, processing controls, and output controls. Input controls are concerned primarily with the observation, recording, and preparation of "good" data. Among the many controls available for the observation and recording phases are objectivity, supervision, feedback, and the use of preprinted forms. Where punched cards are involved, an important control for data accuracy and completeness is the use of the card verifier, although prepunched cards and the use of a drum-control card (to prepunch "fixed" data or skip field-punching in many successive cards) are also possible.

Restricting logical access to the computer is also an important input control. Secret passcodes have been the primary control devices in this regard, although the historical record would suggest that these methods have met with limited success. Personal identification methods, using thumbprints, handprints, voice input, and handwriting analysis are being investigated. Good employee relations and strict control over who is given passcodes continue to be important deterrents to unauthorized computer access.

Processing controls begin once the data reach the computer center itself. The maintenance of batch controls, hash totals, and record counts are common data-acquisition controls, as is the use of editing checks, which test for accuracy and completeness in the individual data fields of the input media. Included among editing checks would be (1) tests of alphabetic, numeric, or alphanumeric field content, (2) test for valid codes, (3) tests of reasonableness of the data magnitudes, (4) tests for algebraic sign (for numeric fields), and (5) tests of completeness (e.g., to guard against unwarranted blank fields). Also in common use is the calculation of check digits, which adds a computed digit to an account number, customer number, or part number, and guards against transposed numbers, misaligned numbers, and just plain wrong numbers in data identification.

Where data manipulation is concerned, the CPU hardware must be checked periodically to assure computational accuracy. Since the computerized accounting information system relies upon the computer program to perform the actual data processing, close attention must also be focused upon the program's accuracy, completeness, and propriety. Supervision of program development and implementation as well as separation of EDP duties during program development, operation, and continual testing are highly recommended. The surprise audit has also proved a useful accounting control, especially where the time element is of prime importance to the company embezzler.

Output controls were discussed within the context of the output medium used. Tape and disk controls are concerned primarily with assuring the accuracy of the encoding process and the maintenance of current information about the file in the file's header and trailer labels. Print controls are of particular concern when bank checks or sensitive output documents are being prepared. Sequence tests of check numbers and the strict regulation of preprinted forms are the principal controls in the output area, although it should be remembered that output is at the tail-end of the processing sequence, and nothing can be done to improve the output if poor data were used to generate it.

Maintaining the physical security of the computer center is vital to the operation of the accounting information system, and controls to assure this security are imperative. Among these controls are: (1) strategic placement of the center equipment, (2) limited employee access, (3) preparation of fall-back procedures (especially the maintenance of back-up files), and (4) purchase of insurance. It was noted that in the past several companies had not implemented such controls adequately, and the results were disastrous.

A special section of the chapter illustrated a number of the aforementioned controls, plus a few new ones, which might be used when preparing a company payroll. Two important characteristics of the payroll system described were: (1) both manual and computerized controls were involved in, and interacted with, the system and (2) not every control mentioned in Chapters 7 and 8 was included. This last point reminds us that not every accounting application is likely to use every control we have discussed. In some cases, a specific control is just not worth its cost (i.e., the control's expected cost exceeds its expected benefits), thereby making it more sensible to do without the control.

DISCUSSION QUESTIONS

8-1. Why are controls for the automated accounting information system sometimes considered even more important than controls for the manual accounting information system?

8-2. What controls might have prevented the three problems discussed in the introductory section of this chapter?

8-3. Within the chapter, it was stated that not all the controls discussed would be advantageous for a particular accounting information system. The general rule is that a specific control should be used only if its benefits exceed its costs. Discuss in greater detail what kinds of benefits these would be.

8-4. "Supervision doesn't always guarantee a control; sometimes it just guarantees a conspirator." Discuss.

8-5. Enumerate the advantages of preprinted source documents, and indicate why each advantage is useful as a control for an accounting information system. Can you think of any disadvantages? Discuss.

8-6. For years, color-coded forms have served as one of the most effective means of differentiating data documents in information systems. To what extent has this control been exploited in automated accounting information systems?

8-7. Jean & Joan Cosmetics has a complete line of beauty products for women and maintains a computerized inventory system. Inventory items are identified by an eight-digit product number, of which the first four digits classify the beauty product by major category (hair, face, skin, eyes, etc.) and the last four digits identify the product itself. Enumerate as many controls as you can which the company might use to assure accuracy in this eight-digit number when updating its inventory-balance file.

8-8. The sales manager of an insurance office called a sales-personnel meeting to discuss the problems he had been having with his sales people filling out the insurance forms. "Ladies and gentlemen," he explained, "you all know how hard our Ms. Wiskovski works around here, and she is too busy with her other chores to correct your mistakes on our intake forms. So from now on, I will dock each person $5 for every mistake we catch on the form." Comment.

8-9. Discuss the method(s) by which greater accuracy can be obtained in keypunched cards. What problems can you foresee in these so-called controls?

8-10. Yolanda and Melba were keypunch operators at Smith and Horngren's Cardboard Box Company. One day, Yolanda said to Melba: "Our boss—that Mr. Hardgrove—is some turkey. But today I'll fix him. I've got a hat pin in my purse and I'm going to use it to stick a hole into every other card I punch! The guys down at the computer center will go crazy trying to figure out why the card reader keeps jamming!" What controls would you suggest for this situation?

8-11. "The security of an accounting information system is only as good as the honesty of the people that run it." Comment.

8-12. What is the difference between logical access to the computer and physical access to the computer? Why is the security of both important?

8-13. Why has it been said that in some circumstances, the implementation of a computerized accounting information system has actually helped, rather than hindered, the would-be company embezzler?

8-14. Discuss the role of a "separation of duties" as a control of the automated accounting information system.

8-15. Discuss the role of the control total in accounting information systems. Why are control totals insufficient to guard against data inaccuracies?

8-16. Donna MacAdam was a computer operator working for the Third National Bank of Fat City. At one point she complained to her friend that she hated her job. "It's a dead-end situation," she said. "Half of the time I'm working night shifts and all the time I just push buttons. I know I'm supposed to type 'YC6' everytime I get an 'ENTER' instruction on the console, but I don't know why I do it. I think I'll quit and become an accountant!" Comment.

8-17. Explain the functions of the unscheduled audit. Why is the element of surprise important?

8-18. "Because a human cannot read what is written on a tape or disk, there is no way to be sure that what is being written is correct." Do you agree? Why or why not?

8-19. Automated data-collection techniques enable the accounting information system to avoid the problems of data transcription and therefore to increase the accuracy of the input. Name several methods of automated data collection and identify the ways in which each contributes to the goals of data accuracy and completeness.

8-20. Why is the area of forms control given so much attention in computer output? After all, what does a company really have to lose if a blank sheet of output or two is missing?

8-21. Discuss the methods of safeguarding the physical assets of the computer center. What extra costs would you anticipate when these controls are used?

8-22. Explain the concept of the grandfather-father-son method of file control. Whom would *you* trust with the grandfather file?

8-23. A computer programmer had a grudge against his company. To get even, he coded a special routine in the mortgage loan program which erased a small, random number of accounts on the tape file every time the program was run. The company did not detect the routine until almost all of its records had been erased. Discuss what controls might have protected this company from its own programmer.

8-24. An accountant working for a medium-sized distributor set up several dummy companies and began directing the computer to write checks to them for fictitious merchandise. He was apprehended only when several of the company executives began to wonder how he could afford a vacation in Acapulco every year. What might have prevented this?

8-25. The "million-dollar" club of computer criminals is an elite list reserved for those embezzlers who have stolen over $1 million from their company with the aid of the company computer. Among them are:

(a) Roswell Stephens, chief teller at the Union Dime Savings Bank in New York. Roswell exploited the bank's file of inactive accounts and made off with $1.5 million. He was apprehended only when police raided his bookmaker and discovered a few of his $30,000 bets.

(b) A Salinas, California, accountant who stole over $1 million from his company by recording excessive costs for material acquisitions and directing the company's computer to pay the difference to his own dummy corporations. He had even programmed the computer to estimate how much he could safely embezzle at any one time without being caught. He was finally apprehended when he got greedy and withdrew more than his own program advised him was safe.

(c) Jerry Neal Schneider, a precocious high school student who began reading the discarded manuals of a Los Angeles telephone company. At 17, he figured out a way to dial into the company's computer directly with his home phone and began directing the computer to ship inventory parts to his own company. He was finally caught when he refused to give his partner a raise and the partner went to the police.

(d) The executives of Equity Funding Corp. of America, who made up magnetic tape records of fictitious insurance policies and sold these to reinsurers as bonafide accounts. A disgruntled employee tipped the hand of the participants in March of 1973.

Many of these cases are discussed in greater detail in Chapter 9 on Computer Crime. For now, however, suggest as many controls as you can which might have prevented these frauds.

8-26. The controls for the Alan Company's payroll example given in the latter part of the chapter outlined a set of procedures by which to assure accuracy and completeness in the data-gathering, data-processing, and check-distribution functions of this application. It is possible that several additional controls besides those mentioned in the payroll discussion might have occurred to you for possible implementation within this application. Suggest several such controls that would assist the accountant in this application.

PROBLEMS

8-27. Compute check digits for the following account numbers using the method described in the chapter.

(a)	123456	(d)	821652
(b)	826431	(e)	356211
(c)	545323	(f)	352253

8-28. A check-digit system uses only every other digit in a 9-digit account number to guard against data errors. The sum of these values is added and then the digits in this sum are added continuously until a single number remains to serve as the check digit. Thus, for the account number 123456789, just the values 2, 4, 6, and 8 are used. Their sum is 20 and the sum of these digits is $2 + 0 = 2$. Hence, "2" becomes the check digit for this account number. Using the above method, compute the check digits for each of the following account numbers.

(a)	375621883	(d)	443216820
(b)	537662115	(e)	956821654
(c)	872216535	(f)	631862477

8-29. A check-digit system uses the odd numbers beginning with 3 to compute a check digit for a four-digit account number as follows. The low-order digit is multiplied by 3, the next low-order digit is multiplied by 5, the next low-order digit is multiplied by 7, and the high-order digit is multiplied by 9. These multiples are then summed and the low-order digit of the sum is used as the check digit. Thus, for the account number 1234, the multiples are $4 \times 3 = 12$, $3 \times 5 = 15$, $2 \times 7 = 14$, and $1 \times 9 = 9$. The sum of these multiples is $12 + 15 + 14 + 9 = 50$, and the check digit is therefore 0. Compute check digits for the following account numbers, using this system.

(a)	4569	(d)	6951
(b)	3827	(e)	1219
(c)	4342	(f)	9995

8-30. The Modulus-11 Check-Digit System. The most common check-digit system in use today is the somewhat complicated modulus-11 check digit system which, for technical reasons, has been shown to be superior to similar systems using an alternate modulus than 11. The system works as follows:

1. Assign weights to each number. The low-order number is given a weight of "2," the next-low-order number is given a weight of "3," and so forth.
2. Multiply each digit in the number by its weight.
3. Add the products computed in step (2) to obtain a single number.
4. Divide the value found in step (3) by 11.
5. Examine the remainder. If the remainder is zero, the check digit is also 0. If the remainder is not zero, subtract the remainder from 11 to obtain the check digit. A check digit of 10 is usually written as "x." *Example:* For account number 123456, for each digit, reading from left to right, the weights are, respectively, 7, 6, 5, 4, 3, and 2. The product of these digits times their respective weights is $1 \times 7 = 7$, $2 \times 6 = 12$, $3 \times 5 = 15$, $4 \times 4 = 16$, $5 \times 3 = 15$, $6 \times 2 = 12$. The sum of these products is 77. When this number is divided by 11, the remainder is 0 and thus the check digit is 0. The new account number is therefore 1234560.

Employee Social Security number	Department number	Employee name	Pay rate—regular hours	Pay rate—overtime hours	Number of regular hours worked	Number of overtime worked	Blank
1 9	10 13	14 38	39 42	43 46	47 50	51 54	55 80

For each number below, perform a similar computation.

(a) 254667   (c) 334886
(b) 765895   (d) 965334

8-31. A computerized payroll system utilizes card input. The format is illustrated above. List a set of editing tests that might be used to assure the accuracy and completeness of the information contained on each card.

8-32. An accounts receivable system uses punched cards to update a master file of magnetic tape records. Five illustrative cards are shown below.

A careful inspection of the values in these five cards will reveal a number of potential errors.

(a) Identify as many errors as you can.
(b) For each error, identify a control that might have been used to catch it.
(c) Using the data below, compute at least one example of each of the following: financial control total, hash total, record count.

8-33. The Alpine Flight Club is an organization of amateur pilots with 182 members. The club owns three airplanes: a Cessna, a Piper, and a Comanche, which it rents out for $15, $18,

Account Number	Trans-action Code[a]	Credit Sale or Cash Receipt Amount	Discount Allowed (Percent)[b]	Discount Allowed (Dollars)	Net Amount
Col. 1–5	Col. 6	Col. 7–12	Col. 13–14	Col. 15–19	Col. 20–25
53162	2	$52.00	(blank)	$1.04	$50.96
53175	1	250000	02	5000	245000
53781	2	2 0095	−2	00000	20095
53192	2	45000	20	9000	360000
S3198	3	4L0.00	02	820	40180

[a]1 = credit sale; 2 = cash receipt.
[b]Assume all sales terms are x/10, n/30, where x is the percent in the column.

Member Number	Billing Date	Plane Code[a]	Hours Logged[b]	Total Charge
Col. 1–3	Col. 4–9	Col. 10	Col. 11–14	Col. 15–20
172	101580	A	5.40	$81.00
195	101780	C	0250	005000
L51	103280	P	320	005760
048	110308	E	0400	080000
391	110580	C	015-	002250

[a]C = Cessna, P = Piper, E = Comanche.

[b]Expressed to nearest hundredth hour, decimal point omitted.

and $20 per hour, respectively, to club members. The club performs its billing with the aid of a punched card system, and a few representative cards are illustrated above.

Required:

(a) Identify the errors in the above cards.

(b) For each error, suggest an editing control that would detect it.

(c) Using the data above, compute at least one example of each of the following: financial control total, hash total, record count.

8-34. Below is a repesentative master file record utilized by the Sterling National Bank to process its customers' checking accounts. Also found below is a representative file segment control record. A separate such segment control record is used for every branch of the bank. This record is the last record of each file segment.

Account numbers consist of a two-digit branch number followed by a six-digit account number. The bank has recently installed an "Automatic Loan Approval" (ALA) feature in which certain customers are permitted to overdraw their accounts. Thus, for approved accounts (ALA flag = 1 in the master file record), the account balance can be negative.

Identification numbers in the segment-control record contain the two-digit branch number, followed by 999999. The account balance field in the control record is the sum of all positive account balances for the corresponding branch accounts. The loan balance field is the sum of all negative account balances for the corresponding branch accounts.

The checking account master file is processed with customer transactions for such customer activities as writing checks, making deposits, changing home addresses, and so forth. Besides updating the account balances,

MASTER RECORD

Account Number	Name	Address	Phone Number	Account Balance	Savings Account Ref. No.	ALA Flag

1 = yes
0 = no

SEGMENT-CONTROL RECORD

Control Record Identifier Field	Branch Name	Number of Accounts this Segment	Account Balance Total	Loan Balance Total

the processing routine performs certain processing-control functions. Among them are:

1. Checking account number field check: the account number should have exactly eight numerical digits as described above. No alphabetic letters or other special symbols are permitted. In addition, the latter six digits of each account number should be 100,000 or larger.
2. Phone number field check: this field should contain a positive, ten-digit numerical number.
3. Checking account balance field check: only numerical information should be found here. In addition, the field can only be negative if the ALA flag is on (i.e., is set to one).
4. Savings account reference number field check: this field can be blank if the customer does not have a savings account with the bank. If the field is not blank, it must contain a nine-digit, numerical value.
5. ALA flag field test: this field can only be zero or one.
6. Segment identification number field test: this field should pass the same tests as the account number in part (1) above.
7. Control total check: the number of records for each branch should equal the "number of accounts" stored in the associated segment-control record. The sum of the positive account balances for the accounts of each branch should equal the "account balance total" in the associated segment-control record. The sum of the negative account balances for the accounts of each branch should equal the "loan balance total" in the associated segment control record.
8. Trailer record processing: the trailer record contains grand-total fields similar to those of the segment control records. At the completion of all processing, the same tests as in (7) should be performed for the entire file.

Prepare a microflowchart for a computer program to perform the above editing and testing. If errors in any of the fields of an account record are detected, the program should print out the information contained in the entire record, along with an error message indicating the type of problem encountered. Cross-footing errors detected by (7) above should be communicated via printed output message indicating the branch and the nature of the problem. A similar attack should be made for problems encountered when processing the trailer record in item (8).

CASE ANALYSES

8-35. *The Lottery**

During the past few years some states have implemented lottery systems as an alternative to raising or levying new taxes. The results from these lotteries have run the gamut from very disappointing to very good. However, it appears that in states where the computer was utilized extensively in the lottery system, the results have been generally good. One of the most important advantages of the computerized system is that the administrator of the lottery can implement extensive control procedures to minimize fraud and deception.

You are a systems analyst employed by a state which has decided to implement a lottery. Your assignment is to analyze the controls in the lottery system considered most successful to date. Below are three tickets which were purchased from the same lottery office. The only additional facts that you have at this time is that these tickets were printed on a central computer and manually distributed to the sales outlets.

Based on this information only, prepare a report describing the possible controls in the lottery systems operations.

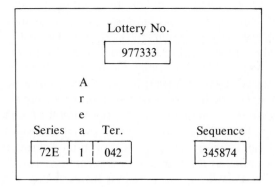

*Used with the permission of John G. Burch, Jr., and Felix R. Strater, Jr., *Information Systems: Theory and Practice* (New York: John Wiley & Sons, Inc., 1979).

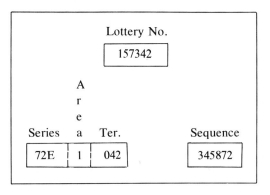

Lottery No.

157342

A
r
e
a

Series	Ter.	Sequence
72E	1	042	345872

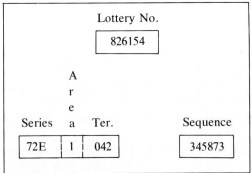

Lottery No.

826154

A
r
e
a

Series	Ter.	Sequence
72E	1	042	345873

8-36. *Airpower Industries*

Airpower Industries, a manufacturer of hand-pump pellet guns, is a company which was started 20 years ago by John Stewart, the company's current president. Airpower Industries had relatively few competitors and its sales had increased consistently each year. Last year, sales exceeded $12 million and a computer system was installed by a national business machine firm to assist the company with its paperwork.

Last month, John Stewart decided to request a review of data-processing control procedures by a well-known CPA firm, Bruce Wilson and Sons. Douglas Shafter, the controller of Airpower Industries, was called to assist the CPA firm with its review. Douglas Shafter was a loyal employee of the company and had been promoted through the ranks as the firm had grown and prospered. He had no formal computer education but was responsible for the operating practices of the company's newly-created EDP system.

Bruce Wilson and Sons assigned its computer specialist, Phillip Marris, to manage the review. During his first meeting with Douglas Shafter,

Mr. Marris requested a tour of the facilities. Mr. Shafter thereupon led the way to the computer center, which was located on the ground floor of the company office building in the offices of the company Personnel Department.

In the computer room, the company programmer and the company system analyst were testing programs and going over the results. In response to an inquiry about developmental responsibilities, Mr. Marris was informed that all programs were tested by the programmer and systems analyst. Based upon their review, the programs were given final approval by these two employees when they were sure everything was in order. A similar procedure was followed for program modifications. As Mr. Shafter and Mr. Marris toured the center, Mr. Shafter pointed with pride to the new computer, which was prominently displayed near the Personnel Department's interviewing rooms. Mr. Shafter pointed out to Mr. Marris that the computer was considered one of the company's most innovative developments. Because almost every employee in the company had to conduct some business with the company personnel office at one time or another, Mr. Shafter explained that the computer placement maximized its visibility and was thought to be a real employee motivator.

Mr. Shafter also showed Mr. Marris the computer tape files and program library. Both the tape files and programs were stored on open shelves in the middle of the computer room. Mr. Shafter explained that such a location was convenient to both operators and programmers, and eliminated such problems as the need for the programmer to ask anyone else for a particular program if modifications were required. In fact, Mr. Shafter went on to explain, this turned out to be very important because the company programmer had just bought a new house and was putting in a lot of overtime on nights and weekends to help pay for it.

When Mr. Marris expressed concern about the possibility of a lost tape file, Mr. Shafter began to chuckle. The company had already thought of that, he explained. Back-up copies of the tapes, along with the transaction tapes needed to re-create current files, were stored with the current copies to guard against that possibility, he said. Thus, even if the original copy of the tape were lost, he noted, there would still be the back-ups.

Computer cards, work tapes, and most of the forms used within the data-processing center (such as purchase orders, payroll checks, and storeroom transfer documents) were stored next to the tape and program library shelves. Phillip Marris noticed that the computer operator was able to halt the computer during the regular processing of accounts receivable. When Phillip Marris asked about the company's insurance program, Douglas Shafter replied that all raw materials for production and the manufacturing equipment were adequately covered, but because the computer hardware was leased, it therefore did not require insurance coverage. Furthermore, when Phillip Marris asked Douglas Shafter about fidelity bonds, he was not aware of what they were. When asked about back-up facilities in emergency procedures, Douglas Shafter said that the maintenance lease of the national business machine company had provided excellent service and was very responsive to the company's needs.

Question

What preventive controls would you recommend to Airpower Industries if you were the CPA reviewing this company's operating procedures?

8-37. *United Airlines Half-Price Coupons*

In June of 1979, United Airlines made its customers a very unusual offer. Every person taking a United Airlines flight in the month of June would be issued a half-price coupon which entitled the bearer to a 50 percent reduction in the full-fare price of any flight taken between July 1, 1979 and December 15, 1979. The purpose of the promotion was to lure travelers back to United Airlines flights after the company had suffered from a devastating strike. An interesting feature of the coupons was that there were very few restrictions on their use. For example, a traveler could take a $30 flight on one of the company's short trips, yet apply the half-fare discount to a second, transcontinental flight from (say) New York to Los Angeles. Further, the ticket itself was not encoded with the name of the passenger. Thus, in effect, such coupons were transferable.

As illustrated below, each coupon was stamped in red with a seven-digit accounting number which was also coded on a perforated stub portion of the ticket. This stub was torn from the ticket coupon at the time of use and affixed to the accounting copy of the passenger's airline ticket. Thus, the affixed stub portion of the coupon indicated that the 50 percent discount had been applied to the price of the passenger's ticket. As with other airlines, all accounting copies of the United Airlines tickets are collected

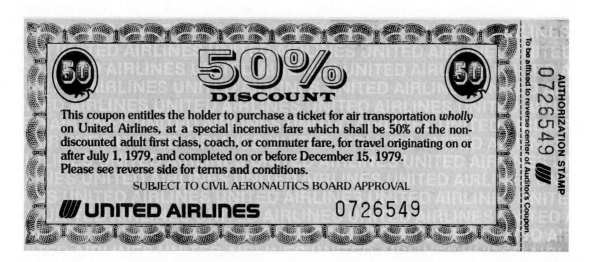

at the company's national accounting headquarters for processing purposes.

Questions

1. What strengths and/or weaknesses do you perceive in the United Airlines discount scheme as described above?
2. For each weakness you mentioned in question (1) above, also identify a means by which the weakness could be avoided.

8-38.   *Olympia Manufacturing Company*

In connection with her examination of the financial statements of the Olympia Manufacturing Company, Laura Lannan, CPA, is reviewing procedures for accumulating direct labor hours. She learns that all production is by job order and that all employees are paid hourly wages, with time-and-one-half for overtime hours.

Olympia's direct labor hour input process for payroll and job-cost determination is summarized in the flowchart below. Steps A and C are performed in timekeeping, step B in the factory operating departments, step D in payroll audit and control, step E in data preparation (keypunch), and step F in computer operations.

Required

1. Redraw the diagram, using familiar system flowcharting symbols.
2. For each input processing steps A through F, cite possible errors or discrepancies which might arise and identify the corresponding control procedure that should be in effect for each error or discrepancy. Use the table organization:

Step	Possible Errors or Discrepancies	Control Procedures

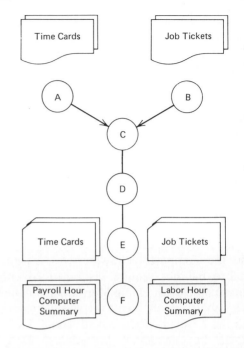

(AICPA Adapted)

8-39.   *Simmons Corporation*

Simmons Corporation is a multi-location retailing concern with stores and warehouses throughout the United States. The company is in the process of designing a new, integrated, computer-based information system. In conjunction with the design of the new system, the management of the company is reviewing the data-processing security to determine what new control features should be incorporated. Two areas of specific concern are (1) confidentiality of company and customer records and (2) safekeeping of computer equipment, files, and EDP facilities.

The new information system will be employed to process all company records which include sales, purchase, financial, budget, customer, creditor, and personnel information. The stores and warehouses will be linked to the main computer at corporate headquarters by a system of remote terminals. This will permit data to be communicated directly to corporate headquarters or to any other location from each location within the terminal network.

At the present time certain reports have restricted distribution because not all levels of management need to receive them or because they contain confidential information. The introduction of remote terminals in the new system may provide access to this restricted data by unauthorized personnel. Simmons top management is concerned that confidential information may become accessible and may be used improperly.

The company also is concerned with potential physical threats to the system, such as sabotage, fire damage, water damage, power failure, or magnetic radiation. Should any of these events occur in the present system and cause a computer shutdown, adequate back-up records are available so that the company could reconstruct necessary information at a reasonable cost on a timely basis. However, with the new system, a computer shutdown would severely limit company activities until the system could become operational again.

Required

A.   Identify and briefly explain the problems Simmons Corporation could experience with respect to the confidentiality of information and records in the new system.

B.   Recommend measures Simmons Corporation could incorporate into the new system which would ensure the confidentiality of information and records in the new system.

C.   What safeguards can Simmons Corporation develop to provide physical security for its (1) computer equipment, (2) files, and (3) EDP facilities?

(CMA Adapted)

9

Computer Crime

Among the important questions that you should be able to answer after reading this chapter are:

1 Why is it difficult to define *computer crime*?
2 Why is there an absence of good data on computer crime?
3 Is computer crime on the *upswing* or on the *downswing*?
4 How was the Equity Funding fraud committed? Was it a computer crime?
5 What characteristics of an individual might be recognized at the time of initial hire which might indicate criminal intelligence?

INTRODUCTION

In 1966, a programmer working with a bank had an overdrawn bank account. Fortunately, or perhaps unfortunately, it was the same bank. He meticulously programmed his IBM 1401 computer to ignore his $300 overdraft, intending to replace the money three days later. But he did such a good job of hiding his "loan" that, four months later, he had increased this amount to over $350. He was caught when the computer broke down, thus earning him the dubious honor of becoming the world's first known computer criminal.

This chapter is about computer crime, frauds, and other irregularities which have occurred in the past, and which, in many instances, can still occur in the future. The connection between computers, computer crime, and accounting information systems is both straightforward and important. Computers tend to concentrate the asset-bearing information of the individual organization into a compact, but highly vulnerable, format. The accounting information system exploits this format for efficiency in data-gathering, data-storage, and data-dissemination. The cost-effectiveness of such an accounting system begins to diminish, however, if it is unprotected and subject to abuse. Thus, the study of computer crime and its deterrents is an important focal point in the maintenance and protection of organizational data within the accounting information system.

For the purposes of discussion, we have chosen to divide this chapter into three logical sections. In the first of these, we take a closer look at some definitions of computer crime, and review what facts are presently available about the incidence and types of computer abuse now on record. In the second section, we examine five specific examples of computer crime. With the exception of the Equity Funding scandal, which has been included in the discussion principally because of its enormity, each of these cases has been selected as a model representing a "class," or category of computer abuse. Accompanying each case is a small "analysis" section which examines the reasons why the computer abuse was not detected through normal processing controls, and an indication of what controls might have been installed to thwart the crime. Because you are already familiar with many accounting controls from the last two chapters, you might want to read the case descriptions first and then decide for yourself what might have been done before turning to the "analysis" sections of the text.

Finally, in the last portion of this chapter, we conclude with a profile of the computer criminal. In this section, we examine those characteristics of individuals involved in computer crime that seem to reappear constantly in the computer-abuse reports, and make some observations about what can be done to avoid computer difficulties in the future.

COMPUTER CRIME—AN OVERVIEW

Computer crime has become a "hot" topic in the field of computerized data processing, and even such prestigious publications as *Fortune* magazine, *Business Week,* and the *Wall Street Journal* have devoted space to reviews, surveys, and general discussions of computer abuse. Pub-

lic interest has also inspired expanded reporting of computer crimes in local newspapers, radio, and television. Because computers and the information systems that use them are still highly technical in nature, however, mass-media coverage has been limited in scope and details. Thus, the most informative reports of computer abuses may still be found in computer trade journals, of which *Computerworld* has been an especially important source.

The number of in-depth surveys of computer abuse conducted to date has been surprisingly small. As discussed in greater detail below, this is partially attributable to the relatively small proportion of computer crime that ever gets detected and the even smaller proportion that ultimately gets reported in sufficient detail to permit accurate classification and evaluation. Most of the analysis which follows is based upon the now-famous studies of Donn B. Parker,* the work of Brandt Allen,† and the work of Lee J. Seidler, Frederick Andrews, and Marc J. Epstein.‡

Computer Crime—What Is It?

A definition of computer crime is elusive. In some circumstances, the use of a computer to deceive for personal gain is clearly an example of what might commonly be termed a *computer crime*. Thus, when a police chief was charged with altering his own driving record through an online computer terminal, there is good reason to call this a computer crime. However, much of what has been termed computer crime has merely involved the computer, but probably would be more accurately classified as other

---

*See Donn B. Parker, *Computer Abuse Assessment*, a monograph available from Stanford Research Institute, Menlo Park, California, 94025, SRI Project 5068, and Donn B. Parker, *Crime by Computer* (New York: Charles Scribner's Sons, 1976). Copyright © 1976 by Donn B. Parker. Used by permission of Charles Scribner's Sons.

†See Brandt Allen, "The Biggest Computer Frauds: Lessons for CPAs," *The Journal of Accountancy*, May 1977, pp. 52–62.

‡See Lee J. Seidler, Frederick Andrews, and Marc J. Epstein, *The Equity Funding Papers, The Anatomy of a Fraud* (New York: John Wiley and Sons, © 1977).

types of crimes. Consider the following cases for example:

1. A programmer changed a dividends-payment program to reduce the dividends of eight stockholders and issue a check to a fictitious person in the total amount of $56,000.

2. A company charged a computer-equipment vendor with fraudulently representing the capacity and capability of a computer system. It charged that the full system was never delivered and did not have adequate software.

3. In a fit of resentment, a keyboard operator shattered a CRT screen with her high-heeled shoe at Orly Airport in France.

4. A credit bureau sent notices to those individuals listed as bad risks in its files. For a fee, the bureau would withhold the damaging credit information and keep it from being put into a larger, computer-based credit system.

5. A computer-dating service was sued because referrals for dates were so few and inappropriate. The new owner of the dating bureau said that no computer was used at that time although the use of a computer was advertised.

The first case, which involved dividend payments, could just as easily be called embezzlement—the computer was just a means toward this end. The second, a computer-equipment case, involves a potential instance of misrepresentation—the item involved in the transaction could just as easily have been a toaster. In the third case, a CRT screen, and not a computer, was damaged. By chance, the unfortunate woman chose a computer-oriented object, instead of a dish or book, upon which to vent her anger. In the fourth case, the attempt to sell credit information was a straightforward attempt to threaten individuals' credit reputations. Perhaps a better description for such a crime would be extortion. Finally, in the last case, the use of a computer to match blind dates was guaranteed when none, in fact, was used.

Clearly, it is questionable to call this a computer crime when there was no computer!

The definition of computer crime is important because it affects how the statistics on such crimes are tallied. For example, the largest computer crime on record—the Equity Funding Scandal—involved the loss of $200 million if only direct company losses are counted, and over $2 billion if indirect losses to other companies and investor losses in common stock and bonds are counted. Either way, these losses are so large that including them as computer-crime losses severely affects the statistics computed about such activities. The question, however, is whether we should "count" the Equity Funding Case in our sample of known computer abuse. At the time of this writing, the classification of the Equity Funding Case as a computer crime is still debatable. We shall look more closely at the Equity Funding Case in a later section of this chapter.

Figure 9-1 lists 15 of the largest computer crimes uncovered to date. The list indicates a summary of the crime itself, the amount of loss, the time frame, the type of scheme involved, the type of computer manipulation, the fraudulent debit used to cover the missing assets, the job position of the primary perpetrator, the total number of perpetrators inside and outside the organization in which the crime was committed, and the means of detection. Several crimes which involved losses in excess of $1 million were excluded from the list because they ran for less than a year, the victim was not the employer, or the fraud methodology was atypical of "common" computer crimes. Notably absent, therefore, is the Equity Funding scandal.

In reviewing the methods and practices of the computer criminal, we find that most are common deceptions which have been tried many times before. Thus, the use of the computer to deceive is simply "a new twist on an old rope." For the 15 cases at hand, for example, over half of them involved a simple transfer of funds through a set of accounts with the dollars ultimately winding up in the hands of the perpetrators. In terms of methodology, therefore, one computer expert has described computer crimes simply as ". . . old wine in new bottles. The technology may be random access and hexa-decimal but the scheme itself should be as familiar to the auditor as debits and credits."*

One of the few types of automated activities that might satisfy the purist as a computer crime involves the theft of computer time or computer programs. Usually, in such instances, both the computer resource itself, and the means by which it is obtained, require an intimate knowledge of computers and computing methodology. The following cases might fall under this category:

1.   European news media reported that a 15-year-old London schoolboy compromised a commercial time-sharing system by obtaining and using operating system program listings to discover privileged user access codes, and was able to take over the time-sharing system.
2.   The owner of a software-leasing company convinced programmers to take copies of programs from their employers and sell them to the software-leasing company which then marketed the software as their own.
3.   A Denver programmer short-circuited his computer 56 times in a misguided attempt to shut down the computer. By the time the programmer was caught, the company had spent half a million dollars attempting to find a hardware failure.
4.   An unknown person gained access to a computer-terminal room by asking the custodian to open the door for him. He picked the locks of the telephones and terminals to gain unauthorized use of time-sharing services.
5.   Two computer and peripheral-equipment manufacturers engaged in charges and countercharges of unfair competition and industrial espionage, including wiretapping and destruction of products and facilities.

*Brandt Allen, "The Biggest Computer Frauds: Lessons for CPAs," *The Journal of Accountancy,* May 1977, p. 60.

Although these cases would appear to qualify clearly as computer crimes, there is still some basis of doubt. Where students are involved in "bugging" the computer center at universities, for example, the crime often has taken on the appearance of a prank. Thus, "challenge," more than "personal gain," is the primary motive. Similarly, in case (3) above, the real problem appeared to be an unstable individual much more than a theft of real property for personal gain. The conclusion is therefore rather disappointing—a clear definition of computer crime is lacking. Until this question is resolved, both our statistics and our understanding of security will be inadequate. In the pages which follow, we present our findings of computer crime as we understand it today.

Computer Crime—
We Don't Have Many Statistics

The statistics on computer crime are notable principally for their absence. Since the computer has been in use commercially (1952), for example, there are less than 700 documented cases of such crime. The likelihood that this figure includes the total number of crimes that have been committed in almost three decades is remote. The fact that there are presently over 200,000 computers and 2.5 million EDP-related employees in the United States adds to this conclusion.

The absence of good data on computer crime becomes even more remarkable when average losses are calculated. Even when excluding the Equity Funding Case, the average loss from a computer crime is $450,000, as compared with only $19,000 in average losses resulting from other types of white-collar crime. Thus, if the perpetrator can get away with it, computer crime pays—and pays big!

An explanation for the absence of complete information on computer crime includes several factors. One possible cause is the fact that a large proportion of the computer crime committed in companies and government agencies is handled as an internal matter. Thus, much of the information about such crimes never reaches the pub-

Figure 9-1

FIFTEEN IMPORTANT COMPUTER CRIMES

Case	Summary	Amount (thousands)	Time Frame (years)	Type of Scheme	Computer Manipulation	Fraudulent Debit	Job Position of Primary Perpetrator	Number of Perpetrators Inside/ Outside	Means of Detection
1	Accountant at west coast department store set up phony vendors, purchases and vouchers.	$ 100	1.3	Disbursements	Unauthorized transactions added	Inventory	Accountant	1/-	Suspicious bank employee
2	Claims reviewer at insurance company prepared false claims payable to friends in a manner that would be paid automatically by the computer.	$ 128	4	Fraudulent claims paid	Unauthorized transactions added	Expense	Claims clerk	1/22	Error made by greedy associate
3	Clerk at storage facility entered false information to computerized inventory system to mask theft of inventory. Shipments then made without billing.	$ 4,000	6	Inventory/billing	Input transactions altered	Inventory	Computer terminal operator	1/13	Physical inventory shortage detected in audit
4	Warehouse employees manipulated computerized inventory system through unauthorized terminal entries to mask inventory thefts.	$ 200	1.5	Inventory	Unauthorized terminal entries	None (inventory records changed as to location)	Warehouse employee(s)	"Several"	Suspicious wife of store manager
5	Accountant at metal fabricating company padded payroll, thereby extracting funds for own use.	$ 100	3	Payroll	Unknown	Expense	Accountant	1/-	IRS investigation
6	Officer of London bank stole funds from inactive customer accounts.	$ 290	5	Account transfers	Unauthorized addition and alteration of transactions	Customer accounts (liability)	Computer liaison officer	1/-	Unknown
7	Bank employee misused online banking system to perpetrate large lapping fraud including unrecorded transactions, altered transactions and unauthorized account transfers.	$ 1,400	3	Lapping	Transactions altered, added and withheld	Customer accounts (liability)	Teller supervisor	1/-	Gambling activities uncovered by police raid

#	Description	Duration	Method	Transaction	Account	Role	Ratio	Discovery
8	Manufacturing company manager designed and installed automated accounting system and used it to steal.	2	Disbursements (also billings fraud)	Transactions altered (also unauthorized transactions)	Inventory (also expense)	Operations manager	1/1	Suspicious associate
9	Customer representatives of large public utility, together with outside associate, erased customer receivables using computer error correction codes; received kickback from customer.	2	Accounts receivable—collections	Unauthorized transactions	Expense (adjusting entry)	Customer service representative	2/1	Suspicious bank employee together with expanded type of scheme
10	Clerk in department store established phony purchases and vouchers paid to friend's company.	3	Disbursements	Unauthorized transactions	Inventory	Accounts clerk	1/1	Suspicious associate
11	Organized crime ring operated check-kiting fraud between two banks using computer room employees who altered deposit memos to record check deposits as available for immediate withdrawal.	4	Kiting (float fraud)	Transactions altered	(Timing)	VP-computer systems (also assistant branch manager)	2/3	Bank messenger failed to deliver checks on time
12	Accountant at large wholesaler established phony vendors through computerized accounting system that he operated.	4	Disbursements	Unauthorized transactions	Inventory	Controller	1/-	Gave up
13	Officer of brokerage house misappropriated company funds through computer system that he controlled.	3	Account transfers	Unauthorized transactions	Revenue account (interest earned)	VP-computer systems	1/-	Unknown
14	Partner at brokerage house transferred funds from firm's accounts to his own.	3	Account transfers	Unauthorized transactions	Expense (via adjusting entry)	Partner-head of computer system	1/-	Unknown
15	Director of publishing subsidiary manipulated computer system to add false sales and block recording of accounts payable—all to improve operating results, thereby securing a position on board of directors.	"Several years"	Padded sales (also unrecorded expense)	Program alterations (also file changes)	Receivables	Director of subsidiary	5/-	Unknown

Source. Brandt Allen, "The Biggest Computer Frauds: Lessons for CPAs," *The Journal of Accountancy*, May 1977. Copyright © 1977 by the American Institute of Certified Public Accountants, Inc.

267

lic domain. A second explanation is that the definition of computer crime is of sufficient ambiguity to forestall an accurate listing. For example, when several thousand employees of one federal government agency were asked to enumerate all the computer crimes that had been detected during the last year, there was only one positive reply. However, when the survey was redistributed to these same employees and asked about deceptions in data or information which eventually would have been computer-processed, or, in fact, had been computer-processed already, there were thousands of responses.

The most obvious explanation for the lack of good computer-crime data, however, and the explanation to which almost all the experts subscribe, is the simple fact that most computer crime just isn't discovered! Thus, the 600-odd cases of verified computer crime now known are just the tip of the iceberg of the total amount of computer crime presently "under way." Because the majority of computer criminals are caught by chance, accident, or just luck, rather than via internal computer controls alone, this fact is really no surprise. Nonetheless, it leaves us wondering what the clever computer criminals are doing right now if we catch only the unlucky ones!

For the reasons enumerated above, we can only consider the presently known cases of computer crime a sample, rather than a population, of modern computer abuse. Although it is possible to derive descriptive statistics from such data, care must be exercised in extrapolating results because there is good reason to believe that the sample is biased by the type of crime likely to be reported, by the problem of estimating losses, and by the influence of civil cases in which both actual and punitive ("punishment") damages are awarded to those seeking action in the courts.

Having stated these difficulties with the data, we must also state that the historical record of computer crime provides a fascinating study in modern criminology. The positions of the perpetrators, the number of accomplices involved in a particular incident, and the methodology of the crimes themselves have attracted the attention

and study of several specialists in the area. Some tentative conclusions about computer crime are presented in the paragraphs below.

The Growth of Computer Crime

Figure 9-2 graphs the incidence of selected computer abuse cases from 1958 until 1978. Omitted from the figure are a number of cases involving student computer abuse at universities, certain business disputes over computer products and services, and a few unverified reports of computer abuse for which there is reason to doubt authenticity. It is unlikely, however, that the absence of these cases from the tally of computer abuse for the years selected in the figure would affect the overall conclusion that the incidence of computer crime is a growing phenomenon. From the years 1966 to 1972, in fact, this growth has been almost geometric in nature. Not only are these increases spectacular, they were also unforeseen. In 1971, for example, the number of known computer crimes totaled approximately 130, and one of the leading computer-crime specialists of the day speculated that this sum would reach the "200 mark" by the year 1980. That figure was in fact reached in 1973, two years later.

In Figure 9-2, the apparent downturn in computer crime in the years 1976 and 1978 is misleading. There is an appreciable lag between the time a computer crime occurs and the time such a crime is reported, verified, and therefore counted in the statistics. Inasmuch as the cutoff date for the study depicted in Figure 9-2 was January 1979, there is good reason to believe that a number of computer-abuse cases still had not been reported for the latter years of the study. Under this assumption, the conclusion that computer crime is on the rise continues to hold.

The seriousness of computer-crime growth is not appreciably lessened by the fact that the number of computers, and the use of computers, in the United States has also grown over the years. From 1965 to 1975, for example, the number of computers in the U.S. has approximately doubled, from 100,000 to 200,000. Coordinating these statistics with the graph, the rate of com-

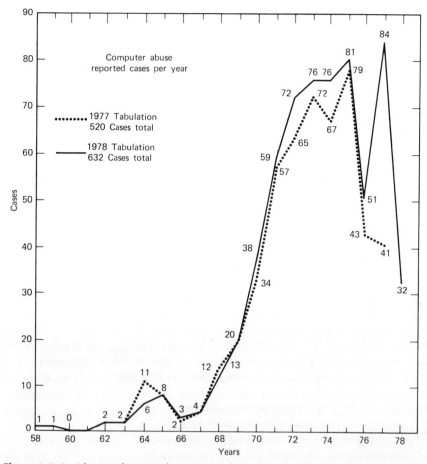

Figure 9-2. Incidence of reported computer abuse cases, to January 1979. (Courtesy of Donn B. Parker, SRI.)

puter crime is found to be approximately 1 reported case per 10,000 computers in 1965, and close to 4 reported cases per 10,000 computers in 1975—still a sizable increase despite an allowance for the larger number of computers available for criminal abuse. Moreover, the 1975 rate of 4 reported cases per 10,000 computers, or 1 reported case for every 2,500 computers, would appear to be unreasonably low, again suggesting that the number of computer-abuse cases reported is suspiciously small relative to the number of potential cases that are likely to occur in these risk environments.

It is interesting to speculate on why computer crime is increasing. Some experts suggest that the increase in computer crime merely parallels the rise in the number of other types of crime during the years 1965 to 1975. Another possibility is that the expanding rate of computer abuse follows the increasing concentration of information regarding business financial assets in computer files, thereby making the practice of computer crime that much more lucrative. Figure 9-3, for example, illustrates the average losses for a sample of known computer crime, categorized by application area. According to these statistics, by far the largest losses were sustained in corporate accounting and inventory-control situations, where the average was $1.3 million. Fraudulent corporate payments to creditors averaged

Figure 9-3
AVERAGE LOSSES FOR A SELECTION OF 150 COMPUTER FRAUDS ($000's)

Type of Fraud	Corporation	Bank/Savings and Loan	State and Local Government	Federal Government
Payments to employees	$ 139	$ 3	$ 14	$33
Payments to other individuals	133	—	487	—
Payments to creditors	324	252	—	56
Accounting/inventory control	1,300	195	a	—
Collections/deposits	43	157	—	—
Billings	6	—	—	—
Miscellaneous	a	—	a	—
Average loss totals for frauds with documented losses	$ 621	$193	$329	$45

[a] Amount of loss unknown.

Source: Brandt Allen, "The Biggest Computer Frauds: Lessons for CPAs," *The Journal of Accountancy,* May 1977, p. 54. Copyright © 1977 by the American Institute of Certified Public Accountants, Inc.

$324,000 and fraudulent corporate payments to employees averaged $139,000. The conclusion seems clear: computer crime involves high stakes.

An additional explanation for the rise of computer abuse may be the impersonality of the crime itself. The perpetrator almost never deals with another individual, just the computer system. This often gives the thief anonymity, plus the dubious satisfaction that he or she is not stealing from an individual, but rather "beating the system." Most computer criminals have been quite emphatic on this point. One bank embezzler who was apprehended after stealing thousands of dollars from inactive bank accounts explained that he never took more than $20,000 from any one account because the accounts were only insured up to $20,000. Other embezzlers have argued that they were only doing on a larger scale what the inventory clerks and stock people were doing in the warehouse, that is, helping themselves to corporate assets as a fringe benefit of their jobs.

A final explanation for the rise in computer abuse may be the growing awareness of the possibilities of computer crime and the publicity that computer crime has attracted in the news media. This is sometimes called a "skyjack syndrome," in which the wide availability of information about an exciting, and seemingly "safe," type of

crime attracts others to try it. This phenomenon would appear to explain a rash of bank frauds in the late 1960s, in which dishonest employees exchanged the deposit slips of customers with deposit slips of their own, thus crediting their own accounts with the deposit money. Since, at that time, bank processing depended only upon the MICR code (see Chapter 4), there was no control over this practice. It is reported, for example, that in the course of a single day, one dishonest bank employee deposited $250,000 in customer funds to his own account, wrote out a single check to himself for $100,000, and was never heard from again.

Conclusions

The most fundamental conclusion which we can draw from computer crime is that at present we know very little about it. The fact that the number of reported cases of computer crime has increased substantially tempts us to conclude that computer crime is on the rise. However, it is not clear whether this is indeed a fact or merely the result of better reporting. It would also appear that computer crimes involve large sums of money. Again, however, whether the averages calculated from our sample of known computer crimes accurately reflect the overall magnitude is speculative.

An understanding of computer crime is perhaps best accomplished not by examining the statistics in the aggregate, but rather by studying selected abuses that have occurred in the past. Thus, in the next section of this chapter, we take a closer look at five specific cases of computer crimes with the hope of learning from the experiences of others.

FIVE BIG COMPUTER CRIMES

As one reads the fascinating accounts of different computer crimes, a pattern of classifications begins to emerge. One type of crime clearly involves vandalism, another the falsification of input data, and yet a third the unauthorized use of output documents. The number of computer crimes that involve the substitution of bogus bank deposit slips for legitimate ones continues to grow each year, as does the programming of instructions which enable embezzlers to steal funds from their bank's inactive accounts or funds from their company's accounts receivable.

In this section of the chapter, we have chosen for analysis five computer crimes which are fairly representative of certain classes of computer fraud *as we know it today*. Of course, whether or not the five cases discussed are actually representative of all computer crime is not known. Moreover, it might reasonably be argued that because each crime is committed by different perpetrators in a different environment, there are no categories: each crime necessarily is unique. Nevertheless, we will discuss each of our computer crimes in the pages that follow.

The Round-Off Trick

Perhaps the most common example of computer fraud is performed in the manipulation of the round-off error which occurs when fractions of a cent are involved in computer computations. Normally, a computer program is instructed to follow the rounding convention you learned as a child in grammar school: round down if the decimal is below .5; round up if the decimal is .5 or greater. Thus, if the interest calculations for two bank accounts were $2.534 and $7.787, the first

account would be credited with a total interest of $2.53 and the second with a total interest of $7.79.

The accumulated error from this rounding is the sum of the actual payments subtracted from the (more accurate) computed payments, or

$$
\begin{array}{ll}
\$10.321 & (= \$2.534 + \$7.787) \\
- \quad 10.32 & (= \quad 2.53 + 7.79\ ) \\
\hline
= \quad .001 &
\end{array}
$$

In general, the accumulated error will be very small since the "round-ups" will offset the "round-downs," leaving an expected value for the accumulated error of zero. A bank can maintain a slush fund of a few dollars in a special account to absorb, or pay out, an accumulation error that results from any particular processing run of its regular accounts.

A programmer performs the round-off trick by ignoring this rounding convention, always rounding down, *and crediting his or her own account with the accumulation error*. Note that for the two accounts above, this error is not $0.001, but $0.011 because the programmer receives four-tenths of a penny from the first account (= $2.534 − $2.53), plus seven-tenths of a penny from the second account (= $7.787 − $7.78). With this system, the programmer will take, on average, a half-cent per account. Thus, the total amount of money that can be stolen in total with this scheme depends upon the number of accounts in the company files and, also, how often these files are updated. A bank with 100,000 accounts, for example, could be expected to generate an accumulation error of $500 *per run*—not bad for a few minutes work of programming! If the bank were to compute interest quarterly, therefore, the total theft would be $2000 per year. If the programmer were lucky enough to work for a savings and loan that compounded interest daily—a common practice today—the yearly net would be approximately $182,500 (= .005 × 100,000 × 365)!

Analysis. The round-off trick is a classic example of the "magic" involved in computer crime. The total interest paid by the bank or savings and loan to each of its customers will differ from the correct amount by at most one penny—a magnitude hardly noticeable to most people today. Moreover, for approximately half of the customers, the interest amount for any given payment period will be exactly correct because a round-off in the downward direction would follow proper convention.

The "magic" part of the round-off trick occurs in the distribution of the accumulation error. This amount will be credited to the account of the dishonest programmer. In effect, therefore, the programmer collects the odd "round-up" pennies which should by rights be credited to the individual accounts that generated them.

The round-off trick can also be used by programmers working for other types of organizations besides banks or savings and loan institutions. An insurance company or any company which issues bonds and is thus responsible for periodic interest payments is a likely target of this scheme. Banks, however, have been a particularly popular target inasmuch as there is a high concentration of wealth, the data processing is performed often, and almost all banks today use computerized methods to service their accounts. Variations of the rounding trick include the embezzlement of interest only on inactive accounts, manipulations of pension-fund interest, and the transient theft of large sums of money just long enough to credit another account with interest payments.

Partial safeguards for the control of manipulations involving interest payments would include the following:

1. Require authorization for program changes. Once a computer program has been written and approved for use, any subsequent changes in that program should require authorization from the programmer's supervisor. A programmer should not have the authority to make program changes unilaterally, and authorized changes should be scrutinized wherever possible. Use of "canned programs" to perform routine data processing also helps because such programs are often maintained by an independent vendor and, in

any event, can always be checked against an original copy to assure their integrity.

2. Separate personnel duties. A programmer should not be permitted to perform the functions of an operator. Thus, for a programmer to write a fictitious program and execute it when such a control was in force would require the collusion of two or more people. Of course, separation of duties cannot assure processing integrity, but it is a useful control nonetheless because collusion requires twice as much dishonesty as when the programmer and computer operator each work alone.

3. Perform complete audits of personnel accounts. With limited resources, auditors rarely scrutinize every account in an accounting information system. However, although a random sample of customer accounts may be sufficient for some purposes, a 100 percent sample of the accounts of employees may be performed if desired. Most bank auditors do this as a matter of course. Also, whenever possible, the audit should be performed on a surprise basis in order to observe data processing during a typical operation cycle.

4. Audit the data processing results. A random sample of accounts should be taken and the data-processing results from the computer run(s) should be compared against manually-prepared results. The computer program(s) can also be audited using methods described in the following chapter.

5. Know your employees. Employees who are in financial trouble, employees who are not challenged by their jobs, and employees who are disgruntled are those most likely to manipulate programs to their own advantage.

6. Perform statistical tests of round-off error. In this case, the proper test would be a "runs test." During normal processing, a random mix of "round-ups" and "round-downs" could be expected, just as a random mix of heads and tails would be

expected when tossing a fair coin. The runs test looks at the number of successive "round-ups" and "round-downs" which occur sequentially. An excessive number of runs in either direction would signal the need for closer observation.

The Equity Funding Case

As the largest scandal involving computer fraud ever recorded, the Equity Funding Case has become the landmark case of computer crime. The fraud itself was uncovered in April 1973, although various illegal activities had been going on for years prior to this date. The total sum of the losses resulting from these activities was enormous. As noted earlier, minimal direct losses to the company have been fixed at approximately $200 million, although figures as high as $2 billion have been quoted if such indirect losses as legal expenses and common stock price declines are included in the total.

Ironically, there is substantial controversy over the question of whether or not the Equity Funding Case is a computer crime. On the one hand we have the Bankruptcy Report of Mr. Robert M. Loeffler, the Trustee, which stated:

Least of all was this a modern "computer" fraud. The computer did not even contain complete records for EFCA's (Equity Funding Corporation of America's) legitimate business—let alone the fraud. For example, the critical records for the company's legitimate funding business were kept on microfiche, and were dealt with entirely by hand. The only record for funding business kept on the computer was an inventory of funding accounts. Entries to book fictitious income were made by manual additions to the books and records in total disregard of the company's computer printouts. . . . Hence, while the computer may have generated a paper "screen" for some aspects of the fraud, in fact the role it played was no bigger and more complicated than that played by the company's adding machines.*

On the other hand, we have the statement of Gleeson Payne, the California State Insurance Commissioner:

This massive fraud was peculiarly a crime of the computer. The computer was the key to the fraud. I would certainly call it a computer fraud. Under the old, hard copy methods of keeping insurance records you . . . couldn't build up bogus records in this kind of volume or in this kind of time. The insurance industry assumed computers were always accurate; computer fraud wasn't expected. Equity was the most advanced in use of computers. Few file cabinets or physical records were found. The computer was the key to the fraud. Auditors have computer programs, but Equity had a secret code which made the computer reveal only real insurance policies. We had a situation in which technology surprised and surpassed our examination system. We do not have a program to audit computers, nor do departments in other states. It is something that must be developed. Our examiners are not equipped to check out a computer run and find out if it is authentic.†

The facts pertinent to our study of Equity Funding begin in 1959 when the Equity Funding Corporation of America was formed for the purpose of selling insurance, mutual funds, and special "funding programs" (described below), which combined features of both mutual-fund and insurance investments. From the start, the major emphasis in the company was an aggressive sales program and the acquisition of other, similar companies—principally through the exchange of common stock. The price of EFCA's shares of common stock thus became very important because higher stock prices placed the company's management in a better position to make favorable deals through acquisitions and mergers. Thus, Equity Funding placed a very strong emphasis on internal company growth. The higher the company's earnings, the more favorably investors viewed the company, and therefore the higher the stock price was bid on the open (stock) market.

Much of the company's hopes for sustained internal growth rested upon its sales of the aforementioned "funding programs." These programs worked as follows. The participant signed up for a ten-year program. The individual purchased shares of selected mutual funds which

---

*See Donn B. Parker, *Crime by Computer* (New York: Charles Scribner's Sons, 1976), pp. 118–174, or Lee J. Seidler, et al., *Ibid*.

†Donn B. Parker, *op. cit.*, p. 119.

were then pledged as collateral for a loan from Equity Funding Corporation. The money from this loan was then applied to the purchase of term life insurance. After the ten-year period, the term insurance expired, and the participant could either renew the program or "cash out." To cash out, the participant either paid off the loan from EFCA directly with cash, or simply sold off a sufficient number of mutual fund shares to cover the insurance costs.

The objective of the funding programs was to take advantage of expected appreciation of the mutual fund shares of stock while at the same time maintaining bona fide life insurance. In this sense, the investor was "to have his cake and eat it too!" Ideally, the appreciation in the mutual fund shares would be high enough to cover (1) interest on the loan made against these shares, (2) the management fees charged against the various transactions involved, and (3) even the term insurance costs. Thus, the investor got "free insurance" and had the potential to make substantial capital gains if the price of the mutual fund shares soared high enough.

The funding programs were of considerable advantage to Equity Funding as well. Although Equity Funding's marketing scheme was not new, the plan had great appeal to investors during the early years when it was marketed and initial sales were high. In addition, the company received commissions on both the mutual fund and life insurance activities of the business. Thus, an investor who bought into a funding program generated a double sale for Equity Funding.

The key to the success of the funding programs was a rising stock market. To the disappointment of the management of EFCA, however, the stock market failed to increase appreciably over the last few years of the first program. The company compounded the problem by writing funding programs without careful attention to their profitability. An overemphasis on sales and an underemphasis on administrative detail caused earnings to suffer and this in turn threatened the acquisition program of the company.

To bolster profits, EFCA management turned to recording commissions on nonexistent loans taken out against fictitious mutual fund programs. This "first phase" of the fraud, identified as the "inflated earnings phase," went on until 1967, and is said to have generated in total over $85 million in bogus earnings. The problem with the system, in addition to the work required to cover up the fraud, was that it necessitated the generation of fictitious funding programs. Each dollar in commission supposedly had been generated from an individual participant in the program. As years went by, it became increasingly difficult to account for these nonexistent programs.

The first phase of the EFCA scandal was definitively noncomputer in nature. The accounting entries perpetuating the hoax were all performed manually, and little effort was made to provide underlying documentation. As the company's cash needs continued to grow, however, EFCA management turned to a second, "foreign phase" of fraud. Within this phase, the company set up a series of offshore subsidiaries whose primary purpose appears to have been nothing more than to act as bogus assets for the parent organization. Through a series of complicated transactions, EFCA's accountants played a complex "shell game" with these subsidiaries, in which assets were double, triple, and even quadruple counted by cleverly transferring them back and forth between the subsidiary companies. At times, EFCA management even went so far as to record the transference of funds from one company to another without recording offsetting amounts to other accounts.

When even these efforts proved to be insufficient, the company turned to a third, "insurance phase" of its fraud. In concept, the scheme was simplicity itself. The company merely sold some of its own fictitious insurance policies from its phase-one activities to other insurance companies! In order to sell something for nothing, however, the company resorted to the perfectly legal practice of "coinsurance." Under this arrangement, the issuing, or primary, insurance company sells a block of insurance policies to a second company called a "coinsurer." The primary company maintains physical control of the actual policies (fortunately for EFCA), and continues to perform the routine data processing.

The coinsurer rarely even sees its policies, and is often simply sent a letter identifying the serial numbers of the policy holders. However, the coinsurer commonly would pay 180 to 190 percent of the first-year premiums for its role in the coinsurance agreement.

The practice of coinsurance is not unknown. It represents a sale to the primary company, which may need cash for other purposes, and an investment to the purchasing company, which may have extra cash and be interested in buying insurance policies from other companies. In the case of Equity Funding and its insurance subsidiary, Equity Funding Life Insurance Company (EFLIC), however, the practice proved to be its downfall. The reason becomes clear when the mechanics of the agreement are understood. EFLIC collected sums equal to 180 or 190 percent of the first year's insurance premiums on the "policies" it had sold its coinsurers. EFLIC, however, was required to forward to these coinsurers the insurance premiums paid by the policy holders. Thus, in the first year of a given sale, the company had to give back nearly $1 for every $2 of its coinsurance business. In subsequent years, as for the first year, EFLIC was expected to forward policy premiums to its coinsurance partners. Because the policies were fictitious in the first place, *there were no premiums*! Thus, the only way the company could stay ahead of the game was to sell yet more bogus policies to coinsurance buyers. This practice had a pyramiding effect and by 1972, the company had incurred $1.7 million in losses associated with its bogus coinsurance transactions. By this time, however, the company was in too deep to quit and the fraud fed upon itself. By April 1973, when the fraud was discovered, nearly two-thirds of the company's 97,000 insurance policies—over 64,000 of them—were phonies!

Analysis. The obvious question that comes to mind when reading about such scandals is: "How did the company ever manage to hide over 64,000 fictitious insurance policies from its auditors?" This is where the computer enters the narrative. All of the company's insurance policies were maintained on magnetic tape files,

and little documentation of any kind was maintained. As noted in the State Insurance Commissioner's report, bogus policies were systematically assigned special policy numbers, and the computer programs used to process the insurance files were simply instructed to ignore these bogus policies.

Occasionally, of course, coinsurance companies would ask for information concerning their policies. Sometimes, Equity Funding would supply the requestor with a list of random digits designed to look like account numbers. Most of the time, however, this was not necessary because the perpetrators at EFLIC had been clever enough to program an occasional death of a fictitious policy holder so as to avoid arousing suspicion. However, when coinsurers asked for a printout of the names and addresses of their policy holders, selected personnel at EFLIC would use a special program to generate the fictitious accounts and randomly use the names of conspirators and friends over and over until the required number of policy holders had been printed.

External auditors for the company were similarly duped. In the early years, the auditors were treated lavishly during their visits and were often entertained in the plush executive suites of the company's fabulous Century City office building in downtown Los Angeles. When the auditors requested the EFCA people to provide them with a sample of insurance policies for checking purposes, the EDP personnel of course made sure that all of the policy numbers in the "random sample" were legitimate policy holders. When the auditors chose their own sample of policy holders for auditing purposes and asked to see hard-copy documents (e.g., insurance policy application forms), however, the auditors were told that those particular documents were being used by another department and would be provided the next morning. The company management team would then stay up at all-night "fraud parties," hand-writing the requested hard-copy documentation.

It is speculative as to how long Equity Funding could have continued its hoax. Certainly, the company had been able to play its hand well beyond the time that an effectively performed audit could have detected the situation as fraud. Thus, it is not surprising to learn that the Equity Funding fraud was not discovered by an audit at all, but rather by a tip from a former EFLIC employee named Ronald Secrist. Secrist's employment had been terminated by the company on March 15, 1973 in an effort to cut payroll costs. On March 7, 1973, just prior to his departure and perhaps in retaliation, he telephoned the New York State Insurance Department and revealed what he knew. Examiners from their Illinois Insurance Department (which shared regulatory responsibility for EFLIC with California) were notified and descended upon Equity Funding shortly thereafter. In a meticulous audit, and acting with the information supplied by Secrist, the hoax was discovered. For EFCA, the jig was up. The world soon learned about the biggest "computer" fraud ever uncovered.

An additional question that might be raised in connection with the fraud is: "How could that many employees at Equity Funding be dishonest?" One answer is that not everyone at the company appears to have been "in" on the fraud. The EDP department maintained two computers: an IBM 360 (later upgraded to an IBM 370) which did most of the routine data processing, and a smaller IBM System/3 which was used principally by EFLIC's actuarial group. Controls within the EDP department were extremely lax. For example, the company maintained an open library, and almost all of the company's master files were set on open racks, available for anyone to borrow, use, and, as it turned out, alter. Similarly, the machine room was run as an *open shop*. Incredibly, any of the employees working for any one of Equity's 100 companies could therefore walk into the machine room at any time to run their own programs on the computer.

EDP requests to tighten up on controls were routinely ignored by top management. Moreover, the actuarial group at the company made frequent use of the insurance policy master tapes, and, as time went on, began to insert fictitious policy records in the master tape. EDP personnel were told that such records were for

"simulation purposes" and they were instructed to ignore these records in legitimate processing runs. At other times, the EDP personnel themselves were requested to insert new policies in the master file. Frank Hyman, manager of the MIS system, reported that, in a typical input run, he often saw that as many as 600 new policies were specially coded because they had been sold at a group rate to a union or some other special organization and required special identification. Only later, when the true use of these records came to light, did many of the programmers and EDP managers with the company realize what had happened.

The TRW Company Credit Data Case

There is a tendency to view the typical computer crime as a situation in which a perpetrator compromises the computer system in order to gain access to a company's physical assets—especially the cash in the company's bank account or the company's inventories stored in the warehouse. A major class of computer crime, however, merely involves illegal access to the information stored within the computer system because such information is valuable in and of itself.

"Valuable-information computer crime" is well-known. In some cases, the information involved is simply a company's computer programs because such software (1) is proprietary (i.e., owned by an independent developer and leased to users), (2) may give the firm a competitive advantage in its industry, and (3) is often worth as much as the company's hardware in terms of development and replacement costs. Thus, several cases of corporate computer espionage involving the theft, or attempted theft, of key programs have been reported in the literature. Because of the difficulty of collecting proof of such espionage when remote terminals are involved, there is every indication that a substantial number of additional cases have gone unreported.

In other situations, the valuable information involved in computer crime has been a company's processing files—information which would be of little value to an outsider, but which is vital to the normal functioning of the company that owns the files. In 1977, for example, one disgruntled EDP employee working for a Netherlands company decided to exploit this fact in retaliation for the organization's failure to promote him. In January of that year, Rodney Cox "kidnapped" both his company's financial tape and disk files, and their backup copies—a total of 594 tapes and 48 disks in all—and held them for over $500,000 ransom. (He was eventually caught by Scotland Yard investigators when his accomplice attempted to pick up the money.)

In the case of TRW, the valuable information was the company's computerized credit data. TRW is the largest credit-rating company in the United States. In 1976, when the fraud was discovered, the company was collecting and disseminating credit information on approximately 50 million individuals. To handle its processing, the company used two IBM 370/158 computers, one IBM 370/155 computer, 380 Datapoint terminals, 2000 teleprinters, and 100 Raytheon CRT terminals. Clients of the company included banks, retail stores, and such credit-conscious concerns as Diner's Club, American Express, Master Charge, Bank Americard, Sears Roebuck, and several leasing establishments.

TRW advised its clients of bad credit risks on the basis of information maintained in its data files. Clearly, however, this file information could be changed. The fraud began when six company employees, including a key TRW clerk in the consumer-relations department, realized this fact and decided that they could sell "good" credit ratings for cash to individuals with bad credit ratings logged in their computer records. The names and addresses of the bad credit risks were already on file—it merely remained to contact these individuals and inform them of a new-found method of altering their records. Accordingly, individuals with bad credit ratings were approached by the TRW employees and offered a "clean bill of health" in return for a management fee.

Those people who decided to buy paid TRW employees "under the table," and the clerk in the consumer-relations department would then input whatever false information was required to reverse the buyer's bad credit rating. In some cases, this required the deletion of unfavorable information already stored in the individual's credit record; in other cases, it required the addition of favorable information. Fees for such services varied from a few hundred dollars to $1500 per individual. Ironically, the TRW clerk who ultimately input the false information to the computer system received only $50 for each altered record. However, the losses resulting from these activities were not so inconsequential. Independent estimates placed this figure close to $1 million.

The principal victims of the fraud were TRW's clients, who acted on credit information that ultimately turned out to be fraudulent. Exactly how many file records were actually altered is difficult to say. Lawyers for the prosecution had documented 16 known cases, but there was reason to believe the number was in excess of 100. Paradoxically, the prosecution had difficulty in acquiring testimonies because the buyers as well as the TRW sellers were technically in violation of the law by conspiring to falsify credit-rating information.

Officials at TRW played down the whole case as a local matter which involved the Federal Trade Commission (FTC) only because of the type of crime involved. A TRW spokesman stated, for example, " . . . this is a nonpublic investigation and we believe it should remain nonpublic as it was intended to be. To us, it's not unusual to have the FTC conducting this type of investigation. It is chartered to enforce the Fair Credit Reporting Act, and it's just doing business as normal as far as we are concerned." The fact that a serious abuse of TRW's file information had occurred gives us pause to wonder, however. How safe is our credit information, especially in the hands of a private, and to a large extent, unregulated, profit-seeking company?

Analysis. There are two key issues here: (1) the propriety of the input information used in updating a specific accounting information system, and (2) the protection afforded both consumer and user in the accuracy and use of credit informa-

277

tion gathered by a private company. With regard to the first point, it is clear that the fraud was successful only because the perpetrators had been able to enter false information to the computerized system. This observation once again points to the importance of controls—for example, the presence of hard-copy validation of credit changes—in order to safeguard the accuracy and completeness of file information. In light of what had already been discovered, the statement of the TRW spokesman about the FTC's investigation carries a note of irony:

We don't believe the investigation is going to lead to any significant results. As far as we're concerned, we're in full compliance with the law. Our measures and our standards have been the highest in the industry. . . . We've always gone beyond the letter of the law in operating policies and procedures.*

The opinion of the prosecuting attorney contrasts sharply with that of the TRW spokesman. He suggested that the entire operation did "not take a great deal of intelligence" and only proved that there are weaknesses in any system. Thus, one is led to the conclusion that "the highest standards in the industry" were insufficient to catch an "unintelligent" fraud. One thing is certain. At the time that the fraud was perpetrated, the security measures of the company were inadequate to control the crime. In fact, as is true of so many cases of computer crime, the six employees involved in the case were caught only by luck: an individual who had been approached with an offer to buy a good credit rating for $600 became angry and called the FBI. Later, the TRW clerk in the consumer relations department decided to turn state's evidence.

The second point involving the protection of the consumer and user of credit information encompasses a much larger issue. In 1970, Congress passed the Fair Credit Reporting Act, which requires that an individual be informed

why he or she is denied credit.† The consumer also has the right to contest the information maintained by the credit-rating company although there is clearly a vast difference between the right to challenge, and the right to change, credit information. TRW reported that since the Fair Credit Reporting Act had gone into effect, consumer inquiries had increased a hundredfold and that at the time the fraud was detected, approximately 200,000 consumers annually were complaining about their credit ratings. The fact that, by TRW's own admission, fully one-third of these inquiries resulted in a file change or update is unsettling. Moreover, how much more information collected by TRW is inaccurate but is simply not being challenged—either because the inaccuracy is not communicated to the individual involved, or because the consumer does not know he or she has recourse through the law—is unknown.

In the United States today, the vast majority of "big-ticket" items such as cars, appliances, stereo equipment and, of course, homes, are purchased on credit. In 1979, there were 100 million outstanding credit cards in the United States. A bad credit rating severely limits the options of the consumer and adversely affects the individual's quality of life. That this quality of life can be damaged so readily by the information on less than 2 inches of magnetic tape is a chilling thought.

Roswell Stephens and the Union Dime Savings Bank Case

Banks are obvious targets of computer fraud and embezzlement because they are prime holders of liquid assets, and also because the banking industry was one of the first to automate its operations. At present, the American banking system processes over 30 billion checks each year, and the cost to clear these checks is in excess of $10 billion. As noted in Chapter 4, banks depend heavily upon the industry's standard MICR code

---

*Molly Upton and E. Drake Lundell, Jr., "Six Charged with Altering TRW Credit Data Files as FBI Breaks L.A. Ring," *Computerworld*, Volume X, No. 37 (September 13, 1976), p. 4.

†See Consumer Credit Protection Act, Section 601, Title 6 of Public Law 91-508, "Federal Deposit Insurance Act," October 26, 1970.

and automated check-processing equipment to keep processing costs low. The potential to eliminate much of the present check writing with the use of Electronic Funds Transfer Systems (EFTS)—which would simply hook up the nation's business computers and automatically record increases or decreases to individual checking accounts—would move us closer to a "cashless" society, but would not lessen our dependency upon the computer to keep track of our check-writing activities. In any case, the potential for computer crime within the banking industry's electronic environment is high and this potential, together with other banking industry factors mentioned earlier in the chapter, have conspired to yield a rich and growing literature of computer abuse in the banking world.

One of the most famous cases of computer bank fraud involved Roswell Stephens, a bank supervisor with the Union Dime Savings Bank in New York City. Heavyset, balding, and the father of two daughters, Roswell was well-liked and was earning a respectable salary in the job which he had held for 9 years. But at 41 years of age, and unbeknownst to all but his bookies, Roswell had a serious gambling problem which was financially destroying him. Thus, after trying to moonlight as a taxi driver at night and finding himself shot at twice, he decided to pursue a "safer" activity and steal from his bank.

The keys to Stephens' embezzlement were his unique position as new-teller trainer, his vast experience in the banking profession, his intimate knowledge of his bank's operating procedures, and his ability to "override" account information in his bank's computer system simply by inputting "corrective" data through his personal terminal. Stephens' position as teller supervisor enabled him to blame obvious discrepancies in customer statements on his new trainees, whereas the additional points listed above enabled him to cover up his other embezzlements. For example, Roswell would take several thousand dollars from his cash drawer and enter a fictitious withdrawal transaction into the computer system to justify the reduction in the account's balance. At the end of the quarter, both

the depositor's balance plus the depositor's interest would be incorrect. The depositor would be mailed a statement from the bank. If the depositor failed to complain, Roswell did nothing. If the depositor did complain, Roswell would blame the problem on an error committed by one of his trainees, pretend to find the discrepancy, and enter a correction—which did little more than steal from another account—through his supervisor's terminal.

Stephens also used a number of other tricks to steal from his bank and support his gambling habit. In one gambit, he would take a valid deposit from a customer, properly credit the customer's account, and then later reverse the transaction and withdraw most, if not all, of the deposit through his terminal for his own use. In another, he would embezzle from the bank by failing to deposit the money customers wished to invest in long-term certificates of deposit. In this latter situation, Stephens would prepare the necessary paperwork for the customer, and the customer would believe that all the necessary steps had been taken to make the deposit. But all this was just for appearance. Stephens would prepare no input for the computer about the transaction, and thus, the bank would have no record of the deposit. Stephens would thus have two years (at a minimum) to "make good" on the money.

Perhaps one of the most interesting ways in which Stephens stole from his bank was through the manipulation of new savings accounts. When a customer wished to open a new passbook account, Stephens would secretly take two new passbooks from the bank vault. The customer would be given the first of these passbooks, with all the prerequisite information clearly showing, but Stephens would carefully enter the transaction under the account number of the second passbook, which he kept for himself. The new deposit would therefore be entered under a different account number than that assigned the customer. Later, at his leisure, Stephens could withdraw all the money from the second account, destroy the corresponding passbook, and eliminate almost all traces of the "switch." Stephens was able to get away with this particular fraud for quite a while because the bank did not appear to keep records of the shiny new passbooks stored in its vaults.

Banks perform numerous tests, counts, and audits to assure processing accuracy and control financial resources, but Stephens, with his superior knowledge of the banking profession in general, and his intimate knowledge of the controls of his own bank in particular, was able to avoid every last one of them. One of the controls of special importance involved the crediting of interest. Because Stephens had withdrawn a great deal of money from selected accounts, the principal balances, and therefore the interest computations, would not match the amounts expected by the bank or anticipated by the bank's customers.

Stephens used several methods to solve his problem. Under one method, for example, he would use his terminal to transfer funds from certain accounts to others to create the appearance of an interest payment when, in fact, the transfer actually involved principal balances. In another method, he would enter interest payments through his terminal, later reversing these transactions after the desired effect had been accomplished. Finally, for those instances in which customers would bring their passbooks into the bank, Stephens would manually enter a fictitious interest payment to the passbook in a hand that shook so much the bank's customers began to fear for the man's health. Of course, the manual entry had absolutely no relationship to the customer's computer-controlled balance, which was unaffected.

The last, particularly effective, ploy that Stephens used to avoid interest-computation scrutiny was to exploit the fact that at the Union Dime Savings Bank, interest payments for passbook accounts were computed on the last day of each quarter of the year, whereas time-deposit account interest was computed two days *after* the last day of the quarter. Stephens would bring the passbook accounts up to their appropriate levels in time for the interest computations, and then, in the two-day lag period, quickly transfer funds from the passbook accounts to the time-deposit accounts in time to receive the proper interest on these latter accounts. In effect, therefore, Stephens was shifting funds through accounts rapidly enough to make his bank pay double interest on the same dollars. In reality, those dollars were long gone at the race track!

Stephens was also able to avoid the scrutiny of the auditors. Normally, the bank auditors always gave him advance notice of their arrival and much of his embezzlement could therefore be covered up in time to avoid detection. He claims that he could almost predict what the auditors were going to do at each moment. In addition, small discrepancies could easily be blamed upon the mistakes of inexperienced tellers who were training under Stephens' supervision. In one fascinating close call, however, an auditor was about to discover a $20,000 shortage in one of Stephens' two cash boxes. Through a stroke of good luck and what had to be a very dextrous sleight of hand, however, Stephens removed the $20,000 which had already been counted from the first cash box, and placed it in the second cash box just in time for the auditor to count it again!

The thing that Stephens could not avoid was discovery through audit confirmation. In such instances, the auditing team selects a random sample of depositors and mails letters of inquiry to the customers requesting a confirmation of their account balances. Because the total number of accounts Stephens was manipulating was relatively small (approximately 50 at any one time), Stephens was lucky enough to avoid detection during the 3½ years that he practiced his deception.

Analysis. Given the background of the foregoing computer cases, it should come as no surprise to learn that Stephens was not caught through banking controls. Rather, his luck ran out when the police raided his bookie and discovered that a bank teller earning $11,000 a year had been placing weekly bets of $30,000! The Union Dime Savings Bank was alerted and a full-scale inquiry was secretly put into effect. Putting "two and two together" and using a massive audit, the bank came up $1.4 million short!

As the largest known bank fraud of its time, the Roswell Stephens Union Dime Savings Bank case has attracted considerable attention. Learning from the incident, the banking industry in general has installed tighter controls which will undoubtedly go far to avoid a repetition of the crimes so successfully executed by Roswell Stephens. (At least this is certainly true for the Union Dime Savings Bank.) Perhaps the easiest control which the Union Dime Savings Bank failed to enforce was the two-week vacation rule. The kinds of activities in which Stephens was engaged required almost constant attention. It is therefore very unlikely that the crime would have gone undetected during his two-week absence when another bank employee would have performed Stephens' job functions. Luckily for Stephens, however, the required vacation rule was never enforced at the Dime and he was able to concentrate on his customer account manipulations undisturbed.

A major area which the bank failed to pursue adequately was the unusually large number of discrepancies that appeared in customer account balances at Stephens' branch bank. A comparison of trainee teller "errors" at this bank with the average number of mistakes at other bank branches surely would have revealed an unusual situation worthy of further investigation. When even routine teller activity would disclose discrepancies in passbook entries as compared with the computer listings, grounds for suspicion become clear. Such discrepancies should have been reported to special investigatory authorities (such as the bank's internal auditors). Requiring that any substantial account balance correction be made with the approval of two responsible individuals, instead of concentrating such authority in the hands of only a single, hard-pressed supervisor, would be an added control. A similar statement regarding joint supervision might be made when accounts were opened and also when accounts were closed, especially for those accounts involving substantial amounts of money.

Random checks of account closings, for example, using a confirmation letter, would have been beneficial. Some banks also mail a "welcome-aboard" letter to new depositors which thanks the customer for his or her patronage and, incidentally, verifies the depositor's account balance. Special letters of inquiry can also be made when suspicious correction transactions are observed in the processing flow.

Lax audit procedures must also be mentioned as a possible reason why Stephens' embezzlement went undetected for so long. As noted in Chapter 8 on computer controls, the surprise audit is a most effective method by which to detect fraud, and, perhaps, serves as a deterrent to its beginnings. Procedure is also important. The auditors were careless when counting Stephens' two cash boxes, enabling him to conceal a $20,000 cash shortage. The auditors should have taken control of both cash boxes simultaneously prior to beginning their count. This procedure would have prevented Stephens from transferring $20,000 from the first cash box to the second cash box after the former box had been counted. Moreover, the bank audit should be thorough and uncompromising, and the validity of all transactions examined should be proven with hard-copy evidence of legitimacy. Close scrutiny of unusual activity in dormant accounts, less-than-active accounts, and time-deposit accounts is especially important because these types of accounts are common targets for computer crime. The advantages of larger samples for audit confirmation are also clear.

The question of whether the computer can be programmed to detect computer crime arises at this point and raises an interesting issue. As noted in the previous chapter, the computer can easily be programmed to test for valid and consistent data, and also to perform certain cross-checking and cross-footing activities to assure processing accuracy. In the present case, however, the input data easily passed all of these tests because the perpetrator was clever enough to construct "good" transaction data initially. The computer can still serve as an aid to fraud control, however, by programming it to perform analyses of funds-transfer transactions, activity-reversal transactions, and other special correction transactions. A pattern of increasing activity in these types of transactions may signal possible problems, and thereby prompt management to take a closer look at probable causes. Thus, the management-by-exception principal may be utilized in such situations.

Jerry Schneider and the Pacific Telephone Company

Our last case deals with the embezzlement of a corporation's inventory of equipment which was accomplished through the manipulation of the company's computer records. Embezzlement is usually perpetrated by an employee within a company because of the detailed knowledge of the computer system required to complete the crime successfully. In the unusual case of the Pacific Telephone Company, however, the computer was not only duped by an outsider, but by a high school student to boot!

Our case begins with Jerry Neal Schneider who, in 1968, was going to a Los Angeles High School and whose walk home from school led him past the back office of the Pacific Telephone and Telegraph Company. The trash cans were always filled with interesting manuals, pamphlets, and memos concerning corporate activity, and on several occasions they contained complete, unopened sets of operating instructions for inventory procurement and storage. Helping himself to these manuals, Jerry proceeded to build a complete library of inventory guides which he eagerly read and decided to use for his own purposes. By 1971, so the story goes, Jerry knew more about the phone company and its supplier, Western Electric, than any other person in either company.

To put his plan into action, Jerry formed his own company, ironically named "Creative Systems Enterprises," rented a 4000 square foot warehouse in West Los Angeles, and for $50 convinced a friend working for the Pacific Telephone Company to sell him a pass key to the phone company's warehouse gates. Then, in a stroke of genius, Jerry went to a telephone company auction and bought a Pacific Telephone Company truck with the company's emblems still painted on the truck's sides. Finally, Jerry bought a touch-tone telephone with which he could order telephone equipment parts by dialing into the company's online equipment-ordering system. Obtaining the identification number and account number of the ordering sites by posing as a supply attendant, Jerry was now all set.

In June 1971, Jerry placed his first order for $30,000 worth of equipment. All went smoothly and by 2 A.M. the following morning, the equipment had been transferred from the telephone company's main warehouses to the identified company delivery site where it would await local pick-up. At 5 A.M., Jerry drove his newly-acquired Pacific Telephone Company truck to the delivery gate, used his newly-acquired pass key to open it, loaded the equipment, signed the bill of lading (indicating receipt of the merchandise), and drove off to his own warehouse. Jerry repeated this activity almost daily for the next seven months. Once at the warehouse, Jerry and his 10 employees would repackage some of the merchandise, and simply label other equipment "Released for Resale" with an official-looking rubber stamp. Jerry's customers were amazed at how quickly he could acquire necessary equipment for them!

To beef up the retail end of his business, Jerry advertised in local trade journals and, of course, was bent on providing good service for his regular customers. In fact, over half of Jerry's business was legitimate; he claims that he only used his "special ordering" techniques when he received a rush order from one of his customers.

Business was so good that Jerry began to look for short cuts to lessen his own work time. One way to cut corners on the job was to get the telephone company to deliver equipment for him, and thus save him the trouble of going out to a delivery site for a pick up. Using his knowledge of the telephone company's delivery system, Jerry began to provide instructions with his orders directing the phone company to deliver merchandise to street locations such as construction sites and warehouses. In one bold stroke, Jerry claims, he even directed the telephone company to deliver a $25,000 switchboard to a manhole in a Los Angeles street at 2 A.M.!

Jerry would also keep track of the reorder point for some of the major pieces of equipment stocked in the phone company's inventory. For any given item, this reorder point represented a critical level of inventory—for example, 20 units—below which the phone company would act to replenish its stock. Knowing these critical reorder points, Jerry would request enough of a particular type of equipment to reduce the phone company's inventory level below the critical reorder point. Jerry would subsequently inform the telephone company that he could supply the depleted equipment and save the telephone company the trouble of reordering through its major supplier. The phone company gratefully purchased back its own equipment from Jerry, never realizing that it was acquiring recycled assets that had never left the original cartons! Jerry repeated this gambit often, turning over equipment at a fast pace.

The end came as Jerry's business continued to bloom, but Jerry's own time commitments began to overburden him. He was attending school at night to please his parents, making "moonlight runs" to the telephone company, and supervising his employees as well. His social life began to suffer and he became depressed. To lighten his work load, therefore, Jerry decided to confide in one of his employees and let him in on the fraud. Jerry's intentions were to let this new employee perform the early morning pickups. At first, things worked well, but eventually, the employee indicated that his $300 per week salary was not high enough and that a $40 a week raise was desired. Jerry refused and the employee threatened to go to the telephone company and reveal all. Jerry fired him and two months later, a very angry ex-employee of Jerry's Creative Systems Enterprises walked into the offices of the Pacific Telephone Company and began to tell a remarkable story.

The investigators couldn't believe their ears at first, but after observing Jerry's operations for a month, they had no choice. On January 2, 1972, a group of investigators from the Los Angeles district attorney's office swooped down on Jerry's warehouse and found thousands of dollars of illegal equipment. For Jerry, the jig was up.

In the aftermath, it remained to determine exactly how much equipment Jerry had stolen from the telephone company. For his own protection, Jerry had kept no records, and wherever possible, Jerry had also taken steps to make sure that the telephone company had no records of his activities either. Because, in some cases, the same equipment had been "stolen" over and over again and had simply been recycled, there was some problem in determining an accurate tally of lost equipment. The Los Angeles District Attorney claimed that Jerry had been caught with equipment worth $8,000, and that in total, close to $125,000 worth of equipment had been taken. The telephone company claimed that identifiable losses were between $65,000 and $75,000, but that the total loss was probably closer to $800,000 or $900,000. Jerry claimed that most of his money had been reinvested into his business and that his own "take" from his illegal activities was just a meager salary.

In any event, Jerry was faced with both a criminal suit of grand theft for the equipment actually discovered in the police raid and a $250,000 civil suit instigated by the Pacific Telephone and Telegraph Company. On July 5, 1972, Superior Court Judge George M. Dell found Jerry guilty of the criminal charges and sentenced him to two months in jail and a $500 fine. On November 26, 1974, Jerry also lost the civil suit. Judge Ernest J. Zack found in favor of the telephone company and required Jerry to pay the company approximately $8500, spread out over five years in equal monthly installments of $141.50.

Analysis. Could Jerry's activities have been thwarted with better computer controls? One thing is clear: limiting access to the telephone company's inventory manuals and computer operating instructions, which originated Jerry's illicit activities, would have done much to prevent what ultimately transpired. It would appear in this matter that simply throwing used, but security-threatening, manuals in the company trash was insufficient to prevent their use and that more elaborate safeguards were necessary to dispose of the sensitive information.

Another key aspect of the fraud was Jerry's access to the telephone company's computer system that controlled the organization's inventories of equipment. As noted in the previous chapter, an important security feature for remote terminal computer systems is the utilization, and frequent changing, of codes that limit computer access to bona fide users. The telephone company had in fact been using such codes and Jerry obtained his initial computer-coded access to the system by posing as a telephone company employee. The fact that another telephone company employee had readily given the secret code to him was obviously an important breach of security with, as it turns out, expensive repercussions.

To guard against unwarranted access to computers from remote terminals, some companies will switch access codes from time to time. With such a policy, the theory is that whatever unauthorized access does occur will be limited to the time the stolen code is being used at the data center. Where tight security is important, the access code may be changed daily, although such a situation is both unusual and expensive. During the active period of his fraud, Jerry claims that the telephone company had in fact changed the time-sharing computer access code three times. Every time the code was changed, however, a news notice was automatically sent to all users through their terminals. In effect, therefore, once the individual was "in" the system, the telephone company itself made sure that the user could stay "in." The importance of communicating code changes through alternate media thus becomes clear, although mailing or phoning users would obviously be more expensive than the "automatic" messages prepared via the terminals.

The telephone company also had certain financial controls with which to limit budget overruns. For example, there were quarterly budgets for each equipment site which represented expected dollar cost figures for equipment handled at any particular site. As it turns out, however, budgeted dollar magnitudes were based upon *maximum*, rather than average, inventory usage. For example, if the budget allowance for site "X" were $100,000, then this amount was automatically paid to Pacific Telephone's supplier, Western Electric, as a matter of course. In actuality, the costs of the equipment flowing through any particular site rarely totalled the budgeted amount, and thus, for our hypothetical site X, this amount might have been $75,000. Jerry knew that as long as the actual cost of equipment flowing through the site stayed below the budget allotment, little accounting analysis was performed. Thus, by carefully shifting his delivery sites, Jerry was able to order his equipment in such a way as to avoid budgetary detection from the phone company. For our hypothetical budgetary example, therefore, Jerry would have been free to order up to $25,000 worth of equipment from the telephone company without attracting attention to his ordering activities.

It is difficult to know if such a crime could ever happen again. Certainly, the odds are slim for a reoccurrence at the Pacific Telephone and Telegraph Company. However, the potential for computer crime in the area of inventory management remains high. Moreover, it seems certain that computer controls will be unable, in and of themselves, to prevent such crime. The need for individuals to read carefully the output listings of inventory-control programs and the necessity for strict employee adherence to security regulations are of equal importance.

There is an interesting postscript to the Jerry Schneider case. When the crime was originally discovered, it was given wide coverage by the media and the newspaper headlines sensationalized the fraud. Upon his release from jail, therefore, Jerry was able to capitalize upon his new-found notoriety and become a management consultant specializing in the computer security area. Today, he is still regarded as one of the leading experts in this area.

A PROFILE OF THE COMPUTER CRIMINAL

There is a school of thought on accounting controls which holds that an accounting information system is only as effective as the people who use the system. Under such a theory, understanding the criminal mind is just as important a step in thwarting computer crime as are the ''mechanical'' computer controls which help deter unauthorized use of accounting information. As a step toward avoiding given types of crimes, criminologists often look for common characteristics in individuals who have committed certain illegal acts as a way of detecting patterns of action or behavior which may identify the problem individual before a crime occurs. A set of such characteristics is called a *profile*. Of course, it is not always possible to construct a profile for a given type of crime. In the case of computer crime, however, there appears to be a remarkable number of similarities among the individuals who have been caught using a computer illegally. A few of these characteristic features of the computer criminal are examined briefly below.

Superior Backgrounds

According to Donn Parker, an expert in the field of computer crime, the best way to identify the potential population of perpetrators is on the basis of the unique skills, knowledge, and experience possessed by the people engaged in computer technology.* Computer criminals tend to be bright, talented, qualified individuals with good intellects and superior educational backgrounds. Ironically, it is usually these very qualifications that enable such individuals to acquire jobs as data-processing employees in the first place. It is obvious, however, that a data-processing employee must be smart enough not only to understand the company computer system but also to recognize its limitations if he or she is going to be able to commit a crime. Thus, high technical qualifications would have to be considered an important characteristic of the computer criminal.

A second fact of possible relevance in the detection of potential computer abusers is the fact that almost all computer criminals are males

*Donn B. Parker, *Crime by Computer* (New York, Charles Scribner's Sons, 1976), p. 45.

under 30 years of age. For example, Jerry Schneider was only 19 years old when he began his operations, although this young an age is unusual even in computer crime. Since a number of computer crime cases involve students, there is undoubtedly some bias in any computation of an average age of the computer criminal. However, the fact that data processing as we know it today is less than 30 years old, and the fact that the special skills required of today's data-processing personnel have only recently been taught in colleges and universities may help to explain the youthfulness of the computer-oriented perpetrator. The fact that young people are often in greater need of money and are often more willing to take a risk may contribute to these reasons.

Morals

The tenet that ''a thief has no morals'' does not seem to hold in the area of computer crime. Most computer criminals consider themselves to be relatively honest people who simply steal with a computer what other employees steal from the filing cabinet. Many perpetrators actually view themselves as long-term borrowers rather than thieves, and several have exercised great care to avoid harming individuals when performing their illegal activities. Alternately, the belief that computer theft involves an impersonal company or ''system'' rather than another individual is often expressed by computer criminals when apprehended, and a large number of these criminals simply claim to be ''victims of fate.''

The element of challenge involved in beating the system is often presented as a rationale for computer abuse. Such an attitude tends to remove the ''crime'' stigma from illegal computer activities, and casts computer abuse more in the role of game-playing rather than a violation of moral conduct. Such an attitude, for example, would probably explain a vast proportion of the student abuse of computer time at colleges and universities. A number of commercial cases of computer abuse also seem to be best explained by this thinking process.

The fact that certain illegal practices are common in the data-processing industry has also

285

been used as a rationale for computer abuse. Thus, tampering with an important bank-processing program might be in technical violation of the law, yet such tampering occurs quite frequently in order to meet computer-implementation deadlines imposed by management. Alternatively, at the civil trial of Fred Darm, who stole a computer program from the computer memory of a rival firm through the use of a remote terminal, the point was made that it was common practice for the programmers of rival firms to "snoop" each other's data files in order to obtain competitive information. Thus, when Fred Darm was apprehended for his offense, not only was he surprised—he was quite offended!

The overwhelming conclusion drawn from such considerations of morality in computer criminals is that the "average" perpetrator tends to be ordinary in his beliefs but unlucky in his position. Thus, the real distinguishing feature of the criminals is that they find themselves in the unfortunate situation of believing that the assets controlled by the computer are within their grasp, and that these assets are available—at least temporarily—for their own use.

Noncriminal Background

The question of criminal background in computer abuse becomes important because of the fear that such abuse may be linked to organized crime. In studies conducted to date, however, very little connection has been shown, although an absence of proof does not necessarily imply an absence of organized crime in the computer field. Obtaining proof is difficult. In one case, for example, a computer perpetrator agreed to turn state's evidence to implicate his underworld brethren, but was gunned down on a street in New York before he could testify.

According to the experts, almost all computer criminals are amateur, first-time offenders rather than professional criminals. Few individuals who have been caught stealing with the aid of a computer have been proud of their activities or considered their embezzlement to be their principal work. Thus, very few of the individuals ap-

prehended for suspicion of computer crimes have a previous criminal record. In a study of 374 cases of computer crime committed prior to 1976, for example, only one case involved an ex-convict. At the time this book went to press, the only additional case involving previously convicted criminals and with which the authors are familiar concerned prisoners at Leavenworth Penitentiary in Kansas. In this fascinating crime, the prisoners learned how to file fraudulent, but acceptable, claims on their federal income tax returns (which even prisoners have to file), thus enabling them to obtain huge bogus refunds. One prisoner was finally caught with a government check for $20,000. (Back to making license plates!)

The identification of the computer criminal as a first-time offender has important implications for EDP control. Screening individuals on the basis of an existing criminal record is insufficient, for example, to avoid computer crime. The stability of the applicant may offer clues as to future behavior, however. The historical record suggests that employee disgruntlement is almost always present in the environment of the computer criminal. Causes vary but the fact remains that an unhappy employee is a very dangerous threat to a vulnerable accounting information system.

Environment

The computer criminal must have an opportunity to commit his or her crime. Thus, we conclude with a telling description of the environment most likely to offer the computer embezzler the ideal circumstances for computer abuse.

The most vulnerable EDP operation is the one which performs financial processing and produces negotiable instruments. Employee and management relations are poor, with a high degree of employee disgruntlement. There is a significant lack of separation of tasks requiring a great amount of trust and responsibility. In other words, employees are given wide-ranging responsibilities with minimal checking or observation of their activities. Employees are unsupervised when they are working in the EDP facilities outside normal hours. This weakness is supported by a number of cases that occurred at night or on weekends when employees, especially programmers, were given access to computers for program development work. The computer application programs lack controls to detect anomalous activities and events. The programs are difficult to test and provide few opportunities for the development of audit trails, the means by which transactions can be traced from the end product back to source data. Finally, there is little or no accounting of use of the computer system. Programmers, computer operators, or any employees can use computer services without any direct accountability. Actual experience shows that any EDP organizations which have some significant combinations of these weaknesses are particularly vulnerable to computer abuse.*

SUMMARY

In this chapter, we have focused our attention on computer crime and its relationship to accounting information systems. For the purpose of discussion, the chapter has been divided into three categories: (1) an overview of what is known about computer crime in general, (2) a brief description of five well-known cases of accounting/computer crimes, and (3) a general profile of the computer criminal.

In the first section, the most fundamental conclusion is that we know very little about computer crime. Less than 700 cases have been reported but there is very good reason to believe that many more cases go unreported and—even worse—undetected. Because most computer criminals are caught by luck, chance, or accident, rather than by controls, our sample of known cases is not random. From our limited information about computer fraud, however, we have drawn two tentative conclusions. The first is that computer crime appears to be growing. The second is that computer crime involves large sums of money, usually much more than comparable white-collar crime.

In the second section, we reviewed five cases: (1) the Round-Off Trick, (2) the Equity Funding Case, (3) the TRW Company Credit Data Case, (4) the Union Dime Savings Bank Case, and (5) the Pacific Telephone Company Case. These cases were chosen for review because of their notoriety and because they represent a type or "class" of computer crime. Thus, the round-off trick was discussed because it has been done many times and because a large number of pro-

*Ibid., p. 40.

cessing applications are vulnerable to this type of manipulation. The Equity Funding Case represents the most costly computer crime known to date, although some would argue that it was not a computer crime at all.

The TRW Company Credit Data Case involved the misuse of credit information stored in the company's computers. Its importance therefore rests in the fact that it is a "valuable information" computer crime. The related question of consumer rights with regard to credit information was also a key issue in this case. The Union Dime Savings Bank case was reviewed as an example of a computer crime in the banking industry. This case is unusual in that Roswell Stephens, the perpetrator, does not fit the image of the typical computer criminal, but the case is fairly representative of the potential abuse in the banking industry. Finally, the Pacific Telephone Company case is a classic example of a computer "ripoff" of equipment which was made possible through the manipulation of computerized accounting records.

The last section of the chapter attempted to construct a profile of the computer criminal. The rationale for this part of the chapter rests in the observation that internal controls have not thwarted major computer crimes and that prior recognition of the computer criminal may therefore prove a better safeguard. In this section of the chapter, we observed that the typical computer criminal is bright, young, typically male, and in possession of a good technical as well as general-educational background. Most computer criminals view themselves as moral and, in fact, most of them are first-time offenders. There is little evidence to support the claim that computer criminals are involved in organized crime.

DISCUSSION QUESTIONS

Unless otherwise stated, all names and incidents in these questions are fictitious.

9-1. Why is a definition of computer crime elusive? Would you be willing to call computer crime a "white-collar" crime? Why or why not?

9-2. Give some examples of computer crime drawn from this chapter, your outside reading, or, perhaps your own experience. What characteristics do your examples have in common?

9-3. Known cases of computer crime have been described as just "the tip of the iceberg." Would you consider this description accurate? Why or why not?

9-4. An historical fact which is not widely known is that in 1856, the manager of the U.S. Patent Office quit his job because he thought that everything which could possibly be invented had already been invented. Would you consider computer crime a "new invention" or is there nothing in "modern" computer crime that would have prevented the manager from quitting?

9-5. Most computer crime is not reported. Give as many reasons as you can why much of this crime is purposely down-played. Do you consider these reasons valid? Discuss several arguments favorable to the reporting of all computer crime.

9-6. Rosemarie Lux was an external auditor for Bill Sandmeyer and Associates, a small, independent CPA firm. She had just finished her audit of the Tracy Company and had found that one of the company's employees had been embezzling from the company's inventory accounts by manipulating inventory records stored on the company's computer system. Discuss what professional reasons would prevent her from making a statement to the press.

9-7. Denny Jacobs, a one-time computer expert and presently the town drunk, had been thrown in the city slammer to "dry out." In one of his more lucid moments, he turned to his fellow drinking partner and cell mate and said "You know, mate, I've just realized that computer controls are really for friends—the crooks are going to get around them anyway." Do you agree? Why or why not?

9-8. According to recent statistics, the odds of a white-collar criminal being convicted of a crime in the courts when caught are 33 to 1. If this is true, why do you suppose that some experts continue to claim that computer crime does pay?

9-9. Why have most computer experts suggested that computer abuse is growing despite the apparent downturn in the number of cases reported in Figure 9-2?

9-10. Banks have been frequent targets of embezzlers and criminal perpetrators because, by definition, banks are large holders of liquid assets. Inasmuch as a good number of bank-swindle cases have involved nothing more complicated than the switch of a deposit slip, why are many of these swindle cases reported as "computer crime"? Would you say that many of these crimes would be better reported as other types of crimes? Discuss.

9-11. There is an old saying that "it takes a thief to catch a thief." How accurate would you say this observation is when applied to the area of computer crime?

9-12. In 1973, the President of the United States imposed a wage and price freeze in this country in order to stabilize the economy and curb inflation. To implement the program, a special Wage and Price Control Board was set up with powers to make exceptions and with a supervisory staff to identify violations. After administering the freeze for a few months, William Simon, the chief executive of the Control Board, stated: "I used to think that 95 percent of the American people are 100 percent honest. I have come to find out that 100 percent of the American people are 95 percent honest." What implications does this observation have for computer crime?

9-13. The Citizen's Capitalist Bank uses a computerized data-processing system to maintain both its checking accounts and its savings accounts. During the last year, there have been a number of complaints from customers that their balances have been in error. Mr. Carl Doyle, the EDP bank manager, has always treated these customers very courteously, and has personally seen to it that the problems have been rectified quickly, sometimes by putting in extra hours after normal quitting time to make the necessary changes. This extra effort has been so helpful to the bank that this year, the bank's top management has made plans to award Mr. Doyle with the "Employee-of-the-Year Award." Comment.

9-14. Explain the "Round-Off Trick." What type of position would an individual have to occupy within a company to successfully perform it? What controls would you recommend to avoid dishonest rounding in a computer?

9-15. Outline the details of the Equity Funding Case. What is meant by the "Inflated Earnings Phase," the "Foreign Phase," and the "Insurance Phase" of the fraud? What would you say was the most fundamental problem which permitted the fraud to go undetected for so long a time period?

9-16. Explain why there is controversy over whether or not the Equity Funding Case was a computer fraud. What is your opinion on the matter?

9-17. What is meant by the term *open shop* at the computer center? Why is an open shop a hazard? What can be done to minimize the dangers of this practice? Why do you suppose business firms or other organizations ever allow an open shop in view of the problems such a policy entails?

9-18. What is meant by the term *valuable information computer crime*? In what way(s) does a grandfather-father-son file system guard against the perpetration of this type of computer abuse? In what way(s) does it fail to guard against such abuse?

9-19. Steven Brown was a computer specialist working for a management consultant firm, and his friend, Dennis Coleman, held a similar job with the local police department. One day, while the two men were having lunch, Dennis said, "You know, Steve, I wish more of you folks would step forward when you uncover a computer fraud—it would sure make my job a lot easier. One of the best ways to control crime is to convince the criminal he can't get away with it. Putting the spotlight on some of these penny-ante computer crooks would probably keep a lot of others from trying their hand at it. Companies that keep these things hush-hush are not doing anyone any favors and, in addition, actually are in technical violation of the law for not reporting it." Comment.

9-20. Identify the key manipulations that enabled Roswell Stephens to steal from the Union Dime Savings Bank. Enumerate as many controls as you can which would have prevented Stephens from getting away with his actions. Would you imagine that such controls are active at your bank? Discuss.

9-21. The TRW Company Credit Data case involves two issues: (1) the propriety of computer-based information, and (2) the protection afforded the consumer in the use of credit information. Identify each of these issues more fully and explain your own position on these matters. Do you feel, for example, that a company has the right to collect, store, and disseminate information about your purchasing activity without your permission?

9-22. What enabled the employees at TRW to get away with their crime? What controls might have prevented the crime from occurring?

9-23. The TRW case has been identified as an unusual case because the information stored on the company's computer files, rather than any liquid assets, was the major target of the perpetrators. From your reading of this and the previous chapter, plus your outside readings, discuss other cases that appear to fall into this category of computer crime.

9-24. In an early portion of this chapter, it was suggested that some experts feel that computer crime is just a "new twist of an old rope." Would you agree or disagree? What bearing does the definition of computer crime have on this issue?

9-25. In a recent news bulletin, it was announced that the FBI has organized a special section of its force to investigate crimes related to the use of computers. What advantages are there in training the employees of a federal agency to investigate the computer crime of a local company? In what way is federal jurisdiction justified? What special skills would you like to see these FBI investigators possess which a keypunch operator or computer operator would not be likely to have?

9-26. With regard to question 9-25 above, envision the following (imaginary) conversation between Mr. Warren Gulko, the FBI computer-division supervisor, and his staff. "Ladies and gentlemen, I am proud to be the supervisor of such an elite and well-trained staff. With your skills I have every confidence that we shall not only catch more computer thieves, but that we shall also prevent more computer crimes." Comment in light of the historical record.

9-27. What makes the Jerry Schneider–Pacific Telephone and Telegraph case unique? Would you say that such a crime might be typical of a number of yet-undiscovered crimes of a similar nature?

9-28. In the Jerry Schneider–Pacific Telephone and Telegraph case, why was there a problem in determining the telephone company's losses? Why is the problem of calculating computer-crime costs actually a general problem of the computer-crime victim?

9-29. In the introduction to this chapter, it was stated that in 1966, a bank employee was caught in the first known case of computer abuse. According to Figure 9-2, however, there were earlier cases. How might this inconsistency logically be reconciled?

9-30. Stripes and Stars Penitentiary had just been granted $100,000 to set up new rehabilitation programs for the inmates. A poll was taken to discover what subject areas were most desired by the prisoners, and "auto-mechanics" and "computer programming" tied for first place. What success would you estimate the data-processing program would be likely to have if one were implemented? (It is up to you to define what is meant by "success.")

9-31. There once was a man from Ann Arbor,
who decided to outsmart his computer.
He faked a transaction,
and much to his satisfaction,
he wound up, in the end, quite richer.
Comment. (Not about the quality of the poetry either!)

9-32. Discuss the motivations for computer crime.

Is all computer crime ultimately for financial gain? Explain.

9-33. Rodney Smallskull was apprehended for grand larceny shortly after he had poured gasoline over his company's central processing unit, igniting both the machine and his trouser leg with a single match. After being taken into custody, Rodney was assigned legal counsel who advised him to plead innocent by reason of temporary insanity. In your opinion, how sound was this advice? (*Hint:* If you wanted to harm a computer center, what would *you* do?)

9-34. In the past several years, there have been many incidents of CPA firms failing to detect major computer crimes committed by the firms' audit clients. Do you feel that these failures normally are caused by the incompetency of the external auditors or the cleverness of the individuals who commit the computer crimes? Discuss.

9-35. What are the lessons to be learned from computer crime, if any? From what you have read in this chapter, would you say that there is such a thing as a "secure" computer system? Discuss.

PROBLEMS

9-36. Zollinger National Bank has 8429 savings accounts, and credits interest to these accounts on a quarterly basis. Deborah Knowlton, one of the bank's assistant programmers, has often considered the use of a round-off "scam" to augment her own savings account balance. Assuming that she could get away with it, how much could she expect to accumulate in her account at the end of a year with such a scheme? Assume daily processing.

9-37. In many companies, there is a great volume of transactions affecting their "accounts receivable" asset account and this account has a large dollar balance. Try to think of an example whereby a computer crime could be committed successfully on a company's accounts receivable. (Assume that the company's accounts receivable subsidiary ledger is maintained on magnetic tape storage media.) Outline in detail the steps to be taken in order to commit a fraud. What internal controls could be established within the company that likely would have prevented the computer crime you have described?

9-38. A recent computer crime case which occurred too late to document in this textbook in detail was the electronic funds transfer scandal allegedly perpetrated by Mark Rifkin at a bank in Los Angeles. Using outside source materials, obtain information about this case and prepare an analysis similar to those for the cases which were presented in this chapter. In your analysis, you should address the following questions: (1) Was this a computer crime? (2) How was the crime committed? (3) What safeguards might have prevented this crime? (4) How was the crime discovered?

9-39. (Library Research) Newspapers and such journals as *DATAMATION* and *Computerworld* are prime sources of computer crime articles. Find a description of a computer crime not already discussed in this chapter and prepare an analysis similar to the cases presented in this chapter.

CASE ANALYSES

9-40. *The Case of the Purloined Computer*

Below is a true account of a computer which was stolen from its company. The story is taken from the March 1979 issue of *The PRINTOUT* (p. 10).

On January 2, Dave Dumas, vice-president of Appliance Parts Company, Inc., came to work at 8:30 a.m. and discovered that his computer system had been stolen from its second-floor home during the New Year's holiday. The system which had been installed for about two years had become a critical part of his business because it was an online system with many terminals located in different parts of his company.

Missing were the main computer, a disk drive, four video display terminals, the system and appli-

cations software disk pack, and all of the operating manuals.

After notifying the police, Dumas called Euclid Lee, the local representative for Triad Systems Corporation. Euclid immediately packed his demonstration system into the back of his station wagon and arrived at the offices of Appliance Parts Co. in time to see the police still conducting their investigation. After receiving police clearance to set up a replacement system, Euclid and his crew installed a fully-operational system in place of the one stolen. Fortunately, Dumas had been operating his data-processing activity according to generally accepted security practices for disaster protection and had a complete set of current files backed up at an off-site location. The combination of management foresight and vendor response enabled APC to come back online by 11:30 that morning.

The stolen computer had been insured against everything—except theft. No one thought it likely that it would be dismantled and purloined from its rather difficult location on the second floor. Euclid called Bill Stevens, president of Triad Systems Corporation, and explained the problem. Stevens decided to replace the original system for APC at one-half Triad's cost. A new system was shipped from California on Wednesday evening of that same week and by Friday was in full operation. Total down time for the Appliance Parts Company, Inc. online system: four hours!

Questions

1. Is this an example of a computer crime? Why or why not?

2. Discuss the controls that might have thwarted this crime. Why do you suppose such controls were not in place?

3. The report is presented here in its entirety. Is such a report sufficient for aggregating good statistics on computer crime? Why or why not?

9-41. *Charles Lasher and Associates*

Of all the programmers working for Charles Lasher and Associates, Ray Williams was probably the most competent and, at the same time, the least motivated. His father, Ray Williams,

Sr., had sent Ray Jr. to the best private schools in the area, and had even managed to pay for Ray's four-year education at Branard College—a considerable expense and one that was more than he could afford. Thus, when his father got Ray a job at Charles Lasher and Associates through an old friend of the family, Ray felt obligated to take it and try to do well.

The problem was that Ray didn't like the work or the work environment. Charles Lasher and Associates was a management consulting firm with branches in several East Coast cities, and several of the company's clients required analysis work done on their various computer files. The Lasher Company's customer representatives, who were not well-versed in computer programming, constantly promised jobs to these clients without allowing enough time for the company's programming staff to complete them. On several occasions, in fact, the entire EDP staff of the company was told to cancel all their plans for the coming weekend because an important client needed some work done immediately and the staff was expected to get the job done "no matter what!" At other times, however, the work would slack off and there would be virtually nothing to do. Usually, nonbusy periods would occur during the summer months when the temperatures rose to the high 80s and the air conditioners decided to stop functioning. At these times, the staff would swelter in the inner, windowless offices assigned to the EDP department, drink coffee, and tell stale jokes that they all had heard from each other "about a million times."

Some of the work that Ray did for the company involved the extraction of selected information from client master files. A common task would be to take a master file containing 10 to 20 thousand accounts receivable records and print out the name and address of those retail accounts which matched a specific customer profile. Thus, for example, a client might ask to have the computer print out those customer accounts who simultaneously had income levels of at least so much, lived in zip-code areas such-and-such, had at least so many children, and had credit ratings of a certain level or higher.

For Ray, the programming aspects of this work were easy, and most of the job actually involved acquiring the detailed specifications of the computer file used in the extraction process and determining what format the client desired for the final report. From this information, Ray could easily scan the client's master file and direct the computer to print out the required information.

Ray knew that the computer files with which he worked contained sensitive data, but at first, he simply did what was asked of him. As time went on, however, Ray became curious why the types of information he was extracting from the files were of interest to the clients, and he began to ask questions. His boss told him that these clients "liked to keep Ray busy," but somehow, Ray didn't think that was the answer. The "moment of truth" actually came from a chance remark of an insurance client, Bob Tomlinson. Tomlinson had brought a tape reel of subscribers to *Business Month* magazine and asked for a profile printout as described above. Bob let slip, however, that his company was planning to use the information as leads for its insurance business. In effect, each name on the file matching the prescribed customer profile was a potential buyer of insurance, and Tomlinson's insurance company planned on contacting each of these customers by mail in hopes of selling them one or more policies. This information struck Ray like a bolt of lightning. "So that's why they want these fool reports," he thought!

At the time that Ray found out about the insurance mailing, he was in a particularly foul mood. He had worked all weekend on another project and he felt that he was being treated unfairly. The fact that he was on salary and thus received no overtime for his troubles especially rankled him. But the news about the insurance mailing started him thinking. There were other insurance companies around. Perhaps they, too, would be interested in the list he had prepared for Tomlinson's company. . . .

In the spring and summer, Ray played softball in a league which included younger guys from around the local neighborhood. One of them was Carl Weeks. Carl worked for Indemnity Life and Casualty Company, a rival insurance company to the company of Bob Tomlinson, and Ray was pretty sure that Carl would be interested in acquiring a copy of the hot leads in the report Ray had just prepared for Tomlinson's company. Thus, at the softball game the following Saturday, Ray casually mentioned to Carl that such a list "could be provided for a price." Carl jumped at the chance and it was agreed that, for $1,000, Ray would deliver such a list the following weekend.

For Ray, printing out the list was a simple matter. On Monday morning, he walked into the computer room and told the computer operator that he needed "one more run" on the Tomlinson Company's *Business Month* file. The computer operator, who was a friendly chap, said, "Sure, Ray—no problem. In fact, I'm a little hung over from a party last night so if you don't mind, here's the tape file; run it yourself while I go get some more coffee."

Ray ran the program and, with the good fortune of the "disappearing computer operator," had no trouble in disposing of all traces of the extra program run. The next weekend, Ray delivered the "extra" computer list to Carl. Carl, in turn handed over $1,000 to Ray in small bills, and then both men retired to the local tavern—ostensibly to celebrate their 15-to-3 loss to their rival softball team. Ray treated.

During the next few months, Ray had a number of similar opportunities. In one instance, for example, an auditor wanted the computer to prepare a list of names and addresses drawn from a computer file for audit-confirmation purposes. For a fee, Ray "fixed" the program so that only those people known to have active, valid accounts were chosen for audit confirmation, thus assuring the auditor of a trouble-free audit-confirmation job. In another instance, Ray got his hands on the Chadwick Department Store accounts receivable file and had the computer print out a list of retail customers who were behind in their payments. He sold this list to a collection agency hungry for business. Using the information obtained from the listing, the agency was

able to convince the Chadwick Store's management that it could do a very efficient job performing its collecting business, and thus landed a "fat" account. In yet a third instance, Ray copied over an entire file belonging to *Woods and Streams* magazine. He then sold copies of this subscription file to rival magazines. In one notable gambit, Ray actually stole the subscription list of a second rival magazine and sold this back to the subscriptions manager of *Woods and Streams*. Neither manager knew that, through Ray, each was "ripping off" the other!

It wasn't until almost a year had gone by that things began to get a little sticky for Ray. Bob Tomlinson had returned to Ray's office several times complaining that the leads acquired from the *Business Month* file "weren't panning out," and that he couldn't understand it. He said the industry was competitive and that most of the insurance customer leads, he was discovering, seemed to have just bought new insurance policies from other companies—especially Indemnity Life and Casualty Company. Bob wondered if Ray knew anything about that.

Questions

1. Why is Ray's work environment conducive to computer crime?

2. Does Ray fit the profile of a computer criminal? Defend your answer.

3. What controls appear to be missing at Charles Lasher and Associates which enable Ray to get away with the things he's been doing? Briefly identify each weakness at the company, and recommend one or more controls that might be used to eliminate this weakness.

4. Bob Tomlinson suspects something. What steps might be taken to confirm the suspicion that there is a security leak at the Lasher Company? What evidence might be collected, assuming it was available? (*Note:* For this last question, you may assume that desirable security controls not discussed in the case have, in fact, been installed at Charles Lasher and Associates.)

10

Auditing the Computerized Accounting Information System

Among the important questions that you should be able to answer after reading this chapter are:

1 What are the differences between internal auditing and external auditing?
2 Under what circumstances could an audit be considered successful even if no system weaknesses or embezzlements were uncovered?
3 How accurate is the analogy of the internal auditor to the police detective?
4 What is the difference between "around-the-computer" auditing and "through-the-computer" auditing?
5 What are the techniques involved in auditing "with the computer?"

INTRODUCTION

Chapters 7 and 8 have stressed the importance of internal controls in the efficient operation of an accounting information system. To make sure that these controls are functioning properly, and to make sure that yet additional controls are not needed, the typical business organization relies on examinations or *audits* of the system as a means of measuring the accounting system's effectiveness. Inasmuch as auditing is usually taught in one or more quarter or semester courses within the typical accounting curriculum, it goes without saying that a single chapter of a book is not sufficient to cover the spectrum of topics involved in a complete audit of an organization. Thus, this chapter will be merely introductory in scope and, because of the complex nature of the auditing function, limited to areas of immediate consequence to accounting information systems. Also, to narrow the chapter discussion still further, we have chosen to focus primarily upon the audit of computerized accounting systems because this area is central to our textbook and, additionally, is a subject that is likely to complement, rather than repeat, the subject coverage of an auditing course.

THE AUDIT FUNCTION

We shall begin our discussion with some introductory comments about the nature of auditing in general, including a discussion that emphasizes the distinction between internal and external auditing, a discussion of the major purposes of the audit, and a discussion of the importance of the audit trail in laying the foundation for the investigative auditor. These comments in turn will provide a context for the more detailed material which follows concerning the methodologies to be used when auditing *around* the computer, auditing *through* the computer, and auditing *with* the computer.

Internal Versus External Auditing

Conventionally, we distinguish between two types of audits: the *internal audit* and the *external audit*. As the names imply, the internal audit is typically performed by the accounting employees of the company itself (i.e., "internally"), whereas the external audit is normally conducted by an accountant (or team of accountants) working for an independent CPA firm. The fact that an audit may be performed internally is somewhat misleading to the uninformed because it conjures images of undesirable self-regulation—like the basketball team which hires its own referees. In actuality, internal auditing positions are staff positions reporting to top management. Thus, whereas an audit might be internal to a company, it is invariably *external* to the corporate department or division being audited. Thus, the objectivity and professionalism required for the auditing function is preserved

whether an internal or external audit is underway.

Although similar in their need for objectivity, internal and external audits are quite different in their operational goals. The internal audit is concerned primarily with employee adherence to company policies and procedures—for example, the use of an official form when preparing payroll vouchers or completing purchase orders. On the other hand, the external audit's chief function is to verify that the financial statements of a firm are fairly and accurately presented—for example, to make sure that generally accepted accounting principles have been used to determine the balance sheet value of the company's unsold inventories.

Although the primary goals of the external and internal audits differ somewhat, they are also quite complementary within the context of accounting information systems. For example, the data-processing controls scrutinized by the internal auditor while observing managerial procedures are in part designed to increase the accuracy of the external financial reports of interest to the external auditor. Similarly, the use of an acceptable method of inventory valuation such as FIFO or LIFO, as required by the external auditor, is likely to be an important corporate policy falling under the domain of the internal auditor.

Most of the discussion that follows regarding the audit of computerized accounting information systems is applicable to both internal and external auditors. Therefore, except where specific reference is made to either the internal auditor or the external auditor, the term "auditor" is used broadly in this chapter to encompass both internal and external auditors.

What an Audit Is Supposed to Do

Webster's *Seventh New Collegiate Dictionary* defines an audit as "a formal or official examination and verification of an account book." This definition tends to give the auditing function a rather drab, examination-like aura. Certainly anyone who has been required to undergo an audit by the Internal Revenue Service has not found a lot to cheer about. In fact, many people still believe that an audit is primarily punitive in nature; i.e., punishment for discovered or suspected wrong-doing. Employees undergoing either internal or external audits for the first time are consequently nervous and uncertain, even to the point of making mistakes in front of auditors that they have never made before. In one notable case, for example, a new computer operator became so flustered when he was informed that the auditors had arrived and were watching him that he mounted the wrong tape on a tape drive and erased two-thirds of the company's accounts receivable records before the error was discovered!

Audits are not intended to punish anybody, and certainly are not supposed to be performed for the purpose of employee intimidation. In the case of the internal audit, for example, we have noted that the principal goal is to ascertain that the company's established policies and procedures are in effect, and that they are sufficient to assure effective operating performance and data-processing completeness. Thus, the easiest and most efficient way for employees to satisfy the internal audit is to provide simple evidence that their jobs are being performed according to company specifications.

Auditing has often been likened to detective work in police investigations. Although this analogy has the advantage of implying professional skill, meticulous attention to details, and perhaps thoroughness, it also has the unfortunate implication that the primary goal is to catch a crook. This is *not* the major purpose of either the internal or external auditor. Of course, it *is* true that many audits have uncovered fraud, but this is typically a byproduct of the investigation rather than an end in itself. Furthermore, it should not be surprising that such activities as embezzlement or theft are discovered in the course of an audit, for clearly such activities must violate company policy and, in covering up the fact that assets have been stolen, result in an overstatement of the true worth of the company. The distinction between what the auditors are *assigned* to do, however, and what they ultimately find, is important and should be kept in mind when audit tasks are being studied.

For the reasons enumerated above, most modern auditors consider themselves accounting consultants in a position to assist managers in their planning and controlling functions rather than "police workers" in search of criminals. In this sense, the auditor is someone interested in verifying the present strengths, safeguards, and controls of the organization's accounting information system, and only as a consequence of the auditor's position, someone who is able to discover potential or existing weaknesses requiring further managerial consideration. For example, the auditor might discover that the addition of a simple edit test in a computer program could enable the company to reject a certain type of erroneous transaction in the processing cycle, or, alternatively, the auditor might suggest (from experience) that a costly control presently used in a client company could be eliminated with little risk. Thus, the fact of the matter is that the auditor is "on management's side," despite the arm's-length relationship which must be maintained in order to assure objectivity in the review process.

Planned Versus Surprise Audits

For the most part, accounting audits must be planned because of the need to coordinate visits to the various accounting activity sites of the company, the need to schedule managerial assistance in providing pertinent documents, the need for computer time to review important computer files and data-processing programs, and so forth. However, both internal and external audits can be performed either on a planned, or surprise, basis.

As the name suggests, the surprise audit is an unscheduled investigation of system activity, in which a company's internal or external auditors completely take over the operations of the systems and check the integrity and accuracy of the current data processing. In his famous book, *The Money Changers* (Doubleday and Company, Garden City, N.Y., 1975), Arthur Hailey describes such a surprise audit at the "First Mercantile American Bank," a fictitious commercial bank with branches scattered throughout a large metropolitan urban area (pp. 86–87):

... An essential part of the audit function was to descend irregularly and without warning on any of the bank's branches. Elaborate precautions were taken to preserve secrecy and any audit staff member who violated it was in serious trouble. Few did, even inadvertently.

For today's maneuver, the score of auditors involved had assembled an hour ago in a salon of a downtown hotel, though even that destination had not been revealed until the latest possible moment. There they were briefed, duties allocated, then inconspicuously, in twos and threes, they had walked toward the main downtown branch of FMA. Until the last few crucial minutes they loitered in lobbies of nearby buildings, strolled casually, or browsed store windows. Then, traditionally, the most junior member of the group had rapped on the bank door to demand admission. As soon as it was gained, the others, like an assembling regiment, fell in behind him.

Now, within the bank, audit team members were at every key position.

Clearly, the element of surprise serves a dual role. On the one hand, it gives the auditors a chance to examine the organization's processing during what is hopefully a typical processing cycle. Thus, there is good reason to expect the data to be fairly representative of daily input, and therefore gives the auditors a good idea of the actual procedures which are presently being used. On the other hand, the element of surprise serves to limit severely the amount of time which the embezzler must have to "cover his tracks." This aspect is crucial to catching systematic processing frauds. As Mr. Hailey explains (p. 87):

A convicted bank embezzler of the 1970s, who successfully concealed his massive defalcations for some twenty years, observed while eventually en route to prison, "The auditors used to come in and do nothing but shoot the breeze for forty minutes. Give me half of that time and I can cover up anything."

The audit department of First Mercantile American, and other large North American banks, took no such chance. Not even five minutes passed after the surprise of the auditors' arrival until they were all in preassigned positions, observing everything.

Resigned, regular staff members of the branch went on to complete their day's work, then to assist the auditors as needed.

Once started, the process would continue through the following week and part of the next. But the most critical portion of the examination would take place within the next few hours.

In the computer machine room, the auditor's approach is similar to that described above for other portions of the bank. The operations of the computer center are taken over by the auditing staff and the input, processing, and output of the computer run(s) are carefully examined. If need be, the contents of a computer program as it resides in computer memory can be "dumped" onto a computer file or a printer page and checked against an authorized version to make sure the program agrees with the documentation in the run manual. This procedure is a long and tedious process, but it is one way to detect irregularities or fraud.

The Importance of a Good Audit Trail

As we have now observed in several earlier chapters, a good audit trail means that a manager or any other employee is able to follow the path of the organization's accounting transactions from their initial source documents to their final disposition on a report. The audit trail is probably the most important preventive control in the accounting information system because it enables management to know what is happening as transactions wind their way through the various phases of manual and computerized data processing. As a result, management is in a position to detect and correct any errors and irregularities occurring during the course of normal accounting activity.

Clearly, a good audit trail is equally important when it comes time to *audit* the accounting information system. Like the concerned manager, the auditor must be able to trace the flow of accounting transactions as these transactions pass through the accounting information system in order to test data-processing accuracy as well as to verify the controls used to safeguard the integrity of the data. Without a good audit trail, the auditor's job is virtually impossible to perform. If the audit trail is obscured, the auditor is similarly left "in the dark."

It was pointed out in Chapter 7 that the introduction of a computer into a company's system often causes audit-trail problems. Prior to the computerized system, transaction processing under the company's manual system was visible to the human eye, making the audit trail relatively easy to follow. When a company's data-processing activities are handled by the computer, however, accounting transactions are processed internally by computer hardware. Because this internalized computer processing is not visible by humans, the audit trail of financial transactions becomes more difficult to follow.

When a real-time accounting information system is used to process data from remote terminals, the audit trail has the potential to be even more difficult to follow. The reasons for this are twofold. First, the physical location of the source-document data and the physical location of the computer that processes these data may be separated by hundreds or even thousands of miles. Thus, discrepancies which appear on a summary listing of processing maintained at the computer center cannot be traced immediately to the source documents which relate to the processed data. In effect, the audit trail has "leaped" a great distance. When the auditor follows an audit trail, therefore, it is also necessary to leap this distance in order to follow the processing logic and information flow involved. To permit the auditor to perform this tracing task successfully, clear identification of transactions and record updating must be available to make the audit path continuous and easy to follow.

The second audit-trail problem related to real-time accounting information systems is the lack of a regular schedule for processing specific types of accounting transactions. In order for a manager to trace a particular business transaction through the computer system, it is necessary to know when that transaction was processed. For example, if a company's sales manager desired information about a sales transaction that took place during the third week of February, and the company utilized a weekly batch-processing computer system, the manager could

trace the transaction in question by looking at the data processing for sales occurring in that week. If the company in the above example utilized a real-time system, however, the sales manager's tracing of the audit trail for the required sales transaction may be more difficult. Assuming the manager knew which terminal location was used to process the sales transaction, the determination of which particular day of the week this transaction was processed could still be extremely hard, obviously causing audit-trail problems.

A popular control used in many organizations' real-time processing systems is the *internal transaction log* maintained by the operating system of the computer. Each time a transaction is processed from remote terminal input, or perhaps each time a terminal requests processing time from the CPU, it is possible to log detailed information about the user and/or the processing request on magnetic disk or tape. Periodically (perhaps daily), the contents of the internal transaction log can be printed out, thereby providing hard-copy data visible to the human eye. This hard-copy printout, containing detailed information about each terminal's input transactions, is a valuable report contributing to the accountant's tracing of each terminal's audit trail of processed transactions. The sales manager in the above example could therefore have obtained the transaction log hard-copy printout of the specific terminal in question for the third week of February.

AUDITING AROUND THE COMPUTER

When computers were first used for accounting data-processing functions, the typical auditor was expected to know very little about automated data processing. The basic auditing approach was to follow the audit trail up to the point at which accounting data entered the computer, and to pick up the trail again when the data reappeared in processed form as computer output. Historically, the auditor paid little attention to the accounting controls which were, or were not, used in the computer processing because it was assumed that the presence of accurate output verified proper processing operations. Thus, as long as the output from the accounting information system was valid and could be traced back to the input from which it was generated, the auditor was satisfied with the data-processing portion of the accounting information system.

To illustrate around-the-computer auditing in greater detail, consider the simplified payroll processing of the Alan Company illustrated in Figure 10-1. As shown in the figure, time cards are punched by employees as they report for work, leave work, take time off for lunch, and so forth. At the end of each week, these time cards are collected and sent to be keypunched into computer cards. These cards are then processed once a week in a batch. A master file of employee records, containing such information as social

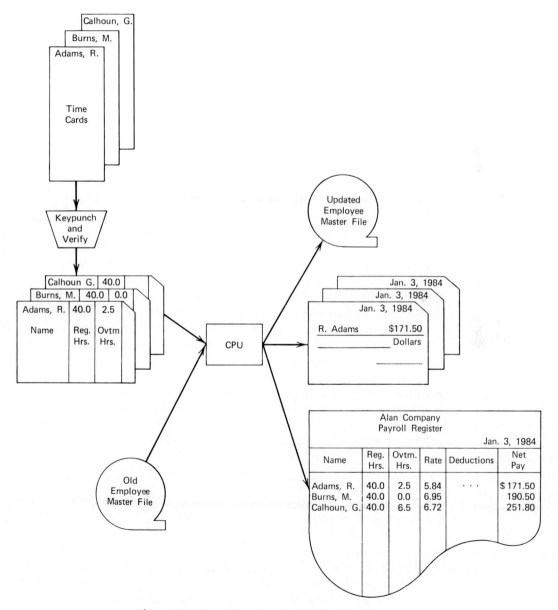

Figure 10-1. Payroll processing for the Alan Company.

security number, name, year-to-date tax with-holdings, and so forth, is also used in the processing. Output from the processing run includes the company's payroll checks, an updated master file, and a "payroll register" indicating what payroll disbursements have been authorized as a result of the computer processing.

The auditor begins with the verification of the source documents—in this case, the Alan Company employee time cards—to check for accuracy and authenticity. Next, the auditor would follow these time cards to the keypunching phase and verify that they are properly transcribed into computer cards in preparation for computer processing. The auditor would then literally walk around the computer to the output and verify, manually, that the payroll checks have been prepared properly. A correct match of the output with the manual calculations performed from the input would thus serve as the audit test. Finally, for completeness, a printout of the payroll master file before and after the processing run takes place would also have to be made to permit the auditor to verify that this file has been updated properly.

When performing a payroll audit, a question naturally arises as to how many employees should be "screened" when checking the computer processing. Because cash disbursements are involved in preparing payroll checks, a verification of the complete set of time cards and punched cards involved in the processing run would be desirable. Where the payroll checks for thousands of employees are involved in a single processing run, however, this task would probably be too time-consuming to perform completely, and only a subset of employees (say, from randomly-selected departments) would be chosen for the audit.

The advantages of around-the-computer auditing include (1) the fact that it is relatively straightforward, (2) the fact that it can be performed with minimum, if any, disturbance of the company records, (3) the fact that it is performed with live (as opposed to artificial) data, (4) the fact that it can be performed completely with the company's existing input and output, (5) the fact

that it requires little skill or training in computers of the auditor, and (6) the fact that it requires little assistance from the accounting or EDP staff. For the above reasons, such auditing is also relatively inexpensive to perform.

The chief disadvantage of around-the-computer auditing is that it does not test enough. In testing controls, the exceptions—not the normal transactions—of a typical processing run are of interest to the auditor, and these are basically overlooked in around-the-computer auditing practice. Consider again the payroll example of Figure 10-1. How will the processing run treat a "nonexistent" employee, especially an employee who has been fired but whose computer payroll record has not yet been removed from the master file? What happens if an "old" employee punched card from week "one" is processed again in week "two's" computer run; will the employee be paid double? What happens if there are two employees with the same name, or by mistake, the same social security number?

As you can see, our around-the-computer audit has ignored the processing controls designed to test these cases, and therefore has the potential to reveal only those system weaknesses that can be detected under normal processing conditions. In this sense, around-the-computer auditing is actually a feedback control rather than a preventive control, and therefore, at best, can be used only to audit the accounting information system "after the fact." It cannot identify problems before they occur.

A further problem with around-the-computer auditing is that audit tests are limited to the manual resources of the auditor. This means, in particular, that auditing cannot be performed in volume. The result is that only a fraction of the transactions involved in a typical computerized processing environment are likely to be scrutinized when around-the-computer auditing is being performed, and these transactions are likely to be perfectly valid, but uninteresting, situations. Thus, we need further tests to investigate the questions of exceptions and completeness, and this requires "through-the-computer" auditing as described below.

AUDITING THROUGH THE COMPUTER

As the name implies, through-the-computer auditing follows the audit trail as it proceeds within the internal-computer-operations phase of automated data processing. Unlike around-the-computer auditing, therefore, through-the-computer auditing attempts to verify the processing controls involved in the accounting information system programs, as well as assure that accurate data processing is performed in the normal course of accounting activity.

Although through-the-computer auditing would, for completeness, also include tests of computer hardware, it is usually assumed that the central processing unit, peripheral tape and disk drives, and other interfacing equipment are functioning properly. This leaves the auditor the principal task of verifying processing logic as opposed to computer accuracy. The three primary methods of through-the-computer auditing are (1) the preparation of a special set of test transactions, called the *test deck,* (2) the validation of computer programs themselves through a variety of specialized auditing techniques to ensure that authorized versions of the accounting programs are, in fact, being used for data-processing purposes, and (3) the use of an *integrated test facility* or ITF. Each of these three methods is discussed at greater length in the paragraphs below.

The Test Deck

It is the auditor's responsibility to develop a set of transactions which tests, as completely as possible, the range of exception situations which might challenge the computer processing of the accounting data under normal processing conditions. Possible exception situations for our payroll application in Figure 10-1, for example, would include (1) out-of-sequence conditions, (2) no-master-file-record-found conditions, (3) invalid employee number, (4) processing wrong input, (5) invalid dates, invalid pay rate, or invalid deduction codes, (6) processing wrong files, (7) use of alphabetic data where numeric data are required, or vice versa, and (8) invalid field relationships—such as a pay-rate amount and a pay-rate code. Of course, these are just examples for our payroll illustration—additional test conditions would be developed on a program-by-program basis as auditing needs dictate. In more sophisticated accounting information systems, it is common to find that an initial set of transaction data will serve as input to more than one processing routine. This makes the development of a suitable test deck that much more difficult inasmuch as the set of exceptions must be expanded to include the possibilities involved for all programs utilizing the input data. The point, however, is that as many different exception situations as possible should be built into the test deck in order to provide a thorough audit test.

Once the auditor has assembled appropriate sample data, they are arranged into test sequence in preparation for computerized data processing. Although card input is certainly possible, such alternate input media as tape, disk, or even remote manual entry via a terminal might also be used. Thus, in this day and age, the term *test deck*—implying that the test data must be card input—is probably misleading. No matter what medium is used for the data input, however, the important thing is to process the transactions utilizing the organization's normal methods in order to test for processing accuracy.

To complete the audit test, the auditor will compare the results obtained from the data-processing test deck transactions with a predetermined set of answers developed by the auditor on an audit work sheet. If the processing results and the work sheet results are not in agreement, further investigation must be made to determine the reasons. It should be pointed out that discrepancies found in an audit test are not always attributable to deficient data processing or the lack of good accounting controls. The use of nonstandard procedures, the introduction of spurious data, the possibility of machine malfunction, or the presence of other random irregularities which might take place during the processing tests are all possible causes of unanticipated results. As far as possible, therefore, the auditor must guard against these situations during auditing operations.

Auditing Computer Programs

A clever programmer can bypass the "perils" of a test deck by substituting a legitimate, but unused, program for a dishonest one when an auditor asks for the processing routine(s) required for the audit. Although there is no 100 percent foolproof way of validating a program, there are four tests that may be used to assist in this task. These are (1) tests of program authorization, (2) control-total tests of the program itself, (3) surprise audits of the program when it is in actual use, and (4) surprise use of an authorized program when data processing is scheduled. Each of these is discussed in greater detail below.

Tests of program authorization. At a typical computer center, the EDP manager is required to make the final approval of all computer programs used in the normal course of the organization's data processing. Of course, the EDP manager may choose to delegate this responsibility to subordinate managers. Furthermore, delegation of responsibility is almost always exercised by the EDP manager when minor changes to existing programs are made on a routine basis. Regardless of how major or minor a program change might be, however, it is the auditor's responsibility to ensure that proper authorization procedures have been formulated and that the organization's employees observe these procedures in the normal course of processing accounting data.

The place to start the validation process is with the documentation found at the EDP subsystem. An efficient organization usually will have internal forms which authorize a change to an existing program or authorize the development of one or more new programs. Included on these forms should be the names of the individual(s) responsible for the work and the signature of the supervisor responsible for approving the final programs. Similarly, there should be forms which indicate that the work has been completed and a signature authorizing the use of the program(s) for present data processing. It is these authorizing signatures which affix responsibility for the data-processing routines and ensure accountability when problems arise. We call this a *responsibility system of computer program development and maintenance.*

The chief purpose of a responsibility system at the computer center is not to affix blame in the event of program failures but to ensure adequate supervisory controls in the critical area of data processing. It is a well-known fact that individuals are more careful and meticulous when they are responsible for a given piece of work. As a result, tighter control both over the development of new programs and changes to existing programs is enhanced and better computer software may thus be anticipated. In this sense, responsibility programming is an important preventive control which should be observed carefully in the course of an EDP audit.

Control-total tests. A *trojan-horse computer program* is a program with a hidden, intentional error—for example, a program that changes its own machine code once it is executed within the central processing unit. Usually, a trojan-horse program is difficult to detect in practice because the typical commercial accounting computer program is thousands of instructions in length and the very few unauthorized instructions which might cause difficulties in the computer program may be hidden anywhere in the programming code. Moreover, a very smart programmer will never change the source language code of an authorized program for illicit purposes; the programmer will almost always use the human-unreadable machine language code for this task.

To guard against unauthorized program tampering, especially at the machine-language level, it is possible to perform certain control-total tests of program authenticity. The most common is a test of length. To perform this test, the auditor obtains the latest version of a program to be verified, and counts the number of bytes or words of computer memory required to store the program in machine language when it resides in the central processing unit of the computer. This length count is then compared with a security table of valid length-counts of all accounting programs at the computer center. Program lengths that do not match these control totals are subjected to further scrutiny.

As described above, a length-count is an excellent test of program security because it is very difficult for an individual to tamper with a computer program in such a way that the "tampered" program length comes out the same as the valid-program length. A similar control-total test would be a check-sum comparison of the total number of source-language instructions in the program. For technical reasons, however, this test is not as efficient as the length-test discussed above. Yet a third test is to treat the machine-language instructions of the program as binary numbers which are added to compute a hash total. In all these tests, the computed control total is compared with a table of security values to determine the validity of the program.

Surprise audits. As the name implies, this test involves the examination of a set of accounting computer programs on a surprise basis. Here, the auditor will appear unannounced at the time that specific processing runs are scheduled, and request duplicate copies of the computer programs just after they have been used to perform their required data-processing tasks. Usually, these programs will be copied onto a spare magnetic tape reel that the auditor brings for this purpose. Once the complete set of programs has been copied, the auditor can compare the "in-use" programs with "authorized" versions which have been acquired previously for checking purposes. This test, by the way, need not be performed "on the spot" at the computer center, but can be performed later if desired.

It might also be noted that manually checking computer programs against their source listings is a very arduous, time-consuming process because thousands of instructions are involved in the coding. Consequently, many auditors use special computerized "comparison" programs. In effect, comparison programs are special computer programs that use source-language accounting programs as input data. The comparison program will compare the "surprised" program (in use at the computer center at the time the surprise audit takes place) with the "authorized program" on a line-by-line (instruction-by-instruction) basis. Unmatched instructions in either program are identified on a discrepancy report and form the basis of further inquiry.

Surprise use. Here again, the auditor visits the computer center unannounced and requests that his or her (authorized) programs be used instead of any others to perform the required data processing. If this request is denied, the reasons for the denial are carefully documented and investigated. If the request is honored, the auditor will then perform the specific accounting tasks required using the alternate programs. Unusual conditions that occur during the processing runs should be carefully scrutinized.

The surprise use of a set of authorized computer programs guards against unwarranted program changes and the use of unwarranted computer files or data input. For example, the authorized program will not be able to access a dummy file as might be used by an illegitimate program because the file-identification instructions of the authorized program will not match those of the bogus tape or disk file. Similarly, if illegitimate data are being processed in a tampered computer program, the authorized version of the program with proper data-testing controls will be able to identify these data on an exception basis.

If desired, the auditor can also run a test deck of special transactions on the "in-use" program at the time the surprise visit is conducted. As suggested above, any special exception conditions contained in the test deck which are not adequately handled by the in-use program will form the basis of further investigation.

Integrated Test Facility (ITF)

The purpose of an integrated test facility is to audit an accounting information system in an operational setting. It works as follows. A set of fictitious accounts is created and appropriate master records are placed on the computer files of the accounting information system. For example, a number of fictitious credit customers might be made up by the auditor and appropriate accounts receivable master records would be placed on the company's accounts receivable computer files. From the standpoint of the auditor, of course, the information contained on these records is for test purposes only. From the standpoint of the company, however, these records represent bonafide credit customers entitled to purchase company goods and services on credit.

To use the integrated test facility, the auditor will introduce artificial transactions into the data processing stream of the accounting information system and have the company routinely handle the business involved. In a truly integrated test facility, this may mean actually having the company ship merchandise (not ordered by anyone) to designated addresses, or billing customers for services not rendered. Because of the amount of work involved, however, the ordered goods will be intercepted at the shipping department and the billing transactions will be reversed at the managerial level. In any event, the auditor's task is to examine the results of the transactions and to determine how well the accounting information system has performed the tasks asked of it. The auditor does this by examining printouts of the computer file records and data-processing runs used to update them, and by comparing the information on these reports with anticipated results. Discrepancies between actual results and anticipated results form the basis of further inquiry.

The greatest advantage of the integrated test facility is that it enables the auditor to examine both the accounting steps and the procedural steps that are used by a company as it processes business transactions. For example, in testing an accounts receivable processing application, the auditor will be able to ascertain (1) how quickly a new customer can order merchandise on credit, (2) how credit sales are approved and processed, (3) how the company reacts to credit customers who exceed their credit limits, (4) how the company bills its customers for merchandise, (5) how sales returns and allowances are handled, and (6) how the company handles delin-

quent accounts. The examination of many different aspects of an accounting application is what is meant by the word "integrated" in the term "integrated test facility." According to those familiar with integrated test facilities, the results can be eye-opening.

The greatest drawback of the integrated test facility is that it introduces artificial transactions in the data-processing stream. For the sake of accuracy in the company's financial statements, however, these transactions must be reversed. There are two principal ways of accomplishing this. The easiest way is with a *filtering system*. By using this method, the artificial test transactions are identified when they are input for processing, and are separated out of the transaction stream for special treatment. Thus, the test transactions are used to update the appropriate accounting records of the company, but are "filtered out" of the data-processing flow as far as further business activities are concerned. This method is relatively straightforward, although it may require a substantive amount of coordinative work between the auditor, the EDP department, and accounting department for implementation. This method is also undesirable because it defeats the integrative nature of the test facility and, therefore, fails to perform important validation functions.

An alternative to the filter approach is to manually reverse the effects of the test transactions at the very end of the accounting cycle. For example, in the accounts receivable illustration, this would mean (among other things) manually reversing the company's final sales figures in the general ledger by the amount of artificial sales generated during the course of the company's audit testing. To the extent that such a procedure requires accountants to directly alter the financial information of its own accounting information system, such an approach may be objectionable to management. However, because this method also enables the auditor to test the accounting information system, it is considered the more desirable.*

*See, for example, John G. Burch, Jr., and Joseph L. Sardinas, Jr., *Computer Control and Audit: A Total Systems Approach* (New York: John Wiley and Sons, 1978), pp. 431–441.

Advantages and Disadvantages of Auditing Through the Computer

As we noted above, the chief advantage of through-the-computer auditing techniques over around-the-computer auditing techniques is that the former enables the auditor to test for computer controls and exceptions, in addition to testing the basic capacity of the computer programs to process normal accounting data. This advantage, in turn, enables the auditor to become more closely involved with the data-processing under scrutiny. As a result, the auditor has the potential to offer a company valuable insights in areas of weakness or areas which could be improved at minimal cost.

Clearly, through-the-computer auditing is a more thorough test of accounting data processing than around-the-computer auditing, and therefore enables the auditors to fulfill their roles more effectively as objective examiners of the accounting information system. This in turn enables the external auditors to provide better services to their clients, or, alternatively, enables the internal auditors to provide better services to their company.

Through-the-computer auditing also has disadvantages. Perhaps the most apparent is that through-the-computer auditing is much more demanding of EDP and accounting resources. For example, special computer time must be set aside for auditing runs with test decks, and EDP subsystem staff must be assigned to the auditor in order to provide computer documentation, library files of computer programs, spare tapes, and so forth. Where data processing is performed on a tight schedule, this requirement of additional resources is often difficult to satisfy.

Through-the-computer auditing demands more technical skills of the auditor. For example, it is difficult to imagine an auditor designing a test deck without at least some knowledge of automated accounting practices and procedures. (The fact that many practitioners in fact lack these skills perhaps explains the high demand for computer-trained auditors in today's job market.)

Although through-the-computer auditing is likely to be more thorough in evaluating the strengths and weaknesses of a given accounting information system, it must also be remembered that, at best, through-the-computer auditing is only a limited test of a complete accounting information system. No test deck is even remotely likely to examine every data possibility and thus, some processing weaknesses are always going to continue undetected. It should be noted, however, that no organization would even want to have a 100 percent audit of all its business transactions—the costs of such an audit would be exorbitant, and certainly not likely to be worth its benefits.

EVALUATING THE EFFECTIVENESS OF CONTROLS

At this point, it should be clear that one of the most important responsibilities of the auditor is to probe the accounting information system for system weaknesses, and where these are found, report such weaknesses to management. In fact, for the external auditor, this reporting is mandatory. Statement on Auditing Standards Number 20, which sets forth standards on "Required Communication of Material Weaknesses in Internal Accounting Control," states for example:

... the independent auditor should communicate to senior management and to the board of directors or its audit committee (or the equivalent level of authority, such as a board of trustees) any material weaknesses that come to his attention during the course of his examination of the financial statements if such weaknesses have not been corrected before they come to his attention. Preferably the auditor's findings should be communicated in a written report to reduce the possibility of misunderstanding. If the auditor's findings are communicated orally, he should document the communication by appropriate notations in his audit working papers.*

Although there is no similar legal requirement binding *internal* auditors to report system weaknesses to management, such a requirement

---

*Auditing Standards Executive Committee, American Institute of Certified Public Accountants, *Statement on Auditing Standards No. 20* (New York: American Institute of Certified Public Accountants, © 1977), p. 3.

is implicit in their positions within the audited company. Thus, both internal and external auditors should present their findings to a responsible organizational staff, and the auditors should accomplish this reporting on a timely basis.

Accounting textbooks have tended to place a great deal of emphasis on the detection and correction of system weaknesses, but much less attention upon system strengths. In a sense, the above is logical because system deficiencies are almost always costly if they are not corrected, whereas system strengths can only contribute in a positive sense toward the efficient operation of accounting functions. However, a myth often prevails that the typical accounting information system cannot have too many controls, and it is important that this myth be dispelled. As we have noted frequently during the last few chapters, specific system controls should be implemented only if their anticipated benefits exceed their anticipated costs.

One method by which the auditor can evaluate the desirability of controls for a particular aspect of accounting data processing is through a *hazard and loss analysis*. A table constructed in the course of this analysis is provided in Figure 10-2. Basically, the idea is to estimate the expected

Figure 10-2

HAZARD AND LOSS ANALYSIS TABLE FOR THE ALAN COMPANY

Hazard (1)	Probability that Hazard Will Occur (level of exposure) (2)	Losses		Expected Losses		Estimated Hazard Control Costs (7)
		Low Estimate (3)	High Estimate (4)	Low (5)	High (6)	
Malfunctions and Human Errors						
Equipment	.05	$100,000	$ 250,000	$ 5,000	$ 12,500	$1,000
Software	.10	10,000	100,000	1,000	10,000	2,000
Programmers	.70	1,000	20,000	700	14,000	8,500
Computer operators	.60	1,000	10,000	600	6,000	4,350
Maintenance	.90	1,000	10,000	900	9,000	2,550
User	.90	1,000	15,000	900	13,500	500
General personnel	.50	1,000	20,000	500	10,000	1,000
Fraud						
Embezzlement	.05	10,000	100,000	500	5,000	250
Confiscation of files	.10	10,000	100,000	1,000	10,000	250
Tapping	.05	10,000	100,000	500	5,000	100
Program changes	.20	5,000	25,000	1,000	5,000	5,000
Power and Communications Failures						
Brownouts and failures	.50	1,000	10,000	500	5,000	6,000
Surges	.30	1,000	50,000	300	15,000	7,500
Line failure	.70	1,000	20,000	700	4,000	1,000
Fire and Natural Disasters						
Fire	.07	100,000	250,000	7,000	17,500	1,250
Sabotage	.20	20,000	60,000	4,000	12,000	2,500
Earthquake	.01	500,000	3,000,000	5,000	30,000	2,750
Flood	.10	500,000	3,000,000	50,000	300,000	3,000
Lightning	.01	10,000	1,000,000	100	10,000	260

losses that might reasonably be anticipated if a given hazard or disaster were to occur, and to compare these expected losses with the cost of providing one or more controls to safeguard against the particular hazard under examination. For those areas in which protection costs are less than anticipated losses, the auditor recommends that the associated preventive controls be implemented. For those areas in which the costs of protection are greater than anticipated losses, the conclusion is that the degree of risk is not high enough to warrant an expenditure for certain preventive controls. Thus, for these latter cases, the auditor recommends that the specific controls not be installed.

To understand how expected losses are computed, it is necessary to examine Figure 10-2 in greater detail. The first column of Figure 10-2 identifies a particular type of hazard, the second column identifies the probability that this hazard will occur, and the third and fourth columns state low and high dollar estimates of losses resulting from the hazard (as provided by appropriate organizational management). Multiplying these "low" and "high" estimates of losses by the probability of such losses (column 2) provides the expected dollar losses of columns five and six. Thus, for example, our table states that the probability of equipment malfunction is .05, that a low estimate of the losses involved in such a difficulty would be $100,000, that a high estimate of losses involved would be $250,000, and that the range of expected costs of these losses would therefore be between $5,000 and $12,500.

The seventh column of the table provides estimates of the costs of providing preventive controls which guard against a particular type of accounting difficulty. These values would either be provided by management or estimated by the auditor. Once the expected losses and the hazard-control costs have been ascertained, a decision regarding whether or not to provide preventive controls for the particular difficulty can be made on a hazard-by-hazard basis. For those hazards whose control costs are less than the low expected loss (column 5), the benefits of the control exceed their costs and the controls should be maintained (or installed). This con-

clusion would apply in our case of equipment malfunction, for example, in which the total estimated costs of guarding against such an occurrence are $1000 but anticipated losses are at least $5000. In effect, $1000 worth of controls are "buying"—or guarding against—at least $5000 worth of anticipated losses—or $5000 worth of benefits—and therefore these controls should be installed.

Where the estimated costs of control exceed the "high" estimate of expected losses, the opposite conclusion would be reached and the controls should not be implemented. Thus, for example, in the case of brownouts and power failures, the control or safeguard (e.g., the maintenance of a stand-by generator) is shown to be too costly ($6000 compared with the "high" expected loss of $5000) and not worth its benefits. In this instance, therefore, the control should not be implemented.

The most difficult decision is the case in which the estimated cost of controlling a particular hazard falls within the range of expected losses. In this instance, the costs of protection would be too great if losses were small, but well worth their costs if losses were high. This is the kind of situation that turns an auditor's hair prematurely white, but in fact, such an event is likely in accounting practice. In these situations, it is the auditor's responsibility to report such findings to management and not to make a recommendation either for or against the implementation of the associated preventive controls. The decision must be made by management.

A hazard-and-loss table is not an easy analysis to prepare. Neither the costs of implementing specific accounting controls nor the losses that might occur in the absence of such controls are always estimatable or, for that matter, even identifiable. Furthermore, because the statistical probabilities required to compute expected losses are not given quantities, but must be estimated subjectively, they are unsettling for decision-making purposes. Finally, the entire analysis is somewhat questionable to the extent that it uses expected losses, which are computed as probabilities times anticipated losses, rather than full losses, for comparative purposes. Thus, for all these reasons, a hazard-and-loss analysis is not a definitive means of evaluating the desirability of specific internal controls. Rather, it is better considered one of the many tools that the auditor may wish to apply in this evaluation process.

AUDITING WITH THE COMPUTER

In addition to auditing *through* the computer in order to verify processing accuracy and the presence of adequate processing controls, auditors can use the computer to assist them in various other auditing tasks. Where an accounting information system has been automated, in fact, auditing *with* the computer is virtually mandatory because the accounting data are stored on computer media and manual access is impossible. However, there are many other positive reasons beyond the need to access computerized accounting data for the use of the computer in performing audit functions.

Perhaps one of the most important of these reasons is auditing efficiency. Kenneth Cadematori reports an excellent illustration.* His assignment was to audit a computerized payroll system, which included (1) the verification of wage rates, (2) the checking of income tax deductions and social security deductions, and (3) the validation of the accuracy of the payroll files with respect to employees who had left, new employees hired, and changes in rates of pay. There were approximately 25,000 employees, whose payroll records were stored on three magnetic tape files. Cadematori estimated that it would have taken over 5000 hours to audit the payroll system manually. Instead, he spent approximately 300 hours to develop a computer program which accomplished the same thing. This program took only two hours to execute on the computer and, once written, was available for years of subsequent auditing use.

*Kenneth Cadematori, "Computer Auditing," *New York CPA*, June 1959, p. 433.

Uses of the Computer

By and large, auditing *with* the computer usually focuses upon the verification of accounting data stored on computer files. Functional tasks along these lines are described in the paragraphs below.

File printouts. An auditor can print the entire contents of a file, or if desired, just those particular file records passing predetermined selection tests. If complete printouts are justified, the auditor can usually make use of tape-to-printer or disk-to-printer utility programs which require no special computer coding by the auditor and can be run on the computer immediately as needed. Inasmuch as the amount of data stored on the typical computer file is likely to be voluminous, however, it usually makes more sense for the auditor to print out the contents of a file on a selective basis. For example, in reviewing the contents of an inventory file, the auditor would probably not wish to see the file records for each inventory item. Instead, the auditor might request only those records for inventory items whose purchase-cost fields (indicating the per-unit costs of the items) exceed a specified cost level.

Where records are to be printed on a selective basis, it is usually necessary to prepare a special program for running in conjunction with the file to be processed. At one point in time, auditors had little recourse but to either write their own programs or do without. Today, most auditors make use of prewritten computer programs (called "generalized auditing packages") which accomplish their desired tasks with a minimum of additional input. These prewritten computer programs are described more fully in a later section of this chapter.

File verification. An auditor can verify the contents of a file by performing such functions as testing for internal consistency, arithmetic checking, cross-footing, computing subtotals, making record counts, and searching for discrepancies. In testing for internal consistency, for example, the auditor can make sure that sequential files are, in fact, in proper, ascending, sequential order, compare redundant data fields of a single record (e.g., a product code and a product description in an inventory-file record) to make sure that the fields are in agreement, compare record key numbers to make sure that they correspond to appropriate file-segment numbers, and so forth. In arithmetic checking, the auditor can reperform any arithmetic computations which were initially made when the record was created—for example, the extension of sales-ticket information within a sales file—to check for accuracy and completeness in file records.

Cross-footing requires that the auditor add a set of figures twice, each time using a different classification of the data. For example, on a computer file containing information about the sales performance of marketing personnel, the sum of a month's sales by all sales representatives should equal the sum of the month's sales by regions. Where cross-footing is not successful, the auditor is obliged to report the discrepancy to management and, where the discrepancy is material in dollar amount, ascertain causes.

Computing subtotals and making record counts have been discussed at length in Chapter 8, and therefore need not be discussed again. This leaves discrepancy reporting. Here, the auditor looks for file records which appear to be exceptions to normal conditions, and he or she requests the computer to print out such records on an individual basis. This type of auditing is an excellent example of our management-by-exception principle which was discussed in Chapter 2. Because the discrepancy report focuses attention only on those items that have failed a specific validity test, it is a very efficient auditing tool.

Most of the audit verification functions described above could be used by the auditor as a basis for preparing a discrepancy report. Some additional examples would include the detection of outdated records on a "current" transactions file, the listing of accounts receivable records for customers whose balances exceeded specified credit limits, and the listing of payroll records for employees whose gross-pay amounts exceeded predetermined pay levels. In each case, the auditor would be concentrating only on those items that fell outside a predetermined range of "normal" values. This does not of course mean that such records are necessarily in error. Rather, such records simply form the *basis* of further inquiry because they are, in some way, unusual, and therefore reasonable targets for auditing scrutiny.

Preparing profiles. Another name for this use of the computer might be "data-reduction techniques" because the primary intent is to categorize the accounting data of a computer file into one or more classifications, or data "strata," for the purpose of reviewing the file's contents. An example, which has been discussed at length in earlier chapters, is the preparation of an aging analysis of accounts receivable. Here, the strata categories are (1) amount of accounts receivable not yet past due, (2) the amount of accounts receivable 1–30 days past due, (3) the amount of accounts receivable 31–60 days past due, and so on. (See Figure 6-5.) Similar profiling of an inventory file, for example, might be used to identify which inventory items require the greatest use of the company's cash asset, which suppliers provide the bulk of the company's production supplies, which of the company's manufacturing divisions make the greatest use of certain types of raw materials, and which suppliers offer cash discounts of greatest advantage to the company.

In addition to "one-dimensional" profiles, in which the contents of a computer file are sorted according to only one categorizing criterion, "two-dimensional" profiles are also possible. For example, a computer file of the Alan Company's sporting goods sales could be categorized both by product type and sales region, as reflected in Figure 10-3. (For illustrative purposes, only a few of the company's products are included in the figure.) A report of this type might be of great value to the vice president of marketing because it would indicate those regional areas in which certain product sales were the

Figure 10-3. A sales report for the Alan Company.

ALAN COMPANY SALES ANALYSIS REPORT

Month of June 1984

Product	Sales Region					
	Northeast	**Southeast**	**Midwest**	**Northwest**	**Southwest**	**Totals**
Baseball gloves	$ 6,431	$ 4,322	$ 3,652	$ 2,587	$ 3,451	$20,443
Baseballs	2,561	7,575	5,431	3,443	2,666	21,676
Golf bags	482	952	2,544	1,295	3,498	8,771
Basketballs	1,382	3,451	6,431	8,436	3,222	22,922
Footballs	4,631	3,321	974	2,139	1,389	12,454
Tennis balls	829	119	1,630	2,884	2,145	7,607
Totals	$16,316	$19,740	$20,662	$20,784	$16,371	$93,873

strongest, and perhaps even more importantly, also indicate those regions in which certain product sales were weakest. The auditor could also make good use of a report of this type. For example, where sales of a particular product were not being reported for a certain marketing region, the two-dimensional report would make this system deficiency obvious because the appropriate table element would be missing.

One especially notable case of profiling was performed by an iron-works manufacturing company that supplied construction materials to local contractors. An audit of the company's business sales over a two-year period revealed the startling fact that 99 percent of the company's sales volume was concentrated in the hands of only 10 customers! Said one manager of the company, "We knew these guys were important, but none of us had any idea they were *that* important!" As a result of this discovery, the company streamlined its customer-support operations to make sure that these "top-ten" clients got first-class service.

Statistical sampling. Rarely is it possible or cost-effective for an auditor to examine 100 percent of the computer records stored on a commercial computer file. Thus, where magnetic tape or disk files are involved, the auditor may also make use of a computer to select a small subset of the computer records for auditing purposes. The size of this sample varies according to the needs of the auditor and is determined through the use of statistical methods beyond the scope of this book. Of more immediate importance are: (1) the reasons that might motivate an auditor to statistically sample a computer file of accounting records, (2) the data-processing implications of such statistical sampling, and (3) the methods used in the various types of sampling processes. Each of these is discussed briefly in the paragraphs below.

Perhaps the most common use of statistical sampling is in confirmation auditing. Here, the auditor is asked to verify the computer-file information through some type of feedback investigation. Where the auditor is primarily concerned with the monetary information of the computer records (as for example in the confirmation of the dollar balances of the computerized accounts receivable subsidiary ledger), this type of sampling is termed *estimation sampling for variables*. Where nonmonetary information is the primary focus (e.g., in verifying that inventory receipts are correctly recorded), this type of sampling is termed *estimation sampling for attributes*.

The most common form of confirmation sampling is *positive confirmation*, in which a selected sample of accounts (e.g., credit-sales customers) are mailed polite letters of inquiry and asked to verify their account-balance information as shown in the letter. A return envelope is customarily enclosed for the convenience of the respondents. Usually, it is possible to have the computer generate the letter, whose format would be standard for each account and can therefore be preprinted. The only information that would vary from letter to letter would be the customer's name and address and, of course, the file-record information to be confirmed— information that should be available directly from the computer file(s) being audited.

With positive confirmation techniques, it is necessary to keep track of which respondents reply to the confirmation letter and which do not. The maintenance of a separate computer file is convenient for this purpose because: (1) the file can be created by the computer at the same time the initial confirmation sample is drawn, (2) the credit customers responding to the confirmation letter can automatically be "checked off" the list of accounts in the sample audit if a machine-readable turnaround document is provided in the original letter of inquiry, (3) a second, follow-up letter of inquiry can be computer-generated in a manner akin to the first letter for those credit customers who have not responded by a specified date, and (4) the automated handling of the confirmation sample permits the auditor to confirm in a cost-effective manner a larger portion of the original computer file than could otherwise be achieved with manual methods.

Negative confirmation is also possible. Here, credit customers are also sent a letter of inquiry, but are asked to respond only if a discrepancy in their account-balance information is noted. The negative confirmation approach is typically used for auditing receivable accounts having relatively small dollar balances. Because negative confirmation is based upon our now-familiar management-by-exceptions principle, it is often more efficient than a positive confirmation approach: valuable auditing efforts, EDP staff time, and management time are devoted entirely to only those accounts requiring investigation. Negative confirmation is also less expensive to perform because only the costs of the return mail for the discrepancies, rather than for all re-

spondents, need be incurred. Finally, with negative confirmation, it is not necessary to maintain a computer file as it was for the positive-confirmation process.

The biggest problem with negative confirmations is that the auditor cannot distinguish between those credit customers whose balances are correct and therefore do not respond, and those customers whose balances are incorrect but do not respond. Where the confirmation mailing is large enough, however, or, where there is a strong incentive for the "discrepancy account" to respond (e.g., a credit-sales customer discovers an unfavorable error or the customer is offered a reward for reporting the error), the negative confirmation may be quite satisfactory.

Beyond positive and negative confirmation sampling, there is also physical confirmation, which requires the auditor to verify account information using some physical process. Where inventory records are involved, for example, the auditor would be required to confirm the inventory account balances by actually visiting the warehouse site and counting the number of units of specific inventory items. In one famous case, auditors were required to examine the holding vats of a vegetable-oil company in order to verify this (liquid) asset of the company. The auditors climbed to the tops of huge holding vats, observed that they were full, and filed a positive report. They never realized that almost all the vats had fake bottoms and that the tanks contained less than 3 feet of oil.

The method by which a sample of the computer file is taken will dictate the type of data processing used to perform this audit task. There are various sampling procedures. Perhaps the most straightforward is the systematic selection of every nth record on the computer file (e.g., every tenth accounts receivable record within the accounts receivable subsidiary ledger file). Where sequential files are involved, the systematic selection process is easy to program and the sample is relatively unbiased. (However, care must be taken that the file does not have a systematic storage feature which would defeat this systematic-selection purpose.) Where a computer file has been arranged in segments—for example, where customer checking account data for multiple branches of a bank are stored as separate, contiguous segments of a file—this sampling technique also automatically assures that the number of elements drawn from each file segment is proportional to the size of the file segment.

Because it is the exceptions that are of special interest to the auditor, audit sampling is often performed on a more discriminatory basis. *Selective sampling techniques* enable the auditor to specify those conditions which will automatically trigger the selection of special records for confirmation purposes. Thus, 100 percent of large, inactive accounts of a bank should be included in an audit because these accounts are especially prone to unauthorized manipulation. Other conditions under which selective sampling might wisely be used would include those general ledger accounts having large or unusual balances, those computer records appearing to have unusual activity, those employee payroll records with an unusual amount of overtime, or those inventory records reflecting unusually high or low inventory turnover rates.

A final, relatively uncommon form of selective sampling is called *discovery sampling*. Here, the auditor looks for at least one example of a particular type of error—for instance, the creation of a fictitious accounts-payable invoice or the creation of a fictitious payroll record. Discovery sampling is difficult to perform unless the auditor knows precisely what is required when searching the computer file. For this reason, and also because neither internal nor external auditors are concerned primarily with the detection of fraud when performing their normal audit functions, discovery sampling will only be implemented when special circumstances appear to warrant it.

The problem with selective sampling when performed on a computer is that it requires special effort to create the computer program necessary to execute the selective process(es). Even the most sophisticated generalized auditing computer program package (discussed below) is lim-ited in what it can do, and thus, the auditors will need special skills if they are to perform the detailed auditing work necessary in the automated accounting environment.

Computer Audit Packages

The need to audit accounting files with the aid of the computer has inspired the development of *generalized auditing packages* (i.e., prewritten computer programs) which enable the auditor to review computer files without continually rewriting processing programs. Almost all large CPA firms have at least one such audit package, and additional packages can be acquired from software suppliers (such as IBM) at relatively little cost to the user.

Most generalized auditing packages are basically file-manipulation programs written in a high-level programming language such as COBOL or RPG. Some representative examples, together with selected operating characteristics, are identified in Figure 10-4. All of these audit packages have the capability to perform basic data-manipulating tasks such as sampling, performing mathematical computations, cross-footing, categorizing, summarizing, performing comparisons, matching fields in separate files, merging two files together, sorting, and printing reports. In each package, the user can specify the input/output media used in the process (e.g., tape, disk, etc.).

Generalized audit packages are more alike than different. Primarily, the differences fall into three areas: (1) what computer hardware the software programs will run on, (2) the number of reports that can be generated in one pass through the computer file being audited, and (3) the number of data fields within a single computer file record which can be accessed and manipulated for auditing purposes. Of these differences, hardware requirements are probably the least restrictive. This is because it is usually possible to reformat a tape or disk file so that the file can be processed on the hardware available to the auditor.

Name	CPA Firm	Hardware Requirements	Number of Output File Requests/Run	Number of Extractable Data Fields/Run
AUDASSIST	Alexander Grant & Co.	Not available	Not available	19
AUDITAPE	Deloitte, Haskins & Sells	IBM 1401, 360, 370; Honeywell 62, 66, 200, 6000; Univac 1100	Not available	12
AUDITPAK II	Coopers & Lybrand	IBM 360, 370	9	No limit
AUDITRONICS 32	Ernst & Whinney	IBM 360, 370; Honeywell with conversions	98	100
STRATA	Touche, Ross & Co.	IBM 360, 370, System 3; Honeywell 2000–4700; Burroughs 2500–4700	20	99
SYSTEM 2170	Peat, Marwick, Mitchell & Co.	IBM 360, 370; Honeywell 2000–4700; Burroughs 2500–4700	5	50

Figure 10-4. Names and selected operating characteristics of six generalized auditing packages.

The number of reports that can be generated, per pass, from a given file is important primarily in terms of resource efficiency. The greater the number of reports that can be generated from a computer file in a single pass, the less computer time and other resources required for the audit. There are only so many reports that an auditor is likely to want from any given file, however, and thus, even the capability of producing two or three reports is often sufficient for auditing purposes.

The last difference identified above is the number of data fields, per record, which the audit program can extract and/or manipulate. This is probably the most crucial of the three differences in generalized audit packages. Certain types of analysis require the use of many fields of data. If the data fields are not available because of this field limitation, the analysis cannot be performed. In commercial accounting applications, a typical computer record on an important master file is likely to have hundreds of data fields. Thus, the larger the number of fields that an audit program can access per record, the more data processing that can be performed in a single pass of the computer file.

SUMMARY

This chapter has discussed the general topic of auditing from the viewpoint of a computerized accounting information system. Although both the internal and external auditor are vitally concerned with the accounting information system, we noted that there are important differences in the goals of internal and external auditing. The external auditor's chief concern is that the financial statements of the company are fairly presented, whereas the internal auditor verifies adherence to company policies and procedures.

The primary goal in the audit of an accounting information system is to evaluate the system's strengths and weaknesses, and to make recommendations where changes seem appropriate. Thus, the intent is not to catch crooks. In the sense that both planned and surprise audits are feedback controls, however, the detection of fraud, should it exist and be material, is a natural by-product of the auditor's investigative responsibilities. It was also noted that a good audit trail is an absolute necessity in the audit process. Because computerized accounting tends to obscure this audit trail, the auditor must make sure that input transactions are traceable throughout the processing cycles. This is especially problematic where real-time data-processing accounting systems are in use because remote input obscures the origin of some transactions, and updating in place on magnetic disk files changes the status of the file records after this updating is accomplished.

There are three approaches to auditing a computerized accounting information system: (1) auditing *around* the computer, (2) auditing *through* the computer, and (3) auditing *with* the computer. Today, and in most cases, auditing *around* the computer is the least viable investigative approach: the auditor must audit *through* the computer and *with* the computer to do a creditable job. The three primary methods of auditing *through* the computer involve: (1) the use of a specially prepared test deck of hypothetical business transactions, (2) the validation of the computer processing programs themselves to assure the accuracy and integrity of the data-processing logic, and (3) the use of an integrated test facility. The test deck examines both the processing capabilities of the accounting information system and the controls that safeguard these capabilities. The procedures involved in the validation of the computer processing programs include (1) tests of program authorization, (2) control-total tests, (3) surprise audits of programs while they are in use, and (4) surprise substitution of auditor-controlled programs for those in use at the computer center. Finally, an integrated test facility enables the auditor to create fictitious accounts and audit an accounting information system on an operational basis.

An auditor may also be asked to evaluate the effectiveness of controls either already installed within the accounting information system or contemplated for the system when design changes are about to be made. A useful device for this evaluation process is a hazard and loss analysis report. For each set of potential hazards, the estimated costs of associated controls are weighed against the expected benefits from these controls. Although the computation of a single benefit figure is possible for each set of controls, this chapter has suggested the alternate computation of a *range* of benefit values, based upon the likelihood of various hazards causing harm to the normal functioning of the accounting information system. We noted that the computation of such a range of benefits makes the ensuing analysis a little more complicated. On the other hand, such an approach is probably more realistic in terms of calculating the true "exposure" of the accounting information system to the various problems that might occur.

When an accountant audits *with* the computer, the computer is used as a tool to assist in the various audit processes. The computer can prepare printouts of magnetic tape and disk files, verify the information on a file and report discrepancies on an exceptions basis, prepare statistical profiles of accounting data (e.g., an aging analysis of accounts receivable), assist in the preparation of confirmation letters to credit customers, and take any number of statistical samples for investigative purposes. Most of the major CPA firms make use of generalized audit packages, that is, prewritten computer programs which perform various auditing tasks and therefore assist auditors in their examination work. Audit packages are written in higher-level source programming languages such as COBOL, and typically require little computer programming skill by the auditor.

DISCUSSION QUESTIONS

10-1. Distinguish between the roles of an internal auditor and an external auditor. Cite at least two examples of auditing procedures that might reasonably be expected of the internal auditor but not the external auditor. If you had your choice, which type of auditor would you rather be? Why?

10-2. "Inasmuch as the internal auditor works for the same company he or she audits, the question of objectivity is a moot point—no sane person is going to blow the whistle on his or her own people." Discuss.

10-3. Bob Hogan worked as an administrative assistant for Janet Cornelius Publishers. Part of Bob's responsibilities included the supervision of the petty cash fund. When the disbursements from the fund failed to match the voucher receipts for the third straight week in a row, Bob's boss called him into his office, told him that his work was "unsatisfactory," and informed him that a full external audit would be required of his department because of his negligence in handling the petty cash fund. Discuss this situation in light of the chapter materials.

10-4. In the text, it was stated that "auditing is like police investigations." In what ways would this analogy make sense? In what ways would this analogy not make sense?

10-5. Discuss some of the advantages of the surprise audit as opposed to a planned audit. What disadvantages are involved in the surprise audit?

10-6. Linda Carr Cosmetics distributes a full line of cosmetics for women, including facial makeup, eyeliners, beauty and skin creams, and so forth. Phil Morena was the company's treasurer. One evening, after consuming an excessive number of Manhattans at his favorite bar, Phil stated to an accountant friend, "You know, ole buddy, you accounting people don't fool anybody. We have both announced and surprise audits at the company, but the only 'surprise' in the surprise audit is how long the auditors will take to finish up. Last year when the auditors 'burst' through the door, for example, we even had baked a cake with their names on it. We went right to coffee instead of wasting time in our accounting office. The whole thing is just a big waste of time." Comment.

10-7. Why is a good audit trail important to both the internal and external auditor? How is the audit trail followed in a real-time processing environment?

10-8. Chia and Corter Enterprises manufactured "antique" furniture, which it then sold to distributors on both coasts. The inventory-

control system kept track of raw materials on a real-time basis. Thus, the inventory records for such items as sheets of stock plywood and hardware were updated on a magnetic disk as issuances and receipts took place. Once a week, the contents of the inventory file were printed out to provide management with current information on the status of the major inventory items. The issuances and receipts slips for the previous week were then destroyed. Because the company had little room for excess paper and because the primary emphasis was on manufacturing and not on paperwork, it had been the practice to empty the week's issuances and receipts slips from the "inventory-activity" hopper once this report had been reviewed by management. Comment from the standpoint of the internal auditor and also from the standpoint of the external auditor.

10-9. Distinguish among the following terms: auditing around the computer, auditing through the computer, and auditing with the computer. Which is least effective in performing an audit of an accounting information system? Justify your answer, providing specific examples of an accounting application of your choice.

10-10. Describe the use of a test deck when auditing through the computer. Why is the term *test deck* somewhat of a misnomer today? Give some examples of exception conditions which a test deck might discover in auditing an accounts receivable accounting information system.

10-11. Why is the assembly of a test deck more difficult when accounting data are accumulated for a data base? Provide an example.

10-12. Describe four methods by which an auditor might audit the computer programs of an accounting information system. Which method do you think would be the easiest to use? Which is the hardest? If you could use but one of the four methods described, which would you choose? Why?

10-13. The Hillside Company is an auditing firm whose auditors are notorious for conducting "merciless" surprise audits. The company's president, Mr. Jackson Suyderhoud, in fact, often bragged about the severity of his firm's scrutiny and the fact that none of the firm's surprise audits lasted less than a month. Said Mr. Suyderhoud, "Hillside prides itself on a thorough, complete job for its clients. If there is any fraud left undetected in a company we audit on a surprise basis, I'll eat it!" Comment.

10-14. Through-the-computer auditing has several advantages over around-the-computer auditing, but it also has some disadvantages. What are some of these disadvantages? For each disadvantage discussed, suggest a method by which the problem might be solved, or at least lessened, without abandoning the through-the-computer approach to conducting audit functions.

10-15. How does an auditor evaluate the internal controls of an automated accounting information system? How is the element of uncertainty handled in the audit examination?

10-16. Mr. Robert Sproule was the one and only internal auditor of a medium-sized communications firm. The company used a computer for most of its accounting applications, and recently, several new software packages had been implemented to handle the increased volume of the company's business. To evaluate the package's control capabilities, Mr. Sproule had performed a cost/benefit study and found that many of the controls were potentially useful, but not clearly cost-effective. The problem, therefore, was what to say in his report. After pondering this question for some time, he decided to recommend almost all the controls on the idea that a company was "better to be safe than sorry." Comment.

10-17. Mr. Joseph Taylor was the head of the accounting department at Pomona Graphics, Inc., a company which specialized in lettering, artwork, and other graphics-design work used in commercial business. Joe was familiar with computer audit techniques but felt a little uncomfortable about the distinction between auditing through the computer and auditing with the computer. Are there any differences? Explain.

10-18. The Pan Pacific Computer Company pur-chases independent computer components which it then uses to manufacture custom-made computer hardware. Since it deals with a number of vendors, it has computerized the accounting procedures for its accounts payables. Describe how an auditor might use an integrated test facility to audit this accounting application.

10-19. How can the auditor verify the contents of a computer file? Describe as many tests as you can. Would the tests for a master file of accounts receivable be the same as the tests for the year-to-date transactions file in this same application? (You might wish to review the detailed discussion of this accounting application in Chapter 6.)

10-20. What is a "profile" as might be generated from an accounting information file? What uses are made of these profiles? Provide an example of a profile that might be generated for each of the following accounting applications: (a) accounts receivable file, (b) accounts payable file, (c) sales file, (d) purchase order file, (e) employee payroll file, and (f) inventory file.

10-21. Discuss the advantages and the disadvantages of the various types of statistical sampling. What purpose(s) does confirmation techniques play in auditing? Are there any circumstances in which an auditor would choose *not* to confirm the contents of a computer file in one of the sampling techniques you mentioned?

10-22. What is a computer generalized auditing package? Why are there so many of them?

10-23. John Wells was an auditor working for the independent accounting firm of Pat Gilbert and Associates. John's training at the local College of Business had been thorough and he loved his job because it gave him an opportunity to use his extensive computer skills in his chosen auditing profession. On one particular job, John was asked to verify the contents of several large computer files. "No problem," he said. "I can write a set of computer programs which can get the job done in a few weeks." His boss replied, "Why not use the company's SCAN program—it should do almost all the verification work for us." John replied that he liked to program and could write as many tests as necessary to get all the verification work done. Comment.

PROBLEMS

10-24. Describe the steps an auditor might take in performing an "around-the-computer" audit of an accounts payable accounting application. Assume that vendor purchase invoice data are recorded on punched cards. These cards are used to produce checks, as illustrated below. What potential weaknesses in this processing system might not be detected by such "around-the-computer" auditing practice? What additional tests in a "through-the-computer" audit might be used to identify the system weaknesses you have outlined in your answer above?

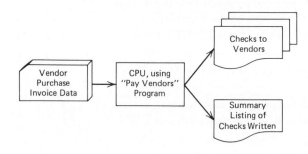

10-25. A CPA accumulates various kinds of evidence upon which to base an opinion on the fairness of financial statements under examination. Among this evidence are confirmations from third parties and written representations from the client.

Required

1. What is an audit confirmation?
2. What characteristics should an audit confirmation possess if a CPA is to consider it as valid evidence?
3. Distinguish between a positive confirmation and a negative confirmation in the auditor's examination of accounts receivable.
4. In confirming an audit client's accounts receivable, what characteristics should be present in the accounts if the CPA is to use negative confirmations?

5. List the information a CPA should solicit in a standard bank confirmation inquiry sent to an audit client's bank.

(AICPA Adapted)

10-26. On page 318 is an order form used by Automated Information Systems, Inc. to sell its computer package called "ASKIT." According to the information on this form:

1. What is ASKIT?
2. What accounting tasks might such a programming system perform for a typical business organization?
3. Interpret the "operating characteristics" indicated in item A of the form. (*Hint:* See Chapter 19.)
4. Why would a user require cards as offered in item (B) instead of a magnetic tape as offered in item (A)?
5. Would the typical commercial company use this form as an invoice as suggested in the form? Why or why not?

CASE ANALYSES

10-27. *Linder Company*

Linder Company is completing the implementation of its new computerized inventory control and purchase order system. Linder's controller wants the controls incorporated into the programs of the new system to be reviewed and evaluated. This is to ensure that all necessary computer controls are included and functioning properly. He respects and has confidence in the system department's work and evaluation procedures, but he would like a separate appraisal of the control procedures by the internal audit department. Hopefully, such a review would reveal any weaknesses or omissions in control procedures and lead to their immediate correction before the system becomes operational.

The internal audit department carefully reviews the input, processing, and output controls when evaluating a new system. When assessing the processing controls incorporated into the programs of new systems applications, the internal auditors regularly employ the technique commonly referred to as "auditing through the computer."

AUTOMATED INFORMATION SYSTEMS, INC.
P. O. BOX 875
HANDSON, PENNSYLVANIA 19040

INVOICE-ORDER FORM FOR ASKIT

"AUTOMATED SEQUENTIAL COMPUTER TO INQUIRE TERMINALS"

AUTHOR: Dr. Johnathan Streffler, University of Pennsylvania
VERSION: September, 1979

This program enables the user to inquire the contents of any magnetic or disk file. The program will indicate the status of a particular master file record, prepare frequency distributions of selected data according to pre-selected data fields, prepare cross-tabulations for aging analysis or salesperson reports, and perform simple linear regressions. Additional support, including error corrections and telephone conversations, is available at two levels to suit processing and support needs (see below, items C and D). Just fill in the form below.

CHECK ITEMS DESIRED BELOW

ITEM	DESCRIPTION	CHARGES
A	Basic programs in source language on magnetic tape, including sample data deck. The tape is a 9-track tape prepared on an IBM 370/168 with the following operating characteristics: DSB-DATA, RECFM=FB, LRECL=80, BLKSIZE=12960, DENSITY=1600 bpi. (University rate: $1,500; Nonuniversity rate: $3,000)	$ _____
B	Card deck instead of above magnetic tape. (University rate: $1,550; Nonuniversity rate: $3,050)	_____
C	Service level (1) for user support. Includes notice of errors, modifications, contributed changes to the program from users, and one year's membership in USER GROUP. (Yearly cost: $25)	_____
D	Service level (2) for user support. Includes all support identified in (C) above, plus 5 hours telephone service to answer specific questions and advise user clients on use of system. (Yearly cost: $200)	_____
	TOTAL AMOUNT	$ _____

Your name: _____

(Payment must accompany order)

Company name: _____

Company address: _____

City/State/Zip Code: _____

SAVE: RETAIN THIS INVOICE FOR YOUR RECORDS. SEND US A COPY WITH TOTAL AMOUNT REMITTED. ORDERS OUTSIDE THE UNITED STATES AND CANADA MUST INCLUDE $15 ADDITION FOR POSTAGE AND HANDLING.

Required

A. Identify the types of controls that should be incorporated into the computer programs of the new system.

B. Explain how the existence of the computer controls and their proper functioning are verified using "auditing-through-the-computer" techniques.

(CMA Adapted)

10-28. *Wholesale Cosmetics*

An auditor is conducting an examination of the financial statements of Wholesale Cosmetics, a distributor with an inventory consisting of thousands of individual items. The distributor keeps its inventory in its own distribution center and in two public warehouses. An inventory computer file is maintained on a computer disk and at the end of each business day the file is updated. Each record of the inventory file contains the following data:

- Item number
- Location of item
- Description of item
- Quantity on hand
- Cost per item
- Date of last purchase
- Date of last sale
- Quantity sold during year

The auditor is planning to observe the distributor's physical count of inventories as of a given date. The auditor will have available a computer tape of the data on the inventory file on the date of the physical count and a general purpose computer software package.

Required

The auditor is planning to perform basic inventory auditing procedures. Identify the basic inventory auditing procedures and describe how the use of the general purpose software package and the tape of the inventory file data might be helpful to the auditor in performing such auditing procedures.

Organize your answer as follows:

Basic inventory auditing procedure	How general purpose computer software package and tape of the inventory file data might be helpful
1. *Observe the physical count, making and recording test counts where applicable.*	*Determining which items are to be test counted by selecting a random sample of a representative number of items from the inventory file as of the date of the physical count.*

(AICPA Adapted)

10-29. *Mark Tick, Auditor Extraordinaire**

The paragraphs below describe an audit of the computer center of the Jim Harmon Company, as performed by Mark Tick, Auditor Extraordinaire.

Driving up to headquarters, Mark could sense he was close to his destination, probably because of the neon sign on the roof indicating that the division's data center was located in the basement of the main building on the river side, which was four inches below flood level.

Mark donned his dark glasses, adjusted his CIA-emblazoned belt buckle, checked his supply of red and blue dual-pointed pencils, and, approaching the receptionist, asked for the data center manager. Without questioning Mark's identity or reason for being there, she informed him that the manager was away from the data center for a few minutes and told him to wait in the computer room.

"We have all our visitors wait there. They seem to be infatuated with the twinkling little lights on the console," she crooned.

"What's a console?" asked Mark.

"It's the thing next to the 10-gallon gas-fired coffee urn," was her reply.

*Adapted from Paul D. Johnson, "Mark Tick's Data Center Audit," *EDPACS*, June 1974, pp. 16–17. Copyright © 1974, Automation Training Center, Inc., Reston, VA. Reprinted with permission.

Mark walked toward the data center, down a hallway crowded with employees on their way to the cafeteria. On both sides of the hall he noticed, without interest, open racks of magnetic tapes labeled neatly with such titles as "Accounts Receivable Master File," "YTD Payroll Master," "Stockholder Records," "General Ledger Summary," etc. He paused for a moment to watch a pickup game of ring toss, noting that the lunch crowd had obtained the rings from the sides of magnetic tape reels.

"Ingenious people," he thought, "finding use for those worthless little rings."

As Mark walked through the keypunch room, he noticed employees drifting into the room and dumping loose source documents into a box labeled "Input." The keypunch operators were taking out handfuls of the documents for punching. Mark, ever alert, recognized that documents were selected in conformity with the generally accepted "Random LIFO" method.

Entering the computer room, Mark waved to the sole occupant, a machine operator who was hastily punching up cards and inserting them in a deck labeled "Payroll Source Code."

"Obviously, a valuable employee," mused Mark. "It's good to see someone putting forth some extra effort."

Mark poured a cup of coffee, and, as he started to count the petty cash, placed it on top of the 4-foot high stack of dust-covered disk packs. He wondered if the small amount of coffee he spilled would stain the floor as it drained through the disks. Noticing that the hot cup was causing the plastic top of the disk to bend a bit, he pulled a few cards from a deck labeled "Daily Sales Update," which was lying on the console, to use for a coaster.

Mark noticed that the machine operator, having run the unnumbered payroll checks through the check signer, was separating the carbons from the checks. The fourth copy of the checks passed neatly into the fiberboard wastebasket as the machine hummed smoothly, giving the operator a chance to have a smoke and discuss with two mailboys who had just entered how much the various vice-presidents were being paid. Mark was impressed with the operator's concern for neatness, displayed by his having run the console log sheets through the shredder as soon as he finished the payroll run. Mark drew an appreciative smile from the operator as he quipped,

"Nobody could make anything out of the gobbledygook the typewriter just printed, so better to destroy it than get buried under it."

Mark saw a box in the corner labeled "To Disaster File" and inquired, "What's this for?"

The operator explained that the maintenance department's foreman allowed the data center to store copies of important programs in the bottom of his locker.

"What type of programs?" asked Mark.

"Well, as far as I know, the only program over there is the one which causes the printer to use millions of little x's to form a nude girl saying "Merry Christmas!" was the reply.

Mark glanced at the bulletin board and immediately got an indication as to how well organized the data center manager was and that he was nobody's fool. The three signs that impressed him the most read:

—"Fairness is our motto. All input is processed on a first-come, first-served basis."

—"This is a data processing operation, not a delivery service. All output for the current week will be placed on the big table in the cafeteria before 4 p.m. each Friday. Help yourself."

—"To expedite processing and cut down on unnecessary paper shuffling, all documents rejected by the computer because of out-of-balance controls or invalid data will be immediately corrected and re-entered by the machine operators."

The data center manager came in and introduced himself to Mark. He apologized for being away so long. He explained that he had had a hard time finding a garden hose long enough to reach into the data center through a hole in the plywood partition separating it from the adjacent boiler room.

"Good idea," Mark said approvingly. "A lot cheaper than buying fire extinguishers for the data center."

"Well, how does the place look?" the manager asked, perspiring slightly in the 90-degree heat.

"Great!" said Mark. "There will be only one item in my report. There is the serious matter of the 47-

cent unexplained shortage in your $5 petty cash fund. Now, as soon as you buy me lunch, I can be off on my next adventure."

Required

Write a critique of this audit, indicating what company procedures and/or auditing procedures could stand improvement, and also indicating what you would recommend to correct the identified weaknesses.

10-30. *Vane Corporation*

The Vane Corporation is a manufacturing concern which has been in business for the past eighteen years. During this period, the company has grown from a very small family-owned operation to a medium-sized manufacturing concern with several departments. Despite this growth, a substantial number of the procedures employed by Vane Corp. have been in effect since the business was started. Just recently Vane Corp. has computerized its payroll function.

The payroll function operates in the following manner. Each worker picks up a weekly time card on Monday morning and writes in his or her name and identification number. These blank cards are kept near the factory entrance. The workers write on the time card the time of their daily arrival and departure. On the following Monday the factory supervisors collect the completed time cards for the previous week and send them to data processing.

In data processing the time cards are used to prepare the weekly time file. This file is processed with the master payroll file which is maintained on magnetic tape according to worker identification number. The checks are written by the computer on the regular checking account and imprinted with the treasurer's signature. After the payroll file is updated and the checks are prepared, the checks are sent to the factory supervisors who distribute them to the workers or hold them for the workers to pick up later if they are absent.

The supervisors notify data processing of new employees and terminations. Any changes in

hourly pay rate or any other changes affecting payroll are usually communicated to data processing by the supervisors.

The workers also complete a job time ticket for each individual job they work on each day. The job time tickets are collected daily and sent to cost accounting where they are used to prepare a cost distribution analysis.

Further analysis of the payroll function reveals the following:

1. A worker's gross wages never exceed $300 per week.
2. Raises never exceed $0.55 per hour for the factory workers.
3. No more than 20 hours of overtime is allowed each week.
4. The factory employs 150 workers in ten departments.

The payroll function has not been operating smoothly for some time, but even more problems have surfaced since the payroll was computerized. The supervisors have indicated that they would like a weekly report indicating worker tardiness, absenteeism, and idle time, so they can determine the amount of productive time lost and the reason for the lost time. The following errors and inconsistencies have been encountered the past few pay periods:

1. A worker's paycheck was not processed properly because he had transposed two numbers in his identification number when he filled out his time card.
2. A worker was issued a check for $1,531.80 when it should have been $153.81.
3. One worker's paycheck was not written, and this error was not detected until the paychecks for that department were distributed by the supervisor.
4. Part of the master payroll file was destroyed when the tape reel was inadvertently mounted on the wrong tape drive and used as a scratch tape. Data processing attempted to re-establish the destroyed portion from original source documents and other records.

5. One worker received a paycheck for an amount considerably larger than he should have. Further investigation revealed that 84 had been punched instead of 48 for hours worked.

6. Several records on the master payroll file were skipped and not included on the updated master payroll file. This was not detected for several pay periods.

7. In processing nonroutine changes, a computer operator included a pay rate increase for one of his friends in the factory. This was discovered by chance by another employee.

Required:

Identify the control weaknesses in the payroll procedure and in the computer processing as it is now conducted by the Vane Corp. Recommend the changes necessary to correct the system. Arrange your answer in the following columnar format.

Control Weaknesses	Recommendations

(CMA Adapted)

10-31.   *The Embarrassed Auditors**

Super Industries is a growing diversified manufacturing firm. Recently, the newly established internal auditing subsystem headed by Mr. C. P. Autrey conducted the first operational audit of the Reda Division. The operational audit involved a comprehensive examination of the existing policies, controls, and procedures in the division. Fundamentally, the audit objective was not to express an opinion on the divisional financial statements but to appraise (in order to improve) the ''economic efficiency of divisional operations in the context of Super Industries' corporate objectives and organization.'' The au-

*Used with the permission of Dr. E. L. Summers, Professor of Accounting, The University of Texas at Austin.

dit recommendations included suggestions for significant changes in inventory policy, plant layout, and budgeting procedures. These recommendations were routinely approved by Super Industries' central management (comprised primarily of engineers). The divisional management was a holdover from Reda's days as a separate company prior to its acquisition ten months earlier by Super. Divisional management was unsure of its relationships with corporate headquarters; accordingly, it implemented the audit recommendations with some misgivings, based in part on a poor understanding of the recommendations.

Unfortunately, Mr. Autrey and his internal auditor were inexperienced in operational auditing and it was later realized that they overlooked some important considerations in developing the audit recommendations. In a short time, inventories and unit manufacturing costs rose sharply in the Reda Division.

Sixteen months after the date of the audit recommendations, the internal auditors returned to Reda. They appraised the division's deteriorating situation and prepared specific recommendations designed to arrest it. Since the audit staff had been enlarged by the employment of three individuals of widely recognized competence and in the meantime had gained valuable experience, they were now making recommendations with much greater confidence. The recommendations were presented by Autrey directly to Reda Divisional Vice-President I. M. Beastly. After studying the recommendations for a few minutes, Beastly reacted:

''Oh, the hell you say! Yes, divisional income is down from new product start-up costs, and our relations with corporate management are bad now anyway. How are we going to justify our capital budget appropriation requests this year if you submit another half-baked audit report that makes us look like monkeys?'' In similar forceful language Beastly told Mr. Autrey that he was responsible for the extra costs since the earlier recommendations were ''no damn good.'' He stated that the internal audit function was not important to the success of the company, and that if the present recommendations were presented to

Super's management without acknowledgment of the auditors' own responsibility for generating the conditions that provoked them, he personally would see to it that "there will be some drastic changes in the internal auditing function at Super Industries."

Autrey was a man of conviction and purpose; nevertheless, he was quite shaken by this ultimatum. He realized that if Beastly's threat could be carried out, the internal audit function would be jeopardized and his own competence questioned. It seemed to him that Beastly had created an issue that would have to be resolved and that "someone would come out the loser." Eventually, the following two positions developed in the internal auditing department out of the debate on this issue.

1. That the report should be revised so as to omit the recommendations challenged. If, by the following year, Reda had not through its own efforts corrected the situation in question, a second report would be prepared to include both the current recommendations and others appropriate at that time.

2. That this year's report should include the current recommendations with no changes. If truth were the ultimate persuader, Super Industries' management would respond to it. Possibly even Beastly would respond to it. If the worst happened, they reasoned, there is a good demand for internal auditors in other firms.

Questions

1. What is the central issue?
2. Which alternative would you recommend? Why?
3. What would you do in this case if you could arbitrate it?

10-32. An Independent Audit

With the consent of your instructor, audit a computerized accounting information system of your choice or as directed in class. In the course of your study, trace the business transactions as they are initially recorded on source documents, as they are fed into a computer, and as they are used to produce managerial reports. Identify system strengths and weaknesses. Document your findings in a complete report.

PART FOUR

Systems Studies for Effective Accounting Information Systems

Accounting information is often required by an organization's management when making business decisions. For this information to be readily available, an accurate and responsive accounting information system must exist within the organization. The chapters up to this point have stressed the accounting information system's contributions to an efficient and effective business information system. Part One's chapters discussed the accounting information system's vital role in managerial planning and controlling activities, Part Two's chapters examined the accounting information system's relevant role in collecting, recording, and storing financial-oriented data needed for managerial decision making, and Part Three's chapters analyzed the accounting information system's important role relating to internal control systems. Part Four's chapters will tie-together many of the previous chapters' materials by examining in considerable depth the work involved when performing a *systems study*, the purpose of which is to develop efficient and effective information systems within organizations.

A system study is often performed because of current problems existing in a company's present information system, thereby resulting in a lack of good decision-making information being provided to management. These problems are frequently the direct or indirect result of weaknesses in the flow of accounting information through the system. Consequently, accountants normally participate in performing a systems study to help an organization solve its problems associated with inefficient information flows to management for its decision-making endeavors. Part Four will thus examine the activities that are essential when performing a systems study of a company's information systems problems, stressing accountants' functions in systems study work. A major part of the discussion in Part Four will assume that accountants are working for a consulting firm and they are participating in systems studies of companies' information systems problems. Furthermore, the emphasis in Part Four's chapters will be on a systems study to convert an organization's manual accounting information system to a computerized accounting information system.

The first step in a system study, called

analysis, will be discussed in Chapter 11. From analysis, strengths and weaknesses in a company's present system are identified. This analysis work leads to the *design* of changes into the company's system so that previously identified weaknesses can be eliminated. The design of changes into a system will thus be examined in Chapter 12. Once design changes have been planned, these changes must be incorporated into the company's system. The subject of *implementing* systems revisions and then *operating* the newly implemented system will be the topic of Chapter 13. This chapter also will briefly discuss the work involved in analyzing the effectiveness of a newly-implemented business information system (i.e., *follow-up studies*) and then making additional systems modifications, if necessary.

Since the subject of follow-up studies of a newly implemented computer system is discussed only briefly in Chapter 13, this phase of a systems study will be stressed in Chapter 14 under the subject of *resource acquisition*. Chapter 14 will discuss the follow-up work on a computerized system which may lead to the acquisition of additional hardware resources, additional software resources, and/or additional personnel resources.

11

Systems Study: The Analysis Phase

Among the important questions that you should be able to answer after reading this chapter are:

1 Why is training in accounting such a valuable "asset" to a management consultant?

2 What is a "management consulting team" and what is the normal role of accountants on this team?

3 Is it necessary for a management consultant to understand human behavior?

4 What is a document flowchart and how does it aid consultants in performing systems analysis work?

5 Because managerial employees should already be familiar with their company's strong and weak points, isn't it a waste of time and money to have a consultant perform a systems survey of the company's strengths and weaknesses?

INTRODUCTION

One common cause of a business organization's operating problems is a breakdown in its accounting information system. This breakdown is the result of such things as delays in communicating financial information to specific managers needing the information included in these reports for decision making, or certain managers never receiving the types of financial information feedback necessary for effective decision making. Obviously, business problems can result from factors other than the failure of the accounting information system (e.g., negative employee attitudes toward their work environment caused by the boring nature of the employees' jobs or the lack of responsibility delegated to them by management). However, because a large majority of an organization's business decisions are based upon accounting information, the failure of an accounting information system to provide relevant and timely managerial information typically will lead to inefficient organizational activities, thereby causing problems for the company.

As discussed in Chapter 1, a systems study involves four major steps (or phases):

1. The *Analysis* of a company's current operating system to determine the system's strong points and weak points.

2. The *Design* of changes into the company's current system so that the system's weak points can be eliminated (or at least minimized) and the strong points maintained.

3. The *Implementation* and *Initial Operation* of the newly designed system within the company.

4. The *Follow-up* analysis of the newly designed system to determine whether the previous weaknesses (or problems) have actually been eliminated so that the system is efficiently operating, thereby contributing toward meeting the company's objectives and goals.

The above four steps of a systems study encompass the "life-cycle" of a business information system. As Figure 11-1 illustrates, this life-cycle reflects the time span during which a company's system is operating on a daily basis and is subsequently revised as a result of some problem (or problems). Each time a newly revised system takes over the company's daily operating activities, a new life-cycle begins.

The dashed-arrows in Figure 11-1 emphasize the fact that follow-up studies of an ongoing system should be a continuous process. Periodically (e.g., every three months, every six months, annually, etc., as determined by management), the

ongoing system should be evaluated to ascertain whether it is still operating efficiently. The continued efficiency of the system means that no further revisions are necessary. Thus, the same system continues its daily functioning. (The route from the follow-up studies solid-arrow back to the system operation on a daily basis is taken.) If the follow-up studies indicate that the previous systems problems have reoccurred and/or new systems problems now exist, however, the route is from the follow-up studies dashed-arrow to the recognition of systems problems (or weaknesses) part of the figure. The complete systems study steps are then repeated.

Even though each of the four major phases of a systems study will be discussed separately in this and the next three chapters, it should be emphasized that in actual practice, there is a certain amount of overlap between these four phases. For example, while management consultants are involved in isolating specific systems weaknesses (the analysis phase), they may simultaneously be considering possible systems changes (the design phase) that will eliminate these weaknesses. Therefore, the subsequent discussion of a systems study will utilize this same approach; that is, while analyzing a specific systems study step, comments may also be included regarding one or more of the other systems study steps.

As mentioned above, many business problems result from a company's lack of effective decision-making information being provided by the accounting information system. For this reason, accountants (especially managerial accountants) are actively involved as management consultants helping organizations solve their current information systems problems. It is important therefore for today's accountants to have a thorough understanding of how to perform a systems study of an organization's business information problems so that they can make positive recommendations to solve these problems.

This current chapter will discuss the analysis phase of a systems study, Chapter 12 will examine the systems study design phase, and Chapter 13 will discuss the remaining two phases: implementation and initial operation, and fol-

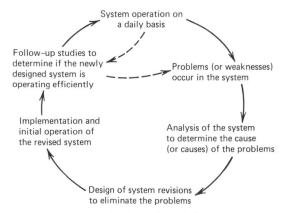

Figure 11-1. Life-cycle of a business information system.

low-up. However, because the follow-up phase is examined only briefly in Chapter 13, this systems study phase will be discussed thoroughly in Chapter 14. After studying these four chapters, a good understanding of how to perform a study of an organization's information systems problems should be acquired.

Because this text has emphasized the computer's role in accounting information systems, the discussion in Chapters 12 and 13 will focus upon the conversion of a company's current manual data-processing system to a computerized data-processing system. Naturally, not all systems studies will involve the conversion from a manual to a computerized information system. For example, a company may already have a batch-processing computer system. The company's management may hire a consulting firm to perform a systems study which analyzes the feasibility of converting to an online, real-time system for processing its accounting data. However, by concentrating on the conceptual and the procedural aspects of a major conversion from a manual to a computerized data-processing system in Chapters 12 and 13, you will be provided a much broader coverage of the systems study field.

Before beginning the discussion of the analysis phase of a systems study, we will first look at the modern technique, called the *systems approach,* used by many management consultants today when performing a systems study.

SYSTEMS APPROACH

The *systems approach* to analyzing a company's current problems and making change recommendations to help solve the problems encompasses two major aspects: (1) approaching a specific organizational problem (or problems) from a broad point of view, and (2) utilizing a consulting team for performing a systems study of an organization's problems. Each of these two aspects is now discussed briefly.

Broad Viewpoint in a Systems Study

When management consultants are hired by an organization to help solve a specific problem, the consultants should take into consideration what effects their recommendations will have on the organization's total system environment. This environment includes all the specific subsystems within the organization as well as the external environment outside of the organization's boundaries.

For example, assume that the actual time required to manufacture basketballs within the Alan Company's production subsystem is continually exceeding the standard time. As a result of these basketball production delays, Alan Company's customers are not receiving their basketball purchases on schedule, as promised by the Alan Company's sales staff. To help solve this basketball production problem, Alan Company's management hires the Reliable Professional Consulting Firm to analyze the problem and to make recommendations for improving the basketball production process. As an accountant, you are assigned the task of reviewing the standard cost accounting system for manufacturing basketballs (i.e., reviewing the raw materials standard, the direct labor standard, and the production overhead standard). Based upon this review, you feel that the major cause of basketball production delays is the inefficient performance by those direct laborers involved in the basketball manufacturing process. This inefficiency was hidden by the loose time standards originally established for basketball production. Even with these loose time standards, the direct laborers' actual hours for basketball production are still exceeding standard hours. Therefore, you recommend to Alan Company's management that employees of higher skill level (who naturally earn higher wages) be used in manufacturing basketballs and that a stricter production time standard be adopted.

Impressed with these observations, Alan Company's management incorporates your suggestions into its basketball production operations. The company soon discovers that with higher-skilled employees manufacturing the basketballs, however, the actual cost per basketball increases considerably, thereby causing management to increase the basketball selling price charged to customers. Because competitors have not increased their basketball selling prices, the basketball sales of the Alan Company drop steadily, causing a decline in the company's total *gross margin* (excess of sales dollars over cost of goods sold) on basketballs sold.

The above example illustrates what can possibly occur when a consultant "tackles" an organization's systems problem from a narrow point of view. As one of the management consultants from the Reliable Professional Consulting Firm, your recommendation to upgrade the skill level requirement of those employees who manufacture basketballs was based upon only the positive effects that would take place within the Alan Company's production subsystem. If, however, you had approached the company's basketball production problem from a broad point of view, you would have considered as well the possible implications of your recommendation on the company's total systems environment. You would have thus studied the prices of basketballs charged by the Alan Company's competitors (an external environmental factor), and attempted to ascertain how the sales of the Alan Company's marketing subsystem (an internal environmental factor) might change as a result of higher priced basketballs.

From the above analysis, you would have learned that the competitive nature of the basketball sales market does not make it feasible for the Alan Company to increase the selling price of basketballs without harming the company's market position. Therefore, rather than recommending higher-skilled employees to manufacture basketballs (which causes the per unit production cost to increase), you might have recommended that the present basketball manufacturing employees be provided additional on-the-job training to increase their production capabilities.

In general, when a change is made in one aspect of a company's system, the change will likely affect other parts of the system. Unless the consultants realize this fact and take into consideration what effect a specific recommendation will have on the total system, their systems study work may be unproductive. Thus, management consultants should always have a "total systems" viewpoint (or "broad" viewpoint) when helping a company solve a current problem. Otherwise, the consultants may solve the specific problem by creating new problems.

Consulting Team in a Systems Study

This aspect of the "systems approach" follows from the above discussion which emphasized the importance of a broad viewpoint when performing a systems study. Because a management consultant normally has specialized training in one particular discipline (e.g., accounting or marketing), the consultant is not expected to be an "expert" in all phases of a company's operations. However, when approaching a systems problem broadly by analyzing the consequences of a specific change recommendation on other operating areas of a client company, knowledge of several disciplines is essential. Therefore, most consulting firms (including the management advisory services departments of CPA firms) hire employees with many different educational backgrounds to work as management consultants on specific client jobs. These individual employees will possess specialized knowledge in such areas as accounting, management, marketing, electronic data processing, psychology (to analyze organizational behavior problems), and engineering (to analyze complex organizational production systems).

Depending upon the expertise required for a specific systems study, the consulting firm sends a team of experts to a company to help solve the company's systems problem (or problems). Just as an efficiently operated system requires coordination and communication among its subsystems, this team of consultants must coordinate the systems study work and must also have good communications among its members in order to perform efficiently for the client company. In the previous discussion of the Alan Company's basketball production problem, for example, the accountant performing the analysis of the company's standard cost accounting system would probably not be qualified to perform the market analysis study of future expected basketball demand as a result of increasing the per unit selling price. Rather, a marketing specialist on the consulting team would undertake this market study. The marketing specialist would communicate his or her findings to the accountant. This input data from the marketing expert could then be used by the accountant in reaching a decision about revisions, if any, within the basketball production process.

It should be emphasized, however, that in a systems study for a small business (e.g., revising the accounting information system for a lawyer who operates a small law office), a consulting team of experts would normally be unnecessary. A knowledgeable accountant from the consulting firm should be able to handle this systems study job alone. On the other hand, a consulting job performed for a major corporation with several divisions would likely require a team of specialized consultants to analyze the corporation's information system and make recommendations regarding this organization's complex systems structure.

Having completed the discussion of the systems approach for performing a consulting job, the remainder of the chapter will concentrate on the *analysis* phase of a systems study. It should be kept in mind that an organization's own employees (e.g., the internal audit staff) might be called upon by management to help solve a specific systems problem. Much of the subsequent discussion of a systems study in Part Four of our text, however, will assume that an outside consulting firm is being hired to perform the systems study work.

SYSTEMS ANALYSIS

The analysis phase of a company's information system life-cycle begins following the recognition of some problems (or weaknesses) in the company's current system (see Figure 11-1), and the company's top management (or possibly the board of directors) decides to hire a consulting firm to help solve its systems problems. The basic purpose of systems analysis is to enable the consultants to familiarize themselves thoroughly with a company's current operating system so that they can eventually make recommendations

for improving the system. Figure 11-2 shows the logical procedures that would be followed by the consultants when performing their systems analysis work. Each of these procedures associated with systems analysis is now discussed on the following pages.

Define the Problem (or Problems)

Before management consultants are able to make any valid recommendations which improve a company's information system, these consultants first must make sure that they comprehend the "real" problem (or problems) of the current system. In the process of hiring consultants to perform a systems study, the company's management will normally tell the consultants what it believes the systems problems are. The consultants, however, should not accept management's comments without doing some preliminary investigation of their own to make sure that management's impressions of the actual problems are correct. In fact, the major factor that may be compounding a company's current information systems problems is management's failure to distinguish the company's *real* problems from the symptoms of these problems. (When people are so close to a situation, it is easy for them to lose sight of what is actually happening!) For example, Alan Company management may be blaming production supervisors for the manufacturing inefficiencies occurring within their departments. In actuality, however, the real problem is the slowness of the company's infor-

Figure 11-2

SYSTEMS ANALYSIS PROCEDURES

Define the Problem (or Problems)
in the Present System

↓

Systems Survey to Acquire Sufficient Information
Relating to Present Systems Problem (or Problems)

↓

Generate Possible Solutions to Solve
the Systems Problem (or Problems)

mation system to provide timely production control reports to these supervisors. By receiving quicker "after the fact" performance reports, the supervisors could have taken immediate action to correct the manufacturing inefficiencies before they became too serious. Thus, the real problem is the information reporting system, whereas a symptom of this problem is the production supervisors' operating performances.

In order for the consultants to define the systems problems of a company, they must first understand the goals (or objectives) of the company's system. It is likely that the company's current problems are caused by certain aspects of the present system failing to accomplish its original planned systems goals. Thus, the consultants must adequately define the goals of the company's system and then, through their subsequent systems survey (to be discussed shortly), attempt to ascertain which goals are being achieved and which goals are not being achieved under the present system. Those factors causing the lack of accomplishment of specific goals hopefully will be detected during the consultants' systems survey work.

For the purposes of this discussion, a company's systems goals can be examined at three levels: (1) general systems goals, (2) top management systems goals, and (3) operating management systems goals. Each of these three goal categories is now briefly analyzed.

General systems goals. This goal category represents, in effect, broad principles of good systems design that should contribute to an effectively operated business information system. Included among these general systems goals are:

1. *Cost awareness.* When designing the system's internal control structure, its report structure, its use of manual or automated data-processing techniques, and so on, the benefits associated with a specific system component should, at a minimum, equal the component's costs.

2. *Relevant output.* The information provided by the system should have a high degree of accuracy, be communicated to management on a timely basis, and be

useful for management's decision-making functions. If output information is to be relevant, the methods used for data gathering (i.e., accumulating the input information) must be reliable. Thus, when the input data for reports are incorrect, the processed output reports are not relevant for management decision making.

3. *Simplistic structure.* If a system is so complex in design that most company employees become frustrated with its structure, the system's potential usefulness may be lost. To obtain the most benefits from an information system, its structure must be as simple as possible so that organizational employees will understand the system's data-processing and reporting capabilities, and be able to use these capabilities when needed.

4. *Flexible structure.* The system should be able to accommodate the changing information needs of management, and should have back-up procedures that permit information processing to continue if a breakdown occurs in the automated data processing equipment. (For instance, if the Alan Company's central processing unit is malfunctioning, alternate manual or automated procedures should be available that will permit data processing to continue until the computer hardware is operating again.) The system should not only be capable of providing decision-making information to management; it should also be able to interact with the company's customers to answer their inquiries. (For example, some credit customers of the Alan Company may telephone to ask questions about their account balances.)

The above general goals are applicable to most organizations' information systems. Each one of them contributes positively to an efficiently operated business information system. It is important that the management consultants ascertain whether the above goals are incorporated into their client company's information system design. The inability of the information system to achieve one or more of these general systems goals may be the cause of the company's present problems.

Top management systems goals. Chapter 2 emphasized that top management is responsible for its organization's long-range planning functions. Top management develops broad, nonoperational goals (e.g., achieving a satisfactory level of net income and manufacturing high quality inventory items) to guide the operations of the entire organization. As discussed in Chapter 3, individual subsystems will submit long-range program proposals which a company's budget committee (this committee includes top management personnel) evaluates for possible implementation into the system. Ongoing programs should be reviewed periodically by the budget committee and decisions made regarding the continuance or discontinuance of these programs.

Since the planning and controlling functions of top management affect the entire organization, it is often difficult to specify the types of decision-making information needed by these top-level managers. Furthermore, much of the information required by top management is for long-range planning and controlling activities and is not available within the organization's internal information system. In carrying out long-range planning functions, top management must have a good deal of external environmental data (including report data on such things as the company's long-range market potential, the future economic outlook for the country and how its company will be affected by inflation, unemployment, etc., and the future effects on company sales from the introduction of new products by competitors) which is not generated internally by the organization's accounting information system. On the other hand, information required by a production supervisor (an operating manager) regarding the efficiency of manufacturing activities can be generated from the company's standard cost accounting system.

Even though it is often difficult to pinpoint the specific information needs of top management, this task is not impossible. The accountant, in the role of budget coordinator, can provide top management executives with long-range planning data to enable them to make effective strategic decisions for the future. Through periodic performance reports (the control function), top management is provided feedback about the effective execution of its long-range plans. Top management must also be informed about the short-range operating performance of the organization's subsystems. After each subsystem's short-range budget has been developed (short-range budget systems were also discussed in Chapter 3), the accountant is then responsible for providing top management with summary information about the individual subsystems' budgetary projections compared with their actual operating results.

Because of the large variety of planning and controlling information required by top management (both internally generated data and externally generated data), it is possible that a company's systems problems can be caused (or at least partially caused) by the system's failure to satisfy top management's information needs. It is therefore essential for the consultants to thoroughly understand the information needs of top management and then attempt to ascertain whether these needs are being satisfied by the company's current information system.

Operating management systems goals. Compared with top management's systems goals discussed above, the information needs of operating management (those managers working within specific organizational subsystems) are normally much easier to ascertain. The decision-making activities of operating managers typically relate to well-defined and narrower organizational areas than those decision-making functions of top management. Also, the majority of operating management's decision-making endeavors are for the current business year (in contrast to top management's long-range decision-making endeavors). Most of the information required for operating managers' decisions can be generated internally as a by-product of processing a company's accounting data (in contrast to top management's need for a large amount of external data which is not internally generated by the accounting information system).

All the above reasons enable the management consultants to have an easier job determining each operating manager's specific information needs and to ascertain whether these needs are being met by the present information system. For example, in order to analyze a manufacturing department's operating efficiency, the department's production manager needs timely responsibility accounting reports comparing the actual raw materials and actual direct labor costs with the predetermined standard costs of these two manufacturing cost items. As a further example, in order to analyze the sales results of specific product lines as well as the performance of the sales staff, a marketing manager requires timely sales reports comparing each salesperson's actual product-line sales with his or her budgeted product-line sales. The discussion of prior chapters indicated that these types of reports required by the production manager and the marketing manager could be processed by the company's EDP subsystem on a "management-by-exception" basis.

When analyzing the systems goals of operating management and deciding whether its information needs are being satisfied, the consultants may find that the client company's accountants are overemphasizing the communication of monetary rather than nonmonetary data to the operating managers. In fact, the accountant's preoccupation with reporting monetary data is sometimes cited as a major criticism of the accounting information system. Because many subsystem managers are likely to make decisions on the basis of nonmonetary data, the accountant performs a disservice by reporting only monetary data to these managers. Most organizations, especially those having a computerized data-processing system, maintain within their information systems both monetary and nonmonetary accounting transaction data. When the accountant draws upon this data to prepare a computerized report for a subsystem manager, however, the report will often include only monetary information. From the subsystem manager's (i.e., the report recipient) point of view, this manager

might better understand (or perceive) the report information and thereby make more effective decisions if the report included nonmonetary information. (Remember, all organizational managers do not have accounting backgrounds!)

To illustrate, assume that the Alan Company maintains detailed data about product-line sales activities. The data includes information regarding each salesperson's budgeted weekly sales quotas (both in sales dollars and in physical units) for specific product-lines and each salesperson's actual weekly sales results (both in sales dollars and in physical units) for specific product-lines. The accountant's instructions to the EDP subsystem for processing weekly sales performance reports are as follows:

Include in these weekly reports information (on a "management-by-exception" basis—the criteria for exceptions are ignored here to simplify the example) about each salesperson's budgeted product-line dollar sales compared with his or her actual product-line dollar sales.

These reports are then analyzed by the marketing managers every week to enable them to ascertain areas of efficiency and inefficiency within the sales function. Because many sales managers think in terms of unit sales data rather than dollar sales data, the reports probably would have more relevance to the managers' decision-making activities if the data contained in them were the budgeted compared with the actual *physical product items* sold rather than the budgeted compared with the actual *sales dollars*. Both the budget projection of unit sales and the actual units sold were part of the Alan Company's data base; however, this nonmonetary information was completely excluded from the sales performance reports.

Nonmonetary rather than monetary reporting to subsystem managers on an exception basis was discussed previously and was illustrated in Chapter 2 (see Figure 2-4). This topic has again been analyzed because of its importance to a systems study. When management consultants are attempting to determine what their client company's systems problems are, they may find that operating managers' feedback reports used in decision making exclude the types of nonmonetary data that would enable these managers to make more effective organizational decisions.

Systems Survey

After determining the client company's systems goals and subsequently defining the system's problem(s), the management consultants then begin an intensive investigation of the company's present information system so that they can discover those system weaknesses that are causing the problem(s). This investigative activity, which thoroughly familiarizes the consultants with their client's current information system, is called the *systems survey*.

During the course of their systems survey work, the consultants should note the strengths as well as the weaknesses in the company's information system. Then, when changes in the system are eventually recommended by the consultants, these recommendations, if implemented, will likely eliminate the system's weak points while continuing to maintain the system's strong points. One of the worst possible mistakes management consultants can make is to ignore the strong points of their client's present system. When this happens, the consultants increase the risk that their recommendations will include systems change suggestions that also eliminate those strengths within the existing information system.

Because each organization's information system design is somewhat different, there is no standard list that describes the techniques for performing a systems survey. Depending upon the unique attributes of their client's information system, the consultants must exercise a degree of creativity in selecting the best methods for gathering reliable information about the strengths and weaknesses of the specific system. Even though the systems survey work performed for individual companies will vary, two of the typical organizational areas that must be investigated in every survey, regardless of the unique aspects of a company's system, are: (1) the human element, and (2) the internal control structure. Each of these systems survey investigative areas is now discussed.

The human element. Even in a highly automated company, employees are a critical element in the success or failure of the company's information system. Therefore, an important part of the systems survey work involves a thorough analysis of employee activities within the client company's information system. Two human element areas of concern to management consultants are: (1) employee involvement in the systems study, and (2) analysis of employee job functions. These two areas are examined below.

Employee involvement. Many people dislike any changes that affect their present life styles. Because the appearance of management consultants on the work scene usually implies changes in a company's system, employees often develop negative attitudes toward these "outside" consultants. Unless the consultants deal directly with this potential human-relations problem during the beginning stages of the systems study, there is a strong likelihood that any change recommendations incorporated into the client company's system will not be effective. In essence, employees are the crucial elements that will determine the effectiveness of a newly implemented system. Since company employees will be directly involved in the daily operations of the new system, the best-designed system "on paper" is likely to fail when implemented if the system does not have wide user support.

Ideally, top management, operating management, and nonmanagerial workers should all play a participative role in the systems study. For example, in addition to top management's involvement in the initial hiring of the consulting team, these high-level executives are also responsible for communicating to the consultants the purpose (or purposes) of the systems study. The systems study purpose may be, for instance, to analyze the feasibility of converting the company's information system from a manual to an automated structure or to analyze problems within the company's production area and examine the feasibility of a major capital expenditure for plant expansion. It is extremely important for top management to have a positive attitude about the potentially valuable services the consultants can provide to its organization. If top management personnel resent "outsiders" coming into their organization and suggesting changes, the likelihood of a successful systems study will be slim. If lower-level employees observe top management's resentment toward the consultants, chances are these employees will quickly lose interest in the consultants' endeavors.

A major task faced by the consultants during the systems survey is to gain the active cooperation of the operating managers and the nonmanagerial employees (including custodians, inventory clerks, bookkeepers, accountants, secretaries, and salespersons). Employee uncertainty about the systems survey activities often creates hostility in those persons who may have the greatest potential to aid in the survey work. If the systems study involves a major overhaul of the company's present system, many employees may become fearful of losing their jobs. (This fear is often the result of rumors among employees regarding job cutbacks.)

In an attempt to avoid the types of problems discussed above, the consultants (as well as their client's top management) should communicate openly with the company's operating managers and nonmanagerial employees from the inception of the systems study. Furthermore, this communication policy should continue throughout all phases of the systems work. Before beginning the systems survey, the consultants should have formal meetings with all the operating managers of the various subsystems in order to explain the scope and purpose of the systems study and the advantages that the contemplated systems change will offer to each operating manager. For example, if the systems study involves the conversion from a manual to an automated data-processing structure, the consultants should explain to the operating managers how the computer will alleviate a large amount of their routine and boring functions, thereby providing them with opportunities for more challenging work. In addition, the consultants should encourage the operating managers (1) to voice their opinions about any weaknesses they perceive in the pres-

ent system, and (2) to provide suggestions for eliminating these weaknesses.

If the purpose of the current systems study is to analyze the feasibility of computerizing the company's manual information system, there is a strong possibility that employee displacement will occur. Rather than avoiding this issue, the consultants should openly admit the likelihood of a work force reduction when the automated system is implemented. In most conversions from a manual to a computerized system, however, there is an opportunity for many employees to be assigned to different jobs within the new system. Assuming that the company's top management supports the retention of as many current employees as possible, the consultants should stress this fact to the operating managers. The company's personnel subsystem can offer training programs to enable displaced employees to perform alternate jobs within the automated system (e.g., a program that trains a typist to become a terminal operator in an online computerized system). Management should provide those employees who will lose their jobs with severance pay and possibly letters of recommendation for available jobs in other organizations.

In a systems study for a large organization, it would be quite time consuming for the consultants to communicate personally all the above information to the many nonmanagerial employees. Therefore, the consultants should encourage individual operating managers to communicate the systems study information to their subordinates. The operating managers can schedule meetings with their workers to provide this information and also answer any questions about the systems study. At these meetings, nonmanagerial employees should be encouraged to cooperate with the consultants and make suggestions to them concerning any revisions they feel would improve the company's information system. Operating managers should stress to their workers the opportunities that the new system will provide for both improving the employees' skill levels and promoting the employees to higher-level jobs.

If a human-relations approach such as described above is followed by the management consultants when interacting with their client company's employees, the entire systems study should progress smoothly. When organizational employees are well informed about the purpose, scope, and contemplated outcome from the systems study, they should have a rational perspective about the consultants' important job in revising their company's information system.

Job analysis. One of the major operating costs in many organizations is for labor. Therefore, as part of a systems survey, the management consultants will often analyze the efficiency of employee job functions (for both office and factory jobs).

Normally, a company's personnel subsystem will have on file job-description information about each of the labor activities. The consultants should acquire copies of these job descriptions to familiarize themselves with the different types of labor skills needed in the company. As discussed in Chapter 7, the assignment of overqualified or underqualified individuals to specific jobs can lead to operational inefficiency. Thus, after the consultants have analyzed the personnel subsystem's job description data, they should then study actual labor assignments within the company to ascertain whether there is a proper *matching* of employee qualifications to job qualifications. Should the consultants find instances where specific job assignments are made to either overqualified or underqualified people, these system weaknesses should be noted for subsequent discussion with top management (or whomever the consultants are reporting to in the organization).

For those job functions that are highly repetitive (such as typing and working on the assembly line of a production plant), the consultants may decide to utilize *work measurement* techniques to evaluate the efficiency of the employees performing these jobs. One popular work measurement technique available for the consultants' use is based upon *average throughput* (i.e., the amount of useful work that can be performed within a specific period of time). With this tech-

nique, the average output results from many individuals working *together* during a typical business day are used as the criteria for evaluating efficient employee performance. The throughput approach avoids the difficulty of having to evaluate a specific employee's individual operating performance. An alternative work measurement technique (in fact, one of the first techniques ever used for evaluating job performance) is called *time-and-motion study*. Under this approach, a repetitive type job is first broken down into the specific tasks required to successfully complete the job. Then, individual employees' operating performances in completing these job tasks are secretly timed with a stopwatch. The time-and-motion study technique is subject to many problems and is thus seldom used today. For instance, a major problem involves the selection of specific employees whose operating performances will be observed. Furthermore, if individual employees are aware that their job functions are being observed, the performance results will likely be misleading because the employees will not be working under normal conditions (i.e., without someone timing their every move).

Work measurement techniques can be a valuable information gathering tool for consultants in companies already having standard cost accounting systems, as well as in those companies planning to implement standards into their cost systems. In the former case, the consultants can utilize throughput procedures as a means of evaluating the reasonableness of their client's existent labor time standards for repetitious job functions. These observations may lead the consultants to conclude that the company's present standards are inaccurate. For the latter situation, the consultants' objective in using throughput procedures is to enable them to derive the specific labor time standards that will be incorporated into their client's newly designed standard cost accounting system.

In a consulting job regarding the possible expansion of a company's production capacity (by purchasing additional manufacturing equipment, by hiring additional production workers, etc.) to meet increased sales demand, the throughput technique can also be an effective analysis tool. The results from this work measurement approach might reveal, for example, that production output within the company's present plant facility is low because of inefficient performance by the "team" of manufacturing employees. Therefore, the consultants could recommend that, as an alternative to plant expansion, the current production workers be given the necessary training to make them more efficient. The improved worker efficiency should cause sufficient production output increases in the existent plant facility to nullify the need for expansion.

The internal control structure. The importance of good internal control within an organization's system has been emphasized in Part Three of this text. Chapter 7 distinguished between *preventive controls* (which are designed to safeguard a company's asset resources from being misused) and *feedback controls* (which are designed to encourage organizational operating efficiency so that management's prescribed policies and goals are achieved). Because weaknesses in an organization's internal control structure can cause major systems problems, the management consultants will normally spend considerable time reviewing their client's internal control system. The following discussion analyzes some of the possible methods available to consultants for gathering systems survey information about the strengths and weaknesses of a company's preventive controls and feedback controls.

Systems survey of preventive controls. A common method employed by consultants in reviewing their client company's preventive control system is to use a questionnaire. It contains a detailed list of questions regarding the preventive controls within each organizational subsystem. These questions are normally stated in such a manner that "yes" answers indicate the existence of the controls within the company's system and "no" answers indicate an absence of these controls within the company's system. Because the same internal control questionnaire is typically used on all consulting jobs, some of the specific questions may not apply to an individual

company's system characteristics. Therefore, in addition to providing columns on the questionnaire for answering either "yes" or "no" to a specific internal control question, the consultants also include a column for answering "not applicable." Finally, space is normally provided for the consultants' "comments" regarding an internal control question. For example, if the consultant wants to further investigate a specific internal control area at a later time, a note of this can be made in the "comments" column.

Figure 11-3 illustrates portions of an internal control questionnaire that might be used by a management consulting team in reviewing the preventive controls within a company's individual subsystems.

The detailed systems survey work required to answer the items on an internal control questionnaire will enable the consultants to become quite knowledgeable of their client's information system. For those questions answered "no," the consultants should attempt to ascertain what negative effects, if any, might result within the client's information system from the absence of the particular controls. After further investigation, the consultants may conclude that major improvements could be made in the company's information system by implementing one or more of these previous nonexistent preventive controls.

Because preventive control systems within a company's accounting and electronic data-processing subsystems have been covered extensively in Part Three of the text, the analysis below will briefly examine some of the important preventive controls within a company's production, marketing, and personnel subsystems. (Our intention is not to explore these subsystems in depth, but rather to discuss a few preventive controls applicable to the subsystems.)

PRODUCTION SUBSYSTEM: One of the important decisions that must be made in the production area is whether to use a perpetual inventory system (in which inventory records are updated each time a transaction occurs which affects the inventory balances), a periodic inventory system (in which inventory records are typically updated only at specific time intervals prior to preparing

Figure 11-3

PORTIONS OF AN INTERNAL CONTROL QUESTIONNAIRE

Questions	Answers			Date & Name[a]	Comments
	Yes	No	Not Applicable		
Subsystem: *Accounting*					
1. Is fidelity bond coverage provided for those employees handling liquid-type assets?					
2. Is there separation of duties between the cash-handling function and the record-keeping function relating to cash?					
3. Is a voucher system with prenumbered checks used for cash disbursement transactions?					
Subsystem: *Production*					
1. Is there separation of duties between the inventory handling function and the record-keeping function relating to inventory?					
2. Is the inventory storage room accessible only to properly authorized employees?					
3. Are periodic physical counts made of the inventory on hand and then reconciled to the inventory records?					
Subsystem: *Marketing*					
1. Are periodic analyses prepared showing each salesperson's product-line sales by territories and by contribution margins?					
2. Is a periodic accounts receivable aging analysis prepared as a means of evaluating credit customers' outstanding balances?					
3. Is proper authorization required by a designated employee (or employees) to write off a customer's account balance as a bad debt?					
Subsystem: *Electronic Data Processing*					
1. Are the job functions of systems analyst, programmer, and operator adequately separated?					
2. Do adequate input controls exist to detect any errors in transferring source document data to computer storage media?					
3. Is each computer run well documented?					
Subsystem: *Personnel*					
1. Are training programs offered to increase the operating efficiency of employees?					
2. Do equitable company-wide policies exist for salary and promotion rewards to subsystem employees?					
3. Is there separation of duties in the payroll preparation and distribution process?					

[a]In addition to including the date (or dates) on which a specific internal control question was investigated and subsequently answered, the particular consultant who performed the investigative work should include his or her initials next to the date. This initialing process thus recognizes the consultant's responsibility for examining the specific internal control area.

financial statements), or a combination of these two systems. For control purposes, a perpetual system is considered superior because it provides day-to-day information about the status of a company's various inventory balances. As a result of having current inventory data, management is able to plan its company's optimal on-hand inventory balances more efficiently. Because the costs of operating a perpetual system are considerably greater than the costs of operating a periodic system, however, many companies choose the latter type of inventory system.

If the consultants are hired to help a company design its inventory control system, these consultants should perform a cost/benefit analysis as a basis for recommending the best inventory system to meet the company's informational needs. Normally, for a company selling high-volume inventory items of small unit cost (e.g., such items as pencils, construction nails, ice cream cones, and paper clips), a periodic rather than a perpetual system is used because the operating costs of updating the inventory accounts each time one of these items is sold (as required by a perpetual system) would likely exceed the system's benefits. On the other hand, a company that sells new automobiles (i.e., inventory items with a large unit cost) would probably favor a perpetual system because the volume of transactions is usually low, and the benefits to management from having daily account balance information regarding these large unit cost items would likely exceed the system's operating costs. Finally, a discount store selling both large unit cost items (e.g., television sets, furniture, and stereos) and small unit cost items (e.g., aspirins, books, and underwear) might use a perpetual system for the large unit cost items and a periodic system for the small unit cost items.

MARKETING SUBSYSTEM: Because an organization's marketing subsystem is usually the major revenue-generating area, serious information systems problems involving the marketing function can adversely affect the organization's continued existence. When attempting to plan its optimal sales mix of product lines for the coming budget year, the company's marketing managers should consider both *volume* and *unit contribution margin* factors. Ignoring one or the other of these factors can be detrimental to the company's sales efforts.

For example, The Safe and Sturdy Car Company manufactures and sells three automobile models (the xy compact, the ty compact, and the zz deluxe) to dealers throughout the country. The company's annual sales budget is based upon the anticipated volume sales of these three models. In comparing the 1984 profit performance with 1983, top management is confused by the fact that even though both sales volume and sales revenue were higher in 1984 than in 1983, net operating income actually declined during 1984. The management consultants, who were hired to investigate this income decline problem, revised the company's sales performance reports by incorporating contribution margin data into the reporting system. Figure 11-4 illustrates the performance report for one of the car company's East Coast sales representatives, "Honest" John Turner, for the year ended December 31, 1984 under both the original and revised reporting structure.

The sales results of the company's other salespeople were similar to John Turner's. For the most part, each salesperson's actual unit sales of car models xy compact and ty compact exceeded his or her budget projection, whereas the actual unit sales of car model zz deluxe were below the budget projection. As shown under the "original reporting structure" in Figure 11-4, John Turner's actual total unit sales and actual total sales revenue generated during 1984 exceeded his budget figures. This same favorable performance also existed when the 1984 operating activities of all the sales staff were combined.

The actual cause of the company's net operating income decline during 1984 is revealed by the consultants' "revised reporting structure" shown in Figure 11-4. As was true for John Turner as well as the other salespersons, the actual unit sales of the car model with the greatest contribution margin per unit (which is model zz deluxe) were considerably below the budget projections. On the other hand, the company's

Figure 11-4

THE SAFE AND STURDY CAR COMPANY SALES PERFORMANCE REPORT OF JOHN TURNER
For the Year Ended December 31, 1984

Original Reporting Structure

Car Model	Unit Sales		Sales Revenue				
	Actual	Budget	Per Unit Selling Price to Dealers	Total Actual Revenue	Total Budgeted Revenue	Variance—	Favorable (Unfavorable)
xy compact	500	450	$2500	$1,250,000	$1,125,000		$125,000
ty compact	300	280	2800	840,000	784,000		56,000
zz deluxe	120	180	2600	312,000	468,000		(156,000)
TOTALS	920	910		$2,402,000	$2,377,000		$ 25,000

Revised Reporting Structure

Car Model	Unit Sales		Contribution Margin (CM)				
	Actual	Budget	Per Unit CM	Total Actual CM	Total Budgeted CM	Variance—	Favorable (Unfavorable)
xy compact	500	450	$ 400	$200,000	$180,000		$ 20,000
ty compact	300	280	500	150,000	140,000		10,000
zz deluxe	120	180	1000	120,000	180,000		(60,000)
TOTALS	920	910		$470,000	$500,000		($30,000)

1983 actual unit sales of model zz deluxe were considerably higher than the 1984 sales of this model. (The 1983 sales data are not provided here.) Because those product items with the largest contribution margin per unit make the largest "contribution" toward covering a company's fixed costs and providing a net operating income, The Safe and Sturdy Car Company's sales volume decline in model zz deluxe automobiles appears to be the major cause of the 1984 net operating income decline.

This example demonstrates the valuable service that consultants can provide as a result of reviewing their client company's information reporting structure. On the surface, The Safe and Sturdy Car Company's sales performance looked good in 1984 because both actual sales volume and actual sales revenue exceeded the 1984 budget as well as exceeded the 1983 sales volume and sales revenue actual results. The company's critical variable, contribution margin per car sold, however, was completely excluded from its reporting structure. The revised reporting system suggested by the consultants emphasized contribution margin data, thereby providing the company's management with relevant information explaining the critical factor causing the 1984 decline in net operating income.

An important preventive control for the marketing subsystem's credit sales activities is to require proper authorization from a designated employee (or employees) before a customer's account balance can be written off as a bad debt. To help safeguard a company's asset resources from improper use, the consultants should ascertain whether or not this preventive control is present. For example, without this control procedure, a customer payment for $100 could be "pocketed" by the company's accountant, followed by his or her recording of the journal entry below:

Allowance for uncollectibles	100	
Accounts receivable		100

The above entry gives the customer full credit for the payment. Rather than debiting the "cash" account for this customer payment, however, the accountant's embezzlement procedure is covered up by giving the impression that the customer's balance was never collected; thus, the debit to the "allowance for uncollectibles" account.

The accountant's fraudulent activity probably could have been prevented by requiring the credit and collection department manager's formal approval for all bad debt write-offs. This control procedure would have hindered the accountant's successful embezzlement of the $100 cash receipt since the debit portion of the preceding journal entry could not have been recorded without approval from the credit and collection department manager. The consultants' recommendation to require formal approval for all uncollectible account write-offs can thus increase the efficiency of their client company's data-processing system.

PERSONNEL SUBSYSTEM: In some companies frequent errors and irregularities occur in their personnel subsystems' payroll preparation and distribution processes. Errors and irregularities occur more often in large organizations in which hundreds or thousands of employees receive weekly paychecks, because the massive volume of data-processing activities required to prepare each week's payroll increases the opportunities for both human processing errors and fraudulent acts. Examples of payroll fraud by company employees include such things as maintaining fictitious names on the payroll, padding the number of hours worked by specific employees, and giving unauthorized salary increases to specific employees.

Because of the increased risk of both human errors and intentional errors in the payroll area, the management consultants will often review, as part of their systems survey work, the preventive control structure surrounding their client's payroll functions. In the processing of payroll transactions, it is quite common to find the payroll processed with the assistance of a computer. Because Chapter 8 discussed some of the relevant controls for computerized payroll sys-

tems, there is no need to reiterate these controls here. The most important factor in the systems survey work regarding payroll functions is that an adequate review of payroll controls be made by the management consultants. Any control weaknesses detected by the consultants during their survey of a company's payroll system should be noted for further investigation. Change recommendations which improve the control structure for payroll activities should contribute to increased efficiency within the company's information system.

Systems survey of feedback controls. It was emphasized in Chapter 7 that timely performance reports under a responsibility accounting system are the principal means by which most organizations achieve feedback control. These performance reports are designed to measure the operating efficiency of various preventive controls within a company. Hopefully, any inefficiencies disclosed by the performance reports would be eliminated as a result of managerial corrective action. For example, within the Alan Company, a timely performance report disclosing significant unfavorable variations between a manufacturing supervisor's standard and actual controllable production costs (controllable costs are the responsibility of the supervisor) will enable immediate managerial action to eliminate or at least reduce these inefficiencies.

If a company's feedback reporting structure is to achieve its control objective, each specific report must be communicated to the manager (or managers) with decision-making authority and responsibility for the subject matter contained in the report. For instance, a report analyzing the causes of direct labor variances in the Alan Company's production plant would be of little use to a marketing manager. Because both the content and the communication network of an organization's reports can significantly affect the efficient performance of its information system, the management consultants normally spend considerable time in systems survey work analyzing their client company's report structure.

A useful tool often employed by consultants

when evaluating a client's information reporting system is a *document flowchart* (which is a special type of *systems flowchart*). The term *document* is used here in a broad sense to include all types of written communications in an organization (e.g., memos from one manager to another, performance reports, purchase orders, sales invoices, and petty cash vouchers). When constructing a document flowchart, some consultants will also include, where applicable, any movement of physical goods (e.g., the movement of inventory from the receiving department to the inventory storeroom in a purchase transaction) and any information flows not involving documents (e.g., a sales clerk telephoning the credit and collection department to check a customer's outstanding receivable balance in a credit sales transaction). As in the preparation of systems flowcharts and program flowcharts, symbols

having conventional meanings are utilized when preparing document flowcharts. Unlike the symbols used for systems and program flowcharts, however, the document flowcharting symbols are not standardized. Figure 11-5 illustrates a popular set of symbols often employed by management consultants when preparing document flowcharts.

In discussing the document flowchart (illustrated in Figure 11-6), assume that Grashoff, Runnels, and Warren is a retail clothing store that updates its inventory accounts weekly. Based upon a computerized inventory exceptions report of items requiring reorder, the purchasing department initiates an inventory acquisition transaction by manually preparing six copies of a purchase order. These copies are distributed as follows: one copy remains in the purchasing department for reference, two copies go to the

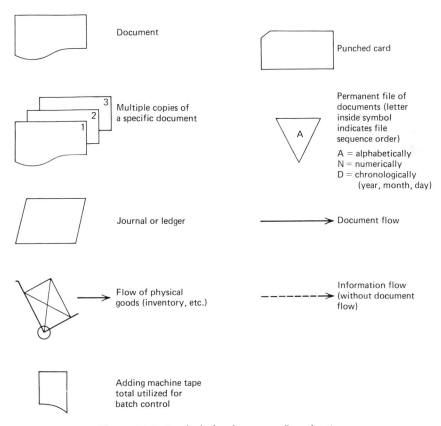

Figure 11-5. Symbols for document flowcharting.

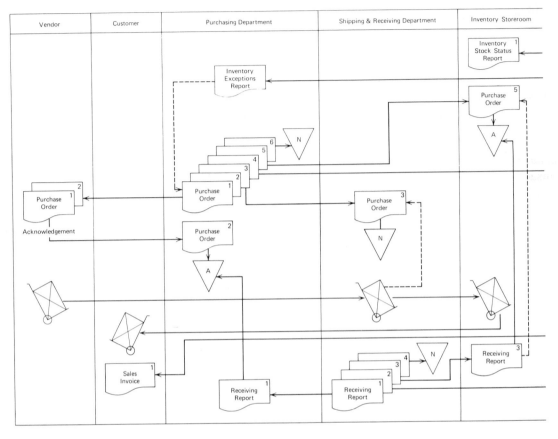

Figure 11-6. Grashoff, Runnels, and Warren document flowchart of inventory processing activities.

vendor (the purchasing department requests the vendor to return one of these copies as acknowledgment of the order—this returned copy is filed alphabetically by vendor name), one copy goes to the shipping and receiving department (so that when inventory shipments arrive, this department can refer back to the applicable purchase order to ascertain whether the goods were actually ordered by the clothing store), one copy goes to the accounting department (so that it is provided advance information about the cash disbursement that will eventually be required for this inventory purchase, thereby contributing to the accounting department's cash planning activities), and one copy goes to the inventory storeroom (so that the storage space required for the future inventory receipt can be planned—this

copy is filed alphabetically according to type of inventory item).

When inventory arrives in the shipping and receiving department, clerks count the goods, compare their count with the quantity indicated on the purchase order, and then prepare four copies of a receiving report. These copies are distributed as follows: one copy remains in the shipping and receiving department for reference, one copy is sent to the purchasing department (so that it is informed about the inventory delivery—this copy is filed with the previously received purchase order acknowledgment copy from the vendor), one copy is sent to the accounting department (so that the inventory receipt can eventually be recorded in the accounting information system—this copy is filed nu-

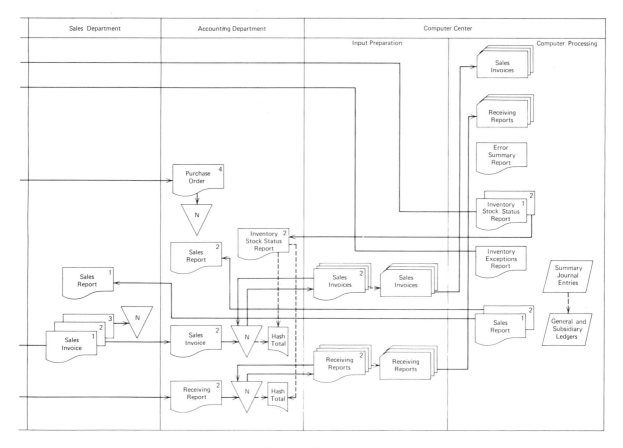

Figure 11-6 (Continued)

merically according to inventory code numbers), and one copy, together with the actual physical goods, is sent to the inventory storeroom (so that the receiving report can be matched to this department's purchase order copy and then filed with the purchase order; the inventory items are stored for future sales).

To simplify this example, we will assume that all the clothing store's sales are cash sales. Therefore, for each sales transaction, three sales invoice copies are prepared. These copies are distributed as follows: one copy remains in the sales department for reference, one copy goes to the customer (together with the clothing items that were purchased), and one copy goes to the accounting department (so that the cash sale and the inventory reduction can be recorded in the accounting information system—this copy is filed numerically according to inventory code numbers).

At the end of each week, the accounting department batches together the week's receiving reports and the week's sales invoices. After accounting department personnel prepare hash control totals of the prenumbered receiving reports and the prenumbered sales invoices, these documents are sent to the computer center. The relevant data from the receiving reports (e.g., code numbers, quantities, and costs of each type of inventory acquired) and the sales invoices (e.g., code numbers, quantities, and selling prices of each type of inventory sold) are keypunched onto punched cards. The output reports from the computer processing of the in-

345

ventory and sales data are: (1) an error summary report indicating any errors occurring in the inventory processing run (e.g., inputting onto a punched card a nonexistent inventory code number for an inventory receipt); the errors disclosed by this report are investigated by EDP personnel and necessary corrections made before the additional output reports are processed, (2) an inventory stock status report indicating the current balance of each inventory item—one copy goes to the inventory storeroom manager and one copy goes to the accounting department (the hash totals for the receiving reports processed and the sales invoices processed are printed out on the stock status report and compared by accounting department personnel with their previously computed hash total data), (3) an inventory exceptions report disclosing inventory items that should be reordered—this report goes to the purchasing department manager, who initiates the preparation of purchase orders, and (4) a sales report by product-line—one copy goes to the sales department manager and one copy goes to the accounting department. The computer also processes summary journal entries for the inventory and cash sales transactions. These entries are then posted to the correct general ledger and subsidiary ledger accounts. (The processing of the accounts payable file for the credit purchases of inventory is performed by another computer run.) Finally, the processed batches of receiving reports and sales invoices are returned to the accounting department for filing.

A document flowchart of the above process for updating the Grashoff, Runnels, and Warren clothing store's inventory accounts is shown in Figure 11-6. (Unless otherwise indicated, the letter "N" inside the "permanent file of documents" symbol means that these particular documents are filed according to their preprinted numbering sequence; e.g., sales invoice number 174 is filed immediately following sales invoice number 173, etc.)

Before the consultants can prepare a document flowchart for a specific information processing activity within their client company's system, they must thoroughly understand this activity. Separate columns of the document flowchart are

used to reflect each entity's involvement in the flow of information through the system function being analyzed. As Figure 11-6 demonstrates, the entities include external parties to the organization (the vendor and the customer) and internal parties involved in the organization's information flow (such as the accounting department and the inventory storeroom). If specific company employees play a major role in particular activities subject to document flowcharting, their names can be reflected within the flowchart's columns.

A document (as well as physical items such as merchandise inventory) initially appears in the specific column of the flowchart where it originated. Any information flow for which there is no document movement is reflected by a "broken line." Written within each document is its name, and for those documents involving multiple copies, numbering of the individual documents is performed. This numbering procedure makes it easier to follow each of these multiple copies' subsequent route through the document flowchart. When specific documents reach their destinations, they are normally filed for future reference.

The document flowcharts prepared by the consultants are often supplemented with more detailed written descriptions of the information flows being analyzed. Also, because the consultants' analysis of their client's feedback reporting structure should include both the flow of information (which is reflected on the document flowchart) and the specific data included within each document (which is not disclosed on the document flowchart), actual copies of all the documents shown on the flowchart should be obtained. The consultants can then compare the informational content of each document with the information needs of each document's recipient (or recipients). This comparison may reveal some weaknesses in the company's information communication flow which would not be revealed by the document flowchart itself. A specific document's data content will have limited value if, based upon the decision-making information required by an organizational employee, the document fails to provide this information, or if it provides unnecessary information to the decision maker. For example, to monitor manufacturing activities, a production supervisor of the Alan Company's baseball manufacturing department may receive a weekly control report comparing actual production costs with standard production costs. However, because the supervisor is likely to perceive the baseball manufacturing department's operating efficiency in terms of physical goods manufactured, this report's decision-making value to the supervisor would probably increase by including an analysis of actual physical units manufactured compared with the standard manufacturing quantity. The production *cost* data could possibly be excluded completely from the supervisor's feedback report of operating efficiency.

Upon completing the Grashoff, Runnels, and Warren clothing store's document flowchart of its inventory processing activities (see Figure 11-6), the consultants will then thoroughly analyze this flowchart data (together with actual copies of the specific documents reflected on the flowchart) for possible information systems weaknesses. For the case at hand, three major weaknesses in the clothing store's inventory processing system were detected by the consultants, as follows (suggestions are also included for eliminating these weaknesses).

1. Under the current system, six copies of a purchase order are manually prepared in the purchasing department after the department receives the inventory exceptions report. To eliminate this time-consuming function and thereby increase the inventory processing system's efficiency, the computer could prepare these purchase orders. Assuming that the clothing store's inventory data were maintained on magnetic tape for batch processing, this tape file could be designed to include the names and addresses of the particular vendors from whom the clothing store acquires its various inventory items. Also contained on the inventory tape file would be the optimal quantity of each inventory item that should be ordered when its balance reaches the reorder point. Then, in addition to computer processing of the weekly inventory exceptions report, individual purchase orders could be printed out by the computer. The only major manual function required would be to place each purchase order in an envelope for mailing. (In fact, it is also possible to mechanize this envelope preparation function.) Rather than including the vendor information (such as the vendor's account number, the vendor's name and address, and the terms of purchase) on the inventory tape file, many companies maintain this information on a special "vendor file," which is a separate magnetic tape file.

If the above suggestion is implemented into the clothing store's inventory processing system, more effective utilization of the store's computer center will result. In fact, another possible suggestion might be to replace the clothing store's present cash registers with point-of-sale recorders (discussed in Chapter 4). These sophisticated cash registers would be online to the store's computer and allow immediate updating of the inventory after each sales transaction. With point-of-sale recorders, the clothing store's management would likely want to switch from magnetic tape to magnetic disk or drum for storing inventory data. Because the costs of converting to and operating an online inventory system would be significant, a complete cost/benefit analysis should be performed before implementing this type system.

2. Under the current system, the copy of the purchase order sent to the shipping and receiving department (purchase order copy number 3 in Figure 11-6) discloses the *quantity* of inventory ordered. As a result, inventory shipments from vendors may not be counted by the clerks working in the shipping and receiving department. These clerks may examine only the specific purchase order relating to an incoming merchandise shipment and then record the designated quantity from the purchase order on the receiving report. The actual inventory quantity received may vary from the purchase order quantity (possibly caused by some of the shipped inventory being lost "in transit" to the company's warehouse), which would go undetected by the clerks. If the physical quantity amount were blacked out on the purchase order copy sent to the shipping and receiving department, this department's em-

ployees would be forced to count each inventory shipment received. After recording the count on the four copies of the receiving report and sending one of these copies to the accounting department (receiving report copy number 2 in Figure 11-6), an employee within the accounting department can then make the comparison of physical quantities shown on the receiving report with physical quantities shown on the purchase order (purchase order copy number 4 in Figure 11-6). The accounting department would be responsible for investigating the causes of any quantity variations on these two documents.

3. Under the current system, inventory deliveries are sent from the shipping and receiving department to the inventory storeroom. Upon receiving these goods, the inventory clerk is not required to sign any document. Therefore, if an inventory shortage occurs at some future date, the inventory clerk (or clerks) may claim that certain inventory items were never received. (The clerks may have taken these items for their own personal use!) To prevent this type of situation from happening, the shipping and receiving department should not release merchandise to the inventory storeroom until the inventory clerk counts the items and then signs his or her name to the shipping and receiving department's copy of the receiving report (receiving report copy number 4 in Figure 11-6). The inventory clerk's signature establishes his or her responsibility for the merchandise and also eliminates the shipping and receiving department's responsibility for the goods. With these procedures incorporated into the clothing store's system, the inventory clerk cannot later claim that he or she failed to receive certain merchandise from the shipping and receiving department.

The above discussion of document flowcharts has provided a good understanding of the valuable contribution that this flowcharting technique can make to the consultants' systems survey work. An organization's systems problems are often caused by inadequate communication of document data to those employees involved in decision-making activities. Or, on the other hand, the organization's systems prob-

lems may result from too much irrelevant document data (not required for decision making) being communicated to specific managerial employees. The document flowchart provides the consultants a logical picture of how the communication flow currently takes place within a specific organizational area. By understanding the types of feedback data required by various employees to execute their assigned organizational functions effectively, the consultants can then thoroughly analyze their previously prepared document flowcharts and determine if these employees' information needs are being satisfied. If the client company's information communication network reveals weaknesses, the consultants can suggest positive systems revisions that will eliminate these weaknesses. Furthermore, as previously discussed, the document flowchart may reveal some inefficiencies in the client company's data-processing methods (e.g., the clothing store's manual rather than computerized preparation of purchase orders). The consultants' suggestions for revising their client company's data-processing methods can increase significantly the operating effectiveness of the information system.

Suggest Possible Solutions

The final aspect of systems analysis is closely related to the consultants' systems survey work. For this reason, the systems survey discussion in the previous section also illustrated the types of solutions that the consultants might recommend to solve their client's systems problems.

As shown in Figure 11-1, the analysis phase of a systems study (discussed in this chapter) is immediately followed by the design phase (discussed in the next chapter). This latter consulting work involves the preparation of detailed systems change proposals that should solve the client company's current problems. Normally, before the consultants begin the detailed, time-consuming job of designing systems changes, they will first discuss possible solution approaches with their client. Because these suggestions are presented to the client prior to beginning any in-depth design work, this systems study procedure is considered part of the consultants' systems analysis function.

For example, after the consultants have completed the first two major steps in systems analysis (defining their client's systems problems and performing the systems survey), they may conclude that the company's major systems problems are caused by the failure of its manual data-processing methods to provide timely managerial decision-making information. Before the consultants "jump into" the detailed work of designing various possible computerized systems to solve the company's current problems, however, they would first discuss their systems analysis conclusions and their suggestions for future changes with the client. These discussions may take place in a formal meeting between the consultants and the company's top management personnel. It is possible that top management will not favor implementing a computerized system into its organization. Top management's negative attitude may be the result of such things as the excessive costs associated with computerization or of many managerial executives' dislike of these enormous electronic machines. If top management's arguments against a computerized system appear to be irrational (e.g., "I am scared to death of the electronic geniuses!"), the consultants should attempt to change these negative attitudes by sound, logical arguments. However, because the consultants are outsiders and the company's top management has, within reasonable limits, the prerogative to do whatever it wants with its system, the consultants' systems revision suggestions may be rejected. If this should happen, top management may ask the consultants to perform some additional systems analysis work so that they can provide some "better" revision suggestions. (Or, top management could politely ask the consultants to discontinue any further systems study work!)

The point of the above example is that management consultants should not begin their detailed systems design work until they get approval from their client. Positive client reaction to the consultants' recommendations will justify the beginning of the next major systems study phase, which is the detailed design of specific changes that should eliminate the weaknesses in the current system. Chapter 12 will examine the consultants' approach to designing changes in their client's information system.

SUMMARY

Modern management consultants utilize a "systems approach" when performing a systems study. Under this approach, the consultants view their client company's information systems problems broadly by considering the positive or negative effects that will likely occur in all organizational areas as a result of a specific systems change recommendation. To utilize the systems approach effectively, a team of management consultants having different specialized knowledge are often involved in performing a systems study.

The first major phase of a systems study is called *systems analysis*. In this analysis phase, the consultants become thoroughly familiar with their client's current operating system so that they can identify the system's strengths and weaknesses. By the time the systems study has been completed, the consultants should be able to introduce systems changes that eliminate the weaknesses and maintain the strengths of their client's information system. The initial task in performing systems analysis is to define the present problem (or problems) that exists in the client company's current information system. A company's systems problems are often caused by the system's failure to achieve its intended goals. Therefore, when attempting to ascertain what the systems problems are, the consultants should define the three levels of their client's systems goals: (1) general systems goals, (2) top management systems goals, and (3) operating management systems goals.

After defining these goals, the next important aspect of systems analysis, called the systems survey, begins. In their survey work, the consultants perform a detailed investigation of the client's present information system to enable them to determine which of the levels of systems goals are not being accomplished. Upon discovering specific systems weaknesses, the consultants should be able to recommend changes that eliminate these weak points in their client's information system. Because an organization's employees (which include top management, operating management, and nonmanagerial workers) often resent outside consultants, the management consultants should be aware of this problem and attempt to deal positively with the employees' negative attitudes. By clearly communicating the purpose of their systems work to the company's employees and by having the employees participate in different aspects of the systems study, the consultants can attempt to achieve positive employee reaction regarding the present systems study. A company's systems problems may be caused by inefficient employee job performance. Therefore, as part of the systems survey work, the consultants might utilize a work measurement technique (e.g., the *average throughput* technique) to evaluate employee operating efficiency in performing repetitive type jobs.

When gathering the systems survey information, consultants normally will spend considerable time examining their client's preventive control system and feedback control system. A popular method used for analyzing the preventive controls is the questionnaire approach. By answering a series of preventive control questions about each organizational subsystem, the consultants are able to identify specific control weaknesses in their client's current system. Recommendations can subsequently be made for eliminating these weaknesses.

An effective tool often employed to evaluate a client's feedback controls is the document flowchart. This flowchart discloses the movement of information (and possibly physical goods as well) in various organizational data-processing activities. Both the document content and the document communication network can be analyzed by the use of this systems survey technique. Any inefficiencies in the client's information processing system should be revealed by the document flowchart. The consultants then will be able to suggest systems revisions to correct these inefficiencies.

Before beginning the intensive systems design

work to eliminate current weaknesses in an information system, the consultants should first communicate to the client company's top management their possible solution (or solutions) to the systems problems. If top management has a positive reaction concerning the proposed solution approach, the consultants can then proceed into the design phase of their systems study.

DISCUSSION QUESTIONS

11-1. The Clean Free Diaper Company has been in business 50 years without completing a single "life-cycle" of its information system. Is this situation good or bad? Explain.

11-2. Discuss the major differences, if any, between the *analysis phase* and the *design phase* of a systems study.

11-3. You have recently graduated from college and successfully passed the CPA examination. You are interested in working as a management consultant and therefore accept a position in the management advisory services department of Koote, Katch, and Kramer (a major public accounting firm). Upon being assigned your first systems study job, you are told by the chief consultant that the "systems approach" will be used in performing the necessary work on the client company's information system. Discuss in detail what the chief consultant means when he or she uses the term *systems approach*. Do you feel that this systems approach will increase or decrease your opportunities for creative thinking when performing the systems study work? Explain.

11-4. Assume that you are one of the partners of a major consulting firm and are responsible for hiring an additional consultant to work in your firm. You feel that this new employee's educational specialty (such as accounting, marketing, personnel, or mathematics) is not too important because the consulting firm already has professional employees with a wide variety of educational backgrounds. You believe, however, that the new employee should have other qualifications. List the *four* most important traits that you would want this newly hired consultant to possess. (*Note:* Trait 1 should be the most important employee characteristic, trait 2 should be the second most important employee characteristic, etc.) For each of these listed traits, indicate why you think the specific trait is important.

11-5. When beginning the analysis phase of a systems study, why is it important to first define the problem (or problems) that exists in the client company's current information system?

11-6. "To enable consultants to define the problem (or problems) that currently exists in their client company's information system, they must first define the goals of the client's system." Do you agree or disagree with the above statement? Discuss.

11-7. Three levels of a client company's systems goals that the management consultants should understand are general systems goals, top management systems goals, and operating management systems goals. If you had to select one of these categories of systems goals as the most important to the effective operation of an organization's information system, which one would you choose? Explain the reasons for your choice.

11-8. The Clayton Gordon Delight Company manufactures and distributes low-priced bottled wines to retailers. You are hired as a management consultant to help this company solve some of its present systems problems. Describe the types of decision-making information that probably would be needed by the company's

a. supervisor of the production plant.
b. top management.
c. marketing manager.

11-9. An organization's accounting information system should be able to communicate relevant decision-making information to both top management and operating management. For which of these two managerial groups is the accountant's communication tasks normally easier? Why?

11-10. At lunch yesterday, Don Wilson was telling his friend, Manny Koral, about the valuable changes that were introduced into his company's system five months ago by the Zebra Consulting Firm. Don indicated that, as a result of these systems changes, his company's net operating income has increased threefold. Manny was so impressed with Don's comments that when he returned to his office after lunch, he immediately called the Zebra Consulting Firm. Manny indicated to the firm's chief consultant that he had heard about the successful consulting work in Don Wilson's company, and that he would therefore like to have the same changes incorporated into his company's system. Do you agree with Manny's reasoning? Explain.

11-11. In most consulting jobs, why wouldn't it be desirable to *completely* eliminate a client's present information system and replace this system with a new one?

11-12. Do you think it is feasible for a consultant to use a work measurement technique such as *average throughput* to evaluate the operating efficiency of a company's top management personnel? Explain.

11-13. At the annual awards banquet of The Society for Consenting Consultants, the guest speaker was Arnold A. Arnstein. Mr. Arnstein has been a practicing management consultant for the past 40 years. In concluding his 3-hour speech, Arnstein made the following comments:

> To be an efficient and effective management consultant in today's sophisticated business world, you must let your client know from the beginning who is the *boss*—which is obviously *you*! Don't waste your time listening to suggestions from the client company's employees. It will only delay the completion of the consulting job. After all, if the client's employees were that bright in the first place, the company would not have requested your services. Should the company's management initially dislike your systems change recommendations, don't worry. As soon as your systems revisions are implemented, management will probably love you for making such valuable contributions to its organization's operating efficiency. Good luck and just remember—the business world could not survive without us consultants!

As a novice management consultant attending the awards banquet, how would you react to Arnold A. Arnstein's closing observations? Explain thoroughly.

11-14. This chapter emphasized that the three major groups of company personnel (top management, operating management, and nonmanagerial workers) should all play a participative role in a management consultant's systems study work. Discuss the type of role that each of these three groups normally would play. If you could have only *one* of these three company personnel groups actively involved in your systems study work (while the other two groups were completely unaware of what was happening), which group would you choose? Why?

11-15. George Beemster, management consultant, is currently performing a systems survey of the Louisville Sales Corporation, which recently installed an off-line electronic computer. The following comments have been extracted from Mr. Beemster's notes on computer operations and the processing and control of shipping notices and customer invoices:

- To minimize inconvenience Louisville converted immediately (without documenting the changes) its existing data-processing system, which utilized tabulating equipment. The computer company supervised the conversion and has provided training to all computer department employees (except keypunch operators) in systems design, operations, and programming.
- Each computer run is assigned to a specific employee, who is responsible for making program changes, running the program, and answering questions. This procedure has the advantage of eliminating the need for records of computer operations because each employee is responsible for his or her own computer runs.
- At least one computer department employee remains in the computer room during office hours, and only computer department employees have keys to the computer room.
- System documentation consists of those materials furnished by the computer company—a set of record formats and program listings. These and the tape library are kept in a corner of the computer department.

- Company products are shipped directly from public warehouses, which forward shipping notices to general accounting. There a billing clerk enters the price of the item and accounts for the numerical sequence of shipping notices from each warehouse. The billing clerk also prepares daily adding machine tapes ("control tapes") of the units shipped and the unit prices.
- Shipping notices and control tapes are forwarded to the computer department for keypunching and processing. Extensions are made on the computer. Output consists of invoices (in six copies) and a daily sales register. The daily sales register shows the aggregate totals of units shipped and unit prices, which the computer operator compares with the control tapes.
- All copies of the invoice are returned to the billing clerk. The clerk mails three copies to the customer, forwards one copy to the warehouse, maintains one copy in a numerical file, and retains one copy in an open invoice file that serves as a detailed accounts receivable record.

Required

Describe weaknesses in internal control over information and data flows and the procedures for processing shipping notices and customer invoices, and recommend improvements in these controls and processing procedures. Organize your answers as follows:

Weakness	Recommended Improvement

(AICPA Adapted)

11-16. As part of their systems survey work, the management consultants normally give considerable attention to the client company's "human element" area. What is meant by the "human element" area and why is it important to the consultants?

11-17. Try to think of several advantages and disadvantages that result from the management consultants' use of a "yes/no" type questionnaire when analyzing the client company's preventive control system. For each item listed, indicate your reasons for including it as either an advantage or a disadvantage.

11-18. A portion of an internal control questionnaire was provided in this chapter (see Figure 11-3). It illustrated a few examples of specific questions that management consultants might investigate when performing their systems survey of a client company's preventive controls. Try to think of some additional questions in each of the five subsystem areas (accounting, production, marketing, electronic data processing, and personnel) that you would expect to find on the consultants' questionnaire. (*Note:* Make any reasonable assumptions you wish about the type of company for which a systems study is being performed.)

11-19. Percy McBridge is one of the three partners of a management consulting firm called Brains Unlimited. The firm's motto is "Your Problem, Our Solution." Percy's consulting firm has recently been hired by the Quick Clothing Store to perform a systems study regarding the store's inventory system. In his first meeting with the clothing store's top management personnel, Percy learned the following facts about the store's business operations.

The Quick Clothing Store sells all types of medium-priced women's apparel (such as dresses, blouses, shoes, and nightgowns). The store utilizes a periodic system for inventory recordkeeping purposes. At least twice a month, some of the salespeople will visually inspect the inventory on hand to determine which inventory items, if any, require reordering. On each December 31 (the end of the store's accounting period), a complete physical count is made of the inventory and reconciled to the inventory accounting records. At the close of the previous calendar year, the comparison of the physical count with the accounting records indicated some major shortages of inventory. For example, the store's records disclosed that 350 pairs of women's dress shoes, model TS66, were in stock as of December 31. However, the physical count by the store's salespeople revealed only 295 pairs of these shoes.

Because of last year's excessive inventory shortages, the Quick Clothing Store wants Percy McBridge's consulting firm to deter-

mine the causes of these shortages and also suggest some possible changes in its inventory system that will eliminate any future inventory discrepancies.

Requirements

Assume that you are Percy McBridge, ace consultant of Brains Unlimited. With the available information provided about the Quick Clothing Store's inventory system, attempt to answer the following questions.

1. Before formally beginning your systems survey work, top management asks your opinion regarding the possible causes of its clothing store's inventory shortages. What response would you give to management at this stage of the systems study?

2. What specific questions would you want to be answered during your systems survey of the clothing store's inventory activities? How would you go about acquiring answers to these questions?

11-20. The treasurer of the Rockhill Company, a corporation that employs approximately 500 workers, recently made the following comments.

I am so happy that our company has finally acquired a computer to handle the payroll-processing activities. Under our previous manual system for payroll preparation, I was always worried about the possibility of either accidental human errors or fraudulent acts occurring in the payroll area. Now, with our computerized payroll system, I no longer have sleepless nights. The computer's sophisticated processing capabilities eliminate the likelihood of either errors or irregularities in our company's weekly payroll.

Do you agree or disagree with the above observations by the Rockhill Company's treasurer? Explain.

11-21. As emphasized in this chapter, document flowcharting is often used by management consultants when performing a systems survey of their client company's feedback controls. Could consultants also utilize a document flowcharting approach in their systems survey work concerning the client's preventive controls? Discuss.

11-22. Discuss some of the possible advantages of

using document flowcharts when gathering systems survey information. Can you think of any alternative information gathering methods that you feel would be superior to the document flowchart technique? If you can, indicate why you believe your suggested method (or methods) is more effective.

11-23. Why is it necessary for consultants to obtain actual copies of the specific documents appearing on their document flowcharts of a client company's information processing activities?

11-24. Are there actually any major differences between a systems analysis and a systems survey? Discuss.

11-25. As shown in Figure 11-2, the final procedure in systems analysis is the consultants' suggestion of possible solutions to solve the client company's systems problem (or problems). Because the consultants are actually recommending changes in the design of their client's present system structure, wouldn't it be more logical to include this final systems analysis procedure as part of the systems design phase of a consulting job? Explain.

11-26. During the beginning stages of a systems study, it is extremely important that the consultants define the information needs of their client company's management. Why?

11-27. Business organizations are required to modify or replace a portion or all of their financial information system in order to keep pace with their growth and to take advantage of improved information technology. The process involved in modifying or replacing an information system, especially if computer equipment is involved, requires a substantial commitment of time and resources. When an organization undertakes a change in its information system, a series of steps or phases is taken. The steps or phases included in a systems study are:

- survey of the existing system.
- analysis of information collected in the survey and development of recommendations for corrective action.
- design of a new or modified system.

- equipment study and acquisition.
- implementation of a new or modified system.

These steps or phases tend to overlap rather than being separate and distinct. In addition, the effort required in each step or phase varies from one systems change to another depending upon such factors as extent of the changes or the need for different equipment.

Required

A. Explain the purpose and reasons for surveying an organization's existing system during a systems study.

B. Identify and explain the general activities and techniques which are commonly used during the systems survey and analysis of information phases of a systems study conducted for a financial information system.

C. The systems survey and analysis of information phases of a financial information systems study are often carried out by a project team composed of a systems analyst, a management accountant, and other persons in the company who would be knowledgeable and helpful in the systems study. What would be the role of the management accountant in these phases of a financial information systems study?

(CMA Adapted)

11-28. You are the management consultant for the Alaska Branch of Far Distributing Company. This branch has substantial annual sales which are billed and collected locally. As a part of your systems survey work, you find that the procedures for handling cash receipts are as follows:

Cash collections on over-the-counter sales and C.O.D. sales are received from the customer or delivery service by the cashier. Upon receipt of cash, the cashier stamps the sales ticket "paid" and files a copy for future reference. The only record of C.O.D. sales is a copy of the sales ticket which is given to the cashier to hold until the cash is received from the delivery service.

Mail is opened by the secretary to the credit manager, and remittances are given to the credit manager for review. The credit manager then places the remittances in a tray on the cashier's desk. At the daily deposit cutoff time, the cashier delivers the checks and cash on hand to the assistant credit manager who prepares remittance lists and makes up the bank deposit which he also takes to the bank. The assistant credit manager also posts remittances to the accounts receivable ledger cards and verifies the cash discount allowable.

You also ascertain that the credit manager obtains approval from the executive office of Far Distributing Company, located in Chicago, to write off uncollectible accounts, and that he has retained in his custody (as of the end of the fiscal year) some remittances that were received on various days during last month.

Required

A. Describe the irregularities that might occur under the procedures now in effect for handling cash collections and remittances.

B. Give procedures that you would recommend to strengthen internal control over cash collections and remittances.

(AICPA Adapted)

PROBLEMS

11-29. Charting, Inc. has hired your consulting firm to perform a systems study. As part of the systems survey work, you determine that the company processes its sales and cash receipts documents in the following manner.

1. *Payment on account.* The mail is opened each morning by a mail clerk in the sales department. The mail clerk prepares a remittance advice (showing customer and amount paid) if one is not received. The checks and remittance advices are then forwarded to the sales department supervisor who reviews each check and forwards the checks and remittance advices to the accounting department supervisor.

The accounting department supervisor, who

also functions as credit manager in approving new credit and all credit limits, reviews all checks for payments on past due accounts and then forwards the checks and remittance advices to the accounts receivable clerk who arranges the advices in alphabetical order. The remittance advices are posted directly to the accounts receivable ledger cards. The checks are endorsed by stamp and totaled. The total is posted to the cash receipts journal. The remittance advices are filed chronologically.

After receiving the cash from the previous day's cash sales, the accounts receivable clerk prepares the daily deposit slip in triplicate. The third copy of the deposit slip is filed by date and the second copy and the original accompany the bank deposit.

2. *Sales.* Sales clerks prepare sales invoices in triplicate. The original and second copy are presented to the cashier. The third copy is retained by the sales clerk in the sales book. When the sale is for cash, the customer pays the sales clerk who presents the money to the cashier with the invoice copies.

A credit sale is approved by the cashier from an approved credit list after the sales clerk prepares the three-part invoice. After receiving the cash or approving the invoice, the cashier validates the original copy of the sales invoice and gives it to the customer. At the end of each day the cashier summarizes the sales and cash received and forwards the cash and the second copy of the sales invoices to the accounts receivable clerk.

The accounts receivable clerk balances the cash received with cash sales invoices and prepares a daily sales summary. The credit sales invoices are posted to the accounts receivable ledger and all invoices are then sent to the inventory control clerk in the sales department for posting to the inventory control cards. After posting, the inventory control clerk files all invoices numerically. The accounts receivable clerk posts the daily sales summary to the cash receipts journal and sales journal and files the sales summaries by date.

The cash from cash sales is combined with the cash received on account to comprise the daily bank deposit.

3. *Bank deposits.* The bank validates the deposit slip and returns the second copy to the accounting department where it is filed by date by the accounts receivable clerk.

Monthly bank statements are reconciled promptly by the accounting department supervisor and filed by date.

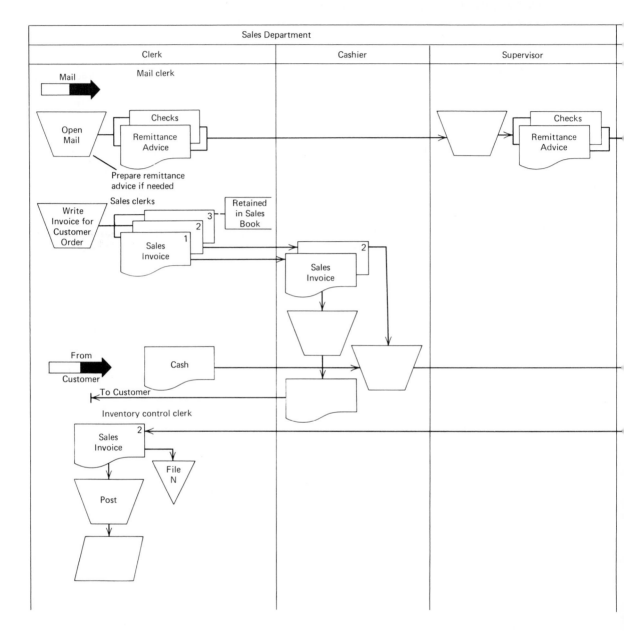

Figure 11-7. Charting Inc. document flowchart for sales and cash receipts.

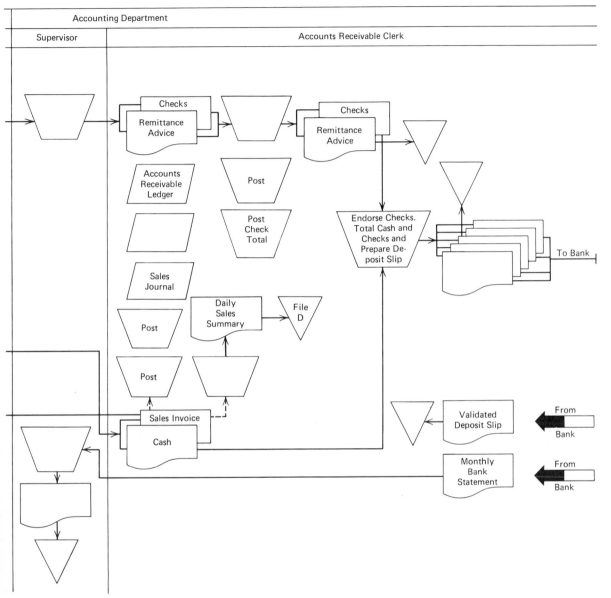

Figure 11-7 (Continued)

Problem Requirement

You recognize that there are weaknesses in the existing system and believe that a chart of information and document flows would be beneficial in evaluating this client's internal control system. Complete the document flowchart in Figure 11-7 for sales and cash receipts of Charting, Inc. by labeling the appropriate symbols and indicating information flows. The chart is complete as to symbols and document flows. The following symbols are used:

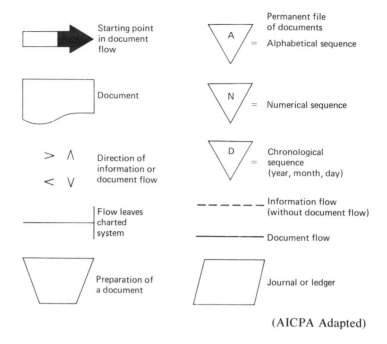

(AICPA Adapted)

11-30. Long, CPA, has been engaged to examine and report on the financial statements of Maylou Corporation. During the review phase of the study of Maylou's system of internal accounting control over purchases, Long was given the following document flowchart for purchases.

Required

A. Identify the procedures, relating to purchase requisitions and purchase orders, that Long would expect to find if Maylou's system of internal accounting control over purchases is effective. For example, pur-

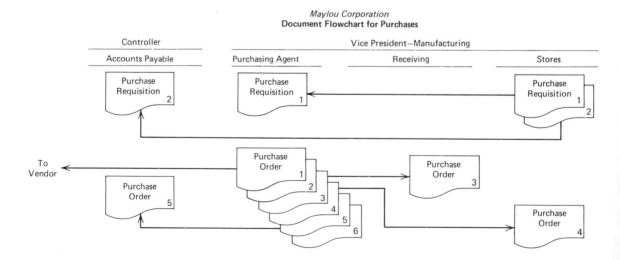

Maylou Corporation
Document Flowchart for Purchases

chase orders are prepared only after giving proper consideration to the time to order and the quantity to order. **Do not comment on the effectiveness of the flow of documents as presented in the flowchart or on separation of duties.**

B. What are the factors to consider in determining:

1. The time to order?
2. The quantity to order?

(AICPA Adapted)

CASE ANALYSES

11-31. *Wright Company*

Wright Company employs a computer-based data processing system for maintaining all company records. The present system was developed in stages over the past five years and has been fully operational for the last 24 months.

When the system was being designed, all department heads were asked to specify the types of information and reports they would need for planning and controlling operations. The systems department attempted to meet the specifications of each department head. Company management specified that certain other reports be prepared for department heads. During the five years of systems development and operation, there have been several changes in the department head positions due to attrition and promotions. The new department heads often made requests for additional reports according to their specifications. The systems department complied with all of these requests. Reports were discontinued only upon request by a department head, and then only if it was not a standard report required by top management. As a result, few reports were in fact discontinued. Consequently, the data processing system was generating a large quantity of reports each reporting period.

Company management became concerned about the quantity of report information that was being produced by the system. The internal audit department was asked to evaluate the effective-

ness of the reports generated by the system. The audit staff determined early in the study that more information was being generated by the data processing system than could be used effectively. They noted the following reactions to this information overload:

1. Many department heads would not act on certain reports during periods of peak activity. The department head would let these reports accumulate with the hope of catching up during a subsequent lull.

2. Some department heads had so many reports that they did not act at all upon the information or they made incorrect decisions because of misuse of the information.

3. Frequently action required by the nature of the report data was not taken until the department head was reminded by someone who needed the decision. These department heads did not appear to have developed a priority system for acting on the information produced by the data processing system.

4. Department heads often would develop the information they needed from alternative, independent sources, rather than utilizing the reports generated by the data processing system. This was often easier than trying to search among the reports for the needed data.

Questions

A. For each one of the above four reactions, indicate whether it contributes positively or negatively toward the Wright Company's operating effectiveness. Explain your answer in each case.

B. For each reaction that you indicated as negative, recommend alternative procedures the Wright Company could employ to eliminate this negative contribution to operating effectiveness.

(CMA Adapted)

11-32. *Duval, Inc.*

Duval, Inc. is a large publicly held corporation that is well known throughout the United States for its products. The corporation has always had good profit margins and excellent earnings. However, Duval has experienced a leveling of sales and a reduced market share in the past two years resulting in a stabilization of profits rather than growth. Despite these trends, the firm has maintained an excellent cash and short-term investment position. The president has called a meeting of the treasurer and the vice-presidents for sales and production to develop alternative strategies for improving Duval's performance. The four individuals form the nucleus of a well organized management team that has worked together for several years to bring success to Duval, Inc.

The sales vice-president suggests that sales levels can be improved by presenting the company's product in a more attractive and appealing package. He also recommends that advertising be increased, and that the current price be maintained. This latter step would have the effect of a price decrease because the prices of most other competing products are rising.

The treasurer is skeptical of maintaining the present price when others are increasing prices since this will curtail revenues, unless this policy provides a competitive advantage. He also points out that the repackaging will increase costs in the near future, at least, because of the start-up costs of a new packing process. He does not favor increasing advertising outright because he is doubtful of the short-run benefit.

The sales vice-president replies that increased, or at least redirected, advertising is necessary to promote the price stability and to take advantage of the new packaging; the combination would provide the company with a competitive advantage. The president adds that the advertising should be studied closely to determine the type of advertising to be used—television, radio, newspaper, magazine. In addition, if television is used, attention must be directed to the type of programs to be sponsored—children's, family, sporting events, news specials, etc.

The production vice-president suggests several possible production improvements, such as a systems study of the manufacturing process to identify changes in the work flow which would cut costs. He suggests operating costs could be further reduced by the purchase of new equipment. The product could be improved by employing a better grade of raw materials and by engineering changes in the fabrication of the product. When queried by the president on the impact of the proposed changes, the production vice-president indicated that the primary benefit would be product performance, but that appearance and safety would also be improved. The sales vice-president and treasurer commented that this would result in increased sales.

The treasurer notes that all the production proposals would increase immediate costs, and this could result in lower profits. If profit performance is going to be improved, the price structure should be examined closely. He recommends that the current level of capital expenditures be maintained unless substantial cost savings can be obtained.

The treasurer further believes that expenditures for research and development should be decreased since previous outlays have not prevented a decrease in Duval's share of the market. The production vice-president agrees that the research and development activities have not proven profitable, but thinks that this is because the research effort was applied in the wrong area. The sales vice-president cautions against any drastic reductions because the packaging change will only provide a temporary advantage in the market; consequently, more effort will have to be devoted to product development.

Focusing on the use of liquid assets and the present high yields on securities, the treasurer suggests that the firm's profitability can be improved by shifting funds from the presently held short-term marketable securities to longer-term, higher-yield securities. He further states that cost reductions would provide more funds for investments. He recognizes that the restructuring of the investments from short-term to long-term would hamper flexibility.

In his summarizing comments, the president

observes that they have a good start and the ideas provide some excellent alternatives. He states,

I think we ought to develop these ideas further and consider other ramifications. For instance, what effect would new equipment and the systems study have on the labor force? Shouldn't we also consider the environmental impact of any plant and product change? We want to appear as a leader in our industry—not a follower.

I note that none of you considered increased community involvement through such groups as the Chamber of Commerce and the United Fund.

The factors you mentioned plus those additional points all should be considered as we reach a decision on the final course of action we will follow.

Questions

A. State explicitly the implied corporate goals being expressed by each of the following:

1. Treasurer
2. Sales vice-president
3. Production vice-president
4. President

B. Compare the types of goals you discussed in (A) above with the corporate goal(s) postulated by the economic theory of the firm.

(CMA Adapted)

12

Systems Study: The Design Phase

Among the important questions that you should be
able to answer after reading this chapter are:

1 **What is a feasibility evaluation and why is its
performance such an important aspect of
the management consultants' systems study
work?**

2 **What are some specific benefits that normally
result when a company converts from a manual to a computerized accounting information system?**

3 **What are some important factors that a company should consider when deciding which
computer manufacturer's (e.g., IBM or Honeywell) hardware and software system to acquire?**

4 **How is a cost/benefit analysis performed for a
proposed computer system?**

5 **Is a service bureau a division of the FBI?**

INTRODUCTION

The "life-cycle" of a business information system was illustrated in the previous chapter (see
Figure 11-1). The existence of a problem (or
problems) within a company's current system
often leads its top management to hire an outside
consulting firm (whose staff of consultants includes accountants) to help solve the problem.
Of the four major phases of a systems study
(which are analysis, design, implementation
and initial operation, and follow-up), only the
analysis phase was discussed in Chapter 11. This
chapter will therefore continue the discussion of
a consulting firm's systems study work by examining the design phase.

The final procedure in systems analysis is the
consultants' suggestions to their client of possible solutions to the company's information systems problem. If the client's top management has
positive reactions toward these suggestions for
change, the consultants can then begin the next
major systems study phase, called *design*. In the
subsequent discussion of systems design, the assumption will be made that the consultants' systems analysis work revealed weaknesses in their
client company's present manual data-processing
methods. For discussion purposes, we shall assume, in particular, that the growth in size and

complexity of the client's business has led to the inability of the manual data-processing system to provide timely informational reports to both top management and operating management for decision making. Therefore, the consultants have suggested that the company consider the possibility of converting to a computerized data-processing system. This suggestion to automate was made at a formal meeting between the consultants and the company's top management executives. Top management's reaction towards a computerized information system was quite favorable, and as a result, the consultants' systems study design phase commences.

SYSTEMS DESIGN

The systems design work relating to the possible acquisition of a computerized data-processing system involves two major activities: (1) the feasibility evaluation, and (2) the preparation of a "systems specifications report" for hardware and software supplier evaluation. The feasibility evaluation is, in effect, a specialized type of systems survey whereby the consultants attempt to determine whether or not it is practical for their client company to convert its present noncomputerized data-processing system to a computerized one. Alternatively, if a company already has an automated system (such as a batch-processing computerized system), the feasibility evaluation might involve the consultants' study of the practicality of converting this system to an online, real-time configuration. The systems specifications report for hardware and software supplier evaluation includes detailed, written descriptions of the specific operating tasks that the consultants' proposed computerized system will perform. This system specifications report is then submitted to hardware and software suppliers (such as IBM, Honeywell, and Burroughs) for their review. These suppliers will subsequently submit hardware and software proposals to the company. Finally, the company's management (usually with the consultants' advice) must decide which supplier's proposal, if any, should be accepted. Each of these two systems design activities is discussed below.

The Feasibility Evaluation

After obtaining a positive response from the client company's top management regarding the conversion of its current manual data-processing system to a computerized data-processing system, the consultants must then begin a detailed feasibility evaluation of different possible computerized systems. The alternatives to be evaluated might include (1) a batch-processing system, (2) an online, real-time processing system, and (3) a combination of these two systems (e.g., a major airline might utilize an online, real-time system when processing flight reservations and a batch-processing system when processing its accounts receivable and accounts payable transactions). For each computerized system under consideration, four feasibility areas must be examined by the consulting team: (1) technical feasibility, (2) operational feasibility, (3) schedule feasibility, and (4) economic feasibility. Because the accountants on the consulting team normally are responsible for the economic feasibility evaluation work, the following discussion of these four feasibility areas will emphasize the economic evaluation phase.

Technical feasibility. This phase of the feasibility evaluation typically is performed by the computer experts on the management consulting team because a thorough understanding of computer hardware and software is essential. The consultants may have developed a preliminary hardware configuration for an envisioned computerized system that would meet their client's information processing needs. Before further steps can be taken to implement this system, however, the consultants must analyze the technological state of the computer industry as well as the technological expertise that currently exists within the client company. Obviously, a suggested computer system would be impractical if the specific hardware and software requirements indicated in the initial design proposal could not be supplied by any one of the computer manufacturers. In addition, the consultants must determine whether the technological skills needed to handle this proposed system either currently exist in their client's operating struc-

363

ture or if they can be acquired in the near future. (This evaluation overlaps into the operational feasibility investigation, to be discussed below.) If a specific computerized system is too sophisticated for a company's employees, it is likely that the system's implementation and subsequent day-to-day operation will be unsuccessful.

Operational feasibility. This area of the feasibility evaluation attempts to ascertain how the newly proposed system will affect the client company's existing operational environment. A company's operational environment includes its current personnel and the many functional activities performed by these employees. The consultants must analyze the capabilities of the client's personnel to perform the specific functions required by the newly proposed system. If additional employees with specialized training are necessary to operate the new system when it is implemented, the consultants should disclose this fact to their client. The need for any training programs to upgrade the skill levels of current personnel should also be considered.

In effect, the operational feasibility analysis is also a human relations study because it is strongly oriented toward "people problems" that are likely to occur in the new system. (For this reason, personnel management specialists on the consulting team often participate in the operational feasibility evaluation.) By considering in advance some of the possible human relations problems, these problems should be avoided. As discussed in Chapter 11, people often have a negative attitude toward change. Because a proposal to convert a company's manual data-processing system to a computerized data-processing system will cause many changes in employee organizational duties, the client company's human resources (i.e., its personnel) must be directly considered before the automated system is implemented. Hopefully, if the client's personnel are kept well-informed about such things as the need for the systems change, how the new system will affect their organizational functions, and so forth, any employee resistance to the systems revisions can be minimized. Also, the employees should be encouraged to make

suggestions regarding changes in the system that they feel are necessary. Unless the human element of a systems change is considered, the best-designed system "on paper" will often be an operational failure when it is implemented.

Recently, for example, a computerized inventory system was installed in a company's large warehouse. After a three-week operational period, top management discovered that there were more processing errors in the new system than there had been in the old manual system. These processing error problems persisted for months. Finally, the company hired a management consultant to perform a systems study. The consultant quickly found the difficulty. The company's system was so mechanized that employees had very little to do but punch buttons. The consultant discovered that the employees were purposely sabotaging the system out of boredom! Since the client's personnel must carry out the day-to-day operations of the system, their positive motivation is an essential prerequisite to the successful functioning of systems revisions.

Schedule feasibility. If the initially designed systems changes are approved by the client company's top management, the consultants must estimate how long it will take for the new system to become operative. Because a major conversion from a manual to a computerized data-processing system could take several years to implement, the client's management should be given an estimate of the time required to make the system operational. The company's top management may visualize a time interval of approximately six months until the revised system is operational. Upon learning that the systems conversion will take several years to implement, top management may decide to reject the systems design proposal for a simpler alternative that can be implemented in a shorter time interval (e.g., a batch-processing computerized system rather than an online computerized database system).

When performing the schedule feasibility analysis, the consultants often utilize a PERT (program evaluation review technique) network to help them coordinate the many activities necessary in the newly designed system. When a systems implementation involves the conversion from a manual to a computerized data-processing system, the computer experts on the management consulting team normally will have a major role in the schedule feasibility work. A PERT network for planning and controlling a systems implementation will be illustrated in Chapter 13.

Economic feasibility. As discussed in Chapter 3 on budgetary accounting information systems, a program proposal for a major capital expenditure should not be approved for implementation until a cost/benefit analysis has been performed. All programs' cost/benefit analyses submitted to the budget committee for review and subsequent acceptance or rejection are ranked according to their *excess present value indexes* (also discussed in Chapter 3). Based upon the number of dollars budgeted for long-range programs, those program proposals with the highest rankings are accepted. Because the consultants' proposal to computerize their client's present manual data-processing system involves a major long-term asset investment, the consulting team's accountants should perform a cost/benefit analysis of this proposal. The program proposal's excess present value index will be ranked with other program proposals' indexes. The budget committee of the client company can then decide whether to accept or reject the consultants' program proposal for computerizing the information processing system. (Of course, the results must also be positive from the other three feasibility areas discussed above before top management will accept the consultants' proposal.)

To illustrate the calculations required in a cost/benefit analysis for the conversion of a company's manual information system to a computerized batch-processing information system, assume that the consultants estimate a four-year useful life for the computerized system proposal. Further assume that the client's opportunity cost is estimated to be 10 percent. Figure 12-1 reflects the cost/benefit analysis performed by the consulting team's accountants on a proposed medium-size computer system for their client. (Ex-

planations of the individual cost and benefit items will follow.)

It should be kept in mind that the consultants might develop a preliminary design of other types of computer systems (e.g., an online, real-time data-base system) in addition to the batch processing proposal discussed here. For each alternative system proposed, a cost/benefit analysis similar to the one in Figure 12-1 would be prepared.

As discussed in Chapter 3, the benefits from a program proposal often are quite difficult to quantify monetarily. Normally, when attempting to project these benefits, a large degree of subjectivity is necessary. Thus, the seven benefit categories listed in Figure 12-1 reflect the accountants' subjective estimates of the monetary advantages from the batch-processing computerized system proposal. Furthermore, because the details of this proposal have not yet been discussed with a hardware and software supplier (which is part of the second major activity in systems design), the costs included in Figure 12-1 are also based upon the accountants' subjective estimates. We will now briefly examine the specific cash benefits and the specific cash costs of the batch processing system proposal.

Cash benefits. The first benefit listed in Figure 12-1 is the savings from reduced employee clerical costs. The computerized system will handle a large number of processing functions (such as the accounting cycle data-processing steps, the preparation of sales analyses, and the preparation of production reports) previously performed manually by organizational employees. Therefore, many of the manual clerical jobs that exist under the present data-processing system (such as accounts receivable bookkeeper and payroll clerk) will be eliminated if the computerized system is implemented. Also, under a manual data-processing system, clerical employees often have to work overtime in order to get reports prepared on schedule. As a result of computerization, most of the previous overtime pay to clerical workers should be eliminated.

Benefits 2, 3, and 4 relate to more productive use of the company's working capital resources

Figure 12-1

COST/BENEFIT ANALYSIS OF COMPUTERIZED SYSTEM PROPOSAL

	Years				
	1[a]	2	3	4	5
Cash Benefits					
1. Reduction in employee clerical costs		$ 950,000	$ 970,000	$ 990,000	$1,300,000
2. Additional return due to reduction in average annual inventory balance plus reduction in lost sales caused by stockouts		350,000	360,000	370,000	400,000
3. Additional return due to reduction in average annual accounts receivable balance and average annual cash balance		27,000	46,000	65,000	84,000
4. Reduction in bad debt write-offs		3,000	4,000	5,000	6,000
5. Better customer services		700,000	750,000	900,000	900,000
6. Better market planning		600,000	625,000	670,000	770,000
7. More efficient management control		900,000	950,000	900,000	1,050,000
Total Benefits		$3,530,000	$3,705,000	$3,900,000	$4,510,000
Cash Costs					
1. Computer hardware and software	$ 600,000	$ 900,000	$ 900,000	$ 900,000	$ 900,000
2. Environment	520,000	9,000	10,000	11,000	12,000
3. Physical installation	90,000				
4. Training	100,000	8,000	8,000	8,500	8,500
5. Programming	240,000	100,000	85,000	85,000	75,000
6. Conversion	1,400,000				
7. Operation		1,180,000	1,500,000	1,500,000	1,600,000
8. Additional systems study work	350,000	20,000	5,000	5,000	5,000
Total Costs	$3,300,000	$2,217,000	$2,508,000	$2,509,500	$2,600,500
Excess of Annual Cash Benefits Over Annual Cash Costs	—	$1,313,000	$1,197,000	$1,390,500	$1,909,500
× present value factors at a 10 percent opportunity cost (see the present value table in Figure B-1 of Appendix B)		× .826	× .751	× .683	× .621
Present Value of Annual Cash Benefits Over Annual Cash Costs		$1,084,538	$ 898,947	$ 949,712	$1,185,800

EXCESS PRESENT VALUE INDEX

= Total Net Cash Flow Present Value/Total Asset Investment Present Value

= ($1,084,538 + $898,947 + $949,712 + $1,185,800)/$3,300,000

= 1.248, or 124.8%

[a]It is assumed that a full year is required to implement this system. Therefore, no benefits occur during the first year. Also, this illustration assumes that because the computer center is not operative until the second year, all the first-year cash costs ($3,300,000) reflect the present value of the total asset investment required for the computer system. The four-year estimated useful life of this information system actually begins in year 2 when the computer center becomes operative.

(i.e., the current assets). A computerized inventory system will enable the company to better control its merchandise inventory activities. Under the present manual inventory system, management reports on quantity balances of specific inventory items may have been prepared infrequently, causing management to be unaware of the updated inventory quantities on hand. This situation may have resulted in too large a physical quantity balance for some inventory items (thereby having excessive dollars invested in these inventory items with the result that the dollars are not being used for more productive investments) and too small a physical quantity balance for other inventory items (thereby increasing the possibility of stockouts and the resultant lost sales; in a production process, a stockout of specific raw materials could cause a stoppage of the entire manufacturing activities). Through timely computer printouts (on an exception basis) of those inventory items that should be replenished, optimal inventory balances hopefully can be maintained. Ordinarily, these timely feedback inventory reports will enable a company to reduce its average annual total investment in inventory as well as reduce the incidence of stockouts.

A possible reason for a large accounts receivable asset balance is the slowness of a company's manual system in preparing and mailing billing statements to customers. (Most credit customers will not pay their account balances until they receive billing statements.) By batching credit sales data and preparing customers' statements on the computer, the company's billing function can be performed faster than with a manual system. Consequently, an individual customer would receive a billing statement much sooner after credit sales transactions have occurred, and the company would thereby receive the cash payment much faster. Thus, a shorter turnaround time (from the time a credit sale is made to the time the cash is collected) would cause the company's average annual accounts receivable balance to decline. The company can then use this cash collection money much sooner for an income-generating investment rather than having the money tied up in the accounts-receivable asset (where a productive

return is not being earned, except for the possible carrying charges billed to the customer).

With the use of a computer, a company is usually able to do a better job of forecasting its future needs for cash. Prior to a computerized system, the company's inability to forecast accurately its future cash requirements may have caused the company's financial managers to attempt to avoid the risk of a cash shortage by maintaining a larger than necessary cash balance. Because cash is a fairly unproductive asset (e.g., you can invest your cash in a savings account and earn an annual return of only approximately 5 or 6 percent), computerized forecasting of future cash requirements for paying bills should provide the company with a more accurate picture of the optimal cash balance that should be maintained. The cash in excess of this optimal balance can then be invested in productive income-generating activities (e.g., purchasing stocks or bonds of another corporation—the return from these investments should be considerably higher than the interest paid on a bank savings account). The computerized forecasting system will thus enable the company to reduce its average annual cash balance.

A computerized data-processing system enables the credit and collection department managers to receive more timely reports on credit customers' past-due account balances. The accounts receivable aging analyses will provide essential information to these credit managers so that they can observe the slowness or promptness of specific customers' cash payments. If, for example, the credit managers felt that the number of accounts which were over 90 days past-due was becoming too large, they could take steps to tighten their company's credit-granting policies. This action should lead to a reduction in the company's bad debt write-offs. Also, by receiving prompt computer printouts of those customers' accounts that are past due, the credit managers can take immediate action to attempt collection of these account balances. If information regarding customers' past-due account balances is slow in being provided to the credit managers (as can occur in a manual data-processing system), these delinquent customers may be more difficult to locate.

They may, for example, have moved to another city without leaving any forwarding addresses. As a result, the company's bad debt write-offs are likely to increase.

Computerization of a company's data-processing system should help in providing better services to customers (benefit number 5 in Figure 12-1). Among these services would be such things as the company's ability to process customers' orders in a fast and efficient manner, the company's ability to respond promptly to customers' questions regarding the present status of their account balances, and the company's ability to provide customers more accurate projections of when the manufacturing work on their purchased production items will be completed. If a company is involved in a highly competitive business, the above customer services should be especially helpful in increasing the organization's sales.

As pointed out in Chapter 3, a computer can greatly aid a company's market planning (benefit number 6 in Figure 12-1). Through the utilization of mathematical sales forecasting models (such as the multivariate forecasting model mentioned in Chapter 3), the company is able to develop more accurate short- and long-range sales projections, thereby contributing to effective budgetary planning. Simulation techniques can also be employed to enable the company's management to generate various possible sales forecasts under differing assumptions regarding changes in key variables. For example, if the Alan Company's budget committee anticipated a significant rise in inflation during the coming year, different expected effects on sporting goods sales from this inflation variable could be incorporated into the company's computer analyses of possible sales projections. Mathematical forecasting models and simulation techniques are difficult, if not impossible, to use without the availability of a computer.

Benefit number 7 (more efficient management control) encompasses all aspects of a company's operational activities. As emphasized throughout this book, the computer's ability to provide timely feedback performance reports on subsystems' actual operations compared with their budgets will enable management to take quicker action to correct areas of significant budget deviation. These faster "after-the-fact" performance reports should contribute to increased operating efficiency within all phases of the company's system.

Cash costs. It is assumed in Figure 12-1 that the company will lease rather than purchase its required hardware and software. The consultants' estimate that this annual fixed-lease cost will be $900,000 (cost item number 1 in Figure 12-1). We are also assuming in Figure 12-1 that this $900,000 annual lease cost will not be incurred in its entirety during year 1. Since year 1 is the period of implementation, the computer hardware and software will not be acquired until several months into the implementation work (thus making the lease cost less than $900,000 for year 1). Most lease agreements with computer suppliers are for a period of at least three years. Lease payments are normally made monthly and the lease covers all maintenance work necessary on the computer system. A major advantage of leasing versus purchasing the computer hardware and software system is the increased flexibility provided the company. At the end of the lease period, the company can cancel the contract for the use of a specific computer system if its data-processing needs have changed. Company management may decide to switch to a more efficient computer system offered by the same or another supplier. Many leasing contracts provide a clause that enables the user, if so desired, to purchase the hardware and software system at a later date. This purchase price is often stated within the lease contract and normally is below the original retail price of the system, thereby giving the user an allowance for prior lease payments.

Cost item number 2 of Figure 12-1 (environment costs) includes all monetary expenditures in initially preparing the company's premises for the computer installation as well as additional site preparation costs that may be necessary in subsequent years during the life of the computer system. As can be seen in Figure 12-1, the first-year costs associated with site preparation are by far the largest ($520,000), and these costs significantly decline in years 2 through 5. Chapter 2 emphasized that many organizations establish their computer center as a separate subsystem apart from the accounting subsystem. Therefore, a specific area within a company's building structure will have to be found for locating the EDP subsystem. (If no current space is available, it may be necessary for the company to construct a new building to house the computer.) Some of the environmental costs associated with a computer installation include offices and conference rooms for computer personnel, air conditioning of the computer center (to ensure more efficient functioning of the computer equipment), electric outlets for providing the proper power voltage requirements to operate the computer equipment, and furniture and fixtures needed in the computer center. The building location in which the computer system is housed should be protected from electrical interference, dust, and any other environmental factors that would deter the system's efficient functioning. For effective internal control, adequate safeguards should exist to prevent unauthorized employees from entering the computer center and using the equipment. (Examples of such safeguards were discussed in Chapter 8.)

Physical installation costs (item number 3 in Figure 12-1) include the expenditures for transporting the computer equipment to the company's premises (even when acquiring a small computer system, for example, the freight costs for transporting this system can be considerable) as well as using cranes or other special equipment to carry the hardware to its specific organizational location, such as the fourteenth floor of the company's building. Cost item number 4, training, is usually high during the first year of computer implementation, but declines significantly in subsequent years (as illustrated in Figure 12-1). Training includes all the costs in preparing the company's present employees as well as newly hired employees to operate the computer system efficiently. The necessary training sessions may be provided to the user company's employees ''at no charge'' by the hardware and software supplier. If the supplier

does not offer training, however, the company will have to incur the costs of sending its employees to outside training programs.

The fifth cost item shown in Figure 12-1 includes all the costs associated with writing specific computer programs to perform a company's data-processing activities, testing the correctness (or logic) of these programs before they are implemented into the system, and making revisions to old programs based upon later design changes in systems operations. One method of testing a company's programs prior to implementation is through simulation. For example, the mathematical logic of an accounts-receivable processing program could be ascertained by creating a fictitious customer with a $300 balance owed the company. If a $50 credit sale to this customer is then assumed, the program will be run with the above data to determine whether the computer printout indicates a $350 updated account balance for the customer. Companies are often able to reduce their programming costs by leasing from the computer suppliers' prewritten, ''canned'' programs (called *proprietary software*) for various data-processing functions. However, these canned program packages may be costly and, in many cases, major modifications are required in the prewritten programs to meet the specific data-processing needs of an organization's system. (Obtaining prewritten programs from computer vendors will be discussed further in Chapter 14.)

The cost of converting a company's current data-processing system to the new one (cost item number 6 in Figure 12-1) depends upon the magnitude of changes involved. For example, if some minor modifications were made in the Alan Company's present batch-processing system, the conversion costs would likely be minimal. However, a conversion from a manual to a computerized system will entail large dollar expenditures to make the new system operative. Among these costs will be monetary expenditures: (1) to transfer a company's financial data from its present storage media to computerized storage media (e.g., transferring the accounts receivable subsidiary ledger data to magnetic tape files), (2) to establish good internal controls for the new computerized system (discussed in Chapter 8), and (3) to test the operations of the new system before it replaces the old system (discussed in Chapter 13 under the implementation phase of a systems study). Thus, the conversion costs associated with a new system are basically set-up type costs which are incurred only in the first year of a new system to enable this system to take over a company's data-processing functions. The next cost category shown in Figure 12-1 (number 7, operation) represents the expenditures necessary to enable the new computerized system to operate on a day-to-day basis once it is implemented. These costs include (1) the salaries of employees working in the EDP subsystem (such as systems analysts, programmers, computer operators, security officers, keypunch operators, tape librarians, etc.), (2) the necessary supplies needed in the EDP subsystem (such as punched cards, magnetic tape, printer paper, etc.), (3) the monthly electricity bill, and (4) the insurance coverage premiums for fire and vandalism.

If the current system proposal is eventually approved for implementation by the company's top management, additional systems study work will be required by the consultants. The cost of this additional work is reflected as cost item number 8 in Figure 12-1. The further work performed by the consultants (for which they will be paid) includes preparing a "systems specifications report" for use in discussions with various hardware and software suppliers regarding specific computer systems to meet their client's needs (discussed later in this chapter), supervising the implementation of the new computer system (discussed in Chapter 13), and performing periodic follow-up tests of the new system's effectiveness after it becomes operative (also discussed in Chapter 13).

Concluding comments on the feasibility evaluation. To enable the consultants to proceed into the next major activity of systems design, the preparation of a systems specifications report for hardware and software supplier evaluation, all four of the feasibility areas (technical, operational, schedule, and economic) must be "feasi-

ble" (i.e., capable of accomplishing within the client company's specific systems goals). Furthermore, top management must have positive reactions regarding each of the feasibility evaluations. For example, if top management personnel (as well as their budget committee) believe that the estimated excess present value index of 124.8 percent for the proposed computer system (see Figure 12-1) is far too low in comparison with the company's other long-range programs, no further consideration of this systems proposal may be warranted. To permit the consultants to provide their client company with a *total* feasibility evaluation analysis, all four feasibility areas must be considered simultaneously. If one or more of these areas (e.g., the technical feasibility) is unable to be accomplished or if top management and various budget committee members have negative feelings about any of the four feasibility evaluations, then the consultants' design proposal is not *totally* feasible. Top management personnel may then ask the consultants to develop an alternate design proposal that would be suitable for their company.

Our assumption here is that the batch processing computer system proposal of the consultants does "pass" the feasibility evaluation stage. We will therefore begin discussing the second major activity of systems design.

Preparation of a Systems Specifications Report for Hardware and Software Supplier Evaluation

This activity of the consultants' systems design work builds upon findings from the feasibility evaluation. The systems specifications report prepared by the consultants contains detailed information about each computerized systems design proposal that meets the feasibility requirements of the client's system. Thus, a detailed systems specifications report would be prepared for the computerized batch-processing system proposal discussed above. If the consultants had also proposed, for example, an online, real-time computer system and this alternate system satisfied the feasibility evaluations, the specifications report would include detailed information regarding this design proposal as well.

The systems specifications report on each design proposal is the focal point for discussions between the consultants and the hardware and software suppliers (also called ''computer vendors''). Before computer vendors such as IBM or Burroughs can submit a specific hardware and software package proposal to the consultants' client, they must first be provided with detailed descriptions of the company's information processing needs. Normally, the consultants will want to receive hardware and software proposals from several different computer suppliers. This will permit the consultants and their client's management to evaluate the pros and cons of each vendor's offerings, with the objective of selecting that proposal which best meets the company's information needs.

Each of the three major stages associated with the hardware and software supplier evaluation process (i.e., preparing a systems specifications report, submitting this report to computer vendors, and selecting a specific computer system based upon each vendor's proposal) is now examined.

Preparing systems specifications report. As indicated above, the systems design work of preparing a systems specifications report builds upon the feasibility evaluation data. This systems design activity is, in actuality, a continuation of the feasibility evaluation process. When the consultants were performing their feasibility survey work, they did not analyze in detail the specifications of each proposed systems design. The detailed work was unnecessary because the purpose of the feasibility evaluation was to ascertain whether or not a computerized data-processing system appeared ''totally feasible'' for the client company. Once this determination was made and assuming that it appeared to be ''totally feasible'' for incorporating a computerized information system into the client's organization, the detailed design work on each system proposal could then be performed. The results of the design work (which are reflected in the ''systems specifications report'') will be provided to computer suppliers so that they will know the specific requirements of the organization's system. This detailed information will enable the computer suppliers to recommend specific hardware and software packages.

Among the information contained in a systems specifications report is:

1. Historical background information about the company's operating activities. Included here would be facts about the types of products manufactured and sold by the company, the financial conditions within the company, the type of building structure occupied by the company, the company's current data-processing methods, the peak volume of data-processing activities, and the types of equipment currently being used in the company's data-processing system. The above information familiarizes the computer hardware and software suppliers with the company's operational environment so that they can make computer systems recommendations.

2. Detailed information about the problem (or problems) in the company's current data-processing system. By understanding the present systems problem, the hardware and software suppliers should have a better idea of what type of specific computer application will eliminate the company's system weaknesses. The consultants may also include information here about how soon they would like to receive the suppliers' recommendations (e.g., two months from the date their report is provided to the computer suppliers), and the approximate date that the final decision will be made by their client regarding which supplier's hardware and software system will be purchased (or leased).

3. Detailed descriptions of the consultants' systems design proposals. As a result of the feasibility evaluations on two or more different types of computer systems (e.g., a batch system, an online, real-time system, and a combination system having some data-processing functions under batch processing and others under online, real-time processing) being quite similar, information about each of these potential systems should be provided to the hardware and software suppliers. For every design proposal, information should be included about such things as the input and the output of specific computer runs (this can best be illustrated by preparing systems

flowcharts for each run), the types of master files needed and the approximate volume of each file, the frequency of updating each master file, the format of each output report, the approximate length of each output report, the types of information included in each report and how often the various reports will be prepared, the organizational managers to whom every report will be distributed, and the company's available space for locating the computer center. This detailed information about each of the consultants' systems proposals should provide the hardware and software suppliers adequate data for making suggestions concerning specific computer systems to handle the company's data processing requirements.

4. An indication of what the consultants expect the hardware and software suppliers to include in their proposals to the company. This section of the systems specifications report, in effect, tells the computer suppliers how detailed they should make these proposals. The company's consultants might request information regarding the following: the speed and size of the central processing unit needed, the type and quantity of input and output hardware units as well as the speed capabilities of these devices, the specific programming language that would be best for the company's system, the availability of compiler programs, the availability of prewritten canned programs that could be used for specific processing activities, the training sessions offered by the suppliers to teach the company's employees the operating details of the new system, the help provided by the suppliers in implementing and testing the new system, the maintenance services available from the suppliers should the hardware have mechanical failures, and the suppliers' provisions for backup data-processing facilities while the hardware is being repaired. The consultants would possibly want the hardware and software suppliers to indicate the costs of their computer system recommendations under both purchase and lease arrangements.

5. Time schedule for implementing the new system. This final section of the report will request the hardware and software suppliers to estimate the number of weeks, months, or years that will be necessary to implement their recommended computer systems into the company.

To demonstrate the types of information contained in a systems specifications report, Figure 12-2 illustrates a systems flowchart reflecting the design of a company's new computerized system for processing fixed asset acquisitions (other than *land*, which is not subject to depreciation) and for recognizing depreciation on these fixed assets. (Explanations will follow.)

The "Accounts Payable Detail File" (created from another computer run) contains information about all credit purchases during the period such as inventory, office supplies, and fixed assets. By using the "Fixed Assets Extraction" program, those credit purchases of fixed assets during the period are reflected on a *fixed assets new purchases on credit report*. Both the "Fixed Assets Extraction" program (which extracts those credit purchases of fixed assets from the accounts payable detail file) and the "Add Cash Purchases" program (which processes the few, if any, fixed assets purchased for cash) are used to create the "New Property File." This file contains information describing all new acquisitions of fixed assets. By then using the "New Property" program with the data from the new property file, a *new property report* and *equipment identification labels* are prepared. A separate identification label is prepared by the computer for each piece of new equipment. For every new item of equipment, its identification label can be attached to the equipment to enable specific identification and control of the fixed asset resource.

The "Property Depreciation" program and the data from the "New Property File" and the "Property Master File" (which contains all fixed asset records other than *land*) are then used to prepare the "Updated Property Master File," the *property book value report* (reflecting the cost *minus* accumulated depreciation on each fixed asset), and the *tax depreciation report*. Because a company may have different depreciation amounts for tax purposes compared with book purposes, the data included in this tax de-

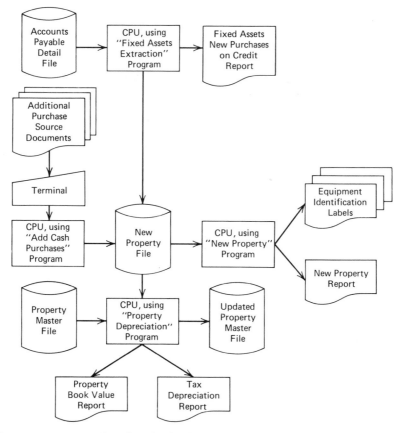

Figure 12-2. Systems flowchart for fixed asset acquisitions and depreciation on fixed assets.

preciation report will be used as input when the company prepares its tax returns for the government.

In addition to the systems flowchart shown in Figure 12-2 being prepared for the systems specifications report, a detailed description of the various files and their contents would also be provided in the specifications report. To illustrate, Figure 12-3 lists some common data that would likely be included for each fixed asset resource within a company's "Property Master File."

Items 1–3 in Figure 12-3 would be obtained from the "Accounts Payable Detail File." The data indicated in items 4–6 are required in order to compute each fixed asset's periodic depreciation. Upon determining a fixed asset's deprecia-

1. Purchase cost of fixed asset.
2. Purchase date of fixed asset.
3. Vendor data (name, address, etc.).
4. Depreciation method selected.
5. Estimated salvage value of fixed asset.
6. Estimated useful life of fixed asset.
7. Insurable value of fixed asset.
8. Book value of fixed asset.
9. Identification number of fixed asset.
10. Description of fixed asset.
11. Classification of fixed asset (for example, factory equipment, office furniture, etc.).
12. Organizational location of fixed asset.
13. Maintenance schedule for fixed asset.

Figure 12-3. Illustration of common data included within property master file.

tion, the asset's *book value* can then be updated (item number 8). Items 9–13 are largely for control purposes. For example, data regarding the maintenance schedule on production equipment (item number 13) are important to ensure that the equipment is properly cared for and thereby operates efficiently whenever it is used by company employees. Without regular maintenance, the equipment's useful life of service would likely be decreased.

Submitting specifications report to computer vendors. Upon finalizing the systems specifications report, the consultants must then decide which of the many hardware and software suppliers should be sent a copy of this report so that they can submit proposals for computer services. The major computer vendors include IBM, Honeywell, Burroughs, Digital Equipment Corporation, Control Data Corporation, and UNIVAC.

The systems specifications report will normally be sent to three or four computer vendors. During the intervening period from the time the report is submitted to the computer vendors until they have their specific proposals completed (which may take as long as three months), the consultants should be available to answer any of the vendors' questions regarding specific aspects of the specifications report. For example, one of the vendors may be confused about the maximum volume of data-processing activities expected in the company. This question must be answered immediately by the consultants (or their client's management) in order to enable the vendor to continue designing the optimal size computer system to meet the company's data-processing requirements.

Selecting a specific computer system. Upon receipt of the hardware and software suppliers' proposals, the difficult task begins of selecting that vendor's proposal (if any) which best meets the client company's data-processing needs. This decision-making activity normally will be performed by both the consultants and their client's top management personnel (as well as budget committee representatives). Each computer ven-

dor submitting a proposal will likely send a representative to the company to discuss its proposed computer system with the consultants and the top management executives. The consultants should act as advisors to management when evaluating the individual proposals because the company's top management has final responsibility for the decision regarding which hardware and software supplier's computer system will be acquired. After evaluating all the proposals, management may possibly decide to acquire its computer system from more than one of the vendors. For instance, the decision may be made to lease the central processing unit as well as the peripheral input-output equipment from Burroughs, and to lease the software from IBM.

The computer specialists on the management consulting team will have the major responsibility for advising the client company about the pros and cons of each supplier's systems proposal. Often, the final decision on which vendor's system to choose is quite difficult because the differences among the proposals may be minimal. Some of the key factors that should be considered when comparing each hardware and software supplier's proposal are:

1. The *performance* capability of each proposed system in relation to the system's cost. It is imperative that a vendor's hardware and software system is capable of processing the company's data within the time schedules desired by the user company's management. Otherwise, delays in providing management with needed output reports will occur once the computer system is operational. The hardware and software operating efficiency of the various proposals may be compared by using what is called the *benchmark problem*. Under this approach, a data-processing task that the company's computer system will eventually have to perform is selected (e.g., weekly batch processing of inventory transactions). Then, with the approval of each computer vendor, some actual transactions which are representative of the data processing task (e.g., purchase transactions that increase the inventory balance and sales transactions that decrease the inventory balance) are processed by each supplier's proposed hardware and software

system. This processing can be performed at the various suppliers' own premises or even on other companies' computers (assuming their systems are identical with the ones being proposed). After this data-processing task is performed on the suppliers' proposed hardware and software systems, comparisons can then be made of each system's operating performance efficiency. The accountants on the consulting team will be concerned principally with analyzing the costs of each vendor's proposed system in relation to the system's performance efficiency. Concerning the cost factors, the accountants should analyze the monetary differences between purchasing and leasing each vendor's hardware and software system. If the company's top management elects to purchase its computer system, the accountants should then advise management on a realistic depreciation program for its newly acquired system.

2. The *modularity* of each proposed system. This refers to the ease with which a proposed computer system can be altered at a later date. For example, the company may initially choose a less expensive, slower central processing unit. Good modularity would enable the company to easily add components to its CPU at some future time in order that changing data-processing requirements can be handled. The company might subsequently want to increase the CPU's size by adding more primary storage or to increase the input-output peripheral equipment. Also, good modularity would enable the company to substitute a disk unit for a tape unit with minimum computer programming changes.

3. The *compatibility* of each proposed system to the company's current data-processing system. This is especially important if the company already has an automated data-processing system and wants to "upgrade" its system; for example, if the Alan Company decides to add an additional CPU to its present computer system. If both the old CPU and the newly acquired CPU can function together effectively and thereby handle the same input data without major program rewrites, good compatibility exists between these two central processing units. As can be seen, compatibility is closely related to modularity (discussed in point 2 above).

4. The *reputation* of the computer vendor as well as the vendor's *support* in implementation and subsequent operation of the system. Obviously, the hardware and software supplier whose system is chosen should have a good reputation in the business community. (It's like buying an unknown brand television set; the initial cost may be smaller than for a familiar brand model, but the later headaches and expenses may be greater when breakdowns occur!) The vendor's support includes such things as training programs to familiarize the company's employees with the unique operating characteristics of the new system, help in implementing and testing the new system, contracts for maintenance on the new system, and providing of backup systems for temporarily processing the company's data if the new system fails to operate. Some computer vendors will provide the above support free of charge, whereas others will bill the company for these services. In computer terminology, the word *bundling* refers to the degree of software support provided to companies by computer vendors without charging additional fees. For example, a computer vendor who provides all software support services to a company free of charge is considered to be *completely bundled*. On the other hand, if the vendor charges the company a fee for each software service it provides, then the hardware and software supplier is *totally unbundled*. Finally, if some vendor software support services are provided without charge and other software support services are provided at a charge, the hardware and software supplier is considered to be *semibundled*.

After each hardware and software supplier has presented its systems proposal to the consultants and their client's management, the specific proposal that best meets the company's data-processing needs should then be selected. As mentioned previously, this decision is the responsibility of the company's top management personnel (with possible advice from budget committee members). It is quite likely, however, that the consultants' recommendation will be given considerable weight in top management's decision-making process.

Once a decision is reached regarding a specific computer system, the next major phase of a systems study begins. This phase encompasses those activities required to implement the new system so that it can take over the day-to-day data-processing functions of the company. We will assume here that the company's top management has selected a complete batch-processing computerized system which will be leased from the computer vendor.

We should mention at this point that because a company acquiring its first computerized data-processing system normally will not have trained computer personnel, the company may decide to negotiate with an independent organization (called a *facilities-management services organization*) to manage its data-processing facilities on a contract basis. The company will typically own or lease its computer hardware and will pay a monthly fee to the facilities-management services organization for providing trained computer personnel to handle its data-processing activities. Banks and insurance companies, for example, are common users of facilities-management services.

By contracting with a facilities-management services organization for data-processing management, a company is thereby freed from the daily operation of its computer center. For the novice company with little or no knowledge of the technical aspects of computers, facilities-management services organizations can also provide assistance in acquiring computer hardware and software, modernizing computer installations, and determining efficient operating policies and procedures. A user of facilities-management services is relieved of such personnel activities as recruiting and training new employees needed for its computer center. Perhaps the greatest disadvantage of using facilities-management services organizations is that control of valuable information is turned over to *outsiders* (i.e., employees of the facilities-management services organization). These outsiders may not be sensitive to the importance of accuracy and security in the daily data-processing tasks assigned to them.

Before beginning the Chapter 13 discussion of the implementation steps for the new batch-processing system, let's assume for a moment that none of the hardware and software suppliers' proposals were satisfactory to the company's top management. The principal reason for management's negative reactions to each supplier's proposal was the *cost* factor. When the consultants performed their economic feasibility evaluation of anticipated cash benefits and anticipated cash costs of various computer design proposals (see the cost/benefit analysis example in Figure 12-1), the excess present value indexes were favorable for several possible computer configurations. Therefore, the hardware and software supplier evaluation stage of the consultants' systems design work began. When each computer vendor's detailed systems proposal was eventually presented to the company's management, however, the specific costs of the individual proposals were considerably higher than the consultants anticipated. At this point, it is possible for the company's top management to do one of three things: (1) request additional systems proposals from other hardware and software suppliers, (2) abandon the idea of converting to a computerized data-processing system, or (3) investigate the acquisition of computerized data-processing services from an outside organization.

Alternative 3 permits the company to obtain computerized processing of its operating data without having to purchase or lease a hardware and software system. The two major types of organizations that provide computerized data-processing services to other companies (called *user* companies) are *service bureaus* and *time-sharing organizations*. Both are discussed briefly below. (Service bureaus and time-sharing organizations will be analyzed further in Chapter 14.)

Service bureaus and time-sharing organizations. It is common for small companies that do not have the volume of transactions to justify acquiring their own computer systems, but yet desire the benefits from computerized data processing, to utilize either a service bureau or time-sharing organization to process their financial data. However, even medium-sized and large companies often find it advantageous to use the services offered by these data-processing organizations. A user company's data-processing costs can be significantly reduced by sharing the computer facilities of service bureau and time-sharing organizations with other users, rather than leasing or purchasing its own computer system.

A service bureau provides users primarily with batch processing of their financial data. The bureau's fee normally is based upon the *time* required to process a company's batch of data. A user company must physically transport its source document input data to the service bureau and subsequently pick up the processed output data. For example, an organization may hire a service bureau to process its semimonthly payroll. Prior to the actual payday (perhaps one or two days), the organization will send its payroll information (employee timecards, any hourly wage rate changes, etc.) to the service bureau. The service bureau will have previously prepared a master file (such as a magnetic tape file) containing relevant payroll information about the organization's employees. The output from the payroll processing run will be a payroll register and the paychecks.

As the above example demonstrates, the organization obtains the benefits from computerized processing of its accounting data without incurring the major costs of purchasing or leasing its own computer system. Other types of financial data (e.g., processing the credit customers' monthly statements) that the organization wishes to have computer processed would also be sent in batches to the service bureau. There are, however, certain disadvantages in the use of a service bureau as opposed to the use of one's own computer system. The principal disadvantage is the data-security problem. The user company must send its important source documents to the outside service bureau organization and there is always the risk that some of these source documents may get lost in transit, be misplaced by the service bureau's employees (e.g., the source

documents may be accidentally processed with another user company's financial transactions), or be fraudulently manipulated. Consequently, before hiring a service bureau to handle its data-processing functions, the user company should inquire about the security features at the service bureau. The user can also establish some of its own controls to detect any loss of source documents either in transit or on the service bureau's premises. An effective user company preventive control would be a hash total control (illustrated in Chapter 7—see Figure 7-1) for its source documents sent to the service bureau. Another disadvantage of having a service bureau process a company's financial data is possible delays in receiving the output information. Due to the backlog of work required on other users' financial data, the service bureau may be unable to process a company's financial transactions in as short a time interval as the company desires.

Whereas a service bureau offers batch processing of financial data, time-sharing organizations provide user companies with online capabilities. Thus, each user company has an online input device (such as a remote keyboard terminal) within its own offices which is directly connected to the time-sharing organization's central processing unit. This online capability permits real-time processing of a company's financial transactions. Rather than physically transporting its source documents to the service bureau for processing, the user company inputs data directly from its own terminal to the time-sharing organization's CPU. In many accounting applications which are processed through a time-sharing organization, the user also requests immediate output reports (e.g., an immediate output report on updated inventory balances). The online, real-time data processing capability offered by time-sharing organizations tends to be more costly than the batch processing methods of service bureaus. If a company desires fast feedback report information for management decision making, however, a time-sharing data-processing organization is likely to be favored over a service bureau data-processing organization. The monthly cost of a time-sharing organization's services includes a fixed cost for the terminal equipment facilities and a variable cost for the communication time (in processing data) between the terminal and the central processing unit. An additional variable cost is for the quantity of file storage used.

Some time-sharing organizations offer their users access to a centralized data base of financial information. For example, a retail store that allows customers to use store credit cards for purchasing merchandise can obtain immediate credit rating facts about individual customers from a time-sharing organization's data base file of credit reference information. This feedback information concerning a specific customer's credit rating will enable the store to evaluate the advisability of granting him or her a credit card.

From a security point of view, a company utilizing a time-sharing organization's services should establish controls that prevent unauthorized employees from entering transactions (which could be fictitious transactions to commit a fraudulent act) on its data terminal. Chapter 8 emphasized that secret password codes can be utilized in an online, real-time system. The code numbers should be known only to the specific organizational employees who are responsible for the input of data on the terminal. As a further means of preventing unauthorized employees from learning the code numbers, many companies change their codes periodically (e.g., weekly or monthly).

Having completed this brief discussion of service bureaus and time-sharing data-processing organizations (which possibly should be considered for the consultants' client company in those situations when the company decides against acquiring its own computer system), we are now ready to examine the remaining two systems study phases—the implementation and initial operation phase, and the follow-up phase. These two phases of a systems study will be discussed in the next chapter.

SUMMARY

This chapter has continued the discussion of the systems study area (which started in Chapter 11) by analyzing the *design* phase of systems study work. At the beginning of this chapter we assumed that a company's top management personnel were in favor of converting their present data-processing system from a manual to a computerized system. Therefore, the consultants began the phase of their systems study called *design*.

The first major activity in systems design is the feasibility evaluation concerning the acquisition of a computerized data-processing system. Four types of feasibility are investigated by the consultants: (1) technical feasibility, (2) operational feasibility, (3) schedule feasibility, and (4) economic feasibility. The accountants on the management consulting team are involved principally in the economic feasibility evaluation. Here, a cost/benefit analysis is performed on each preliminary design proposal for computerizing the company's manual system. A proposed computer system will be worthy of further consideration only if the findings from all four feasibility evaluations are positive.

The second major activity in systems design is to prepare a systems specifications report for hardware and software supplier evaluation. This report contains detailed information about each design proposal that satisfies the feasibility requirements. The specifications report is sent to various computer suppliers to use as the basis for their submission of specific hardware and software proposals to the company. When computer system proposals are received from each hardware and software supplier, the consultants will advise their client's management as to which proposal, if any, should be accepted. Upon accepting a specific hardware and software supplier's proposal, the *implementation* and *initial operation* systems study phase commences. (This phase will be examined in Chapter 13.) On the other hand, if none of the computer vendors' proposals are acceptable to management, one possible alternative is for the company to acquire computerized data-processing services from an outside organization. The two major types of organizations that perform computerized data-processing work for other companies are service bureaus (which offer principally batch-processing services) and time-sharing organizations (which offer online data-processing services). By utilizing either a service bureau or time-sharing organization, a company is able to obtain computerized processing of its financial data without having to incur the major costs associated with purchasing or leasing its own hardware and software system.

DISCUSSION QUESTIONS

12-1. One of the benefits that normally results from computerizing a company's previous manual data-processing system is a reduction in the company's average annual accounts receivable balance. How is this average annual accounts receivable balance reduction usually accomplished, and why is the receivable reduction considered beneficial to a company?

12-2. As discussed in the chapter, simulation techniques can be used to test a company's computer programs before the programs are implemented into the company's system. A simulation technique for testing the mathematical logic of a company's accounts-receivable processing program was illustrated in this chapter. Try to think of several additional simulation techniques that might be employed to test a company's computer programs for processing other types of accounting transactions.

12-3. Why does the design phase of a systems study follow the analysis phase?

12-4. What is the purpose of the feasibility evaluation activity of systems design work? Should the feasibility evaluation activity precede or follow the preparation of a systems specifications report for hardware and software supplier evaluation? Explain.

12-5. As part of their systems design work, management consultants should examine four feasibility areas. Discuss the reason (or reasons) for evaluating each of these feasibility areas.

12-6. Discuss some of the annual cash benefits and annual cash costs that a company would normally have from converting its manual data-processing system to a computerized batch-processing system.

12-7. "In order for the consultants to begin the work of preparing a systems specifications report for hardware and software supplier evaluation, their design proposal must be totally feasible." Discuss the meaning of this statement.

12-8. Howard Berry, management consultant for the International Consulting Organization, has just completed a feasibility evaluation regarding the conversion of his client company's batch-processing computerized system to an online, real-time system. The results from his technical, operational, and schedule feasibility evaluations were all positive. However, the economic feasibility evaluation outcome was quite negative. In your opinion, what course of action should now be taken by Howard Berry?

12-9. What is the purpose of a "systems specifications report"? In what ways, if any, does the data included in this report differ from the data accumulated by the consultants during their feasibility evaluation work?

12-10. Henry Heron is the owner of a minor league baseball team. His team has completed 60 games of its 140-game schedule. Henry is currently worried about two major problems: (1) the low attendance at home games, and (2) the strong possibility that many of his cashiers working at the ticket windows are pocketing portions of each game's cash receipts. To help solve these problems, Henry has hired an outside consultant, Ozzie Seaver. Regarding the low attendance problem, Ozzie is told by the baseball team's traveling secretary that many promotional activities have been tried in an effort to draw fans to the home games. Most of these promotions, however, turned out to be financial disasters. For example, at one of last week's games, every paying customer was given a baseball autographed by the team. Even though a large crowd came to the ball park for this promotional event, the cost per baseball (approximately $2.50) exceeded the average ticket price paid by each customer (approximately $2.25) attending that night's game. Regarding the problem with the cashiers, the only suggestion that has been made by the baseball team's management is to fire all the present cashiers and hire a completely new crew.

Assuming that you are Ozzie Seaver, what are some possible suggestions that you could offer to solve the baseball team's two systems problems?

12-11. In each of the following hypothetical cases, indicate a method of data processing that you would recommend, and the reasons why. State both the advantages and shortcomings of your recommended methods.*

Case 1: A small supply company which handles 300 different inventory items, and processes most orders by mail. On the average 30 orders are processed daily. This company has 40 employees.

Case 2: A medium-sized medical clinic which has on its staff 25 physicians, 15 technicians, 46 nurses, and 30 administrative and clerical personnel. On the average, the clinic handles 450 patients per day who either pay for their treatment through an insurance program (government or private) or have a charge account. That is, few patients pay cash.

Case 3: A large, nationwide supply company which has in its warehouses from 20,000 to 30,000 different inventory items. Ninety percent of its orders are placed by telephone where most of the customers wish to know if the items requested are on hand for immediate delivery. Most customers will not accept backorders. The company employs 4000 people.

Case 4: A large motel organization has 300 motels scattered across the nation.

Case 5: A large manufacturing company has 16 plants and 175 warehouses throughout the country. In addition to general administrative data-processing requirements (the company employs 26,000 people and has 40,000 customers), the company implements many management science techniques such as PERT, linear programming, forecasting, inventory control, and so forth.

*Used with the permission of John G. Burch, Jr. and Felix R. Strater, Jr., *Information Systems: Theory and Practice*, John Wiley & Sons, Inc., © 1979.

12-12. The data contained within a systems specifications report includes "detailed information about the problem (or problems) in a company's current data-processing system." Why is it necessary to include the above type of information in the systems specifications report that a consultant prepares for his or her client company?

12-13. Distinguish between a service bureau and a time-sharing organization. Under what circumstances might a specific company elect to utilize the facilities offered by a service bureau or a time-sharing organization.

12-14. Discuss some of the relevant factors that should be considered by a company's consultants and top management personnel when they are comparing proposals from various hardware and software suppliers for converting the company's manual data-processing system to a batch-processing computerized system. (*Note:* For each named factor, make sure to indicate why it is important to the decision-making process of selecting a specific hardware and software supplier's computer system.)

12-15. The following terms were analyzed in this chapter: the benchmark problem, the modularity capability, and the compatibility of a system. Discuss the importance of each when a company is trying to decide which hardware and software vendor's computer system to acquire.

12-16. A company can either purchase or lease its hardware and software system from a computer vendor. If you were a management consultant for an organization that was acquiring its first computerized system, what are some of the important factors that you should consider when recommending to the company's management either the purchasing or the leasing of the automated system?

12-17. Ed Meld, employed by the AAZ Consulting Firm, was asked by his friend Burt Bones (who is the general manager and majority stockholder of the Pacific Worldwinds, a professional football team) to design an online, real-time computer system for "the more efficient operation of the football franchise."

Ed was quite confused because he could not think of any possible uses for an online, real-time system within the operational activities of a football team (or any other type of athletic team). Assume that you are also employed at the AAZ Consulting Firm. Provide several suggestions to Ed concerning specific areas of athletic teams' (football teams, baseball teams, etc.) information systems where an online, real-time computer configuration might be beneficial to managerial decision making.

12-18. Sandown Power and Light Company (SP&L Co.) is an electric utility in the southwest United States. The demand for electricity is quite seasonal in the area served by SP&L Co. due to the heavy use of air conditioning during the summer months. Currently, customers are billed monthly for the amount of electricity consumed during the previous month. The rates charged by SP&L Co. for the consumption of electricity are the same for all volume levels.

SP&L Co.'s assistant to the financial vice president has suggested that the company adopt an equal monthly billing system. Under this plan, a customer's total annual electrical needs would be estimated for the coming year from past experience; the customer would be billed on the first of each month for one-twelfth of the estimated annual amount. At the end of the billing year the customer would be billed for the amount of electricity consumed in excess of the annual estimate or receive reimbursement for the under-usage. Consequently, the customer would receive a bill for the same amount each month and then either an additional bill or reimbursement, depending upon his usage of electricity, at the end of the twelfth month. SP&L Co.'s rate structure for electricity consumption will not change with the new billing system.

The billing cycle would begin in November and end with October. The annual "settlement" would occur at the end of October.

Required

A. Discuss the advantages and disadvantages

of an equal monthly billing system for Sandown Power and Light Company, including in your discussion the effect(s) on SP&L's cash flow, accounts receivable balances, and profitability.

B. If you were a residential customer of SP&L Co. and had been offered a choice between the new equal monthly billing system and the current billing system, what would be the important factors that you would consider before reaching a decision as to which billing system to select?

(CMA Adapted)

12-19. Rockland Company is a large printing firm with about 500 outstanding customer accounts at any one time.

The Credit and Collections Department of the Sales Division is responsible for granting credit, which includes evaluating the credit worthiness of new customers and reviewing the credit status of current customers. This department is also responsible for any follow-up calls to customers who may be slow or delinquent in paying their accounts. The recording of sales and subsequent payments on account and maintenance of subsidiary account records are among the responsibilities of the company's accounting department.

Periodically, the amount of the allowance account to be deducted from the "Accounts Receivable" on the balance sheet should be reviewed to be sure that it does reflect a reasonable estimate of the amount of the uncollectible accounts included in the accounts receivable balance. A careful and comprehensive review of this allowance account would seem to require input from both the credit and collections and accounting departments.

The balance of the "Allowance for Uncollectible Accounts Receivable" account appearing in Rockland Co.'s financial statements is the result of

1. the current year provision for uncollectible accounts, calculated by applying a percentage to the amount of credit sales,
2. the actual customer accounts determined to be uncollectible and written off, and

3. the allowance account balance at the beginning of the year.

Required

Present the program you would recommend to review the adequacy of the "Allowance for Uncollectible Accounts Receivable" account. In your recommended program identify the information and analyses which could best be provided by:

1. the accounting department
2. the credit and collections department

(CMA Adapted)

PROBLEMS

12-20. Bonn Company recently reorganized its computer and data-processing activities. The small installations located within the accounting departments at its plants and subsidiaries have been replaced with a single data-processing department at corporate headquarters responsible for the operations of a newly acquired large-scale computer system. The new department has been in operation for two years and has been regularly producing reliable and timely data for the past twelve months.

Because the department has focused its activities on converting applications to the new system and producing reports for the plant and subsidiary managements, little attention has been devoted to the costs of the department. Now that the department's activities are operating relatively smoothly, company management has requested that the departmental manager recommend a cost accumulation system to facilitate cost control and the development of suitable rates to charge users for service.

For the past two years, the departmental costs have been recorded in one account. The costs have then been allocated to user departments on the basis of computer time used. The following schedule reports the costs and charging rate for 1984.

Data Processing Department
Costs for the Year Ended December 31, 1984

(1) Salaries and benefits	$ 622,600
(2) Supplies	40,000
(3) Equipment maintenance contracts	15,000
(4) Insurance	25,000
(5) Heat and air-conditioning	36,000
(6) Electricity	50,000
(7) Equipment and furniture depreciation	285,400
(8) Building improvements depreciation	10,000
(9) Building occupancy and security	39,300
(10) Corporate administrative charges	52,700
Total costs	$1,176,000

Computer hours for user processing*	2,750
Hourly rate ($1,176,000 ÷ 2,750) $	428

*Use of available computer hours

Testing and debugging programs	250
Set-up of jobs	500
Processing jobs	2,750
Down-time for maintenance	750
Idle time	742
	4,992

The department manager recommends that the department costs be accumulated by five activity centers within the department: Systems Analysis, Programming, Data Preparation, Computer Operations (processing), and Administration. He then suggests that the costs of the Administration activity should be allocated to the other four activity centers before a separate rate for charging users is developed for each of the first four activities.

The manager made the following observations regarding the charges to the several subsidiary accounts within the department after reviewing the details of the accounts:

1. Salaries and benefits—records the salary and benefit costs of all employees in the department.
2. Supplies—records punched card costs, paper costs for printers, and a small amount for miscellaneous other costs.

3. Equipment maintenance contracts—records charges for maintenance contracts; all equipment is covered by maintenance contracts.

4. Insurance—records cost of insurance covering the equipment and the furniture.

5. Heat and air-conditioning—records a charge from the corporate heating and air-conditioning department estimated to be the incremental costs to meet the special needs of the computer department.

6. Electricity—records the charge for electricity based upon a separate meter within the department.

7. Equipment and furniture depreciation—records the depreciation charges for all owned equipment and furniture within the department.

8. Building improvements depreciation—records the depreciation charges for the building changes required to provide proper environmental control and electrical service for the computer equipment.

9. Building occupancy and security—records the computer department's share of the depreciation, maintenance, heat, and security costs of the building; these costs are allocated to the department on the basis of square feet occupied.

10. Corporate administrative charges—records the computer department's share of the corporate administrative costs. They are allocated to the department on the basis of number of employees in the department.

Required

A. For each of the ten cost items, state whether or not it should be distributed to the five activity centers, and for each cost item which should be distributed, recommend the basis upon which it should be distributed. Justify your conclusion in each case.

B. Assume that the costs of the Computer Operations (processing) activity will be charged to the user departments on the basis of computer hours. Using the analysis of computer utilization shown as a footnote to the department cost schedule presented in the problem, determine the total number of hours that should be employed to determine the charging rate for Computer Operations (processing). Justify your answer.

(CMA Adapted)

12-21. The Wing Commander of a tactical fighter wing has requested the implementation of a formal information system to assist him in evaluating the quality of aircrew members. Although there are many factors related to determining an individual's quality level, it has been recommended that one source of objective data is from the testing process administered by the Standardization/Evaluation Section in the fighter wing. Each flightcrew member is tested periodically either by an instrument check or by a tactical/proficiency check to detect violations of standardized operating procedures or errors in judgment. The result of a test is either pass or fail and discrepancies such as single engine landing, dangerous pass, incorrect holding pattern, and so forth, are noted where applicable. A general feeling exists in the Standardization/Evaluation Section that if these reports were prepared and distributed in a timely fashion, the Wing Commander could take swift corrective action to prevent a hazardous practice or critical weakness from occurring. Further analysis indicates that such a report can be prepared daily, five days a week throughout the year, at a cost of $14.10 per report. This time period for reporting is judged acceptable by the Standardization/Evaluation Section.

While there are many benefits anticipated from implementing such a system in terms of preventing the loss of aircrew member lives and the loss of aircraft property, as well as increasing the effectiveness of the fighter wing, the Wing Commander has requested that all new information systems be initially justified on pure economic grounds before other considerations are evaluated. As the management consultant assigned to this project, you have decided to take the approach that the proposed system will help reduce the rate of major accidents from 2% to 1.5% (as similar systems have done elsewhere, to economically justify their implementation). From your investigation, you have gathered the following statistics concerning major accidents:

Cost of Major Accident

Certain Costs:	
Aircraft	$1,600,000
Accident investigation	6,000
Property damage (impact point)	2,000
Total	$1,608,000

Possible Costs (both crewmembers are lost)	
Invested training in crewmembers	
2 @ $25,000	$ 50,000
Survivors benefits and mortuary costs	
2 @ $50,000	100,000
Total	$150,000

Probability of crew loss is .25

Required

Can the proposed system be economically justified using this approach? Explain. Identify other economic factors not considered in this problem.*

CASE ANALYSES

12-22. *Control By Knight*

John Knight founded the Newworld Company over thirty years ago. Although he has relied heavily upon advice from other members of management, he has made all of the important decisions for the company. Newworld has been successful, experiencing steady growth in its early years and very rapid growth in recent years. During this period of rapid growth Knight has experienced difficulty in keeping up with the many decisions that needed to be made. He feels that he is losing "control" of the company's progress.

Regular discussions regarding his concern have been held with George Armet, the company executive vice-president. As a result of these discussions, Armet has studied possible alternative organizational structures to the present highly centralized functional organization.

*Used with the permission of John G. Burch, Jr. and Felix R. Strater, Jr., *Information Systems: Theory and Practice*, John Wiley & Sons, Inc., © 1979.

In a carefully prepared proposal, Armet recommends that the company reorganize according to its two product lines because the technology and marketing methods are quite different. The plastic products require different manufacturing skills and equipment from the brass products. The change could be easily accomplished because the products are manufactured in different plants. The marketing effort is also segregated along product lines within the sales function. The number of executive positions would not change, although the duties of the positions would change. There would no longer be the need for a vice-president for manufacturing or a vice-president for sales. Those positions would be replaced with a vice-president for each of the two product lines. Armet acknowledges that there may be personnel problems at the top management level because the current vice-presidents may not be competent to manage within the new structure.

The proposal also contained the recommendations that some of the decision-making power, long held by John Knight, be transferred to the new vice-presidents. Armet argued that this would be good for the company. The new vice-presidents would be more aware of the problems and solution alternatives of their respective product lines because they are closer to the operations. Fewer decisions will be required of each man than now are required of John Knight; this would reduce the time between problem recognition and implementation of the solution. Armet further argued that distributing the decision-making power would improve the creativity and spirit of company management.

Knight is intrigued by the proposal and the prospect that it would make the company more manageable. However, the proposal did not spell out clearly which decisions should be transferred and which should remain with the president. He requested Armet to prepare a supplemental memorandum specifying the decisions to be delegated to the vice-presidents.

The memorandum presented the recommended decision areas, explaining in each case how the new vice-presidents would be closer to the situation and thereby be able to make prompt, sound decisions. The following list summarizes Armet's recommendations:

1. Sales
   a. Price policy
   b. Promotional strategy
   c. Credit policy
2. Operations
   a. Manufacturing procedures
   b. Labor negotiations
3. Development of existing product lines
4. Capital investment decision—up to amounts not exceeding the division "depreciation flow" plus 25 percent of its "after-tax income" (excluding ventures into new fields).

The corporate management would be responsible for overall corporate development. Also, they would allocate the remaining available cash flow for dividends, for investment projects above the limits prescribed, and for investments into new ventures.

Questions

A. Does the company have the characteristics needed for decentralized profit centers? Briefly explain your answer.

B. Mr. Knight believes that the proposal, as presented, will not work. In his judgment the corporate level management will be unable to control effectively the destiny of the firm because the proposal grants too much investment freedom to the new divisions. Do you agree with Mr. Knight that effective control over the future of the firm cannot be maintained at corporate level if the capital rationing is shared in the manner specified in the proposal? Support your answer with appropriate discussion including a recommended alternative procedure if you agree with Mr. Knight.

(CMA Adapted)

12-23. *Polynesian Textile Company*

Background

The Polynesian Textile Company, located in Hawaii, first started business in 1954. Initially, the company was primarily a family operation. However, during the 1950s and 1960s, business had been good, and the company expanded rapidly. The firm finally incorporated in 1970.

Although the Polynesian Textile Company had grown in size, the products and services it provides in 1984 are basically the same as those offered in 1954. The Polynesian Textile Company manufactures Hawaiian fabrics in its three production plants. The fabric is sold to various local outlets; e.g., ready-to-wear "muu-muu" and "aloha shirt" manufacturers, and retail department stores.

Organizational Structure

There are two major functional divisions in the organization. They are the production and marketing/sales departments. The production and marketing/sales functions are supported by several administrative departments: accounting, research and development, legal staff, and public relations. The organization chart is depicted in Figure 12-4.

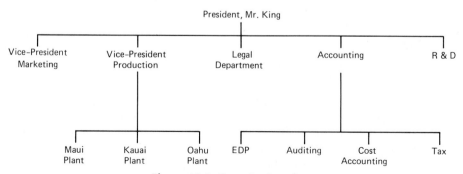

Figure 12-4. Organization chart.

Computer Acquisition

Upon the advice of the firm's controller, Mr. Bob Shade, Polynesian Textile acquired and implemented a computer system in 1968. Bob Shade convinced the president, Mr. King, that a computer could facilitate the processing of routine and clerical activities. Because the computer was to be used primarily in accounting/financial applications, the controller was given primary jurisdiction over the operation of the computerized system.

Mr. King was pleased with Bob Shade's work with the computer system. Ever since the computer's installation, Polynesian Textile has experienced a reduction in its operating costs.

Even though most of the company's data-processing activities are handled by the computer, the computer center still is not operating at full capacity. At the present time, the computer time is allocated as follows:

1.	Accounting applications	65%
2.	Research and development	7%
3.	Production	5%
4.	Marketing	6%
5.	Idle time	17%

Bob Shade, as well as Mr. King, is anxious to increase the utilization of the computer to full capacity. Both men have noticed recently that the cost savings generated by the computer center are slowing down. They believe that by decreasing the amount of idle computer time, the company can increase its rate of return from the computer investment. Therefore, Shade and King are looking for computer applications that would facilitate efficient and effective operations within the entire organization.

Increasing Nonfinancial Applications

Mr. King recently attended a conference on computer applications for business organizations. At this conference, nonfinancial applications of the computer were discussed. Excited about the conference discussions, Mr. King wants to decrease the idle capacity time of his company's computer system by utilizing the computer for nonfinancial applications.

Mr. King discussed some of the ideas presented at the conference with Bob Shade. The following week the memorandum below was sent to all King's managers.

TO: All Managerial Employees
FROM: Mr. King, President
RE: Utilization of Computer Facilities

Did you realize that our computer facilities and computer staff can help you with planning and controlling your divisional operations? Computer applications in nonfinancial areas are feasible and can be profitable for the whole organization.

If you have an operational area which could be facilitated by the computer, please do not hesitate to talk to our controller, Bob Shade. He will be able to explain the capabilities of our computer system. Moreover, he can help you develop programs for your particular project.

I am encouraging all of you to think of ways in which the computer facilities can be useful to your department.

Conversation Between Mr. King and Bob Shade

Six months after the memorandum was distributed, Mr. King and Bob Shade had the following conversation.

MR. KING: I don't understand it. Following the initial installation of the computer, we experienced significant reductions in our processing and operating costs. Yet, by expanding the computer applications to nonfinancial areas, we have not experienced comparable cost savings.

MR. SHADE: My department has tried to give the nonfinancial user departments as much help in developing programs and suggesting potential applications as possible. In fact, I have designated a staff member to help these operating departments. His job is solely to facilitate coordination between the accounting department and the other user departments.

MR. KING: Well, according to the conference speakers, we should be reaping benefits equal to or exceeding those experienced from computerizing our financial applications. Something must be wrong!

The Investigation

Mr. King hired an outside consultant, John Dole, to investigate the existing situation and to make change recommendations.

After reviewing the standard computer procedures and departmental policies with the controller and the EDP manager, the consultant talked to some of the organization's personnel. Presented below are excerpts of his conversations with the production manager and the marketing manager.

Conversation Between Mr. Dole and Mr. Cooke (production manager)

MR. DOLE: How useful do you think computer applications are for your department?

MR. COOKE: I really haven't given it much thought. Mr. King was talking to me about using the computer for inventory control, but I just don't have the time right now to explore all the possible computer applications. All I know is that the accounting department sends me a lot of reports . . . more than I know what to do with. My time is limited. Therefore, I only glance at a portion of what accounting sends me. What do I need another set of reports for? Furthermore, I have indicated to Bob Shade that I would like to receive production reports expressed in quantities rather than in dollar figures. He said that he would see what could be done, but nothing has happened so far. If he can't accommodate me in this one small request, how could he be of much help in designing programs outside of the accounting area?

Conversation Between Mr. Dole and Mr. Bishop (marketing manager)

MR. DOLE: What do you think about increasing your department's use of computer applications?

MR. BISHOP: I can see great possibilities for increased computer applications for my department. Especially in the area of decision making, the computer could help us in a function such as sales forecasting.

Unfortunately, the accounting department often vetoes our proposed applications. If our projects are not rejected, they are usually given a low priority rating. The reasons for denial are many. The major argument given by the accounting department for rejecting our project proposals is that these projects will not provide a direct economic benefit to the company.

I think our controller is too wrapped up with efficiency. In the long run, the company will suffer if Shade continues limiting the types of applications processed by the computer.

Recommendations

After talking to these various people, the consultant felt that he could provide several recommendations to Mr. King for solving the existing problem(s).

Questions

A.   Assuming that you are the consultant, John Dole, define the problem(s) that exist in Polynesian Textile Company. What do you feel are the causes of the problem(s)?

B.   As John Dole, what would you recommend to solve the company's problem(s)?

12-24.   *Merriman Company*

Thomas Dauton is Manager of Reports in the office of Senior Vice-President Frank Lee of the Merriman Company. Until five months ago Lee was a regional vice-president in charge of manufacturing operations for Region 8 of the company, and Dauton was his assistant. At that time Lee was promoted to the newly created position, Senior Vice-President, and given the responsibility for all of Merriman's manufacturing operations. Twelve regional manufacturing vice-presidents report to him.

Lee has visited each region since taking over his new job and Dauton has accompanied him on most of these trips. Relations with each regional vice-president, as Dauton observes them, range from fairly cool to enthusiastic cooperation. Lee's replacement in Region 8 had been one of Lee's stronger assistants; each of the other eleven regional vice-presidents has been in his job for at least six months (and as long as ten years) before Lee's promotion. The least enthusiastic greeting came from the regional vice-president who was the other most likely candidate for Senior Vice-President. Dauton also noted that one other regional vice-president appeared uninterested in the visit and did not seem enthusiastic about the new organizational arrangement; this regional vice-president has been in his present position for eight years and is due to retire within the next eighteen months.

Each regional manufacturing vice-president is required to file a monthly report which contains detailed comparisons of budgeted and actual cost and production for the previous month and an explanation of the differences from budget. Prior to Lee's appointment as Senior Vice-President of Manufacturing, these reports had been sent by the tenth of the following month to the Executive Vice-President for Operations, a member of the three-man President's Office of the Corporation. The reports are still due in the President's Office by the tenth of the following month, but Lee now receives the reports first. The twelve regional reports are then submitted by Lee, along with his own summary and narrative, to the President's Office.

This new reporting arrangement was Lee's idea and he insists that the summary be carefully prepared before it is submitted to the President's Office. The company policy guide, as yet unchanged, requires the regional vice-presidents to submit their reports by the tenth day. Lee has asked the regional vice-presidents to submit the reports by the seventh of the month. This will allow Dauton adequate time to prepare the analysis for Lee's review before it is submitted to the President's Office. The request is not unreasonable as the company recently installed an efficient computer-based information system which can get the necessary information to the regional vice-presidents by the fourth day.

The regional vice-presidents have acknowl-

edged the request and have agreed to try to meet the schedule requested by Lee. Two regions, however, have not met the schedule for the past three months even though Dauton is sure they could with a little effort. He believes one region is not cooperating because its vice-president is still irked at not being promoted to the Senior Vice-President position. The office for this region has called each of the last three months on the seventh day to say the report was not ready but would be ready on the tenth day. The other report, from the region headed by the near retirement vice-president, has arrived on the tenth day each month but no notice or explanation of the delay has been given.

This past month Lee made it clear to Dauton that he wanted the report he would submit to the President's Office ready for his review by noon on the ninth day, rather than late on the tenth day. The reports from all but the two regions mentioned arrived early on the seventh day. Dauton waited until the eighth day before drafting the report hoping that the two recalcitrant division reports would arrive. When the reports did not arrive, Dauton called his counterparts in the divisions to get what information he could so that he could complete his draft of the report. From these informal sources plus the regular reports of the other divisions, he was able to complete the draft on time. The final report, more carefully prepared than in prior months, was ready for the President's Office by noon on the tenth day. The details which had been acquired by phone for the two divisions were verified when their reports were received. The report was delivered by mid-afternoon to the President's Office.

Required

A.   Identify and discuss the organizational and behavioral factors which cause the difficulties Frank Lee and Thomas Dauton are experiencing in preparing monthly a complete and timely summary report for the President's Office.

B.   How should Frank Lee and Thomas Dauton proceed to improve the reporting process? Be sure your answer includes recognition of organizational structure, authority and responsibility, and communication and motivation factors.

(CMA Adapted)

12-25. *Ferguson & Son Mfg. Company*

Tom Emory and Jim Morris strolled back to their plant from the administrative offices of Ferguson & Son Mfg. Company. Tom was manager of the machine shop in the company's factory; Jim was manager of the equipment maintenance department.

The men had just attended the monthly performance evaluation meeting for plant department heads. These meetings had been held on the third Tuesday of each month since Robert Ferguson, Jr., the president's son, had become plant manager a year earlier.

As they were walking Tom Emory spoke. "Boy, I hate those meetings! I never know whether my department's accounting reports will show good or bad performance. I'm beginning to expect the worst. If the accountants say I saved the company a dollar, I'm called 'Sir,' but if I spend even a little too much—boy, do I get in trouble. I don't know if I can hold on until I retire."

Tom had just received the worst evaluation he had ever received in his long career with Ferguson & Son. He was the most respected of the experienced machinists in the company. He had been with Ferguson & Son for many years and was promoted to supervisor of the machine shop when the company expanded and moved to its present location. The president (Robert Ferguson, Sr.) had often stated that the company's success was due to the high quality of the work of machinists like Emory. As supervisor, Tom stressed the importance of craftsmanship and told his workers that he wanted no sloppy work coming from his department.

When Robert Ferguson, Jr. became the plant manager, he directed that monthly performance comparisons be made between actual and budgeted costs for each department. The departmental budgets were intended to encourage the supervisors to reduce inefficiencies and to seek cost reduction opportunities. The company controller was instructed to have his staff "tighten" the budget slightly whenever a department attained its budget in a given month; this was done to reinforce the plant supervisor's desire to reduce costs. The young plant manager often stressed the importance of continued progress toward attaining the budget; he also made it known that he kept a file of these performance reports for future reference when he succeeded his father.

Tom Emory's conversation with Jim Morris continued as follows:

Emory: "I really don't understand. We've worked so hard to get up to budget and the minute we make it they tighten the budget on us. We can't work any faster and still maintain quality. I think my men are ready to quit trying. Besides, those reports don't tell the whole story. We always seem to be interrupting the big jobs for all those small rush orders. All that setup and machine adjustment time is killing us. And quite frankly, Jim, you were no help. When our hydraulic press broke down last month, your people were nowhere to be found. We had to take it apart ourselves and got stuck with all that idle time."

Morris: "I'm sorry about that, Tom, but you know my department has had trouble making budget, too. We were running well beyond budget at the time of that problem, and if we'd spent a day on that old machine, we would never have made it up. Instead we made the scheduled inspections of the fork-lift trucks because we knew we could do those in less than the budgeted time."

Emory: "Well, Jim, at least you have some options. I'm locked into what the scheduling department assigns to me and you know they're being harassed by sales for those special orders. Incidentally, why didn't your report show all the supplies you guys wasted last month when you were working in Bill's department?"

Morris: "We're not out of the woods on that deal yet. We charged the maximum we could to our other work and haven't even reported some of it yet."

Emory: "Well, I'm glad you have a way of getting out of the pressure. The accountants seem to know everything that's happening in my department, sometimes even before I do. I thought all that budget and accounting stuff was supposed to help, but it just gets me into trouble. Its all a big pain. I'm trying to put out quality work; they're trying to save pennies."

Tom Emory's performance report for the month in question is reproduced below. Actual production volume for the month was at the budgeted level.

MACHINE SHOP—OCTOBER 1984
T. Emory, Supervisor

	Budget	Actual	Variances
Direct labor	$ 39,600	$ 39,850	$ 250 U
Direct materials	231,000	231,075	75 U
Depreciation—equipment	3,000	3,000	0
Depreciation—buildings	6,000	6,000	0
Power	900	860	40 F
Maintenance	400	410	10 U
Supervision	1,500	1,500	0
Idle-time	0	1,800	1,800 U
Set-up labor	680	2,432	1,752 U
Miscellaneous	2,900	3,300	400 U
	$285,980	$290,227	$4,247 U

Required

A.   Identify the problems which appear to exist in Ferguson & Son Mfg. Company's budgetary control system and explain how the problems are likely to reduce the effectiveness of the system.

B.   Explain how Ferguson & Son Mfg. Company's budgetary control system could be revised to improve its effectiveness.

(CMA Adapted)

12-26.   *The Reddon Company*

The Reddon Company manufactures and sells plastic products. The company management believes a successful firm should have formally stated objectives. Financial and output goals have been established for all departments and the departments are evaluated against those goals. In addition, the company aggressively seeks new products to support its goal of growth.

Early in 1984 Cupot Inc. offered to sell its design and preliminary engineering studies for a plastic sewing machine housing to Reddon. Cupot management had concluded that the product was too remote from its normal product lines and, equally important, would require manufacturing expertise not possessed by Cupot.

Reddon management requested the marketing department to research the sales potential of the sewing machine housing. The product development department, a department of the product division, studied the production problems of the product. Both departments concluded that it was feasible to add the housing to the company's product line. However, each observed that problems could be encountered because this was a new market for Reddon and that a modification of current manufacturing techniques and processes would be required. In spite of these warnings, Reddon management purchased the idea from Cupot and authorized the project late in 1984.

Management concluded that the marketing and manufacturing requirements were of sufficient complexity to require a project team to bring the product into being. This was a new management technique for Reddon. George Aldon, an experienced sales manager with a strong manufacturing background, was chosen to head the project team. He was selected to head the team because he had been with the company for many years, and was well known and well liked by most people in the company. This was important because the project team had no resources of its own and would have to rely on regular departments to get the work completed.

Aldon was permitted to select one person from the sales, manufacturing, and financial management departments to make a four-person project team. The project team was charged with the planning, coordination, and successful introduction of the sewing machine housing. The three team members were responsible for developing the schedule of services needed, serving as liaison with their former areas, and evaluating the work done by the regular departments. All members of the team would return to their departments when the team completed its task of guiding the new product through its first year of sales.

The project team developed a schedule of events and activities leading to the introduction of this new product in late 1985. Included in the schedule were timetables for the development of a sales program, the modification of the manufacturing facilities, and the sample production run. Financial requirements and budget revision schedules were also prepared.

The product was not ready for introduction in late 1985 as planned. The sales program was not yet finalized, nor were the manufacturing modifications complete. The departments had worked on the project whenever time was available in the regular work schedules. The department heads stated that they were unable to do more because no adjustment in the available resources had been made. Although the project team had prepared a financial requirements schedule, this schedule was not ready when the company budget was adopted. Consequently, the financial requirements were not incorporated into the budget.

George Aldon was disappointed that the team was unable to meet the planned introduction date. This was the first assignment he had failed to complete successfully. He attributed the lack of success to the departmental managers who regularly failed to meet the deadlines in the original timetables. The other members of the project team worked hard but, in Aldon's opinion, were not forceful enough when dealing with their former departments.

Required

A. Describe the potential advantages of the project approach to the development of a new product.

B. Using the information which you are provided about the Reddon Company, describe the probable circumstances that caused the project to be late.

(CMA Adapted)

13

Systems Study: The Implementation and Initial Operation Phase, and the Follow-up Phase

Among the important questions that you should be able to answer after reading this chapter are:

1 How can a PERT network aid management consultants in planning and controlling the implementation of their client company's new accounting information system?

2 Of what importance is a PERT network's "critical path" to the successful implementation of a company's new accounting information system?

3 How can errors be prevented when converting accounting data from manual storage media to computer storage media?

4 What is a modular systems conversion?

5 Can the consultants' systems study work for a client company *ever* be finished?

INTRODUCTION

As discussed in Chapter 11, the existence of a systems problem (or problems) starts the "life-cycle" activities associated with a company's business information system (see Figure 11-1). In an effort to solve its information systems problem (or problems), the company's management will often hire outside consultants to perform a systems study. The first major phase of the consultants' systems study work (examined in Chapter 11) is called *analysis*. Through their analysis work, the consultants will identify the strengths and weaknesses of the client company's present information system. By isolating the weaknesses within the company's system, the consultants can then recommend systems revisions that should correct these inefficiencies. The discussion of Chapter 11 concluded that the major systems problems detected by the consultants were the result of the client company's manual data-processing system's failure to provide timely managerial decision-making information. Therefore, the consultants suggested that their client acquire a computer system to help solve the current data-processing problems.

Based upon the systems analysis findings, the consultants then begin the second major systems study phase, the *design* phase (discussed in Chapter 12). In their design work, the consultants examine the feasibility of replacing the client company's present data-processing system with a computerized system. A *specifications report* describing feasible computer design proposals is prepared and submitted to hardware and software vendors. Each vendor will subsequently develop specific computer proposals for the company's system. The computer vendor's proposal that best satisfies the company's data-processing needs is selected. The Chapter 12 discussion concluded that the consultants' client company elected to lease a batch-processing computerized system from a hardware and software supplier.

Once a specific computer system is chosen, the consultants then begin the third major phase of their systems study work, the *implementation* and *initial operation* of the new computer system. Within a few months after the completion of this third systems study step, the fourth (and final) systems study phase, the *follow-up* analysis, is performed.

This chapter will continue where Chapter 12 ended by discussing the consultants' required systems work to implement and thus enable initial operation of their client company's computerized batch-processing system. The consultants' follow-up analysis work on a newly implemented system will also be examined briefly in the current chapter. However, an intensive discussion of the follow-up phase of a systems study will be postponed until Chapter 14. Thus, by the conclusion of Chapter 14, the entire "life-cycle" of a business information system will have been thoroughly discussed within the text (Chapters 11–14).

SYSTEMS IMPLEMENTATION AND INITIAL OPERATION

This step in the systems study is often called the "action" phase because the recommended changes from the prior analysis and design work are now put into operation. In order to implement the necessary changes into an organization's system efficiently, the consultants must do considerable planning and controlling. A systems implementation ordinarily involves the performance of several specific activities to convert a company's present system to the newly designed one. These activities must be performed in a logical sequence. Thus, some activities must be completed before other activities can commence. On the other hand, the implementation of certain activities can occur simultaneously (or in "parallel"). Unless the consultants plan the systems implementation project logically, project coordination may suffer and/or the completion of the systems implementation may be unreasonably prolonged.

As specific activities are being performed, the consultants can provide feedback reports to management which compare the actual implementation time with the estimated implementation time. These control reports enable both the consultants and company management to be aware of any delays in implementing specific activities (the actual time exceeding the original estimated time) and what effect, if any, the delays may have on the entire implementation process. For example, if a specific implementation activity is behind schedule, the consultants may allocate additional human resources to this activity to speed up its completion. Or, if another activity is proceeding ahead of schedule, the resources working on this activity may be reduced.

Because of the importance of good planning and controlling when implementing systems changes, many consultants utilize a PERT (Program Evaluation and Review Technique) network for scheduling the sequence of activities that must be performed in the implementation

393

phase of a systems study. Using PERT, a diagram reflecting the logical sequence of systems implementation activities is prepared. The time required for implementing each activity is estimated and included in the PERT diagram. When introducing some minor revisions into a company's present system (e.g., changing the formats of certain computerized feedback reports within the Alan Company) or implementing a new system into a *small* company, the consultants typically will not use a PERT network for guiding the implementation activities because the number of required activities will be minimal. For a major systems conversion involving a large number of implementation activities, however, the development of a PERT network can be a valuable tool for planning and controlling the consultants' systems implementation work.

The time required to implement the various activities in a systems change is based upon reasonable estimates for each work segment. Because the future involves uncertainty, there is always the risk that the actual time required to implement a specific activity will vary from the estimated time. Because of this uncertainty regarding the actual time interval for implementing specific systems conversion activities, statistical probabilities can be incorporated into the PERT network analysis. Quantitative analysis example 2 in Appendix A illustrates the use of statistical probability theory in a PERT network diagram. To emphasize the systems implementation process (and de-emphasize the mathematics), the following discussion of a PERT network's use in planning and controlling the revision of a company's current system will ignore the use of statistical probabilities in estimating the completion time for implementing a new system.

In our discussion of PERT below, the reader should keep in mind that the drawing of a PERT network diagram is only a *tool* to aid the consultants in their systems implementation work. The "heart" of systems implementation is performing the specific activities required to implement systems revisions successfully. In fact, even though we will first discuss PERT before beginning a detailed examination of the activities required to implement systems changes, it

should be noted that, in actual practice, the development of a PERT network and the determination of the detailed work that must be performed to implement successfully each activity in a systems change are executed "hand-in-hand." After all, how can you develop a logical sequence of systems implementation activities without knowing the detailed work required for each activity?

PERT Network for Systems Implementation

From the systems design discussion of Chapter 12, it should be remembered that the consultants and their client company's top management reached a decision to convert the company's manual data-processing system to a batch-processing computerized system. Figure 13-1 describes the various activities, the consultants' estimates of the time required to implement each activity, and the predecessor activities (i.e., those activities, if any, that must be completed before a specific activity can commence) for converting the client's present information system to a medium-sized, computerized batch-processing system. Based upon the data in Figure 13-1, a PERT network of the systems implementation process is then prepared, as illustrated in Figure 13-2. (Explanations will follow.)

The arrows on the PERT network designate the activities required to implement the computer system. (In this PERT network figure, the length of each arrow has no relationship to the estimated completion time for an activity.) Conventionally, these arrows flow from left to right. The circles (called *nodes*) with numbers inside represent events. The events signal either the start or the completion of specific activities and do not absorb any time. Event 1 is the beginning of the implementation process. Since neither activity A nor activity B requires any predecessor activities (see Figure 13-1), both of these activities can commence simultaneously at node 1. Since activity B is expected to be implemented before activity A (14 weeks for activity B compared with 19 weeks for activity A), the completion of activity B is reflected as event 2 in Figure 13-2. Once node 2 is reached, ac-

Figure 13-1

SYSTEMS IMPLEMENTATION ACTIVITIES

Activity	Estimated Time (in weeks)	Predecessor Activities	Description of Activity[a]
A	19	None	Prepare the physical site location for the delivery of the computer system.
B	14	None	Determine the necessary functional changes in the system.
C	2	B	Select and assign personnel.
D	6	C	Train personnel.
E	1	A	Acquire and install the computer equipment.
F	7	B	Establish controls and standards.
G	6	E, F	Convert data files to computer storage media.
H	6	E, F	Acquire computer programs.
I	5	H	Test computer programs.
J	26	D, G, I	Test new system's operational capabilities by parallel conversion and eliminate old system.

[a]Each of these activities will be discussed later in the chapter.

tivities C and F can begin. Node 3 indicates the completion of activities C and B, requiring an estimated 16 weeks (from Figure 13-2, 14 weeks for activity B plus 2 weeks for activity C). Activity A's completion, estimated to require 19 weeks, is designated as the fourth event in the implementation process. Node 5, the completion of activities B and F as well as the completion of activities A and E, will be reached in an estimated 21 weeks. Since both of these routes must be completed to reach node 5, and route B,F (14 weeks + 7 weeks = 21 weeks) is estimated to require more time than route A,E (19 weeks + 1 week = 20 weeks), the former's route time of 21 weeks is the earliest possible time that node 5 can be reached. Because the approach used in computing the estimated number of weeks to reach each of the remaining network events is the same as that discussed above, no further computations will be illustrated here. (For your information, however, node 6 will be reached in an estimated 27 weeks, node 7 will be reached in an estimated 32 weeks, and node 8 will be reached in an estimated 58 weeks.)

From the viewpoint of successfully meeting the systems implementation schedule (starting at event 1 and finishing at event 8 in Figure 13-2), the consultants must monitor closely that sequence of activities which is expected to require the longest period of time through the network. In order to determine the network's most time-consuming sequence of activities, each path's estimated time duration from event 1 to event 8 is computed, as follows:

$$A–E–H–I–J = 57 \text{ weeks } (19 + 1 + 6 + 5 + 26)$$
$$A–E–G–J \quad = 52 \text{ weeks } (19 + 1 + 6 + 26)$$
$$B–F–H–I–J = 58 \text{ weeks } (14 + 7 + 6 + 5 + 26)$$
$$B–F–G–J \quad = 53 \text{ weeks } (14 + 7 + 6 + 26)$$
$$B–C–D–J \quad = 48 \text{ weeks } (14 + 2 + 6 + 26)$$

The most time-consuming network path is thus B – F – H – I – J (requiring an estimated 58 weeks) and it is called the *critical path*. The term *critical* is used for each activity within this longest path through the network because any delays in implementing a critical-path activity will delay the entire implementation project. Thus, it is extremely important that the consultants as well as their client company's top management closely monitor the performance of each critical-path activity so that delays in implementing these activities can be avoided. For the noncritical activities (i.e., those activities not on the critical path), time delays can occur in their implementation without a delay in implementing the entire system. Thus, management does not have to monitor these noncritical path activities as closely as the critical-path activities.

The term *slack time* is used to indicate the amount of delay time that can occur in non-

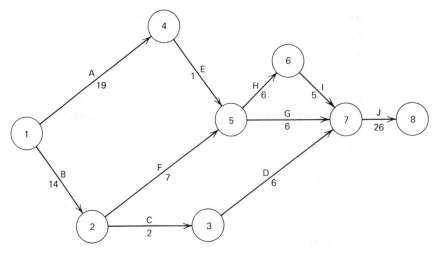

Figure 13-2. PERT network of systems implementation process.

critical path activities and still not delay the estimated completion time (58 weeks in our example) of the entire systems implementation project. Obviously, the greater the slack time for a noncritical activity, the less closely that activity has to be monitored. Because there cannot be any delays in critical-path activities without causing a time delay in completing the project's entire implementation, the slack time for any critical-path activity is always *zero*.

To illustrate the computation of the slack time for a noncritical path activity, assume that top management wanted to know how much delay could occur in completing activity G (an estimated time of 6 weeks in Figure 13-1) without causing the systems implementation project to extend beyond 58 weeks (the critical path time estimate). When determining the slack time of a noncritical path activity, you must compute the activity's earliest possible completion time and its latest possible completion time. The difference between these two time estimates represents the activity's slack time. From Figure 13-2, the earliest possible completion time for activity G is 27 weeks (activity B + activity F + activity G = 14 + 7 + 6). The latest possible completion time for activity G is determined by taking the project's total estimated implementation time (which is the total critical path time) and subtracting from this figure the estimated times re-

quired for all activities performed after activity G. Thus, the latest time for completing activity G is 32 weeks [58 weeks estimated for implementing entire project *minus* 26 weeks estimated for implementing activity J (the only activity performed after activity G)]. In other words, because activity J requires 26 weeks, the maximum number of weeks into the project for implementing activity G without causing the entire project implementation to take longer than 58 weeks is 32 weeks (32 weeks + 26 weeks for activity J = 58 weeks). For example, if it took 39 weeks to reach the completion of activity G and thus be at event 7, then the earliest possible completion time for the entire implementation project would be 65 weeks (39 weeks + 26 weeks for activity J). This 65-week implementation period would result in a 7-week delay from the original critical path estimate of 58 weeks. The slack time for activity G is therefore 5 weeks (32 weeks for the latest possible completion time *minus* 27 weeks for the earliest possible completion time).

The above discussion has attempted to analyze briefly the valuable information that can be obtained by using a PERT network for planning and controlling a systems implementation project. In order to develop the network, the consultants have to plan the logical sequence of activities that must be performed to implement their systems changes successfully. By closely monitor-

396

ing through PERT the actual implementation time required compared with the estimated implementation time required for each critical-path activity and also being aware of the slack time permitted for noncritical path activities, the PERT network is a useful control mechanism for the consultants and for their client's top management during the actual systems installation process.

The PERT network of Figure 13-2 had only one critical path. It should be noted, however, that it is possible to have more than one critical path of activities when implementing a new system; for example, the total estimated times for completing the two longest routes through the PERT network may be identical, resulting in two critical paths. Also, if the actual completion times for various implementation activities should vary significantly from their estimated completion times, it is possible for the critical path itself to change at some point during the implementation process.

Having discussed the use of PERT as a tool for systems implementation, we will now examine each of the activities required (see Figure 13-1) to convert the company's manual data-processing system to a computerized batch-processing system.

Activity A: Prepare the Physical Site

When introducing a computerized data-processing system into an organization for the first time, the work required to prepare the physical site location for the subsequent delivery of the computer system can be quite time consuming (approximately 19 weeks in Figure 13-1). The consulting team's accountants will be especially concerned about the incremental costs (i.e., those costs that will increase as a result of a specific activity) associated with physical site preparation. If the company already has available building space for the computer center and this space is neither being used currently nor anticipated to be used in the future for any other organizational activities, then the incremental cost of utilizing the physical space is zero. However, the building area designated for the com-

puter center may be occupied or plans may exist for its future use in other organizational functions. In this case, the incremental cost of using the specific space area for the computer center is the opportunity cost of being unable to use the area for the other intended purposes.

The company may even decide to construct additional building space to house the new computer center. The costs of performing this construction work would be classified as incremental costs. Additional incremental costs that are normally required in preparing the physical site location include the costs for air conditioning, for electrical outlets, for a library to store data files and computer programs, and for furniture and fixtures (many of these costs were mentioned in Chapter 12). The number of entrances and exits to the computer room should be minimized to prevent the entry of unauthorized employees.

Activity B: Determine the Functional Changes

Included in this implementation activity is the consultants' analysis of job function changes caused by the computerized system and their analysis of the types of data that will be processed and reported by the new computerized system.

The automated system likely will eliminate certain jobs that existed under the old manual system (such as accounts-receivable bookkeeping for preparing the monthly customer billing statements) and will also create new jobs (such as computer programming). The manner of performing the work tasks may change even for those job functions that are not eliminated. For example, under the Alan Company's old manual system, the inventory bookkeeper maintained a handwritten subsidiary ledger disclosing the balances of each inventory item. This ledger was updated monthly by the bookkeeper from the various sales and purchase invoices and receiving reports. With the Alan Company's batch-processing computer system, however, the inventory bookkeeper will review for accuracy the copies of the sales and purchase invoices and the inventory receiving reports, then send them to the EDP center where the data from these source documents (such as the code numbers and quantities of inventory items sold and purchased) are transferred to computer storage media (such as magnetic tape or magnetic disk) and processed to update the various inventory account balances.

The types of transactions—for example, inventory transactions, cash transactions, and accounts receivable transactions—that will be processed by the computer center and the manner in which the transaction data will be stored must be analyzed by the consulting team's accountants. For instance, a decision may have been made initially to record and store inventory transaction data on magnetic tape according to inventory code numbers. A weekly transaction tape of inventory activities (sales and purchases) would be prepared and processed with the master inventory tape file in order to update the inventory balances and print out purchase orders for those inventory items reaching their reorder points. For control purposes, a grandfather-father-son system of tape files may be maintained. After further discussions with the hardware and software vendor, however, the consulting team's accountants may decide to have the inventory transaction data recorded and stored on magnetic disk.

The format of the output reports from the inventory processing functions must also be ascertained. This determination requires an analysis of both the specific information to be included on output reports as well as those employees who will receive copies of these reports. To determine which employees should receive output reports and the data that should be included on the reports, the accountants on the consulting team must be familiar with the employees' organizational functions and the decision-making information they require to perform their functions. A specific report should not be distributed to employees unless they need the report information to execute their duties effectively. For example, the raw materials inventory report distributed to the Alan Company's purchasing agent (who is responsible for placing orders for additional sporting goods raw material inventory items) may be prepared on an exception basis, disclosing only those inventory items requiring reorder. On the other hand, the Alan Company's basketball production manager's output report may include information about the current balances of every basketball manufacturing raw material inventory item. If, for instance, a major production order of basketballs is scheduled in four weeks, this detailed inventory report will enable the production manager to ascertain whether an adequate supply of specific types of raw materials needed for basketball manufacturing is currently available for processing the future order. If sufficient balances of certain raw materials are not on hand, the basketball production manager can then request the purchasing agent to order these specific raw material inventory items immediately.

Activity C: Select and Assign Personnel

After determining the necessary functional changes required in the new computer system (activity B above), the consultants will be able to write job descriptions for the various employee work activities under the revised system. Based upon these job descriptions, the personnel subsystem of the consultants' client company will be principally responsible for selecting the necessary employees and assigning them to specific job functions. The selection and assignment of personnel to organizational jobs is one of the most important activities in the systems implementation process. As emphasized throughout this book, competent and motivated employees are essential to an effectively-operated system.

When converting from a manual to a computerized data-processing system, false rumors often circulate among employees about the jobs and the personnel that will be eliminated, thus causing low employee morale. To prevent this motivational problem from occurring, the consultants and their client's management should communicate openly with the employees regarding the creation of new jobs and the elimination of present jobs. Those employees whose jobs are either eliminated or materially altered as a result of the revised system should be given first opportunity to apply for the newly created job functions. As discussed under activity D below, employees often can be trained to perform the new job duties required by the revised system. For example, with a minimum amount of instruction, a typist can be trained as a keypunch operator.

Some of the highly technical job functions (e.g., computer programming and systems analysis) that must be performed in the new system may be impossible to fill with the company's present personnel. Consequently, the personnel subsystem's employees will have to seek qualified individuals from outside the organizational boundaries. The hardware and software vendor can often aid the company in locating personnel with the specialized knowledge needed to perform computer-related job functions. The topic of personnel acquisition will be examined further in Chapter 14.

The employees who will be terminated by the company should receive ample notice so that they can secure other jobs before their current employment ends. Because the entire implementation process normally takes many months to complete, providing terminated employees with ample notices of their job displacements should not be difficult. If possible, these employees should be given some time off with pay (perhaps a few days or even a week) to look for other positions while they are still working for the company. The company's top management may consider giving early retirement to those employees who have been with the company for many years and are nearing retirement.

Activity D: Train Personnel

Both the consultants and the employee representatives from the computer vendor will normally participate in training the company's personnel to operate the newly designed computerized system efficiently. Seminars should be provided for many of the company's employees to make them aware of the various advantages offered by the new computer system. Specific procedural training should be given to those employees whose job functions are altered as a result of the systems revisions. This training can take place in either a classroom environment or the actual on-the-job environment. When using classroom procedures, simulation is a popular learning technique. Through simulation, the employees learn operational functions by performing their new duties on artificially created data that are representative of the actual data with which they will eventually work on their jobs.

Training will also be required for those newly hired employees already possessing specialized knowledge of computer systems. The training sessions will be designed to teach the EDP subsystem's computer specialists the most effective ways of utilizing the automated system within their company's operating environment. Even if the computer equipment has not yet been installed on the company's premises (activity E below), the hardware and software supplier's personnel can provide this training within their own building facility.

Before the employees are taught their specific organizational tasks, they should be provided an initial overview of how their jobs fit into the entire company structure. This knowledge will give each employee a good understanding of his or her contribution to the company's goals. As a result, the employees should have a better grasp of the meaning and significance of specific tasks, thus motivating them to perform these job duties successfully.

Activity E: Acquire and Install Computer Equipment

After preparing the physical site location for the new computer system (activity A), the hardware equipment must be acquired from the computer vendor. This equipment includes the central processing unit, the input and output devices, and the secondary storage devices. (The acquisition of additional hardware for a company's previously implemented computer system will be discussed in Chapter 14.) The hardware and software vendor's employees normally will have the major responsibility for installing the computer equipment into the company's system. Computer specialists on the management consulting team and/or the client company's employees may also participate in these installation activities.

Activity F: Establish Controls and Standards

Upon determining the functional changes for the new system (activity B), necessary controls and standards must be established. The accountants on the consulting team should have an important role in this systems implementation activity.

Chapter 7 emphasized that an effective internal control system should safeguard an organization's asset resources from misuse and should encourage operating efficiency so that management's prescribed policies and goals are achieved. Safeguarding a company's assets is accomplished through such preventive controls as a good audit trail and the separation of related organizational functions.

As discussed further in Chapter 7, the introduction of a computer into an organization's system often causes difficulty in following the audit trail of accounting transactions. The consulting team's accountants should make sure that adequate documentation exists which describes the operating features of the new system. Good documentation contributes to an effective audit trail. Based upon an analysis of the anticipated costs compared with the anticipated benefits of specific controls, many of the computerized controls discussed in Chapter 8 should be incorporated into the revised system. The newly implemented system will cause changes in some of the employees' job duties, as was emphasized previously. As old job functions are eliminated and new job functions are created, the accountants on the consulting team should strive for good separation of duties when company personnel are assigned to specific job activities under the revised system. For these new job functions (such as computer programming), standards of employee performance should be established.

Operational efficiency is evaluated through feedback controls such as a responsibility accounting system and timely performance reports (both of these controls were discussed in Chapter 7). The responsibility accounting structure should be revised based upon the operating changes introduced into the company's system. A major function of timely performance reports is to aid in the evaluation of employee efficiency in meeting job standards. Because the new system will cause a change in job duties and performance standards for many of the employees, the accountants must redesign their client company's performance reporting system so that it continues to measure employee operating efficiency fairly.

Activity G: Convert Data Files

Under the company's old manual system, its data files of accounting information were maintained on traditional storage media. For example, the information about each general ledger account was recorded manually in a bound book containing preprinted ledger paper, a separate page being used for each account. Separate ledger books were also utilized for the accounts receivable and accounts payable subsidiary ledger information. Data regarding the balances of individual inventory items (both raw materials for production and finished goods) were kept in an inventory subsidiary ledger.

Each of these data files must now be converted to computer storage media. Because the company is implementing a batch-processing system, a storage medium such as magnetic tape would be used. Any revised standards (established in activity F above) affecting a data file should be incorporated into the file at the time of conversion. For example, the computerized processing of the company's cost accounting production reports will cause a change in the dollar amount of allocated standard overhead charged to work-in-process and finished goods inventories. Under the previous manual system, the standard overhead charged to production included an allocated share of the cost accountants' (who prepared the production reports manually) salaries. Because production reports will now be prepared by the computer rather than by the company's cost accountants, a new standard overhead amount relating to report preparation must be determined.

This standard will then be incorporated into the inventory production master file.

When converting the manual data files to computer storage media, care must be taken to assure that no errors occur during the conversion process. For example, when the accounts receivable subsidiary ledger book is converted to a magnetic tape master file, it is important that each customer's correct account number be transferred to the tape file. Because the newly established computer file will serve as the basis for all future credit-sales processing activity, the need for complete accuracy is imperative when creating this file. As a means of detecting the transfer of inaccurate customer account numbers to the new computer master file, a hash total of these account numbers can be accumulated from the subsidiary ledger book. At the completion of the conversion to magnetic tape, a hash total of customer account numbers computed from this new master tape file can be compared with the originally determined hash total from the subsidiary ledger book. These two hash totals should be identical. Any discrepancies between the separately computed hash total numbers must be investigated. Many of the additional controls discussed in Chapter 8—for example, editing checks, control totals, and field checks—can also be used advantageously when establishing computer files for accounting applications.

If the company desires a high degree of integration among its various master files of accounting information, it must somehow coordinate the accounting data contained within these files in a meaningful way. One approach (as discussed in Chapter 5) would be to develop an integrated data base of accounting data in which the data required by various users would all be consolidated in the company's data-base files. An alternate approach would be to coordinate the master files through a *supervisory index file*. The index file would contain the storage addresses of the various master files and serve to link these master files together. Thus, when managers require different types of accounting information (such as inventory and sales information) for specific decision-making endeavors, they can obtain the needed information simultaneously from the several master files through the use of the supervisory index file.

During processing runs to update the company's master files for accounting activities, transaction files often are used to update master files. When updating the master files, there is always the risk of errors that cause master file data to be destroyed (e.g., writing over a portion of a magnetic tape master file). To provide security against the destruction of master file data, backup files containing the master file information are normally maintained. For example, as discussed previously in the text, the grandfather-father-son system of backup file information might be utilized.

Activity H: Acquire Computer Programs

For each of the processing functions to be handled by the company's computerized system, programs must be available in such computer languages as COBOL, FORTRAN, or BASIC. Compiler programs (acquired from the hardware and software supplier) will then be used to convert the programs into machine language.

In the past few years, hardware and software vendors have made great strides in developing software packages for use by companies when performing their computerized data-processing functions. These software packages can be purchased or leased by companies, and the packages include prewritten "canned programs" for handling such accounting applications as inventory processing and accounts receivable processing. As mentioned in Chapter 12, canned programs which are leased from hardware and software vendors are called proprietary software. (The topic of proprietary software will be discussed in Chapter 14.) Because proprietary software packages are written for the mass-market and each company's specific data-processing needs will be somewhat different, a proprietary software package normally requires various modifications before it can be used within a company's system.

Due to the current popularity of hardware and software vendors' proprietary software packages among companies implementing a new computer system or modifying a present computer system, we will assume in this chapter that the company implementing a new batch-processing system will lease prewritten programs from a computer vendor. It should be noted, however, that if a company did elect to develop from "scratch" its own computer programs (called *in-house development*), this activity in the systems implementation process would likely be performed prior to activity E (acquire and install computer equipment). The development of computer programs is very time consuming and often requires many months to perform. Therefore, the company probably would not want to acquire and install its computer equipment first and then allow this expensive equipment to remain idle for months until the computer programs were developed.

The process of obtaining and making modifications to a hardware and software vendor's proprietary software package will often take considerably less time (estimated at 6 weeks in Figure 13-1) than developing computer programs from scratch. (An extensive analysis of software acquisition will be provided in Chapter 14. At that time, many of the variables involved in a company's choice between acquiring a proprietary software package and developing its own computer programs will be discussed.) Thus, we will assume that the computer equipment was acquired and installed (activity E) and the controls and standards of the new system were established (activity F) prior to acquiring the proprietary software.

When making modifications to a hardware and software supplier's prewritten canned programs, it is important for a company to have its controls and standards already established. For example, one of the important considerations by the accountants on the consulting team when initially establishing their client company's feedback controls was the types of information that should be included in performance reports to specific managers. Having made this determination in activity F, the prewritten computer canned programs can then be modified (normally with help from the hardware and software vendor's staff of computer experts) to enable the managers to obtain their needed decision-making information. As another example, when the credit managers'

information needs for effective decision making were being evaluated, the consulting team's accountants determined that the weekly feedback aging analysis report (prepared on an exception basis) for these managers should include only information about those credit customers' account balances that are more than 60-days past due. In modifying the proprietary software program which processes the company's weekly accounts receivable aging analysis report, the above information concerning the content of the credit managers' exception report must be known.

Activity I: Test Computer Programs

After the computer programs have been acquired (activity H above), the logic of all modified programs must be adequately tested before these programs can be used in the day-to-day processing functions of the company. This testing activity on the computer programs is called *debugging* because the objective is to eliminate the errors (or "bugs") in the modified programs. As discussed in Chapter 12, "simulation" is quite useful for testing the logic of a company's computer programs. The hardware and software vendor's staff of computer experts normally will aid the consultants in testing these computer programs.

Failure to test the newly acquired computer programs adequately could lead to disastrous consequences. Assuming that programming errors go undetected and the programs are used to process the company's actual operating data, the output report information from the specific processing runs would be incorrect. The subsequent use of these incorrect output reports for management decision making, and so forth, would obviously be detrimental to the company's present and future operating success!

Activity J: Test New System and Eliminate Old System

At this stage, all the prior systems implementation activities have been completed and the new system should be ready to take over the company's processing functions. As yet, however, the new system has not passed the final test of being able to process correctly the company's *real-world* operating data. Therefore, rather than immediately eliminating the old system by replacing it with the newly designed system (the *direct conversion* method discussed later), many companies utilize a gradual approach when implementing their new systems into practice.

A popular operational testing method for introducing a new system into a company's day-to-day processing activities is called *parallel conversion*. Using this method, both the old system and the new system operate simultaneously (or "in parallel") for a certain period of time. Thus, all of the company's processing activities are handled independently by both systems. The resultant outputs from each system are then compared and any differences reconciled. Assuming that the old system's processing accuracy is already well-established from prior years of company use, those output discrepancies between the old system and the new system will likely be attributable to errors in the latter system. The causes of these errors can be investigated and revisions made in the final design of the new system.

The time necessary for parallel conversion (assumed to be 26 weeks in Figure 13-1) depends upon the number of processing discrepancies detected and the time required to make revisions in the new system. In addition to testing for processing discrepancies under the parallel conversion method, the implemented controls of the new system (established in activity F) should also be observed and tested to make sure they are functioning as originally planned. For example, if a "check-digit" control (discussed in Chapter 8) for inventory account numbers was implemented into the computer system, the consultants should evaluate the effectiveness of this processing control by reviewing the handling of those incorrectly coded inventory account numbers detected by the "check-digit" control.

When the consultants are satisfied with the operational functioning of the new system, this system completely replaces the old system in handling the company's data-processing activities. A major advantage of parallel conversion is that the company's data-processing activities

are protected from a possible failure in the new system. Because the old system remains in operation during the parallel conversion period, it will continue to process the company's data correctly even if processing errors occur within the new system.

The obvious disadvantage of the parallel conversion method is the cost factor. Because each accounting transaction is processed by both the old system and the new system throughout the parallel conversion period, company facilities and personnel must be available to handle the dual processing work. This dual processing of all transactions often leads to considerable overtime work by the company's employees.

The opposite of a parallel conversion is called a *direct conversion*. Under this conversion method, the old system is immediately discontinued at the time the new system is implemented, and the new system "sinks or swims." Direct conversion compared with parallel conversion is thus a relatively inexpensive systems implementation approach. The direct conversion method might be employed under any one of the following circumstances: (1) the old system has so many weaknesses that a parallel conversion would serve no useful purpose, (2) the revisions to be implemented into the company's system are either very minor or simple—which would undoubtedly not be true when converting from a manual to a computerized data-processing system, or (3) the new systems design differs drastically from the old system, thereby making comparisons between the two systems meaningless.

One additional systems implementation method is called *modular conversion* (or the *pilot conversion* approach). When utilizing this method, a specific data-processing activity (e.g., batch processing of all inventory transactions) is broken down into smaller units, called modules. The implementation of the new data-processing activity is then executed on a "piecemeal" basis for the specific units associated with the activity.

To illustrate the modular conversion method, assume that a company has five separate divisions that purchase and sell inventory. Using modular conversion, each of these divisions' inventory transactions would be treated as a specific unit (or module). A new batch-processing computerized inventory system would be implemented for one of the five divisions. After satisfactorily testing the inventory system's operation in this division, the batch-processing system could then be implemented for the second division. Successful results in the second division would lead to the system's implementation for the third division, and so on. The major advantage of modular conversion is that specific problems discovered in a new system can be corrected prior to further implementation activities. A possible drawback of using modular conversion is the long time period normally required to complete the entire implementation process.

Regardless of which conversion method is used, activity J's work results in the disappearance of the old system and the emergence of the new system to handle a company's data-processing functions. After completing activity J, some management consultants might feel that their systems study work is finished. However, they would be wrong! The final aspect of a systems study, called the *follow-up* phase, is discussed in the next section of this chapter.

SYSTEMS FOLLOW-UP

As emphasized in Chapter 11, a company's information system should contribute toward three levels of goals: (1) general systems goals such as a simplistic structure and a flexible structure, (2) top management systems goals, and (3) operating management systems goals. When goals are not being achieved in any of these three levels within the company's current operational system, problems (or weaknesses) normally occur in the system. Management consultants may then be hired to help solve the problems by performing a systems study for their client company.

The consultants' initially implemented system should be designed to eliminate the problems of the old system. As the new system operates on a day-to-day basis, however, the company's original systems problems may reoccur or new

problems may surface. Therefore, after the initially implemented system has been in operation for a few months, representatives from the management consulting firm should return to their client company's premises to evaluate the new system's effectiveness in contributing toward the three levels of goals mentioned above.

The consultant's follow-up analysis work on the implemented batch-processing computerized system discussed in this chapter might include the following activities: (1) talk with top management personnel and operating management personnel about their satisfaction with the output reports (both the content and the timeliness of these reports) received from the computer center, (2) evaluate the systems controls to ascertain whether they are functioning properly, (3) observe some of the employees' work performances to ascertain whether the employees are executing their assigned job functions correctly, and (4) evaluate whether data-preparation functions as well as processing functions are being performed efficiently, and also determine if output schedules for reports (both internal and external reports) under the new computer system are being met.

As Figure 11-1 (see Chapter 11) illustrated, the follow-up studies can lead in one of two directions in the "life-cycle" of a company's information system. If the consultants are satisfied as a result of their follow-up work that the initially implemented system has eliminated the company's previous information systems problems, no further revisions are required. Thus, the new system continues processing the company's daily transactions (the solid-arrow from the follow-up studies description in Figure 11-1). On the other hand, if the consultants' follow-up analysis reveals that problems still exist in the newly implemented system, the systems study steps (analysis, design, implementation and initial operation, and follow-up studies) must be repeated in an attempt to solve these problems (the dashed-arrow from the follow-up studies description in Figure 11-1). Hopefully, the resultant revisions will eliminate the systems problems, thereby contributing toward the achievement of the company's general systems goals, top management systems goals, and operating management systems goals.

The dashed-arrow in Figure 11-1 from the system operation on a daily basis to the follow-up studies indicates that the follow-up phase of a systems study should continue throughout the life of a company's system. Even though an information system is currently satisfying the company's needs, this may not be the case at some future time. For example, because of increased competition or new governmental regulations, the information needs of top management personnel may change. To satisfy top management's new information requirements, the company's system will have to be modified.

As indicated in Chapter 11, the consultants should periodically return to their client's company (e.g., every six months) to ascertain whether the current information system is still satisfying the organization's needs. These periodic reviews will normally lead to few, if any, revisions in the company's data-processing system. However, the follow-up work and resultant modifications to a computerized information system can become quite involved. Therefore, the subject of follow-up analyses of existent computerized information systems will be examined extensively in Chapter 14 on resource acquisition.

SUMMARY

Following the decision to acquire a specific computer system, the *implementation* and *initial operation* phase of the systems study begins. A useful tool often employed by consultants for planning and controlling the systems implementation project is PERT. By preparing a PERT network diagram which reflects the logical sequence of conversion activities and the time estimates for performing these activities, the implementation of a new system should proceed in an efficient manner. To avoid delays when implementing the new system, the sequence of conversion activities requiring the most time (called the critical-path activities) should be

closely monitored by both the consultants and their client's top management. If more time than originally estimated is necessary to implement any critical-path activity, then the completion of the entire systems conversion work will be delayed. The end result will be a delay in the initial operation of the new system.

The final phase of a systems study is called *follow-up* analysis. The objective of this systems study work is to evaluate whether or not the newly implemented system has solved the company's previous information systems problems and is therefore meeting the informational needs of the organization's management. After the new system has been functioning for a few months, the consultants will evaluate the system's effectiveness in accomplishing its intended purpose (or purposes). If the revised system has failed to solve previous systems problems or possibly caused new problems, further changes are required. The consultants will then repeat their systems study steps in order to make the necessary revisions. Follow-up reviews by the consultants should be performed periodically throughout the system's life to determine if further changes are necessary.

DISCUSSION QUESTIONS

13-1. When a company acquires a computerized data-processing system for the first time, what are some of the company's incremental costs that normally are incurred during the preparation of the physical site?

13-2. Tommy Solton has just finished the implementation of an online, real-time system for his client, The Archy Bald Company. Tommy works as a management consultant in the firm called Consultants For Success. At a cocktail party the other night, Tommy was bragging to one of his friends about how efficient he was in performing the systems study work for The Archy Bald Company. Tommy's comments were as follows:

> The company's president, Archy B. Bald, was very frustrated with the slowness of reports

coming from his organization's manual data-processing system. About three days before I was contacted by Bald, I read an advertisement in a trade journal about IBM's new 1984-model on-line, real-time computer system. Therefore, as soon as I arrived at The Archy Bald Company to discuss my potential systems job, I immediately showed this advertisement to Mr. Bald. He was so excited that he immediately hired me to supervise the implementation of the online system. The next day I contacted the IBM people and a short time thereafter, the new computer system was delivered and implemented into the company. Before the company's employees knew what had happened, their old and outdated manual system had been replaced by this superior computerized system. Bald was so pleased with my speed in implementing the new system that he paid me an extra $500 over the fee I charged his company. I deserved this extra money, of course, because Bald's new accounting information system should function so efficiently that he will never need to call me back for further work.

What are your reactions to Tommy Solton's above comments?

13-3. Jordan Finance Company opened four personal loan offices in neighboring cities on January 2, 1984. Small cash loans are made to borrowers who repay the principal with interest in monthly installments over a period not exceeding two years. Ralph Jordan, president of the company, uses one of the offices as a central office and visits the other offices periodically for supervision and internal auditing purposes.

Mr. Jordan is concerned about the honesty of his employees. He came to your office in December 1984 and stated, ''I want to engage you to install a system to prohibit employees from embezzling cash.'' He also stated, ''Until I went into business for myself I worked for a nationwide loan company with 500 offices and I'm familiar with that company's system of accounting and internal control. I want to describe that system so you can install it for me because it will absolutely prevent fraud.''

Required

a. How would you advise Mr. Jordan about his request that you install the large com-

pany's system of accounting and internal control for his firm? Discuss.

b. How would you respond to the suggestion that the new system would prevent embezzlement? Discuss.

(AICPA Adapted)

13-4. Curtis Company operates in a five-county industrial area. The company employs a manual system for all its record keeping except payroll; the payroll is processed by a local service bureau. Other applications have not been computerized because they could not be cost-justified previously.

The company's sales have grown at an increasing rate over the past five years. With this substantial growth rate, a computer-based system seemed more practical. Consequently, Curtis Company managers engaged the management consulting department of their public accounting firm to conduct a feasibility study for converting their record-keeping system to a computer-based system. The accounting firm reported that a computer-based system would improve the company's record-keeping system and still provide material cost savings.

Therefore, Curtis Company decided to develop a computer-based system for its records. Curtis hired a person with experience in systems development as manager of systems and data processing. His responsibilities are to oversee the entire systems operation with special emphasis on the development of the new system.

Required

Describe the major steps that should be undertaken to develop and implement Curtis Company's new computer-based system.

(CMA Adapted)

13-5. The following statement was made in this chapter: ''The follow-up phase of a systems study should continue throughout the life of a company's system.'' What is the meaning of the preceding statement? Do you agree or disagree with this statement? Why?

13-6. The Len Hoss Consulting Firm is currently in

the process of completing the systems implementation activities for converting the Samuel Company's manual data-processing system to an online computerized system. The major reason for eliminating the manual system was its slowness in providing needed reports to Samuel Company managers. Because of unexpected delays in performing specific implementation activities, the Len Hoss Consulting Firm's chief consultant, Stanly Dungfield, is concerned about meeting the scheduled implementation completion date. The only remaining implementation activity to perform is the testing of the new computer system by parallel conversion and the subsequent elimination of the old manual system. Stanly's assistant, Katie Fignery, has suggested that the original estimated date for completing the new system's implementation still could be met if direct conversion rather than parallel conversion were used.

Assuming that you are Stanly Dungfield, how would you react to Katie Fignery's suggestion? Discuss.

13-7. Al Hedge recently graduated from college and is working as a management consultant for the Diamond Consulting Firm. Al's first major consulting assignment involved a systems study to convert the Bogie Company's manual system for processing accounts receivable and inventory transactions to batch-processing computerized methods. Upon performing the analysis and design phases of the systems work, Al and his consulting team were ready to implement the newly designed system. Markus Williams, the chief consultant supervising the Bogie Company's systems work, assigned Al the job of preparing a PERT network diagram for the system implementation activities. Because Al is unfamiliar with PERT networks, he has asked Percy Sneed (who has been with the Diamond Consulting Firm for five years) to advise him regarding the preparation of a PERT network diagram.

Assuming that you are Percy Sneed, first explain to Al Hedge the advantages, if any, of utilizing a PERT network diagram in systems implementation. Second, describe for Al

Hedge the procedures that should be used to prepare the PERT network diagram for implementing the necessary changes into the Bogie Company's system.

13-8. When converting a company's manual data-processing system to a computerized system, two of the implementation activities required are: (1) establish controls and standards, and (2) convert data files to computer storage media. What is the rationale for performing implementation activity (1) before implementation activity (2)?

13-9. One of the important implementation activities that must be performed when converting a company's manual system to a computerized system is "determining the necessary functional changes in the system." Describe some of the functional changes in a company's system that would likely be necessary when management consultants perform this systems implementation activity. (*Note:* Because you are not provided with detailed information about an actual systems change, your discussion will have to be in general terms. Feel free, however, to make any reasonable assumptions about an imaginary company that is currently undergoing functional changes.)

13-10. What is the purpose of the follow-up analysis phase of a systems study? Describe some of the specific activities that management consultants would perform in their follow-up work.

13-11. *Required:*

For each of the three situations identify the problem, discuss the issues, and recommend the action to be taken by the named employees—Don Kline, John Wood, and Tim Spencer.

a. The Majina Plant of Reed Manufacturing Co. produces automotive components and accessories. Recently Don Kline has been assigned to the accounting department at the Majina Plant. Kline spent a great deal of time reviewing the plant's operations, operating procedures, and reporting practices in order to become familiar with the plant's activities.

During this review period, Kline discovered an inconsistency in the reporting of production and finished goods inventory to corporate headquarters. The normal rejection rate on components manufactured at the Majina Plant was 5 percent. The production reports indicate that Majina's experience during periods of normal production activity was much better than this rate. Yet when reporting to corporate headquarters, Majina reported spoiled units at above 5 percent rather than the lesser quantity of actual units spoiled.

Further analysis disclosed that the units representing the difference between the actual and reported defective rates were stockpiled in the plant warehouse for future disposition. The plant would release these units whenever they were needed. These "extra" units proved convenient especially when the plant was asked to operate at a higher than normal production rate or when there was an unexpected order to be filled. Under such circumstances extra demands were placed on Majina manufacturing facilities. This usually resulted in a larger than normal defective rate. The "stockpiled" units could then be released to offset the large spoilage rate.

By the end of the year Majina's inventory and production records were in agreement with the actual activities. Don Kline was concerned about the reporting discrepancies which occurred throughout the year.

b. Olson Company is a small manufacturer of jewelry. Although most of Olson's jewelry is sold directly to retailers, its fine jewelry is sold on a consignment basis to jewelry stores.

Olson Company's jewelry was well known for its excellent quality. The company's operations have been profitable in the past. Recently, the company has expanded its operations and, as a result, has experienced some cash flow problems. In October 1984, Olson Company applied to the Merchants Union Bank for a loan to finance the acquisition of raw materials to be used in making jewelry. The bank was familiar with the company and its operations. As part of its normal procedure, the bank required Olson Company to submit its audited financial statements for the past year (1983) and unaudited statements for the 9-month period ending September 30, 1984.

John Wood, manager of the accounting department, was on vacation when the 9-month financial statements were prepared and submitted with the loan application. Upon Wood's return the company treasurer asked him to review the financial statements and pending loan application. During this review Wood noted that the revenues appeared disproportionately large and the inventory of finished goods unusually small. After further checking he discovered that the sales reflected revenue from jewelry still out on consignment at the end of September. The error resulted in a material overstatement of income. By the date when the loan is expected to be approved, however, a large part of the consigned goods probably will be sold.

c. Daton Community Hospital is a 140-bed hospital serving a community of 75,000 people. The hospital employs bookkeeping machines to maintain its accounts receivable and other related accounting records. The hospital administrator believes the hospital's volume is great enough to justify the use of computerized record keeping. However, he does not think the hospital should acquire its own computer system at this time.

A member of the accounting department who had some systems experience was assigned the responsibility of surveying the service bureaus in the area. After considerable study he recommended that the hospital should seriously consider Compudat, Inc. The administrator confirmed that Compudat was a growing and well-respected service bureau by checking with business organizations that were using or had used Compudat's services. Preliminary arrangements were made with Compudat to begin designing a system for Daton Community Hospital, and the accountant who made the recommendation was named project manager.

Tim Spencer, a member of the administrator's staff, was given the responsibility of monitoring the progress of the conversion to computerized billing. At a meeting between Spencer and the project manager, the project manager reported that the work was progressing as planned. The project manager further commented, "Compudat's work is very professional and progressing on schedule. I'm not surprised because my cousin Max, who owns Compudat, is well qualified in systems and computer operations. He has been able to put together an excellent staff in a short period of time. I'm so convinced of his ability that I provided him with 25 percent of his capital needs in the form of a long-term loan."

Tim Spencer asked the project manager if the administrator was aware of his family ties with Compudat, Inc. The project manager stated that he did not know because the topic had never been discussed in their conversations. Spencer has heard from others that work is progressing smoothly on the new system.

(CMA Adapted)

13-12. Appliance City (a discount store selling all types of home appliances such as toasters, ovens, etc.) has recently acquired a computer system for handling its customer billings, its inventory records, and other accounting functions. The following notice appeared on the employee bulletin board:

> TO: Appliance City Bookkeeping
> Department Employees
> FROM: Monroe Cycle, President
> REGARDING: Job Termination
>
> It is my sad duty to inform each of you that by the end of this work week, your services as employees will no longer be needed at Appliance City. Our new computer system for processing accounting transactions eliminates the functional duties which you have been performing for the company. I am aware of the loyal services performed by many of you to help foster Appliance City's sales growth. However, modern computer technology cannot be given a back seat in our company's future growth plans. I hope that each one of you will feel free to drop by the store any time and say hello.

Required

a. Comment upon the technique used by Appliance City's president to notify the bookkeeping department's employees of their termination. If you disagree with the president's method of notifying his terminated employees, what would you do differently?

b. Discuss some possible alternative steps that might have been taken by Appliance City's president instead of terminating all the bookkeeping department employees. (Note: In answering this part of the question, make any reasonable assumptions regarding Appliance City's system.)

13-13. Three different methods for implementing a new system into an organization were analyzed in this chapter—modular conversion, parallel conversion, and direct conversion. Discuss the advantages and the disadvantages of using each of these three systems implementation methods.

13-14. A new batch-processing computer system is currently being implemented into the Monarch Company. Bob See, president of the Monarch Company, is concerned about the fact that many of the implementation activities are requiring more time to complete than originally estimated by the company's consultants. To hasten the implementation process, See has asked the consultants to postpone the establishment of systems controls and standards until after the new computer system has become operative. Assume that you are one of the consultants participating in the implementation of the Monarch Company's computerized system. How would you react to the request made by Bob See? Explain.

13-15. When implementing an online, real-time computer system to replace a company's previous manual data-processing system, one of the important implementation activities is to convert the data files. Why is this implementation activity necessary? Give several specific illustrations of how accounting data files would be converted. (*Note:* Make any assumptions that you feel are necessary regarding the operational characteristics of the company for which the computerized system is being implemented.)

13-16. In your opinion, which one of the four major systems study phases (analysis, design, implementation and initial operation, and follow-up) would you consider the most difficult to perform? Why?

13-17. When converting a company's manual data-processing system to a computerized system, two of the required implementation activities are: (1) establish controls and standards, and (2) acquire computer programs. What is the rationale for performing implementation activity (1) before implementation activity (2)?

PROBLEMS

13-18. The Dryfus Company specializes in large construction projects. The company management regularly employs the Program Evaluation and Review Technique (PERT) in planning and controlling its construction projects. The following schedule of separable activities and their expected completion times have been developed for an office building which is to be constructed by Dryfus Company.

Activity Description	Predecessor Activity	Expected Activity Completion Time (in Weeks)
a. Excavation	—	2
b. Foundation	a	3
c. Underground utilities	a	7
d. Rough plumbing	b	4
e. Framing	b	5
f. Roofing	e	3
g. Electrical work	f	3
h. Interior walls	d,g	4
i. Finish plumbing	h	2
j. Exterior finishing	f	6
k. Landscaping	c,i,j	2

Required

Identify the critical path for this project and determine the expected project completion time in weeks.

(CMA Adapted)

13-19. Edward Jones is responsible for finding a suitable building and establishing a new convenience grocery store for Thrift-Mart, Inc. Jones enumerated the specific activities that had to be performed and the estimated time to complete each activity. In addition, he prepared a PERT network diagram, which appears below, to aid in the coordination of the activities. The list of activities to locate a building and establish a new store is as follows:

Activity Number	Description of Activity	Estimated Time Required
1-2	Find building	4 weeks
2-3	Negotiate rental terms	2 weeks
3-4	Draft lease	4 weeks
2-5	Prepare store plans	4 weeks
5-6	Select and order fixtures	1 week
6-4	Delivery of fixtures	6 weeks
4-8	Install fixtures	3 weeks
5-7	Hire staff	5 weeks
7-8	Train staff	4 weeks
8-9	Receive inventory	2 weeks
9-10	Stock shelves	1 week

Required

A. Identify the critical path for finding and establishing the new convenience store.

B. Edward Jones would like to finish the store two weeks earlier than indicated by the schedule, and as a result, he is considering several alternatives. One such alternative is to convince the fixture manufacturer to deliver the fixtures in four weeks rather than in six weeks. Should Jones arrange for the manufacturer to deliver the fixtures in four weeks if the sole advantage of this schedule change is to open the store two weeks early? Justify your answer.

C. A project such as the one illustrated by the PERT network diagram for the new convenience store cannot be implemented unless the required resources are available at the required dates. What additional information does Jones need to administer the proposed project properly?

(CMA Adapted)

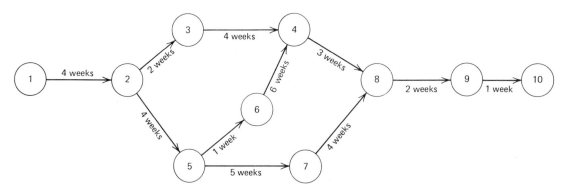

CASE ANALYSES

13-20. *Wenrock's Use of Delmo's Computer System*

Delmo Inc. is a wholesale distributor of automotive parts which serves customers in the states east of the Mississippi River. The company has grown during the last 25 years from a small regional distributorship to its present size.

The states are divided into eight separate territories in order to service Delmo customers adequately. Delmo salespersons regularly call upon current and prospective customers in each of the territories. Delmo customers are of four general types:

1. Automotive parts stores.
2. Hardware stores with an automotive parts section.
3. Independent garage owners.
4. Buying groups for garages and filling stations.

Because Delmo Inc. must stock such a large variety and quantity of automotive parts to accommodate its customers, the company acquired its own computer system very early and implemented an inventory control system first. Other applications such as cash receipts and disbursements, sales analysis, accounts receivable, payroll, and accounts payable have since been added.

Delmo's inventory control system is comprised of an integrated purchase ordering and perpetual inventory system. Each item of inventory is identified by an inventory code number; the code number identifies both the product line and the item itself. When the quantity-on-hand for an item falls below the specified stock level, a purchase order is automatically generated by the computer. The purchase order is sent to the vendor after approval by the purchasing manager. All receipts, issues, and returns are entered into the computer daily. A printout for all inventory items within product lines showing receipts, issues, and current balance is prepared weekly. However, current

status for a particular item carried in the inventory can be obtained daily if desired.

Sales orders are filled within 48 hours of receipt. Sales invoices are prepared by the computer the same day that the merchandise is shipped. At the end of each month, several reports are produced which summarize the monthly sales. The current month's sales and year-to-date sales by product line, territory, and customer class are compared with the same figures from the previous year. In addition, reports showing only the monthly figures for product line within territory and customer class within territory are prepared. In all cases the reports provide summarized data; i.e., detailed data such as sales by individual customers or product are not listed. Terms of 2/10, net 30 are standard for all of Delmo's customers.

Customers' accounts receivable are updated daily for sales, sales returns and allowances, and payments on account. Monthly statements are computer prepared and mailed following completion of entries for the last day of the month. Each Friday a schedule is prepared showing the total amount of accounts receivable outstanding by age—current accounts (0–30 days), slightly past-due accounts (31–90 days), and long overdue accounts (over 90 days).

Delmo Inc. recently acquired Wenrock Company, a wholesale distributor of tools and light equipment. In addition to servicing the same type of customers as Delmo, Wenrock also sells to equipment rental shops. Wenrock's sales region is not as extensive as Delmo's but the Delmo management has encouraged Wenrock to expand the distribution of its product to all of Delmo's sales territories.

Wenrock Company uses a computer service bureau to aid in its accounting functions. For example, certain inventory activities are recorded by the service bureau. Each item carried by Wenrock is assigned a product code number which identifies the product and the product line. Data regarding shipments received from manufacturers, shipments to customers (sales), and any other physical inventory changes are delivered to the service bureau daily, and the service bureau updates Wenrock's inventory records. A weekly inventory listing showing beginning balance, receipts, issues, and ending balance for each item in the inventory is provided to Wenrock on Monday morning.

Wenrock furnishes the service bureau with information about each sale of merchandise to a customer. The service bureau prepares a five-part invoice and records the sales in its records. This processing is done at night, and all copies of each invoice are delivered to Wenrock the next morning. At the end of the month, the service bureau provides Wenrock with a sales report classified by product line showing the sales in units and dollars for each item sold. Wenrock's sales terms are 2/10, net 30.

The accounts receivable function still is handled by Wenrock's bookkeeper. Two copies of the invoice are mailed to the customer. Two of the remaining copies are filed—one numerically and the other alphabetically by customer. The alphabetic file represents the accounts receivable file. When a customer's payment is received, the invoice is marked "paid" and placed in a paid invoice file in alphabetic order. The bookkeeper mails monthly statements according to the following schedule:

10th of the month	A-G
20th of the month	H-O
30th of the month	P-Z

The final copy of the invoice is included with the merchandise when it is shipped.

Wenrock has continued to use its present accounting system and supplies Delmo management with monthly financial information developed from this system. However, Delmo management is anxious to have Wenrock use its computer and its information system because this will reduce accounting and computer costs, make the financial reports of Wenrock more useful to Delmo management, and provide Wenrock personnel with better information to manage the company.

At the time Delmo acquired Wenrock, it also hired a new marketing manager with experience in both product areas. The new manager wants Wenrock to organize its sales force using the same territorial distribution as Delmo to facilitate the management of the two sales forces.

The new manager also believes that more useful sales information should be provided to individual salespersons and to the marketing department. While the monthly sales reports currently prepared provide adequate summary data, the manager would like additional details to aid the sales personnel.

The acquisition of Wenrock Company and expansion of its sales to a larger geographic area has created a cash strain on Delmo Inc., particularly in the short run. Consequently, cash management has become much more important than in prior years. A weekly report which presents a reliable estimate of daily cash receipts is needed. The treasurer heard that a local company had improved its cash forecasting system by studying the timing of customers' payments on account to see if a discernible payment pattern existed. The payment pattern became the model that was applied to outstanding invoices to estimate the daily cash receipts for the next week. The treasurer thinks that this is a good approach and wonders if it can be done at Delmo.

Questions

A. Identify and briefly describe the additional data Wenrock Company must collect and furnish in order to use the Delmo data-processing system. Also, identify the data, if any, currently accumulated by Wenrock which no longer will be needed due to the conversion to the Delmo system.

B. Using only the data currently available from the Delmo data-processing system, what additional reports could be prepared that would be useful to the marketing manager and the individual salespersons? Briefly explain how each report would be useful to the sales personnel.

C. If Delmo Inc. were to use a cash forecasting system similar to the one suggested by the treasurer, describe:
1. The data currently available in the system which would be used in preparing such a forecast.
2. The additional data that must be generated.

3. The modifications, if any, that would be required in the Delmo data-processing system.

(CMA Adapted)

13-21. *Westside Electric Company*

The production manager, chief accountant, marketing manager, and president of Westside Electric Company are discussing the feasibility and the desirability of changing their batch-processing system to an online, real-time system. Westside Electric is a medium-sized firm that manufactures small electrical equipment. Its business is centered in Los Angeles.

Presented below is an excerpt from their conversation.

PRESIDENT: After reading this article in the *Harvard Business Review* on the benefits of a real-time system, I think we should seriously consider changing our present system to an online, real-time system. Our operations are large enough so that we probably could benefit from a simple real-time system. I was thinking of a three terminal arrangement . . . something like this:

Warehouse terminal ⟷ ⟶ [CPU] ⟵ [On line file storage]
Factory terminal ⟷ ⟶
Main office terminal ⟷ ⟶

MARKETING MANAGER: You know, a real-time system could give us a tremendous competitive advantage. Under this automated design, a perpetual inventory system could easily be implemented. Then, with each order placed, the inventory files could be immediately updated. My sales staff would thus be able to know at any point in time how much stock we have available for sale.

CHIEF ACCOUNTANT: If the general ledger and accounts receivable subsidiary ledger are also online, the accounts within these two ledgers could be updated at the time orders are placed. This will facilitate invoice processing. Moreover, the billing and collection process will probably be faster.

PRODUCTION MANAGER: Not only that, but if the information from invoices could be transmitted through a data terminal to our warehouse, we could speed up delivery to the customers. A faster turnover would certainly be beneficial to the whole organization.

PRESIDENT: The *Harvard Business Review* article also indicated that with an online system, you are able to immediately test the outcomes of various decision alternatives. This can help us with our planning process. . . . I can see that the real-time system will be extremely beneficial to us. Shall I call in the IBM people to see what kind of package they can give us?

CHIEF ACCOUNTANT: But, wait a minute! Installing a real-time computer system is a big undertaking. I understand that the costs associated with the hardware and software of a real-time system as well as the operating costs are far more than with our present batch-processing system.

MARKETING MANAGER: You accountants are always worried about costs. Surely, in the long run, the benefits from the real-time system will exceed any of the associated costs. After all, many of the larger firms already have installed real-time systems. I haven't heard anything negative about their automated systems.

CHIEF ACCOUNTANT: But it's more than the cost aspect that I'm worried about. What about the control of the system? For example, how am I to monitor the use of the terminals? How can my internal auditing staff make sure that only authorized personnel have access to the terminals? You know that if someone inputs incorrect data accidentally or intentionally, our files will be contaminated. With so many input points, it will be difficult, if not impossible, to track down errors. Under batch processing, we have control over the computer hardware, so the unauthorized personnel problem is minimal. Furthermore, because similar transactions are

413

PRODUCTION MANAGER:
processed at one time, we can easily pinpoint any mistakes in the input data.

I think you're exaggerating the security aspect of a real-time system. Granted there must be security precautions, but let's not go overboard.

CHIEF ACCOUNTANT:
Well, let me tell you, if incorrect data are input and you make decisions using the invalid data, your effectiveness as a manager will be significantly reduced. The real-time system can make a major contribution to our operations, but until this security and data reliability aspect can be controlled, I don't think we should implement such a system.

PRESIDENT:
There's more controversy to this proposal than I anticipated. Let me think about what all of you have said. If you have any more input, I want to hear from you.

Questions

A. Assuming that the president is still strongly in favor of implementing an online, real-time system, what would be his next step?

B. One of the management accountant's major functions is to maintain good internal control within his or her organization. Are the chief accountant's concerns about security and data reliability warranted? Why or why not? Are there ways to overcome security and data reliability problems? Discuss.

14

Systems Study: Resource Acquisition

Among the important questions that you should be able to answer after reading this chapter are:

1 What resources are vital to the accounting information system and why is their maintenance an ongoing task?
2 Why is resource acquisition important to the organization that already has an accounting information system?
3 Why would a company buy a second computer?

4 How can you test a second programming package without interfering with the processing of the first?
5 What is important when "shopping" for a software package? How are such packages evaluated?

INTRODUCTION

The computerization of the accounting information system represents the beginning, not the culmination, of a system's life cycle. During the normal course of activity, the EDP center staff, the individuals who provide data to the information system, and the individuals who use the processed data flowing from the information system will learn how to use the system effectively, identify weaknesses (such as unforeseen processing errors), and in general gain experience with the system at hand. Thus, it is natural that, in the course of time, follow-up studies of an accounting information system will reveal areas for improvement. Some of the improvements are called "maintenance," which consists of correcting problems that are detected during the normal course of processing activity. Other types of improvements, however, involve the realization that yet one more task or processing activity might be added to the existing information system at great advantage.

We have chosen to treat this special topic of accounting information system improvement as a separate chapter entitled "Resource Acquisition," because at some point the improvement desired in the system will call for an acquisition expenditure decision. Thus, the follow-up phase of a system's study includes not only the identification of unforeseen system weaknesses, but also cost/benefit analyses of how such weaknesses can be corrected. Three possibilities present themselves. Sometimes, the correction is a minor one, as for example, when asking a programmer to spend a few hours changing the format on an accounting report. At other times, the cost outlay is considerable and greater care must be exercised in making a judicious decision. (A complete cost/benefit analysis, as discussed and illustrated in Chapter 12, would likely be performed if a major cost expenditure was anticipated for making the system improvements.) Finally, in the extreme, an idea for system improvement assumes such magnitude as to cause EDP management to consider scrapping its entire hardware or software network in favor of a more modern, cost-effective system.

In this chapter we shall examine the problem of resource acquisition from the standpoint of the company that now has a computerized accounting information system but has an opportunity to acquire additional system support at additional cost. In particular, therefore, we assume that the prerequisite hardware and software for an accounting information system is present but that further processing is contemplated. To achieve this processing, the firm must acquire additional hardware resources, additional software resources, and possibly additional personnel resources. It should be noted that a company's hired management consultants, as part of their systems study follow-up analysis work (discussed in Chapter 13), would likely play a major role in a decision regarding the company's acquisition of additional resources. This chapter assumes, however, that resource acquisition decisions are made by a firm's own employees rather than by outside management consultants.

In the present chapter, we examine the acquisition of hardware, software, and personnel resources under separate headings in the discussions below. This categorization is somewhat misleading, however, because the decisions to acquire these resources are rarely independent considerations. Our breakdown is merely for the sake of convenience in presentation.

HARDWARE ACQUISITION

The technological advances which have taken place in the computer industry during the last 10 years have been so fast and so revolutionary that almost any central processing unit purchased before 1976 is now an antiquated machine. Computer costs have followed a similar course. Just as a $100 pocket calculator of a few years ago can now be bought for $10.99, computer costs have been reduced by a similar *order of magnitude*! Thus, it is not surprising to find that the managers of many large data-processing centers are continually in the market for new equipment—they cannot afford not to be!

Today there are many options available to the computer center interested in acquiring additional hardware. Besides the simple purchase of computer equipment, the firm may rent, lease, or lease with option to buy. Because there are significantly different tax factors associated with each of these possibilities, the decision becomes complicated. Chapters 11 and 12 have discussed the major considerations required in the overall assessment process when acquiring a complete new system. Thus, we shall focus here primarily upon the problem of hardware acquisition from the standpoint of system improvement. At times, this system improvement will require little more than the acquisition of an extra terminal or tape drive. Alternatively, however, there are other occasions when management considers such a large expansion of its data-processing activities that a more radical approach than the simple acquisition of additional peripheral equipment seems necessary. We examine both of these possibilities in the paragraphs below.

Single-Item Hardware Acquisition

Figure 14-1 lists representative prices for several common pieces of computer equipment likely to be considered as add-on acquisitions to an already

	Typical Prices
Disk drive	$1,050–$2,250
Tape drive	600– 1,000
CPU memory (256K)	400– 900
Card reader	150– 900
Printer	400– 2,200
CRT terminal	50– 150

Figure 14-1. Lease prices for selected computer hardware (12-month lease, including maintenance.)

existing computer installation. These prices are for a standard 12-month contract which includes maintenance. Given the fact that a tape drive or disk drive costs almost $1000 a month to lease, for example, it is clear that peripheral machinery is not inexpensive. Thus, although such a dollar amount would not represent a very large proportion of the operating budget of a typical commercial computer installation (a rough rule of thumb is 1 percent of a company's retail business), it is certainly large enough to warrant a careful analysis of needs before making an acquisition decision.

The reasons why an EDP center might wish to expand its inventory of processing equipment are many and varied. An extra tape drive, for example, might permit the purchase of a more efficient sorting program which, in turn, might significantly reduce the processing time required for an accounts-receivable application. Similarly, the acquisition of an additional disk drive might permit the user to switch to a more productive operating system, enabling a larger number of terminals to use the computer simultaneously for such applications as an online bank-teller system or an inventory-control system. Finally, because almost all central processing units are "I/O bound" (i.e., "input/output bound"), meaning that they can compute faster than their peripherals can read or write, it is common to find computer center personnel shopping for an extra disk drive or printer in order to increase the productive utilization of the computer center's CPU. The list goes on and on, but by now you get the idea.

At times, the justification for the acquisition of additional hardware is clear and the acquisition

decision is thus primarily contingent upon the budget of the computer center. At other times, however, the reasons for further hardware expenditures are not so obvious, and a careful analysis of the utilization of existing hardware may be in order. A convenient way to monitor the use of a company's computer equipment is a *run log of equipment utilization* as illustrated in Figure 14-2. This log can be updated manually by the computer operator, or, if necessary, reconstructed from the system console log of the central processor. Note that the primary function of the equipment-utilization log is simply to keep track of what computer equipment is being used when. An entire day's use of all the machinery of the computer center may be recorded on a single page, or a few pages, if desired.

It might be mentioned that some operating systems come with optional *hardware-monitor modules* built into them. These modules automatically keep a record of what peripheral equipment is being used each second the central processor is in operation. Printouts showing equipment utilization, number of input/output operations, and even the number of parity errors and automatic tape-cleaning operations can be obtained. In larger computer centers supporting time-sharing operations and more than 20 disk drives, the manual maintenance of an equipment run log is virtually impossible. In these circumstances, the hardware monitor of the operating system is the only effective way the computer center can accurately log equipment utilization.

There is an interesting story about an EDP manager who switched jobs from one computer installation to another. When he first arrived at his new location, his subordinates submitted a request for the acquisition of an additional tape drive. Before agreeing to the subordinates' wishes, the new manager had his computer operators maintain an equipment run log for a month in order to determine the utilization of the existing equipment. The tabulations revealed not only that the additional tape drive was unnecessary, but that two existing tape drives could be returned to the manufacturer and still fulfill the center's data-processing needs completely!

417

RUN LOG

ALAN COMPANY
125 King Street
Honolulu, Hawaii 96822

Operator _Susan Chandler_   Employee I.D. No. _532-65-2133_

Date(s) _January 21, 1984_

Time (hour) AM	Tape Drives				Disk Drives					Card Read/Punch		Printer		
	1	2	3	4	1	2	3	4	5	1	2	1	2	3
00:00–00:15	✓	✓			✓					✓		✓	✓	
00:15–00:30	✓	✓	✓	✓	✓	✓	✓			✓		✓	✓	✓
00:30–00:45	✓	✓			✓	✓		✓			✓	✓	✓	✓
00:45–01:00		✓			✓		✓			✓		✓	✓	
01:00–01:15		✓		✓		✓	✓			✓	✓	✓		
. . . .														
23:45–24:00														
Total Times														

Figure 14-2. A Run Log of Equipment Utilization. Check marks indicate use during the time period.

Once the decision to obtain a new piece of data-processing equipment has been made, it remains to decide upon a make or model. In the past, there has been a strong tendency for processing centers to exhibit a *one-vendor syndrome* when it comes to hardware purchases, that is, to buy or lease additional equipment from the manufacturer of the installation's existing hardware. At one time, this often made sense because the computer equipment of different manufacturers were rarely compatible with each other and complicated interfacing made "mixing" peripheral equipment too costly.

Today, this interface reservation would no longer seem to be a problem. There are many vendors of reliable hardware that are "plug-to-plug" (i.e., electronically) compatible with IBM, Burroughs, or Control Data Corporation equip-ment. Thus, it is usually wise for the user to examine carefully what is available on the open market and weigh the decision on the basis of needs, costs, and availability of equipment maintenance.

Systems Acquisition

Inasmuch as Chapters 11–13 have examined systems acquisition in depth, we shall not repeat those discussions here. Rather, our purpose at this point is to suggest that a company need not simply upgrade its existing accounting information system hardware in order to accommodate additional processing requirements. Three other possibilities would be: (1) to acquire a second central processor and additional input/output equipment, enabling the computer center to share the additional processing burden between two units, (2) to acquire a "dedicated" computer system that would be used exclusively for one processing application, and (3) to rent processing time from an external computer center. Each of these three possibilities is discussed briefly below.

The second computer. The acquisition of an additional central processing unit (alternative 1) often makes sense when an organization is seriously contemplating large processing expansions that are expected to overload the existing system. The University of California at Berkeley, for example, successfully used two interlocking Control Data Corporation central processing units for years: one unit performed data-processing computations, whereas the other handled the many remote terminal requests and input/output tasks required by the University's information system network.

There is also a strong used-computer market in which to shop for second-hand equipment. Some of this equipment can be very cost-effective to a computer installation that does not require highly sophisticated technology to accomplish its processing goals. Like any other piece of used equipment, of course, an older central processing unit is likely to need more repairs and will therefore carry a more costly maintenance contract. Nonetheless, if the acquisition price is low enough and processing feasibility for the equipment's use appears likely, the late-model CPU may be a good option. Thus, at least in the late 1960s, several computer experts convinced corporate data-processing managers to trade in their newly acquired IBM 370 equipment and reacquire older, but at least at that time, cost-effective IBM 360's.

Dedicated computer systems. A dedicated computer system (alternative 2) is a computer system that is used for one primary data-processing function. For example, a bank will sometimes use a dedicated computer as an inquiry system for customers interested in confirming their account balances. The bank will delegate other data-processing functions to a different computer system that is more appropriate for batched (as opposed to online) data-processing tasks. Dedicated computer systems are often smaller than large, general-purpose computer systems because their uses are more limited and their tasks are constrained to one type of data-processing function. As a result, the total cost of dedicated computer systems may be less than the marginal cost of upgrading a medium-sized computer system to a larger computer system. In some instances, it just makes more sense for a company to acquire an entire additional system, albeit a small one, than upgrade its existing facilities.

An especially convenient type of dedicated computer system is the so-called *turn-key computer system*. This type of system comes complete with both hardware and compatible software specifically developed for a particular set of processing tasks and is thus a complete, independent processing entity unto itself. The convenience of acquiring such a computer system rests in the avoidance of any coordination efforts with existing hardware equipment or software packages. Therefore, the purchaser is ready to begin data processing just as soon as the equipment is installed. In this sense, the new computer system is analogous to a new car that has been readied for use—the purchaser simply "turns the key" and starts out.

The acquisition of a dedicated computer system offers several advantages. One is the aforementioned cost factor. Another is that the acquisition of the dedicated system has the potential to cause minimal disruption of normal data processing—the new computer system can be acquired, tested, and implemented on an independent basis. This avoids the risk of "contaminating" a company's day-to-day processing of "live" accounting transactions. Finally, the acquisition of a dedicated system may yield valuable insights into the processing tasks involved in an accounting application. In the course of evaluating the merits of a dedicated computer system for processing inventory transactions, for example, a utility company in Hawaii discovered that its old, card-handling system created a lag of almost three weeks from the time that the initial inventory data was prepared to when the inventory records were finally updated in a master file. The acquisition of a dedicated computer system to process the company's inventory transactions in real time assured the utility company that its inventory balances would be updated immediately when inventory transactions took place.

Dedicated computer systems also have their drawbacks. These computer systems tend to be more limited in what they can do, constrained in how much peripheral equipment can be added to the CPU "mainframe," and restricted in the kinds of programming languages and other software support that can be utilized in the data-processing environment. Another consideration is the fact that dedicated hardware is flexible but dedicated software often is not. Thus, for example, the software written for an inventory-processing system to run on a small computer is usually inefficient when run on a larger computer system. (The acquisition of inflexible programming support is definitely not recommended, although it sometimes proves a necessary evil.) A final negative factor is the observation that, by definition, dedicated systems provide little opportunity for interfacing with other accounting information system software. Thus, for example, if a company's inventory-processing software package were to be run in a dedicated environment, there would be limited opportunity for this accounting application to interface with the general ledger accounting system run on the company's main computer system. In addition, the inventory information stored on the files of the dedicated system may not be available for use in a generalized accounting information system data base.

The fact that both positive and negative arguments can be made for the dedicated computer system should prompt management to look carefully at the particular requirements involved in its data-processing applications. Most of the techniques discussed in the preceding chapters on systems study (Chapters 11–13) apply to the analysis, design, and implementation of the smaller, dedicated accounting information systems. Rather than review the techniques again, the reader is referred back to these chapters for criteria important to such a decision as acquiring a dedicated computer system.

Service bureaus and time-sharing organizations. The opportunity to rent processing time on an "outside" computer (alternative 3) is often exploited by both large and small business firms. Usually, the external hardware is owned by a service bureau (discussed in Chapter 12), which is in business specifically to sell computer processing time. Special arrangements, however, between any two companies (one having a computer and the other not having a computer) are also observed in practice.

Service bureaus are excellent sources of computing power when additional hardware and software is contemplated for the expanding computer center. For example, the service bureau is often a good source of modern software which the service bureau can make available to its clients at nominal charge. Companies can thus use this software either on an experimental basis or on a continuous one if desired. This feature is therefore especially advantageous to the firm interested in acquiring new software and wishing to try it out first.

Even when an organization has purchased new software already, the service bureau may come in handy. For example, the service bureau having prior experience with the particular software acquired can be consulted for advice or asked to modify the package's programs to meet the needs of the user organization. The service bureau may also be able to provide such additional support as (1) add-on programs that interface with the user's software package and that accomplish certain additional accounting functions, (2) training for the user-organization's personnel, and (3) paper forms and other printed matter.

Many companies choose to maintain their own computer centers and, at the same time, use a service bureau on a continuous basis for some of their data-processing requirements. For example, if a company were interested in using a new accounts payable accounting package but felt it would not use this accounting package often enough to justify its long-term purchase or lease, the company might turn to a service bureau, thereby incurring a smaller fee which would be paid only for the package's use. Similarly, if the company wished to use a software package that could not be run on the company's present hardware configuration, but could be implemented on the hardware of the service bureau, the company might turn to the service bureau for assistance. Finally, if a company were working its own computer center around the clock, yet wished to execute additional programs (such as a program to process monthly billings) on a routine basis, the service bureau might serve as a useful source of additional computing power.

Many of the preceding comments would also apply to time-sharing organizations (discussed in Chapter 12). Time-sharing organizations are often more limited in the types of computer programs available, however, and most do not employ large programming staffs for software development or modification. Nonetheless, time-sharing organizations would be especially attractive to companies wishing to expand their computer capabilities in the direction of online computing services. For example, a company wishing to computerize its perpetual inventory system functions might consider a remote-terminal network linked to a time-sharing computer. Even if the terminals were scattered around the country, the computer system would link these terminals together in a unified information system. As a result, current information regarding the balances of individual inventory items would be available to the company at all times. In addition, the company's management would have current information concerning the cost of merchandise sold from its sales transactions.

Like service bureaus, time-sharing organizations have the potential to be cost-effective for companies with limited-data processing budgets and no real need to purchase their own computers. At one point in time, the economies of scale in the large computer systems operated by time-sharing organizations gave rise to the concept of the *computer utility*. The idea was for the time-sharing organization to act like a telephone company or electric company, metering out computer services over telephone lines and billing customers much like any other utility. However, several factors have conspired to keep the vision of the computer utility from becoming a reality. Among these are: (1) the variability in the needs of individual users, (2) the problems of data security, and (3) the advent of very inexpensive minicomputers and microcomputers. Of the above factors, perhaps the most telling has been the advent of inexpensive minicomputers and microcomputers. As detailed more thoroughly in the next chapter, such computer systems have reduced the costs of computer power to the point where it is often cheaper to buy an entire minicomputer and install it at the local site of the user than to acquire computer services from a time-sharing organization.

SOFTWARE ACQUISITION

The previous chapters on systems study have stressed the importance of good software to perform the processing tasks required by the accounting information system. Often, in fact, it is the presence or absence of good software application programs that proves to be the crucial factor in the selection of one hardware manufacturer's equipment over another. Thus, for example, one computer manufacturer may have superior hardware in terms of processing capability but still lose sales to the manufacturer of "weaker" equipment with better-developed software. The discussion of software acquisition is relevant either to a company implementing its first computer system or to a company making modifications to its previously-implemented computer system as part of the follow-up analysis work performed in a systems study.

The acquisition, development, and/or maintenance of computer programs for the accounting information system is a continuing process in almost all active EDP centers. In the United States, for example, it is estimated that over 1 percent of our gross national product—over $10 billion—is spent on software each year. In addition, surveys of software users reveal that the software budget of the typical user of electronic data processing systems is rising by 20 percent each year.

Usually, a company will begin with a comparatively "bare bones" system, adapting it to the company's processing needs and acquiring additional software support as time and resources permit. Because typical EDP centers of companies have at least as much money invested in software support as they do in hardware, it is clear that software acquisition is an activity that involves important resource decisions. In this section, we analyze factors important to these decisions.

For the purposes of discussion, it is convenient to group all computer-program software into three major categories: (1) operating systems, (2) utility programs, and (3) application programs. Of these three categories, the first has traditionally been the exclusive domain of the hardware manufacturers. This is because the hardware manufacturer usually develops systems software in parallel with hardware, and therefore has time to work on improved versions of its operating systems before such software actually reaches the market. Thus, generally speaking, very few companies develop their own operating systems. In recent years, however, both the hardware manufacturers and the users of EDP systems themselves have sometimes modified acquired operating system programs in order to accommodate special idiosyncrasies of a particular computer center. One of the most common modifications, for example, is to revise the operating system to cause a third (or fourth) generation operating system to "emulate," that is, simulate, the behavior of a second (or third) generation system in order to permit companies with "old" software to run their programs on newer, more efficient machines. Thus, emulation eases the transition to higher-generation equipment.

The biggest market in software products, however, lies in utility and application programs (i.e., our second and third categories of computer programming support). In these areas, hardware manufacturers, software-development houses, and even individual user companies of EDP systems have been able to develop good software

products. Thus, in the last few years, the supplier market for these products has been growing and becoming increasingly more competitive. As a result, it is now possible to purchase (or lease) a sorting program or an accounts payable routine from a large number of vendors.

From the perspective of the individual EDP center, the basic software decision is whether to purchase (or lease) an already developed package (i.e., proprietary software) from an independent vendor or to develop a particular software system "in-house" (i.e., by the user company itself). The software-acquisition decision is a classic case of the make-or-buy decision especially in the area of application programs. All other things being equal, of course, the choice is simple: acquire the most effective system (based upon its expected costs versus its expected benefits) whether this means an in-house development job or an external acquisition. Because all other things rarely are "equal," however, it is necessary to look further into the factors that weigh heavily in the decision-making process. We examine proprietary software and in-house development in the discussions below.

Advantages of Acquiring Software from an Independent Vendor

The advantages of acquiring proprietary software would include (1) low risk, (2) lower cost, (3) shorter implementation time, (4) standardization, (5) internal control, and of course, (6) avoidance of an in-house effort. Each of these advantages is described briefly below.

"Low risk" refers to the likelihood of the company that sells the software going out of business. At one point in time, most software vendors depended upon program software sales not only for their revenues, but also for their very existence. Many of these software companies were small in size and had limited, easily outdated products. Consequently, the software vendors often went bankrupt, thereby making recourse to their assistance extremely risky in the event of software problems. In some instances, an absence of documentation for some of this software and a buyer's fear that the software company would not stand behind its product added to these risks. As a result, EDP users were very hesitant to purchase programming packages from independent software vendors, even though the software was often of superior quality. Thus, earlier EDP users looked to the big hardware manufacturer in the (sometimes mistaken) belief that at least the hardware company would be around to service its products when trouble developed. Ironically, history has revealed that such confidence in the "big" hardware manufacturers has often been misplaced. For example, G.E., RCA, and Xerox corporations each spent millions of dollars to develop, manufacture, and promote their own computer equipment, only to pull out of the computer market several years later when anticipated profits failed to materialize. Companies that were then utilizing RCA or Xerox equipment were faced with limited future hardware support or software support.

Today, it would appear that many of the above-mentioned fears no longer apply. Most experts in the field recognize the software-development field as a legitimate, thriving industry in its own right, and recent surveys indicate that program packages developed by independent software houses are often preferred, in terms of quality, to packages developed by hardware manufacturers. Many hundreds of such software houses are operating profitably today.

"Lower cost" refers to the purchase price of the proprietary software in comparison with an in-house development effort to write and document the same set of programs. A commonly quoted ratio is a purchase-cost amount of one-fifth the developmental figure. Thus, as a general rule of thumb, it will cost a company five times as much to write its own software package as it will to buy a comparable system on the open market. It would stand to reason that purchase costs would be cheaper than development costs inasmuch as the software vendor is able to spread the development costs over more users, thus enabling a lower cost-per-package. Because almost all user companies require FORTRAN or COBOL compilers, sorting routines, and elementary statistical packages, these items tend

to be fairly inexpensive to acquire, whereas highly specialized inventory-control packages or integrated accounting routines—for example, routines that simultaneously process a company's credit sales transactions, update the accounts receivable subsidiary ledger, and update the inventory file as well as compute the cost of merchandise sold relating to the sales transactions—tend to be comparatively more expensive to acquire.

"Lower cost" also refers to the fact that the software vendor's price is a "known-in-advance" charge to the user. Sometimes, this is a one-time fee but more often it is a monthly rental agreement or lease contract of specified duration. Usually, the agreement or lease includes a limited "maintenance contract." The maintenance contract guarantees a restricted amount of modification work to be performed by the vendor on the purchased system to correct errors which are detected during the course of the software's use. The contract also usually guarantees continued maintenance for a specified period beyond the acquisition date. It should be noted, however, that there is nothing necessarily standard about such agreements and both the buyer and seller are free to negotiate whatever contract they wish.

"Shorter implementation time" refers to the fact that most of the software vendor's programs have been pretested and that the documentation is already available prior to purchase. Thus, implementation problems are usually limited to compatibility constraints with the user company's present hardware and software systems. This does not mean that any new computer package written for a company's existing equipment is ready for use "off the shelf," but rather that the software vendor is likely to have anticipated the user's needs and that the package may be expected to perform according to the specifications outlined by the seller.

"Standardization" means that the programs are usually written in conformance with "standard" programming procedures and that adequate documentation will be available for the user company to (1) understand the individual programs comprising the package, and (2) make modifications as necessary. Standardization normally suggests a certain degree of conformance of the programming package with existing vendor software perhaps already in use by the potential buyer. For example, a company might start out with a simple general ledger accounting system developed by an independent vendor for an IBM System/34 computer. Later, it might be advantageous for this company to purchase a specific inventory-processing package from this same vendor because the new package could also run on the System/34 computer and could also be expected to interface easily with the existing accounting programs.

Standardization also assures the user company that the processing effort—for example, preparing the payroll—will always be performed the same way regardless of the location of the processing system. This means both uniform accounting procedures and consistent output listings. For companies with multiple EDP centers scattered across the country, this type of standardization is sometimes invaluable.

We have discussed the importance of internal control in Chapters 7–10. Programs that handle sensitive data must be secured from unauthorized use. This security is especially important in a time-sharing and/or remote-terminal environment. Similarly, programs that process financial data must be free of both accidental and intentional error, and must also provide for both internal and external auditing. Because such features are required by a variety of potential data-processing users, the purchased packages are likely to contain many of these important security features as a matter of course.

"Avoidance of an in-house effort" has been listed as a separate category because of several factors. As noted above, in-house development is usually more costly than commercial purchases, and this, in and of itself, may be sufficient to motivate the user company toward the purchase decision. However, the purchase option may be the only option if the programming expertise required for the development job is not available in a company and/or the company's EDP budget cannot be expanded to permit acquisition of additional developmental staff.

Another consideration is the fact that in-house developmental projects are notoriously overoptimistic in what can be done with the time and resources allotted the programming effort. In one project, for example, all the software for a planned two-year systems-development job familiar to the authors had not been completed by the fifth year of effort, even with the addition of two extra systems analysts! This situation is not unusual in the history of systems development.

Advantages of In-House Development

The merits of acquiring proprietary software are considerable but the acquisition of proprietary software also has drawbacks. Because the disadvantages of acquiring proprietary software are also the advantages of in-house software development, we shall take a positive attitude and look at the problem from this latter perspective. Among the arguments favorable to in-house software development are: (1) advantages of "custom" work, (2) cost, (3) avoidance of proprietary software revisions to conform to company standards, (4) assurance of system compatibility, (5) minimization of start-up costs and training costs at implementation time, and (6) higher EDP morale. Each of these advantages is examined in greater detail below.

Perhaps the most important advantage of the in-house developmental effort is that it is a custom job. For certain specialized applications, of course, the in-house programming effort may be the only choice available. But even if this were not the case, the in-house option still has the advantage of providing the user just what processing is desired in just the proper amounts. Thus, the user does not pay for unnecessary frills or options and, of course, the user company is also free to design whatever unique features are needed in its organization. Moreover, because the effort is performed in-house, changes and additions are also likely to be easier to make because the programming expertise required for such alterations already resides within the user company's EDP staff. Maintenance becomes easier for the same reason. Finally, because the user's EDP staff is familiar with the system, training and implementation can be performed in parallel with the developmental effort. Thus, staffing requirements for the new system can be forecast in advance, suggestions from employees within the system can be incorporated into the system while it is still under development, weaknesses in the new system can be corrected more easily, and so forth.

In the previous discussion regarding the acquisition of software from an independent vendor, "lower cost" was considered to be one of the advantages. However, in specific situations, the cost of an in-house effort may still prove to be cheaper in the long run. For example, rarely can an accounting package be bought from a software vendor, "thrown" on the company computer, and run directly "off the shelf." Rather, revisions must almost always be made to make the package programs conform to company standards, file structures, input/output equipment configurations, and so forth. In a *DATA-MATION* survey of nearly 500 EDP users of proprietary software, for example, only 16 percent indicated that their acquisition did not require modification, whereas 29 percent indicated that the package required modification by the software vendor, and 55 percent indicated that the package required modification by the user.* Little can be inferred from the 29–55 split between vendor modifications and user modifications because much of this depends upon the initial contract agreement. However, the fact that a very clear majority of users find that additional programming effort must be expended in order to bring a particular application programming system "on board" means that, on average, additional resources beyond the initial purchase expenditure must be included in the cost calculations for a given package acquisition. The conclusion: it *can* cost more to purchase and make extensive modification to a proprietary software programming package than to develop the same system in-house.

Because proprietary software is written for the mass market, there is no assurance that any particular package will be compatible with a user company's other application programs. The in-house effort assures system compatibility. Thus, such considerations as successful data-file interface (to assure that the system can use the company's existing files in their present form) and hardware limitations (e.g., CPU and input/output capacities) are not a problem with the in-house effort because the software programs are designed with these constraints in mind. Proprietary software may not have this compatibility.

Systems compatibility must also include a volume dimension. For example, it usually does not make sense for a company to acquire an externally-prepared accounts receivable program written for a large data-processing user with 50,000 accounts if the intended application presently processes one-tenth of this volume. Of course, room for expansion is important in any data-processing system, and the accountant is wise to allow for a reasonable increase in processing volume as projections of future data flows might warrant. However, processing programs for large-scale users are rarely cost-effective for the small-scale data processor; these programs usually require peripheral hardware and software which the small-scale user would find too expensive to acquire. For example, an article in *Computerworld* reported that 14 international airline companies installed an airlines reservation system software package which the vendor had developed and sold previously to several domestic lines. After implementation, it was found that the system was operating at only one-third of anticipated capacity and had necessitated far more hardware than was actually needed.†

The problem of start-up costs and training costs associated with new systems have been discussed in previous systems study chapters, and thus need not be analyzed again here. There is little doubt that such costs will be incurred no matter which new software system (i.e., proprietary or in-house) is acquired. The real ques-

---

*Daniel J. Tanner, "User Ratings of Software Packages," *DATAMATION* (December 1975), pp. 138–154.

†"14 Airlines Pan IBM on Software," *Computerworld*, Volume 1, No. 9 (February 19, 1975).

tion is not under which option such costs can be avoided but rather, assuming equal benefits, under which option these costs can be minimized. For reasons mentioned above, it would appear that the in-house strategy may have a "start-up," or "training" advantage. For example, there is much to be said for the convenience of having immediate access to the programmers and systems analysts who designed the system, and being able to rely upon dedicated company personnel to provide instructional support and guidance during the initial implementation and subsequent operation of the new system.

Our last advantage of in-house development is higher EDP morale. For a particular EDP installation, of course, it is possible that the present staff of programmers are so busy that they would welcome the purchase of proprietary software and thereby avoid the additional responsibility of a new system development. However, this is not always the case. Avoiding the in-house effort is sometimes considered a management "vote-of-no-confidence," and in isolated cases may actually bring about a reduction in the size of the existing programming staff. Moreover, there is the "not-invented-here" syndrome—an attitude held by many programmers and organizational systems analysts that only an in-house effort will truly serve the processing needs of the company installation(s). This attitude undoubtedly has inspired some programmers to call proprietary software "out-house" programming. In any event, however, it is clear that the decision to pursue a system-developmental effort in-house is a vote of confidence for the company's existing team of programmers and systems analysts. Morale is positively affected, and this consideration in and of itself may sometimes tilt the decision toward the in-house project.

The Selection Process

If the individuals involved in the follow-up analysis of a company's accounting information system prefer to enter the market for a software package, still further decisions must be made regarding a choice of software supplier. The number of independent vendors that offer reliable products has grown over the years, thereby expanding the software for application programs and utility programs.

A richer variety of software has led to more difficult decision-making from the standpoint of the user company because there are more alternative program packages to evaluate. Cost, of course, continues to be an important constraint in the final decision, but cost, in turn, is dependent upon a myriad of other factors that affect the implementation and ultimate operating performance of the system under study. Among such other factors are: (1) reliability, (2) compatibility, (3) security, (4) flexibility, (5) training, (6) maintenance, and (7) recoverability. Because we have discussed all of these factors within the context of systems study in the prior three chapters as well as in the present chapter, we shall not dwell on them here. Of greater importance from the standpoint of the user company is how to tell whether a given software package meets minimal levels of performance in each of the above seven dimensions when the potential purchaser or lessee has never used the package before.

At a minimum, a company interested in acquiring additional software can ask for a detailed prospectus of the vendor's product. Normally, this documentation will provide detailed information concerning the hardware and software needed to run the system, volume constraints, and the nature and extent of support which the potential user can expect from the software vendor. Experts suggest that the potential user prepare a checklist of needs and performance requirements in advance so that several competitive products can be evaluated with uniform criteria. Thus, for example, an organization with three disk drives and which is presently in the market for an accounts receivable package would probably eliminate from further consideration those proprietary-software packages that required four or more disk drives.

For situations in which two or more software packages are able to meet minimal performance specifications, a further evaluation using a point-scoring method can be made to determine the best choice. A typical approach would be to allocate 100 points among those factors considered critical for the particular software application under study, giving more potential points to those areas considered most important by the user. For example, a company considering the acquisition of a payroll accounting system might use a scheme awarding (at most) 25 points to "reliability," 20 points to "compatibility," 10 points to "security," 20 points to "flexibility," 10 points to "training," and 15 points to "recoverability." The company would then proceed to rate the software candidates with this scoring system, choosing that accounting package with the highest aggregate score. Cost can also be included as an evaluation factor in the analysis if competing products are not equivalent on a cost basis.

To illustrate the point-scoring system for the evaluation of accounting information system software, suppose that the Alan Company has decided to acquire a new accounts payable computer-software package. A committee of Alan Company personnel is formed and a survey of user requirements is taken. Thus, the committee has interviewed members of the accounting department, the purchasing department, and even the receiving department to ascertain which characteristics in the evaluation process it should consider most important. These items are listed on the left margin of Figure 14-3.

For simplicity, assume that two proprietary software packages have been identified which appear to satisfy the requirements of the users interviewed in the company's initial survey. (The identification of more than two packages would not change the analysis appre-

Category	Possible Points	Vendor A	Vendor B
I. Ease of Use	40		
(a) Operations	8	8	7
(b) Administration interface	8	5	4
(c) Customer service	8	2	6
(d) Response time	8	8	3
(e) Amount of input required per transaction	8	8	2
II. Ease of Conversion	30		
(a) Adherence to company reporting	10	10	7
(b) Business services	10	6	6
(c) Interface with existing general ledger package	10	8	0
III. Vendor Support	30		
(a) Back-up in case of loss or disaster	6	6	5
(b) Programming assistance for changes	6	6	6
(c) Training	6	5	0
(d) Software upgrade support	6	3	3
(e) Miscellaneous support	6	2	4
Totals		77	53

Figure 14-3. The point scores awarded two software vendors in the Alan Company's evaluation of accounts payable computer systems.

ciably, however.) One of these packages is marketed by vendor A, the other by vendor B. Both lease for about the same cost, so price is not an issue. Therefore in evaluating these packages, the members of the committee have decided upon three major decision criteria: (1) "ease of use," (2) "ease of conversion" (to the Alan Company's existing accounting information system), and (3) "vendor support." On the basis of its earlier survey, the committee has further decided to weight "ease of use" by 40 points, "ease of conversion" by 30 points, and "vendor support" by 30 points. Weights for subcategories such as "adherence-to-company-reporting" within the general category "ease of conversion" are determined on an equal-weight basis. Thus, for example, with three subcategories under "ease of conversion," each subcategory is weighted as one-third the total weight of the general (ease-of-conversion) category, or in this case, 10 points apiece.

The weights identified above are maximum values that can be assigned to each subcategory element identified in the evaluation. The actual number of points to be awarded each vendor package for a given subcategory will be dependent upon the software package's individual merit. For example, a software package whose output reports would have to be completely revised in order to make them compatible with the informational needs of the user company would be given an actual score of zero for the "adherence-to-company-reporting" subcategory. On the other hand, a package whose report formats were already perfectly acceptable to management would be awarded the highest possible score for the same "adherence-to-company-reporting" subcategory, or in this case, 10 points.

Figure 14-3 illustrates a set of possible ratings for our hypothetical evaluation problem. After all of these points have been awarded, the scores are summed to obtain a final score for each software vendor. In this case, vendor A's final score of 77 turns out to be considerably higher than Vendor B's final score of 53. Thus, in this case, the Alan Company should acquire the computer software package of vendor A. It might

also be pointed out that if both vendor scores were low, the company might choose to acquire neither software package. In this instance, it would probably serve the company's best interests to search further for suitable accounting software.

Although costs were not formally considered in the preceding example, such an evaluation criterion can easily be added to the analysis. In the extreme, of course, it is possible to make cost the *only* evaluation criterion. In this case, the basis for the decision is simple: choose the vendor with the cheapest package. More typically, however, cost is but *one* of the important criteria usually considered in the evaluation of a software package. In these latter circumstances, it is possible to treat cost as a separate evaluation category, assign "cost" the point-score weight considered appropriate for its relative importance in the overall decision, and proceed as outlined above.

The recommendations that result from such point-scoring evaluations are sometimes surprising even to the participants themselves. For example, one EDP manager reported that he had been placed in charge of acquiring an accounts receivable package for his medium-sized company and that he had narrowed the choice to two possibilities: a large hardware manufacturer's (the XYZ Company) software package and an alternative software product developed by a small, but reputable, independent software house. The EDP manager knew that it would be a simple matter to gain budgetary approval for the hardware manufacturer's product inasmuch as XYZ's position in the data-processing field was well known to the manager's superiors and the executive staff of the company trusted XYZ products. Management's unfamiliarity with the products of the alternative software house would make managerial approval of the alternative product more difficult. Thus, at first glance, the XYZ Company choice seemed obvious.

As a conscientious worker, however, the EDP manager decided to perform an objective evaluation. He therefore quizzed the potential users of the new system to determine needs and requirements, created weights for a point-scoring evaluation, and directed his own staff to rate the two packages according to the criteria developed in his survey. To everyone's surprise, the alternative software product won by a wide margin! The independent software house's system turned out to have twice the number of desirable features as the XYZ Company alternative, and was also cheaper to acquire. The EDP manager used the point-scoring evaluation results to justify the alternative purchase in his report to top management, and successfully acquired the product to everyone's satisfaction.

Not every software acquisition necessarily has a happy ending. Some software products look good on paper but turn out to be "dogs" when placed in actual use. Thus, the real "acid test" of proprietary software lies in "hands-on" experience with the software product under study. Acquiring such experience without risk is difficult, but not impossible. Some software vendors are willing to let potential users try their products free, or at nominal cost, for a 30-, 60-, or even 90-day trial period. Usually, the company testing the software product will run its old programs and the new programs in parallel so that unforeseen problems with the new system will not affect the company's normal operations. Some software vendors will even make their own computer equipment available to the potential user company for testing purposes in order to avoid tying up the potential user's equipment, in order to render assistance to the new user, and of course, in order to make sure the potential user is aware of all the advantages of the vendor's product(s). Experience with a software product is one of the most efficient types of software evaluation. Thus, when acquiring software packages for accounting information systems, testing before buying is a good idea.

PERSONNEL ACQUISITION

Ultimately, it is people who are responsible for the care and feeding of the accounting information system. Moreover, it is people who must ultimately make use of the valuable information that the accounting system generates. Thus, personnel comprise a key resource which affects the success or failure of the accounting information system. Individuals are needed for a myriad of positions ranging from key-entry operators and data coders to programmers, budget analysts, cost accountants, systems analysts, and data-processing managers. Both men and women prove equally competent in performing the necessary responsibilities in these positions and, because of the rapid technological advancements in the field of automated accounting, it is one of the most dynamic careers open to young people today. We shall look more closely at career opportunities momentarily. First, however, we shall turn our attention to the general problem of personnel acquisition for the accounting information system.

Usually, recognizing the need for "extra help" when expanding the activities within the computer center is fairly straightforward. For example, the decision to add an extra work shift in order to accommodate the data-processing requirements of a new accounting application package automatically carries the need for an extra computer operator, perhaps an extra programmer to be on duty in case of emergencies, and an extra accountant who understands the accounting concepts and procedures associated with this new accounting application package. Similarly, the acquisition of a new payroll-processing system will simultaneously require at least one full-time programmer to perform necessary maintenance and to implement the changes initiated by the system's users. Thus, generally speaking, the acquisition of either new hardware or new software will imply the need for additional personnel, or at least additional hours of staff time, and therefore automatically require the incurrence of additional staffing costs.

From the standpoint of the organization seeking to hire additional personnel support for its computerized accounting information system, the most important qualifications are almost always experience and technical competence. For example, computer operators and key-entry personnel are expected to know the functions of specific pieces of equipment, and the organization's job-specification descriptions usually pinpoint how many years of experience with what hardware and/or software is desired. Although the number of years of experience required of a job applicant is a somewhat arbitrary figure, there can be little doubt but that experience is crucial in the hiring of personnel. Similarly, with regard to technological expertise, knowledge of specific programming languages is critical when hiring programmers, and sometimes, familiarity with specific types of software such as utility programs, data bases, or operating systems is also required.

Most companies use general aptitude tests and specialized data-processing tests to screen prospective employees. In the United States, the Computer Programmer Aptitude Battery (or CPAB) and the Programmer Aptitude Test (or PAT) have been used extensively in an attempt to measure the ability of an individual to perform vital data-processing tasks. Included in such tests are (1) exercises in recognizing letter sequences, (2) exercises in manipulating algebraic terms, (3) tasks requiring rapid approximations to numerical calculations, (4) exercises in flowcharting, (5) exercises requiring the subject to draw inferences from stated facts, and (6) general tests of reasoning, analytical skills, and verbal expression. Several of the larger companies in the United States have their own specialized examinations as well.

In addition to the above "technical" tests, many companies also use standardized psychological tests to augment the review profile of prospective employees. In a survey of 581 United States and Canadian firms employing a total of 25,000 programmers and systems analysts, for example, it was found that 70 percent of these organizations used psychological tests of one kind or another.* The most common were the Wonderlic Personnel Test, the Thurstone Test of Mental Alertness, and the Otis Quick Scoring Mental Abilities Test.

An alternative to hiring additional staff to perform certain data-processing tasks is to *con-*

*Peter Saville and Dan Simpson, "Selection Testing for Computer Staff," *Data Processing* (September–October 1973), pp. 318–323.

tract the work out to another firm, and some companies have found such an alternative attractive. In the case of programmers and/or systems analysts developing new systems, advantages of contracting would include the fact that (1) the contracting company avoids the paperwork, salary payments, and other responsibilities attendant with a hiring commitment, (2) the contracting company will usually pay a fixed fee regardless of how much work ultimately goes into the contracted data-processing project, (3) the debugging, testing, and other developmental work is usually performed on alternate hardware and therefore does not tie up the contracting company's computer, and (4) the contracting company may acquire technical expertise not available within its own staff. Hiring part-time or temporary help has also proven quite beneficial to companies with substantial seasonal fluctuations in data-processing volume, enabling the organization to obtain needed assistance during "rush times" but avoid expensive payrolls during "lulls."

There are also disadvantages to work contracting. Security problems would be one. The need to specify precisely what is required from the outside contractor is a second disadvantage. Because contract work is not cheap, expense would be a third disadvantage. In short, therefore, the decision to contract programming work "outside" has both pros and cons. Hard-and-fast guidelines are difficult to establish; it is necessary to examine each individual company's data-processing needs on a case-by-case basis.

Careers in Automated Accounting Information Systems

At the time this book was written, there were over 2.5 million people working in jobs connected with computers and computerized data processing. Although not all of these jobs were accounting oriented, it is hard to imagine the data-processing center of even the smallest computer installation not performing at least one accounting function. Thus, the need for trained individuals to assist in the areas of data generation, data processing, and information-dissemination for accounting information systems appears clear. At least in the near future, therefore, the prospects for employment in the area of automated accounting information systems are extremely good. Large auditing firms, manufacturing firms, and governmental agencies visit college and university campuses regularly in search of potential employees possessing an understanding of both accounting and computers.

Many companies offer extensive training programs once the new recruit is hired. Most noticeable would be the training courses of the computer hardware manufacturers, although the large auditing firms also run extensive training classes designed to assist individuals to function in an automated data-processing environment. "Generalized training" is rarely standard, however. Thus, some new hirees have been disappointed to find themselves in short courses designed to give them the minimal background they will need to accomplish the tasks required of a specific project rather than in more general courses which offer instruction in the broad concepts associated with performing a systems study.

Earning potential is also of interest in the area of automated accounting information systems. Partly because the supply of skilled personnel has not kept pace with the demand, increments in salary levels have more than outpaced inflation. Moreover, once the young college graduate is hired, the chances for advancement are quite good. Thus, in short, it is the authors' belief that a career in automated accounting information systems is a very promising one.

SUMMARY

The acquisition of a computerized accounting information system is part of the follow-up study work in a system's life cycle. This chapter has focused upon resource acquisition for the operational accounting information system and has categorized "resources" into three major areas: "hardware," "software," and "personnel." It was noted, however, that this categorization was convenient but also misleading; it is almost impossible to consider an expenditure in one of these areas without simultaneously examining an investment in each of the other two.

Our discussion of hardware focused upon such things as (1) the acquisition of additional peripheral equipment like additional tape drives, disk drives, or printers, (2) the acquisition of a second computer system (possibly a dedicated computer system), and (3) the use of a service bureau or time-sharing organization. Service bureaus, for example, are advisable for an organization with limited capital, limited programming expertise, or the need for extra processing time on a computer.

The section on software acquisition discussed the importance of programming support for the ongoing accounting information system. It was noted that a high percentage of the typical investment in a data-processing system is for software, and that this software must be maintained, updated, and modified if it is to remain useful to management. The chief decision that must be made in the area of software acquisition is whether to develop the software in-house or to acquire the software from an independent vendor (i.e., proprietary software). The proprietary software option has the advantages of low risk, lower cost, shorter implementation time, standardization, internal control, and avoidance of in-house development. The in-house development option has such advantages as custom work, assurance of compliance to company standards, minimization of start-up and training costs associated with external systems, and higher staff morale. If the decision is made to acquire proprietary software, a further choice must sometimes be made between competing software systems offered by vendors. It was recommended that in such circumstances, a survey of needs be made and that a point-scoring method be used to determine the best software package from among the alternatives.

The last section of the chapter on personnel acquisition recognized the importance of a trained staff to operate an automated accounting information system. In this discussion, the need for individual competence in automated accounting information systems was stressed, and it was observed that a number of general psychological tests as well as technical tests have traditionally been used to screen applicants for jobs involving automated systems. Career opportunities in accounting information systems are both promising and rewarding, at least at the time this book was written.

DISCUSSION QUESTIONS

14-1. Are the decisions relating to hardware acquisition, software acquisition, and personnel acquisition independent, or are they somehow connected? Discuss, giving specific examples of either independence, or dependence, among these three elements.

14-2. Discuss the importance of cost in the resource-acquisition process. Why is cost often considered only one of many factors in the decision analysis?

14-3. There are significantly different income-tax treatments associated with lease versus purchase plans for hardware and software resource acquisitions. Drawing from your previous courses in accounting, identify the important tax advantages and disadvantages that would be expected with each option.

14-4. What factors should be considered in the decision to lease a tape drive or disk drive from a computer hardware manufacturer? What reasons might the EDP manager have for seeking to acquire yet additional hardware equipment?

14-5. What is the meaning of the statement: "Most central processors are I/O bound"? What is the implication of "I/O bound" to a company in terms of resource acquisition?

14-6. Discuss the use of the equipment log or hardware monitor as an aid in the hardware-acquisition decision process. Could such logs or monitors be utilized for software acquisition? Discuss.

14-7. What is meant by the "one-vendor syndrome"? Does such a term apply equally to hardware as well as software, or is there a difference? Is there such a thing as "two-vendor syndrome?"

14-8. Tom Henry, the planning vice-president of Elaine Dolgin's Dress Company, had just been presented an expenditure proposal from his EDP processing manager, Lee Tracy. As the vice-president began to read the report, he realized that his right-hand person was suggesting that the company purchase a second computer system for its data processing. Throwing the report down on his desk, he roared to his secretary: "Get that woman in here! Buying another computer system is the last thing this company needs!" What possible justification could Lee Tracy have had for acquiring a second computer system if the company already had one?

14-9. Of what value is the "used" computer market in the area of resource acquisition? Is buying a used computer much like buying a used car—that is, like buying "someone else's headache"?

14-10. What is meant by a "dedicated" computer system? What is meant by a "turn-key" computer system? Discuss the pros and cons of acquiring such systems.

14-11. Why is good software considered crucial in the selection of hardware systems?

14-12. What is meant by the term *software support*? What factors would determine whether software support was "good" or "bad"?

14-13. Why have computer operating systems generally been developed by hardware manufacturers, whereas utility programs and application programs have also been developed by independent software vendors?

14-14. Discuss the acquisition of computer software as a make-or-buy decision. What are the advantages of the "make" option? What are the advantages of the "buy" option?

14-15. What is meant by "recoverability" in computer programs? Why might such a factor be important to a data-processing center?

14-16. Charles Sterling Portwood, III, was the well-respected head of the Pan Pacific Computer Company. The company had flowered from a proprietorship organization in 1975 to a partnership organization (with three partners) in 1983. The company had recently acquired a small business computer to perform some of its data-processing functions, and Lance O'Neal, a company employee, had been put in charge of acquiring a payroll software package. After a week's searching, Lance reported to his boss, "CP, I think I've found just the right thing for us. This payroll system will run on anything from a small computer up to a million-dollar central processor and handle the payroll for up to 10,000 employees. If we buy it tonight, I can probably have it running by tomorrow in time for the end-of-the-month payroll." Comment.

14-17. Why do some programmers call proprietary software "out-house software?"

14-18. What criteria are important in the selection of proprietary software? Would such criteria apply equally to the acquisition of a payroll-processing package and an inventory-control package?

14-19. How can a company interested in the software package of a particular vendor acquire "hands-on" experience before committing itself to a lease or purchase contract? What advantages and disadvantages might be involved in each of the ideas you have suggested?

14-20. Describe the point-scoring method of evaluating computer software. Could such a method also be used when evaluating computer hardware? What drawbacks can you foresee in the use of such an evaluation mechanism?

14-21. Why are the requirements for new personnel so closely associated with the acquisition of new computer hardware and/or software? Can you think of any hardware and software acquisition situations in which no new personnel would likely be required? Discuss.

14-22. Discuss the use of psychological, general aptitude, and specialized data-processing tests in screening programmer and system-analyst job applicants. What are the advantages and disadvantages of using such tests? Would you call such tests discriminatory? Why or why not?

14-23. In the text, it was stated that an alternative to hiring additional staff was to contract the work

out. Would you imagine that contracting would always be possible? What jobs would you say are better performed in-house and which jobs would you say are better performed on a contract basis?

14-24. In this chapter it was suggested that "security" might be one of the drawbacks in contract work involving accounting information systems. Elaborate on some of the security risks that might be involved in the area of contract work. Could security precautions ever be a reason to contract as well as a reason not to contract? Discuss.

14-25. At the most recent conference of Automated Accountants Anonymous, a local data-processing manager remarked: "When it comes to hardware or software acquisition, you never have to look further than IBM. Whenever possible, I even try to hire IBMers away from their jobs because I know what a great training program they have." Comment in light of the discussions in this chapter.

PROBLEMS

14-26. The Watson Research Corporation is interested in purchasing a new computerized accounts receivable billing package for its data-processing center. After an initial survey of requirements, Hong Sohn, the EDP manager, has found that ease of use, ease of conversion, and vendor support are the three characteristics considered most important to the new system's users. Two proprietary software packages appear to satisfy minimal levels of performance in these areas: one available from Integrated Bytes and Macros (vendor A), and one from American Teletype and Telegraphy (vendor B). Assume for the moment that both firms are reputable companies and that the costs involved in the acquisition of the two products are, for all intents and purposes, equivalent.

To assist him in a final decision, Mr. Sohn decides to perform a 60-point evaluation analysis. Selected members of his staff are formed into a committee for this purpose, and the two systems are rated as shown below. (A value of "5" is the highest score for a given category and a value of "1" is the lowest score for a given category.)

	Vendor A	Vendor B
I. Ease of Use		
(a) Operations	5	4
(b) Administration Interface	2	3
(c) Customer Services	1	4
(d) File Structures	3	1
II. Ease of Conversion		
(a) Adherence to Company Reporting	1	2
(b) Business Services	2	3
(c) Interface with Existing Accounts Receivable Package	1	3
III. Vendor Support		
(a) Back-up in Case of Loss or Disaster	5	5
(b) Programming Assistance for Changes	4	3
(c) Training of Users	5	2
(d) Hardware Upgrade Support	4	1
(e) Miscellaneous Support	3	2

Required

A. Suppose that the ease-of-use criterion were given a weight of "20," the ease-of-conversion criterion were given a weight of "15," and the vendor support criterion were given a weight of "25." Which system would be recommended according to the results of this evaluation?

B. What problems can you foresee in obtaining these weights and in allowing a committee, as opposed to an individual, to perform this type of analysis?

14-27. Refer to Problem 14-26 above. Suppose the two packages were not the same cost, but that Integrated Bytes and Macros' package cost approximately $15,000, whereas American Teletype and Telegraphy's cost approximately $10,000. In addition, suppose that "weights"

for the evaluations were (1) ease of use—30 percent, (2) ease of conversion—20 percent, (3) vendor support—25 percent and (4) cost—25 percent. Perform a reevaluation of the two systems and make a recommendation. (*Hint*: To convert the acquisition costs to a point scale, assume that a total of 25 points are to be divided between the two products in inverse proportion to cost.)

14-28. (Library Research) To attract clients, service bureaus often advertise in such publications as *Datamation, Computerworld,* and the *Journal of Systems Management*. Local newspapers and more technical trade publications are also likely sources of such advertisements. Find three advertisements by service bureaus and compare them. What special services appear to be emphasized in each advertisement? What kinds of features offered by these service bureaus would motivate customers to choose one service bureau over another?

14-29. (Library Research) What are the salary levels of programmers and systems analysts in your area of the country? What companies are hiring people with these skills in your locality? What are the fringe benefits? Do the hiring companies offer special training classes or on-the-job training? Is there opportunity for advancement in these jobs?

14-30. (Library Research) Bring into class copies of three programming or systems-analyst job descriptions. Using the class set as a data base, compare those jobs that are local with those that would require an individual to move to another part of the country. Are there any distinguishing differences?

14-31. (Library Research) Using the informational sources suggested in Problem 14-28 above, find three advertisements for the same type of accounting application software (e.g., three advertisements for payroll packages) and compare them for apparent desirability. Do all three software applications appear to do the same job? Are there more output reports provided with one software system as opposed to the others? Is one software system cheaper than the others? Can the three software systems all run on the same types of computers or is one or more of the systems limited to a specific hardware configuration?

14-32. The Giant S Manufacturing Corporation leases a small computer configuration for $1,200 a month. This payment includes machine usage for up to 176 hours per month and all hardware maintenance. Each metered hour of computer usage in excess of this base (176 hours per month) incurs a charge equal to 10% of the hourly rate for a base hour. The cost of operating personnel for the computer has been calculated at $9.50 per hour. Historically, the corporation has realized .8 of a computer usage hour for each operating personnel hour reported. Supply costs are estimated at $1100 per month. Lastly, the data processing center is assessed a monthly charge of $900 for use of building, utilities, management fees, etc. The Manager of Data Processing, Sandra Widener, estimates that 300 hours per month will be metered during the next year.

Required

A. Calculate the budget for the Giant S Manufacturing Corporation's data processing center for the next year.
B. Calculate the monthly budget.
C. Calculate the expected cost per operating hour.*

14-33. Refer to Problem 14-32 above. Betty Larance, the Manager of Systems and Programming for the Giant S Manufacturing Corporation, is in the process of completing an investigation for computerizing a manual accounts payable system. Thus far the following statistics have been determined: (1) $14,000 annually in clerical cost savings can be realized if the computer is utilized, (2) 25 meter hours per month will be required if the computer is utilized, and (3) supply costs will not differ significantly whether the computer is used or not.

Required:

Based on the data provided here and the calculations you performed in Problem 14-32, determine the following:

A. The cost of using the computer for processing accounts payable, based on the budgeted hourly cost.
B. The actual cost which would be incurred by Giant S if accounts payable was processed on the computer.
C. What would be your recommendation, based solely on the calculations that you have performed?†

CASE ANALYSIS

14-34. *Hawaii Teachers Association*

Hawaii Teachers Association (HTA) is a collective bargaining unit that represents approximately 9000 teachers employed by the State of Hawaii. The main functions of HTA are: (1) to negotiate employment contracts for public school teachers with the State, (2) to represent teachers in their grievance procedures, and (3) to develop and implement programs for enhancement of teachers' rights and status.

For these purposes, HTA employs about 15 professional staff workers and 20 clerical staff workers. Professional staff is engaged mostly in contacting teachers to assist them in their grievance procedures and to survey specific needs of school teachers. They also contact state officials and legislators to advocate teachers' interests in the state education administration. Accordingly, their work involves a lot of traveling throughout the state and the nation. The work of the clerical staff is to arrange professional staff's travel, to prepare research and survey papers, and to type various contract drafts, fliers, and newsletters. As a result, the clerical staff uses a large volume of paper and office supplies, and uses various kinds of office equipment such as a copying machine, mimeo and duplicator, collator, folder, inserter, and postage machine.

Sources of funds for HTA are: (1) a general fund that is collected from all bargaining unit members as a service fee and (2) a special fund that is provided by the national affiliate. Therefore, HTA must adhere strictly to the budgetary limits established for various funds. However, there is a difficult problem in controlling staff travel and office supplies. To cope with this problem, management has set forth detailed procedures for its accounting functions.

An accounting clerk or other staff worker who contemplates any office supply purchase or travel expenditure must fill out four copies of a purchase order on which he or she lists the name of the supplier, the items to be purchased (or itinerary of travel), and the estimated cost. The purchase order is then submitted for the approval of the Program Director, the Support Service Director, and the Executive Director. These directors examine the purchase order in light of their budget and organization objectives, and either approve or veto the expenditure.

If the expenditure is approved, the purchase order is routed to the Accounting Department where one copy is filed alphabetically until an invoice is received. A second copy is filed numerically for control purposes. The originator of the purchase order keeps a third copy, and he or she sends out a fourth copy of the approved purchase order to the outside supplier.

After office supplies are delivered or travel is completed, the supplier prepares and sends an invoice to the HTA office. In the Accounting Department, the invoice is compared with the approved purchase order. If there is no discrepancy between these two documents, the invoice is paid, the transaction is recorded in the cash disbursements journal, and these documents are stored alphabetically in a file cabinet. Transactions recorded in the purchases journal, the cash disbursements journal, and other journals are posted monthly to the general ledger. From these accounting records the monthly financial statements as well as the monthly expense reports are prepared and presented to the Executive Director, the Support Service Director, and the Program Director.

Management is not satisfied with the results of these accounting procedures because the information provided by the expense reports is not detailed enough to insure proper control and the reports are not available in time for controlling those staff members whose expenses exceed their monthly budget allotment. As a result, management has computerized its accounting procedures by using a service bureau for data processing.

Under the new system, accounting procedures remain virtually the same as before except that all transactions are recorded on coding sheets instead of journals. These coding sheets are forwarded to the service bureau where they are keypunched on punched cards for further processing. With this computerization, more detailed information is now available as to which HTA employee spends how much, for what purpose, from which fund, and what the balance is in each fund. Management's purpose to conduct timely control on employee expenses is not fulfilled yet, however, because it now takes more time than before to code all transaction data on a coding sheet. And often the service bureau is not able to finish accounting work in time due to an increased workload which occurs at the end of each pay period. As a result, the management of HTA is considering the purchase or rental of a small computer such as IBM System/3, Wang System, or one of several other brands. Management wants rapid and instant processing of HTA's accounting data.

Questions

1. Draw a document flowchart of the HTA's accounting procedures surrounding purchase orders.
2. What improvement(s) can you suggest to expedite preparation of the financial statements and monthly expense reports without using a computer?
3. HTA is having problems in getting timely reports even after computerization. What can you suggest to expedite the coding work of the Accounting Department?
4. Discuss the feasibility of the purchase or rental of a small computer system by HTA.

PART FIVE

Special Topics Related to Accounting Information Systems

Chapter 15
Accounting Information Systems for Small Business

Chapter 16
Accounting Information Systems for Service and Not-For-Profit Organizations

Three specific types of organizations that have not been discussed in prior chapters are the small business organization, the service organization, and the not-for-profit organization. (Of course, it is possible for either a service organization or a not-for-profit organization to have many of the same characteristics as a small business organization.) To function effectively in today's economic society, each of these three types of organizations needs a good accounting information system. Therefore, Chapter 15 will discuss accounting information systems for small business organizations, whereas Chapter 16 will examine accounting information systems for service and not-for-profit organizations.

Because the costs of computer hardware and software systems have been lowered in the past several years, many small companies are now able to afford computerized systems of their own for processing accounting data. Thus, in discussing the small business firm in Chapter 15, we will look at some of the various types of computer systems (such as minicomputers and microcomputers) that can satisfy the data-processing needs of small business organizations. In the Chapter 16 discussion of service organizations (e.g., law firms, CPA firms, and restaurants) and not-for-profit organizations (e.g., public universities, police departments, and federal government agencies), we will analyze some of the unique operating characteristics of these two types of organizations. In addition, several of the budgetary attributes associated with service and not-for-profit organizations will be discussed.

15

Accounting Information Systems for Small Business

Among the important questions that you should be able to answer after reading this chapter are:

1 **What is meant by the term *small* in small business?**

2 **What are the informational needs of the small business and how do these needs differ from those of the larger organization?**

3 **What is a matrix accounting system? Why is such a system especially suited for the small business?**

4 **Why have some companies treated the programmable calculator more as a Christmas gift for managers than as a serious computa-** **tional device for the processing of accounting information?**

5 **How should the small business choose the computer hardware and software for an automated accounting information system? Are there other alternatives available to the small business besides the purchase or lease of expensive computer products?**

INTRODUCTION

There was a time when a computer was just like a fancy car—only the very rich could afford one. Thus, in the "old days," say between 1955 and 1965, a computer was cost-effective only for those organizations that required data processing in large volumes. This virtually eliminated small businesses from using automated processing, thus making the computer a status symbol for big businesses. Today, modern technology has reduced the cost of computer systems to the point where almost anyone can afford to lease or buy a computer of some kind. The results have been nothing short of a miniature revolution in the area of data processing for the smaller organization because automated accounting is now cost-effective even for the company with a limited volume of financial transactions and records. In this chapter, we discuss this revolution in greater detail, looking especially at the alternative types of automated data processing available to the smaller user, and examining those computerized accounting applications that appear to be suitable for implementation on a limited scale.

Before turning to these discussions, however, it is advisable perhaps to make clear what we mean by "small business." The definition is provided by the Small Business Administration of the federal government and depends upon the type of work involved. For example, in manufacturing, the classification is based upon the number of employees within a certain type of industry. Thus, apparel and textile companies are regarded as "small" if they have no more than 250 employees, whereas for producers of aircraft and ammunition, the number is 1500 employees. In the service industries, the criterion is dollar volume of sales: a maximum of $7.5 million for department stores and groceries, $6.5 million for auto dealers, $2 million for most other retailers, $9.5 million for general contractors, and $9.5 million for most wholesalers. Thus, "small business" does not necessarily imply "tiny business." It just means "not large." As we have defined them, there are nearly 9 million small businesses in the United States. This represents 95 percent of all businesses, over 50 percent of the entire national payroll, and about 30 percent of the gross national product.

Small companies tend to be more flexible than larger companies in the ways they do business, but they are also more vulnerable to unfavorable turns in the economy. Although it is tempting to joke that the major needs of the small business are money, money, and more money, the fact remains that small businesses often find themselves in financial binds because of increasing costs on the one hand, and downward competitive pressures on prices for their goods and services on the other. Business failures, which are disproportionately high in small businesses, are an important element in the total turnover (liquidations, take-overs, mergers, etc.) within the business population.

One of the primary causes of small business failures is a simple lack of accounting information of one kind or another. Examples would include an inability to forecast cash needs, incomplete information regarding the balances of individual merchandise inventory items, inadequate

communication between the small business and its suppliers, and a weak audit trail of transactions. In some instances, the necessary accounting data are being collected—but at too slow a pace to be of much use. In the sections of the chapter that follow, therefore, we examine the informational needs of small businesses and those accounting methods and machines particularly designed to meet small business needs in an efficient, cost-effective manner.

DESIGNING AN ACCOUNTING INFORMATION SYSTEM FOR A SMALL BUSINESS

The owners of small businesses are prone to look upon accounting as a time-consuming nuisance or, at best, an inconvenience. They seem to feel that only large companies need a formal accounting information system. Because of this misconception, many of these owners attempt to remain in operation without any specific system of accounting, or with a system inadequate for their organizations' needs.

It is true that many small businesses do not need elaborate financial reporting systems because they have a low volume of accounting transactions as compared with larger organizations, and they need not devote a large amount of resources to record-keeping operations. However, these businesses still need a functional accounting system that provides timely information to internal decision makers and to external parties such as stockholders, creditors, government tax agencies, and various governmental regulatory agencies such as the Securities and Exchange Commission. Complete, accurate, and timely accounting information should help to keep a small business solvent and profitable.

The average small business often does not collect the type of information needed to make crucial managerial decisions. Thus, the first step in the design of an accounting information system for the small business is the same as for a large organization: a survey and an assessment of managerial information needs. Based upon a cost/benefit analysis of several data-processing alternatives, however, a small business organization may conclude that no automated type of system is justified. The organization may then return to its conventional manual system of journals and ledgers for accumulating accounting information. A small business could save time and effort in recording and classifying its financial transactions by using a *matrix accounting system* to replace the conventional journals and ledgers. An example of a small company's matrix accounting system is presented below.

A Matrix Accounting Information System*

Assume that the Mike Por Company is a small proprietorship organization that sells office supplies. Its January 1, 1984 trial balance is shown in Figure 15-1. (Small numbers have been used intentionally in this example to simplify the presentation.)

The Por Company uses a perpetual inventory system. Its January transactions are

1. Sold merchandise on account at a $350 retail price. Cost of this merchandise to the Por Company, $140.
2. Paid the January store rent, $75.
3. Paid the January salary to part-time employee, $100.
4. Received $50 in payment of an account receivable.
5. Paid $200 of the accounts payable liabilities.

Based upon the January 1 trial balance and the above transactions, the matrix in Figure 15-2 is prepared. (Explanations will follow.)

The matrix columns are for recording debits, and the rows are for recording credits. Since a debit or credit may occur in each account, all of the accounts are listed in both columns and rows. The same debit and credit rules for increasing and decreasing accounts are used with a matrix accounting system: (1) asset and expense account increases are recorded in columns (debits) and decreases in rows (credits), and (2) liability, owner's equity, and revenue account increases

*This discussion is taken from Stephen A. Moscove, *Accounting Fundamentals: A Self-Instructional Approach* (Reston Publishing Company, Reston, Va., © 1977).

Figure 15-1

MIKE POR COMPANY
Trial Balance
January 1, 1984

Cash	$ 500	
Accounts receivable	400	
Merchandise inventory	2800	
Accounts payable		$1400
Mike Por, capital		2300
	$3700	$3700

are recorded in rows (credits) and decreases in columns (debits).

Each rectangular box within the matrix is called a *cell*. For discussion purposes, these cells are numbered. Based upon the Por Company's trial balance (see Figure 15-1), the January 1 account balances are entered in their proper cells. Since the asset accounts have debit balances, the cash, accounts receivable, and merchandise inventory balances are recorded in column cells 1, 2, and 3, respectively. The liability and owner's equity accounts reflect credit balances and are, therefore, recorded in row cells 48 and 60, respectively.

After these account balances have been recognized, the January transactions are then recorded in the matrix cells. Each transaction is illustrated in Figure 15-3. (If adjusting entries are required at the end of an accounting period, they are recorded within the proper matrix cells in the same manner as the journal entries described in Figure 15-3.)

When a conventional accounting system with journals and ledgers is used, the recorded journal entries are posted to general ledger accounts in order that each account balance can be determined. A matrix accounting system does not require all this work. Rather, an account balance is computed by adding the "column" and "row" monetary items for the account and then subtracting the smaller total from the larger one to determine its balance. For example, the cash column total is $550 (cell number 121) and its row total is $375 (cell number 22). The cash account

Figure 15-2

MIKE POR COMPANY

January Matrix

Rows for Credits			Columns for Debits: Assets (Increases) — Cash (1)	Assets (Increases) — Accounts receivable (2)	Assets (Increases) — Merchandise inventory (3)	Liabilities (Decreases) — Accounts payable (4)	Owner's Equity (Decreases) — Mike Por, capital (5)	Revenues (Decreases) and Expenses (Increases) — Sales (6)	Revenues (Decreases) and Expenses (Increases) — Cost of merchandise sold (7)	Revenues (Decreases) and Expenses (Increases) — Salaries expense (8)	Revenues (Decreases) and Expenses (Increases) — Rent expense (9)	Row Totals (10)	January 31, 1984 Account Balances (11)
January 1, 1984 Account Balances →			500	400	2800								
Assets (Decreases)	Cash	(12)	(13)	(14)	(15)	(16) (5) 200	(17)	(18)	(19)	(20) (3) 100	(21) (2) 75	(22) 375	(23) —
Assets (Decreases)	Accounts receivable	(24)	(25) (4) 50	(26)	(27)	(28)	(29)	(30)	(31)	(32)	(33)	(34) 50	(35) —
Assets (Decreases)	Merchandise inventory	(36)	(37)	(38)	(39)	(40)	(41)	(42)	(43) (1) 140	(44)	(45)	(46) 140	(47) —
Liabilities (Increases)	Accounts payable 1400	(48)	(49)	(50)	(51)	(52)	(53)	(54)	(55)	(56)	(57)	(58) 1400	(59) 1200
Owner's Equity (Increases)	Mike Por, capital 2300	(60)	(61)	(62)	(63)	(64)	(65)	(66)	(67)	(68)	(69)	(70) 2300	(71) 2300
Revenues (Increases) and Expenses (Decreases)	Sales	(72)	(73)	(74) (1) 350	(75)	(76)	(77)	(78)	(79)	(80)	(81)	(82) 350	(83) 350
Revenues (Increases) and Expenses (Decreases)	Cost of merchandise sold	(84)	(85)	(86)	(87)	(88)	(89)	(90)	(91)	(92)	(93)	(94) —	(95) —
Revenues (Increases) and Expenses (Decreases)	Salaries expense	(96)	(97)	(98)	(99)	(100)	(101)	(102)	(103)	(104)	(105)	(106) —	(107) —
Revenues (Increases) and Expenses (Decreases)	Rent expense	(108)	(109)	(110)	(111)	(112)	(113)	(114)	(115)	(116)	(117)	(118) —	(119) —
Column Totals		(120)	(121) 550	(122) 750	(123) 2800	(124) 200	(125) —	(126) —	(127) 140	(128) 100	(129) 75	(130) 4615	(131) —
January 31, 1984 Account Balances		(132)	(133) 175	(134) 700	(135) 2660	(136) —	(137) —	(138) —	(139) 140	(140) 100	(141) 75	(142) —	(143) 3850

Transaction 1

In journal form, this transaction would have been recorded as

Accounts receivable	350	
Sales		350
Cost of merchandise sold	140	
Merchandise inventory		140

Cell number 74 reflects the first entry. This cell is in the accounts receivable debit column and sales credit row. Since the Por Company uses a perpetual inventory system, the second entry is also required. It is recorded in matrix cell number 43 (the cost of merchandise sold debit column and merchandise inventory credit row).

Transaction 2

In journal form, this transaction would have been recorded as

Rent expense	75	
Cash		75

Cell number 21 represents this entry (the rent expense debit column and cash credit row).

Transaction 3

In journal form, this transaction would have been recorded as

Salaries expense	100	
Cash		100

This salary payment is recorded in cell number 20 (the salaries expense debit column and cash credit row).

Transaction 4

In journal form, this transaction would have been recorded as

Cash	50	
Accounts receivable		50

Matrix cell 25 reflects this entry (the cash debit column and accounts receivable credit row).

Transaction 5

In journal form, this transaction would have been recorded as

Accounts payable	200	
Cash		200

This liability payment is recorded in cell number 16 (the accounts payable debit column and cash credit row).

Figure 15-3. January Transactions of the Mike Por Company.

therefore has a January 31 debit balance of $175 ($550 − $375). This is shown in cell number 133. The same process is followed to determine each account balance. Since matrix columns reflect debits, the monetary balances of the asset and expense accounts (having debit balances) appear in columns. The matrix rows represent credits. Thus, the dollar balances of the liability, owner's equity, and revenue accounts (having credit balances) are reported in rows. For example, the $1200 accounts payable liability balance is shown in matrix cell number 59 [$1400 row total (cell number 58) *less* $200 column total (cell number 124)].

The $4615 in cell number 130 is a "check figure" showing that the total of the column items (the debits) equals the total of the row items (the credits). Before preparing financial statements, a company should determine that its accounts with debit balances equal the accounts with credit balances. To accomplish this, a "trial balance" is prepared. Under a matrix accounting system, a separate trial balance is unnecessary since the equality of debit and credit account balances can be ascertained directly from the matrix. Cell number 143 on the Por Company's matrix reflects its trial balance results. The January 31 *debit* account balances from the "column" financial items (asset and expense accounts) are added. Their total is $3850. Then the January 31 *credit* account balances from the "row" financial items (liability, owner's equity, and revenue accounts) are added. Since this total is also $3850, the Por Company's trial balance is finished.

443

The financial statements can now be prepared. Based upon the account balances disclosed in the Por Company's January matrix, its month-end income statement and balance sheet are presented in Figures 15-4 and 15-5. The matrix cell number of each financial item is shown in parentheses.

The Por Company's February accounting transactions are recorded on a new matrix in the same manner as the January transactions. The January 31 asset and liability account balances are reported as the February 1 balances on this matrix. With a system of journals and ledgers, the revenue and expense account balances would have been closed into the owner's equity account at the end of January. Since journal entries are not utilized under a matrix system, the Por Company's January net income is added to the "Mike Por, capital" account. The resulting $2335 (see the owner's equity section of Figure 15-5) is then reflected as the February 1 balance of the "Mike Por, capital" account on the February matrix. Each revenue and expense account would have a zero balance to begin this new accounting period.

A matrix system is practical only for those organizations having a low volume of financial transactions. It eliminates the need for journals and ledgers, and is thus quite efficient for small businesses. Moreover, the matrix organization of accounting data is also a natural link between a manual and a computerized accounting information system. To better understand this link, we next turn our attention to the possibility of automating the accounting procedures with computer-type equipment.

COMPUTERIZING THE SMALL BUSINESS

Early computer-based systems saw the payroll function as the most common and fundamental application of automated data processing. But other accounting functions, such as recording cash receipts, processing accounts payable and accounts receivable, maintaining inventory records, and preparing bank reconciliations have since been computerized and offer the small business an attractive alternative to the manual approach.

In addition to some of these basic accounting functions, computerization has allowed the small firm to obtain assistance in operational aspects of the firm. Many sales and inventory functions, for example, have been automated to allow a more scientific analysis of the internal operations of the firm than was possible with manual procedures. Applications such as inventory purchasing and receiving, inventory forecasting and control, production scheduling, labor distribution, and job-order costing have been computerized, and canned programs are often available from computer vendors together with the computer hardware.

All of the above benefits from computerization are possible to the small business—but what are the specific computer alternatives? We shall explore three of them: (1) programmable cal-

Figure 15-4

MIKE POR COMPANY
Income Statement
For the Month Ended January 31, 1984

Revenues		
Retail price of merchandise sold		$350 (cell 83)
Less: *Operating Expenses*		
Cost of merchandise sold	$140 (cell 139)	
Salaries expense	100 (cell 140)	
Rent expense	75 (cell 141)	
Total operating expenses		315
Net income		$ 35

Figure 15-5

MIKE POR COMPANY
Balance Sheet
January 31, 1984

ASSETS		LIABILITIES & OWNER'S EQUITY		
Current assets		Current liabilities		
Cash	$ 175 (cell 133)	Accounts payable		$1200 (cell 59)
Accounts		Owner's equity		
receivable	700 (cell 134)	Mike Por,		
Merchandise		capital, Jan. 1	$2300 (cell 71)	
inventory	2660 (cell 135)	*Plus:* Net In-		
		come for Jan.	35	
		Mike Por,		
		capital, Jan. 31		2335
		Total liabilities and		
Total assets	$3535	owner's equity		$3535

culators, (2) microcomputers and minicomputers, and (3) small-business computers.

Programmable Calculators

Despite their small size and limited processing capabilities, many small businesses are discovering that a programmable calculator can be a useful management tool. In fact, the programmable calculator is becoming just as "hot" among some managers as the standard pocket calculator already has become among individual consumers. In the past decade, programmable calculators have grown from fancy adding machines that had a few special function keys to very powerful and flexible interactive calculating systems. Like computers, programmable calculators now have a wide range of peripheral devices available such as card readers, tape readers, and card punches. A programmable calculator can perform many of the same functions as a small computer, but of course a programmable calculator does not cost nearly as much.

Today, managers are using programmables to attack complex problems involving multistep procedures (such as discounting future cash flows). However, these machines stop short of handling high-volume, repetitive data-processing jobs such as preparing a payroll. Among the more common applications of programmable calculators are investment analysis, production scheduling, and inventory control. Businesses not only use programs offered by the manufacturers of programmables but also write their own specific programs.

Prices of programmable calculators vary with the size of their memory and the sophistication of their input-output devices. Many of the programmables, manufactured by such companies as Hewlett-Packard Co. and Texas Instruments, Inc., are priced under $100, and the fact that they are "personal" possessions small enough to fit into a pocket means that they are even more accessible and economical than minicomputers or time-sharing systems. Executives with a small programmable calculator, for example, can run computations in a few minutes that otherwise would take hours to calculate by hand. Because the programmable calculator is so portable and immediately available to their owners, such instruments are of special use to both the executives of large corporations who require fast answers and the executives of small businesses who are on limited budgets.

The primary disadvantage of programmable calculators is that they are limited in what they can do. The number and type of instructions within their instruction sets tend to be small and very few of the programmables can prepare a company's output reports in acceptable formats for decision-making by external and internal parties. Also, at the time this book was written, programmable-calculator manufacturers made very little provision for the permanent storage of such data sets as customer records, and almost all input to the programmable calculator had to be performed manually. Thus, whereas the programmable calculator is extremely useful for on-site calculations and the execution of simple programs requiring little input data, the programmable calculator is not useful for repetitive processing of accounting transactions. For this reason, many companies have considered the programmable calculator as a bonus or Christmas gift for executive employees, but have looked much more closely at minicomputers, microcomputers, and small-business computers for their information processing needs. We examine these types of computers in the following pages.

Minicomputers and Microcomputers

Previously, the term *minicomputer* was used to describe a very small computer costing under $20,000 and utilizing a central processing memory with less than 8K bytes of storage. Alternatively, the term *microcomputer* was used to describe a computer of yet smaller dimensions—that is, a computer costing under $10,000 and having even more limited CPU storage. Modern technology, however, has blurred the distinction between the minicomputer and the microcomputer. Today, it is possible to buy very small computers with considerably more internal storage capacity, more external storage options, and additional general processing capacity for considerably less money than the figures quoted above. Thus, the terms *minicomputer* and *microcomputer* have lost their descriptive power and in the discussions that follow, we shall use the term *minicomputer* to refer to both types of systems.

The force behind the emergence of minicomputer systems is the continuing price plunge of semiconductor circuits. Such circuits—

thousands of transistors on a single chip of silicon—make up the logic and memory circuits of most computers. As semiconductor makers squeeze more and more circuits on a chip, the costs per circuit falls, making it economically feasible to increase computer power and simultaneously decrease costs.

Today, tiny microprocessors (which do the "thinking" for minicomputers) are so inexpensive that virtually every major household appliance or major business machine is soon likely to have one. The automotive manufacturers are putting microprocessors in new cars to monitor ignition systems. Microwave ovens use them to control baking. Copier machines now have them to coordinate duplicating and to serve as a diagnostic should paper jams or drops in ink level occur. In one especially interesting application, Exxon Corporation has recently coupled a minicomputer to its new business typewriter. The computer "remembers" what has been keyed into the machine, thus enabling the typist to correct mistakes and then reprint the entire page. The computer in the typewriter is also a *word processor*, meaning that the machine will automatically scan each line before typing, make a decision about word length, and then design the entire output so that there is both left and right text alignment. The processor even knows how to hyphenate words!

A common application of microprocessors is in the use of smart terminals. As discussed in Chapter 4, the smart terminal acts as an input device to a central processor, perhaps on a remote basis. The processing feature of the terminal enables the machine to perform on a "stand-alone" basis when simple computations are needed. In this mode, the terminal acts much like a programmable calculator. However, when operating as a transmission device, the microprocessing portion of the smart terminal can also be used to monitor data, assemble and disassemble messages, edit input codes, test for improper computer access, and coordinate transmission activity between the terminal itself and the central processing unit to which it is connected. This microprocessing capability is especially exploited by banks using smart terminals at teller windows, manufacturing companies using online inventory control systems, credit-card authorization systems supporting an online inquiry capability, and hospitals requiring an extensive communication network between the various care and support departments of the medical facility.

Computers that are used primarily for a specific data-processing application such as inventory processing or accounts receivable processing are called "dedicated computers" (discussed in Chapter 14). The importance of minicomputers for performing specific data-processing functions is illustrated by the phenomenal growth in the use of minicomputers as dedicated computers. In 1971, for example, only about 15 percent of all minicomputers were used as dedicated machines. By 1975, over half the minicomputers were dedicated computers. By the time this book is published, it is likely that as many as 75 percent of all minicomputers will be used as dedicated computers.

Minicomputers are also being used extensively in the business world as small, but complete, data-processing systems. Chapter 14 has already discussed the concept of the turn-key computer system, and such systems are ideal for small businesses with limited computer expertise.

In accounting, the minicomputer would naturally extend the flexibility of the matrix accounting system as discussed previously. To understand this extension, refer to Figure 15-2, and imagine that the Por Company was using a minicomputer to process its accounting transactions. In this application, each cell of the accounting matrix would be represented by a memory location of computer storage. At the beginning of each month for the Mike Por Company, these memory locations would be empty —except for the cells containing the dollar balances carried over from the previous month for the asset, liability, and owner's equity accounts.

When utilizing a minicomputer, entries to the accounting matrix would be made more or less as before: for each transaction, the proper matrix cell would be identified and the appropriate dollar amount recorded for the business transaction. With a manual approach, each entry would be recorded by hand on a sheet of paper. With a minicomputer, the number of the cell would be keyed into the computer through the minicomputer console, followed by the transaction amount. The console video terminal would screen each entry for verification, perform certain edit tests, and confirm each recording operation after the transaction had been entered.

One advantage of the computerized version of the accounting matrix over the manual one is that cross-footing could be performed continuously, and virtually instantaneously. Every time an entry was made to the accounting matrix, the sum of the rows and the sum of the columns of the matrix would be computed in a fraction of a second and compared to assure processing accuracy. Any errors detected by this procedure would be communicated to the operator.

A second advantage of the computerized system over the manual one is realized at the end of the accounting period when certain additional processing tasks must be performed. For example, through specifying the format of the income statement and balance sheet (by identifying which cells were to be included and which figures were to be added or subtracted), the Mike Por Company could have its minicomputer prepare these important financial statements. (A printer would be desirable with the minicomputer for preparing financial statements, although it would be a simple matter for an employee to copy the figures from a video screen if a printer were not available.) Of course, as discussed before, all accounting processes could be done by hand. Barring abnormalities in the computer hardware and software, however, the minicomputer will be much faster, and 100 percent accurate.

As the minicomputer industry has matured and proliferated, more emphasis has been placed on modular systems, with add-on CPU storage a primary selling factor. As presented in Figure 15-6, which illustrates the cost of several representative systems, minicomputer prices vary. Also, typical of the minicomputers, is the availability of several external storage options and printer options. As noted in Chapter 18, the "floppy disk" has proven especially popular as

Figure 15-6

PRICES OF SELECTED MINICOMPUTERS

Manufacturer	Model	Base Price	Monthly Maintenance	CPU Memory Capacity of Basic Model
Century Computer	200 Series	$16,500	$200	32K
Data General	Eclipse S/130	11,000	145	32K
Datapoint	Diskette 1100	12,880	47	16K
General Automation	GA-16/460	11,000	140	64K
GRI	9950	6,410	257	8K
Hewlett-Packard	HP 1000	7,425	126	64K
Lockheed Electronics	Sue 1110	10,780	NA*	32K
Perkin-Elmer	Interdata 7/32	11,659	NA*	64K
Raytheon	RDS-5000	15,000	250	32K
Texas Instruments	980B	5,150	95	16K
Westinghouse	W-2500	8,500	140	32K

*Not Available

Source: "Minicomputer and Microcomputer Survey," *DATAMATION,* Volume 24, No. 8 (August 1978), pp. 112–127. Reprinted with permission of DATAMATION® Magazine, © Copyright by Technical Publishing Company, A Dun and Bradstreet Company, 1978—all rights reserved.

an inexpensive and convenient way for small-scale computers to store data in a machine-readable, cost-effective manner. Cassette-tape external storage, which utilizes the cassette-tape cartridges familiar to the stereo enthusiast, is less popular, but still used extensively with minicomputer systems.

Software support is slowly catching up with hardware advances in the minicomputer industry. At one time, for example, minicomputers were undesirable to many business organizations because these computers had to be programmed in assembler-level languages and were marketed mainly by "lots-of-luck" manufacturers—the buyer paid for the machine and the manufacturer wished him lots of luck! All that has changed now. Almost all minicomputers have at least one higher-level language compiler—usually BASIC—"hard-wired" to the central processing unit, thus giving the programmer an opportunity to code in a familiar programming language. More importantly, the minicomputer industry finally has realized that the provision of good software support is the key to a successful marketing effort. Because the small business can now afford a minicomputer, computer manufacturers have focused their software-support ef-

forts on this unsophisticated, but highly lucrative, small-business market. Thus, minicomputer software packages are available for such familiar accounting applications as payroll, accounts receivable, accounts payable, general ledger, and inventory processing at an additional cost to users.

Advantages and disadvantages of the minicomputer. Certainly price would rank high on the list of advantages of the minicomputer. The fact that many minicomputer systems now have good software support for common accounting applications and therefore can be installed as complete, turn-key systems is also important. By corollary, minicomputers can be dedicated to specific accounting applications and enable a company to "go time-sharing" but still retain a second, batch-processing system for other accounting uses.

Until recently, the biggest drawback of the minicomputer was the lack of software support. While this problem is being rectified, small business is still at a software disadvantage with a minicomputer if more than very common accounting software applications are required. This software support problem is also compounded by the fact that most of the smaller systems can handle at most one or two computer programming languages. Thus, for example, it is possible to acquire a minicomputer system which is programmable in BASIC, but it is unlikely that such a system would also be able to run programs written in COBOL or PL/1.

Peripheral support is another area of importance. High-quality peripheral equipment that at one time was available only with larger computers is now available on minis. However, minicomputers are usually limited in *how many* printers, tape drives, and disk drives can be attached to any given CPU. The exact number will vary from manufacturer to manufacturer, of course, but there is always a point at which the user must switch to a larger computer. Where flexibility for growth is important, the acquisition of a larger computer must be considered.

Throughput is yet another consideration. This is the time required for a given computer system to complete a set of processing jobs. Throughput is not as great on minis as on larger computers. Reasons for this are mainly attributable to the fact that minicomputers use computer words of 18 bits or less. This means that all data transfers and arithmetic operations are performed on less-than-normal-sized "chunks" of information. Thus, to perform a "standard" 32-bit operation, a minicomputer must work nearly twice as hard as a larger, 32-bit-word, machine. All this slows down effective throughput. Because data-processing applications in large business organizations such as accounts receivable billing operations often involve a high volume of transactions, minicomputer throughput is rarely acceptable. For the small business with a limited amount of data-processing work, however, the minicomputer may be sufficient.

Small-Business Computers

From programmable calculators and minicomputers, we move up in technology, power, and price to what is commonly called the *small-business computer*. The term small-business computer causes a certain amount of confusion because it is often used very loosely to refer to a wide range of equipment with as wide a range in price. For example, Douglas Moore (writing in *Data Processing*) points out that "one machine may come under several headings." The NCR 399, for example, has been classified as a small business computer, as a business minicomputer, and as an office computer, while NCR itself generally refers to the 399 as an accounting computer.*

To clarify this situation, we shall define a small business computer as a computer with more internal storage and peripheral devices than minicomputers, and with programs already available for processing accounting applications like payroll, accounts receivable, and inventory. Small business computer systems are typified by popular systems such as the IBM System/3 (there are currently about 40,000 of these in use), IBM System 32, Burroughs' B1700, Honeywell Series 61, and NCR 615-50. Figure 15-7 illustrates a typical system—a CADO System 40—which is geared especially to the small business. Note in particular the availability of two full (132) column impact printers and 19 megabytes (19 million bytes) of external, floppy-disk storage—features that (at the time this book was written) would be excessive for a minicomputer. In the figure, "ROM" stands for "read-only memory" whereas "RAM" stands for "random-access memory."

The monthly rental prices of small-business computer systems are usually well under $2,000 and selling prices are in the $20,000 to $100,000 range. In 1980, there were about 90 firms supplying small computer systems. Figure 15-8 lists five of these small computer models, together with some processing capabilities. The business manager who should be concerned with small-business computers probably already has some accounting machines to assist with billing functions. Although different businesses have different requirements, as a rule of thumb, companies with 200 employees and $500,000 in capital can normally justify the costs of their own small-business computer installations.

*Douglas Moore, "An Introduction to Small Business Systems," *Data Processing* (November–December 1974), p. 407.

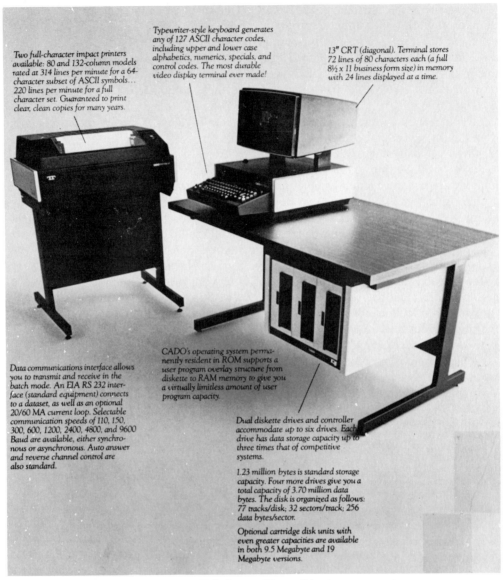

Typewriter-style keyboard generates any of 127 ASCII character codes, including upper and lower case alphabetics, numerics, specials, and control codes. The most durable video display terminal ever made!

Two full-character impact printers available: 80 and 132-column models rated at 314 lines per minute for a 64-character subset of ASCII symbols... 220 lines per minute for a full character set. Guaranteed to print clear, clean copies for many years.

13" CRT (diagonal). Terminal stores 72 lines of 80 characters each (a full 8½ x 11 business form size) in memory with 24 lines displayed at a time.

Data communications interface allows you to transmit and receive in the batch mode. An EIA RS 232 interface (standard equipment) connects to a dataset, as well as an optional 20/60 MA current loop. Selectable communication speeds of 110, 150, 300, 600, 1200, 2400, 4800, and 9600 Baud are available, either synchronous or asynchronous. Auto answer and reverse channel control are also standard.

CADO's operating system permanently resident in ROM supports a user program overlay structure from diskette to RAM memory to give you a virtually limitless amount of user program capacity.

Dual diskette drives and controller accommodate up to six drives. Each drive has data storage capacity up to three times that of competitive systems.

1.23 million bytes is standard storage capacity. Four more drives give you a total capacity of 3.70 million data bytes. The disk is organized as follows: 77 tracks/disk; 32 sectors/track; 256 data bytes/sector.

Optional cartridge disk units with even greater capacities are available in both 9.5 Megabyte and 19 Megabyte versions.

Figure 15-7. A CADO System 40 small-business computer.

The fact that programming expertise is not likely to reside in the typical small business means that the manufacturers of small business machines must anticipate the informational needs of small-business management and provide for these needs in software support. In the area of accounting, this has led to the development of integrated accounting systems that may be purchased by the small business and used for such important accounting applications as (1) accounts receivable processing and preparing customer billing statements, (2) inventory processing, (3) accounts payable processing, (4) cash forecasting and other budgeting functions, and (5) payroll. The accounting programs are integrated in the sense that several programs are likely to use the same set of disk or tape files, and are likely to have standardized input and out-

Figure 15-8

OPERATING CHARACTERISTICS FOR FIVE SMALL, GENERAL PURPOSE COMPUTERS

Manufacturer	Data General	Digital Equipment	Honeywell	IBM	Sperry Univac
Model	Nova/3	PDP 11/34	Level 6-4X	Series/1	V77-600
Main Storage (CPU Memory)	8K–64K	16K–64K	16K–2000K	16–256K	32K–2000K
CPU Word Length	16 bits	16 bits	16 bits	16 bits	16 bits
Maximum Number of Channels	64	unlimited	1024	1	32
Language Support	ALGOL, BASIC, FORTRAN	APL, BASIC, COBOL, FORTRAN, RPG	COBOL, FORTRAN, RPG	COBOL, FORTRAN, PL/1	BASIC, COBOL, FORTRAN
Typical System Price Range (Thousands)	$5–$70	$10–$100	$10–$47	$12–$100	$80–$150

Source: "Minicomputer and Microcomputer Survey," *DATAMATION*, Volume 24, No. 8 (August 1978), pp. 112–127. Reprinted with permission of DATAMATION® Magazine, © Copyright by Technical Publishing Company, A Dun and Bradstreet Company, 1978—all rights reserved.

put formatting. Consistent, easily-understood programming documentation may also be expected.

Figures 15-9 and 15-10 illustrate reports from a typical small-business system which were processed on a Burroughs B80 small-business computer. Figure 15-9 illustrates two reports that would be used for inventory control. Note that the "Buyer's Guide" will answer such fundamental questions as (1) "Do we have to place an order?" (2) "How many widgets do we currently have on hand?" (3) "When did we last receive a shipment?" (4) "Which vendor usually supplies this item?" (5) "How many of these items have we ordered to date?". Similarly, the "Potential Excess Stock on Hand Report" can answer such questions as (1) "Where is there excess inventory?" (2) "How much excess money do we have tied up in extra inventory stock?" (3) "How many periods can we go before a new order would be required?" (4) "Are our reorder points or safety stock values poorly determined?" (5) "Is the lead time realistic?" and so forth.

Figure 15-10 illustrates two potential reports for an accounts payable application. Questions that can be answered by the "Cash Requirements Report" include: (1) "How much money is currently due?" (2) "How much money is due in the future?" (3) "Are there any invoices overdue?" (4) "How much discount should be taken?" (5) "How much discount will be lost?" (6) "Should payment be made in foreign currency?" (7) "Should only partial payment be made?" and (8) "Which companies must we pay first, and for which companies can we delay payment?". Similarly, for the "Periodic Liabilities Forecast" we can answer a number of questions, but by now you get the idea.

Advantages and disadvantages of the small-business computer. Probably the most important advantage of the small-business computer is the likelihood of obtaining greater software support than with a minicomputer. Many of the manufacturers of small-business computers have developed sophisticated software accounting packages that are likely to be well-suited to the needs of the limited-scale data processor. Pre-printed forms for such computer outputs as financial statements and cash disbursements checks usually are available with small-business computer software packages, as well as a more sophisticated library of subroutines and statistical application programs. Finally, the small-business computer buyer may anticipate better

ABC COMPANY

BUYER'S GUIDE

PRD CAT	STOCK NUMBER DESCRIPTION-REFERENCE	VNDR NO	STD ORD QTY	RE-ORDER PT	STOCK AVAILABLE ON ORDER	BALANCES ON HAND	SAFTY STK	UNIT AVG CST	UNIT RPL CST	CURRENT ISS PER TO DTE	CURRENT ISS YEAR TO DTE	PREVIOUS ISS PER TO DTE	PREVIOUS ISS YEAR TO DTE	DATE LAST ISSUE	DATE LAST RECEIPT	LEAD TIME DAYS
004	12415710 SCREWDRIVER 6"	2141678	250	500	755	755	100	1-185	1-193	703	1-203	479	1-090	02 25 7-	02 10 7-	015
004	12415730 SCREWDRIVER 8" **	2141678	250	500	383 / 500	983	500	1-3152	1-32	613	1-251	534	906	02 13 7-	01 28 7-	015
004	12415740 SCREWDRIVER 10" **	2141678	250	500	450	450	200	1-47	1-5215	345	612	476	820	02 27 7-	02 20 7-	015
004	12415750 SCREWDRIVER 12" **	2141678	250	500	315	315	200	1-6554	1-6554	282	571	321	530	02 26 7-	02 26 7-	021

ABC COMPANY

POTENTIAL EXCESS STOCK ON 03 01 8-

PRD CAT	STOCK NUMBER DESCRIPTION-REFERENCE	NET ISSUES THIS YEAR CURRENT PER	NET ISSUES THIS YEAR CURRENT YEAR TO DATE	NET ISSUES LAST YEAR CURRENT PER	NET ISSUES LAST YEAR YEAR TO DATE	QUANTITY ON HAND	QUANTITY ON ORDER	NO OF PROS ISS ON HND PER	NO OF PROS ISS YR TO DATE	THEORETICAL MAX QTY OH	STANDARD ORDER QTY	POTENTIAL EXCESS QUANTITY CURRENT PER	POTENTIAL EXCESS QUANTITY YEAR TO DATE	POTENTIAL EXCESS VALUE CURRENT PER	POTENTIAL EXCESS VALUE YEAR TO DATE	LEAD TIME DAYS
004	12415710 SCREWDRIVER 6"	703	1,203	479	1,090	755		1.1	1.3	350	250	405	253	480	300	015
004	12416101 PLIERS 6"	12	31	8	41	75		6.3	4.8	40	20	35	49	111	156	021
004	12447401 PLIERS 8"	423	792	520	1,025	1,295		3.1	3.3	600	200	695	712	2,853	2,923	021
004	12447601 PLIERS 10"	363	699	203	509	801		2.2	2.3	200	100	601	637	2,545	2,698	021

TOTAL PRODUCT CATEGORY 004   5,989 / 6,077

GRAND TOTALS   78,436 / 105,295

Figure 15-9. Two inventory control reports for a small business system. (Forms courtesy of Burroughs Corporation.)

DATE 03 20 8-

ABC COMPANY

ACCOUNTS PAYABLE
CASH REQUIREMENTS

TRANS CTRL NO	PC	INVOICE NUMBER	INVOICE DATE	INVOICE DUE DATE	GROSS AMOUNT	DISCOUNT ALLOWABLE	NET AMOUNT DUE CURRENT 03 20 7-	FUTURE 03 31 7-
2000030		***RICHARDSON DIVISION***						
214		A534567	03 15 7-	03 25 7-	500.00	10.00	490.00	
				TOTAL VENDOR	500.00	10.00	490.00	.00
2900680		***URBAN OFFICE SUPPLIES***						
176		60139	02 18 7-	03 18 7-	300.00	.00	300.00 *	
							300.00 *	.00
4000618		***ROBERTS METALS***						
198		A06194	03 05 7-	03 15 7-	325.00	6.50 *	325.00	
230		A06896	03 19 7-	03 29 7-	400.00	8.00	392.00	
				TOTAL VENDOR	725.00	8.00	717.00	.00
8000618		***KUROSAKA ELECTRONICS***						
217	1	30619-1	03 10 7-	04 10 7-	166.67	.00	166.67	
217	2	30619-2	03 10 7-	05 10 7-	166.67	.00	166.67	
217	3	30619-3	03 10 7-	06 10 7-	166.66	.00	166.66	
					500.00	.00	500.00	

```
                                    * DISCOUNT       .00  * PAST DUE
                                      TO BE LOST
```

DATE 03 19 8-

ABC COMPANY
ACCOUNTS PAYABLE
PERIODIC LIABILITIES FORECAST

TRANS CTRL NO	CHECK NO	TRN ST	INVOICE NUMBER	---0--- 03 10	---1--- 03 20	---2--- 03 31	---3--- 04 11	---4--- 04 22	---5--- 05 03	---6--- 05 14	---7--- 05 25	---8--- 06 05	---9--- 06 16
4000618			***ROBERTS METALS***										
198			INVOIC A06194	325.00									
230			INVOIC A06896		400.00								
			VENDOR TOTALS	325.00	400.00								
8000618			***KUROSAKA ELECTRONICS***										
217		1	INVOIC 30619-1			166.67							
217		2	INVOIC 30619-2						166.67				
217		3	INVOIC 30619-3									166.66	
			VENDOR TOTALS			166.67						166.66	
			GRAND TOTALS	3,750.00	2,800.00	166.67	1,300.00	700.00	816.67	800.00	375.00	666.66	425.00

Figure 15-10. Two accounts payable reports for a small business system. (Forms courtesy of Burroughs Corporation.)

software maintenance and other types of programming assistance.

The fact that the small-business computer is larger and can usually do more than a minicomputer should also be noted. Size is particularly important when growth is taken into consideration. Many of the computer manufacturers take special care to develop computer hardware and software which eases the transition from one of their small-business machines to one of their larger models. Thus, it is much easier for a company to "switch-over" from an IBM System/32 to an IBM System/34 than it would be for the company to switch from an IBM System 5100—a minicomputer—to an IBM System/34. The reason is that the System/34 supports card-input much like the System/32 whereas the 5100 is a real-time, keyboard-entry machine.

On the negative side, small-business computers are obviously more expensive than minicomputers and are also likely to be slower than larger computers. The number of small-business computers available today is much greater than just a few years ago. With such a wide choice of equipment, how is the small business to decide which particular computer system to lease or buy? Before jumping in and spending $10,000, $20,000, or even $100,000, the small-business manager should also examine the possibility of renting time on the computer of a service bureau or time-sharing organization. Since these options have already been discussed in Chapters 12 and 14, they will not be analyzed further here. However, the fact that the small-business computer will be costly and will also require a substantial change in operating procedures (compared with manual methods) must still be considered in the decision to acquire a small business computer.

THE SELECTION PROCESS FOR
THE SMALL BUSINESS

The formation of a computer-evaluation committee is a good approach to use in solving the problem of computer model selection. For the small business, the computer-evaluation committee may consist of just one individual, or it may consist of many individuals representing the various interests of the company. For example, each of the following individuals could make a major contribution to the computer-selection process:

1. Representatives from the user group(s) requiring data-processing services.
2. Technical experts, such as data-processing planners and systems personnel, to prepare requests for computer vendor proposals.
3. Accounting personnel to prepare cost/benefit analyses of various proposals and to evaluate procurement alternatives.
4. Legal representatives to protect the rights of the company in contracts with vendors and to seek legal remedies in the event of default by vendors.

The committee's first job is to analyze the company's actual data-processing needs. To determine the size of computer system required, the committee must ascertain if the company is meeting its present data-processing objectives and also attempt to project the company's future data-processing needs. More important though, the committee must be able to communicate its company's data-processing needs into the systems specifications report (discussed in Chapter 12) which is submitted to hardware and software vendors as a basis for these vendors' subsequent computer proposals.

Not all businesses need to computerize. William G. Barry, President of Cooper Data Systems, believes that a great number of small businesses are still approaching automation for prestige value. "The problem," he states, "is related to the old mystique of the computer. Seventy-five percent of the time, the computer decision is an emotional one and not a good business decision."*

Alan Liebert, who has spent a career designing cost-effective computer systems, emphasizes the care that is necessary when acquiring a computer

*Ralph M. Stair, Jr. and Barry Render, "The Computer Service Industry," *Metro New Orleans Business* (May 1975).

system. For the company that has decided to computerize, Liebert has the following advice:

1. Don't be in a hurry to spend money.
2. Carefully select the best computer and peripheral equipment for your needs.
3. Look at the financial implications of your selection.
4. Don't try new applications purely for sex appeal—cost justify them.†

Knowledge and experience in data processing are essential to assure effective selection, installation, and use of data-processing equipment. Because such an acquisition usually requires a substantial dollar investment, management involvement is a "must" for effective utilization of computer equipment. This involvement should start with detailed studies of a company's data-processing alternatives and should continue long after a computer system choice is made.

SUMMARY

This chapter has examined computerized accounting information systems for the small business. The most important factor for the small business in search of a more efficient accounting information system is an assessment of needs. Once these needs have been determined, budget restrictions will probably dictate the type of system that will be implemented. One possibility is to employ a manual accounting matrix system. Today, however, it is difficult to imagine a company that would not benefit from some sort of electronic data processing. The choices include programmable calculators, minicomputers and small-business computers. Prices for the programmables are under $100, prices for the minicomputers presently range between a few hundred dollars and perhaps $20,000, and the prices of small business computers usually are greater than $20,000 but generally well under $100,000.

The process of selecting the "best" accounting information system for the small business should follow the same pattern discussed elsewhere in this text (specifically, Chapters 11–14) for a

---

†Alan Liebert, "Reducing the Cost of Computing," *Data Processing* (November–December 1973), p. 390.

larger company. Beyond an understanding of informational needs, the small business should acquire familiarity with computer technology, solicit proposals from hardware and software vendors, and weigh the evidence carefully before making a final choice of a specific data-processing system.

DISCUSSION QUESTIONS

15-1. How small is "small business"? Would the million-dollar-a-year manufacturing company be included on a list of small businesses?

15-2. Why is the small business of today able to buy or lease a computer, whereas it was not in the past? Is there such a thing as a small business that is too tiny to use some type of automated data processing? Discuss.

15-3. Ma and Pa Smallfield have worked all their lives in their own grocery store, which is located in a small town near Kent, Ohio. Outside of Sally Peterson, the checkout girl, and an occasional part-time stock boy or two, the Smallfields are the only employees. Recently, Pa Smallfield was approached by a computer salesman from nearby Smokeville. The salesman was hoping to get Ma and Pa interested in leasing a small minicomputer to help keep their records. Not wishing to push the Smallfields into a hasty decision, the salesman left some literature and promised to return a week later. The couple pondered over pictures of the new-fangled device and debated the issue.

Ma Smallfield, ever the more open-minded of the two, liked the idea very much. "It's just what we need," she said, "to help us with the paper work."

"Fiddlesticks," replied Pa. "We've gotten along just fine without one of those Rube Goldbergs for the last 30 years, and I see no reason to start now. Do you realize that if we go ahead and get one of those "misty-computers," or whatever those things are, we probably wouldn't need Sam Peterson, your cousin's brother-in-law, to do the books. I'd sure hate to fire Sam. Sam's wife has been laid up in the hospital, you know, and they need the money. Besides, I kinda like havin' Sam come around once a month and play checkers after he's through with the books. I vote no." Comment.

15-4. What are the factors that influence the "computerization" of the small business? What are the pitfalls to avoid?

15-5. Describe the process by which a small business might decide to purchase a particular computer. How does this process differ from that which should be used in acquiring the computer hardware for a large company's information system?

15-6. Describe the differences between a programmable calculator and a minicomputer. Which type of computer system might best be used by: (a) a real estate broker, (b) a small CPA firm, (c) an engineer working on a small problem, (d) a student, and (e) a minor league baseball team.

15-7. "The minicomputer is causing a revolution in computer manufacturing. Yet, the typical consumer does not know about this revolution." How can you explain this fact?

15-8. A number of companies such as Radio Shack and Heathkit now make available "computers" with 48K memories and video screen input/output devices. Would you classify such computers as programmable calculators, minicomputers, or small-business computers? Discuss.

15-9. In the chapter, it was stated that "the force behind the emergence of the new computer systems is the continuing price plunge of semiconductor circuits." Explain this statement in greater detail.

15-10. What is a "dedicated computer system?" What is a "turn-key" computer system? How are these terms related to each other? How are these terms related to minicomputers?

15-11. Food-processing companies use dedicated minicomputers to monitor the heat in boilers, the position of valves, and the flow of liquid through pipes. What advantages might there be in such use and what "decisions" would such computers make?

15-12. What are the advantages and the disadvan-

tages of acquiring a minicomputer from the standpoint of the small business? Why would a business buy or lease a minicomputer when it could also buy several programmable calculators for the same money?

15-13. Explain the difficulties in classifying computers as "microcomputers," "minicomputers," and "small-business computers." Would you prefer to keep the meaning of these three terms distinct or would you prefer to call all "nonlarge" computers "minicomputers?" Justify your answer.

15-14. How important is computer software to the small business? Why don't most small businesses write their own computer programs?

15-15. In the text, it was noted that many accounting information systems using small-business computers were "integrated." What does this term mean, and why would integration concern the small business?

15-16. Examine the Accounts Payable Periodic Liabilities Report illustrated in Figure 15-10. Discuss as many uses as you can for such a report. Which personnel within a small company would need the information contained in this report?

15-17. What is a matrix accounting system? What advantage(s), if any, might a matrix accounting system offer a small business as compared with a conventional manual system of journals and ledgers?

15-18. How might the use of a matrix accounting system lead in a natural way to the use of a minicomputer or small-business computer?

PROBLEMS

15-19. Refer to Figure 15-9. Design a computer file record that would enable a computer program to print out the reports illustrated in the figure. The order in which you list the data fields is not as important as the completeness of your list. What additional fields beyond those you have listed already would be desirable in the computer record?

15-20. Refer to Figure 15-10. Design a computer file record that would enable a computer program to print out the reports illustrated in the figure. The order in which you list the data fields is not as important as the completeness of your list. What additional fields beyond those you have listed already would be desirable in the computer record?

15-21. Alex Road operates a part-time plumbing business a few hours each week. His business is called the Clean Sewer Company. Because of the small volume of transactions, Mr. Road uses a matrix accounting system to accumulate his company's monetary data for monthly financial statements. The Clean Sewer Company's June 1, 1984 trial balance is shown below.

Cash	$ 700	
Accounts receivable	300	
Plumbing equipment	800	
Accumulated depreciation—		
plumbing equipment		$ 500
Accounts payable		200
Alex Road, capital		1100
	$1800	$1800

The company's June 1984 accounting transactions are:

June 1 Paid the June store rent, $300.

June 5 Provided plumbing services to a customer and received $600 cash.

June 10 Paid $75 of the accounts payable liabilities.

June 17 Provided plumbing services to a customer and billed him $200.

June 23 Collected $100 from an accounts receivable customer.

June 30 Paid the June utilities bill on the store, $75.

June 30 Paid the part-time employee his monthly salary, $250 (ignore social security taxes and other deductions).

June 30 Recognized the monthly depreciation on the plumbing equipment, $25.

Requirements

Perform the following accounting functions for the Clean Sewer Company.

A. Utilizing a matrix system, record the Clean Sewer Company's June 1984 accounting transactions within its matrix.

B. Using the data from the Clean Sewer Company's completed June matrix, prepare the company's June 1984 financial statements (i.e., its income statement and its balance sheet).

15-22. (Library Research) From such publications as *Datamation, Computerworld*, or some other source, obtain copies of an advertisement for a programmable calculator, an advertisement for a minicomputer, and an advertisement for a small-business computer. What features appear to distinguish one machine from the other? What types of accounting functions could be performed on the smallest machine as well as on each of the two larger machines?

CASE ANALYSES

15-23. *Ward's Farm*

Ward's Farm is a 3000 acre grain farm located in White County, near Carmi, Illinois. Paul Ward, the owner, has been farming since 1971. He initially purchased 325 acres and has made the following land purchases since then: 300 acres in 1975, 150 acres in 1978, 1000 acres in 1979, 900 acres in 1982, and 325 acres in 1984. The cost of farm land has inflated over the years so that although Mr. Ward has a total investment of $919,000, the land is currently valued at $2,950,000.

The farm is separated into 48 different fields averaging over 60 acres per field. Several larger fields exceed 100 acres, whereas others run 10 to 12 acres. The farm also covers several types of terrain and has several types of soil. Some of the land is high and hilly, some of the land is low and claylike, and the rest is humus-rich prairie soil. Fertilizer mixes are determined by type of soil and type of grain to be planted. Mr. Ward now determines mix by his experienced "rules of thumb."

The equipment used on the farm consists of nine tractors (farm-type), three combines with assorted grain heads, four tandem-axle grain bed trucks, one tractor-trailer, three pickup trucks, and numerous discs, plows, wagons, and assorted tractor and hand tools. Additionally, the farm has three equipment storage barns, an equipment maintenance shed, and a 165,000 bushel grain elevator/drier. The equipment and buildings have an estimated worth of $625,000.

Mr. Ward employs five full-time farm hands, a mechanic, a bookkeeper, and has contracted part-time accounting/tax assistance with a local CPA firm in Carmi. All employees are salaried. The farm hands are paid $12,000 a year, as is the bookkeeper. The mechanic is paid $15,000 annually and the CPA contract costs are $8,250 a year.

In 1984, the farm produced 25,300 bushels of wheat, 68,800 bushels of soybeans, and 119,000 bushels of yellow corn. The gross income was $681,321 with Mr. Ward's net income after taxes being $57,500.

Ray Ward, Mr. Ward's son, has just returned from college. He knows that the farm is profitable but feels that proper work scheduling and implementation of proper internal controls could increase profitability and reduce his father's workload even more. He also knows that his father still thinks of the farm as a small business which requires only a knowledge of farming for proper management. There are no controls over parts inventory, no schedules for preventive maintenance, and no scientific application of crop rotation or crop food principles.

Questions

1. Some people still think of farming as small, family-run operations, but the average farm today exceeds 200 acres. Large corporate farms seem to be the development of the future. With this in mind, what are some data-processing areas where the capability of the computer could assist farm owners in their accounting functions?

2. Given the limited information above, recommend a cost-effective approach to computerizing some of the accounting functions suggested in the case description.

15-24. *Papakolea Country Club*

Papakolea Country Club is a small golf facility that has grown from a 9-hole golf course at its inception in 1938, to its present 18-hole status. Other facilities include a paddle tennis court, shuffleboard, lawn sports, and a modest club house with a small bar and snack shop. The pro shop is operated by the golf professional. All other facilities are under the control of the club manager, who is guided by a board of directors.

The membership is made up of 350 regular members and 150 social members. The club is located in a suburban environment. The membership is primarily made up of "self-made" small business entrepreneurs who do not have a great deal of sophistication in the planning and control techniques of a business concern.

Management personnel of the club have been very basic in their approach, choosing to "fly by the seat of their pants." Salary levels in the management area have not justified or attracted high-level management personnel. In addition, the board of directors, elected from the club membership, serve two-year terms. This fact and normal membership attrition give very little continuity to the board.

Existing operating departments are: (1) golf, which has sub-functions of golf-course operations, carts, pro shop, and lockers, and (2) the snack bar and liquor bar. Staff functions of administration, promotions, and maintenance are also an integral part of the club operation. Revenues and expenses attributable to these two operating departments vary according to season and the degree of activity generated by the current board of directors in the way of tournaments, social functions, and the like. The largest source of revenues is from initiation fees and monthly dues.

The current practice with regard to accounting records is for the manager and the office assistant to accumulate monthly documents and forward them to a small bookkeeping service which subsequently furnishes an income statement and balance sheet to the club manager and board of directors. These financial statements are received by the twentieth of the month following the previous month's operations. The statements are hard to interpret and provide no comparative basis for analysis. Because of the lack of information and the lack of timeliness provided by the financial reports, it is difficult for the club to define objectives for future operations, measure the efficiency of operations, and generally plan and control the club's financial matters.

You have been hired by the club as an independent consultant. A review of the existing state of affairs has revealed the facts disclosed above. As an initial means to alleviate the club's problems, you are thinking of implementing an operational budget with resultant performance reports.

Required

1. Design a basic format for the operational budget.
2. As a tool to assist in implementing the budget system, enumerate the ways in which the budgetary system will assist the club management, board of directors, and membership.
3. As a consultant you have been queried on the appropriateness of installing an EDP system to help the club in its accounting functions. Discuss from a positive and negative point of view how a computer application would or would not provide assistance to the club's accounting information system.

16

Accounting Information Systems for Service and Not-for-Profit Organizations

Among the important questions that you should be able to answer after reading this chapter are:

1 What are some common accounting information systems problems in a service organization such as a law firm or a medical clinic?

2 Why doesn't a service organization such as a consulting firm have a "merchandise inventory" asset on its balance sheet?

3 Why are the budgetary planning and controlling systems in service organizations typically less effective than the budgetary systems in nonservice organizations?

4 Why is effective budgetary planning and controlling more important in a not-for-profit organization such as a state university than in a profit-oriented organization?

5 Would a hospital be classified as a service organization, a not-for-profit organization, or a combination of both types of organizations?

INTRODUCTION

Up to this point, little attention has been given to either service organizations (such as law firms, CPA firms, consulting firms, medical clinics, and restaurants) or not-for-profit organizations (such as governmental organizations and religious organizations). A service organization normally provides "intangible services" rather than "tangible goods" to its customers and is a profit-oriented organization. Since a not-for-profit organization (sometimes called a *nonprofit* organization) also typically provides "intangible services" to its customers, the not-for-profit organization is a type of service organization. However, by definition, not-for-profit organizations are not profit-oriented. These organizations' successes are evaluated based upon their contributions to the public welfare.

This chapter will analyze some of the major operating aspects of both service organizations and not-for-profit organizations. Since many college graduates will be employed by either a service organization or a not-for-profit organization, an entire chapter covering these two types of organizations is essential. Primary attention will be devoted to discussing those accounting information systems characteristics that are unique to the service and the not-for-profit organizations.

SERVICE ORGANIZATIONS

The term *service organization* encompasses a wide variety of business establishments that provide services to consumers. Included within the service organization classification of business entities are restaurants, hotels, barber and beauty shops, law firms, CPA firms, consulting firms, motion picture and television studios, and athletic organizations such as professional baseball or football teams.

Compared with organizations that provide tangible goods (such as an automobile manufacturer) to their customers, service organizations have several unique operating characteristics. Some of these characteristics are now examined.

Unique Characteristics of Service Organizations

The distinguishing characteristics of most service organizations include: (1) the absence of an inventory of saleable merchandise, (2) the importance of professional employees, (3) the difficulty in measuring the quantity and quality of output, and (4) the smallness of size. Each of these four service-organization attributes is discussed below.

The absence of merchandise inventory. This characteristic can greatly affect the revenue-earning activities of a service organization. A manufacturer of tangible goods (such as the Alan Company which manufactures sporting goods) builds up an inventory of merchandise for both current and future sales. This inventory serves as a buffer against future possible sales fluctuations. For example, if the Alan Company expects next month's basketball sales to exceed the basketball manufacturing capacity of the plant, the company can increase the current month's basketball production. Alternatively, if the Alan Company loses some sporting goods sales this month as a result of poor marketing efforts, perhaps these sales can be made up in subsequent months (for instance, through more efficient marketing programs).

Most service organizations cannot manufacture an inventory of merchandise for present and future sales. The so-called "inventory" that a service organization sells in its revenue-earning endeavors consists of the services that the organization's employees provide to customers. These services cannot be accumulated in an inventory. Therefore, any failure today to earn revenues from services cannot directly be made up tomorrow or next month. The revenue lost from not providing the services today has a high probability of never being earned. For example, on a Saturday night, the Fine Taste Restaurant may have to turn away some customers because all the available table space has been reserved. These customers will likely make reservations at another food establishment, causing the Fine Taste Restaurant to lose forever the revenues that could have been earned from the customers that evening. Of course, the customers turned away on Saturday night may make reservations for Sunday night or next weekend at the Fine Taste Restaurant. The point, however, is that a service organization such as a restaurant is unable to stockpile an inventory to meet fluctuations in sales demand. The Fine Taste Restaurant may have 75 percent of its dining tables unoccupied on Monday night, whereas the demand for dining tables on Saturday night may exceed the supply. Ideally, the restaurant's management could plan an inventory buildup of customer dining services Monday night and then sell these services Saturday night. Obviously, this type of inventory buildup would be impossible.

The importance of professional employees. In many service organizations, the most important "asset resources" are the specialized skills of their personnel. True, skilled employees are also important to the efficient operation of a nonservice organization such as a manufacturing firm. But, for a large number of service organizations, the *only* product offered is the professional talents of their human resources. For example, a law firm could not function properly without trained lawyers. Similarly, how could a professional football team operate without the talents of its athletes?

The measurement of quantity and quality of output. In a manufacturing firm such as the Alan Company, the organization's accountants can develop both quantity and quality standards for the manufactured inventory items. If the actual physical quantity of manufactured sporting goods within a specified time period varies significantly from the predetermined standard production quantity, management-by-exception reports can be prepared to disclose these variations. Furthermore, as the Alan Company's tangible sporting goods inventory items come off the assembly line, quality control experts can inspect the merchandise for defective items. Thus, any defective merchandise can be discovered before it is sold to customers.

Quantity and quality standards of output are difficult, if not impossible, to measure in most service organizations because a tangible output product does not exist. A further problem when attempting to establish output quantity standards in a service organization is the fact that much of the work performed is nonrepetitive, thereby making it extremely difficult to develop a standard quantity of output for a specified period of work time. In an 8-hour work day, for example, a lawyer may talk to four different clients with four completely different problems. (One of the clients may be facing a murder charge, whereas another client is filing for a divorce!) The lawyer may consult with each of these clients for approximately two hours. However, the number of hours spent with a client is no indication of the quantity of actual services provided to the client since the services (the legal advice) are an intangible product. Because each client's problems are unique, any attempt to establish a quantity standard of legal services per hour would be very difficult. Furthermore, because no tangible prod-

uct (whose quality level can be physically inspected) results from the lawyer's services, any attempt to establish a quality standard of output would be highly subjective. For example, the client facing a murder charge may receive a 20- to 30-year prison sentence. The lawyer may feel that he or she performed a "brilliant" defense because the client could have received a life sentence. The client, on the other hand, may be quite dissatisfied with the lawyer's work because this client expected to receive only a 10-year prison sentence. The debate concerning the lawyer's quality of performance could continue indefinitely without being resolved.

The difficulty of establishing a quality standard of performance for professional workers (whether an accountant, a lawyer, an engineer, or a doctor) and then determining whether or not this standard has been met is probably the major factor causing the number of negligence suits filed against professional individuals. If, for example, a doctor performs heart surgery on a patient and the patient subsequently dies, the deceased person's family may sue the doctor for negligence. Because of the difficulty involved in assessing the quality of care provided to this deceased patient, the matter of negligence is often a subjective issue.

The smallness of size. This characteristic does not apply to all service organizations. (For example, some CPA firms have 500 or more partners and have offices in over 100 cities.) However, many service organizations are relatively small business firms that operate from a single office. Service organizations' smallness of size enables such companies' top management personnel to exercise close control over day-to-day operating activities rather than having to delegate this control function to lower-level managers (as is done in large organizations).

From a cost/benefit standpoint, the limited daily volume of financial transactions that occur in most small service organizations would not justify these companies having large and expensive computerized data-processing systems. However, because of the stiff competition that often exists among several service firms in the same geographical location (e.g., it is common to find 100 or more small restaurants within many cities' boundaries) and the resultant need for timely information which contributes to more efficient and effective decision-making, many service organizations utilize some form of automated data processing. A restaurant, for example, may hire a service bureau or a time-sharing organization to process its monthly sales, inventory of food supplies, and accounts payable data. As we have already discussed in Chapter 15, it is also quite common for small companies to acquire their own minicomputer systems. Chapter 15 emphasized that minicomputers are inexpensive and can be utilized very effectively for many accounting data-processing functions of the small business firm. For instance, it is important for a restaurant to have timely data about the current balances of the many inventory food items in stock so that an additional quantity of a specific inventory item can be reordered when its balance gets too low. Otherwise, the food service firm may run out of a needed inventory item (such as hamburger meat) before it can be replenished. As a consequence, the restaurant would be unable to fill customers' requests, possibly causing these customers to take their business to the restaurant across the street. To obtain timely inventory data and avoid a problem such as the above, the restaurant might purchase a minicomputer for maintaining food inventory information rather than continuing to utilize its manual inventory record-keeping system.

In the past several years, various types of minicomputer systems have been developed to meet the specific data-processing needs of small service organizations. For example, a minicomputer system called the "dental management computer system" has been designed by Praxis Ltd. for use by dentists who have their own small medical firms to service patients. This computer system includes a 12-inch CRT video display terminal, a high-speed printer, a 10 megabyte dual hard disk storage unit, a central processing unit, and dental software packages. The dental management computer system is capable of performing seven major data-processing functions: personal communication, appointment book, pa-

tient records maintenance, accounts receivable, disbursements, general ledger, and payroll. Figure 16-1 reflects a schematic diagram of the specific data-processing activities that the minicomputer system can perform within each one of the seven above-mentioned functions. (The diagram also indicates the types of "maintenance and utilities" functions that the system is able to execute.)

Having analyzed several of the operating characteristics found in most service organizations, we will now discuss some specific budgetary planning and controlling attributes that are common to many service type business firms.

Budgetary Attributes of Service Organizations

Most service organizations' budgetary planning and controlling systems are not as effective as the budgetary systems of those business firms that manufacture and sell tangible goods. Among the principal reasons for service organizations often having ineffective budget planning and controlling systems are: (1) the smaller investment in long-term tangible assets, (2) the difficulty in defining operational goals, and (3) the difficulty in evaluating performance. Each of these three reasons is examined in greater detail below.

The smaller investment in long-term tangible assets. As discussed in Chapter 3, most long-range budgetary planning decisions involve the evaluation of alternative program proposals, each one of which requires a major dollar investment in long-term assets (e.g., a new building or new machinery). Because of the large cost involved in acquiring long-term tangible assets such as a building or additional machinery and the difficulty of reversing the acquisition decision once it is made, many organizations will perform rather sophisticated long-range budgetary planning prior to committing themselves to long-term asset investments. For each major long-term asset investment under consideration, an organization should compare the present value of the total expected net cash flows from the asset's use with the present value of the total expected cash investment necessary to acquire the asset (in

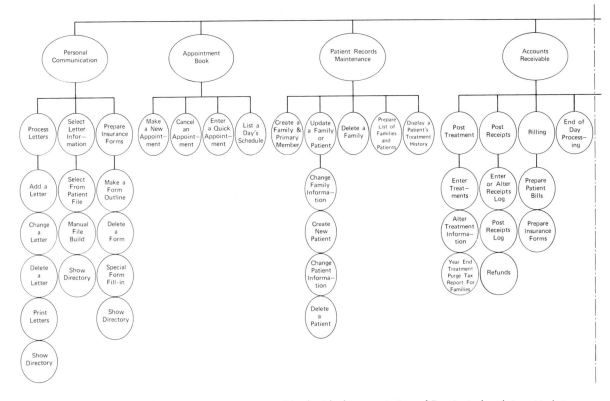

Figure 16-1. Dental management computer system. (Used with the permission of Praxis, Ltd., Alpine, Utah.)

other words, employ the "excess present value index" method discussed in Chapter 3). Then, those investment alternatives having the largest expected excess present value indexes are selected for implementation.

For the typical service organization, however, the principal assets in both the long-run and in the short-run are people rather than things. (There are exceptions, of course, such as a hotel with its major dollar investment in a building facility.) As a result, the only long-range budgetary planning commonly performed in many service organizations (such as those law firms, CPA firms, restaurants, and athletic organizations that lease rather than purchase their building facilities) are forecasts of long-range employee staffing needs. However, even when projecting long-range staffing needs, most service organizations do not use formal quantitative methods (such as the "excess present value index" method) in the budgetary planning of their future

labor requirements. Rather, a service organization's top management will often hire additional personnel based upon highly subjective judgments about the firm's current and future staffing needs. One major reason for this subjective and normally less-effective budgetary approach in service organizations is the difficulty of quantifying the anticipated benefits from hiring additional staff. On the other hand, a manufacturing firm considering the acquisition of new production equipment can attempt to measure the benefits from this equipment (although not easily measured) by analyzing the additional tangible goods that the equipment will be able to manufacture and then estimating the additional revenue that will be earned from selling the goods produced.

A second major reason for less-effective long-range budgetary planning methods in service organizations is the result of the increased flexibility of these organizations in reversing a previous

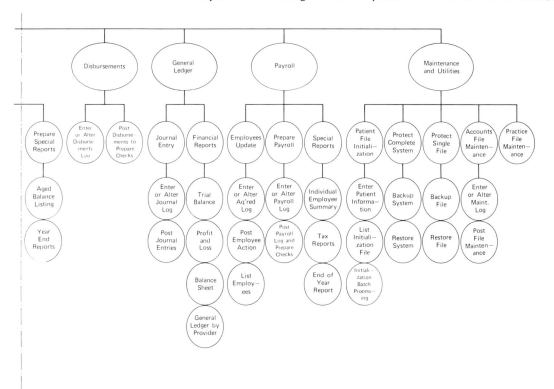

Figure 16-1 (Continued)

long-range budget decision. For example, if a CPA firm hires two additional staff members and subsequently (say a year later) the two employees' services are no longer needed, the CPA firm's top management can terminate their employment without great difficulty and cost to the firm. However, if a manufacturing organization acquires additional machinery costing $150,000 and a year later realizes that this equipment is unnecessary, the difficulty and cost of reversing the previous decision (i.e., to acquire the equipment) could be detrimental to the success of the organization's operating activities.

The difficulty in defining operational goals. As has been previously emphasized in the text, the development of a budgetary system requires that an organization's long-range nonoperational multiplicity of goals first be established. Then, based upon these nonoperational goals (such as achieving a satisfactory level of net income,

achieving a high quality of manufactured inventory items, etc.), the organization develops its short-range and long-range operational budgets. For business firms that manufacture and sell tangible goods and normally have a major investment in long-term tangible assets, the budgeted level of net income performance can be based upon a satisfactory "return-on-assets employed" (i.e., net income ÷ total assets). However, for a service organization, the quantity of tangible assets required to earn a satisfactory net income is often minimal. Rather, the major resource that contributes to many service organizations' income earning capabilities is the *skills* of their professional staff (e.g., the skills of the accountants in a CPA firm, the skills of the doctors in a medical firm, etc.). Because it is difficult, if not impossible, to quantify monetarily the skills of a service organization's professional staff, the determination of a satisfactory "return-on-assets employed" operational goal monetary

465

measure for budgetary planning is unattainable. Without a monetarily determined asset base from which a satisfactory level of income performance can be planned, budget forecasting of the service organization's acceptable future income level is an extremely difficult task.

In its budgetary planning, a manufacturing firm can establish a "quality level" operational goal for its inventory and then plan the production process (e.g., purchase the proper quality of raw materials to be used in the manufacturing activities) so that this pre-established quality level can be achieved. As discussed earlier in the chapter, the products sold by most service organizations are of an "intangible" rather than a "tangible" nature (such as the systems change recommendations provided to a client by a consulting firm). Therefore, any efforts by a service organization to develop pre-established operational quality goals for its intangible products involve considerable subjectivity.

Another factor that makes defining operational goals quite difficult (especially in professional service organizations such as law firms, CPA firms, and medical clinics) is the motivation of the professional staff. A professional (a doctor, a lawyer, an accountant, etc.) often has motivational goals that point in two conflicting directions: (1) goals that contribute to the operational success of the business firm where he or she works, and (2) goals that contribute to the professional's recognition by colleagues. The former goals are positively related to the goals of the professional worker's organization, whereas the professional worker's latter goals may be inconsistent with the goals of the organization. For example, during a doctor's normal 8 hour work day in a medical clinic, approximately 6 of these hours may be devoted to patient care, while the other 2 hours may be devoted to the doctor's own personal research endeavors. The 6 hours during which the doctor is working with patients contribute directly to the medical clinic's profit goal because the doctor's services earn revenue for the clinic. However, the direct contribution that the doctor makes to the medical clinic's goals during the 2 hours which are devoted to research may be questionable. If the research work

enables the doctor to publish several articles in professional medical journals, this doctor will receive positive recognition from colleagues. But, during the 2-hour daily research period, the doctor is not earning any clinic revenues, which otherwise could be earned if the medical doctor were seeing patients. Thus, the work time that is spent on research could actually be inconsistent with the medical clinic's profit goal. (Of course, if the doctor becomes well-known from the research activities, more patients may start coming to the medical clinic, thereby causing the clinic's net income to increase significantly!) When a service organization attempts to establish operational goals as the basis for budgetary planning, it becomes very difficult to forecast what positive effects might accrue to the organization as a result of the employees' professional recognition goals.

The difficulty in evaluating performance. Chapters 2 and 3 discussed the importance of timely performance reports which disclose significant variations between budget projections and actual results. The information from these control reports enables a company's management to investigate any significant budget variations and institute corrective action.

The difficulty in evaluating a service organization's operating performance arises from the previously discussed reason (which was "the difficulty in defining operational goals") why these types of organizations have less effective budgetary systems. It is a vicious circle with no escaping! In order to develop an effective budgetary planning system, a business firm first must clarify its operational goals. If an organization is unable to define its operational goals formally (as is true in many service organizations), the process of preparing financial budgets becomes extremely difficult. Without reliable, available budget data which can be compared with actual operating data, any attempt to evaluate the efficiency or inefficiency of the business firm's operational performance is therefore a difficult undertaking. Even in specific situations where a fairly reliable budget projection can be made for a service organization's operating activities, the evaluation of the organization's subsequent efficient or inefficient performance is usually still quite difficult.

For example, a consulting firm's top management may be able to estimate that approximately 350 hours will be necessary to perform a systems study for its client company. Based upon this estimate, the consulting firm's budget planners can develop financial forecasts of the expected costs and revenues from performing the consulting job. When the systems study work is finished, the budget projections can be compared with the actual results. However, these comparisons do not reveal the true efficiency or inefficiency of the consulting firm's services to its client. The consulting firm did not provide the client company any "tangible product" whose quality could be examined. Rather, an "intangible product" (the systems change recommendations) resulted from the consulting firm's work activities. Since there are often so many variables beyond the consulting firm's control which determine the effectiveness of its client company's new system (variables such as the competency of the client's employees and the financial stability of the client company), any attempt to evaluate the efficiency or inefficiency of the consultants' systems change recommendations will be very subjective. Furthermore, the newly designed system may have to operate for several years before an evaluation can be made of the system's effectiveness in contributing to the client company's goals.

Concluding Comments on Service Organizations

Accounting information systems face a major challenge due to the unique characteristics of service organizations. The main reason for this challenge is that most service organizations provide their customers with intangible products in which quantity and quality standards are difficult to measure. The measurement problems associated with service organizations are partly the result of the historical development of cost accounting systems. The cost accounting field was originally developed to aid manufacturing companies in accumulating the costs of their work-in-process and finished goods inventories for financial statement reporting. Methods of establishing standards and of reporting variances from standard performance were designed for manufacturing companies' tangible inventory items.

Only in recent years have accountants started to look at some of the measurement problems in service organizations and to recognize the need for cost accounting systems in these types of business firms whose principal assets are often the skills of employees. Some accountants have attempted to measure the value of a service organization's human resource asset. In those service organizations where the employees' professional skills are the major "products" sold, a monetarily-measured human resource asset would be equivalent to a manufacturing or a retail firm's monetarily measured merchandise inventory asset.

Having completed the discussion of service organizations, we now turn our attention to not-for-profit organizations and some of the major operating aspects associated with these types of organizations.

NOT-FOR-PROFIT ORGANIZATIONS

The various types of organizations we have discussed throughout the book were assumed to have the earning of a satisfactory net income as one of their goals. A not-for-profit organization, on the other hand (e.g., a governmental organization such as a public hospital, a state university, a police department, or a fire department), exists primarily to provide services for the protection and betterment of society, and does not have a profit goal.

In the previous analysis of service organizations we discussed several unique characteristics that typically distinguish a service organization from an organization that sells tangible goods. This same type of approach will again be used in examining not-for-profit organizations. Thus, we will now look at some of the specific characteristics which distinguish a not-for-profit organization from a profit-oriented business firm.

Unique Characteristics of Not-for-Profit Organizations

The distinguishing characteristics of most not-for-profit organizations include: (1) a service organization usually staffed by professional employees, (2) a lack of a profit measure, (3) a smaller role of the market mechanism, and (4) a political emphasis. Each of the above-named not-for-profit organization attributes are discussed on the following pages.

A service organization usually staffed by professional employees. Many not-for-profit organizations are similar to service organizations in that (1) the not-for-profit organizations also provide their customers intangible services rather than tangible goods, and (2) the professional skills of the not-for-profit organizations' employees are the most important asset resources. For example, the major asset of relevance to a state university is the knowledge possessed by the educational institution's faculty. In addition, the principal product offered by a state university is an intangible service called "education." It should be emphasized here that whereas a state or city publicly financed educational institution (which is financed through taxpayers' income tax payments, etc.) is a not-for-profit type organization, a privately operated school is profit-oriented and would thus be classified as a service organization. Similarly, a publicly financed hospital or medical clinic is a not-for-profit organization, whereas a privately operated hospital or medical clinic has a profit goal and is therefore considered a service organization.

Since the provision of intangible services to customers and the importance of professional employees exist both in service and not-for-profit organizations, many of the previously-discussed unique characteristics of service organizations also apply to not-for-profit organizations. Most not-for-profit organizations are unable to accumulate an inventory of merchandise for current and future sales, and these types of organizations often have difficulty measuring the quantity and quality of their output. For example, a church cannot build up an inventory of religious inspirational motivation to offer its members, and it is normally quite difficult to measure the quantity and quality of the output from the church. Earlier in this chapter we discussed the systems' problems faced by a service organization from being unable to accumulate an inventory of saleable goods and from the organization's difficulty in measuring its quantity and quality of output. These same systems problems (which will not be discussed again here) can also occur in a not-for-profit organization having no inventory of saleable goods and having difficulty in measuring its quantity and quality of output.

A lack of a profit measure. As we emphasized in Chapter 3 on budgetary accounting information systems, a profit-oriented business organization is able to measure both its inputs (costs or expenses) and its outputs (revenues) monetarily. The organization's operating effectiveness can then be evaluated based upon the extent to which its outputs exceed its inputs (which accountants call a "net income"). For most not-for-profit organizations, however, inputs can be measured monetarily but outputs are difficult, if not impossible, to quantify in monetary terms. Without a monetary measure of both the inputs and the outputs from a specific organizational activity, a profit measure for evaluating the activity's effectiveness cannot be obtained. True, a not-for-profit organization, by definition, does not have a profit goal. However, in order to survive and continue its principal goal of providing useful services to society, a not-for-profit organization should have as one of its goals a "break-even" operating performance level (i.e., that level of performance where the input expenses exactly equal the output revenues).

The inability to measure the output performance monetarily makes it very difficult to evaluate several proposed courses of action that a not-for-profit organization might pursue. Consider the case of a city government that is attempting to evaluate two program alternatives for possible implementation: (1) expand the police department by hiring five additional law-enforcement officers, or (2) expand the fire department by hiring five additional fire-fighters. Ideally, a cost/benefit analysis (as discussed and illustrated in Chapter 3) should be performed on each alternative so that the alternative with the greatest benefits in relation to costs can be selected. Approximate costs can be reasonably estimated for the two alternatives above. The costs of the individual programs will include such things as the anticipated annual salaries and fringe benefits provided to the law-enforcement officers under the one program and the fire-fighters under the other program. However, any attempt to measure monetarily the anticipated benefits (or *outputs*) from each program alternative would be extremely difficult. After all, how can one place a monetary measure on the value of protecting a citizen's life and personal property as a result of hiring additional law enforcement officers or measure monetarily the value of protecting a citizen's life and personal property as a result of hiring additional fire-fighters? Because of the difficulties encountered by many not-for-profit organizations when attempting to determine the monetary benefits from program proposals, highly subjective means are often used in selecting specific programs for implementation.

A smaller role of the market mechanism. The typical profit-oriented business firm operates in a highly competitive market environment and must evaluate consumers' demands for goods and services continually. Profit-oriented organizations must also be highly concerned about cost efficiency so that they can sell their products or services at a competitive price and earn a profit on their various revenue-producing activities.

On the other hand, many not-for-profit organizations are only slightly, if at all, affected by competition, and the not-for-profit organizations typically need not be as concerned about consumers' demands for specific goods and services as profit-oriented firms. For example, a publicly financed university usually will offer educational programs to the residents of its state at a substantially smaller cost than either a private university or a publicly financed university in another state (because the residents would have to pay the higher out-of-state tuition if they elected to attend another state's university). Due to the rising costs of education and the

limited number of dollars that many families have for sending their children to college, a publicly financed university normally will have little, if any, competition regarding the educational opportunities offered in its state. This lack of competition from other educational institutions often causes a publicly financed university to give minimal attention to its consumers' (i.e., the students') demands. Courses within various curricula may be designed for faculty members' subject interests rather than for students' requests for topic coverage. The publicly financed educational institution's lack of competition still permits the school to attract adequate student "consumers" even though little or no attention is given to the students' curricula demands.

The continued survival of a not-for-profit organization is not dependent upon earning an income. As a result, some not-for-profit organizations are unconcerned about cost efficiency and they have weak feedback control systems for evaluating the effectiveness of operational performance. A major reason for a lack of effective feedback controls in some governmental organizations, for example, is that the *owners* of these not-for-profit organizations are actually the taxpayers. Because taxpayers are a diverse group of people who do not directly evaluate the day-to-day operating performance of a governmental organization, inefficiencies that occur within a particular governmental organization may go unnoticed by the taxpayers.

The market competition encountered by a profit-oriented organization and the desire to increase periodic income performance ordinarily causes the organization to institute promotional activities that attract more customers, thereby resulting in more sales revenue. However, many not-for-profit organizations, whose annual operating budgets are fixed by appropriations (such as in governmental organizations), must sometimes turn customers away. Because of their fixed annual budget appropriations, many publicly financed universities, for example, place a quota on the number of students admitted each year. Consequently, some potential student "customers" are typically refused admission to these universities each year.

469

A political emphasis. Politics has a major impact on the operational environment of many not-for-profit organizations (especially governmental organizations). In governmental agencies (whether a city, state, or federal agency) where the "top management" personnel are elected by the voters, executives are often selected for reasons other than their managerial abilities. The reasons may range from the political candidates' pleasing personalities to their financial standing. A negative consequence may be that once the individuals are elected to office, their lack of managerial skills can lead to inefficiency within the particular governmental agency.

Another negative aspect of governmental organizations' operating activities is that these institutions must function within the framework of specific statutes enacted by legislators. As a result, a not-for-profit governmental organization often has less flexibility in its operational activities than a profit-oriented organization. Once statutes are established which control the types of activities that a governmental organization can perform, it is normally very difficult and time consuming to subsequently change these statutes.

Having discussed the important operating characteristics common to many not-for-profit organizations, we will now turn our attention to a few of the specific budgetary planning and controlling attributes that often exist in not-for-profit organizations.

Budgetary Attributes of Not-for-Profit Organizations

The following analysis of not-for-profit organizations' budgetary systems will center around the two principal forms of budgeting performed in these types of organizations: (1) long-range budgeting for time intervals beyond the coming one-year period, and (2) short-range budgeting for the coming one-year period.

Long-range budgeting. The use of cost/benefit analysis with zero-based budget reviews (thoroughly discussed in Chapter 3) is a popular technique for evaluating long-range budgetary pro-

grams of profit-oriented organizations. Through this cost/benefit analysis technique, a profit-oriented organization's limited asset resources can be allocated to the most productive program proposals. Not-for-profit organizations also have limited asset resources for implementing long-range budget program proposals. Furthermore, not-for-profit organizations should strive to utilize their limited asset resources in ways that will contribute most effectively to the protection and betterment of society. As a result, many not-for-profit organizations (especially governmental organizations) also employ formal long-range budgetary techniques such as cost/benefit analyses in evaluating program proposals for subsequent implementation. In fact, the federal government started formal use of the cost/benefit analysis technique with zero-based budget reviews many years before profit-oriented organizations were utilizing this long-range budgetary technique. The term *Planning-Programming-Budgeting System (PPBS)* was coined to designate the federal government's cost/benefit analysis approach to long-range budgeting.

As discussed above, a not-for-profit organization's long-range program proposals should be directed towards the protection and betterment of society. Thus, when performing a cost/benefit analysis of a specific program proposal, the anticipated costs and benefits to society must be quantified monetarily. In most cases, however, a monetary determination of society's benefits from a long-range program is very difficult to make. For example, a department of the federal government may be proposing a program to subsidize automobile manufacturers for the costs of installing safety devices on cars. This program's principal benefits would result from the reduced number of automobile accident deaths. Therefore, in performing a cost/benefit analysis of the automobile safety program proposal, the value of saving a human life in an automobile accident must be monetarily quantified. Obviously, the quantification in monetary terms of a person's life would be extremely difficult, thereby making the decision regarding the acceptance or rejection of the proposed safety program quite difficult.

Short-range budgeting. The establishment of a good short-range budgetary planning and controlling system is normally more important in a not-for-profit organization than in a profit-oriented organization. The reason for the added importance of good short-range budgetary planning and controlling in not-for-profit organizations is the result of the fixed rather than flexible nature of most not-for-profit organizations' 12-month budgets. In a profit-oriented organization, flexibility is normally built into its budgetary system (see Chapter 3). Thus, as the budget year unfolds and management determines that some budgetary costs were underestimated, the profit-oriented organization can revise its budget projections and allocate more dollars to specific expenditures.

However, in a not-for-profit organization, budgetary revisions are difficult, if not impossible, to implement once the budget year begins. For example, in a governmental organization such as a publicly financed state university, the educational institution's annual operating budgets are approved by the state legislators and the governor. If subsequent operations under the approved budgets reveal that actual costs will be higher than anticipated in specific areas of the university, additional budgetary appropriations normally will be impossible to obtain. Because these additional appropriations would require legislative action and the state legislators would not be in session (because legislative sessions for budget approval typically are held only once a year), the university would have to live with its original budgets. Thus, in those not-for-profit organizations subject to *fixed* (also called *static*) budgets, good short-range planning is necessary to obtain accurate budget projections for the coming year. Hopefully, effective budgetary planning will avoid a situation such as the one described above in which the state university's budgeted costs were inadequate to meet actual operating needs. Of course, effective budgetary control is also an essential element that contributes to a not-for-profit organization's actual operating costs being within the original budget appropriations. In the budgetary control area, a computerized data-processing system can play a valuable role. Through timely computerized reports which disclose operational areas where a not-for-profit organization's actual costs exceed original budget appropriations, management can immediately investigate and initiate corrective action before these actual expenditures get too far out of hand.

A further difficulty often encountered in not-for-profit organizations' budgetary systems is the absence of a monetary measure of output accomplishments (such as the sales revenue earned by the Alan Company from selling its sporting goods). For example, a city police department does not bill citizens when law enforcement officers investigate burglaries at their homes. (Of course, citizens pay indirectly for the police services through taxes!) Traditional budgeting typically is centered around the planning of both inputs (costs or expenses) and outputs (revenues) in monetary terms. Since monetary output measures may not exist in certain not-for-profit organizations, alternative quantitative output measures will therefore be needed. A common nonmonetary output performance measure used in some not-for-profit organizations' short-range budget systems is a *process measure* (i.e., a measure relating to a specific "activity" performed by an organization's employees). For instance, within a police department's short-range budget system, one possible process measure could be the number of traffic tickets issued per month by each law enforcement officer. At month's end, traffic citations actually issued by a law enforcement officer could be compared with his or her budgeted number of traffic citations to be issued. It should be kept in mind, however, that a specific officer is not necessarily inefficient merely because the actual issued traffic tickets are below the budgeted number in any one month. It may be that people are just driving more carefully!

Concluding Comments on Not-for-Profit Organizations

The major challenge that accounting information systems face regarding not-for-profit organizations is the difficulty in evaluating the operating performances of these organizations. Because we are all taxpayers who provide financial support for many not-for-profit organizations, we are entitled to receive informational reports that disclose whether or not our tax dollars are being used efficiently and effectively.

The lack of a profit measure in not-for-profit organizations makes it difficult for accounting information systems to report on the operational effectiveness of these organizations. Conventional accounting information systems are designed to measure organizational performance by comparing monetary inputs with monetary outputs. But, in many not-for-profit organizations, monetary output measures do not exist (discussed above). As a result, these organizations' accountants must develop alternative nonmonetary measures (such as a *process measure*) of output performance, and the alternative measures often are inferior to monetary performance indicators. The inferiority of nonmonetary output measures is due to the fact that the evaluation of a not-for-profit organization's operational activities cannot be performed with a common measuring unit. That is, because a not-for-profit organization's inputs are measured in dollars, ideally the organization's outputs should also be measured in dollars. This would enable a realistic evaluation of performance because the output accomplishments could be related to the input efforts with an identical measuring unit—dollars. However, since many not-for-profit organizations' output accomplishments are measured on a nonmonetary basis, whereas their input efforts are measured on a monetary basis, any attempt to evaluate the organizations' operating performances on the basis of these two dissimilar measuring devices (dollars and nondollars) can be quite difficult.

SUMMARY

Several important operating aspects of service organizations (e.g., restaurants, law firms, consulting firms, and CPA firms) and not-for-profit organizations (e.g., governmental organizations) were analyzed in this chapter. The discussion of service and not-for-profit organizations centered around many of the accounting information systems problems that occur because of the unique characteristics that are typical of these two types of organizations.

Service organizations' employees are often professionally trained individuals who provide "intangible services" to the organizations' customers. As a result of most service organizations selling intangible commodities (such as legal advice from a law firm or systems revision advice from a consulting firm) rather than tangible goods, these organizations are unable to build up an inventory of their products for current and future sales. In addition, the intangible characteristic of many service organizations' revenue-producing output makes it quite difficult to develop predetermined quantity and quality standards for this output. Regarding budgetary planning and controlling, several reasons were discussed as to why service organizations normally have less-effective budget systems than organizations that manufacture and sell tangible goods. Included among these reasons were the minimal long-term tangible asset investments required by most service organizations (which therefore make sophisticated long-range budget techniques unnecessary) and the difficulty in defining the operational goals of most service organizations, which is an essential first step in establishing effective budgetary accounting information systems.

Not-for-profit organizations have several characteristics that are similar to service organizations. Most not-for-profit organizations, for example, also offer their customers intangible services and hire professionally trained employees. On the other hand, a service organization has a profit goal, whereas, by definition, a not-for-profit organization lacks a profit orientation (other than achieving a "break-even" performance level). In many not-for-profit organizations, monetary quantification is feasible for their inputs but not their outputs. The unavailability of monetary output measures often makes it difficult to establish effective budget systems within a not-for-profit organization. In the area of long-range budgeting, for example, not-for-profit organizations often utilize cost/benefit analyses in evaluating program proposals for implementation. To evaluate each program proposal effectively, however, both the costs and the benefits must be subject to monetary quantification. For many program proposals of a not-for-profit organization, only the cost inputs can be monetarily quantified. Since the benefit outputs are typically difficult, if not impossible, to quantify in monetary terms, the decision-making process regarding which programs to accept and which to reject can be perplexing. Upon the approval of not-for-profit organizations' short-range budgets, these budgets are normally fixed rather than being subject to later change. Therefore, good short-range budgetary planning is important in a not-for-profit organization so that reasonably accurate annual budget projections can be initially prepared. Monetary measures of output performance for short-range budgetary planning and controlling often are nonexistent in a not-for-profit organization. As an alternative, a nonmonetary indicator such as a *process measure* may have to be used in developing the organization's short-range budgets.

DISCUSSION QUESTIONS

16-1. Four unique characteristics of service organizations were discussed in this chapter. Of these four characteristics, which one do you feel causes the greatest problem for a service organization's accounting information system? Explain.

16-2. Why isn't it possible for a service organization such as a law firm to have a "merchandise inventory" asset? What effect (or effects) does the absence of a "merchandise inventory" asset have on a service organization's revenue earning activities?

16-3. Why is it very difficult to establish quantity and quality standards in most service organizations? If you were an accountant given the responsibility for establishing quantity and quality standards for the food served in an exclusive restaurant, which one of these two types of standards do you feel would be more difficult to determine? Why?

16-4. Jack Butcher is a well-recognized heart surgeon who has been employed at the Healthy House Medical Clinic for the past ten years. During a recent luncheon, Doctor Jack (as he is called by his friends) made the following comments to his wife:

> Here I am a successful surgeon and currently facing a $100,000 malpractice suit from one of my patients. I talked to our clinic's accountants this morning and they indicated that very little information from the accounting system could help my court defense. A major revision of our accounting information system is definitely needed and fast so that when other clinic doctors are facing court action from patients at some future time, these doctors will be able to call upon our accountants for help!

Do you agree or disagree with Doctor Jack's comment regarding the clinic's accounting information system? Discuss.

16-5. The Spicy Pizza Parlor has been in operation for the past six months. The restaurant currently utilizes a manual system for processing such accounting transactions as the weekly payroll for its ten employees, the monthly payments to creditors for the purchase of ingredients used in cooking pizzas, the acquisition of additional food ingredients when the balances of specific ingredients get too low, and the payment of the monthly rent and utilities bill. The Spicy Pizza Parlor's owner, Don Bartenfelder, feels that business is so good that a computer should be acquired for processing the restaurant's accounting transactions. The pizza parlor's monthly sales have been gradually increasing during each of the six months that the business has been functioning (e.g., last month's sales were $7000—a $500 sales increase over the previous month). Don believes that the improved information that could be provided by a computerized data-processing system would cause the future operating performance of his restaurant to increase considerably.

Assume that you are a consultant hired by Don Bartenfelder to help him plan the necessary changes in the restaurant's current accounting information system. With the limited information provided here about the restaurant's operations, indicate the procedures you would use in evaluating the pizza parlor's data-processing needs. (*Note:* You can make any reasonable assumptions necessary concerning the restaurant's operating activities.) What type of data-processing system (a manual system, a purchased or leased online, real-time computerized system from a hardware and software vendor, etc.) would probably be best suited to handle the restaurant's financial transactions? Discuss.

16-6. The following idea was expressed in the chapter: "For the typical service organization, the principal assets in both the long-run and in the short-run are people rather than tangible assets." Discuss the implications of this statement to a service organization's budgetary planning and controlling system.

16-7. Bill Hunt, a partner in the law firm of Hunt, Jacobs, and Bogle, made the following statement during a recent luncheon speech he gave to the Busy Budgeters of America:

> Our law firm recognizes the important role that good budgetary planning and controlling plays in an organization's operational success. All of the partners in our firm participate in developing detailed annual operating budgets. However, when it comes to long-range budgeting, very little, if any, financial projecting is performed. I think the reasons for our lack of attention to long-range budgeting are obvious to all of you.

What do you believe are the obvious reasons for the lack of attention that Bill Hunt's law firm gives to long-range budgeting?

16-8. Discuss some of the factors that typically make it more difficult to define the operational goals of a service organization. How, if at all, does the difficulty in defining a service organization's operational goals affect the organization's budgetary planning and controlling system?

16-9. A major goal common to all universities is the provision of quality education. To help achieve this goal, a university should include in its budgetary planning system adequate provisions for faculty salaries, classroom teaching aids such as overhead projectors and video tape machines, and so forth. What do you think would be the employment goals of faculty members working at a university? For each one of the goals you mentioned, indicate (and give reasons) why you feel the specific goal would contribute positively or negatively to the university's goal of a high-quality student education.

16-10. Do the types of workers employed in an organization (e.g., assembly-line workers in a manufacturing plant compared with accountants in a consulting firm) affect the organization's budgetary planning and controlling activities? Discuss.

16-11. The town of Commuter Park operates a private parking lot near the railroad station for the benefit of town residents. The guard on duty issues annual pre-numbered parking stickers to residents who submit an application form and show evidence of residency. The sticker is affixed to the auto and allows the resident to park anywhere in the lot for 12 hours if 4 quarters are placed in the parking meter. Applications are maintained in the guard office at the lot. The guard checks to see that only residents are using the lot and that no resident has parked without paying the required meter fee.

Once a week the guard on duty, who has a master key for all meters, takes the coins from the meters and places them in a locked steel box. The guard delivers the box to the town storage building where it is opened, and the coins are counted manually by a storage department clerk who records the total cash counted on a "Weekly Cash Report." This report is sent to the town accounting department. The storage department clerk puts the cash in a safe and on the following day the cash is picked up by the town's treasurer, who manually recounts the cash, prepares the bank deposit slip, and delivers the deposit to the bank. The deposit slip, authenticated by the bank teller, is sent to the accounting department where it is filed with the "Weekly Cash Report."

Required

Describe weaknesses in the existing system and recommend one or more improvements for each of the weaknesses to strengthen the internal control over the parking lot cash receipts.

Organize your answers as follows:

Weakness	Recommended Improvement(s)

(AICPA Adapted)

16-12. Two major types of not-for-profit organizations are a publicly financed university and a publicly financed hospital. For each one of these organizational types, discuss some data-processing functions of the organization for which: (1) an online, real-time computerized system would likely be most beneficial, and (2) a batch-computerized system would likely be most beneficial.

16-13. Discuss some of the major operating characteristics that are similar and dissimilar in a service organization such as a consulting firm and in a not-for-profit organization such as a police department.

16-14. Would a college be classified as a service organization, a not-for-profit organization, or a combination of both types of organizations? Explain.

16-15. It was emphasized in the chapter that most not-for-profit organizations lack a profit measure. What effect (or effects), if any, does this lack of a profit measure have on a not-for-profit organization's short- and long-range budgetary planning and controlling system?

16-16. From the viewpoint of society, do you feel that the lack of market competition which many not-for-profit organizations enjoy is good or bad? Explain with a few examples of specific not-for-profit organizations and their positive or negative effects on society.

16-17. The operational environment of a city government unit such as the police department is influenced by politics. Try to think of some positive and negative effects that may occur within the police department's system because of the political impact on the department's operational environment.

16-18. The following statement was made in the chapter: "The establishment of a good short-range budgetary planning and controlling system is normally more important in a not-for-profit organization than in a profit-oriented organization." Do you agree or disagree with this statement? Explain.

16-19. Why might a not-for-profit organization utilize a "process measure" in its short-range budgetary system? For each of the following not-for-profit organizations, suggest possible process measures that might be used in its short-range budgetary system: (a) a city fire department, (b) a publicly financed state university, (c) a publicly financed state museum, and (d) a cancer research institute.

16-20. Why is long-range budgetary planning usually more difficult to perform in a not-for-profit organization than in a profit-oriented organization?

16-21. Joan Moward, the mayor of Green Grass City, has convinced the city council that a new pollution-control department is necessary to preserve the town's clean environment. The city's budget committee is currently meeting to discuss the pollution-control department's short- and long-range budgetary system. Assuming that you are a member of Green Grass City's budget committee, discuss some of the difficulties that the committee might face in its budgetary planning and controlling activities associated with the pollution-control department's short- and long-range budget system. (*Note:* Make any reasonable assumptions you feel are necessary regarding the specific functions that the newly established pollution-control department will perform.)

16-22. The board of trustees of a local church has asked you to review its accounting procedures. As a part of this review, you have prepared the following comments relating to the collections made at weekly services and the record-keeping for members' pledges and contributions:

The church's board of trustees has delegated responsibility for financial management and audit of the financial records to the finance committee. This group prepares the annual budget and approves major disbursements but is not involved in collections or record-keeping. No audit has been considered necessary in recent years because the same trusted employee has kept church records and served as financial secretary for 15 years.

The collection at the weekly service is taken by a team of ushers. The head usher counts the collection in the church office following each service. He then places the collection and a notation of the amount counted in the church safe. Next morning the financial secretary opens the safe and recounts the collection. He withholds about $100 to meet cash expenditures during the coming week and deposits the remainder of the collection intact. In order to facilitate the deposit, members who contribute by check are asked to draw their checks to "cash."

At their request, a few members are furnished prenumbered and predated envelopes in which to insert their weekly contributions. The head usher removes the cash from the envelopes so that it can be counted with the loose cash included in the collection. He immediately discards the envelopes. No record is maintained of issuance or return of the envelopes, and the envelope system is not encouraged.

Each member is asked to prepare a contribution pledge card annually. The pledge is regarded as a moral commitment by the member to contribute a stated weekly amount. Based upon the amounts shown on the pledge cards, the financial secretary furnishes a letter to requesting members to support the tax deductibility of their contributions.

Required

Describe the weaknesses and recommend improvements in procedures for:

a. Collections made at weekly services.
b. Record-keeping for members' pledges and contributions.

Organize your answers as follows:

Weakness	Recommended Improvement(s)

(AICPA Adapted)

PROBLEMS

16-23. Each month the department heads of the National Association of Trade Stores receive a financial report of the performance of their departments for the previous month. The report is generally distributed around the 16th or 17th of the month. Although the association is a not-for-profit trade and educational association, it does attempt to generate revenues from a variety of activities to supplement the member dues. The association has several income-producing departments: research, education, publications, and promotion consulting services. As a general rule, each department is expected to be self-supporting, and the department head is responsible for both the generation of revenue and the control of costs for the department.

As an example of the monthly department report, the March 1984 report of the education department is presented on page 477 with the comment of the accounting department.

The annual revenue target, which becomes the revenue budget, is established by the executive director and the association's board of directors. The annual and monthly expense budgets are then developed at the beginning of the year by the department heads for all costs except rent, utilities and janitorial services, equipment depreciation, and allocated general administration. The amounts for these cost items are supplied by the accounting department. The monthly budget figures for revenues are also determined by the department heads at the beginning of the year. The monthly budget amounts for revenues and expenses are not revised during the year.

For example, the following changes in operations have taken place but the monthly budgets have not been revised: (1) a new home-study course was introduced in February, one month earlier than scheduled; (2) a number of the week-long courses were postponed in February and March and rescheduled for April and May; and (3) the related promotion effort—heavy direct-mail adver-

National Association of Trade Stores
Education Department
Report for the Month of March 1984

	Budget			Actual			Variance		Variance as a Percent of Budget	
	Person Days or Units	$	%	Person Days or Units	$	%	Person Days or Units	$	Person Days or Units	%
Revenue										
Week-long courses	1500	$225,000	71.4%	1250	$187,500	66.4%	(250)	$(37,500)	(16.6)%	(16.6)%
One-day seminars	50	15,000	4.8	17	5,100	1.8	(33)	(9,900)	(66.0)	(66.0)
Home-study courses	1000	75,000	23.8	1100	89,700	31.8	100	14,700	10.0	19.6
		$315,000	100.0%		$282,300	100.0%		$(32,700)		(10.4)%
Expenses										
Salaries		$174,000	55.2%		$167,000	59.1%		$ 7,000		4.0%
Course material		35,500	11.3		34,670	12.3		830		2.3
Supplies, telegraph, and telephone		4,000	1.3		4,200	1.5		(200)		(5.0)
Rent, utilities and janitorial services		7,000	2.2		7,000	2.5		—		—
Equipment depreciation		700	.2		700	.2		—		—
Allocated general administration		5,000	1.6		5,000	1.8		—		—
Temporary office help		5,000	1.6		3,750	1.3		1,250		25.0
Contract employees		15,000	4.8		18,500	6.6		(3,500)		(23.3)
Travel		12,000	3.8		11,500	4.1		500		4.2
Dues and meetings		500	.2		500	.2		—		—
Promotion and postage		32,000	10.1		36,500	12.9		(4,500)		(14.1)
Total expenses		$290,700	92.3%		$289,320	102.5%		$ 1,380		0.5%
Contribution to the Association		$ 24,300	7.7%		$ (7,020)	(2.5)%		$(31,320)		(128.9)%

Comment: The department did not make its budget this month. There was a major short-fall in the week-long course revenues. Although salaries were lower than budget, this saving was entirely consumed by overexpenditure in contract employees and promotion. Further effort is needed to increase revenues and to hold down expenses.

tising in the two months prior to a course offering—was likewise rescheduled.

Required

Identify and briefly discuss the good and bad features of the monthly information communication report presented for the Education Department in terms of:

A. its form and appearance in presenting the operating performance of the education department, and

B. its content in providing useful information to the department head for managing the education department.

Include in your discussion the changes you would recommend to improve the report as a communication device.

(CMA Adapted)

16-24. The Argon County Hospital is located in the county seat. Argon County is a well-known summer resort area. Its population doubles during the vacation months (May–August), and hospital activity more than doubles during these months. The hospital is organized into several departments. Although it is relatively small, its pleasant surroundings have attracted a well-trained and competent medical staff.

An administrator was hired a year ago to improve the business activities of the hospital. Among the new ideas he has introduced is responsibility accounting. This program was announced along with quarterly cost reports supplied to department heads. Previously, cost data were presented to department heads infrequently. Excerpts from the announcement and the report received by the laundry supervisor follow.

> The hospital has adopted a responsibility accounting system. From now on you will receive quarterly reports comparing the costs of operating your department with budgeted costs. The reports will highlight the differences (variations) so you can zero in on the departures from budgeted costs. (This is called *management by exception.*) Responsibility accounting means you are accountable for keeping the costs in your department within the budget. The variations from the budget will help you identify what costs are out of line and the size of the variations will indicate which ones are the most important. Your first such report accompanies this announcement.

The annual budget for 1984 was constructed by the new administrator. Quarterly budgets were computed as one-fourth of the annual budget. The administrator compiled the budget from analysis of the prior three years' costs. The analysis showed that all costs increased each year, with more rapid increases between the second and third year. He considered establishing the budget at an average of the prior three years' costs, hoping that the installation of the system would reduce costs to this level. However, in view of the rapidly increasing prices, he finally chose 1983 costs less 3% for the 1984 budget. The activity level measured by patient days and pounds of laundry processed was set at 1983 volume, which was approximately equal to the volume of each of the past three years.

Required

A. Comment on the method used to construct the budget.
B. What information should be communicated by variations from budgets?
C. Recast the budget to reflect responsibility accounting, assuming the following:
    1. Laundry labor, supplies, water and water heating and softening, and maintenance are variable costs. The remaining costs are fixed.

Argon County Hospital
Performance Report—Laundry Department
July–September 1984

	Budget	Actual	(Over) Under Budget	Percentage (Over) Under Budget
Patient days	9,500	11,900	(2,400)	(25)
Pounds of laundry processed	125,000	156,000	(31,000)	(25)
Costs				
Laundry labor	$ 9,000	$12,500	$(3,500)	(39)
Supplies	1,100	1,875	(775)	(70)
Water and water heating and softening	1,700	2,500	(800)	(47)
Maintenance	1,400	2,200	(800)	(57)
Supervisor's salary	3,150	3,750	(600)	(19)
Allocated administration costs	4,000	5,000	(1,000)	(25)
Equipment depreciation	1,200	1,250	(50)	(4)
	$21,550	$29,075	$(7,525)	(35)

Administrator's comments: Costs are significantly above budget for the quarter. Particular attention needs to be paid to labor, supplies, and maintenance.

2. Actual prices are expected to be approximately 20% above the levels in the budget prepared by the hospital administrator.

(CMA Adapted)

CASE ANALYSES

16-25. *Conflict at Boyd College*

College Publications (CP) was established in 1970 by the president of Boyd College to advance the quality and effectiveness of the college's graphic communications. CP provides professional editing, designing, and planning services to all academic and administrative units requesting help in the publication of catalogs, brochures, booklets, posters, and other forms of printed material. CP is under the vice-president for public affairs, employs a professional staff of 20, and has an annual operating budget of $500,000.

To encourage the use of CP's services, the costs of operating CP have not been allocated or charged to units requesting services. Instead, these operating costs are included in central administration overhead. However, to maintain as much uniformity as possible in the content and design of the college's publications, all items submitted to CP for publication are reviewed and approved by CP. Thus, CP can reject or require the complete revision of a unit's publication. The number of copies for each publication is determined jointly by CP and the unit requesting service.

During the last two years Boyd College has experienced considerable financial pressure. Inflation has increased operating costs, a downturn in the stock market has reduced endowment income, and various governmental agencies have cut back on research support. During the spring of 1984, the president of the college established a number of task forces to review various aspects of the college's operations. These task forces collectively concluded that there was a need to emphasize and promote fiscal responsibility among administrative and academic units. Consequently, the task force on publications recommended the use of a charge-back system in which user units pay for services requested from CP.

In the fall of 1984, the president issued a memorandum requiring the use of a charge-back system for the services of CP. The memorandum stated that the purpose of the new system was "to put control and responsibility for publication expenditures where the benefits were received and to make academic and administrative units more aware of the publication costs they were incurring." The memorandum suggested that the costs of operating CP be charged back to user units on the basis of actual hours used in servicing their publication needs.

The academic and administrative units that purchased publication services through CP were generally pleased with the president's memorandum, even though they had some reservations about how the charge-back rate would be calculated. They had not been happy about having to obtain CP's approval in purchasing publication services. Their major complaint had been that CP imposed excessively high standards that resulted in overly expensive publications.

The director of CP was very upset about the president's memorandum. He believed that the charge-back system was a political maneuver by the president to get the task force pressures off his back. He believed that the task force had paid too much attention to publication costs and that the new system would reduce the effectiveness of CP to the college as a whole. He also was upset that the president took unilateral action in establishing the new system. He believed that it was a big jump from the memorandum to the installation of the new system and he was concerned about whether the new system would achieve the desired results.

Questions

1. What are the likely motivational and operational effects of the new system on:
   A. academic and administrative units requesting and using the services of CP?

B.   College Publications?

C.   Boyd College?

2.   Evaluate the president's methods for instituting an organizational change with respect to College Publications.

(CMA Adapted)

16-26.   *City System**

The purpose of a city is to provide public services desired or demanded by its citizens. These services or functions, of which there are many, include such things as: (1) protection of the citizens from those who break the law, (2) provision of water and sanitary services, and (3) provision for the transportation of people and goods. The total of these functions can be broadly grouped into four sectors: (1) public safety, (2) human resource development, (3) public finance, and (4) physical and economical development.

Present Conditions

In cities, as in any large complex organization, there is a multiplicity of requirements for the same information. Too frequently, however, these requirements are satisfied by each user independently collecting and storing data for himself. The tax assessor, the fire department, and the building inspector, for example, all require similar information about buildings, including such things as: (1) address, (2) dimensions, (3) construction type, (4) number of access ways, etc. Frequently, in many cities, there are a vast number of people whose job it is to "massage" data, putting it into a form useful for managerial decisions ranging from "what are my budget requirements for next year" to "which of the traffic signals should have preventive maintenance performed."

There is a preponderance of the latter type inquiry which, in many instances, requires routine decisions but which, at the same time, occupies so much of a manager's time. By way of examples, such decisions include: (1) designation of which properties in the city should be reappraised, (2) scheduling vehicles and equipment for preventive maintenance, and (3) preparation of lists of those people who should be sent notifications of their failure to pay tickets.

Requirements for Proposed Municipal Information System

1.   Furnish information to top management, operating management, and other users necessary to carry out the day-to-day activities.

2.   Provide a means to interface the system with outside organizations or special districts including: (a) independent school boards, (b) water districts, (c) citizen or civic organizations, and (d) economic development districts. In addition, the system must also be responsive to the many reporting demands of the Federal Government.

Questions

Assume that you are a systems analyst for a consulting firm. Answer the following questions.

1.   Conceptualize, in broad terms, the kind of Municipal Information System you propose. Draw any schematics and write all narratives that you feel are necessary in communicating your systems design. Be as specific as you can, but bear in mind that this design is introductory in nature.

2.   Prepare, in addition to your conceptual systems design, a complete report on some of the benefits that you envision will accrue to the city should the mayor and others commission you for the development and implementation of the information system. Be specific.

3.   Prepare a list of questions that you intend to ask the mayor and divisional heads in your meeting with them.

4.   Enumerate the advantages as well as the disadvantages of your proposed system.

*Used with the permission of John G. Burch, Jr. and Felix R. Strater, Jr, *Information Systems: Theory and Practice*, John Wiley & Sons, Inc., © 1979.

PART SIX

Comprehensive Cases

Accounting information systems within a computerized environment have been stressed throughout this book. Effective tools to help students better understand the dynamic area of accounting information systems are "real-world" cases which illustrate actual problems that have occurred in companies' systems.

Short cases have been provided within most of our book's 19 chapters. As a means of emphasizing the practical application of many of the concepts stressed in the text, this section will present five comprehensive cases that require extensive analysis. There is no one correct solution to any case. Rather, the cases are designed to stimulate class discussions that will bring forth creative ideas.

The five comprehensive cases are completely independent of each other. Thus, one or more of them can be excluded if so desired. Presented below is a brief description of the five cases.

Case 1
VANCOUVER RECREATIONAL PRODUCTS
This case concerns a company that is having problems with its present data-processing system. An extensive systems study job is performed to determine whether or not a computerized system should be implemented into the company.

Case 2
AQUA SPRAY
This case deals with the recommendation of changes in a company's accounting information system for processing inventory and sales transactions as well as suggesting recommendations for maintaining control over inventory activities. In addition, evaluation is required of data-processing equipment alternatives to handle the company's inventory and sales transactions.

Case 3
LAUB GROUP, INCORPORATED
This case concerns a company that is currently using a service bureau to process its accounting information. An evaluation is required of: (1) the company's accounting information system in meeting management's decision-making needs, and (2) the company's control procedures associated with accounts receivable and accounts payable. In addition, consideration is required as to whether the company should purchase or lease its own computer and the types of procedures and controls that should be incorporated into a computerized accounting information system.

Case 4
STATE CONSUMER REPORTING BUREAU
This case involves the data-processing requirements of a collection agency. A team of management consultants has proposed a computerized accounting information system to replace the organization's manual system. Questions remain regarding what kinds of information the collection agency should maintain in its data base, and the advantages and disadvantages of the proposed computerized system.

Case 5
PARADISE HOTEL
This case concerns the front-desk operations of a medium-sized hotel. Problems with some of the front-desk operations have prompted management to consider the use of a real-time computerized data-processing system to replace the front-desk's manual system. A management consultant has outlined how the new computer system will work. It is not clear, however, what computer files will be required in this new system or how these files will be used to accomplish the accounting functions of the front-office staff. A lack of accounting controls also bothers the hotel manager responsible for the front-desk system.

CASE 1

Vancouver Recreational Products*

Company Background

Vancouver Recreational Products (V.R.P.), a privately owned company, has the exclusive distributorship for motorized recreation vehicles across Canada. The company name has been associated with motorized recreation sales for some 60 years, with the different retail outlets operating as separate companies.

The partners, Tom Jones and Henry Leeds, operate the business out of Vancouver although 70% of the volume sales (100 dealers across Canada) is in the eastern provinces. Their warehouse for vehicle parts distribution is located in Toronto and employs 18 people. The Vancouver headquarters has a staff of 12. In addition to the partners, most of the general responsibility is in the hands of Malcolm Redford, the office manager.

Annual sales for the company during 1983 were approximately $9 million. Replacement parts sales generally accounted for 10–15% of total sales. Vehicle sales for 1983 were around 2,000 units with the largest volume occurring during the summer months. Vehicle inventory on hand at any one time might be 800 units, stored in warehouses at four centers (i.e., Toronto, Montreal, Winnipeg and Vancouver). Replacement parts inventory is approximately 12,000–13,000 units, having a value between $600,000 and $1,000,000.

The company supplies retailers and also sells

---

*This case was prepared by Associate Professor Albert S. Dexter and Moira E. Barnett, Arthur Andersen & Company, as the basis for class discussion.

Copyright © 1978, The University of British Columbia. Case materials of the Faculty of Commerce and Business Administration of the University of British Columbia are for the purpose of classroom discussion. They do not attempt to illustrate examples of effective or ineffective handling of administrative practices. The materials presented here were provided by a firm that wishes to remain anonymous; thus, the names of the company and personnel are disguised. Revised June 1978.

Distributed by the Intercollegiate Case Clearing House, Soldiers Field, Boston, Mass. 02163. All rights reserved to the contributors. Printed in the U.S.A.

directly to 18–25 major buyers of the vehicles, including some provincial police departments and some divisions of the R.C.M.P. (i.e., the Royal Canadian Mounted Police). The police seemed to prefer the large powerful vehicles. Although some Japanese manufacturers had begun competing lately, Tom felt that this competitive threat was relatively minor, with straying customers eventually returning to purchase V.R.P.'s product once more.

Day to day operations of Vancouver Recreational Products were handled by Malcolm Redford or one of the partners with expertise in the accounting and control areas being obtained from outside the company through the company auditors. No senior management positions existed in the Toronto office, so decisions emanated from Vancouver.

Events Leading to the First System Outline

As early as 1982, Tom Jones saw the need not only for improvement in the accounting and inventory systems, but also for having sufficient planning to make any system changeover as smooth as possible.

Tom spent a great deal of time analyzing and then outlining what he considered to be the problems and the needs of the company in the area of data processing. He realized that automation could well be the answer to various areas of concern but also felt that these decisions could not be made without outside guidance.

The method of handling product inventory was a major contributing factor in the consideration of automating all data processing. Inventory was divided into two main categories—vehicles and parts. All parts were stored in the Toronto warehouse so all parts activity emanated from there. Regular orders to the factory were placed once a week, with rush orders occurring once or twice a week. An average of 50 dealer inquiries on items took place daily. Dealers sent invoices to the warehouse, or orders were taken over the phone or by Telex (in which case invoices were completed at the warehouse). Parts inventory was controlled by means of a Cardex (index card) system.

Vehicles, by model and color, were warehoused at four locations. Control over the release of vehicles (after payment was received or credit checked) was in the Vancouver or Toronto offices. Vehicle inventory control was kept manually in Vancouver and Telexed to Toronto daily. A serial register was maintained of all vehicles in stock.

Telex was also used to release vehicles from warehouses, and Telex was needed to advise Vancouver of the serial number of the vehicle that was released.

An NCR bookkeeping machine was used to post accounts receivable, prepare statements, post accounts payable, and update the general ledger accounts. Other systems (warranties and payroll) as well as sales analysis were handled manually. Reports for management, (cash flow, parts inventory, budgeting, sales) were obtainable but unfortunately not on a timely basis. The monthly reports needed by Tom Jones and Henry Leeds, such as cash flow, budgeting, unit sales, and profitability statements, were produced two or three weeks after month's end. Tom and Henry had no correct idea of how well they were doing on the present orders. Tom felt that if this information were timely and easily accessible, their management decisions would be greatly enhanced.

During 1982, Tom was re-evaluating the existing systems as they related to their changing environment. With the geographic diversity of the operation and its rate of growth, the manual record keeping and control systems were not adequate in all cases. It appeared to Tom that with proper monitoring of parts inventory procedures the inventory value in the short run could be greatly reduced, thus reducing carrying costs. In the long run, inventory turnover could be improved. This type of control would require the hiring of an extra person in Toronto, or finding a way to control more efficiently from the remote Head Office. It also appeared, however, that the Cardex inventory system would be unable to handle any increase in volume—largely due to physical limitations of such a method.

Tom was concerned about the cost involved in using the Telex as extensively as the inventory system required, and also was worried about the duplication of work and records between the Vancouver and Toronto locations. Tom also felt that the efficiency of manual control over inventory levels and warranty claims was further reduced due to the complexity of both procedures. For example, warranty claims submitted by dealers to the Vancouver office were checked against a warranty registration file and then the dealers were credited. Claims were prepared and batched and then sent to the factory. Manual maintenance of the vehicle file and warranty claim file were a tedious procedure. This system was showing signs of being unable to handle the increased volume of transactions.

Both Tom and Henry felt that their biggest problem was the backorders of the parts inventory. The process was a people-dependent routine, and thus was prone to error. The error rate at times reached 15–20% of the file. Staff turnover, because of the routine nature of the clerical tasks, was also a problem. Tom discussed the backorder problem with Henry. An order from a dealer was written on an invoice and transferred to the card for the Cardex machine; unfilled amounts were backordered; receipts coming in from the factory had to be matched against backorders by dealers in FIFO order sequence to produce a packing slip. This packing slip process could add a dimension of complexity to any automated system. One packing slip was produced per dealer rather than one packing slip per order. It seemed to Tom that if an automated system could improve parts inventory processing, it should be given serious consideration.

Tom gave some thought to the problems and needs of the company in the area of data processing. As one of the alternatives to solving VRP's problem was computer usage in some form, Tom attempted to find out what the industry had to offer. Thus, as early as 1982, Vancouver Recreational Products was "in the market" for an automated data processing system. Tom discovered that there was no shortage of computer salespeople; however, glossy photographs of sleek machinery did not answer his questions:

"Does this machine meet the needs of our company?"

"Is the machine large enough? . . . too large . . .?"

"Should the hardware be in Toronto (where the parts and accessories were stored) or in Vancouver (location of the head office and the majority of present manual systems)?"

"What price range can be justified on a cost/benefit basis?"

"How can I make sure that the automated system will do what I want it to do?"

The last question was crucial. Tom had witnessed small companies "get burned" to some degree in the purchase of a "minicomputer," and could recall stories of small accounting systems sitting idle on the controller's desk. Although these systems were capable of handling all the functions of the firm, nobody knew how! Stories of too much hardware, outdated hardware, or lack of expansion capabilities were numerous, and Tom was sure of one thing: time and money were best spent in research *prior* to making the critical choice of an automated system.

Initial System Description and Requirements

During 1983, Tom spent much time gleaning information from different sources (e.g., computer users, university texts, and computer science graduates). Because the parts inventory system was the area most in need of attention, Tom contacted the factory's parts division personnel, and they in turn spoke to their own systems people. As a result, Tom received literature on the newly released NCR hardware and software packages—NCR system 8200. Tom also contacted other vendors. Munroe and DEC set up demonstrations for Tom at the headquarters in Vancouver, and IBM invited him to a demonstration at their office. In the Munroe situation however, after fairly impressive displays of the magnetic stripe card machine's capabilities, it was apparent on questioning that their system could not handle Vancouver Recreational Products' inventory set-up. The Munroe system was better designed for the smaller accounting envi-

ronment. Tom had difficulties in communicating the problems, as this vendor was quite prepared to squeeze Vancouver Recreational Products' situation to fit their available software. Upon Tom's explanation of the backorder problem however, Munroe's salesmen weren't able to show how their company's system could be applied to solve it. In the DEC case, the software would be handled by a separate software house whose experience was largely in scientific applications. Tom felt very uncomfortable with the prospect of buying a piece of hardware without backup on business software support. In the IBM situation, Tom felt somewhat overwhelmed by the presentation and therefore unable to confidently judge the true capabilities of the system. Upon reflection, Tom viewed the vendor experience as too time consuming for the benefits gained. He believed strongly that it took much more prior preparation than he had done to relate well to the vendors. Without some considerable preparation he would simply be putting too much faith in the vendors' statements of what they could do for him.

Tom felt no nearer to being able to make a decision, and he realized that in order to obtain a system that would achieve his company's objectives, the data-processing requirements had to be detailed as completely as possible. It was at this point that he compiled a seven-page outline of the company's present system and his expectations for any proposed automated system. The document is summarized and presented in Exhibits 1, 2, and 3. Tom made use of textbooks as

Exhibit 1

OBJECTIVES

1. Improved control and elimination of duplication
2. Instantly updated inventory
3. A constantly balanced accounts receivable—automatic posting and instantaneous updating
4. Reports for management, both marketing and financial
5. Ability to obtain current status as well as historical information quickly through centralization of files
6. In-house control
7. Reserve capacity
8. The ability to update and add to the system

Exhibit 2

APPLICATIONS AND VOLUME

Billing and Accounts Receivable

Volumes:
1. 1,000 Invoices per month
     400 Vancouver
     600 Toronto
2. 5 lines per invoice
3. 100 Customer Accounts

Applications:
1. Customer Invoicing
   (a) Parts
   (b) Vehicle
2. Customer statement preparation
3. Cash receipts and adjustments
4. Aging Analysis

Inventory Control

Volumes:
1. 18,000 Item Parts Inventory—Active 12,000
   (a) 10 digit numbers;
       i.e., 43506-62 P.A.
2. 20 Item Unit Inventory (vehicle)
   (a) 12 models
   (b) 5 colors

Accounts Payable

Volumes:
1. 165 Supplier Accounts
2. 500 Supplier Invoices per month
3. 250 Checks per month

Applications:
1. Check Writing
2. Vendor Record Updating
3. Accounts Distribution
4. Vendor Analysis

General Ledger

Volumes:
1. 14 Salaried Employees paid Bi-weekly—Vancouver
   1 Hourly Employee paid Bi-weekly—Vancouver
2. 12 Salaried Employees paid Bi-weekly—Toronto
   1 Hourly Employee paid Bi-weekly—Toronto

Applications:
1. Payroll Check Writing
2. Payroll Register
3. Statutory Reporting

Sales Analysis

Volumes:
1. Dealers
2. Item Unit Inventory

Applications:
1. Sales by Dealer—Unit Dollars
2. Sales by Unit
3. Sales by Parts Dollar
4. Sales by Dealer to Consumer
5. Warranty by Model
6. Warranty by Dealer

Exhibit 3

OVERVIEW OF DESIRED SYSTEM

Sales orders generated at the dealer level could be entered through a sales order system to produce a packing list which is sent to the warehouse for filling. Quantities in the inventory are reserved, and backorders would be established at the time the order is entered.

Outstanding order lists and backorder lists by part number and dealer should be produced upon demand.

When these orders are shipped, a copy of the packing list is returned from the warehouse and these orders are marked for invoicing in the system.

The invoicing system would handle pre-billing situations as well as credit memos.

Output by Destination

Invoices	—Customer
Invoice Journal	—Accounting
Customer List	—Sales/Accounting
Sales Data	—Sales Analysis Module
Shipped Items	—Inventory Module
Receivable Outstanding	—Accounts Receivable Module

1. Accounts receivable to accept manual input.
2. As cash received on account is posted, it should also be posted to the general ledger system.
3. Monthly customer statements and an aging analysis are produced.
4. A dealer volume report by area should be produced.
5. A purchasing module would provide the method of producing purchase orders and keeping track of stocks on order and received. It would also be used to make entries to accounts payable and the general ledger. A list of purchase orders would be able to be run when necessary.

Note: Within the systems overview, Tom included more detail on input methods and output requirements such as reports, statements, and checks.

well as advice from people in the EDP industry.

Tom's documentation concluded with topics about which the possible vendors should supply details, as shown in Exhibit 4.

Consulting Assistance

For the next few months, other items of importance took precedence over the data processing problems.

Early in 1984, the company's auditors of some 30 years standing, Smythe, Hunter, Robinson, and MacKay, suggested that Tom make use of the services offered by their management consultants, Smythe, Hunter, and Associates. Recognizing that Vancouver Recreational Products lacked the expertise in the field of electronic data processing, Tom agreed to discuss developments to date with Oliver Carruthers, a management consultant of Smythe, Hunter, and Associates. In March 1984, Oliver was retained by Vancouver Recreational Products to look at the present system and suggest what he felt was needed. Tom forwarded the documentation he had drawn up to Oliver. It was obvious to Oliver that Tom had done a great deal of mental and written preparation regarding the needs of the company. However, Tom made it clear that he would be open to any feasible suggestions that Oliver put forward.

Oliver visited V.R.P. in order to do an initial

Exhibit 4

SOME QUESTIONS FOR VENDORS

1. *Discount Storage Requirements*
   Customer Master File
   Dealer Master File
   Inventory Master File
   Invoice File
   Sales Detail File
   Sales Summary File
   Accounts Receivable File
   Vendor Master File
   Accounts Payable File
   General Ledger Transactions File
   Financial Statement Table File
   Payroll Master File
   System Software

2. *Hardware Recommended and Pricing*
   MODEL   DESCRIPTION   PURCHASE   MAINTENANCE

3. *Monthly lease (Purchase Option ?)*

4. *Anticipated Line Cost*
   (a) Assuming Toronto hookup in future
   (b) Assuming Discount Mailing or Shipping

5. *Maintenance*
   (a) Warranty—Parts and Labor
   (b) Monthly and Yearly Rate
   (c) Parts, Labor, Calls, and Preventative
       Maintenance

6. *Environment Requirements*

7. *Application Software*
   (a) Required Software Costs
   (b) Optional Modules
   (c) Software Backup and Support

8. *Discount Package Price List*

9. *Future Expansion Options*

10. *Education*

11. *Language*—Program Language Options

evaluation of the situation. After a two week study of the operation from the Vancouver end, Oliver wrote to Tom in March 1984, formalizing some of their discussions and giving some preliminary conclusions. Parts of this letter have been reproduced in Appendix 1 on the next page.

Because of V.R.P.'s remote locations, it appeared that an in-house system would offer greater flexibility, control, and accessibility than a service bureau. Oliver felt that the "purchase price for the hardware and programs" would be in the $65,000 to $100,000 range. He outlined potential areas of savings, largely for Telex, telephone, and inventory carrying charges. Details of cost savings are given in the excerpts from the letter in Appendix 1 of this case.

Oliver had further discussions with Tom in order to obtain a better perspective of Vancouver Recreational Products' operations.

In April 1984, Tom received further correspondence from Oliver confirming the decision that Vancouver Recreation Products would proceed with the next step in the selection of a suitable computer system. Having completed the initial feasibility study, Oliver was convinced of the need for, and cost justification of, an automated system. He suggested vendors who marketed the size system that would suit Vancouver Recreational Products' needs. Tom now took the opportunity to see demonstrations of some other companies' existing systems that both paralleled their own and had an inventory system of even greater complexity than theirs. Tom felt the experience of seeing other similar users of equipment was very worthwhile in his learning process.

Oliver's services for the initial investigation, culminating in the findings outlined in his March letter had cost V.R.P. $800. In the April correspondence, Oliver estimated that his assistance in preparing a "Request for Proposal" and helping select a vendor "would not exceed $4,500." This step in the process would necessitate Oliver becoming more conversant with present clerical procedures and accounting methods. To do this he would need to spend time with people both in Toronto and Vancouver.

Further, should Tom require Oliver's involvement during the implementation phase of the proceedings, the charge would likely be another $4,500. In both cases Oliver stated: ". . . if it appears that the charges are going to go higher, I will discuss it with you in advance."

Tom realized he now had to assess the work Oliver had done, decide on his continuing involvement, and decide just how far this involvement should go. Oliver had certainly brought some organization into the decision process. In Tom's opinion, Oliver had assisted him without overwhelming him. Tom felt the $800 had been well spent but was unsure regarding further commitment.

Tom pondered the present situation. Oliver had made contact with five suppliers he felt worthy of consideration, had arranged some demonstrations of hardware and software for Tom, and had presented Tom with some detail on what price range and characteristics he should look for in a system. Now Tom faced the decision of whether to let Oliver proceed; and if so, whether he was prepared to spend $4,500, $9,000 (or perhaps even more) on the project; or whether to take over himself once again, armed with new found knowledge and awareness.

APPENDIX 1

Excerpts from Oliver's letter to Tom dated March 25, 1984.

This letter will serve to confirm our various discussions and also to report on my progress over the past two weeks.

Previously, we have agreed on the following points:

a. A computer system of some size or sort is required for at least the inventory control problem provided that it can be justified on the combined basis of increased control and reduced investment in inventory.

b. The computer, because of management location and control considerations, must be located in the Vancouver area instead of Toronto.

c. We should attempt to purchase or lease a complete package of hardware, software, programming, and hardware maintenance from a single supplier, and it would be preferable if the supplier was represented in both Toronto and Vancouver.

d. Although the factory's system division is anxious to co-operate in any way, we do not want to go so far as becoming a part of their system.

I have talked to four potential suppliers so far in general terms only and have reached the following conclusions:

a. The configuration involves a small CPU with disk storage, a printer and a CRT terminal in Vancouver, and a remote CRT and printer in Toronto.

b. The purchase price for the hardware and programs will be in the $65,000 to $100,000 range with hardware maintenance about $200 to $400 per month.

c. The competition between suppliers at this level of computer is fairly intense and there should not be any problem negotiating a fair price.

Some possible areas of cost savings are shown below. The true savings cannot be measured until after the computer system is installed, but one can see the potential:

a. Telephone and Telex—Of the $28,000 per year, about $5,600 is related to inventory and invoicing problems. We should be able to cut that by at least 60% for a cost reduction of $3,360 per year.

b. Inventory carrying charges—At last year-end, inventory value was $950,000. At a 10% rate, carrying charges equal $95,000. If that were cut by 1/3, the potential yearly savings would be about $31,600.

c. Staff savings—At present, 5 to 6 people are working full-time on inventory bookkeeping, invoicing, etc. With 6 people at $12,000 including fringe benefits gives a $72,000 annual cost. It may be possible to reduce that to as low as 3 people. Savings could therefore be $36,000 annually.

d. Inventory storage space reduction.

In addition to the equipment costs, the communication between Vancouver and Toronto must also be considered. I have done some preliminary investigation and found that a "Dataroute" hook-up to Toronto for 13 3/4 hrs./day, 7 days a week costs $876/month (which can be partly offset by the reduced telephone and telex costs shown above).

I will be arranging a demonstration for you of at least two suppliers' hardware and standard inventory packages to give you some idea of what is available in the marketplace. We can then decide what the next step is and whether I will have to go to Toronto to look at the warehouse operation.

Discussion Topics

1. Thoroughly describe the circumstances that led Vancouver Recreational Products to consider the need for changing its current data processing procedures.

2. Evaluate the systems study work performed by Tom Jones. This evaluation should include an analysis of Exhibits 1, 2, 3, and 4.

3. Assuming that you are Tom Jones, what decision would you make regarding the continued involvement of Oliver Carruthers in V.R.P.'s systems study work? Thoroughly explain your reasoning.

4. Based upon the available information provided in this case about Vancouver Recreational Products, attempt to design a data-processing system that would fit the needs of the company. (*Note:* Make any reasonable assumptions about the company's operations that you consider necessary.)

CASE 2

*Aqua Spray**

Company Background

History. Aqua Spray, a Milwaukee based firm, was founded in 1964 by Andrew and June Digrovani. The sole product at this time, an underground sprinkler system, was marketed from a store at 1728 North Mayfair Road. The product line was gradually expanded to include inground and above ground swimming pools, pool tables, game tables and artificial Christmas trees. In 1977, the company purchased a store at 9900 West Capital Drive in Milwaukee where it moved its entire operation. In 1983, Aqua Spray rented a facility at 1300 South 108th St. in West Allis. In 1984, an additional outlet was acquired at 6112 South 27th St. in Greenfield. All administrative functions are centralized at the Capital Drive store.

*This case study was prepared by Professor Kailas J. Rao for class discussion rather than to illustrate effective or ineffective handling of inventory and sales systems. Copyright © 1977 by Kailas J. Rao. Presented at a Case Workshop and distributed by the Intercollegiate Case Clearing House, Soldiers Field, Boston, Mass. 02163. All rights reserved to the contributors. Printed in the U.S.A.

Since 1964, gross sales have been increasing an average of 10% a year, with total sales for the fiscal year ended March 1984 approximately $1,800,000. The corporation is considering expanding to other outlets if market conditions permit.

Aqua Spray functions primarily in the capacity of a retailer and contractor. However, it sells chemicals for swimming pools on both a retail and wholesale basis. The firm experiences a very seasonal business due to the nature of its products. To illustrate this, sales items have been divided by product group, sales period, and percentage of total sales as follows:

Product Group	Sales Period	Percent of Sales
1. Underground sprinkler systems	April thru September	5%
2. Swimming pools		
a) Above ground	February thru September	25%
b) Inground	January thru June	25%
3. Pool tables, air hockey, football, ping pong and accessories	All year	30%
4. Christmas trees	October thru December	10%
5. Chemicals	May thru September	5%

Aqua Spray's current operations center around its president and founder, Mr. Andrew Digrovani (see Exhibit 1). Mr. Digrovani is responsible for purchase authorizations, pricing policy, advertising, personnel and finance (including the function of treasurer). June Digrovani, the corporation Vice-President, and Mr. William Frankle, the corporation expediter and set-up man, are primarily responsible for the corporation's inground pool division. All the work is subcontracted through Swimming Pool Services. The Board of Directors is composed of Andrew and June Digrovani.

The three store managers meet frequently with the president and are responsible for store set up, personnel control and sales. Payments to store managers are on a salary plus commission basis. Salespersons receive only a commission. They are allowed to draw a stated amount of their commission against a drawing account. The entire sales staff, with the exception of the store managers, are part time, with additional help being hired during the summer.

The firm is currently experiencing competition from Allied Pools, American Pool Table Company, M & M Sporting Goods, and Pool Park.

Systems Description and Problem Definition

The sales processing system of Aqua Spray (see Exhibit 2) begins with the preparation of a sales invoice by the salesman upon receipt of a customer order. Two types of sales invoices are in use. One is a three part invoice used for small ticket items. The other, a four part invoice, is only used for large items which must be shipped.

The last copy of either invoice is given to the customer as a receipt. In the case of the four part invoice, the third copy is filed at the store of sale pending shipping of the merchandise when it becomes the bill of lading. The first and second copy are sent to bookkeeping and inventory control at the Capital Drive store on a daily basis. In inventory control the quantity of sales (as well as purchases) of above ground swimming pools are recorded by model in inventory control ledger I. The firm plans to expand this to include pool tables as well. This ledger is set up in the following manner. It contains five columns for each model of above ground swimming pool. These columns are date, order number (the number stamped on each prenumbered purchase order and sales invoice), received (purchases), delivered (sales) and a running balance. In this way a perpetual count can be maintained on above ground swimming pools in inventory. The invoices are then filed alphabetically.

In bookkeeping, Pat McDonough, a former public accountant, posts sales by store and product classification. The sales invoices are then filed alphabetically and act as the accounts re-

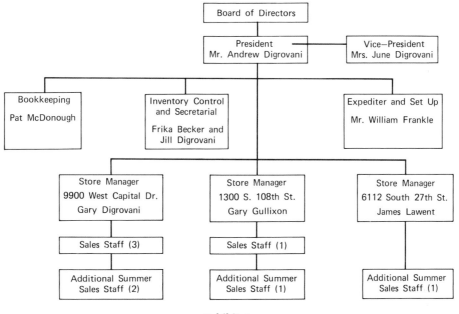

Exhibit 1
ORGANIZATION CHART

ceivable subsidiary ledger. All large receivables are financed through a local finance company.

Expenses are likewise segregated by store and classification in a cash disbursements journal. Sales and expenses are then posted by store on a monthly basis to the general ledger. From the general ledger a monthly statement of profit and loss is prepared for each store. This statement contains the following revenue and expense classifications; above ground pools, inground pools, sprinklers, sprinkler service, pool tables, Christmas trees, greenhouses, spas, miscellaneous, cost of goods sold, rent, heat, utilities, truck and auto, insurance, salaries, commissions, taxes (including payroll), dues and subscriptions, personal property tax, interest, maintenance, travel and entertainment, bad debts, cash over and short, and unclassified. Other revenue items such as interest and investment income are then added in to reach the bottom line figure. Cost of goods sold is based on an estimated percentage of sales, currently 67%. To simplify the making of entries, the firm employs a chart of accounts.

In the purchasing system (see Exhibit 3) a three part purchase order is prepared by the in-ventory clerk upon authorization by the president. At this time an entry is made in inventory control ledger II by the inventory clerk who records the quantities and prices of items ordered. This ledger contains both retail prices and quantities of *all* inventory items broken down by product type. This ledger has four headings for each product. These are: on hand, on order, received and sold. The on hand figures are arrived at through a bimonthly physical inventory count. The quantities sold are determined by subtracting the latest physical inventory from the total of on hand and received merchandise. Figures from the sales invoices are not used in determining sales for the two month period (for purposes of this ledger) between physical counts.

Part one of the purchase order is then mailed to the vendor. Part two is sent to bookkeeping where it is filed pending receipt of the vendor invoice. Part three is sent to receiving where it is filed pending receipt of the merchandise. Although the firm has no specific receiving department, each store manager is responsible for merchandise deliveries to his or her respective stores. Merchandise is currently sent by vendors

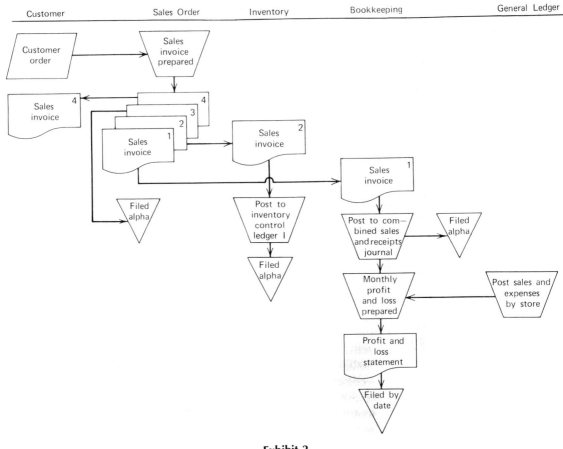

Exhibit 2
SALES PROCESSING FLOWCHART

to both the Capital and 108th St. stores as well as the corporation warehouse.

The vendor invoice is mailed directly to book-keeping. At this time it is compared to the purchase order. If both documents agree, the totals are posted to separate accounts payable and purchases journals. These invoices are recorded alphabetically by vendor and include the invoice number. Accounts payable are aged weekly so that no purchase discounts are lost.

Checks are now prepared, each with two copies. The check itself is mailed to the vendor. Copy one of the check is used to post payment to the accounts payable and cash disbursements journals. The check number is also entered in both journals. Copy one is then attached to the purchase order and vendor invoice and filed al-

phabetically by vendor. Copy two of the check is filed by check number pending receipt of the monthly bank statement for reconciliation purposes.

When merchandise is received by the firm, the store manager compares the purchase order to the packing list and the merchandise. If the documents are in agreement with the shipment, the purchase order is forwarded to inventory control where the purchase quantities are posted to inventory control ledgers I and II as well as a special buying journal maintained by the inventory clerk to assist in planning future purchases. The purchase order is then disposed of.

The present inventory control system is repetitive and poorly coordinated with sales processing. With the exception of above ground

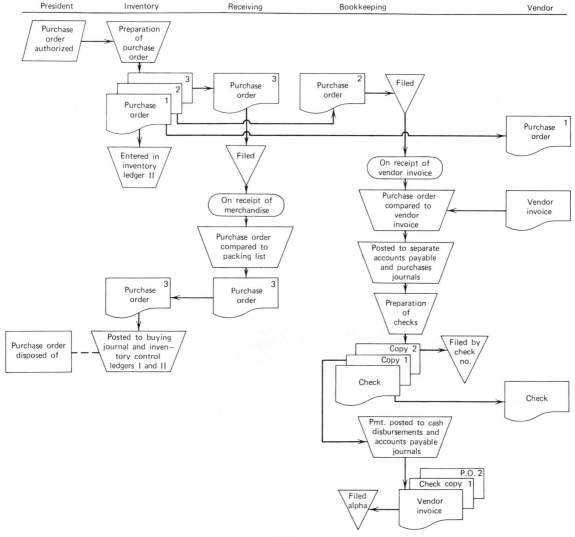

Exhibit 3
PURCHASING FLOWCHART

swimming pools, the current system can provide only a rough figure on inventory shrinkage. The firm is currently unable to determine what quantities are on hand at a given store on a given date, except through a physical count. For this reason, even if an accurate shrinkage figure could be determined, it could not be determined which sales outlets are responsible. This information is desirable for purposes of store manager evaluation. The president also desires a more detailed breakdown of sales by store.

Discussion Topics

1. Thoroughly describe the weaknesses that exist in Aqua Spray's present system for processing sales (Exhibit 2) and for processing inventory purchases (Exhibit 3).

2. Recommend design modifications for Aqua Spray's current sales processing and inventory purchasing systems in order to coordinate these two systems. (*Note:* To clearly reflect your design modifications, it would be quite useful to draw

493

flowcharts of your recommended sales processing and inventory purchasing systems.)

3. The accounting procedures for processing sales transactions and inventory purchase transactions are presently performed manually by Aqua Spray's bookkeeping function. Based upon the limited information available about the company's sales and inventory purchase transactions, recommend some possible data-processing hardware and software systems that might be preferable to Aqua Spray's current manual system. For each suggested data-processing system, indicate both the positive and the negative aspects of your suggestion.

CASE 3

Laub Group, Incorporated*

Company Background

Laub Group, Incorporated is a relatively small insurance agency which matches its private and commercial customers' desired coverage with the insurance policies offered by various companies. The initial capital contribution of $3,349 grew to $55,646 in 1979 and has since remained constant. Losses from 1974 to 1979 increased until they reached $93,936 in 1979 (retained deficit of $330,610), but profits were made in the last two years. (See Exhibit 1 for revenue and profit/loss trends.) Total assets held by the company in 1982 equaled $1,427,223, of which $897,649 were current.

In 1938, Mr. Rudolf A. Laub formed the Rudolf A. Laub Agency at 825 North Jefferson Street, Milwaukee, WI. The agency moved to the Wells Building of Milwaukee in 1947, and continued to operate as a sole proprietorship until its incorporation as the Rudolf A. Laub Agency, Inc., on February 1, 1970. After Rudolf Laub passed away in early March of 1973, his son,

*This case was prepared by Professor Kailas J. Rao as a basis for class discussion rather than to illustrate either effective or ineffective handling of administrative problems. Copyright © 1977 by Kailas J. Rao. Presented at a Case Workshop and distributed by the Intercollegiate Case Clearing House, Soldiers Field, Boston, Mass. 02163. All rights reserved to the contributors. Printed in the U.S.A.

Raymond, purchased the business from his father's estate executors, assumed the duties and responsibilities of president, and changed the company's name to Laub Agency, Incorporated. Mr. Raymond Laub subsequently expanded both the amount and kinds of insurance written to include: underwriting property, liability and crime protection, employee benefit and bonding coverage for commercial accounts, plus auto, home, and health protection for individuals.

Growth of the company was accomplished by the acquisition of various Milwaukee insurance concerns in 1975 and other similar organizations throughout Wisconsin thereafter. At this time, Mr. Laub again altered the name of his firm to Laub Group, Inc., to reflect the consolidation with the following insurance agencies: Warner Insurance Agency (Milwaukee—3/4/75); and Jensen and Phillips Agency, Inc. (Janesville—1/22/75). Presently, Laub Group also has major subsidiaries in Wausau (acquired on 2/19/82), Madison (2/1/79), and Racine and Appleton (both acquired on 6/1/82). Laub Group, Inc. now represents thirty independent insurance companies (see Exhibit 2 for a complete list). On January 1, 1983, Laub Group, Incorporated's Milwaukee office at 324 E. Wisconsin Avenue assumed control over all subsidiary and branch cash payments and receipts. Also, coordination of all consolidated operations became the responsibility of the home office executives.

Of the 61 company employees, 23 are subsidiary sales and office staff, and 4 part-time employees perform similar services for the branches.

The majority of workers are stationed in the Milwaukee home office, since most of the agency's customers are located in this area. They are supervised by an executive staff consisting of the president, executive vice-president, senior vice-president, and the administrative vice-president.

The home office is composed of three distinct operating divisions. Customers are solicited by the producers, who determine the individual or group's insurance needs and suitable coverage. The office staff then submits all insurance applications to one of the thirty companies they repre-

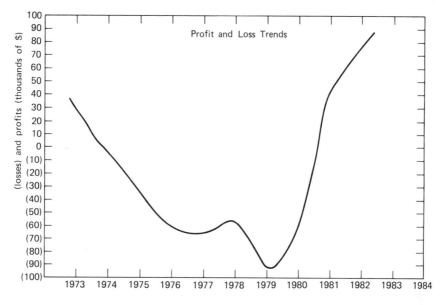

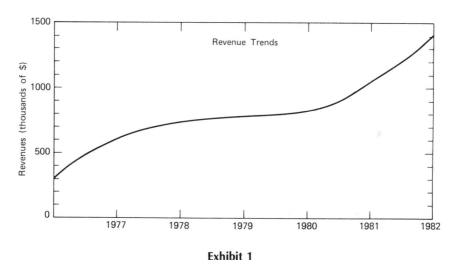

Exhibit 1
REVENUE & PROFIT/LOSS TRENDS

sent for policy approval. Once a client has been accepted, an invoice is prepared by the producer and sent to the accounting department, where the transaction is properly processed and recorded. (See Organizational Chart, Exhibit 3.)

Our analysis is mainly concerned with the accounting department, which consists of four employees and is managed by Mr. Wayne Seidens. Mr. Seidens, who was recently appointed to his position as accounting manager, is responsible for the preparation of all financial reports, cash flow, daily bank balance summaries, branch payroll, and the collection of premiums on overdue accounts. To assist him in these functions, Mrs. Virginia Van Buskirk and her staff prepare invoices, type checks, file reports, post cash and accounts receivable entries, etc. Mrs. Van Buskirk personally reconciles all bank balances and updates the accounts receivable journal for the consolidated entity.

495

Exhibit 2

COMPANIES LAUB GROUP, INCORPORATED REPRESENTS

Aetna Insurance	Hartford Steam Boiler
Aetna Life and Casualty	Home
American States	INA Insurance
Atlantic Companies	Kemper Group
Chubb and Son	Maryland American General
Connecticut General	New Hampshire
Connecticut Mutual Life	Northwestern National
Continental Assurance	Ohio Casualty
Continental Insurance	Reliance Companies
CNA Insurance	Safeco
Fidelity and Deposit	St. Paul
Fireman's Fund American	Time Insurance
General Casualty	Tower
Great American	U.S. Fidelity and Guaranty
Hartford Group	Zurich American

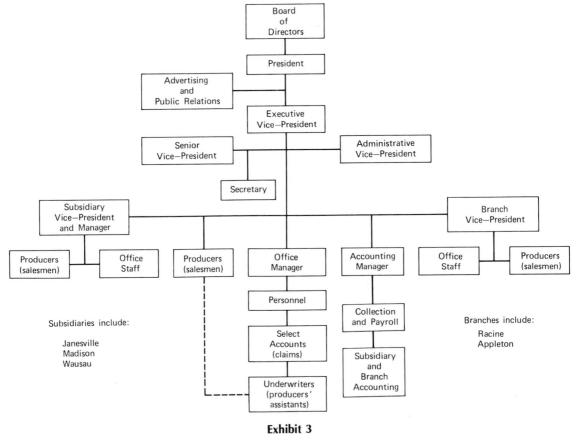

Exhibit 3

LAUB GROUP, INC.

ORGANIZATIONAL CHART

Detailed Description of the Problem

All of Laub Group, Inc.'s monthly reports are compiled by Agency Records Control, Inc. (ARC) in Texas. Any information which should be included in these periodic reports must be submitted to ARC by Laub on the first working day of the following month. This requirement forces subsidiaries and branches to close their books several days before the end of the month to allow for delivery to Milwaukee. Any relevant transactions which occur after closing must be posted manually to be reflected in the financial summaries. Currently, these adjustments are not made. With this lack of proper cutoff, the monthly statements produced by the software package do not accurately represent Laub Group, Inc.'s financial position and may not be a reliable source of information for decision making.

The insurance agency's accounting information system inputs consist of invoices, a cash received sheet, check copies, and a journal entry form to record general items. Most data is generated through the invoices, including the customer's name, the customer's identification number, the salesperson, the insurance company's respective commissions and numbers, the type of policy, the premiums due, and the month the invoice was entered into the system.

The invoice consists of an original and three copies. The original is mailed to the customer, and two copies are filed manually in the bookkeeping and accounts receivable aging file. The remaining copy is sent to ARC. Once received by ARC, the invoice initiates the process of updating the subsidiary, branch, or home office's respective account, the Z-ledger (a general summary of all transactions), and the 3500 account. The 3500 account is used to consolidate and control all of Laub's cash payments and receipts. This information, along with data submitted through the cash received forms, journal entry forms, new account lists, and checks, is coordinated into various summaries, ledgers, and statements. These reports are then mailed to Laub Group, Inc., where they are reviewed by management and subsequently filed in the accounting department. (See Exhibit 4 for a diagram of this accounting information system's inputs and outputs.)

Few errors occur when ARC processes the insurance agency's financial data; however, the sales staff occasionally make mistakes while filling out invoices. Any errors that may arise in the preparation of an invoice cannot be corrected once it is received by ARC. When discovered, the error may be rectified only by submitting an adjustments sheet containing the proper entry with the following month's inputs. Often errors cannot be discovered until the processed reports are returned from Texas seven to ten days after the month's end. This time lag between sending data and receiving the various reports, coupled with the delay in correcting errors subsequently detected, reduces the processed reports' usefulness.

The current accounting information system does not provide an accurate aging of accounts receivable. Customer account balances are now separated by ARC according to the invoices' entry dates. Premiums are due on or before the policy's effective date with a thirty day grace period. Considering that an invoice may be entered well in advance of the date policy coverage becomes effective, the accounts receivable analysis cannot be used to determine which customers are actually behind in their payments.

Another inconsistency exists between the reports which Laub Group, Inc. desires and those sent by ARC. Along with the monthly report data, ARC also prepares quarterly and year-end statements. However, many of these statements are rarely used by management, and are usually discarded or added to the growing volume of filed data. The agency also desires additional reports not currently produced by the computer, such as a profit and loss statement with budget comparisons, a breakdown of salespersons' expenses, and a sources and uses of funds statement.

Discussion Topics

1. Indicate the strengths and weaknesses that you feel exist in Laub Group, Incorporated's present

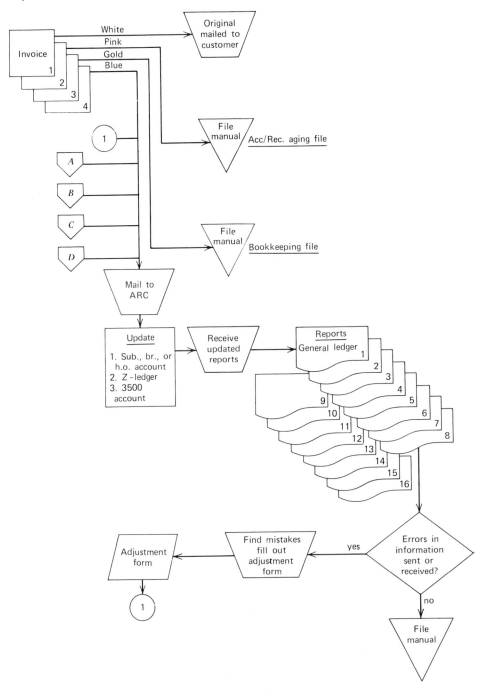

Exhibit 4
LAUB GROUP, INC.
FLOWCHART OF INPUTS AND OUTPUTS

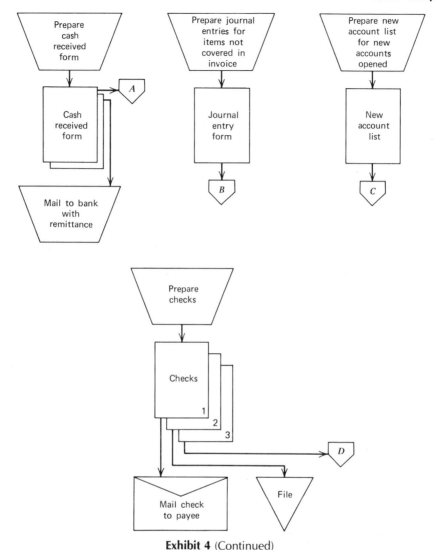

Exhibit 4 (Continued)

accounting information system. (These strengths and weaknesses should encompass both specific accounting procedures as well as internal controls.) Regarding each strength or weakness described, indicate your reason(s) for considering it as such.

2. Raymond Laub would like his company to examine the possibility of purchasing or leasing its own computer rather than having Agency Records Control, Inc. continue to process the company's accounting data. Describe in detail the systems study work that should be performed by Laub

Group, Incorporated in order to reach a decision regarding the purchase or lease of a computer.

3. Based upon the systems study work referred to in (2) above, assume that Laub Group, Incorporated has decided to acquire its own computer. Making any assumptions you consider reasonable, describe in detail the processing procedures and the controls for handling accounts receivable and accounts payable activities on the company's new computer system. (For example, if you think that customer cash payment transactions should be batched semi-monthly for computer processing,

then describe the types of hardware and software that should exist, the specific procedures for batching the transaction data, the types of controls to maintain, the specific format of output reports, etc.)

CASE 4

State Consumer Reporting Bureau*

On June 1, 1980, Mr. Robert Markson, president of the State Consumer Reporting Bureau, retained two consultants to assist him in developing methods for handling State's information processing needs. In their initial session with Mr. Markson, the following information was presented which the consultants felt was particularly relevant.

Company Background

Founded in December, 1962 by Mr. Robert Markson, State Consumer Reporting Bureau is a customer collection agency. Various retail stores in Metropolitan Boston give them delinquent accounts receivable. Through a combination of collection letters, telephone follow-ups and, in a few extreme cases, personal visits, the company's collection department attempts to collect the overdue amounts. In about 50 percent of the cases they are successful. The other 50 percent are either dropped (if the amounts involved are less than $100) or are turned over to the attorneys in the legal department, who file suit against the customer and legally press the matter to a conclusion. The company is paid a fixed percentage on every dollar collected. This percentage increases if legal action must be taken on an account. Currently, the company is trying to collect on approximately 4,000 accounts. New customers' accounts are received at a rate of 500 a month. The firm employs two attorneys, six collectors, and three secretaries, in addition to Mr. Markson.

*Copyright © 1966 by the President and Fellows of Harvard College. Reproduced by permission. This case was prepared by F. Warren McFarlan under the supervision of John Dearden.

Company System for Collection Action

When new customer accounts arrive at State Consumer, a collection card is prepared by a secretary. This is given to Mr. Irwin Gannich, the company's attorney. Considering such things as the amount due, the store where the sale was made, the elapsed time since the last payment on the account, and previous collection action taken by the store, he decides if immediate collection action is necessary or whether the collection department should be given the account.

If the account is sent to the collection department, the collection card is given to a secretary, who automatically mails the delinquent account the first of the company's four collection letters. Designed to frighten the customer into paying, these letters are printed up by a local printing company. The secretary takes the letter and types the following information in the proper places:

a.   the customer's name and address,
b.   the store where he or she incurred the bill, and
c.   the amount of the bill.

The secretary types up an envelope for the letter, mails it, and makes note of the type of letter mailed to the customer and its date on the collection card. The collection card is then routed to one of the six collectors in the collection department.

In general, each collector is responsible for a certain section of the alphabet. Cards of customers whose last names begin with the letters A-E would be given to collector #1, etc. For certain stores, however, continuity of approach makes it desirable that the same collector handle all accounts for this store. Thus collector #1 is responsible for customers whose last names begin with letters A-E plus all accounts of the Central Garden Florist Shop.

Upon receiving a collection card, a collector takes no action on it for five days. At the end of this period, if no payment is received, he or she telephones the customer. At the collector's discretion, he or she may also order the mailing of the second, third and fourth collection letters. A record of all telephone conversations, letters mailed, promises made, and payments given is kept on the collection card. Mr. Markson, in speaking of the collection card, noted:

> This record of information is our collection department's most important tool. They use the customer's past performances as a guide in effective bargaining. When a customer knows you are acquainted with his past activities, he takes you more seriously. Past addresses too may give clues on people who move to another location, leaving no forwarding address. Take away their history record and collection effectiveness is reduced by 60 percent. Any information processing system must be designed around the preservation of this information for the collector.

Many of the cards are completely covered with notations and have a second one stapled to them. These collection cards are filed alphabetically in a box on the collector's desk. If after 45 days the customer shows complete inaction, the collector automatically turns the card over to the legal department. Similarly, if the collector feels payments are dragging too slowly, he or she refers the account to the legal department.

In talking about the collectors, Mr. Markson said:

> . . . the role of the collector at State is similar to that of a blue collar assembly worker. They are the company's primary revenue producer, and it is their effectiveness that keeps us in business. It is similar to a detective game and they view it as a contest between themselves and the customer.

Company System for Customer Payments

The collector negotiates a payback agreement with the customer. In some cases the customer will make a lump sum payment. The majority of the time, however, an installment payback scheme is worked out, sometimes stretching over six or more months.

The collections may be received in three different ways:

1. The customer comes to State's office and makes a payment. He or she is given a receipt and the money is placed in an envelope with the customer's name on it.

2. The customer mails a payment to State (about a third of these payments are cash). The envelopes are checked to make sure the customer's name is on the outside.

3. The customer makes a payment at the store where the purchase was acquired. Within six days after the payment the store sends a notice to State Consumer, giving the customer's name, amount of payment and date it was made. This notice is placed in an envelope with the customer's name on the outside.

Each day the envelopes are taken to the collection room and a secretary gathers the necessary collection cards. The secretary first posts the amount and date of payment on them. Then, the secretary lists each customer's name, date and amount of payment on a yellow collection sheet (separate ones for each store) for payments made to State and on blue collection sheets (separate ones for each store) for payments made to the store. The secretary then returns the collection cards to the collection room and files them in the individual collector's box.

The collection sheets are filed away until the end of the month. They are then gathered and each store is mailed a copy of its collections, together with a summary stating how much it collected and how much State collected. This information is used to calculate State's commission.

The legal collections are handled separately from those of the collection department, and separate, more complete statements are sent by the legal department to the stores. Presently the company has two attorneys. They divide the legal business between themselves and initiate a series of letters and telephone calls which culminates in the customer being brought into court if he takes no payment action.

When payments are received at State, in most cases the secretary can quickly sort the legal payments from the collection department payments. This is because State supplies return mail envelopes to the customers which are stamped legal if it is an account in legal. About 20 percent of the legal mail is not identified as such and is sent to the collection department. If the collection card is not found there, the envelope is forwarded to legal.

Information Processing Requirements

Mr. Markson then made the following remarks which seemed particularly relevant to the two consultants:

> I am not worried about our ability to operate efficiently at the current level of operations. Our current performance from both a cost and efficiency viewpoint is satisfactory. What concerns me is our internal capacity for handling growth. If I thought we could handle it, within six months we would be receiving new customer accounts at the rate of 5,000 per month. Organizing and expanding the collection staff is not a major problem. Neither do finances pose a real threat. What is worrying me is the fear of drowning ourselves in a flood of paper work so that we could neither service the accounts nor produce timely statements for the stores. This could do lasting harm to the firm's prospects. Before we get this additional business, we must be set up to handle it.

Mr. Markson then introduced the two consultants to Miss Duncan, the office manager. During the course of the morning she made the following comments:

> The present system seems to work all right. The only real bottleneck is finding out where a customer's card is. When we get a telephone call I don't always know whether the card is in the collection room, legal, or with the man on the road. . . . Yes, we have our man out collecting all the time. Every Monday I give him 50 collection cards. I mark them down so if someone calls I won't spend all day trying to find a card that isn't in the office. Mr. Markson is sold on the idea of automation, so it is coming. It is only a matter of time. I'll do my best . . . a lot of people don't care for the idea. They have been in the collection business for 30 years and never seen anything like it.

Recommendations

The two management consultants hired by the company have studied the problem carefully and have recommended an automated, magnetic-tape system utilizing three major files: (1) a claims file of accounts sent to State for collection, (2) a client master file, and (3) a history file of the company's accounts. The claims file and client file records are illustrated on page 503.

Claims file master records, containing information about the customers, the client-stores involved, and the credit sales involved, are each followed by detail (payment) records representing customers' activities to pay their debts. The client file master records simply contain name and address information of those client-stores sending collection accounts to the company, plus a cycle (review) date. The history file records (not shown) would serve to replace the collection cards of the company. As such, this file would contain the same kind of information as was originally entered by hand on the collection card previously described.

The proposed system would perform the collections operations of the State Consumer Reporting Bureau in four (or more) processing routines as follows:

1. In Processing Run No. 1, new account claims would be punched on cards, edited, and added to the claims file. At the same time, initial letters of inquiry would be sent to customers requesting payments. Finally, in this run, a summary report would be prepared for management review, copies of which would be forwarded to the individual company collection agents.

2. In Processing Run No. 2, payment information (also initially punched on cards) would be added to the claims file as detail records. Updating the account balance information in the claims file would also be performed. Follow-up letters would be sent to those new customers who had yet to make payments on their accounts. A summary report would be prepared and distributed in similar fashion to Run No. 1.

3. Processing Run No. 3 would use the claims file to prepare billing statements for clients. Summary information for each of State's

Claims File Master Record

Client Number (Store)	Cus- tomer Number	Claim Number	Cus- tomer Name	Cus- tomer Address	Initial Amt. of Claim	Amt. Presently Owed	Cycle Code	Collec- tion Code	Letters Sent Code	Dispo- sition Code

Cycle Code:
1 = immediate
2 = collection
dept. (for
payback
agreement)

Disposition Code:
1 = pending
2 = paid up
3 = sent to
legal dept.

Letters Sent Code:
1 = first letter
2 = second letter
3 = third letter
4 = fourth letter

Claims File Detail (Payment) Record

Client Number (Store)	Claim Number	Cus- tomer Number	Amount of Payment	Date of Payment	Pay- ment Code

Payment Code:
1 = payment to State
2 = payment to client store

Client File Master Record

Client Number (Store)	Client Name	Address	Cycle Date

clients would be prepared indicating the total amount of collections received, the total amount due State, the total amount due the client, and so forth. This processing run would also purge the claims file of bills paid off by the customers, and transfer certain summary information to the company's history file.

4. Processing Run No. 4 would prepare an aging analysis of pending claims for each client of the company.

Discussion Topics

1. Prepare a systems flowchart for each of the four separate processing routines described above. How often should each one of these four processing routines be performed? Explain.

2. Design the record layout of the company's history file records.

3. What additional information might be added to the fields in the claims file master records? What information might be dropped?

4. What additional types of management information might be obtained from the four processing routines which were not available heretofore but which might now be generated with the proposed collections system?

5. Describe the advantages to State Consumer Reporting Bureau of the proposed automated system over the existing manual system. What disadvantages does the new system create for State?

CASE 5

Paradise Hotel

Company Background

The Paradise Hotel is an independent, medium-sized hotel catering to the middle class market. Because the hotel lacks the prestigious image of a national chain hotel, it is necessary to depend on satisfied customers to return on their future trips and to tell their friends about the hotel. Mr. Williams, the General Manager of the hotel, claims that Paradise Hotel has a consistent above-average occupany rate compared with other independent hotels because all employees are trained to provide good service and because the management spends so much effort in follow-up work such as sending thank-you letters and promotional materials to previous guests.

Being confident of the capability of a very experienced front-desk staff, the General Manager is increasingly concerned over the front-desk staff's complaints of the difficulty in organizing their work. There are two front-desk clerks in the day shift, two clerks in the swing shift, and one clerk in the "graveyard" shift. The responsibilities of front-desk clerks include reservations, check-in and check-out procedures, cashiering, switchboard operation, providing information for hotel guests, safekeeping keys and valuables for hotel guests, and various other chores when guests seek service or help from the front desk.

Front Desk Operational Problems

Several problems plagued the front-desk operations. One such problem involved the housekeeping operations. At the close of each shift, the housekeeping department would send a list of checked-out rooms that were cleaned by the maids. The clerk responsible would then update the room inventory sheet so that the next shift would start with complete inventory information. However, the front-desk clerks had no idea what rooms were cleaned *during* the shift.

A second problem concerned the restaurant, gift shop, and laundry department. The supervisors of these operations would forward signed guest bills to the front office twice during a shift listing the different charges to the hotel guests. There were cases when a guest checked out before the front-desk clerk received the billing information that would list the charges for services. In such cases, the hotel would have to send a bill to the guest's residence. It turned out that few people who received such bills bothered to send any payment or response. The uncollected sales plus extra clerical and mailing costs involved in the collection process amounted to an average of $64,000 per year, or approximately 1.5 percent of total hotel revenues.

In view of the above problems, two months ago Mr. Williams ordered a change in operations. These changes required the maids to call the front office every half-hour to inform the front office of rooms cleaned, and required the different departments (such as food service) to call the front office as soon as a charge to a hotel guest was made. Since the change, the front-desk staff has been complaining that they are kept so busy manually posting the room inventory sheet and the hotel guests accounts that they cannot perform their other tasks.

Paradise Hotel has recently computerized its accounting operations by installing an IBM System 370 computer. The new accounting system works extremely satisfactorily in preparing the hotel payroll and in preparing the hotel's financial statements. Mr. Williams suspects that the front-office operations could also be improved through computerization. He contacted Mr. Parks, the systems analyst who had designed the computerized accounting system for Paradise Hotel, and Mr. Parks agreed to do a systems study of the front-office operations.

Mr. Parks spent two weeks observing the front-desk clerks performing their tasks. He noted that as a customer comes in and asks for a room with certain facilities, the front-office clerk checks the room inventory sheet to see whether such a room is available. If it is not, the clerk suggests an alternate room listed on the room inventory sheet as available. If the alternate room is satisfactory, the customer completes a registration card that requires information on name, address, number of persons in the room, hotel room number, room rate, check-in date, and check-out date. (See Exhibit 1.) The customer is given the room key and the check-in procedure is completed. The front-desk clerk then prepares a guest ledger card for the customer who has just checked in. The purpose of the guest ledger card is to record all the charge transactions pertaining to the guest's account. Every time a front-desk clerk receives a call from a revenue-producing department informing him or her of a charge incurred by a guest, the clerk takes the guest's ledger card out from the card file and records the amount on the ledger card. (See Exhibit 2.) Charges are also entered in the cash register in the front office. The tape from the cash register is transferred to the accounting department at the end of a day for auditing and account posting. Because a guest may decide to leave at any moment, the hotel guests' accounts must be complete, accurate, and up-to-the-minute. The front-desk clerk is also responsible

for entering on the Front Office Cash Sheet all receipts and disbursements that he or she made. (See Exhibit 3.) At the end of their shift, the clerks rule off their sections of the cash sheet, summarize their own transactions, and count their cash on hand. When a guest checks out, the front-desk clerk totals the amount on the guest ledger card and collects the balance due from the guest. The check-out date is entered on the guest registration card, which is then transferred from the active file in the front office to the history file in the sales department.

The Recommended System

After his two-week study, Mr. Parks concluded that efficient information flow and efficient transaction-recording procedures were the most important requirements of a good front-office system. He recommended that the hotel install a terminal at the front office and a com-

PARADISE HOTEL

REGISTRATION CARD

Date _____

Name _____

Street & No. _____

City _____ State _____

Room	Rate	Arrived	No. in Party	Departed	Remark

Room Clerk Initial

Exhibit 1

PARADISE HOTEL

GUEST LEDGER CARD

Name _____ Room No. _____

Date of Arrival _____   Room Rate per Day $ _____
Date of Departure _____   No. Guests _____

Date	Brought Forward			TOTAL
Rooms				
Meals				
Beverages				
Local Phone				
L.D. Phone				
Laundry				
Miscellaneous				
Cash Adv.				
Telegrams				
Transfer				
Total Chgs. Today				
Previous Balance				
TOTAL				
Less Cash				
Balance Due				

Exhibit 2

puterized data-processing system to handle the paperwork. This system is described below.

After a guest fills out the registration card, the clerk inputs the data through a terminal, thereby establishing a new computer record. All records are arranged and stored according to room numbers. No ledger cards are prepared because all business transactions between the guest and the hotel are keyed in through computer terminals located at the hotel's restaurant, gift shop, and laundry. At the end of a shift, the computer calculates the total amount of cash receipts and dis-

bursements and the cash balance so that the clerks can reconcile their on-hand cash to the computer records. At the end of the day, the computer calculates the total sales, total accounts receivable, total cash receipts, and total cash disbursements, and automatically updates the various hotel guest accounts within the accounting information system. When a guest checks out, the computer calculates the total balance due from the guest after the clerk has keyed in the room number and depressed the "Total" key on the terminal. When a clerk depresses a

Exhibit 3

| **PH** | FRONT DESK CASH SHEET | | | | | | | | | Date _____ | | | |

Room No.	Name	Room Charge	Food and Beverages	Phone	Long Distance	Laundry	Gift Shop	Cash	Miscellaneous		Paid Out	
									Item	$	Item	$

"Paid-in-Full" key, the computer prints out a receipt for the guest and the record is removed from the file. The registration card is then transferred to the history file in the sales department.

The computer also stores all room inventory information which is available to the front-office clerk through the terminal. When a clerk receives information from the housekeeping department on the rooms cleaned, he or she inputs the information through the front-desk terminal instead of the room inventory sheet.

Mr. Parks estimates that the system will cost $22,000 to install, including training costs. Maintenance will be under $5,000 per year. The system is expected to be adequate for the present volume of business at Paradise Hotel, and for all foreseeable future volumes of business.

Discussion Topics

1. Prepare a document flowchart for the computerized front-desk operations of the Paradise Hotel, as described above.

2. Using any format you like, document how the check-in process, the room-inventory process, the check-out process, and the front-office recording of hotel guests' transactions would function under the computerized version of the front-desk operations.

3. Describe how the proposed computerized system would solve some of the problems of the front desk at Paradise Hotel.

4. When reviewing Mr. Parks' recommendations, Mr. Williams noted that it would be useful to save the information about check-out guests in a guest history file. Evaluate this suggestion. What uses might such a file serve?

5. Including the guest-history file, describe the computer files required for Paradise Hotel's accounting information system. For each file, indicate how the file would be organized, how long the file would be retained, and how the file would be updated. Also, for each file, indicate what specific information would be stored in a typical file record.

PART SEVEN SUPPLEMENT

Computer Hardware and Software

Chapter 17
Computer Hardware: The Central Processing Unit and Input/Output Equipment

Chapter 18
Secondary Storage Devices and Systems Documentation

Chapter 19
Computer Software

This section is designed for students who lack a basic knowledge of electronic data processing and for those who wish to review fundamental EDP concepts. In the introduction to Part Two, we indicated that Part Seven should be covered before beginning Chapter 4. Even for the students who have had prior exposure to computer concepts, a reading of Chapters 17–19 would still be useful as a review of computer fundamentals, terminology, and so forth. Chapters 17 and 18 will emphasize the *hardware* aspects of computer systems, including an examination of input, output, and storage equipment, and the ways in which this equipment can be used to process and store financial-oriented data.

The subject of system flowcharting is also discussed in Chapter 18. Although this subject is technically a software concept, the system flowchart is intimately related to the secondary storage media of the computer system. Thus, Chapter 18 also discusses the manner by which a system flowchart documents the flow of data through the computer files and data-processing phases of the accounting information system.

Chapter 19 is devoted to the topic of computer *software*. The emphasis in this chapter is on computer programming and systems documentation. The discussions on computer programming include a review of the various levels of computer programming languages, and stress the advantages and disadvantages of using BASIC, FORTRAN, or COBOL in the computerized accounting information system. A detailed analysis of these three computer languages is included in Appendix C.

Chapter 19 also stresses the importance of systems documentation in defining the role of the accounting information system in the gathering, processing, storing, and distributing of accounting data. Accountants serving as auditors or systems analysts rely heavily upon such documentation in their examinations. Chapter 19 therefore discusses the characteristics of good systems documentation and tries to identify those documentation aids which are of particular importance to the accounting information system.

17

Computer Hardware: The Central Processing Unit and Input/Output Equipment

Among the important questions that you should be able to answer after reading this chapter are:

1 Why should an accountant be concerned with computer hardware?
2 What is the difference between computer hardware and computer software?
3 What computer equipment is typically found in the computer machine room?
4 What rationale could there possibly be for a data-processing manager to state, "I always like to stay one generation *behind* at my computer center"?
5 Why is computer communication equipment important to an accounting information system?

INTRODUCTION

Since much of today's accounting is performed with the aid of a computer, it is essential that the modern accountant possess a basic understanding of the computer's functions, capabilities, and limitations. It is interesting to note that this requirement was not always so. For many years, the accountant was able to ignore the computer data processing by following the audit trail up to the input portion of the system and picking up the trail again on the other (output) side of the computer system. Today, enough accounting information systems have been computerized and enough computer problems have transpired to convince just about everyone that the accountant must understand how a computer interacts with an accounting information system. Thus, one reason why the accountant should understand the basics of computer hardware and software is because they are vital to the verification of the accuracy and completeness of the data processing.

Fortunately, it is not necessary that the accountant be part engineer in order to follow the logic of the accounting process as it flows through the computer system. In fact, very few programmers, data-processing supervisors, or even computer operators fully understand the detailed hardware operations of a recent model computing machine. What is required, however, is a working knowledge of the computer's hardware and software so that certain, fairly straightforward tests of processing accuracy may be performed and so that the accountant is able to exploit the enormous processing potential offered by modern computer technology. This present chapter and the next examine the computer hardware with which the modern accountant should be familiar. Chapter 19 will then discuss how the computer software utilizes this hardware in the accounting information system.

THE COMPUTER FACILITY

For reasons of convenience, most computer equipment is found in a common location, often a single large room called the *machine room*. During the 1960s, the machine rooms of many large businesses were located in the company's ground floor showroom window. In part, this location was logical because early computer equipment was heavy, and also because there was a certain amount of prestige attached to the company that could boast of a bustling computer center. With the advent of cheaper, lighter, and smaller computers, a perceived need for greater security, and the realization that a showroom computer center displaces a valuable retail sales location, the machine room of the 1980s has moved out of the view of the person on the street and, in many cases, even out of the view of the company programmers who program the computer itself.

Regardless of where the computer facility is physically located, it is likely to resemble, in concept, the machine configuration schematically depicted in Figure 17-1. Conceptually, the system may be divided into five major components: (1) the central processing unit (CPU),

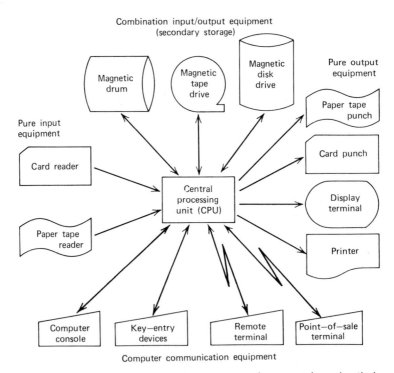

Figure 17-1. A schematic of a computer center (see Chapter 18 for a detailed explanation of symbols).

(2) pure input equipment, (3) pure output equipment, (4) computer communications equipment, and (5) combination input/output (I/O), or "secondary storage," equipment. We shall discuss the first four of these here, deferring a detailed discussion of the fifth category until Chapter 18.

The heart of the computer system is the *central processing unit* which, as the name implies, performs most of the data processing itself and also supervises the functions of the other machines under its control. These "other machines" usually physically surround the central processor, and are therefore also known as *peripheral equipment*.

As suggested by Figure 17-1, most peripheral equipment is electronically connected to the CPU by wires or cables. Usually, these cables are thick and cumbersome, which is the reason that most machine rooms have raised flooring to accommodate them. Equipment directly under the supervision of the CPU via such cables, or *channels*, is also called *online equipment* because it has communication access to the CPU. Technically speaking, therefore, even remote terminals which can communicate with a central processing unit via a telephone line would be classified as online devices. Not all computer equipment is online, however. *Off-line equipment*, such as keypunch machines (for punching cards), card verifiers, card sorters, and so forth, have no direct hook-up with the CPU and for this reason, often are found in areas other than the machine room.

Pure input equipment provides data directly to the central processor. Probably the most common input mechanism is the card reader, although paper tape readers, specialized terminals, and certain optical scanners also perform this pure-input function. We shall take a closer look at some of these devices shortly.

Pure output equipment includes such devices as printers, card punches, paper tape punches, cathode ray tube (CRT) terminal screens, and typewriter terminals. What distinguishes this equipment from the others is their inability to provide data to the CPU. Pure output equipment can only accept data from the central processing unit and transform it to another form such as a punched card or printed document. Although pure output equipment is more limited in capability than other types of equipment in this sense, it is nonetheless very important to the functioning of the accounting information system because it is one of the primary means by which to verify the data-processing performance of the computer facility.

Computer communications equipment enables individuals to communicate directly with the computer and/or the computer's online files. One of the oldest forms of such communications equipment is the typewriter-like computer console used by the computer operator. With it, the computer operator can direct the central processing unit to begin or "abort" a data-processing task, access data from a secondary storage device, or display the contents of the CPU's own computer memory (discussed below). Other forms of computer communications devices include keyboard terminals, point-of-sale terminals, automated bank-teller terminals, and key entry devices. Computer communications equipment is one of the most rapidly developing areas of computer technology, and this development has had a profound impact on the way in which accounting data is accessed, stored, and processed. Thus, like the other types of computer equipment discussed above, we shall be taking a closer look at computer communications devices in a later portion of this chapter.

Finally, *combination input/output equipment* includes such devices as magnetic tape drives, disk drives, magnetic drums, and mass storage devices. All of this equipment is capable of both sending and receiving data to and from the CPU. Since all of these devices have the capability to store large quantities of data, they are therefore also known as *secondary storage devices*. These machines will occupy a central role in our discussion of computer hardware because they are responsible for maintaining the basic files of accounting information systems. We examine them in detail in Chapter 18.

The CPU, online, and off-line equipment found in and around the computing center constitutes the bulk of what is commonly called *computer hardware*. This is distinguishable from such items as source documents, punched cards, computer programs, printed output documents, and the like, which together comprise *computer software*. Although the differences between hardware and software would appear straightforward (after all, who would confuse a program listing with a 500-pound computer?), modern technology has begun to blur even this simple distinction. The ambiguity arises because at present some computer software is being used to perform the functions normally considered those of computer hardware. To label this hybrid development, the computer industry uses the term *firmware*. So, whereas before it was safe enough to call hardware and software complete opposites, it is now better to think of them as settings on a continuum, with hardware on the left, software on the right, and firmware somewhere in the middle.

THE CENTRAL PROCESSING UNIT

As mentioned previously, the heart of the computer system is the central processing unit. Not only is it usually the most expensive piece of equipment at the computer center, but virtually no other online equipment can work without it! Thus, in effect, the CPU is crucial to the computer system in much the same way that an engine is crucial to the automobile. Without a doubt, the CPU is a complex machine. If you were to remove the panels of the machine itself, you are not likely to see a more impressive set of wires, circuits, and other electronics. Thus, if you would like to learn about how the CPU operates, one way *not* to do it is to try and take it apart like a toaster!

Conceptually, the CPU can be divided into three major parts: *the main memory section*, the *arithmetic-logic section*, and the *supervisory-control section*. All are physically contained within the "mainframe" of the CPU itself, although, as you shall see, their functions are quite different. The electronic circuitry used in these three sections of the CPU has been used to define the genealogy of computer development in general. First-generation equipment (starting roughly in 1954) used vacuum tubes exclusively, generated enormous amounts of heat, and consequently required large amounts of electric power, air conditioning, and space requirements. Second-generation equipment (1959–1964) replaced the vacuum tubes with transistors and other solid-state circuitry, cost less, required less space and electrical power, and were substantially smaller and more reliable. IBM's announcement of its System/360 series computers in 1964 ushered in the third generation. These machines used microelectronic circuitry printed on tiny silicon chips or wafers generally known as *integrated circuitry*. Again, an increase in processing speed and a reduction in cost and size were obtained. Finally, in the 1970s, some (but not all) data processors recognized a fourth generation of computers with the introduction of several new types of circuitry including MST (Monolithic Systems Technology), LSI (Large-Scale Integration), and MOSFET (Metal Oxide Silicon Field Effect Transistor) circuitry, as well as the introduction of semiconductor memories. In the 1980s, computer experts are talking about a fifth generation of supercomputers.

Memory Section

Probably the easiest part of the CPU to understand is the memory section. This would be analogous to the memory of a home calculator, except that the home calculator has only one or two memories whereas a typical computer has many thousands. In fact, because the memory capacity of older computers usually determined how much "work" they could do, computer memory was often a primary measure of a CPU's performance capability.

The physical process by which computers store information in their memories has changed considerably over the years, and with this change, the name ascribed to the storage itself. The earliest computers for example were typically *analog computers* which transformed data into electrical current and stored it as electrical voltage in computer memory. Thus, the term "analog" indicated that the magnitude of the voltage in each of the memory compartments of the computer was analogous to the magnitude of the data values that these memory cells stored.

Most computer storage today is accomplished digitally, that is, by discrete (unit-by-unit) counting processes that utilize a binary number system. A description of the binary number system may be found in Appendix D. The earliest digital memories used vacuum tubes, which in turn have been replaced by *magnetic core* (iron-ferrite donuts which were magnetized in either a clockwise or counterclockwise direction), and later by thin film or monolithic (microscopic integrated) circuitry. Research in cryogenic (temperature-controlled) storage and laser (also called "bubble") storage has made even more-advanced storage techniques possible today. A technical explanation of how each of these storage systems works is beyond the scope of this book and, fortunately, need not concern us here. Of greater importance is the concept of primary storage of some type within the CPU itself, and its distinction from the other elements of the CPU.

Logically, the fundamental unit of storage in all digital computers is the *binary digit* or *bit*. Just as a light bulb can be turned on or off, a bit (no matter what physical process is used to represent it) has two and only two settings: "on" and "off." By identifying the number "1" with the "on" position and the number "0" with the "off" position, the digital computer has the ability to store numbers and letters using a binary code. Thus, by grouping bits together, a computer is able to store decimal-equivalent numbers or character symbols internally, albeit in binary format.

Most computer manufacturers use an 8-bit group called a *byte* to form a single character (such as a letter or number) of computerized data. Thus, the memory capacities of most computers are typically measured in *kilobytes* (abbreviated KB or just K) or *megabytes* (abbreviated MB or just M). Although "kilo" means one thousand in the metric system, the electronic data processing industry uses K to represent 2^8 or 1024. Thus, one kilobyte of computer storage is exactly 1024 storage locations. A megabyte of computer storage is roughly 1 million storage lo-

cations. The memory capacities of the smallest computers (i.e., minicomputers) are usually 64K or less; the memory capacities of the largest full-sized computers are 2M or more.

Each unit of storage in the central processing unit has a unique location and can therefore be assigned a unique physical address. This physical address is much like the number on the door of a hotel room, and is used in much the same fashion. When a guest is to be located at a hotel, the individual's room number is first determined and then called. Similarly, when data is required from the memory locations of the central processing unit, the address of the data is determined first and then used to access the storage location wherein the data resides.

For internal representation, a computer will sometimes require more than one byte of computer storage for a single data item. In such instances, it is common to group bytes together to form *computer words*. However, there is no industry standard for a computer word. Minicomputers use as little as two bytes to form a computer word. The IBM standard is four bytes. Control Data Corporation has relied on a 60-bit computer word.

Arithmetic-Logic Section

Most central processing units cannot manipulate data directly while it resides in computer memory. For this reason, tasks such as addition, subtraction, multiplication, division, and comparison must be performed in the arithmetic-logic section of the CPU. For example, if we desire to add two numbers together via the computer, we must first write a computer program to store these numbers in separate storage locations of CPU memory, then transfer one of them to a specific register (a special data-manipulating memory of the CPU found in the arithmetic-logic unit), then access the second number from memory and add it to the first, and finally, store the results by transferring the answer from the register to a third memory location of CPU storage. If we want to *see* the result physically, additional instructions would be required to print the answer with an output device.

Admittedly, the steps by which a computer performs simple arithmetic functions would appear to be unnecessarily cumbersome. In fact, the above description might suggest to you either how efficient humans are or, alternatively, how simple and robot-like a computer is. In defense of the computer, we should keep in mind that a modern computer's "cycle speed", that is, its ability to execute a single instruction (such as an addition or data transfer) is currently measured in *billionths of a second* (called *nanoseconds*). Thus, although it *is* true that a computer executes instructions in a mechanical, robot-like manner, certain very fast computers can also execute as many as 800 million such instructions a second! Although accounting information systems rarely require such speeds, the excellent processing capabilities of modern CPUs are nonetheless important to accounting information systems because accounting data can be processed as quickly as it is accessed. In short, there is "no waiting" once the accounting data is inside the memory of the CPU.

Supervisory-Control Section

The third and last component of the CPU is the supervisory-control section. As implied by its name, the supervisory-control section acts like the supervisor on the loading platform, overseeing operations and making sure that things are done in a proper and orderly fashion. Among its other responsibilities, the supervisory-control section determines the order in which computer-program instructions are executed, acts as a switchboard operator when several users wish to access the computer simultaneously, and also coordinates the activities of the computer center's peripheral equipment as it performs the input, output, and storage tasks dictated by the computer programs stored in the CPU. If the supervisory-control section of the CPU strikes you as a kind of "boss" of operations for the computer system as a whole, you have the right idea.

Large, Small, and Used Central Processing Units

As noted above, computer storage is an important factor in determining the overall power of a given system. For example, the more CPU memory the computer system has, the more information it can store at one time and, therefore, the more processing it can do without having to seek additional data from external sources. Most computer manufacturers supply central processing systems with several memory options. Thus, a computer facility which feels that it does not need extensive main memory can buy or lease a computer with a relatively small amount of "main-frame" storage at first, and then, later, add additional storage as the need arises. However, there is a limit to this process. Eventually, the computer user may be forced to switch to a larger system.

The great strides that have been made in the area of computer technology have also encouraged data-processing centers to acquire several computers to take advantage of newer, more cost-effective equipment. For example, one data-processing manager explained that he had two fairly large computers in his center—one on a long-term lease and the other on a short-term lease. He paid more for the flexibility of a short-term lease, he said, but figured that the cost savings from the superior computer equipment he hoped would be developed in the next two or three years, and for which he would trade his short-term computer, would more than offset the higher short-term lease rates.

As an alternate to the acquisition of a larger system, many computer users have found it advantageous to diversify into several smaller, sometimes interlocking, computer systems. One reason for pursuing a multimachine information system instead of a larger, single CPU is that modern technology has made the small, limited capacity system relatively inexpensive. Thus, for data processors who are involved primarily in a large number of nonintegrated, or marginally integrated, data-processing applications, the replacement (or augmentation) of a large computer system with several smaller ones can be both efficient and cost-effective. For example, among the functions performed by the Alan Company's electronic data-processing subsystem are the weekly preparation of its payroll and the weekly updating of its sporting goods inventory. Since these two accounting functions are performed independently of one another, the Alan Company eventually may want to augment its current large CPU with a separate, smaller computer system for its inventory-control function.

Technology plays an important role in the decision to purchase more than one central processing unit. For example, the Alan Company might wish to keep inventory records on a *real-time basis*—that is, to update and inquiry its inventory records from remote terminals instantaneously as needed. Thus, the Alan Company might consider the acquisition of a real-time computer system in addition to its older system in order to support this real-time inquiry capability. The acquisition of two different systems makes this possible. The fact that newer, real-time computer systems have been decreasing in price would probably make such a possibility cost-effective.

Another reason why a trend toward smaller systems has developed in recent years is because of the relatively large number of hardware manufacturers that offer them (at present more than over 80 firms). This is a complete reversal of the situation just a decade ago when there were only a few important hardware manufacturers in the United States. Today, the computer-on-a-chip is a reality (Figure 17-2), meaning that even a fairly intelligent hobbyist can build a computer from parts bought "off the shelf" from a computer "grocery" store. Of course, the computer system that the business organization would buy from the small computer manufacturer still is likely to be considerably more sophisticated than that of the hobbyist. Yet, the fact remains that a dollar's worth of computing power in 1971 sells for less than 10 cents today. Thus, at present, it is possible to buy several smaller computer systems for what it once cost for a single medium- or large-sized computer system.

Customarily, the smaller of the small-sized computer systems are called minicomputers. Almost all have limited memory capacities (averaging about 32,000 storage locations) and relatively inexpensive purchase or lease prices. Most cost less than $20,000. Minicomputers are highly flexible machines that are easily adapted to various types of applications and usually are inexpensive to operate. They are particularly well-suited to a single application, such as the maintenance of a computerized inventory system or an accounts receivable system.

The biggest problems with minicomputers are the limitations in what they can do. For example, some are programmable only in a single programming language. In addition, they are slow in execution, inflexible as to the number and types of peripheral equipment that can be attached to them, and are subject to an accelerated rate of obsolescence which is caused by the rapid technological developments in the area. For all these drawbacks, however, minicomputers represent one of the fastest-growing segments of the computer market, and have proven especially popular with small businesses. For this reason, we examine minicomputers in greater detail in Chapter 15.

Another interesting feature of today's computer hardware market is the used-machine market. There are large numbers of third-generation, second-generation, and even first-generation equipment that are still being used for normal data-processing tasks in accounting, marketing, production, and so forth. The explanation is *cost*. Older machines are sometimes cheaper to buy, cheaper to lease, and cheaper to repair than certain newer machines. In addition, they are often more familiar to the EDP staff and may therefore be more cost-effective to operate. As one data-processing manager stated, "I always try to stay one generation *behind* at my computer center because I'm sure *that* hardware works!"

In addition to hardware considerations, there are also software considerations. Conversion costs incurred in the transfer to a new computer model always involve the modification of programs, operating systems, and the like. Although these items involve a one-time expenditure, their

Figure 17-2. A computer-on-a-chip held between fingers. (Photo Courtesy of IBM.)

costs nonetheless can be considerable, especially if the additional costs of temporarily operating two computer systems simultaneously are included in the cost analysis. In the end, it is sometimes more desirable to seek another, used machine than to completely change to a newer one.

An interesting compromise between the purchase of new equipment and the maintenance of old equipment is the process of *emulation*. Here, the EDP manager acquires a new central processor which is then programmed to *emulate* the characteristics of the computer center's old hardware. For example, in one computer-processing task, the new CPU may be directed to access data formerly stored on magnetic tape.

With an emulation approach, the central processor performs the requested task, never realizing that, in reality, the required data is stored on a magnetic disk.

The process of emulation is important to accounting information systems because it enables the EDP staff to provide continuous data-processing services to accounting-information users while the computer center hardware is in a state of transition. Thus, while new computer software is being developed to exploit the improved hardware capabilities of a new computer system, the older software can be used on a "business-as-usual" basis to provide necessary reports, payroll checks, and so forth. This approach therefore minimizes disruptions and permits the orderly transition of the computer center's operations from one hardware system to another.

The Central Processing Unit, Concluded

In conclusion, the central processing unit is the focus of the computer facility because it performs the actual data processing. Often, it is the most expensive piece of equipment on the floor and is sometimes the determinant of what can and cannot be done by the computer center. For all this capability, however, the CPU cannot operate alone. Data must be supplied to it by input equipment, and output equipment is required to enable the central processor to communicate its results in an intelligible format. Further, for reasons that will be made clearer in the following chapters, the CPU also relies heavily upon the storage capacities of such media as magnetic tape and disks. The next sections of the chapter discuss input, output, and computer communications peripheral equipment in greater detail.

PURE INPUT EQUIPMENT

The primary function of pure input equipment is to provide data to the central processing unit. Among the more popular forms of input equipment are punched card readers, punched paper tape readers, and optical scanners. Of these, the punched card reader is by far the most important in terms of representative data processing in the United States, although processing through remote punched paper tape readers has been growing in popularity in recent years. For these reasons, we shall limit our discussion to these two types of input mechanisms.

Punched Card Readers

Virtually every computer center has a card reader, which is often found in combination with a card punch (Figure 17-3). Card readers interpret the holes punched in the computer card either through wire sensors or optics, and communicate this information via a channel to the central processing unit. Only valid cards using a recognizable punched code are accepted by the card reader. Bad cards (i.e., cards with too many punches in the same column, cards that are mutilated, etc.) are stacked in a reject hopper, and the detection of a bad card may also require operator intervention. Figure 17-4 compares the input speeds of typical card readers with those of other common input and output devices. Although slow in comparison with magnetic tape or disk input, punched-card input is decidedly faster than manual input.

It is likely that the punched card will always play some role in accounting information systems because of its value as a *turn-around document*. A turn-around document is a document that is output by the computer system, sent to an individual, and then returned for subsequent data processing. Punched cards serving as customer bills, employee payroll checks, and audit-confirmation notices are examples of such documents used in accounting information systems. Thus, although punched cards are used less often to provide information initially to the computer (key-entry devices and point-of-sale terminals are often used instead), punched cards still serve a vital role in many accounting information systems. The use of punched cards both as turn-around documents and as a data medium in accounting information systems is explored in greater depth in Chapter 4.

Punched Paper Tape Readers

Punched paper tape readers generally use paper tape that has been wound on spools first. An example of a paper tape reader is provided in Figure 17-5. The exact process by which punched paper tape is encoded and deciphered is discussed in detail in Chapter 4. The data on paper tape can be accessed at speeds ranging from 100 to 2000 characters per second. As illustrated in Figure 17-4, this is not as fast as card readers. Because paper tape readers are often cheaper than card readers, this can be of some importance to the cost-conscious company interested in acquiring inexpensive input devices.

Punched paper tape readers are often used in conjunction with remote terminals to transmit accounting data over telephone or telegraph

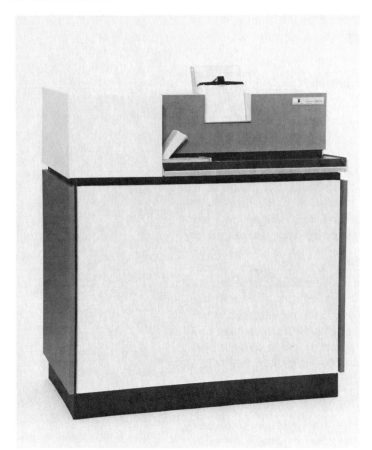

Figure 17-3. A card reader/punch. (Photo Courtesy of Mohawk Data Sciences.)

lines. For example, Western Union uses paper tape as a data-transmission medium. Similarly, a punched paper tape device that has been attached to a cash register can encode paper tape at the same time that the register is used. The tape may then be fed into a punched paper tape reader for transmission to the computer center for data processing.

PURE OUTPUT EQUIPMENT

As the name implies, pure output equipment accepts information from the central processing unit and converts it to an alternate form (e.g., a printed report) for off-line storage or distribution to information users. Of the three links (input, processing, and output) in the data-processing chain, output has tended to be the most time-consuming. Therefore, it has also been the link of primary focus in the study of increasing data-processing efficiency, at least in terms of data-processing speed.

From the remarks at the beginning of the chapter, it should be clear that there are many types of output devices, including card punches, printers, paper tape punches, visual display terminals, and typewriter terminals, as well as many other forms of specialized output-designated forms of equipment. For space reasons, however, we shall limit our study to only two types of output devices: card punches and printers.

Figure 17-4

A COMPARISON OF INPUT/OUTPUT SPEEDS FOR SELECTED MEDIA*

Input and Output Devices

Media	Device	Input	Output	Unit of Measurement	Typical Rates of Speed		
					Low	Medium	High
Punched cards	Card reader	X		Cards/minute	100	600	2,000
	Card punch		X	Cards/minute	100	300	500
Paper tape	Tape reader	X		Characters/ second	100	350	2,000
	Tape punch		X	Characters/ second	20	100	300
Magnetic ink	Reader	X		Documents/ minute	750	1,200	2,500
Paper	Optical scanner	X		Documents/ minute	100	300	1,500
	Printer		X	Lines/minute	300	600	18,000
	Terminal	X	X	Characters/ second	10	30	120
Cathode ray tube	Display		X	Characters/ second	250	1,000	10,000
Microfilm	COM		X	Thousand characters/ second	30	60	500

Secondary Storage Devices

Media	Device	Storage Capacity	Range of Transfer Rates, Thousands of Characters per Second		
			Low	Medium	High
Magnetic tape	Tape drive	172 million characters per tape	15	200	1,000
Magnetic disk	Disk drive	100 million characters per pack	250	885	3,000
Magnetic drum	Drum storage unit	4 million characters per high-speed drum	275	800	1,200
Mass storage	Mass storage device	Up to 472 billion characters	806	806	885

*The secondary storage devices are discussed at length in Chapter 18.

Figure 17-5. A punched paper tape reader. (Photo Courtesy of IBM.)

Card Punches

Although it may be housed in the same cabinet as the card reader (Figure 17-3), the card punch is a pure output device and, therefore, logically distinct from the card reader. Also, because of the physical process involved, punching cards is substantially slower than reading them. For listing or summary reports, punched-card output is not a popular output medium since card decks are bulky and usually require a second processing phase to interpret (i.e., to print) whatever information has been punched in them. (This printing job is often performed by an *interpreter*—a piece of off-line equipment.) For example, if the Alan Company were to utilize punched-card storage for its accounts receivable subsidiary ledger (consisting of several thousand credit customer accounts), the thousands of cards required to reflect the company's ledger would be both bulky and inefficient.

Common accounting applications using punched-card output would include computerized payroll checks, address envelope inserts, accounts receivable billings (such as for credit sales, mortgage coupons, and utility billings), and company dividend or proxy communications. As noted above, almost all of these punched cards are examples of *turn-around documents* since the output medium is sent away and later returned to serve as input media in a new phase of data processing.

Printers

The great bulk of computer output is performed on high-speed printers, making these devices almost as valuable as the CPU in terms of producing human-readable information. Virtually all computers can "think" (i.e., process data) faster than they can write—or, in this case, print. For this reason, most medium and large computer systems have several printers connected to the CPU to share the output "workload." Today, only a very small computer installation would be likely to have only one printer.

There are two types of printers: impact printers and nonimpact printers. Each is discussed below.

Impact printers. Impact printers work much like a typewriter in that a letter or number is formed by physically striking the output sheet with a character-forming device. Chain printers utilize five sets of teletype characters (such as those found on the hammers of a typewriter) which are arranged on a chain much like a bicycle chain (Figure 17-6). To create a line of output, the chain is passed between a set of hammers and the output sheet. The hammers strike the chain at the appropriate time, forming a character on the printed page. The chain is cycled past the hammers until a complete print line has been formed. Then the process repeats itself for the next line.

Wheelprinters (Figure 17-7) utilize one or more printwheels, each of which contains a complete set of print characters. Each printwheel is spun until the proper character is aligned with the printed page, and the page is struck from behind, forcing the paper to impact with the assembled print line.

Matrix printers form print characters from a set of wires. For example, 35 wires arranged in a 5 by 7 matrix are used to form a given print character. The ends of the selected wires are pressed against the print page to form the desired print symbol. Figure 17-8 is an example of how the digit 5 might be formed using this type of printer. The print matrix travels along the line of the paper to print the desired output line.

Nonimpact printers. Nonimpact printers utilize either a chemical process or an electronic photocopying process similar to that of reproducing machines. These print techniques are technically beyond the scope of this text. However, their advantages in terms of speed should not be overlooked. Because the mechanical action of the impact printer is eliminated, nonimpact printers can print a whole page at a time, thus greatly increasing the printing efficiency of this output device. In fact, an electronic printer has an output capability of 64,000 lines per minute!

The output speed of printers is important to the accounting information system because many accounting applications require large volumes of printed output. For example, a payroll processing task will require that a payroll check be prepared for each one of potentially thousands of employees. Similarly, in an accounts-receivable application, a separate bill must be prepared for each customer. Because for both of these applications, several printed lines must be made for each employee or customer, the total number of printed lines for the processing runs tends to become very large. Situations requiring thousands, hundreds of thousands, and even millions of lines are common in business applications today. To avoid slowdowns caused by these large processing volumes, high-speed printing is essential.

COMPUTER COMMUNICATIONS EQUIPMENT

As explained earlier in this chapter, computer communications equipment enables an individual to communicate directly with a central processing unit and/or the CPU's online computer files. Examples include computer consoles, key-entry devices, computer terminals, and various kinds of specialized communications equipment such as point-of-sale terminals and automated bank-teller terminals. Even a pushbutton telephone would technically qualify as a piece of computer communications equipment since it is now possible to use telephones (either by themselves, or with special attachments called *modems*) to perform input/output operations with computer systems set up for this purpose.

The development of new kinds of computer communications equipment has caused something of a data-access-and-retrieval revolution in the field of data processing. This revolution may be attributable primarily to the fact that with such equipment, the transmission of data to and from the computer center can now be performed on a remote basis. This means that accounting data can be collected at its source and fed directly to a computer without having to carry documents, computer cards, and so forth, from one physical location to another. Rather, data transmission over regular and specialized telephone lines has permitted companies to decentralize their data-gathering operations simply by installing appropriate data-transmission equipment at such strategic locations as accounting offices, warehouses, or small retail outlets. Sav-

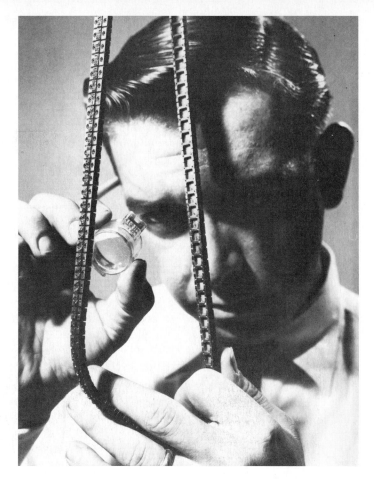

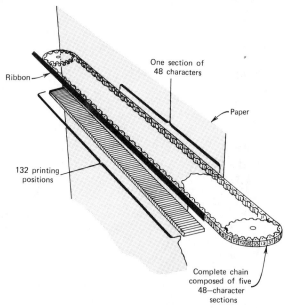

Figure 17-6. A print chain. (Photos Courtesy of IBM.)

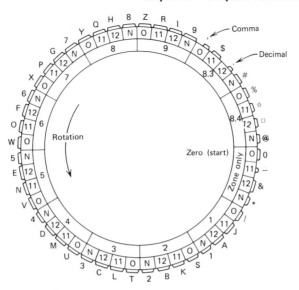

Figure 17-7. A print wheel.

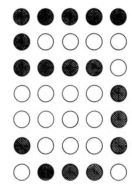

Figure 17-8. The dot selection for the number "5" as written by a matrix printer.

ings in both time and money have resulted, enabling computer systems in general, and accounting systems in particular, to become more responsive and more cost-effective gatherers, processors, and disseminators of (accounting) information.

Telephone companies have also assisted in the computer-communications development by providing specialized communication services for data transmission purposes. For example, telephone networks such as *Telenet* enable users of various computers and computer-communications equipment to transmit data to each other via telephone lines, or, in some cases, even by communications satellites. Further, because of space-age technological advances in the way data can now be coded and then transmitted, the long-distance rates for such services are now orders of magnitude cheaper than normal, voice-grade services. As a result, computer communications equipment has become a viable form of data collection and transmission.

The advantages of computer communications equipment have inspired more serious attention

525

to two interesting informational concepts: (1) the *paperless office* and (2) *electronic mail*. The rationale behind the paperless office is simply that paper documents are no longer the most cost-effective way to transmit and/or store information. Paper documents, it is argued, clutter the work environment, are expensive to mail, take up storage space, are often maintained for unnecessary reference purposes, and actually decrease productivity because they must be filled out, reviewed, and filed. Modern technology would help to avoid all these problems by automating our data-gathering, data-recording, and data-retrieval tasks, and replacing paper forms with information stored on computer files. The use of computer communications equipment is an important step in this general direction.

The concept of electronic mail is related to the idea of the paperless office in that, again, physical paper handling would be reduced by replacing letters and envelopes with electronic signals transmitted over computer communication lines. Here, cost savings may be anticipated because (1) stationery costs would decrease, (2) word-processing equipment (which enables the user to edit correspondence, adjust margins, and even spell properly) can be attached to the data-transmission equipment, (3) physical transportation costs are eliminated and replaced with cheaper electronic transmission costs, and (4) response times for important correspondence would shorten.

The implications of electronic mail to accounting information systems are very important. Invoices can be sent directly to customers, for example, and immediate signaling of their receipt and/or correctness would be possible. Requests for information would no longer be necessary because inquiries could be answered immediately via the data-transmission lines. Electronic funds transfer systems, in which dollars were paid from one financial institution to another using electronic accounting instead of physical transport, is yet another possibility. In short, therefore, electronic mail is an exciting, although as yet relatively undeveloped, concept of relevance to accounting information systems. Whether the potentials of electronic mail as suggested here will be fully or even partially realized had yet to be determined at the time this book went to press.

SUMMARY

Computer hardware is a basic tool of the modern accounting information system. Thus, the professional accountant needs to understand computer hardware in order to be a good accounting systems analyst, budgeting expert, auditor, or management consultant. A technical understanding of computer hardware is not required, but a working knowledge of the different types of data-processing machines is fundamental to a complete grasp of computerized accounting information systems.

The computer facility is comprised of five basic types of equipment: the central processing unit (CPU), pure input equipment, pure output equipment, communications equipment, and combination input/output (secondary storage) equipment. The CPU is the "brains" of the computer center, directing the other online equipment under its control, and performing the bulk of the actual data processing. The CPU is internally composed of three major components: the memory section, the arithmetic-logic section, and the supervisory-control section. Each component performs a different set of functions, all of which are necessary for the efficient operation of the computer center in general, and the processing of accounting data in particular.

Pure input equipment only provides data to the central processing unit. Card readers, paper tape readers, and optical scanners are examples. Similarly, pure output equipment only accepts data from the CPU and transfers this data to some form of output medium. Printers, card punches, paper tape punches, and display terminals are common forms of pure output devices.

Communications equipment enables the accountant to communicate directly with the computer and/or the computer's files. Examples include the computer's console, various types of terminals, and various types of key-entry devices. This chapter has focused primarily upon the implications and potential of communication equipment. Detailed discussions of terminals and key-entry devices may be found in Chapter 4.

DISCUSSION QUESTIONS

17-1. Why is an understanding of computer hardware important to the accountant?

17-2. What is the difference between computer hardware and computer software?

17-3. What are the five categories of computer equipment, and what distinguishes one type from the other?

17-4. Is a central processing unit really "central?" Why or why not?

17-5. Name the three sections of the central processing unit and describe the functions of each.

17-6. What is the difference between "online" computer equipment and "off-line" computer equipment? Give several examples of each type of equipment.

17-7. Why is the central processing unit sometimes called the "heart" of the computer center?

17-8. In what ways is the memory of a computer like the memory of a human being? In what ways is it different?

17-9. Describe the concept of location addresses in the CPU. How are these addresses similar to street addresses? How are they different?

17-10. One central processing unit said to another, "I'd like to have a 'word' with you!" Is it the same "word" that you and I might exchange? Explain.

17-11. The computer has been described in this chapter as both a "robot" and a "brain." In what ways is the computer like each of these?

17-12. Why is it conceptually more desirable to consider the computer "word" as a fundamental unit of storage in the central processing unit despite the fact that, in reality, it is a "bit"?

17-13. In the text, it was noted that there has been a recent trend toward the acquisition of several smaller, more limited computers as opposed to one very large one. Discuss some reasons why this trend has developed and identify

some factors that might have a bearing upon such a decision.

17-14. Why buy a used computer when you can get a new one for less?

17-15. What are the basic advantages and disadvantages of minicomputers?

17-16. Decide the following argument between Mr. McAllister and Mr. Thacker:

McALLISTER: The trend in computers these days is toward bigger, more sophisticated machinery. Why, nowadays, the larger CPU can do the work of hundreds of smaller machines and still have time to twiddle its thumbs. The cost of processing has been reduced substantially, too, in these larger models. Like every other form of big business, there are economies to scale.

THACKER: McAllister, you have your head in the sand. If you weren't so impressed with CPU size, you'd see that what the minicomputers lack in capacity is more than offset in flexibility and price. True, you can't attach an unlimited number of peripherals to the minicomputer's CPU, but so what? You can buy a few extra minicomputers for the price of renting a single large-scale system.

17-17. "Worrying about the hardware of a computer is like worrying about the hardware in my car—that is, unnecessary. I certainly don't have to understand the details of my engine's crankshaft in order to drive my car, and in similar fashion, there is little reason for me to understand the components of the central processing unit." Do you agree? Discuss.

17-18. According to the text, computers can think faster than they can write if only one printer is available to perform the output function. But what if there were two, three, or even four printers available for the output task? Discuss.

17-19. Why are punched cards commonly used as "turn-around" documents?

17-20. What types of equipment would be classified as computer communications equipment? Why is such equipment important to accounting information systems?

17-21. Explain the concepts of the "paperless office" and "electronic mail." What advantages would the paperless office and electronic mail have for accounting information systems? Can you think of any disadvantages?

17-22. In the text, it was stated that developments in

the area of computer communications have caused something of a revolution in the area of data processing. Give accounting examples that might be used to bolster this argument. How do you reconcile the growth of computer communications equipment, which tends to *centralize* the information flow from remote data sources to a central computer, with the parallel growth of small computers and minicomputers, which tends to *decentralize* the flow of information? Discuss.

17-23. Are the following terms synonyms, antonyms, or unrelated? Identify each.

(a) cable—channel

(b) online—off-line

(c) CPU—CRT

17-24. Recent surveys indicate that most business data processing today uses third-generation equipment to perform second-generation type processing tasks. Inasmuch as we are presently in the fourth generation of computer machinery how do you account for this apparent paradox?

PROBLEMS

17-25. Using an IBM standard, how many bytes are needed to construct four computer words? How many bits would this include?

17-26. Are the following considered pure input equipment, pure output equipment, or combination input/output equipment?

(a) card punch   (g) magnetic drum

(b) card reader   (h) magnetic tape drive

(c) CRT screen   (i) mass storage device

(d) printer   (j) paper tape reader

(e) disk drive   (k) paper tape punch

(f) keyboard terminal

17-27. Which component of the central processing unit performs each of the following functions?

(a) determines the order in which instructions are executed

(b) multiplication

(c) coordinates the peripheral equipment as input, output and storage tasks are performed

(d) stores data in unique locations

(e) compares two data values to decide which is the larger

(f) provides a transient "rest-place" for data being transferred from one computer medium to another (e.g., card-to-magnetic tape)

(g) signals the computer operator that a processing function has been completed.

17-28. Mr. Donald Sawicki is trying to decide between a card reader, magnetic tape drive, or magnetic disk to use as an input medium for his processing needs. Which of these would be able to input data the fastest? (*Hint:* Compute transmission speeds in terms of characters per second.)

17-29. Convert the following rates of speed for each device listed below into an equivalent number of cards-per-minute. In all cases, assume that a card is 80 characters in length.

(a) card reader @ 10 cards/sec

(b) paper tape reader @ 100 char/sec

(c) console typewriter @ 30 char/sec

(d) CRT screen @ 8000 char/sec

(e) COM @ 200,000 char/sec

(f) magnetic disk @ 500,000 char/sec

(g) magnetic drum @ 1,100,000 char/sec

17-30. The Ron Murphy Company of Lewiston, Idaho, uses computer cards to help process its mail orders. A separate card is prepared for each item requested in each order. Direct costs for this operation include the following:

(a) monthly rental of keypunch machines, $100 each

(b) monthly rental of card verifiers, $100 each

(c) monthly salary of keypunch operators and verifiers, $800 each

(d) cost per box of computer cards, $6.50

The company gets about 500 orders per week. Each order is different, of course, but on average requires 5 different items. Also, on average, each item requires 50 keystrokes on the keypunch machine. Once data has been punched on the computer cards, the cards are forwarded to a verification station for checking. About half the information on each card must also be verified for coding accuracy. The error rate is approximately 10 percent. For simplicity, assume that all errors are corrected the first time they are returned to the keypunch station. A box of computer cards consists of 2000 cards.

Required

A. Assume that there are exactly 4 weeks in a month and that the average operator can keypunch 2000 strokes per hour. How many keypunches and card verifiers would be required for this task?

B. Compute the monthly cost for this operation, using your answer in part A above.

18

Secondary Storage Devices and Systems Documentation

Among the important questions that you should be able to answer after reading this chapter are:

1 Why are magnetic tape and magnetic disk storage important to the accounting information system?

2 What is parity and what is its relevance to accounting data?

3 What are the major differences between magnetic tape and magnetic disk, and what are the implications of these differences from the standpoint of storing and accessing accounting data?

4 What is a mass storage device? Why is it useful to accounting information systems?

5 How is a system flowchart used to document the flow of data through an accounting information system?

INTRODUCTION

The memory of the central processing unit is too expensive and too limited to serve the entire storage needs of the typical business organization. Thus, most accounting information systems also make extensive use of secondary storage such as magnetic tapes or magnetic disks to maintain computer-readable accounting information. Common to most devices is the ability to store such information on a removable storage medium, such as a reel of magnetic tape or a disk pack, thereby greatly increasing the amount of information that can be made available to the central processing unit *through a single machine device*. Since well over 90 percent of all present accounting data processing utilizes magnetic tape or disk storage, we shall take the opportunity to examine these two types of storage media in detail in this chapter. Magnetic drums and mass storage systems (MSSs) do not play an important role in most typical accounting information systems. Thus, we shall examine these types of secondary storage devices in a somewhat cursory manner.

In the discussions that follow, emphasis has been placed upon the *format* of data as it might reside on magnetic tape or magnetic disk. From the standpoint of the accountant, formatting is important because it is a measure of storage efficiency, resource utilization, and occasionally even computer-system compatibility. The discussions on data formatting also set the stage for the subject of accounting information data bases as covered in Chapter 5.

In a final portion of this chapter, we shall look at systems documentation. Among other things, the system flowchart documents the use of magnetic tape files and disk files within the accounting information system, and traces their utilization in the various data-processing tasks involved in accounting applications. Although technically a software concept, system flowcharts are intimately connected with the computer hardware and computer files of the accounting information system. Thus, as a matter of convenience, we have chosen to include this topic in the present chapter.

MAGNETIC TAPE SYSTEMS

With the exception of its relatively greater width (1/2-inch), the magnetic tape used by the computer system closely resembles the standard recording tape used on the home tape recorder. One side of the tape is dull due to a coating of magnetic oxide, the other side is shiny. Only the dull side is used for recording; the shiny side serves as backing.

Magnetic recording tape is wound on reels that usually have metallic cores and plastic sides. A standard reel measures 10½ inches in diameter and contains 2400 feet of magnetic tape. Half-reels of 1200 feet and "hypertape" lengths of 3600 feet are also available. Regardless of the reel size, however, not all of the tape length is available for data storage. A certain amount of leader tape is set aside for threading on a *take-up reel* (Figure 18-1) and a similar amount of tape is reserved at the end of the mag-

netic tape for permanent anchoring on the reel. A *load marker* separates the leader or take-up portion of the magnetic tape from the data-recording portion, and an *end-of-reel marker* performs the same function for the anchoring portion of the magnetic tape.

All reading and writing of magnetic tape is done via machine—the tape drive. Figure 18-1 (bottom) is a schematic. For the particular tape drive illustrated in this figure, the supply reel is mounted on the left and the take-up reel is mounted on the right. (This configuration differs from manufacturer to manufacturer.) The tape drive passes through several drive capstans (wheels) which guide the tape to and from the reading/recording station. This station is called the *read/write head assembly*. In effect, the tape's path through the mechanism is much like that of a film strip through a home movie projector, except that home movie film has sprocket holes for gear teeth whereas magnetic computer tape is continuous and smooth. The vacuum columns in the tape drive found on either side of the read/write head assembly permit slack in the tape. These columns eliminate the precise coordination that would otherwise be required to turn all the capstans and both tape reels simultaneously when passing the tape through the system. Sensors in the vacuum columns keep the correct amount of tape slack in either column.

Magnetic Tape Coding

The actual coding of magnetic tape (Figure 18-2) is performed by magnetizing microscopic portions of the tape called binary digits or bits. The bits of the magnetic tape system can assume only one of two positions—magnetized or unmagnetized ("on" or "off")—and are created by polarizing the tape area of the bit. Magnetic tape is divided into *channels* or *tracks,* and one vertical column (i.e., a set of bits at the same position on each of the tracks) is used to represent a single character. Figure 18-2 illustrates the coding for a seven-track tape. The letter "K," for example, consists of magnetized bits in tracks labeled 2 and B; the "comma" symbol has "on" bits in tracks 1, 2, 8, and A; the number "6" uses

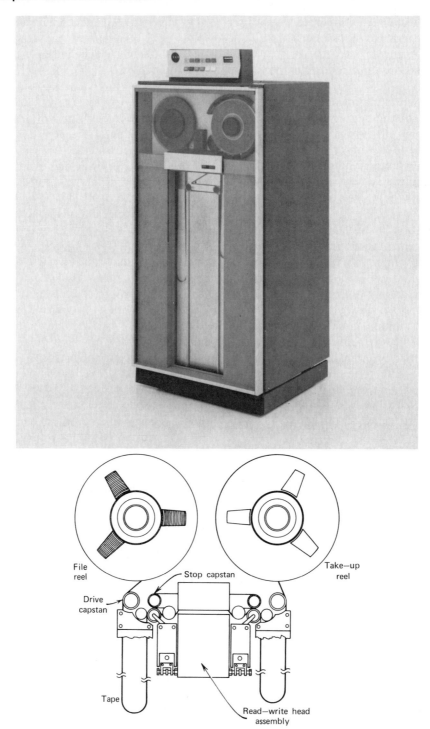

Figure 18-1. A magnetic tape drive (upper diagram), and a schematic of the tape reels, drive capstans, and read/write head assembly (lower diagram). (Photo Courtesy of IBM.)

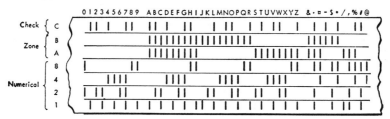

Figure 18-2. Seven-channel (track) magnetic tape coding.

bits in tracks 2 and 4; and so forth. Although the coding system might appear random at first, there is actually a systematic encoding procedure using a combination of low-order tracks (the first four "numeric" tracks of the tape) and high-order tracks (the remaining two "zone" or "letter" tracks) of the tape. Note, for example, that the numbers encoded on the tape do not utilize the zone tracks, the letters "A" through "I" utilize both zone tracks, the letters "J" through "R" utilize only the "B" track, whereas the letters "S" through "Z" utilize only the "A" track. Within each of these series (numbers 1–9, letters A–I, J–R, or S–Z), a binary counting sequence in the numeric tracks may be observed. (Exceptions to this general rule are the number zero and the special symbols such as the dollar sign, period, etc.)

As you may have guessed already, the parity channel (track C) of the tape does not encode information but serves as a check on the other bits comprising the character on the tape. Figure 18-2 illustrates a tape using "even parity." With even parity, the number of magnetized bits for each character in the informational portion of the tape (i.e., in tracks 1, 2, 4, 8, A, and B) is counted. If this number is even, the parity bit is not affected. If this number is odd, the parity bit is magnetized, bringing the total number of "on" bits in the character to an even number. Thus, for example, the letter K does not use the parity bit in its code because the informational bits already total an even number, whereas the percent symbol does. In fact, if you carefully examine the number of magnetized bits in each character of the figure, you will find that all of them will have an even number of "on" bits, the parity bit being on or off as required to accomplish this even-total objective.

Some computer manufacturers prefer to utilize an "odd parity" control system instead. As the name implies, odd parity requires that the total number of bits comprising the character be an odd number. Thus, for those characters whose informational bits total an odd number already, the parity bit is not affected; for those characters whose informational bits total an even number, the parity bit is magnetized, bringing the total bit count to an odd number.

Parity is used to check the accuracy of each character as it is written onto, or read from, magnetic tape. Every time a data transfer is performed, hardware in the tape drive tests each character for proper parity. This is called a *parity check*. When a parity error is encountered, either certain error routines are automatically executed by the computer operating system (see Chapter 19), or the computer operator is called. Thus, magnetic tape has a built-in control feature to assure the accuracy of the information written on this media: no bits can be "dropped" accidentally in the encoding or reading process and go undetected by the system. (Of course no parity error would be detected if two bits were simultaneously lost in the same reading or writing operation. However, the probability of this event is negligible.)

Where accounting data is involved, parity testing is an important hardware control. Since most accounting data will be maintained on magnetic tape or magnetic disk, it is important that the computer system have safeguards that assure accuracy in the transmission of this data from tape or disk to the CPU (or elsewhere). The loss of a single bit has the potential to change a financial figure by an order of magnitude. Parity checking performs this vital control purpose.

More recently, computer manufacturers have

begun to manufacture tape drives that divide the tape width into nine channels instead of seven (see Figure 18-3). Of the nine channels, eight are set aside for encoding data and the ninth serves as the parity test. The advantage of the nine-track format over the seven-track format rests in the larger number of characters that can be represented within a single column of the tape. A seven-track tape can represent only $2^6 = 64$ different characters (two bit settings for each of six informational tracks), whereas a nine-track tape can represent $2^8 = 256$ characters (two bit settings for each of eight informational tracks).

A second advantage of the nine-track tape lies in its ability to represent pure numerical data in a more efficient, *packed-decimal format*. This means that two numbers, instead of one letter or other special symbol, are stored in a single column (eight bits) of the tape. Such formatting is made possible because any one of the decimal numbers (zero through nine) requires only four bits in binary representation (see Appendix D). Thus, using packed-decimal storage instead of "normal" representation cuts the storage requirements in half. When large amounts of numerical data are involved, such as in many typical accounting applications, the savings can be considerable.

Magnetic tape, like home recording tape, may be recorded at different speeds, thus varying the density of the information on this medium. Common densities are 200, 556, 800, and 1600 characters per inch (cpi), although densities as high as 6250 characters per inch are currently possible. As compared with punched cards, the advantages of magnetic tape at these higher densities should be obvious: a standard, 7-pound reel of magnetic tape has the capacity to store the equivalent of over 2 million punched cards' worth of data!

Magnetic Tape Formats

The characters written on magnetic tape are grouped together logically to form data *fields* (e.g., individual numbers grouped together to form a social security number), which in turn are aggregated to form computer *records*. An illustrative employee record is provided in Figure 18-4. In an accounting application, a record is the basic unit of information, containing all the data about one employee, one type of inventory product, one customer's savings account, and so forth. Finally, a set of common records is called a *computer file*.

On magnetic tape, there is no limit on the size of a record, although records in excess of 3000 characters are rare. Figure 18-4 illustrates a tape record for an employee file as might be used in preparing the weekly payroll. Notice especially the large amount of space that has been left for name and address information. If *fixed-length records* are used, in which the same amount of space is reserved for each employee, then such fields must be large enough to accommodate the longest possible name or address. *Variable-length records*, which might set aside only as much room as is actually needed for each employee, would obviously conserve storage space. (The choice of fixed-length versus vari-

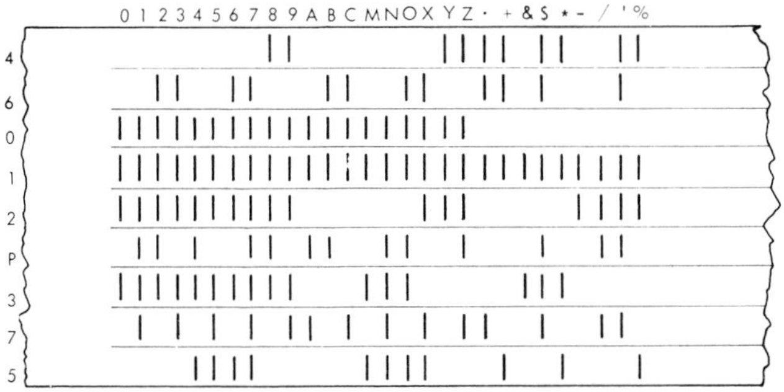

Figure 18-3. Nine-channel (track) magnetic tape coding.

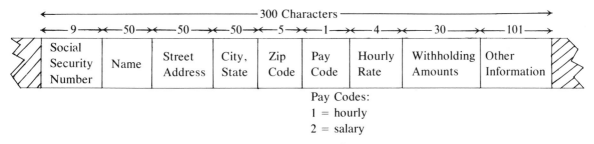

<table>
<tr><td></td><td colspan="9">─────────────────────── 300 Characters ───────────────────────────</td><td></td></tr>
</table>

	9	50	50	50	5	1	4	30	101	
	Social Security Number	Name	Street Address	City, State	Zip Code	Pay Code	Hourly Rate	Withholding Amounts	Other Information	

Pay Codes:
1 = hourly
2 = salary

Figure 18-4. An employee file record on magnetic tape.

able-length records in the design of a tape file is a user option.)

To separate one record from another on the magnetic tape, the tape system uses an *inter-record gap (IRG)* as illustrated in Figure 18-5. Such a gap is required to enable the tape drive to "skid" to a stop after each record has been accessed, and also to gather momentum when commencing to read the next record in the sequence. Although this might seem like a large space requirement, a standard inter-record gap is typically only 3/4-inch in length.

Despite its relatively small size, the inter-record gap is large enough to cause problems. Consider, for example, a hypothetical tape file that has been written at a tape density of 800 characters per inch and that stores fixed-length records each of size 400 characters. The result is a tape file consisting of records each 1/2-inch in length (400 divided by 800) separated by inter-record gaps each 3/4-inch in length. The problem: instead of records separated by inter-record gaps, we really have inter-record gaps separated by records! Most of the tape is wasted with "filler."

The solution to this problem is to *block records*, that is, to place more than one employee record between two inter-record gaps. For example, we might decide on a "blocking factor" of four. This means that we would combine four

of our employee records into one, and have the tape device write out this single block of records as a unit. We gain a considerable savings of space this way because three inter-record gaps are eliminated for every four records written on the file. Figure 18-6 illustrates the results. To distinguish between the individual employee records on the one hand and information between two inter-record gaps on the other, we call the individual employee records *logical records* and the information between two inter-record gaps a *physical record*. Thus, in Figure 18-6 we have four logical records within one physical record. Figure 18-5 represents *unblocked records*, in which there is no distinction between logical records and physical records.

To compute the amount of magnetic tape required for a file of records, the exact record format, blocking factor, and recording density of the tape must be known in advance. For example, suppose that the inventory records of the Alan Company were each 300 characters in length, and that 10,000 records were to be recorded as a magnetic tape file. Using an unblocked record format and a tape density of 800 characters per inch, each record would require 3/8-inch of tape (300 divided by 800). Each record would also require an inter-record gap of 3/4-inch, bringing the total length required for each record to 3/8-inch plus 3/4-inch or 9/8-inches of magnetic tape.

Figure 18-5. Employee records separated by inter-record gaps (IRG's).

535

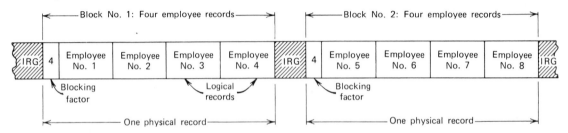

Figure 18-6. Eight employee records (logical records) blocked into two physical records.

Therefore, the total file of 10,000 records would require approximately 10,000 times 9/8-inches or 11,250 inches (937.5 feet) of recording tape.

For comparison, it is instructive to examine the possibility of blocking records. Suppose, for example, that four inventory records were blocked together (blocking factor of four). Our 10,000 logical records would therefore require 2,500 physical records on the tape file. Also, each group of four logical records would require 3/8 times 4 or 3/2 inches of tape. One inter-record gap would be required for each block of four records, bringing the length of each set of four records to 3/2 plus 3/4-inch or 9/4-inches of tape. The total file of 10,000 logical records would, therefore, require 9/4 times 2500 physical records or 5625 inches (468.8 feet) of recording tape—a considerable savings of space in comparison with the previous example.

In addition to the application records (e.g., employee or inventory records) stored on magnetic tape, the tape file usually contains two special records: a *header record* which is the first record on the file, and a *trailer record* which is the last record on the file. Often, these records follow standard formats established by the computer manufacturer and are also known as *header labels* and *trailer labels*. Figure 18-7 illustrates a standard header label for IBM. The purpose of both the header label and the trailer label is to maintain control information about the file. For example, the file's creator normally specifies a file name (e.g., "EMPLOYEE PERSONNEL" file), a file-creation date, and an expiration date for a magnetic tape file, and this information is stored in the header label of the file. Similarly, the number of physical records on the file, the number of logical records on the file,

and certain file control totals are normally stored as part of the trailer label information to serve as data-processing controls each time the magnetic tape file is accessed. Data-processing controls are examined in depth in Chapter 8.

Magnetic tape drive manufacturers have not standardized the length or format of header labels or trailer labels. In general, however, such labels are not especially long—IBM's standard tape file label is only 80 characters in length, for example. Thus, in computing the storage requirements of records written on magnetic tape, minimal allowance is necessary for header or trailer records.

Cassette Tapes

A cassette tape is much like the cartridge recording tape familiar to home stereo owners except that the recording tape on the cassette is magnetically enhanced for greater recording densities. Both "four-track" and "eight-track" versions of these cartridge tapes are available, although these names refer primarily to the size of the cartridge rather than the number of recording channels on the tape's width. Cassette tapes are inserted into, and removed from, cartridge tape drives, thus enabling the user to "flop" them in and out of the access machine. Unlike some magnetic tape, therefore, cassette tape does not require manual tape threading when mounting the tape onto its tape drive. A single cartridge of tape holds about 562 feet of tape and can store up to two million characters of data.

Cassette tape is recorded in much the same manner as standard magnetic recording tape, with tiny polarized bits recorded in channels along the length of the tape. Most cassette tapes,

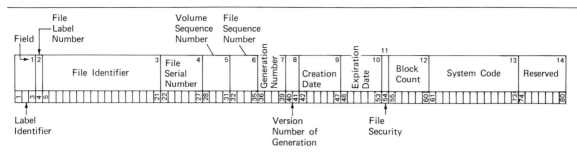

The standard tape file label format and contents are as follows:

FIELD	NAME AND LENGTH	DESCRIPTION
1.	*LABEL IDENTIFIER* 3 bytes, EBCDIC	Identifies the type of label HDR = Header—beginning of a data file EOF = End of File—end of a set of data EOV = End of Volume—end of the physical reel
2.	*FILE LABEL NUMBER* 1 byte, EBCDIC	always a 1
3.	*FILE IDENTIFIER* 17 bytes, EBCDIC	uniquely identifies the entire file, may contain only printable character.
4.	*FILE SERIAL NUMBER* 6 bytes, EBCDIC	uniquely identifies a file/volume relationship. This field is identical to the Volume Serial Number in the volume label of the first or only volume of a multi-volume file or a multi-file set. This field will normally be numeric (000001 to 999999) but may contain any six alphameric characters.
5.	*VOLUME SEQUENCE NUMBER* 4 bytes	indicates the order of a volume in a given file or multi-file set. This number must be numeric (0000–9999). Multiple volumes of an output file will be numbered in consecutive sequence.
6.	*FILE SEQUENCE NUMBER* 4 bytes	assigns numeric sequence to a file within a multi-file set.
7.	*GENERATION NUMBER* 4 bytes	numerically identifies the various editions of the file.
8.	*VERSION NUMBER OF GENERATION* 2 bytes	indicates the version of a generation of a file.
9.	*CREATION DATE* 6 bytes	indicates the year and the day of the year that the file was created:

Position	Code	Meaning
1	blank	none
2–3	00–99	Year
4–6	001–366	Day of Year

(e.g., January 31, 1985, would be entered as 85031).

FIELD	NAME AND LENGTH	DESCRIPTION
10.	*EXPIRATION DATE* 6 bytes	indicates the year and the day of the year when the file may become a scratch tape. The format of this field is identical to Field 9. On a multi-file reel, processed sequentially, all files are considered to expire on the same day.
11.	*FILE SECURITY* 1 byte	indicates security status of the file. 0 = no security protection 1 = security protection. Additional identification of the file is required before it can be processed.
12.	*BLOCK COUNT* 6 bytes	indicates the number of data blocks written on the file from the last header label to the first trailer label, exclusive of tape marks. Count does not include checkpoint records. This field is used in trailer labels.
13.	*SYSTEM CODE* 13 bytes	uniquely identifies the programming system.
14.	*RESERVED* 7 bytes	Reserved. Should be recorded as blanks.

Figure 18-7. An IBM standard header label for a magnetic tape file. (Courtesy, IBM Corp.)

however, are used in conjunction with minicomputers, whereas standard magnetic recording tape is not. The relatively small recording capacities and slower reading and writing speeds make cassette tapes unsuitable for large commercial applications so these tapes are limited to small-scale systems. Their costs are also considerably lower than standard magnetic tape systems, thereby making cassettes cost-effective for small businesses and other limited types of accounting information systems.

Advantages and Disadvantages of Magnetic Tape

In comparison with punched cards, magnetic tape offers several advantages. It is obviously more compact and, in addition, it is much faster as an input media. (Figure 17-4 of Chapter 17, which compares the input/output speeds of a number of peripheral devices, gives some idea of this processing advantage.) Further, because of the tape's continuous recording surface, information need not be broken up into 80-character segments as it is for cards. Finally, once information is written on tape, its order is permanent, in contrast to the card file which can be shuffled or dropped accidentally.

The chief disadvantage of tape in comparison with cards is its inflexibility. Deletions or insertions of records on the tape file are impossible without rewriting the entire file, and any physical problem in reading or writing an early part of the file is usually sufficient to hamper the acquisition or placement of any data on subsequent portions of the file. A second major problem with magnetic tape is that it is unreadable to the human eye. Thus, any information stored on the tape is not directly accessible to the individual. Rather, it must be translated with the assistance of computer machinery—usually a central processing unit and a printer. The wide diversity of possible tape formats and recording densities may also cause some difficulty when personnel unfamiliar with a particular tape reel attempt to run it on a tape drive for the first time.

Even with these problems, however, magnetic tape has proven to be the most popular form of secondary storage at the computer center. Although this popularity may eventually wane in favor of disks, there is little question at this time that tape systems will continue to be with us for some years to come.

MAGNETIC DISK SYSTEMS

As illustrated in Figure 18-8, a magnetic disk closely resembles a stereo record, that is, a platter about 20 inches in diameter. Recording takes place on both sides of the disk, whose surfaces are smooth and coated with an oxide similar to that of magnetic tape. Also, as with magnetic tape, this coating can be polarized to form the "on" and "off" bits of a binary code.

Usually, several disks are permanently mounted on a common spindle to form a "disk pack" (see Figure 18-9). For example, an IBM 3336 disk pack consists of ten disks. Both sides of all but the top disk (to avoid dust) are used for recording data, resulting in a total of 19 recording surfaces.

To read the information on a disk, the entire pack is mounted on a *disk drive* which spins the pack very quickly on its spindle. Actual reading or writing on the disk is performed through special *read/write heads* attached to the drive. There is a separate head for each recording surface of the disk pack, but (for most disk drives) all the read/write heads are attached to a common arm. The arm moves all read/write heads simultaneously to position any one of them for encoding or deciphering.

Early disk drives, which could accept only a single disk pack at a time, have now given way to the multiple disk system of the type illustrated in Figure 18-10. The IBM 3330 System shown, for example, simultaneously spins 8 disk packs plus a spare (in case one fails). For this particular system, one disk pack has a storage capacity of 100 million characters, thereby bringing the total storage capacity of the system to 800 million characters. However, since each pack of the disk drive is removable and may be replaced with an alternate pack, the amount of storage that can eventually be brought online to the CPU through the disk system is virtually limitless.

Like other types of computer storage devices,

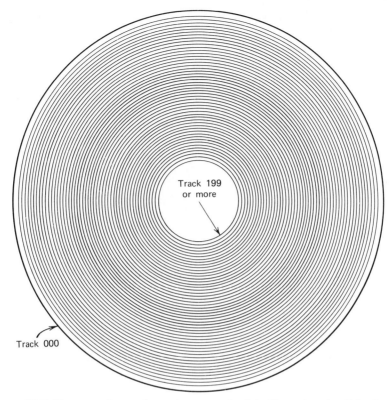

Figure 18-8. The recording surface of a magnetic disk, illustrating the disk's logical tracks.

disk systems are not standardized but vary in dimensions from manufacturer to manufacturer. Disk diameters, for example, vary in size from 14 inches to 36 inches, and the number of disk platters per pack ranges from 10 to 20. This characteristic makes the interchange of disk packs between unlike machines impossible.

Magnetic Disk Coding

The recording surface of a disk was illustrated in Figure 18-8. The surface is divided into concentric (not spiraling) circles, or "tracks," each of which is just wide enough to encode one bit of information. Encoding an entire character therefore takes place in sequential groups of bits along the circumference of the track. IBM and certain others use a standard eight-bit byte for this purpose, although this choice is not universal. To distinguish the "end" bit of one character

from the "beginning" bit of another, the disk drive performs a counting process as the bits are either accessed or written along the circumference of the track. Like magnetic tape, magnetic disks also employ parity bits for data processing control.

Although the physical size of the outermost track on a disk may be several times that of the innermost track (i.e., the one closest to the spindle), most disk systems are designed to store the same amount of information on each disk track of the pack. This remarkable result is made possible through the automatic adjustment of the bit densities around the circumference of the utilized tracks. Thus, for most present-day disk systems, the capacity of a particular track on the disk pack is independent of its physical location within the disk itself. For an IBM 2311 disk system, the standard track has a capacity of approximately 3000 characters (bytes) of information.

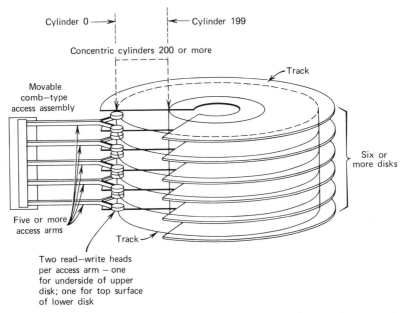

Figure 18-9. Magnetic disks on a common spindle (spindle not shown). (Photo Courtesy of IBM.)

Figure 18-10. IBM 3300 direct access storage facility. (Courtesy, IBM Corp.)

The larger IBM 2314 system can store as many as 7000 characters on a single track. The disk systems of other manufacturers have still different track capacities.

Magnetic Disk Formats

Informational records that are stored on magnetic disks are like records stored on magnetic tape in that every physical record on the disk is separated from every other physical record by an inter-record gap. However, since the disk pack spins continuously on its spindle, this gap is not needed for start-up or slow-down purposes as was the case for the inter-record gaps of magnetic tape. Rather, the gaps are needed only to distinguish one record from another on the same track. Figure 18-11 illustrates this. Blocked records, in which more than one logical record (e.g., an employee record) is stored within one physical record (i.e., stored between two inter-record gaps) are also possible.

The physical characteristics of the disk system make it possible to directly place, or find, a record on a disk pack. This is because each record may be placed at a unique storage location with an address which completely identifies the position of a record on this recording medium. This is why disk systems are also known as *direct-access storage devices (DASD's)*. Disk systems are not the only type of storage device to possess an addressing capability, but they are by far the most popular form of such devices.

A disk address is made up of three components: a cylinder number, a surface number, and a record count. These may be likened to the city, street, and house number of a postal address. If the employee records of the Alan Company were stored as direct-access records on a magnetic disk, for example, one such record might be located at address 12345. This might mean "cylinder 123, surface 4, record count 5."

A *cylinder* is a vertically aligned set of tracks on a disk pack that can be accessed simultaneously by the read/write head of a disk storage device. Thus, for an IBM 2314 disk system with 19 recording disk surfaces, the outermost track on each disk surface (19 tracks in all) would comprise the first cylinder. If we called this cylinder 1, then the next-outermost track on each disk surface of the pack would be cylinder 2, and so forth. The innermost cylinder on each disk

541

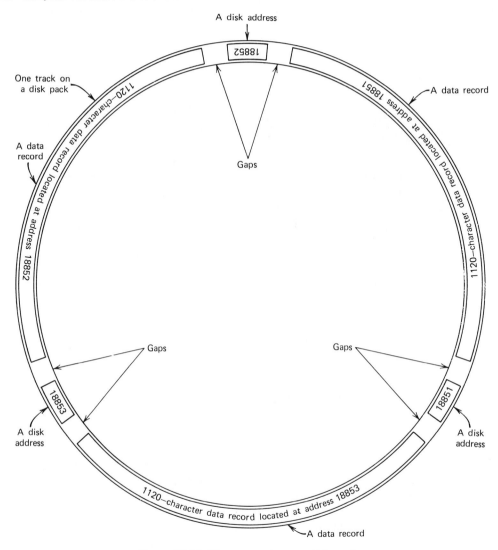

Figure 18-11. Three records on a disk track.

(i.e., the one made up of all disk tracks closest to the spindle on each recording surface) would become cylinder 199 (or whatever the high-order track is numbered—see Figure 18-9). Cylinder 123, which is the cylinder of interest in our example, would be the 123rd track on each recording surface of the disk pack.

The surface number of the disk address identifies the track within the cylinder upon which the record resides. Surface 1 would be the topmost recording surface, surface 2 the next-topmost recording surface, and so forth. The surface or track address of our employee record is, therefore, the fourth recording surface on the pack.

The record count portion of the disk address identifies the position of the record on the already-identified track of the disk pack. A record count of 1 would designate the first record on the track, 2 the second record track, and so on. Since the address of the example employee record is 5, this record would be stored as the fifth record on the track.

Figure 18-11 contains three representative records on a disk. The address 18852 would represent cylinder 188, surface 5, record count 2. Can you interpret the other addresses in the figure? The fact that each record on a disk is locatable through a unique record address means that all this information is immediately accessible to the user (through the computer).

Floppy Disks

Floppy disks are about the size and shape of 45 rpm stereo records and perform much the same functions as the full-sized magnetic disk systems described above. Floppy disks derive their name from the fact that they are not stacked rigidly on a common spindle, but are used as individual platters to record computer file information.

The information stored on a floppy disk is encoded with a floppy disk drive. These drives are about the size of a normal shoe box, and four or five such drives can fit easily under a standard-sized desk. Figure 15-7 in Chapter 15 is an example. To use a floppy disk, an individual platter is inserted into a narrow slit in the disk drive. The drive itself will automatically mount the disk on a rotating spindle in readiness for reading or writing once the user has "flopped" the disk into place.

Like cassette tapes, floppy disks are used primarily with minicomputers. However, the storage capacity of a cassette tape is considerably more than the storage capacity of a floppy disk. A typical floppy disk can store only 500,000 characters (i.e., one half *megabyte*) of information on both sides of a single platter. However, a floppy disk can be used as a direct access device in much the same way as a standard disk system. Thus, the floppy disk has the advantage of a direct access inquiry system—a system that is not possible for tapes. In accounting systems in which customer accounts are to be stored on file and where it is necessary to examine the record of a specific account quickly, this advantage is very important. Thus, because of their direct-access capabilities, floppy disks usually are preferred to cassette tapes on accounting-oriented minicomputer systems.

Advantages and Disadvantages of Magnetic Disks

One distinct advantage of disk storage over magnetic tape storage is the direct-access (also called *random-access*) capability of the disk system. The fact that records may be assigned a unique address on the disk means that a disk file is especially suited to online applications, such as airline reservations or police records, in which immediate access to information is required. Thus, whereas a record sought from a tape file requires a long and arduous sequential search procedure through the file on a record-by-record basis, a disk record may be accessed immediately once its address is known.

For a similar reason, updating a file of disk records is generally much easier than updating a file of magnetic tape records. For example, if the Alan Company maintained a magnetic tape file of employee records organized by social security number, then the hiring of only one employee would necessitate recopying the entire tape file in order to insert the new record in its appropriate, sequential position in the file. In contrast, a disk record can be added to a direct-access file at any time; it is not necessary to recopy the entire file for this purpose.

Magnetic disks have faster data transfer rates as compared with tape systems, again making the disk the more popular recording medium when response time becomes important. A significant application of this property has been the use of disk systems as a kind of auxiliary memory storage for the CPU, an approach usually known as *virtual memory*. With this technique, the storage capability of the disk is used to augment the primary memory of the central processing unit, and information is swapped (transferred) back and forth between the two units as though they were a single, large memory. Because the data swapping is handled by the supervisory/control portion of the system (or the software programs of the computer center's operating system), the use of virtual storage is not apparent to the programmer. The end result is to make the memory of the central processing unit appear as though it were much bigger than it actually is. Processing capability is enhanced accordingly.

543

Disks also have their drawbacks. One problem is cost. Magnetic disk storage is more expensive than magnetic tape storage and thus, magnetic tape usually has been the recording medium of choice when a large amount of bulk storage is involved. For example, a single disk pack may cost up to 100 times as much as a single full reel of magnetic tape.

One might argue that the disk pack is still cheaper than the tape reel if it were to hold proportionately more records. In actuality, however, this is not true. A full reel of magnetic tape can store more than 20 million characters, depending upon the recording density and type of records involved, but an IBM 2314 disk pack can store, at most, 100 million characters. Thus, although a disk pack can store five times more information than a reel of magnetic tape, it usually costs more than five times as much to purchase.

A final drawback of disks, as compared with magnetic tapes, is that disk packs are bulky. The physical width of the recording tape reel is less than an inch, and full reels of tape tend to be compact even when placed in protective covers of heavy plastic. Since the computer library (where tape reels and disk packs are stored) of a fairly active computer center is likely to have thousands of computer files, the use of magnetic tape (as opposed to disk) implies an important physical space savings to the computer center.

MAGNETIC DRUMS

As noted above, magnetic disks are not the only storage devices to possess an addressing capability. Magnetic drums (Figure 18-12) are also direct-access storage devices, although they are not as popular as disk storage. As suggested by the figure, a magnetic drum utilizes a large cylindrical recording surface which is coated with an oxide coating, and which can be magnetized in much the same fashion as a tape or disk system. Conceptually, the smooth sides of the cylinder are divided into tracks which wrap around the cylinder, and records are stored on a portion of a particular track.

Unlike many disk packs, magnetic drums are

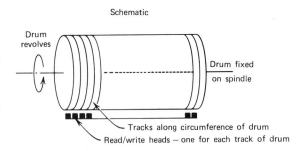

Figure 18-12. A schematic of a magnetic drum.

permanently mounted on a rotating spindle. To access information written on the drum, or alternatively to write out new information, a separate read/write head is available for each track of the system. Accessing the desired record is therefore performed through the selection of the proper read/write head and a counting operation as the track spins under the head. Because a drum has a fixed-position read/write head which does not have to be moved physically to access a record on the system, the access time required to gather information from a drum is somewhat faster than that of a disk. However, unless access time is an overwhelming consideration, the relatively greater storage capacity and lower cost of the disk system makes it a more desirable storage media.

MASS STORAGE DEVICES

As previously emphasized, magnetic tapes are desirable for their relatively cheaper storage capability, whereas disks are desirable because the data stored on them is available to the CPU on a direct-access basis. IBM's 3850 Mass Storage System (MSS) attempts to gain the advantages of both of these devices by interfacing a large magnetic tape system with a disk facility.

Figure 18-13 illustrates the fundamental idea. The basis of the mass storage system is a set of data cartridges that physically resides in storage cells within the IBM 3850 facility. Each cartridge is approximately 4 inches long and 2 inches in diameter, and contains a spool of magnetic tape 770 inches long and slightly less than 4 inches

Figure 18-13. The access mechanism and magnetic tape cartridges of an IBM 3850 mass storage device. (Photo Courtesy of IBM.)

wide. Although relatively short in length, this tape is recorded at high density, enabling each cartridge to store 50 million bytes (characters) of data. The complete storage capacity of the system depends upon the number of such cartridges purchased with the facility, but the capacity ranges from 35 to 472 billion bytes of information. (Obviously, the mass storage system is for large-scale data processors!)

When information is to be read or written on one of the tape cartridges of the mass storage system, the cartridge is physically lifted out of its cell by one of two mechanical arms and mounted on a data reading/recording mechanism within the MSS facility. There, the tape is automatically threaded and the data on the tape is accessed (or written). Rather than transmitting the data directly to the computer, however, the MSS actually copies the contents of the entire data cartridge onto a disk first. This process is called *staging*. Once the data has been staged, it becomes available to the central processing unit on a direct-access basis from the disk. Thus, for example, the Alan Company's file of sporting goods inventory items could be stored cheaply as magnetic tape records, yet processed as direct-access records when the need arises.

The MSS facility enjoys a number of advantages. One is simply its capacity to hold a large amount of data within a single data-storage medium. A second is the fact that this large amount of data is online and, therefore, directly accessible to application programs run on the central processing system. (The alternate procedure of requiring computer-operator intervention to mount tapes or disk packs physically on drives is thus eliminated.) A third advantage is the possible elimination of the librarian function of the computer center—the MSS is the library. The most important disadvantage of mass storage devices is their cost. Unless a data-processing center has need of a great deal of online data storage, such systems are not likely to be cost effective.

DOCUMENTING THE FLOW OF ACCOUNTING INFORMATION WITH SYSTEM FLOWCHARTS

The flow of data in computerized accounting information systems is normally documented in block diagrams called *system flowcharts*. The symbols used in the system flowchart (Figure 18-14) are industry conventions standardized by the National Bureau of Standards (Standard x3.5), although some companies have elected to use flowchart conventions of their own. For the most part, however, professional programmers and systems analysts use the rounded, "Q-like" symbol to represent a file of tape records, the rectangular, corner-cut symbol to represent a file of punched cards, and so forth. Although technically a software concept, system flowcharts that document computerized accounting information systems almost always involve the use of magnetic tape files and/or magnetic disk files. Thus, it is convenient to discuss the concept of system flowcharts in this chapter.

It is easiest to understand system flowcharts by studying their use in a typical accounting application. A classic example is the company payroll. A system flowchart is illustrated in Figure 18-15 and explained in detail below.

Suppose that the Alan Company prepares a weekly payroll for those employees working at one of its production facilities. The basic employee information is maintained on a payroll master file which is stored on magnetic disk. There is one record on the magnetic disk file for each employee at the facility, and each record contains such basic information as employee social security number, name, address, deduction codes, etc., as illustrated in Figure 18-4. Those employees who work on an hourly basis have hourly pay rate information stored in their payroll records. Those employees who are on salary have weekly salary information stored in their payroll records. The payroll file is organized in ascending sequence, according to employee social security number.

During the course of the week, any changes to the payroll master file are keyed directly onto a disk through a terminal located in the personnel office. Such changes would reflect (1) modification of pay rates for employees given raises or promotions, (2) increases or decreases in the number of income-tax exemptions, (3) individual revisions to payroll savings plans, (4) employee changes of name and/or address, and so forth. At the end of each week, all the changes requested by the Alan Company's personnel office would be taken from the temporary disk file and sorted in ascending employee social security number sequence. The resulting sorted disk file of payroll changes would then be input together with the payroll master file to alter the master file payroll records as desired.

Once the modifications to the payroll master file have been made, the Alan Company would then be in a position to prepare the weekly payroll. At the end of each week, time cards from the various departments within the company facility would be collected and brought to the computer center. At first, the information found on the time cards would simply be transferred onto a magnetic disk file. Here, the time-card information would be sorted into ascending social security number sequence. After this sorting process has taken place, the actual payroll checks can be prepared in a separate processing phase.

Figure 18-15 documents the payroll narrative described above in a system flowchart. The flow of information on the upper left-hand side of the figure begins with the payroll change requests made by the personnel department. The keying operation that transfers the change requests directly to the disk is called an *online job entry system*. This keying operation, the sorting of these change requests on a weekly basis, and the use of these change requests to update the employee master file are depicted in sequence reading down the left-hand portion of the systems flowchart.

The upper right-hand side of the figure traces the time-card data through the payroll system. Employee time-card data is keyed onto a disk file and eventually sorted into social-security-number sequence. Finally, in the lower portion of the figure, the updated payroll master

Processing A major processing function.	Input/ output Any type of medium or data.
Punched card A variety of punched cards including stubs.	Punched paper tape
Document Paper documents and reports of all varieties.	Transmittal tape A proof or adding maching tape or similar batch – control information.
Magnetic tape	Online storage
Offline storage	Display Information displayed by plotters or video devices.
Collate Forming one or more sets of items from two or more other sets.	Sorting An operation on sorting or collating equipment.
Manual input Information supplied to or by a computer utilizing an online device.	Magnetic disk
Manual operation A manual offline operation not requiring mechanical aid.	Auxiliary operation A machine operation supplementing the main processing function
Keying operation An operation utilizing a key – driven device.	Communication link The electronic transmission of information from one location to another via communication lines.

Figure 18-14. System flowcharting symbols. (Courtesy, IBM Corp.)

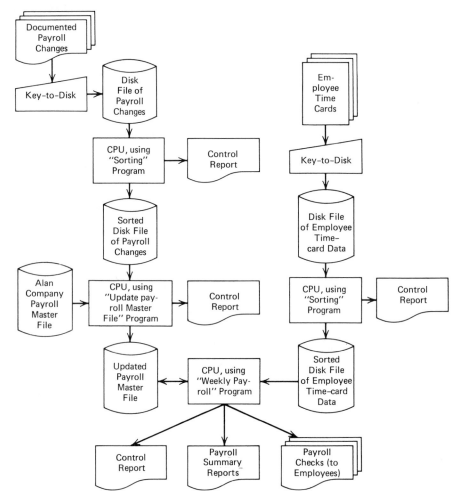

Figure 18-15. System flowchart for computerized processing of the Alan Company payroll.

file and the sorted disk file of employee time-card data are ready for use in preparing the weekly payroll.

Each time that a file is sorted or updated, note that a separate computer processing step using the central processing unit is required. (The computer programs used to perform this processing are discussed in general terms in the next chapter.) Thus, the change requests made by the personnel department update the payroll master file in one processing phase, the time-card data is sorted in a second processing phase, and payroll is prepared in yet a third processing phase. Generally speaking, this is the way data processing

proceeds in almost all accounting information system applications: one step at a time.

A second thing to notice about the system flowchart is that each processing phase of the payroll usually involves the preparation of one or more "control reports." These reports provide processing-control information and help the Alan Company staff involved in the payroll correct errors as they are detected by the processing system.

A final thing to notice about the system flowchart is that it represents a flow of (payroll) information through the various processing phases of the accounting system: the acquisition of accounting data on a timely, accurate, cost-effective basis and the processing of this data into useful information. This point is discussed in greater depth in Chapter 4 on the collection and storage of accounting data.

The above example has been simplified to introduce the fundamentals of flowcharting on an elementary level. System flowcharts are very important to accounting information systems because they document the flow of information through the computerized portion of the accounting subsystem's data processing and, therefore, trace the audit trail. Accountants use these flowcharts to familiarize themselves with new accounting applications, to help them identify an accounting information system's strengths and weaknesses, and to assist them in their roles as auditors and management consultants. In recognition of this, both the American Institute of Certified Public Accountants and the National Association of Accountants have consistently included test questions in their professional examinations that require a working knowledge of system flowcharts.

SUMMARY

Secondary storage equipment, or combination input/output equipment, is capable of both sending and receiving information to and from the CPU. The most popular forms of secondary storage devices are magnetic tape and disk systems, although magnetic drums and mass storage devices are also used to augment the storage capability of the central processing unit. All of these devices store data by magnetizing tiny spots, or bits, on their recording surfaces, which are then grouped together to form characters and numbers. These characters and numbers are aggregated in turn to form data records which comprise the basic unit of information on the file. An example of an employee master file for a payroll application was provided, although files of accounts receivable records, inventory records, bank account records, and so forth, are equally good illustrations of the file concept.

Records stored on secondary storage devices are separated from one another by inter-record gaps. To avoid wasting space, however, several records are sometimes grouped together in order to place more information between two such gaps. In these instances, several logical records are said to be blocked in a single physical record. The practice of blocking records is not a function of the type of secondary storage device used, but is performed at the discretion of the file designer.

A fundamental distinction has been made between sequential-access devices such as magnetic tape drives, and direct-access storage devices (DASD's) such as magnetic disks or drums. In the former, records are stored sequentially on the recording medium. In the latter, each physical record is assigned a unique address on the storage device. Thus, whereas it is necessary to search for a sequential file record, a record stored on a magnetic disk or drum may be accessed directly once the physical address of the record is known.

The final portion of this chapter discussed the concept of system flowcharting. A primary goal of system flowcharts is to depict the flow of accounting information through the processing cycles of accounting applications. We have illustrated this technique with a simplified payroll application that might be used by the Alan Company at one of its production facilities. In this example, the flow of master-file change requests from the personnel department and the time-card data from employee work stations was traced through various processing cycles by using a comprehensive system flowchart. The end result of the data processing was the preparation of weekly payroll checks for the Alan Company employees.

DISCUSSION QUESTIONS

18-1.   Why use secondary storage at all? Why not just keep everything in the memory section of the central processing unit where it will be immediately available?

18-2.   Magnetic tape has been likened to home recording tape, home movie projector film, and punched cards. In what ways are these anal-

549

ogies accurate? In what ways are they inaccurate?

18-3. What is the difference between seven-track magnetic tape and nine-track magnetic tape? (*Hint:* The answer is not "two tracks.") What are the advantages of one over the other?

18-4. Suppose you were a magnetic tape drive just learning how to read a magnetic tape record. You turn to your friend, unit two, for help and ask: "Am I on the right track?" What is unit two's response likely to be? (*Hint:* Not "bleep.")

18-5. Discuss the purpose and placement of header labels and trailer labels on magnetic tape files. What additional information not discussed in the chapter would likely be found in these labels?

18-6. Explain the process of "blocking." What advantage(s) would blocking have for an accounting information system?

18-7. "Fixed length records are more orderly; variable length records are more flexible." Would you agree? Why or why not?

18-8. What factors should be considered in order to compute the space requirements of a collection of magnetic tape records on a reel of tape?

18-9. A file of magnetic tape records is too large to fit on a single reel of tape. What can be done? What implication does this have for the header label information on the magnetic tape reel?

18-10. "Show me a deck of punched cards and I'll show you a file that is better recorded as a magnetic tape file." Comment.

18-11. In what ways are the tracks of a disk similar to the tracks of magnetic tape? In what ways are they different?

18-12. Describe the address system of a disk pack. Why is it roughly equivalent to that of a postal address?

18-13. Why is updating a magnetic disk file often easier than updating a magnetic tape file?

18-14. Magnetic disks are faster, more flexible, and have greater storage capacity than magnetic tapes. Why do firms ever bother with tape if this is so?

18-15. Although magnetic disks are "direct-access" devices, they can also be used to store se-

quential files. Suppose such a sequential file required 40 tracks on a disk pack with 20 recording surfaces (10 individual disks). Would this sequential file best be stored on 40 tracks of the same recording surface or some other way and why?

18-16. How does a magnetic drum store accounting data? Also, of what advantage is it for the drum to be permanently mounted on its drive?

18-17. The Horwitz and McBride Company is a retail clothing store that sells apparel for men and women. The company's accounts receivable subsidiary ledger is maintained on magnetic tape. Every Friday, the week's credit sales to customers as well as the cash collections from credit customers are input into the computer to update the accounts receivable tape file. On the last working day of each month, the computer prints out individual customer statements, which are then mailed to the credit customers.

The clothing store's management is considering the use of punched card storage rather than magnetic tape storage for its accounts receivable subsidiary ledger data. Discuss some of the possible arguments against making this computer storage media change.

18-18. Which of the following devices is the fastest secondary storage device? Which is the slowest?
a. magnetic disk
b. magnetic drum
c. magnetic tape

18-19. Give a complete definition of the following terms:
a. record
b. inter-record gap
c. blocking
d. logical record
e. physical record

18-20. Are the following devices sequential-access devices or direct-access devices?
a. magnetic drum
b. magnetic tape drive
c. magnetic disk

18-21. Explain the following terms with respect to magnetic disks:
a. disk pack

b.   disk drive

c.   disk address

d.   track

e.   virtual memory

18-22. The Tim Lochary Company uses magnetic disk, magnetic drum, and magnetic tape storage. Why do you think the company feels it is desirable to use all three types of storage media?

18-23. Would a magnetic tape file system or direct-access magnetic disk system more likely be used in the following applications? Why?

a.   hospital billing system

b.   airline reservations

c.   FBI file of missing persons

d.   sporting goods store inventory control

PROBLEMS*

18-24. The Bill J. Keenan Company keeps its employee records on a magnetic tape file. The file has been written at a tape density of 556 characters per inch, each fixed-length unblocked record being of size 300. Assume that standard inter-record gaps of 3/4 inch are used, and the company has 15,000 employees.

a.   What is the length of each logical record? Each physical record?

b.   How long is the entire tape file?

c.   Is the company using this file system as efficiently as possible? Why or why not? Do you think the company should change this system? If so, how?

18-25. Suppose, in Problem 18-24, the Paul Keenan Company decides to use a blocking factor of 4.

a.   How long is each logical record now? Each physical record?

b.   How much space on the tape would be saved by using this blocking factor?

18-26. Given the following information, compute the amount of tape needed to create a complete magnetic tape file.

Record format: 400 characters each; fixed length

Blocking factor: none

*Additional problems and cases involving computer files and system flowcharts may be found in Chapter 5.

Recording density: 1600 CPI

Number of records: 20,000

18-27. How would your answer change in Problem 18-26 if there were a blocking factor of 4?

18-28. Arrange the following list of devices in ascending order by input/output speed (using highest speeds):

a.   card reader

b.   card punch

c.   paper tape reader

d.   paper tape punch

e.   magnetic tape

f.   magnetic disk

g.   CRT

h.   magnetic drum

i.   COM

(*Hint:* See Figure 17-4 of Chapter 17.)

18-29. The Worthley National Bank has 100,000 checking accounts at its National City office. These accounts are maintained as a master file of 1200 characters each.

(a) If the bank were to punch every account on cards, how many cards would be needed for *each* account?

(b) How many cards would be needed for all 100,000 accounts?

(c) Suppose the bank were to store the records on magnetic tape. How many *feet* of tape would be required, using an unblocked record format and a tape density of 800 characters per inch?

(d) Answer part (c) if the records were blocked, using a blocking factor of 8 and a tape density of 800 characters per inch.

18-30. The Salsberg Hospital Supply Company has approximately 15,000 inventory items that it maintains on a tape file. Each record has a fixed length of 400 characters.

(a) Suppose that, to create a new master file record, the information must first be punched out on computer cards. How many cards would be required for *one* new record?

(b) Using your answer to part (a), compute how many cards would be required to recreate the entire file of 15,000 words.

(c) How many feet of magnetic tape would be required to store the entire file of inventory records? Assume a blocking factor of 10 and a tape density of 800 characters per inch.

18-31. The Kritchman Sales Service maintains a mailing list of addresses of 200,000 "upper-income" residents in the New York metropolitan area. Each name and address is stored as an unblocked, variable-length record on magnetic tape using a tape density of 800 characters per inch. The smallest record is only 100 characters in length. The largest is 300 characters in length. An average length would be 160 characters.

(a) Approximately how many feet of tape would be required for this file if a magnetic tape file were used?

(b) What would be an upper limit as to the amount of magnetic tape, in feet, required for this file?

18-32. The Gary Welter Company uses a computerized general ledger accounting system to prepare its monthly trial balance. On a weekly basis, the company uses its accounts receivable disk file, its accounts payable disk file, its payroll disk file, its assets and depreciation schedule disk file, and its cash transactions file to update its general ledger disk file. The output from its weekly processing includes a General Ledger Listing Report, a General Ledger Processing Report, and an updated general ledger disk file. The updated general ledger file is then copied so that a back-up file is available should need for one arise.

At the end of each month, the most recent copy of the general ledger disk file is used to prepare a trial balance. The general ledger file is used in a "Monthly Closing Processing Run" to prepare a trial balance and a

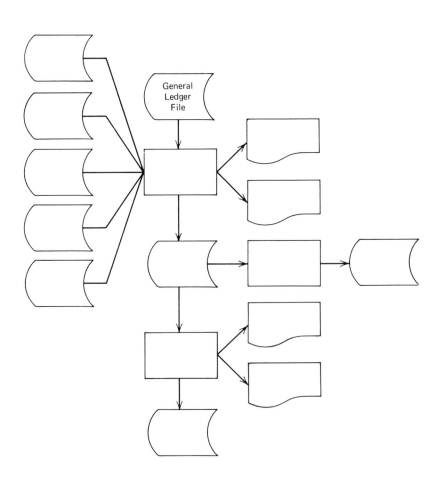

"Monthly Closing Processing Report." The new general ledger disk file output from this data processing is used the next week as the entire processing sequence is repeated.

The figure on page 552 outlines this processing cycle in a system flowchart. However, the descriptions for each symbol have been omitted from all but one symbol in the flowchart. Using the description of the Gary Welter Company's general ledger accounting system provided above, complete the flowchart by writing a description in each symbol.

CASE ANALYSIS

18-33. *Wallace Manufacturing Company*

Production control at Wallace Manufacturing Company operates as follows. Every Wednesday, the production-control manager, the manufacturing-operations foreman, and the vice president of production meet to plan the production for the coming week. A list of products and quantities to produce is prepared, typed by the vice-president's secretary, and then keyed directly into a computer terminal in the production-control manager's office. As the products are keyed in, the computer automatically checks the company's inventory file to make sure that the finished product desired is not already over-stocked, and also checks to make sure that enough raw materials are available to produce the amount of finished product desired. If all is in order, the planned-production requirements are logged onto a production-request file on computer disk, and a hard-copy document is printed for each member of the planning team and delivered on Thursday of each week.

Each Friday, the production-request file is merged with an open production orders file, which contains all production orders not completed to date. At the same time, the computer

prepares a card deck of operations cards and a job-step listing. Each punched card represents one processing step or operations step in the manufacturing sequence for the production of finished product. A computer listing is also prepared which summarizes these job steps for all products scheduled for production in the coming week.

The punched cards slip into special envelopes affixed to the sides of work bins which roll from job-step site to job-step site, and are color-coded by major operation type. As each job step is completed, the associated card is pulled from its envelope and sent directly to data processing. Here, the cards are batched and processed on a daily basis. Initially, the cards are simply re-written on magnetic tape. Next, they are sorted by production batch number and coordinated with the open production orders file to update this file. At the same time, the computer prints an operations summary report, listing those operations that have been completed, by product number, and also listing those production orders still pending.

Required

A. Describe in some detail the types of inventory files that the Wallace Company must have in order to provide the information identified above.

B. Is the open production order file likely to be a sequential file or a direct-access file? Why?

C. What information is likely to be found on the job-step cards? Why are such cards placed on the *outside* of the work bins in special envelopes? What additional information might be collected from the job-step sites through the use of these cards?

D. Draw a system flowchart that documents the production activities described above.

E. Suggest at least one improvement for the information system described above.

19

Computer Software

Among the important questions that you should be able to answer after reading this chapter are:

1 What is the difference between a system flow-chart and a program flowchart?
2 Because the most elementary programming language is machine language, why do very few people use it?
3 Why is COBOL often considered the accountant's choice of programming languages?
4 Documentation merely describes the actual accounting information system. Because documentation therefore requires extra work that is largely unproductive, why bother with it?
5 Why are many of the control features vital to the security of an accounting task not outlined in the documentation?

INTRODUCTION

Computer software controls the hardware of the computer system and describes how this control takes place. Virtually all computer software can be divided into two major categories: programming and documentation. Both are vital to the efficient operation of the data processing function, although the accountant is usually more involved with the latter than the former. Our purpose in this chapter is to introduce both programming and documentation software, emphasizing those aspects of each that are of special importance to the accounting information system.

There are several reasons why accountants are especially concerned with computer software. One of the most important of these reasons stems from the concept of internal control. In accounting information systems, it is important that adequate safeguards be written into computer programs to assure accuracy and completeness in the execution of data-processing tasks. Thus, the accountant's concern with the software of the accounting information system is, in part, attributable to the need for adequate controls in computer programs.

A second interest in the software of the accounting information system becomes apparent in the consideration of the functions and responsibilities of internal or external auditors. Broadly speaking, the auditor must answer the fundamental question: what are the strengths and weaknesses of the accounting information system(s) under study, and what should be done by way of improvement? Related questions on a more operational level include: (1) Are the accounting information system's controls sufficient? (2) Does the accounting information system adequately serve the needs of the system's user? (3) Is accounting data being collected in a timely, accurate fashion? (4) Is the system guilty of "overkill"—that is, providing more information than the system's users need or utilizing computer hardware or software which is not cost-effective? To answer such questions, the auditor must review both the computer programs and the related documentation of the accounting information systems under review before well-defined recommendations can be made.

Accountants are sometimes asked to serve on advisory boards or review boards when a company is contemplating major changes in policy and/or procedures. Where such changes involve accounting information systems, as, for example, in the decision to switch from one accounting software application to another, it is important that the accountants be familiar with the implications of such changes to the company's present accounting operations. This familiarity can be acquired, in part, from an understanding of the computer programs and related documentation of the company's accounting infor-

mation system. Thus, a third reason why computer software is important to accountants stems from their role in systems analysis and design work. (This topic is explored in detail in Chapters 11 and 12.)

There are still other reasons why accountants might concern themselves with the software of the accounting information system, but by now, the importance of computer software should be clear. A common question concerns the degree to which an individual must understand the *technical* details of computer programming and systems analysis in order to understand software fundamentals. In general, it is not necessary for accountants to be very experienced programmers, although more and more accounting positions require some basic familiarity with programming concepts. Therefore, in terms of programming coverage, we shall not endeavor to teach such languages as BASIC, FORTRAN, or COBOL. These are rightfully reserved for a data-processing course where they can be studied in detail. Rather, we shall merely identify the rudiments of program planning, preparation, and maintenance, and focus on programming language differences, advantages, and disadvantages. Appendix C has been provided for those interested in a more detailed analysis of BASIC, FORTRAN, and COBOL.

In addition to an analysis of programming, this chapter will also concentrate upon the documentation aspects of computer software. Accountants are almost invariably exposed to such documentation in their roles as internal or external auditors, financial planners, or management consultants. For example, good documentation provides the signposts of the audit trail by which the accountant traces the flow of data through the accounting information system. Thus, an understanding of the role and functioning of system and program documentation is vital to the professional accountant.

PROGRAM PREPARATION

Computer programs are specially-coded instructions that direct the operations of the central processing unit and dictate the order in which the data processing takes place. Historically, a given data-processing task starts out as a manual one. At some point, however, an analysis is made of the task and the decision to automate begins what is customarily called the *life cycle* of the computer program—or set of programs—that performs the (formerly manual) data-processing task.

The actual development of computer programs begins with a proposal that states the processing objectives and indicates how these processing objectives are to be attained. In commercial applications, this proposal is usually formalized, with non-EDP subsystems being required to submit written request forms to the EDP subsystem for review and approval. At times, a single individual—such as the EDP manager—is responsible for authorizing program development. More commonly, however, a committee of individuals performs this authorization function.

Once a data-processing task has been approved for development, it is submitted to a project leader who becomes responsible for the work. If the data processing task is large, the project leader's task will include the supervision of programmers working under his or her direction. If the data processing task is a relatively small one, the project leader may simply work alone.

For each program to be developed in the software project, a number of logic devices may be developed first to help plan the processing sequence(s). One such logic device is a *decision table*, which outlines the potential conditions and actions to be taken in the data processing environment. Case 19-23 at the end of this chapter examines decision tables in detail. To outline the logic of the data-processing flow, two types of flowcharts usually are developed: *system flowcharts*, which show the computer hardware and file requirements of the programs, and *program flowcharts*, which illustrate how the computer programs accommodate the processing requirements of the task(s) in question. Each of these flowchart concepts is described in greater detail below.

System Flowcharts

As we discussed in the previous chapter, system flowcharts document the hardware and file requirements of the accounting information system. They also illustrate the flow of accounting data through the various processing steps of a particular accounting application. System flowcharts almost never include the complete formats of the input and output media used in the data processing. This is because most commercial processing applications involve card, tape, and/or disk records that are much too detailed to be presented in the flowchart. Thus, further systems documentation is required to identify fully the form and type of information used in the typical automated accounting applications. We shall pick up this point again, therefore, in the documentation section of this chapter.

The system flowchart serves not only as a documentation aid by clearly describing a specific system, but also serves as a planning tool when designing new accounting information systems. For example, the number of files that must be accessed simultaneously in order to process the accounting data helps to identify the type of hardware configuration (i.e., the number of tape drives, disk drives, and so forth) required. Since understanding the flow of financial information is crucial in the design of accounting information systems, this is no small advantage. The system flowchart also serves to help document the audit trail by tracing the flow of transaction data as it enters the accounting information system and winds its way through the various data-processing phases of the system. These points are studied in detail in Chapter 5.

Program Flowcharts

A program flowchart outlines the logic sequence of a particular computer program and diagrams the order in which the data processing is to take place. Once such a flowchart has been designed, it is usually shown to a supervisor for approval. Upon approval, the program flowchart is then used as a "blueprint" for coding the computer program itself. After the program has been completed, it is advisable to check it against the flow-chart to make sure that everything is in order.

Figure 19-1 provides examples of the common *programming flowchart symbols* used in commercial application programming today. The stricter the adherence to these symbols, the easier it is for one programmer to communicate with another.

To illustrate the use of programming symbols in program flowcharts, consider first Figure 19-2, which is a *system flowchart* for the reporting of sales of the Alan Company, using card input. Figure 19-3 is a *program flowchart* that documents the data-processing logic for this sales-report application. Both the starting point and the stopping point of the program flowchart in Figure 19-3 are clear because of the presence of the oval "termination" symbols in the diagram. Note also that the logic sequence in the diagram flows from the top of the page to the bottom of the page in accord with standard flowcharting convention. To make sure that this order is understood, however, it is also customary to place little arrows on the lines connecting the flowcharting symbols for clarity.

As a documentation aid, it is important that the program flowchart uses recognizable processing symbols. Special templates with the standard symbols of the profession may be purchased for this purpose, and are often used by programmers and system analysts. Such templates are relatively inexpensive to purchase and their conformance to industry standards assures accuracy in documentation. Their use also speeds the documentation effort.

Our close attention to the logic sequence in the flowchart is attributable to the fact that the logic sequence of the flowchart dictates the order in which processing tasks are performed once the accounting data is accessed by the central processing unit. Thus, for the illustration at hand, a card is first read, the information is then processed, and finally the output printed, in this order. The end-of-file ("last-account") test is performed at the end of each card-processing cycle to make sure that the final card in the card file has been included in the processing run.

The flowchart illustrated in Figure 19-3 provides a good idea of what is to be done in general terms, and in what sequence the required tasks are to be performed. However, the program flowchart as illustrated does not give much detail. For example, we know that the program will compute tax and totals, but the flowchart does not illustrate exactly how these computations are to be performed. For this reason, we would have to consider the flowchart in Figure 19-3 as a *macro program flowchart*—that is, a program flowchart that provides an overview of the data-processing logic, but one that does not indicate the detailed programming logic necessary to carry out a processing task. This type of logic is shown in the *micro program flowchart* as illustrated in Figure 19-4.

In Figure 19-4, a more precise description of the steps necessary to complete our sales-ticket extension task may be found. First, a control total is initialized to zero. Next, the program enters a *processing loop,* in which the data processing for each sales transaction is outlined. The steps in this data processing include: (1) the computation of the sales amount (price times quantity), (2) the computation of the sales tax (= .03 times sales amount), (3) the computation of the billing amount (= sales amount + sales tax), (4) the addition of the billing amount to the running control total, and (5) the printing of the sales amount, sales tax, and total bill as a detail item on one line of the output sales report. This completes the processing for one sales card. At the end of the processing loop for each sales card, the program tests to see if the card just processed is the last card in the card deck. If it is, the program "exits" from the processing loop, prints the running control total, and stops. If the card just processed is not the last card in the card deck, the program reenters the processing loop, accesses another sales card, and repeats the processing steps outlined above for a new sales card.

The micro program flowchart provides detail at the expense of space. Because most real-life accounting programs are hundreds of times more complicated than the illustration at hand, micro

Symbol	Represents
	Processing A group of program instructions which perform a processing function of the program.
	Input/output Any function of an input/output device (making information available for processing, recording processing information, tape positioning, etc.)
	Decision The decision function used to document points in the program where a branch to alternate paths is possible based upon variable conditions.
	Preparation An instruction or group of instructions which changes the program.
	Predefined process A group of operations not detailed in the particular set of flowcharts.
	Terminal The beginning, end, or a point of interruption in a program.
	Connector An entry to, or an exit from, another part of the program flowchart.
	Offpage connector A connector used instead of the connector symbol to designate entry to, or exit from, a page.
∧ ∨ <>	**Flow direction** The direction of processing or data flow.
	Annotation The addition of descriptive comments or explanatory notes as clarification.

Figure 19-1. Program flowchart symbols.

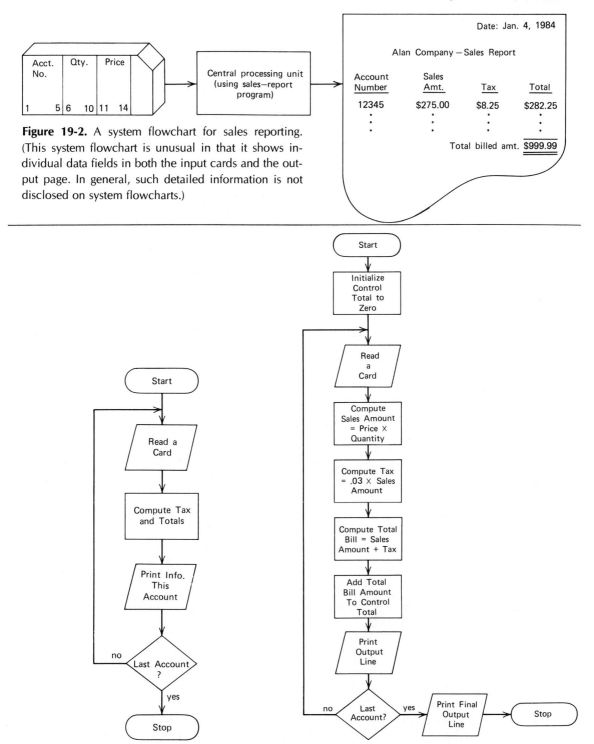

Figure 19-2. A system flowchart for sales reporting. (This system flowchart is unusual in that it shows individual data fields in both the input cards and the output page. In general, such detailed information is not disclosed on system flowcharts.)

Figure 19-3. A program flowchart that might be used to prepare a sales report.

Figure 19-4. A micro program flowchart based on the macro flowchart of Figure 19-3.

program flowcharts are cumbersome and can easily confuse the reader who is not familiar with the overall processing task in question. As you might imagine, therefore, it is customary to develop a macro program flowchart first when designing computer programs. Upon the approval of the macro flowchart by the development supervisor, the individual programmer then develops micro level flowcharts on a routine-by-routine basis. Common examples of such routines, or "subroutines," would include: (1) edit tests, which check the validity of incoming accounting data, (2) computational procedures, such as the calculation of payroll amounts and deductions, and (3) error routines, which enable processing programs to recover from such problems as faulty data or processing interruptions.

Computer programs which are organized carefully in modular fashion are called *structured programs*, and the process by which these computer programs are developed is called *structured programming*. Structured programming enables systems analysts to develop programs more quickly because programmer responsibilities can be assigned on a module-by-module (i.e., portion-by-portion) basis, and also because the programs can be tested, corrected, and documented on a module-by-module basis. This structuring is also important to the accounting information system because processing controls become more identifiable in structured programs and because the documentation for structured programs has the potential to be more easily understood.

PROGRAMMING

Once a computer programming task has been approved, designed, and flowcharted, it must be coded in a programming language intelligible to the computer. Despite science-fiction stories of computer intelligence, computers are perfect robots, doing exactly what they are told no matter how menial, boring, or counterproductive the job. The computer program provides the instructions that control the data access, processing, and output responsibilities comprising the bulk of computerized accounting activity. Thus, it is

virtually meaningless to say that "the computer made a mistake." Outside of a very rare hardware failure, the error is always the mistake of the programming instructions which direct the computer in its appointed task(s).

The history of the development of computer programming languages roughly parallels the history of computer hardware. In particular, there are several levels, or "generations," of programming languages just as there are several generations of computer hardware. The most elementary is machine language, which is written (and stored) in a binary code and which is immediately understandable by the hardware of the central processing unit. Next in the hierarchy is assembler language, which uses English letters and arabic numbers, but which must be translated into machine language before it can be executed by the computer. Finally, at the top of the hierarchy, are the familiar high-level languages such as BASIC, FORTRAN, and COBOL.

In the paragraphs that follow, we shall review each of these levels of programming languages in greater detail, including the specialized job-control languages, and explain why each of these might be of interest to the accountant. Following these discussions, we shall review the three most popular programming languages used in accounting applications today: BASIC, FORTRAN, and COBOL. In this latter study, our examination largely will be exploratory and comparative; we shall not endeavor to teach these languages. However, a detailed discussion of the use of these three languages can be found in Appendix C.

Machine-Level Language

All computers execute instructions expressed in machine languages. The machine language of one computer manufacturer will differ from that of another computer manufacturer, but all machine-level languages are elementary in nature and are expressed in a binary code, that is, a series of ones and zeros. Figure 19-5 provides an example of a machine language as it might be written for an IBM 370 computer. This particular illustration computes the expression: $E =$

Figure 19-5

THE IBM 370 MACHINE LANGUAGE REQUIRED TO COMPUTE THE EXPRESSION $E = (A*B-C)/D$

Operation Code	Register Number[a]	Data Address[b]			Comments
		X_2	B_2	D_2	
0101 1000	0001	0000	1100	1100 1110 1000	Transfer the value of A to register 1.
0101 1100	0001	0000	1100	1100 1110 1100	Multiply register 1 by B.
0101 1011	0001	0000	1100	1100 1111 0000	Subtract C from register 1.
0101 1101	0001	0000	1100	1100 1111 0100	Divide register 1 by D.
0101 0000	0001	0000	1100	1100 1111 1000	Store the result as the value of E in computer memory.

[a]A register is a data-manipulating memory of the CPU's arithmetic-logic unit. In an IBM 370, there are 16 such registers, and a particular one must be specified when transferring data to the arithmetic-logic unit.

[b]For IBM 370 equipment, a data address is expressed in terms of a base register (B_2), a displacement amount (D_2), and an index register (X_2). These items together are used to compute the storage location of a single piece of data. These technical aspects of data addressing are beyond the scope of this text.

$(A*B-C)/D$. (The asterisk is being used here as a multiplication symbol. The slash represents division.)

Note that each instruction in the figure utilizes the same format, starting with an operation code that identifies the particular task to be performed, and followed by one or more computer addresses that identify the location of the data to be manipulated. This formatting makes programming more systematic and also makes it easier for the computer hardware to interpret the different instructions.

As in all levels of computer language, the instructions of the machine language code are executed in the order in which they are encountered. Thus, the first step in our machine-language program would be to retrieve the values of A from its storage location in CPU memory and place it in a register of the arithmetic-logic unit. Next, the value of B would be retrieved from its storage location and multiplied times the value of A in the register. Next the value of C would be similarly obtained and subtracted from the product of A times B already available in the register. Finally, the value of D would be taken, divided into the number sitting in the register ($=A*B-C$), and the results stored in a separate memory location as our answer E. It should be understood that this example is just a *portion* of an actual program. Instructions prior to the ones listed in the figure would be required to initialize the CPU's memory locations with the actual values of A, B, C, and D, and still additional instructions (which would follow those illustrated) would be necessary to print out the result.

Assembler Language

Very few programmers write computer programs in machine language. This is because it is very confusing, and even mentally painful, to code instructions in nothing but zeros and ones. Thus, to assist computer programmers to do their jobs more efficiently, the hardware manufacturers quickly developed assembler languages as a more convenient alternative to machine languages.

In assembler languages, symbols (principally letters) are used in place of binary digits to represent the operation codes and addresses of the machine instruction. Figure 19-6 provides an example, using the same computational problem

Figure 19-6

THE IBM 370 ASSEMBLER LANGUAGE REQUIRED TO
COMPUTE THE EXPRESSION $E = (A*B - C)/D$.

Instruction			Comments
Name	Operation	Operand[a]	
COMPUTE	L	R1, A	Transfer the value of A from storage to register 1.
	M	R1, B	Multiply register 1 by B.
	S	R1, C	Subtract C.
	D	R1, D	Divide by D.
	ST	R1, E	Store the results as the value of E in computer memory.

[a]This field is analogous to the "Register Number" and "Data Address" fields of Figure 19-5.

discussed in the last section, that is, the calculation of $E = (A*B - C)/D$. Note in Figure 19-6 that the assembly language instruction code uses a *mnemonic* to represent the required operation, that is, one or more letters that assist the programmer in remembering what the code represents. Thus, the mnemonic L stands for "Load" (a register), the mnemonic ST means "Store" (from a register), and so forth.

Also note that the symbols A, B, C, and D, are here being used to represent *locations* in computer memory. Thus, the first instruction in Figure 19-6 means "take the *contents* of the storage location symbolically known as A and place this in register no. 1"; the second instruction requires that the value of register no. 1 be multiplied by the *contents* of storage location B; the third instruction requires that the contents of storage location C be subtracted from register no. 1; the fourth instruction requires that the value in register no. 1 be divided by the contents of storage location D; and the fifth instruction requires that the value in register no. 1 be stored as the contents of storage location E. As before, it should be understood that this is just a portion of an ac-

tual program. Additional instructions to perform initialization of the data values (A, B, C, and D) and printing of results would have to be added to the coding to complete the program.

From the standpoint of the programmer, assembler language is a vast improvement over machine language. One reason for this is because it is much easier for humans to use alphabetic mnemonics instead of binary instruction codes when telling the computer how to process data. A second reason is that, with assembler language, the programmer can identify the *contents of a storage location* with the same symbol representing a *value in a formula*. Thus, for example, the symbol "A" in the formula $E = (A*B - C)/D$ represents a value when written on paper. As we have seen above, however, the programmer can also use this symbol to represent the contents of a particular storage location. The direct correspondence between a lettered value in a formula and a data value in computer storage makes programming easier.

Historically, the use of assembler languages has resulted in much faster completion of program coding and "debugging" (correcting programming errors) as compared with machine-language programming. Thus, programmer efficiency is enhanced. Later, the advantages that initially made assembler-language programming easier apply to the programming effort when modifications are required.

High-Level Programming Languages

High-level programming languages include such languages as FORTRAN (standing for Formula Translation), COBOL (Common Business Oriented Language), BASIC (Beginner's All Purpose Symbolic Instruction Code), APL (A Programming Language), PL/1 (Programming Language #1), GPSS (General Purpose Simulation System) and RPG (Report Program Generator). There are still others. As you can tell, most of these names are *acronyms* (i.e., words constructed from the first letter, or first few letters, of a term or phrase). Of all of these programming languages, COBOL is by far the most popular business language.

The distinction between assembler languages on the one hand and higher-level languages on the other is determined in part by their different correspondences to machine language. As we have already noted, assembler languages substitute *alphabetic* or *alphanumeric* (i.e., both numbered and lettered) mnemonics for binary code when expressing computer instructions. Thus, there is a close correspondence between assembler and machine language on an instruction-by-instruction basis. Higher-level programming languages tend to use single, "macro" instructions, each of which translates to several machine-level instructions when readied for computer execution. For example, instead of the five machine-language instructions (Figure 19-5) or the five assembler-language instructions (Figure 19-6) required to compute $E = (A*B-C)/D$, BASIC would use the single instruction:

$$\text{LET } E = (A*B-C)/D$$

Thus, the instructions of high-level programming languages tend to be more powerful in what they can do, and therefore attain a higher level of processing capability in their usage.

From the standpoint of the accountant, the chief advantages of high-level programming languages over machine or assembler languages are that they are usually easy to learn, and therefore easier to code, than assembler languages or machine languages, and that they are largely *machine independent*. One of the reasons why high-level languages are easier to learn is because many of them are *procedure-oriented*. For example, in FORTRAN, mathematical expressions are coded very much like they are handwritten. Thus, it is easy to code mathematical formulas in FORTRAN because FORTRAN is procedurally oriented to this task. COBOL does not enjoy the mathematical advantages of FORTRAN. Yet it, too, is fairly easy to learn, largely because many of its instructions closely resemble the prose of the English language. In this sense, COBOL programs are partially self-documenting—a very important characteristic in situations where accounting files and auditing procedures play major roles.

To say that high-level languages are *machine*

independent is to say that they are not limited to the central processing unit of a particular computer manufacturer for execution. In fact, high-level language programs such as COBOL programs may be run on any computer as long as a special translation program, called a *compiler*, is available to convert these programs into machine code. Because a compiler is nothing more than another computer program that uses the initial (or *source-language*) program as input and compiles a machine-language program, or *object program,* as output, a company's programmers could write a program in any source language they desired as long as they first took the trouble to acquire a suitable compiler. In point of fact, most businesses prefer to write or purchase their accounting information systems computer programs in as few programming languages as possible. This desire for consistency in turn limits the number of different compilers that any particular computing center is likely to have, and therefore, the number of different programming languages "supported" by a particular business firm's EDP subsystem. Many businesses use COBOL exclusively.

Recent advances in computer technology have provided two other important advantages of high-level languages over assembler or machine-coded languages. The first of these is the vast improvement in *error diagnostics* generated by present-day compilers. These diagnostics identify the grammar, syntax, and other mechanical-type coding mistakes that represent a misuse in language construction. For example, if we had coded the expression $E = (A*B-C)/D$ in FORTRAN as

statement number	coded expression
350	$E = (A*B-C/D$

in "the old days," we could have gotten back the compiler error message:

GRAMMATICAL ERROR IN LINE 350.

This certainly informs us that a mistake was made, but provides little information about the nature of the mistake, or how it should be remedied. Had the same FORTRAN instruction been translated by a modern compiler, however, the likely error diagnostic returned would read something like:

MISSING CLOSING PARENTHESIS IN LINE 350

which is clearly much more informative, and therefore more useful for corrective action.

The second advance in source-level programming is the use of interactive terminals in the "debugging," that is, program-correction, process. BASIC has been particularly successful in this regard. When programming in "interactive mode," the programmer sits down at an on-line terminal and enters instructions sequentially on a line-by-line basis. Each time a new instruction is entered, the compiler at the computer scans the instruction for proper programming-language syntax and grammar, as illustrated in the preceding example. When the compiler detects an error, an error message is immediately returned to the programmer through the terminal, enabling the programmer to correct the mistake "on the spot." Thus, by the time the programmer is through entering all of his or her instructions, a complete program, free of almost all mechanical errors, is at hand. System commands at the terminal may then be used either to store the program, execute it, have it punched out on a set of computer cards, or transfer it to any recording medium that suits the programmer's needs.

BASIC, FORTRAN, and COBOL: A Comparison

Of the many computer languages that have been developed over the years, BASIC, FORTRAN, and COBOL have proved to be the most popular in business and commercial applications. For this reason, we take the opportunity to look closely at these languages here.

BASIC. Of the three principal programming languages discussed in this chapter, BASIC is usually considered the easiest to learn. Originated at Dartmouth College on an experimental basis, BASIC closely resembles FORTRAN in syntax and grammar. For example, the arithmetic expression $E = (A*B-C)/D$ would be coded in BASIC as

$$\text{LET } E = (A*B-C)/D$$

which is much like the FORTRAN coding of this expression as discussed above. BASIC has some distinct advantages over FORTRAN, however. One advantage is that BASIC uses very simple input and output instructions. This fact, coupled with BASIC's programming simplicity, makes BASIC a popular programming language for the minicomputer and microcomputer systems likely to be used by individuals unsophisticated in data-processing techniques. Another advantage is that BASIC is structured in such a way that it is particularly well-suited for use as a *time-sharing language,* that is, a programming language in which several programmers interact with the computer at the same time. This second advantage implies, in turn, that BASIC programs can be designed, tested, debugged, and executed from remote terminals. In fact, today, it is possible for programmers to rent or buy terminals the size of briefcases, connect them to a computer via their home telephones, and write computer programs while sipping iced tea in a hammock!

A third advantage of BASIC is that it frees the programmer from much of the file-definition statements and other initialization instructions required by FORTRAN and COBOL. Such statements are often called language "overhead," and thus BASIC is sometimes described as a programming language that has a very small overhead. This is not to say that BASIC cannot do file processing, but rather that BASIC can do such processing in a minimum number of coded instructions. Because, in general, the fewer the instructions required in a program the faster the program can be tested, debugged, and documented, BASIC has a potential to increase programmer productivity.

FORTRAN. FORTRAN is a little more complicated than BASIC, but there are many similarities. Historically, FORTRAN is one of the world's oldest high-level languages, although its age is still less than 30 years. Since newer and more sophisticated programming languages such as APL and PL/1 are being developed all the time, the fact that FORTRAN is still used extensively today is remarkable. Part of this longevity is explained by the evolutionary nature of the language itself. Elementary FORTRAN quickly gave way to an improved version called FORTRAN II. At the time this book went to print, the most common version of FORTRAN in use was FORTRAN IV—a version of FORTRAN that has been expanded and modified to better serve the programming needs of current data processing.

FORTRAN's durability may perhaps be explained in part by its usefulness as a calculating language. As its name suggests, FORTRAN is excellent for formula translation. Its use in countless scientific and military applications testifies to its wide applicability in solving complex quantitative problems. However, many businesses have also found data-processing tasks well-suited for expression in FORTRAN. For example, if the Alan Company desired weekly analyses of operating production costs, FORTRAN might be the best programming language to use because the calculations necessary to satisfy management's cost accounting information needs could be expressed easily in FORTRAN statements.

FORTRAN also suffers some drawbacks. Like BASIC, it does not express instructions in English, or English-like prose, but rather in equation format which nonquantitatively-oriented people find difficult to understand. In contrast to BASIC, FORTRAN requires more overhead instructions. Therefore, FORTRAN programs tend to be longer in size and potentially more prone to initial errors than BASIC programs. Although FORTRAN programs *can* be written and tested on a time-sharing basis, very few computer centers support FORTRAN compilers in a time-sharing mode. Thus, for the most part, FORTRAN programs to be tested must be submitted as a data-processing task to be run at the computer center as time permits. This tends to slow down the *turnaround time* (time between programmer submission of the program and its return from the computer center with error diagnostics), and therefore, the debugging process in general.

A final problem with FORTRAN is that it is not particularly well-suited for processing files. Both BASIC and COBOL are superior in this regard. Where relatively complicated accounting files are involved, COBOL would be especially favored. Thus, since file handling constitutes such a very large portion of business data processing, FORTRAN suffers a great disadvantage in commercial applications.

COBOL. COBOL enjoys wide popularity in business data processing. Undoubtedly its prose-like expression has contributed to this popularity. COBOL statements closely resemble the instructions of everyday English. For example, the expression $E = (A*B-C)/D$ would be coded in COBOL as follows (the letters "F" and "G" below are used as temporary storage locations for performing the computations):

MULTIPLY A BY B GIVING F.
SUBTRACT C FROM F GIVING G.
DIVIDE G BY D GIVING E.

Such instructions make the COBOL program easy to understand for nonquantitatively-oriented people, and may thus enable even a novice to understand (in part) the work of an experienced COBOL programmer. Moreover, as we have noted earlier, the English context of the COBOL program means in effect that the programming language is, to a point, self-documenting.

Unlike BASIC or FORTRAN, COBOL has a precisely-defined program structure consisting of four major divisions: IDENTIFICATION, ENVIRONMENT, DATA, and PROCEDURE. Each is discussed briefly in Appendix C and need not concern us here. It is important to realize, however, that COBOL's structure imposes rigidity in programming construction which has both advantages and disadvantages.

On the plus side, a rigid program structure guarantees a certain degree of uniformity in expression which increases the program's comprehensibility and aids in documentation. For example, one programmer could immediately identify which data-processing files were required in the COBOL program written by a second programmer by looking directly at the program's DATA division. Moreover, the programmer could also identify precisely what fields were in each of the records on these files for the same reason. Program structure also tends to make common instructions fairly standard to code, thus increasing programmer productivity.

The chief disadvantage of a rigid programming structure is that it increases language overhead. COBOL is notoriously demanding of a large number of statements that do not help the execution of the data-processing task. For example, in defining the file records discussed above, COBOL requires that a separate line of the coding be devoted to the description of each field of each record on the file. Thus, if a given COBOL program were required to process three different types of records, each of which had 50 fields, the programmer would be forced to use 150 lines of coding just to describe these fields! In contrast, the corresponding FORTRAN or BASIC coding would require only five or six lines of code. For this reason, the length of COBOL programs tends to dwarf those of BASIC or FORTRAN. The potential for coding errors is thus increased.

One final disadvantage of COBOL is that it is almost always tested and debugged in batch (i.e., noninteractive) mode. Thus, like FORTRAN, turnaround time is slow compared with BASIC, and programmer productivity tends to be hampered.

Despite its demanding enumeration of input/output data, COBOL is often the preferred programming language for file processing because it is so explicit in its treatment of file record fields. This consideration is especially important in the business environment, in which file-handling is often crucial to the data-processing requirements of the commercial enterprise. Also, COBOL language, being written in instructions that closely resemble simple English paragraphs and sentences, enables the accountant to trace the data processing to be performed by the computer.

Job Control Languages

At most computer installations, the programs run on the central processing unit are executed under the supervision of a set of programs called the "operating system." Job control language provides a means of communication between the program and the operating system, enabling the programmer to tell the operating system (through the program) what kind of processing is desired and how the processing is to be carried out. Thus, for example, job control language (or JCL) enables a programmer to identify the processing job as a FORTRAN program that requires compilation, a COBOL program to be stored on a disk file, a BASIC program to be executed, a set of cards to be transferred to tape, a file of magnetic tape records to be sorted, or possibly a magnetic disk file of old employee records to be listed on the printer and then erased from the disk.

In addition to identifying the type of job to be performed, JCL also identifies the physical equipment involved in a data-processing task. Thus, job control instructions might direct the central processing unit to use tape drive #3 in a magnetic-tape sort operation, disk drive #7 in a listing operation, and so forth. Among other advantages, JCL is useful because it enables the programmer to write a computer program as a machine-independent entity, and to decide on specific processing machines separately. This advantage is especially attractive when, for example, the tape drive normally used for a given processing task breaks down and an alternate one must be utilized in its place. JCL can identify the new machine in a single instruction.

Job control language is expressed as either special terminal instructions input to the computer on a real-time basis, or as special instructions punched in special JCL computer cards if a card deck is used. Commonly, the terminal instructions are called *system commands*, whereas the punched cards are called *job control cards*. In either case, however, the objective is basically the same: to enable the user to communicate with the operating system.

Each hardware manufacturer has its own operating systems and therefore its own type of job control language. In fact, some manufacturers have several different operating systems available for the same central processing unit, and the choice of one system over the other is usually dependent upon the type of processing to be performed. Therefore, the computer center which decides to switch hardware from that of one computer manufacturer to that of another is virtually assured of having to learn a new job control language.

TYPES OF COMPUTER PROGRAMS USED BY ACCOUNTING INFORMATION SYSTEMS

Once computer programs have been designed, flowcharted, coded, and debugged, they are formally added to the library of the computer center where they are retained until further notice. Usually, they are stored as *object programs*, that is, programs that have already been translated into machine language by a suitable compiler, and are therefore available for immediate execution. This storage mode thus avoids the inevitable compilation which would otherwise have to be performed repeatedly if the programs were simply maintained in their original, source-language format.

The computer programs stored at the library of the computer center may be divided into four convenient subcategories for the purposes of discussion. These categories are: (1) *application programs*, (2) *utility programs*, (3) *canned programs*, and (4) *operating systems programs*. Each is discussed in greater detail below.

Application Programs

These computer programs perform the data-processing tasks peculiar to the individual company. Thus, the programs that process mortgage loans for a bank, the programs that handle the accounts payable transactions of a retail department store, or the programs that process the payroll at an assembly plant would all be examples of application programs. At one time, most application programs were developed on a custom basis by each data-processing center as requested by the data user of the company. For reasons that we shall discuss in greater detail below and also in the chapter on Resource Acquisition, a large proportion of a company's application programs are now purchased "externally," that is, from computer manufacturers or software-development houses.

Probably the most common type of business applications program found in the commercial computer library would be a company's file-update programs. These programs are designed to alter the records of an existing file to reflect changes in the status of the information contained therein. A good example would be a bank's computer file of customer checking-account records, in which each customer's balance would be updated at the end of each business day with the deposits, withdrawals, and other transactions comprising the customer's activity. Most of the computer programs of an accounting information system would be classified as application programs.

Utility Programs

Utility programs are computer programs that are usually supplied by computer manufacturers or software companies to perform common data processing tasks. One typical requirement is the transfer of data from one storage medium to another: tape-to-tape, card-to-tape, tape-to-disk, disk-to-printer, and so forth. Another requirement would be the sorting of tape or disk records into a desired sequence. A third requirement would be the merging of two sorted tape or disk files into one.

Utility programs generally are easy to use, efficient to operate, and inexpensive to acquire. Only the most limited computer center is likely to be without them. Many hardware manufacturers supply free commercial utility programs to EDP centers as an inducement to lease or purchase their computers. However, recent judicial decisions have made such practices questionable and now, such utility programs usually must be purchased independently of the computer hardware.

Canned Programs

Canned programs are much like utility programs in that they are usually acquired from external sources (such as software houses) for a fee. Unlike utility programs, which for the most part simply transfer data, however, canned programs typically perform some kind of data analysis. Examples of canned programs would include data reduction routines, which compute the statistical properties of a large set of data (means, medians, modes, etc.), and financial analysis routines, which compute such things as net present values and financial ratios.

Over the years, there has been a tendency for computer manufacturers and software houses to offer such programs in sets, or program "packages," which perform a large number of related tasks within a general functional area. For example, IBM's MPS (Mathematical Programming System) Package solves many different types of mathematical programming problems and the University of California, Los Angeles' BMD (Bio-Medical) Package performs many different types of statistical tests.

In addition to data-processing routines, some companies have specialized in providing computerized data to industry subscribers. Although their product would not accurately qualify as canned programs, these data sets serve much the same purpose—enabling the user to purchase the computer work of others and therefore avoid doing (or in this case coding) the work again. Perhaps among the best-known of such services would be the CompuStat magnetic tapes made available by Standard and Poor, Inc., which provide the complete record of the daily trades of stocks on the New York Stock Exchange.

Finally, in addition to the common library routines and data sets commercially available today, some software developers offer large-scale programming packages that comprise a complete data-processing subsystem. Today, for example, banks may purchase the programs necessary to process their installment loans, manufacturers may presently purchase the programs necessary for complete maintenance of their inventory records, and retail stores may presently purchase the programs necessary to execute their accounts receivable billing functions. Many of these packages are also available on a lease basis. Although most of these programs would also be considered "application programs," the fact that they are widely available and can be purchased or leased "off the shelf" has prompted us to discuss them as "canned programs."

Operating System Programs

Operating system programs, often called just the *operating system*, coordinate the activities of the central processing unit with peripheral input and output equipment. Operating system (OS) programs have highest priority on the CPU but serve primarily to maintain the orderly transition of computer execution and control from one processing task to the next. For example, if an applications program—let us say a file-maintenance program—required execution, the application program's lead job-control instructions would communicate the program's requirements to the operating system. The operating system would translate the JCL instructions and, if possible, accommodate the job request. Thus, the OS programs would check to see if the CPU were free and, if so, turn processing control over to the file-maintenance program. If the CPU were otherwise occupied, the operating system could temporarily store the file-maintenance program on a disk, maintaining it with other job requests in a queue until processing resources were available.

Other jobs performed by the operating system would include: (1) the allocation of computer time to competing programs when more than one job request was recognized and the system was operating in "multiprogramming mode," (2) the execution of error routines when such problems as parity errors, data transmission errors, or other input/output abnormalities were detected, (3) the maintenance of simple library subroutines (e.g., the calculation of a square root) and the provision of these subroutines when required by processing programs, (4) the "swapping" of data back and forth between the CPU and disk storage when virtual memory systems are in operation, and (5) the reporting of all I/O activities to machine-operator personnel through the CPU system console. This last task results in a hard-copy document called the *system log*—a listing that has proved invaluable in the detection of computer thefts because it documents who used the CPU when.

Operating systems automate many of the tasks formerly performed by the human computer operator. For example, prior to the use of such sophisticated programs, the operator had to reset computer console switches manually every time a new computer job was to be performed, backspace and retry a magnetic tape reading every time a magnetic tape parity error was detected, and manually sort through job requests to determine the priority of processing tasks required at the center. In effect, operating systems perform all these functions via computer control, plus a great deal more, thus automating this work and making the computing center that much more productive. Today, it is inconceivable to find all but the very smallest and most primitive computer systems functioning without some kind of operating system.

DOCUMENTATION

The individual programs written in one or more of the programming languages discussed above comprise the *programming* software of the accounting information system. The documentation includes all the flowcharts, written descriptions, and other communication aids that enable one systems analyst to outline the software and hardware requirements of the accounting information system for the benefit of another. Obviously, the system and program flowcharts discussed above play a key role in this communication process, but they are not the only means by which this documentation is performed. Equally vital are such items as file descriptions, record layouts, program input and output requirements, machine-operator instructions, and security features. Together, these items comprise a kind of sophisticated instruction set that enables the data processor to use,

and in the course of time, modify, the application programs. In fact, this documentation is considered so important that most companies will not pay software houses for programs which have been written on a contractual basis until both the program(s), *and the documentation*, have been completed to the satisfaction of the buyer. For these reasons, we shall discuss such documentation more thoroughly in the sections that follow.

To illustrate our discussion, let us continue our sales-ticket extension example as discussed in the first part of this chapter and illustrated in Figures 19-3 and 19-4. The information concerning each sales transaction is punched on a single punched card, and this information is used to generate the Alan Company's sales report. To make this problem a little more interesting, let us assume that the Alan Company's sales manager would like the sales report with customer purchases listed in ascending account-number sequence.

The requirement for account-number order in the sales report will require a sequence sort on the customer account number prior to printing the report. To accomplish this, it is easiest to take the (large) deck of sales transaction cards and first transfer the data to magnetic tape using a utility program. Once this task is accomplished, a second utility program can be used to sort the (magnetic tape) sales records into ascending customer account-number sequence. Finally, with the sales records in proper sequence, the report-generating program—that is, the application program—may commence to print the sales report.

Figure 19-7 illustrates the system flowchart for these tasks. Note that the computer is required for three separate jobs: (1) the initial transfer of data from cards to tape, (2) the sorting of the magnetic tape records into ascending account-number sequence, and (3) the actual processing of the data for the final sales report. Although this computer usage might seem extravagant, it still would be much faster than sorting the sales-transaction cards by hand, or using an off-line card sorter. Moreover, job-control language would permit the execution of

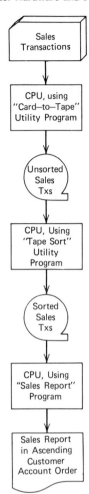

Figure 19-7. A system flowchart for preparing a sales report in ascending customer account order.

these three processing steps automatically, so that very little computer-operator intervention would be required.

The system flowchart cannot tell us all that we would like to know about our processing routines. Further documentation is necessary to describe the files used, record layouts, input and output requirements, machine operator instructions and security features. Each of these is discussed in greater detail below.

File Descriptions

Although the general file requirements of the various programs comprising the accounting in-

formation system are made known through the system flowcharts, specific information is lacking. The format of the header record and trailer record for each file must be specified, outlining such information as file names, creation date, cycle time (i.e., run periodicity), expiration date, record counts, and so forth. The physical composition of the file—particularly the size of each logical record and the number of logical records within each physical record (i.e., the blocking factor)—must be given. The manner by which the file is organized (sequential versus nonsequential method) must be identified. If records are to be stored on magnetic tape, the choice of seven-track tape versus nine-track tape must be known, as well as the recording density and parity type ("odd" or "even"). If records are stored on magnetic disk as a direct-access file, the manner by which disk addresses are determined would have to be described. Since the file will be maintained in the library of the computer center, its physical shelf location should also be identified, or at least the manner by which it can be found in the center's library. Finally, because each file in the accounting information system has the potential to be used by several programs, the exact names of these programs (e.g., the "Inventory Parts Update Program") and the specific file information utilized by each is helpful, especially when design changes are contemplated.

To document all this, it is customary for data-processing centers to use preprinted documentation forms such as those illustrated in Figures 19-8, 19-9, and 19-10. These forms have been filled out to document our sales-extension problem. Documentation forms standardize the recording of pertinent data-processing information and help the programmer or systems analyst in the documentation effort. Looking over the form in Figure 19-8, a few items are worth noting. For example, both of the magnetic tape files are used as input and output files. This is because of their positions in the processing sequence. The unsorted sales transactions file is an *output* from the card-to-tape utility run, but it turns around and becomes an *input* to the sorting run. Similarly, the sorted sales transactions file is an *output* from the sorting run, but turns around and becomes an

Alan Company Data Services	Title	I.D. No.	Creation	Cycle	Manager
	SALES REPORT	34526	10-15-78	WEEKLY	R. RAPOZA

System Identification

Equipment:	Printer	Card Reader	Card Punch	Paper Tape	MICR	OCR	Tape Drive	Disk Drive
Number Needed:	1	1					2	
Unit Address(es):	#8	#5					#3, #4	

System Requirements

Mode*	Media**	Unit	File Name	Description	Retention Cycle
I	C	#5	SALES 01	PUNCHED SALES TRANSACTIONS	3 DAYS
I,O	T	#3	WORK 01	UNSORTED SALES TRANSACTIONS	0 DAYS
I,O	T	#4	WORK 02	SORTED SALES TRANSACTIONS	30 DAYS

*I = Input, O = Output   **T = Tape, D = Disk, C = Card, P = Paper Tape

Tape/Disk Recording Information

File Name	Storage Shelf	Organization	Creation Date	Date Expir.	Blocking Factor	Phys. Rec. Size	Log. Rec. Size	Tape Info.		
								Tracks	Density	Parity
WORK 01	W	SEQUENTIAL	RUN DATE	RUN DATE	20	280	14	9	800	ODD
WORK 02	W	SEQUENTIAL	RUN DATE	DEC. 31	20	280	14	9	800	ODD

Place special instructions, identify other users, here:

1) SORTED SALES TRANSACTIONS TAPE USED AS INPUT FILE FOR
   BILLING RUN.

Figure 19-8. Systems documentation form for the Alan Company.

input to the sales report run. The slashes in the names of these files (WØRK01 and WØRK02) distinguish between the letter "o" and the number zero.

A second noteworthy item is the retention-cycle entries for these tape files. The first of these files—the unsorted sales transactions file—is used primarily to take advantage of the faster input/output speeds of tape media as compared with punched-card media. Thus, there is little reason to save this file once the customer information has been recopied in ascending sequence on the second magnetic tape file. The sorted transactions file is another matter. This file might be used further, for example in the maintenance of a year-to-date sales file. For this reason, the file might be saved. A retention cycle of 30 days is therefore entered on the documentation form.

Record Layouts

Record layouts describe the field content of each logical record of each input, output, and storage file of the accounting system. For example, Figure 18-4 of Chapter 18 provides a layout of a mag-

netic tape record. To assist system designers in documenting such layouts, special preprinted forms such as the one illustrated in Figure 19-9 may be used.

Note that the record layout is actually a multi-purpose document. In addition to its use as a description of the fields in a record, the record layout also serves to identify the record key (i.e., the numerical information by which the file is organized).

Program Input and Output Requirements

The system flowchart gives a general idea of what is involved in a given processing run, but further information about program input and output is required: Does the program require blank cards for card punching? Must special preprinted forms be readied on the printer prior to program execution? Will a "scratch tape" (a magnetic tape used for temporary secondary storage, e.g., when sorting records) be needed? Upon what particular disk drive should a given disk pack, containing a program-required file, be mounted? These are the kinds of questions that

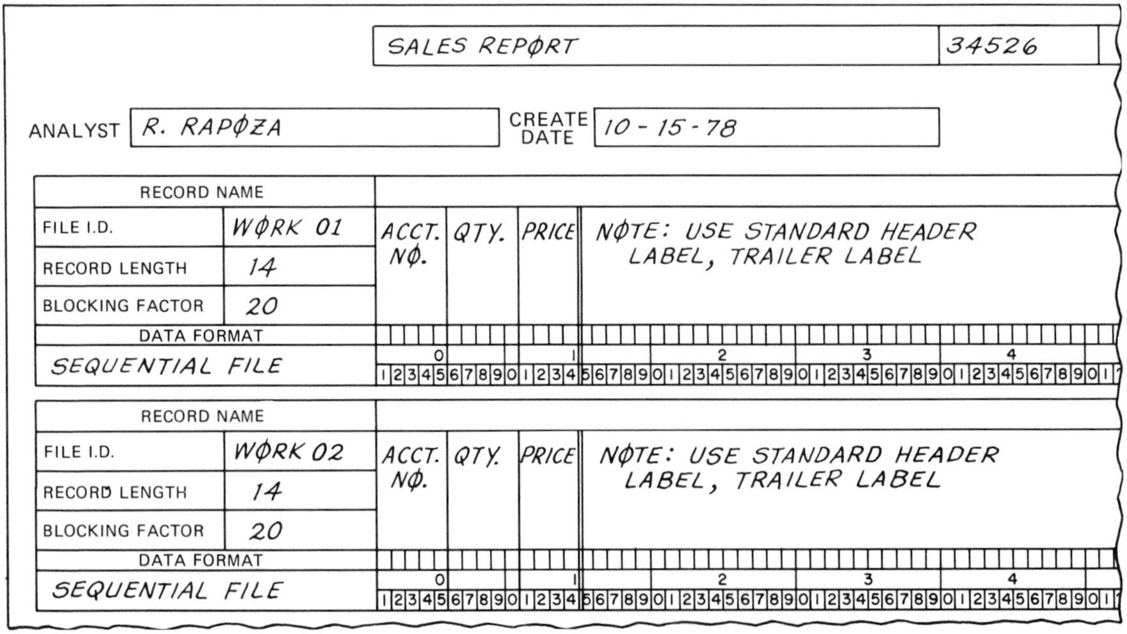

Figure 19-9. A portion of a preprinted record layout form, as it might be used to document the magnetic tape files required to prepare a sales report.

should be answered in the input/output specifications portion of the documentation.

Machine Operator Instructions

It is the machine operator who coordinates the hardware and software requirements of the accounting information system programs on a daily basis. Instructions provided in the system manual, such as those illustrated in Figure 19-10 for our sales-ticket example, explain for any given data-processing task which tape reels and disk packs are required, where they are to be mounted at processing commencement, and what is to be done with the output. Usually, programs provided to the operator for execution have been thoroughly tested and their use is routine. Occasionally, however, an unusual set

Alan Company
Data Services

Title	I.D. No.	Creation	Cycle	Manager
SALES REPORT	34526	10-15-78	WEEKLY	R. RAPOZA

Operator Instructions

1) NORMAL SCHEDULE FOR THIS JOB IS WEEKLY.

2) JOB SHOULD BE COMPLETED BY 10 PM, FRIDAY.

3) USE JOB-CONTROL CARD WITH CURRENT PROCESSING DATE.

4) MOUNT SCRATCH TAPE ON UNIT #3.

5) MOUNT A SAVABLE TAPE ON UNIT #4.

6) CHECK "SYSOUT-A" ON COMPUTER CONSOLE LOG FOR NORMAL
   END OF JOB.

7) LABEL TAPE REEL ON UNIT #4 "SORTED SALES TICKETS
   FOR WEEK ENDING XX-XX-XX." STORE ON SHELF
   5 OF TAPE LIBRARY.

8) SEND OUTPUT LISTING ("SALES REPORT") TO
   MARKETING DEPARTMENT MONDAY MORNING.

9) IN EMERGENCY, CALL BOB MUSIK AT 365-3255.

Figure 19-10. Instructions for the computer operator.

of data requires processing for which the normal routines of the program are not prepared. When a computer encounters data or other problems for which it has not been programmed (e.g., taking the square root of a negative number) processing is immediately halted, the machine operator is notified of the problem via a systems error message on the CPU console, and the CPU goes into a "wait state." At such times, the instructions left to the machine operator become crucial.

If the data processing is not too urgent, it is sometimes possible to permit the operator to abort (terminate) the program and proceed with the next job on the schedule. Information concerning the "hang-up" is gathered and submitted to the machine operations manager for communication to EDP personnel for review and correction. More often than not, however, the problem occurs in a vital, daily-run program which is executed around 3:00 A.M. In these latter instances, the documentation should include the phone number of the *bomb-out programmer* or other person to be notified in such an emergency. (An all-night investigation almost invariably follows.)

Security Features

The security aspect of information processing has become a subject of increasing popularity of late. This is partly attributable to the fact that computer "rip-offs" attract a natural human interest and partly because they are exceedingly lucrative for the amount of effort expended. For these reasons, we have dealt extensively with the topic of computer security in Chapter 8, which details how to safeguard computer processing, and Chapter 9, which discusses computer crime.

Naturally, not all security measures implemented in the data-processing system will be found in the documentation; to do so would be tantamount to designing a blueprint for a computer crime. However, what should be outlined clearly in the documentation would be such items as: (1) the names of key personnel having access to secret password codes, (2) the prenumbered forms (purchase orders, sales invoices, etc.) to be used in given processing routines and

which personnel are authorized to use these forms, (3) the names of the employees who have keys to the computer center library (where computer files and programs are stored), (4) the identity of the computer programs requiring access to sensitive computer files, and (5) the names of EDP personnel authorized to make program modifications.

SUMMARY

This chapter has reviewed the topic of computer software, which we have discussed under the headings of computer programming and computer documentation. The development of a computer program starts with the recognition that a job can be performed more efficiently if it is computer-automated. A system flowchart is then developed which indicates the hardware configuration required and the flow of information from one storage medium to another. Following this, a macro program flowchart is developed which outlines in broad terms the processing logic of the program. Finally, a micro program flowchart is designed for each routine in the macro flowchart, providing detailed information about the data processing. In order to make their meanings clear, both system flowcharts and program flowcharts utilize standard processing symbols and follow conventional flowcharting techniques.

Once the program flowchart has been prepared in sufficient detail, it serves as an outline for coding a computer language. There are three levels of such languages: machine languages, assembler languages, and high-level languages. Of the three, high-level languages such as BASIC, COBOL, or FORTRAN are by far the most popular today, although it should be remembered that, ultimately, all programs *must* be translated into machine language before they can be executed on the central processing unit. BASIC and FORTRAN have the advantage of being easy to learn and use, and BASIC is particularly well-suited for use on a real-time basis. Because much of business data processing involves the creation, updating, and maintenance of disk and tape files (a set of tasks in which COBOL excels),

COBOL is the principal commercial data-processing language.

The computer center maintains a large number of computer programs in its library. Some of these programs are likely to have been developed by the programmers working for the computer center. Others may have been purchased from external sources such as hardware manufacturers or software companies. Application programs perform such data-processing tasks as file-maintenance and report generation. Utility programs transfer data records from one storage medium to another and perform certain other "standard" processing tasks, whereas canned programs are usually externally-written computer programs acquired for the purpose of data processing. Finally, computer operating systems perform supervisory and coordinative functions at the computer center.

Program documentation involves the description of computer programs and related software. Included in such documentation are the system and program flowcharts described above, file descriptions of data records used in the processing routines, record layouts, input/output requirements, machine operator instructions, and an enumeration of certain security features of the programs themselves. Whereas some of this information is fairly technical, virtually all of it is vital to the accountant.

DISCUSSION QUESTIONS

19-1. Describe the advantages of using a system flowchart.

19-2. Describe the advantages of using program flowcharts.

19-3. Why are the names FORTRAN, COBOL, and BASIC used to describe three high-level programming languages?

19-4. Explain the advantages of BASIC, COBOL, and FORTRAN programming languages discussed in this chapter.

19-5. If high-level languages are supposed to make programming easier, why are there so many of them? Wouldn't it be much easier to have just one programming language?

19-6. Good flowcharting technique requires the observance of certain conventions. What are these conventions and why are they important?

19-7. Explain the difference between a system flowchart and a program flowchart.

19-8. Explain the difference between a macro program flowchart and a micro program flowchart.

19-9. Because no one programs in machine language today, why would anyone, especially an accountant, ever bother with it?

19-10. In the context of the present chapter, what is a computer register?

19-11. We have seen that a variable in FORTRAN actually represents the address of a specific storage location of the central processing unit in which a data value resides. Use this fact to explain why the (algebraically impossible) expression $N = N + 1$ is completely legitimate in FORTRAN or BASIC

19-12. What is the meaning and purpose of JCL?

19-13. Why is the system flowchart insufficient as a description of the computer files used in a data-processing run?

19-14. In your opinion, could the record layout portion of the documentation be included in the file descriptions' portion?

19-15. Why bother to write down machine operator instructions? Why not just call the operator and state what you want?

19-16. Since security is so important to the computer center, why are some of the security features of the accounting information system *not* documented as a normal documentation activity?

PROBLEMS

19-17. Modify the programming flowchart of Figure 19-4 so that it will compute the following additional financial totals for all sales transactions processed: (a) total sales amount before tax, and (b) total amount of sales tax.

19-18. You are given three numbers a, b, and c. Develop a detailed micro program flowchart which would enable you to determine which number was the smallest, which number was the next smallest, and which number was the largest.

Assume that all three numbers are different, and that the output required is a single line of three numbers in ascending sequence. How is this exercise related to the general problem of sorting? How is the general problem of sorting related to accounting information systems?

19-19. Suttor Industries is a maker of women's apparel and sportswear. To get some idea of how many accounts were being paid by the company's accounts payable processing system, the firm's chief executive officer, Lucile Suttor, has asked the company's programmer, Joanne Trucko, to design a computer program. Joanne is given the documentation describing the company's disk file of accounts payable records, which stores all the accounts payable for the present month. "Joanne," said Lucille Suttor, "I'd like to know how many accounts we pay, and what the average payment is for each account."

Reading the documentation describing the accounts payable file, Joanne discovers that the disk file contains one record for each account, and that each record contains the total amount owed to the account. Further, because the number of accounts varies somewhat from one month to the next, the total number of records on the file is not available in the documentation.

Required

a. Design a system flowchart describing the computer processing necessary to ascertain the information required by Lucille Suttor.

b. Assist Joanne Trucko by designing a detailed micro flowchart which would illustrate the processing logic by which Joanne could ascertain the accounts payable information required by the company's chief executive officer.

19-20. The order-writing department at the James Dueberry Company is managed by Frank Fox. The department keeps two types of computer files: (1) a customer file of authorized credit customers, and (2) a product file of items currently sold by the company.

Both of these files are direct-access files stored on magnetic disks. Customer orders are handwritten on order forms with the James Dueberry name at the top and "item lines" for quantity, item number, and total amount desired for each product ordered by the customer below the name.

When customer orders are received, Frank Fox directs someone to input the information at one of the department's computer terminals. After the information has been input, the computer program immediately adds the information to a computerized "order" file and prepares five copies of the customer order. The first is sent back to Frank's department, the others are sent elsewhere.

Required

a. Design a system flowchart that documents the accounting data processing described above.

b. Design a program flowchart that would indicate how each complete customer order input to the computer would be processed.

19-21. The Alan Company maintains a set of disk records for an employee file. On page 577 is a flowchart for printing selected records from this file, using punched card input. A set of descriptions for the various processing symbols is also provided. For each processing symbol of the flowchart, select the most appropriate description and write this inside the symbol. In addition, fill in one or more letters for the circles (processing connectors).

19-22. Many cash registers have a built-in change-making feature that automatically computes the number and type of coins to be returned to a customer making a cash purchase. Design a micro program flowchart that outlines the processing logic for this change-making activity. You may assume that the flowchart need only make change for a dollar payment. The results of your processing logic should indicate how many quarters, how many dimes, how many nickels, and how many pennies should be returned to the customer so as to return the *least number of coins.*

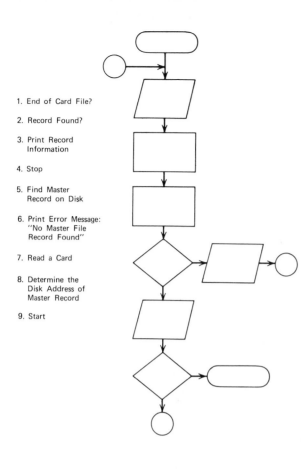

1. End of Card File?

2. Record Found?

3. Print Record
   Information

4. Stop

5. Find Master
   Record on Disk

6. Print Error Message:
   "No Master File
   Record Found"

7. Read a Card

8. Determine the
   Disk Address of
   Master Record

9. Start

CASE ANALYSES

19-23. *Decision Tables for Accounts Receivable Processing*

A decision table is a special analytical device often used by programmers and system analysts to outline the action to be taken for each potential condition in a data-processing environment. To illustrate, imagine a credit union that pays interest to its depositors at the rate of 7 percent per annum. Accounts of less than $5 are not paid any interest. Accounts of more than $1000 that have been with the union more than 1 year also get paid a bonus of ½ percent. At the end of the year, when interest is to be credited to each account, the decision table below outlines the data-processing decisions involved in this accounting application.

Note that the decision table consists of four parts: (1) the condition stub that outlines the potential conditions of the application; (2) the action stub that outlines the potential actions to be taken in the application; (3) the condition entries that depict all of the possible combinations of conditions likely to occur; and (4) the action entries that outline the action to be taken for each combination of conditions. The rules set forth the combination of conditions that may occur and what action is to be taken for each.

DECISION TABLE

		Rules			
Conditions:	1	2	3	4	
Account under $5	x				
Account $5 or more		x			
Account less than $1000		x			
Account $1000 or more			x	x	
Account 1 year old or less			x		
Account more than 1 year old				x	
Actions: ·					
Pay no interest	x				
Pay 7 percent interest		x	x		
Pay bonus of ½ percent interest				x	

Condition Stub ... Condition Entries

Action Stub ... Action Entries

One application of decision table analysis would be for processing accounts receivable. For example, imagine that the Kenneth Garmon Company, an office products distributor, must decide what to do with delinquent credit-sales accounts. Mr. Barton Orange, the credit manager, has divided up the accounts into the following categories: (1) accounts not past due, (2) accounts 30 days or less past due, (3) accounts 31 to 60 days past due, (4) accounts 61 to 90 days past due, and (5) accounts over 90 days past due. For simplicity, assume that all transactions for each account fall neatly into the same category.

Mr. Orange decides what to do about these customer accounts based on the history of the account in general, and also the activity that has transpired during the account's delinquency period. Sometimes, for example, the customer will not communicate at all. At other times, however, the customer will either write to state that a check is forthcoming or even make a partial payment. Mr. Orange has tended to be most understanding of the customers who make partial payments because he considers such payments to be acts of good faith. Mr. Orange has tended to be less understanding of the customers who only promise to pay or of the customers who simply do not respond to follow-up bills from the company.

Mr. Orange has four potential actions to take in the case of credit delinquency. First, he can simply wait (i.e., do nothing). Second, he can send an initial letter to the customer, inquiring about the problem in bill payment and requesting written notification of a payment schedule if payment has not already been made. Third, he can send a follow-up letter of inquiry, indicating that a collection agency will be given the account if immediate payment is not forthcoming. Fourth, he can turn the account over to a collection agency. Of course, Mr. Orange prefers to use one of the first three actions rather than turn the account over to a collection agency because his company only receives half of the total bill if the collection agency becomes involved in the collection process.

Required

A. Design an efficient decision table for the Kenneth Garmon Company and provide a set of reasonable decision rules for Mr. Orange to follow. For the present, ignore the influence of a customer's credit history.

B. Expand the decision analysis you have prepared in part (A) to include the credit history of the customer accounts. You are free to make any assumptions you wish about how this history might be evaluated by Mr. Orange.

19-24. *Hiyawatha University*

Hiyawatha University has recently computerized its payroll operations and employee checks are to be mailed out every month. Each check is to have the gross amount, itemized deductions, and payment amount, in dollars and cents, as well as the employee's name and address. Information for the processing will be read in from cards. The amount of payment is the number of hours worked times the hourly rate of pay (adjusted for overtime if any), less federal and state withholding taxes, company retirement and social security deductions, and (optional) medical plan payments. The following codes indicate the processing:

entry	code	meaning
1. payment rate code	A	no overtime bonus
	B	"time-and-a-half" for all work over 40 hours
	C	"time-and-a-half" for first 10 hours overtime, double hourly pay for all work over 50 hours
2. federal income tax withholding	X	9.5% of gross pay (10.8% if married)
	Y	13.5% of gross pay (14.8% if married)

entry	code	meaning
	Z	18.2% of gross pay (19.5% if married)
3. state with-holding	S	5.3% of gross pay
	T	8.7% of gross pay
4. social security	—	5.5% of gross pay—all employees
5. retirement	1	7.1% of gross pay
	2	9.6% of gross pay
6. medical plan	(blank)	none—no deductions
	H	HMSA plan, $6.92/month
	K	Kaiser plan, $5.09/month

The data card would be as follows:

column(s)	information
1–15	employee name
16–30	first line of address
31–45	second line of address
46–60	third line of address, if any
61–65	number of hours worked (may be a noninteger number)
66–70	hourly rate of pay expressed to tenths of a cent)
71	marriage status (1 = single, 2 = married)
72	payment rate code
73	federal income tax withholding code
74	retirement code
75	state withholding code
76	medical plan code

Required

A. Draw a system flowchart for this processing.

B. Prepare a macro flowchart of the *major* processing requirements of the problem.

C. Prepare a micro flowchart indicating the detailed logic of this problem's processing requirements.

D. Draw a picture of the input card as might be used for documentation purposes for this program.

E. Draw a picture of the output check as might be used for documentation purposes for this program.

19-25. *Statistics for the Accountant*

Suppose you are given N observations, X_1, X_2, . . . X_N, as for example, the grades of N students. Rather than enumerate all N observations, it is sometimes convenient to use the mean, median, or mode. The mean, $\bar{X}$, is the average $(= (\Sigma_{i=1}^{N} X_i)/N)$. The median is the value of one observation, X_m, such that approximately half the observations are values that fall above X_m, and half fall below X_m. The mode is the most commonly-observed value in the sample.

Another descriptive statistic is the variance. Computationally, the variance is computed as $[\Sigma_{i=1}^{N} (X_i - \bar{X})^2]/(N - 1)$. This statistic may be considered a measure of dispersion because the more "spread out" the values of X_i are from the mean, the larger the variance. Conversely, if all values of X_i were the same, the variance would be zero.

Suppose you are asked to design a program that would:

a. read a set of data cards, with one number—a student grade—on each card. Each number would be stored in a separate storage location in computer memory. (*Note:* You will have to count these cards to determine the sample size N);

b. find the largest observation;

c. find the smallest observation;

d. compute the mean;

e. compute the variance;

f. print out the results on a printer.

Required

Design a micro program flowchart in sufficient detail to indicate the logic required to perform the above data processing.

APPENDIXES

APPENDIX A

Quantitative Analysis Examples

EXAMPLE 1: LINEAR PROGRAMMING

Problem Situation

Two products of particular importance to the Alan Company are baseballs and golf balls. Both products are packaged in boxes of one dozen balls each, and both are manufactured by the company in conformance with professional specifications. Demand for these two products has been strong and the company can sell as much as it can produce per year. Management has made long-range plans to expand its manufacturing capabilities. For the present, however, the Alan Company must try to meet its sales requirements with present production facilities. Two production areas of particular importance are the winding machines, which manufacture the cores for both baseballs and golf balls, and the inspection stations, where inspectors must examine finished products. Each winding machine can make either three dozen baseball cores or nine dozen golf ball cores per hour. Each inspector can examine either eight dozen finished baseballs or four dozen finished golf balls per hour. Accountants from the accounting subsystem have provided the following cost figures and selling prices for each dozen baseballs and for each dozen golf balls:

	Baseballs	*Golf Balls*
Direct variable costs	$3.20	$2.75
Allocated fixed costs	1.60	1.30
Selling price	6.80	6.45

Problem Requirement

Using linear programming, determine how many dozen baseballs and golf balls the Alan Company should manufacture per hour to make optimum use of its valuable winding-machine time and inspection time.

Problem Solution

Step 1: Define the Decision Variables. In this problem, we wish to decide how many baseballs (in dozens) and how many golf balls (in dozens) to produce per hour. Thus, let

x = the number of baseballs to produce/hour (in dozens)

y = the number of golf balls to produce/hour (in dozens)

Step 2: Define the Alan Company's Objective Function. The Alan Company's objective is to make the most effective use of its resources associated with production. The company can do this by deciding the most desirable number of baseballs and golf balls to produce per hour. The more profitable the mix of baseballs and golf balls the company produces and sells, of course, the more efficient its utilization of resources. For this problem, therefore, the company should try to maximize the contribution margin, M, of its two products, or

$$\text{Maximize } M = \$3.60x + \$3.70y$$

The contribution margin of each product is computed as the difference between the selling price of each product and its variable cost. The contribution margin for baseballs, therefore, is $6.80 minus $3.20, or $3.60. The contribution margin for golf balls is $6.45 minus $2.75, or $3.70. Allocated fixed costs for both products are ignored. This is because fixed costs do not vary

583

with the level of production volume and are thus irrelevant to the production mix decision.

Step 3: Define the Linear Programming Problem's Constraints. For the purposes of formulation, it is perhaps easiest to convert baseball production and golf ball production into fractions of an hour per dozen. The winding machine can wind either three dozen baseballs or nine dozen golf balls per hour. Thus, it will take the winding machine 1/3 hour to wind one dozen baseballs and 1/9 hour to wind one dozen golf balls. Similarly, it takes an inspector one hour to inspect either eight dozen baseballs or four dozen golf balls. Therefore, an inspector will take 1/8 hour to inspect one dozen baseballs and 1/4 hour to inspect one dozen golf balls.

With these conversions made, it is now a straightforward matter to formulate the mathematical production constraints. We have defined the variable x to be the number of baseballs to produce per hour (in dozens) and the variable y to be the number of golf balls to produce per hour (in dozens). Thus, the constraint

$$\frac{1}{3}x + \frac{1}{9}y \leq 1 \quad \text{(winding constraint)}$$

says that the amount of time it takes the winding machine to produce one dozen baseballs (1/3 hour) times the number of baseballs produced (x), plus the amount of time it takes the winding machine to produce one dozen golf balls (1/9 hour) times the number of golf balls produced (y), must be less than or equal to the amount of time allotted, or one hour. We use one hour because we wish to know how many dozen baseballs and how many dozen golf balls to produce for each unit of time. We shall return to this point after we have solved this problem.

We can formulate a constraint for inspection time in a fashion similar to the winding constraint. It will take an inspector 1/8 hour to inspect a dozen baseballs and 1/4 hour to inspect a dozen golf balls. Thus, the constraint

$$\frac{1}{8}x + \frac{1}{4}y \leq 1 \quad \text{(inspection constraint)}$$

states that the time spent inspecting baseballs (1/8x) plus the time spent inspecting golf balls (1/4y) must be less than or equal to the total time allotted, or one hour.

We are almost finished. A final set of constraints that are somewhat intuitive, although not explicitly stated in the problem, are the *nonnegativity conditions:* $x \geq 0$, $y \geq 0$. The constraint $x \geq 0$ states that we shall produce either a positive number of baseballs or nothing: we cannot produce a negative number of baseballs. Similarly, the constraint $y \geq 0$ states that we shall produce either a positive number of golf balls or nothing: we cannot produce a negative number of golf balls.

We have now completed our formulation. Summarizing, we have

Maximize $M = \$3.60x + \$3.70y$

Subject to:

$$\frac{1}{3}x + \frac{1}{9}y \leq 1 \quad \text{(winding constraint)}$$

$$\frac{1}{8}x + \frac{1}{4}y \leq 1 \quad \text{(inspection constraint)}$$

$$x \geq 0 \qquad y \geq 0 \quad \text{(nonnegativity conditions)}$$

Step 4: Graph the Constraints. Linear programming problems involving three or more variables are solved with algebraic techniques such as the *Simplex Method* which are beyond the scope of this book. Linear programming problems of only two variables such as the Alan Company's production problem may be solved with simple graphs. Thus, here, we can use a two-dimensional grid to help us determine the optimal number of baseballs and golf balls to produce for the Alan Company.

First, let us consider the nonnegativity conditions, $x \geq 0$ and $y \geq 0$. These conditions restrict the linear programming problem to the upper, right-hand quadrant of a graph, as illustrated in Figure A-1. Thus, we need not worry about the other three quadrants because in each of the other quadrants, at least one of the two variables is negative.

Next, let us consider the winding constraint. This constraint is the inequality: $1/3x + 1/9y \leq 1$. To plot an inequality like this, first consider this constraint in the equality form: $1/3x + 1/9y = 1$. This is easy to plot. For example, if $x = 0$, then $y = 9$. Alternatively, if $y = 0$, then $x = 3$. We now have two points with which to determine a straight line; that is, the point ($x = 0$, $y = 9$) and the point ($x = 3$, $y = 0$). Connecting these two points, we have the line segment $1/3x + 1/9y = 1$. This line has been plotted in Figure A-1 as shown.

The winding constraint is not an equality but an inequality. As a result, all the points *below* the line segment $1/3x + 1/9y = 1$ will also satisfy the constraint. For example, the point ($x = 2$, $y = 2$) or point P in the figure will also satisfy the constraint because $1/3(2) + 1/9(2)$ equals $8/9$, which is also less than 1. Thus, we observe that an inequality constraint determines an entire area of points, each of which will satisfy the constraint: $1/3x + 1/9y \leq 1$. This area has been shaded in Figure A-1.

Points that satisfy the constraints of a linear programming problem are said to be *feasible*

points, or *feasible solutions*, to a linear programming problem. If the Alan Company had only this one winding constraint, then the area shaded in Figure A-1 would be the set of feasible solutions to the linear programming problem.

The Alan Company, however, has two production constraints. Thus, it remains for us to consider the inspection constraint: $1/8x + 1/4y \leq 1$. This is handled in exactly the same way as the winding constraint and thus need not be detailed here. However, in Figure A-2, we have plotted both the winding constraint and the inspection constraint.

The set of points that simultaneously satisfy both constraints in Figure A-2 has been shaded. This area is called the *feasible region*. Note that only points within the feasible region satisfy both constraints. Points such as point Q or point R in Figure A-2 will only satisfy one of the constraints and are therefore not feasible (i.e., these points are *infeasible*). Clearly, if an optimal solution

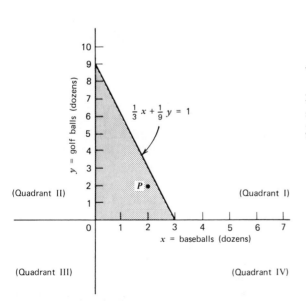

Figure A-1. The set of points (x, y) that satisfies the Alan Company's winding constraint: $1/3x + 1/9y \leq 1$.

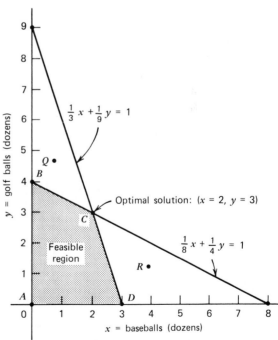

Figure A-2. The feasible region and optimal solution for the Alan Company's production problem.

585

exists to our linear programming problem, we shall find it in this feasible region.

Step 5: Determine an Optimal Solution. The feasible region contains an infinite number of points. But, if an optimal solution to a linear programming problem exists, we know that it will lie in this area. How can we narrow down the possibilities?

The answer to our question lies in the fact that optimal solutions to linear programming problems always are found at the corners of the boundaries of the feasible region. Referring to Figure A-2, we note that there are four such *corner points* for the problem at hand. They have been labeled point A ($x = 0$, $y = 0$), point B ($x = 0$, $y = 4$), point C ($x = 2$, $y = 3$), and point D ($x = 3$, $y = 0$). The coordinates of point C were determined by solving the two simultaneous equations:

$$\frac{1}{3}x + \frac{1}{9}y = 1 \quad \text{and} \quad \frac{1}{8}x + \frac{1}{4}y = 1$$

(i.e., the constraint equations expressed as equalities). These four corner points are also called *extreme points.* By theorem, if an optimal solution exists to a linear programming problem, at least one corner point or extreme point will be optimum.

Since we have only four corner points for this linear programming problem, it is a simple matter to test all four points to find the optimum. The analysis is shown below.

Point	$x =$	$y =$	Objective Function Value: $\$3.60x + \$3.70y =$
A	0	0	$ 0.00
B	0	4	14.80
C	2	3	18.30 ←
D	3	0	10.80

We are trying to maximize the value of the objective function. Therefore, we choose as the optimal solution point C ($x = 2$, $y = 3$) because this point maximizes the contribution margin of the objective function at $18.30 per hour. The values of $x = 2$ and $y = 3$ means that the Alan Company should produce two dozen baseballs

per hour and three dozen golf balls per hour. In so doing, the company will maximize its contribution margin on these two products and thus make optimal use of its winding machine time and its inspection time.

This completes our analysis of the Alan Company's production problem. In reviewing the results, four items should be stressed. The first item is that, for this particular linear programming problem, the optimal solution occurred at point C, which happened to be the corner point or extreme point furthest from the origin. This was coincidence. In other linear programming problems, an alternate point such as point B, point D, or even point A may be optimal. You cannot tell from the geometry of the problem which corner point will be optimum. Rather, you must test each point in the linear programming problem's objective function to determine the corner point that is optimum.

The second item involves the fact that our solution came out to nice whole numbers: $x = 2$ and $y = 3$. This does not always happen. Solutions to linear programming problems often come out in decimals or fractions of units. Thus, a linear programming problem's optimal solution is not wrong if it results in partial units. However, when this happens, the question arises: can you round? The answer depends on the particular linear programming problem under study. Sometimes, rounding will be all right. At other times—especially when rounding up—the results will turn out to violate the constraints or result in suboptimal solutions. Linear programming problems that are required to yield solutions in whole numbers are called *integer programming problems.* This subject is studied at length in advanced operations research courses but is beyond the scope of our analysis here.

The third item involves the fact that our present solution requires the Alan Company to split winding machine time and inspection time between two products each hour. In real-life situations, of course, it would be unlikely that the Alan Company would divide each hour of its winding machine time into time spent winding baseballs and time spent winding golf balls. Such a policy would be disruptive and therefore inefficient. However, our optimal solution to the linear programming problem formulated above is still valid because it tells us the *relative* number of baseballs and golf balls to make on the winding machine as well as to inspect at the company's inspection station. As long as the Alan Company makes baseballs and golf balls in the ratio 2:3 (that is, makes two dozen baseballs for every three dozen golf balls), the company will still use its resources in the most efficient manner. How this production is ultimately performed is immaterial.

Our last item concerns the resource constraints. In the formulation above, it was implicitly assumed that winding machine time and inspection time were valuable, but not severely limited in amount. This assumption enabled us to consider a typical hour of production time as the basic unit of measurement for our productive resources. If the *total* amount of winding machine time and the *total* amount of inspection time had been limited, however, an alternate linear programming formulation would have been necessary to express these facts. In this latter situation, the winding-machine constraint would have stated that the amount of time used on the winding machine must be less than or equal to the total winding machine time available, not one hour. A similar formulation would have been made for the inspection constraint. We did not assume limits on the total amount of winding machine time or inspection time available, and thus proceeded with the type of analysis performed in this problem example.

EXAMPLE 2: PERT WITH STATISTICAL PROBABILITIES

Problem Situation

John Beltcher, management consultant, is preparing to begin the implementation phase of a systems study that his consulting firm is performing for the Big Red Company. There are six activities (A through F) that must be performed to carry out the necessary revisions in Big Red Company's system. Regarding these six implementation activities, John has estimated three possible completion times (i.e., a pessimistic

time estimate, a most-likely time estimate, and an optimistic time estimate) for implementing each activity. Figure A-3 shows John's implementation time estimates as well as any predecessor activities for each of the six activities.

Problem Requirement

The Big Red Company's top management is concerned about how many weeks it will take John Beltcher's consulting firm to implement the systems revisions. Also, Big Red's management is worried about the cost to the company of having its various asset resources working on the systems implementation and therefore not working on regular company operating functions. The top management executives of Big Red Company have approached John Beltcher with two questions: (1) Assuming that Big Red Company's management would like the systems revisions to be implemented within the next 52 weeks, what is the probability of completing the systems implementation activities in 52 weeks or less? (2) Assuming that the estimated cost to the Big Red Company of having its asset resources working on the systems implementation is $1500 per week, and further assuming that the company's top management does not want the total cost of asset resources employed in the systems work to exceed $69,000, what is the probability that the total asset resources cost associated with the systems implementation activities will be $69,000 or less?

Activity	A	B	C	D	E	F
Pessimistic time estimate	24	19	8	30	15	17
Most-likely time estimate	12	10	5	12	9	14
Optimistic time estimate	6	7	2	12	3	11
Predecessor activities	None	None	A	B	C,D	E

Figure A-3. Pessimistic, most-likely, and optimistic estimates of completion times for six activities of a system implementation (all numbers in weeks).

587

Problem Solution

Since three time estimates are given for implementing each of the six activities (see Figure A-3) the first step is to compute a weighted average for each activity. The following formula is commonly used to determine the expected time required to implement activities when three different time estimates are given for each activity: Activity Completion Time $= (a + 4m + b)/6$, where a is the optimistic time estimate, b is the pessimistic time estimate, and m is the most-likely time estimate. The "most-likely time estimate" is closer to what the actual implementation time is estimated to be; therefore, it is given a weight of 4 in the formula, whereas the optimistic and pessimistic time estimates are each given a weight of 1 (the coefficients of a and b in the formula are 1). Using the formula above, the weighted average for the completion time of each activity would be:

the completion of one activity and/or the commencement of a new activity.

To estimate the completion time of the entire project, it is necessary to examine the various paths through the network. The shortest completion time of the entire project is determined by the longest path through the network. This longest path is termed the *critical path* because delays in the completion of these activities will delay the completion time of the project as a whole. For the problem at hand, an examination of the PERT network diagram reveals that the *critical path* is B-D-E-F, a total of 49 weeks $(= 11 + 15 + 9 + 14)$.

Because the activity time estimates on the PERT network diagram are weighted averages, there is a possibility that the actual time required to implement each activity will vary from the expected (i.e., average) implementation time. In statistics, the term *standard deviation* is used to measure relative dispersion (or amount of varia-

Activity	A	B	C	D	E	F
Expected completion time	13 weeks	11 weeks	5 weeks	15 weeks	9 weeks	14 weeks

For example, to compute the weighted average for activity A, we have:

$$\frac{[a + 4m + b]}{6} = \frac{[6 + 4(12) + 24]}{6} = \frac{78}{6} = 13$$

To confirm these values, compute the expected completion times for each of the remaining activities B through F to see if your answers agree with the figures above.

Once the expected completion time for each activity has been determined, a PERT network with these figures can be drawn in a diagram. Such a network for the present example is illustrated in Figure A-4. Note that the "precedence relationships" of the activities, as set forth in Figure A-3, must also be used to determine the sequence of activities in the diagram. Following PERT convention, the lines or "arcs" drawn in Figure A-4 represent activities, and the circles or "nodes" of Figure A-4 represent events—that is,

tion) from an arithmetic average (or mean). Thus, for each of the six implementation activities, a standard deviation can be computed using the following formula:

$$\text{Standard Deviation of an Activity} = \frac{(b - a)}{6}$$

where b is the pessimistic time estimate and a is the optimistic time estimate.

Employing the above formula, the standard deviations for activities A through F would be:

Activity	A	B	C	D	E	F
Standard deviation	3	2	1	3	2	1

Because the estimated project completion time (which is the critical path of 49 weeks) was computed with the use of weighted-average times, there is a possibility that the actual project com-

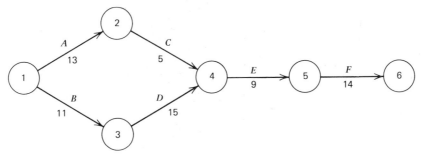

Figure A-4. A PERT network.

pletion time will vary from the expected completion time. Consequently, it is now necessary to determine the standard deviation of the total project completion time from the 49-week weighted-average project completion time. This can be done using the following formula:

Standard deviation of project =

$$\sqrt{\begin{array}{l}\text{Summation of the squares}\\ \text{of all critical path}\\ \text{activities' standard}\\ \text{deviations}\end{array}}$$

The standard deviation of the completion time of the Big Red Company's systems implementation project would thus be:

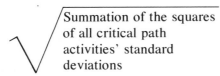

To answer the first question asked by Big Red Company's top management concerning the probability of completing the systems implementation activities in 52 weeks or less, we must compute the number of standard deviations of our *given time* (which is 52 weeks) from our *expected time* (which is 49 weeks—the critical path time estimate) and then associate the result with a probability value. In statistics, the term *z-score* is used to reflect the number of standard deviations of a given time from an expected time and is determined from the following formula

$$z = \frac{\text{(given time } - \text{ expected time)}}{\text{standard deviation of project}}$$

The *z*-score for Big Red Company's systems implementation project would thus be computed as follows:

$$z = \frac{(52 \text{ weeks } - 49 \text{ weeks})}{4.24 \text{ (computed above)}} = .7$$

The .7 *z*-score must now be converted to a probability. This is accomplished by using a statistical table that reflects areas under a normal bell-shaped curve. A table of probabilities associated with *z*-score values under the normal curve is shown in Figure A-5.

From the Figure A-5 table, it can be seen that a *z*-score of .7 gives a probability factor of .75804. Thus, John Beltcher's consulting firm is now able to tell Big Red Company's top management that there is a 76 percent probability (rounded off) that the systems implementation project will be finished in 52 weeks or less.

To answer the second question asked by Big Red Company's top management regarding the probability that the total asset resources cost associated with the systems implementation activities will be $69,000 or less, we must first compute the number of weeks of systems implementation work that will result in an asset resources cost of $69,000. Since *problem requirement 2* assumes a per-week cost of $1500, the total number of systems implementation weeks required to incur a $69,000 asset resources cost is therefore *46* ($69,000 *divided by* $1,500). In our formula for computing a *z*-score, the 46 becomes the *given time* and the *z*-score is computed as

$$z = \frac{(46 \text{ weeks } - 49 \text{ weeks})}{4.24} = -.7$$

Figure A-5

AREAS UNDER THE NORMAL CURVE

z^a	P^b	z^a	P^b	z^a	P^b	z^a	P^b
−3.0	.00135	−1.4	.08076	0.2	.57926	1.8	.96407
−2.9	.00187	−1.3	.09680	0.3	.61791	1.9	.97128
−2.8	.00256	−1.2	.11507	0.4	.65542	2.0	.97725
−2.7	.00347	−1.1	.13567	0.5	.69146	2.1	.98214
−2.6	.00466	−1.0	.15866	0.6	.72575	2.2	.98610
−2.5	.00621	−0.9	.18406	0.7	.75804	2.3	.98928
−2.4	.00820	−0.8	.21186	0.8	.78814	2.4	.99180
−2.3	.01072	−0.7	.24196	0.9	.81594	2.5	.99379
−2.2	.01390	−0.6	.27425	1.0	.84134	2.6	.99534
−2.1	.01786	−0.5	.30854	1.1	.86433	2.7	.99653
−2.0	.02275	−0.4	.34458	1.2	.88493	2.8	.99744
−1.9	.02872	−0.3	.38209	1.3	.90320	2.9	.99813
−1.8	.03593	−0.2	.42074	1.4	.91924	3.0	.99865
−1.7	.04457	−0.1	.46017	1.5	.93319		
−1.6	.05480	0.0	.50000	1.6	.94520		
−1.5	.06681	0.1	.53983	1.7	.95543		

[a] z is the number of standard deviations from the mean.

[b] P is the probability that the actual value of the variable will be z or less.

Looking up the value of −.7 in Figure A-5, we obtain a probability factor of .24196. Thus, John Beltcher's consulting firm is now able to tell Big Red Company's top management that there is a 24 percent probability (rounded off) that the total asset resources cost associated with the systems implementation project will be $69,000 or less.

APPENDIX B

Present Value Tables and Illustrations of Present Value Computational Analysis

PRESENT VALUE TABLES

Figure B-1

PRESENT VALUE OF $1

Years	5%	6%	8%	10%	12%	14%	15%	16%	18%	20%	22%	24%	25%
1	0.952	0.943	0.926	0.909	0.893	0.877	0.870	0.862	0.847	0.833	0.820	0.806	0.800
2	0.907	0.890	0.857	0.826	0.797	0.769	0.756	0.743	0.718	0.694	0.672	0.650	0.640
3	0.864	0.840	0.794	0.751	0.712	0.675	0.658	0.641	0.609	0.579	0.551	0.524	0.512
4	0.823	0.792	0.735	0.683	0.636	0.592	0.572	0.552	0.516	0.482	0.451	0.423	0.410
5	0.784	0.747	0.681	0.621	0.567	0.519	0.497	0.476	0.437	0.402	0.370	0.341	0.328
6	0.746	0.705	0.630	0.564	0.507	0.456	0.432	0.410	0.370	0.335	0.303	0.275	0.262
7	0.711	0.665	0.583	0.513	0.452	0.400	0.376	0.354	0.314	0.279	0.249	0.222	0.210
8	0.677	0.627	0.540	0.467	0.404	0.351	0.327	0.305	0.266	0.233	0.204	0.179	0.168
9	0.645	0.592	0.500	0.424	0.361	0.308	0.284	0.263	0.225	0.194	0.167	0.144	0.134
10	0.614	0.558	0.463	0.386	0.322	0.270	0.247	0.227	0.191	0.162	0.137	0.116	0.107
11	0.585	0.527	0.429	0.350	0.287	0.237	0.215	0.195	0.162	0.135	0.112	0.094	0.086
12	0.557	0.497	0.397	0.319	0.257	0.208	0.187	0.168	0.137	0.112	0.092	0.076	0.069
13	0.530	0.469	0.368	0.290	0.229	0.182	0.163	0.145	0.116	0.093	0.075	0.061	0.055
14	0.505	0.442	0.340	0.263	0.205	0.160	0.141	0.125	0.099	0.078	0.062	0.049	0.044
15	0.481	0.417	0.315	0.239	0.183	0.140	0.123	0.108	0.084	0.065	0.051	0.040	0.035
16	0.458	0.394	0.292	0.218	0.163	0.123	0.107	0.093	0.071	0.054	0.042	0.032	0.028
17	0.436	0.371	0.270	0.198	0.146	0.108	0.093	0.080	0.060	0.045	0.034	0.026	0.023
18	0.416	0.350	0.250	0.180	0.130	0.095	0.081	0.069	0.051	0.038	0.028	0.021	0.018
19	0.396	0.331	0.232	0.164	0.116	0.083	0.070	0.060	0.043	0.031	0.023	0.017	0.014
20	0.377	0.312	0.215	0.149	0.104	0.073	0.061	0.051	0.037	0.026	0.019	0.014	0.012

Figure B-2

PRESENT VALUE OF $1 RECEIVED ANNUALLY FOR N YEARS

Years (N)	5%	6%	8%	10%	12%	14%	15%	16%	18%	20%	22%	24%	25%
1	0.952	0.943	0.926	0.909	0.893	0.877	0.870	0.862	0.847	0.833	0.820	0.806	0.800
2	1.859	1.833	1.783	1.736	1.690	1.647	1.626	1.605	1.566	1.528	1.492	1.457	1.440
3	2.723	2.673	2.577	2.487	2.402	2.322	2.283	2.246	2.174	2.106	2.042	1.981	1.952
4	3.546	3.465	3.312	3.169	3.037	2.914	2.855	2.798	2.690	2.589	2.494	2.404	2.362
5	4.330	4.212	3.993	3.791	3.605	3.433	3.352	3.274	3.127	2.991	2.864	2.745	2.689
6	5.076	4.917	4.623	4.355	4.111	3.889	3.784	3.685	3.498	3.326	3.167	3.020	2.951
7	5.786	5.582	5.206	4.868	4.564	4.288	4.160	4.039	3.812	3.605	3.416	3.242	3.161
8	6.463	6.210	5.747	5.335	4.968	4.639	4.487	4.344	4.078	3.837	3.619	3.421	3.329
9	7.108	6.802	6.247	5.759	5.328	4.946	4.772	4.607	4.303	4.031	3.786	3.566	3.463
10	7.722	7.360	6.710	6.145	5.650	5.216	5.019	4.833	4.494	4.192	3.923	3.682	3.571
11	8.306	7.887	7.139	6.495	5.937	5.453	5.234	5.029	4.656	4.327	4.035	3.776	3.656
12	8.863	8.384	7.536	6.814	6.194	5.660	5.421	5.197	4.793	4.439	4.127	3.851	3.725
13	9.394	8.853	7.904	7.103	6.424	5.842	5.583	5.342	4.910	4.533	4.203	3.912	3.780
14	9.899	9.295	8.244	7.367	6.628	6.002	5.724	5.468	5.008	4.611	4.265	3.962	3.824
15	10.380	9.712	8.559	7.606	6.811	6.142	5.847	5.575	5.092	4.675	4.315	4.001	3.859
16	10.838	10.106	8.851	7.824	6.974	6.265	5.954	5.669	5.162	4.730	4.357	4.033	3.887
17	11.274	10.477	9.122	8.022	7.120	6.373	6.047	5.749	5.222	4.775	4.391	4.059	3.910
18	11.690	10.828	9.372	8.201	7.250	6.467	6.128	5.818	5.273	4.812	4.419	4.080	3.928
19	12.085	11.158	9.604	8.365	7.366	6.550	6.198	5.877	5.316	4.844	4.442	4.097	3.942
20	12.462	11.470	9.818	8.514	7.469	6.623	6.259	5.929	5.353	4.870	4.460	4.110	3.954

PRESENT VALUE COMPUTATIONAL EXAMPLES

To illustrate the computation of present value, suppose you wanted to invest just enough money in the bank (which pays 6 percent annual interest) at the beginning of the year to enable you to withdraw $1 (after interest) at year's end. How much money must you therefore invest? To solve this problem, let X be the (unknown) investment amount and r be the annual interest rate (which is based upon the compounding of interest). The following computation is made.

$$\text{Investment} + \text{Interest} = \$X + \$X(r) = \$X(1 + r)$$

$$\$1 = \$X(1 + .06)$$
$$\$1 = \$X(1.06), \text{ or}$$

$$\$X = \frac{\$1}{(1.06)} = \underline{\underline{\$.943}}$$

Thus, you should invest roughly 94 cents in the bank at the beginning of the year to permit you to withdraw $1 at the end of the year. The present value of $1 received one year hence (using a 6 percent interest rate) is therefore $.943.

A similar analysis can be made if you wanted to find that investment amount that would enable you to withdraw $1 two years hence. Again, let X be the unknown investment amount and r the annual interest rate (which is still assumed to be 6 percent). You already know that the total amount of the investment plus interest at the end of one year would be $X(1 + r)$. The total amount of investment plus interest at the end of the second year would therefore be this amount again multiplied by $(1 + r)$, or $X(1 + r)^2$. Thus, to solve for the investment amount required at the beginning of the first year, you have

$$\$1 = \$X(1 + r)^2$$
$$\$1 = \$X(1.06)^2, \text{ or}$$

$$\$X = \frac{\$1}{(1.06)^2} = \underline{\underline{\$.890}}$$

Therefore, if you were to invest 89 cents in the bank (which pays 6 percent annual interest) at the beginning of year one, then, by the end of the second year, you would have accumulated sufficient interest on this investment to enable you to withdraw a total of $1. The present value of $1 received two years hence (using a 6 percent interest rate) is thus $.89.

From the previous two examples, it should be clear that the computation of a present value is dependent upon (1) the rate of interest r, and (2) the number of years between making the investment and ultimate repayment. For a one-year investment, the present value of $1 was computed from the term $\$1/(1 + r)^1$, and for a two-year investment, the present value of $1 was computed from the term $\$1/(1 + r)^2$. Similarly, the present value of $1 in a three-year investment would be computed from the term $\$1/(1 + r)^3$, in a four-year investment, from the term $\$1/(1 + r)^4$, and, in an n-year investment, from the term $\$1/(1 + r)^n$. These values are easily computed, but because it is inefficient to recompute them every time you wish to solve a new problem, a convenient table of such terms, called *discount factors,* may be found in Figure B-1 of this appendix for various interest rates and various years of investment. Note that we have already derived two entries in the figure's table—the first two numbers under the 6 percent column: .943 and .890. Note also that the numbers under each column *diminish* as you go down the column. This reflects the fact that the longer you must wait for the repayment of an investment at any interest rate, the less that investment return (of $1) is worth to you today.

A slightly different problem often found in investment analysis is the computation of the present value of a uniform series of payments (called an *annuity*) spread out over a number of years. For example, suppose you wished to invest enough money in the bank (paying 6 percent annual interest) to enable you to withdraw $1 at the end of the first year, and a second dollar at the end of the second year. How much money would you have to invest in the bank at the beginning of the first year?

Actually, this problem has already been almost solved by you. You know that at 6 percent annual interest, the present value of $1 paid a year hence is $.943 and the present value of $1 paid two years hence is $.890. Therefore, the present value of this uniform series of dollar payments received at the end of two consecutive years must be the sum of these, or $1.833 ($.943 + $.890). You would thus have to invest approximately $1.83 in the bank at the beginning of the first year. Similarly, if you wanted to compute the present value of a uniform series of dollar payments over three consecutive years at 6 percent annual compound interest, you would add the discount factors from Figure B-1 for years one, two, and three, obtaining a present value of $2.673 ($.943 + $.890 + $.840).

Because the computation of the present value of a uniform series of annual dollar payments is as mechanical as the computation of a single payment, it is convenient to create another table similar to Figure B-1. This is accomplished in Figure B-2. Thus, for example, at 6 percent annual interest, the first present value number in the table of Figure B-2 is the same $.943 as in Figure B-1, but the present value for two years is our previously-computed $1.833 and the present value for three years is our previously computed $2.673. At different annual interest rates, other present values of uniform $1 payments are easily found in similar fashion.

Although these present-value tables are based upon $1 payments, it is quite easy to use the $1 discount factors when dealing with problems involving payments of any dollar magnitude. Once you know the appropriate $1 discount factor, it is a simple matter of multiplying this discount factor by the specific dollar magnitude involved. For example, if the bank pays 8 percent annual interest and you wanted to withdraw $1000 at the end of one year, you would have to invest $926 ($.926 from Figure B-1 × $1000) in the bank at the beginning of the year.

APPENDIX C

Examples of Computer Programs Written in COBOL, BASIC, and FORTRAN

This appendix illustrates the use of third-level programming languages to write computer programs. For illustration we have chosen the sales-ticket problem as discussed in the first part of Chapter 19. In this problem, sales-ticket information is punched into computer cards, and the computer—following the instructions of a computer program—is used to prepare a sales report. The sales-ticket information, as it might be punched on a computer card, is illustrated in Figure C-1. The output document, or sales report, would contain the account number for each sales ticket (i.e., each computer card), the sales amount, the sales tax, and the total billed amount. Not including the headings, the output might appear as follows:

Account Number	Sales Amount	Tax	Total
12345	$200.00	$6.00	$206.00

The processing logic for this problem has already been discussed in Chapter 19. First, a macro program flowchart is developed to outline the general structure of the problem's processing requirements. Then a more detailed micro program flowchart is developed to assist the programmer in the actual coding effort. This latter flowchart may be found in Figure 19-4, and is repeated here as Figure C-2. In the paragraphs that follow, we examine how this processing might be accomplished with COBOL, BASIC, and FOR-TRAN computer programs.

THE SALES-TICKET PROBLEM IN COBOL*

The COBOL computer program for the sales-ticket problem is illustrated in Figure C-3. In this program, several additional instructions would be necessary to actually execute this program on a computer. Because these instructions are not essential to a basic understanding of the nature of COBOL as a programming language, they have been omitted.

It may be seen that the overall program is divided into the identification, environment, data, and procedure divisions, captions for which may be seen on lines 01, 03, 06, and 19 of Figure C-3. The identification division is the shortest, serving only to give the program a name.

The other three divisions are closely related. The environment division tells the computer which input and output units are to be used in this data processing, and the file of data to be associated with each. The data division sets out space in the computer's memory as required by the data records and items, and indicates the relationship existing between items of data. Finally, the procedure division contains the actual commands causing the computer to read, process, and write data. These three divisions merit a more careful examination than is required by the identification division.

*The COBOL material in Appendix C has been used with the permission of Fritz McCameron, *COBOL Logic and Programming,* rev. ed. (Homewood, Ill.: Richard D. Irwin, 1970), pp. 13–15. Copyright © by Richard D. Irwin, Inc.

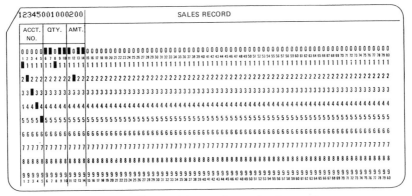

Figure C-1. The card format for a sales transaction.

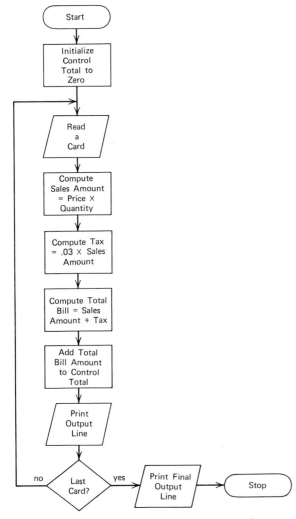

Figure C-2. A micro flowchart for processing sales transactions.

Environment Division

On line 04 in Figure C-3 may be seen a major component of the environment division. Here a command instructs the computer to "SELECT SALES-FILE, ASSIGN TØ 'CARDIN' UTILITY." This informs the computer that a file, named SALES-FILE, is to be processed through a certain data input unit, called CARDIN. This problem assumes CARDIN to be the name assigned to the card reader.

A similar command assigns the file called EXTENDED-SALES-FILE to the computer unit named PRINTØUT, which is assumed to be a printer unit. Thus, through the environment division, the computer is informed which input-output units are to be used and the files associated with each.

Data Division

This program segment, in turn, tells the computer the appearance of each of the files mentioned above. A code symbol, FD, to the left of the associated name tells the computer that a file is being named. An example of this may be seen on line 07 of Figure C-3, where the SALES-FILE is mentioned.

The code symbol 01 on line 08 of the same figure, preceding the name SALES-TICKET, indicates to the computer that within the SALES-FILE are to be found records called SALES-TICKET. This relationship is implied by the symbols and the order in which the names are written.

595

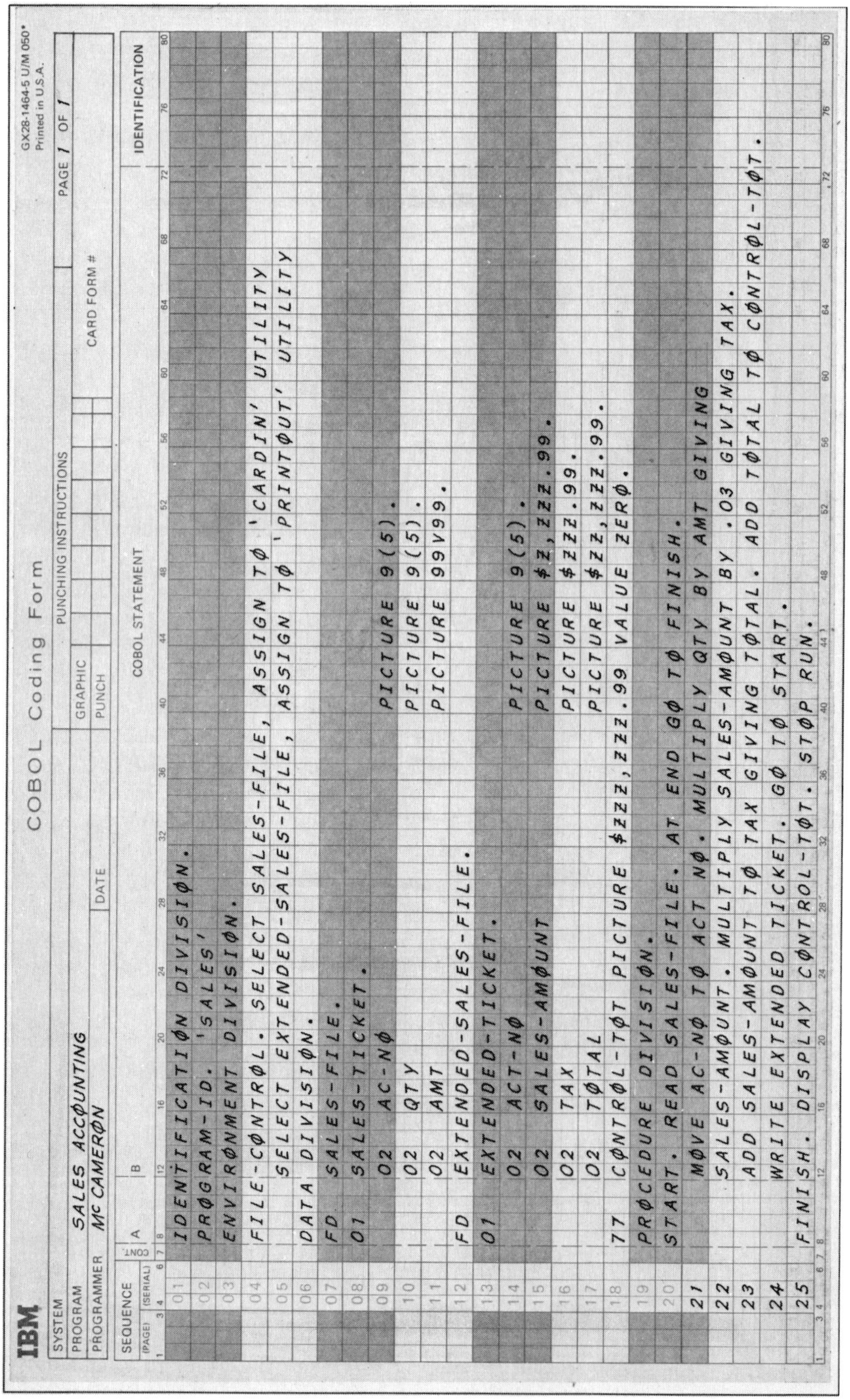

IBM COBOL Coding Form

GX28-1464-5 U/M 050* Printed in U.S.A.

SYSTEM | PROGRAM: SALES ACCØUNTING | PROGRAMMER: Mc CAMERØN | DATE | PUNCHING INSTRUCTIONS: GRAPHIC, PUNCH | CARD FORM # | PAGE 1 OF 1

SEQUENCE (PAGE) (SERIAL) | CONT. | A | B | COBOL STATEMENT | IDENTIFICATION

```
01  IDENTIFICATIØN DIVISIØN.
02  PRØGRAM-ID. 'SALES'.
03  ENVIRØNMENT DIVISIØN.
04  FILE-CØNTRØL. SELECT SALES-FILE, ASSIGN TØ 'CARDIN' UTILITY
05      SELECT EXTENDED-SALES-FILE, ASSIGN TØ 'PRINTØUT' UTILITY
06  DATA DIVISIØN.
07  FD  SALES-FILE.
08  01  SALES-TICKET.
09      02  AC-NØ                       PICTURE 9(5).
10      02  QTY                         PICTURE 9(5).
11      02  AMT                         PICTURE 99V99.
12  FD  EXTENDED-SALES-FILE.
13  01  EXTENDED-TICKET.
14      02  ACT-NØ                      PICTURE 9(5).
15      02  SALES-AMØUNT                PICTURE $Z,ZZZ.99.
16      02  TAX                         PICTURE $ZZZ.99.
17      02  TØTAL                       PICTURE $ZZ,ZZZ.99.
18  77  CØNTRØL-TØT PICTURE $ZZZ,ZZZ.99 VALUE ZERØ.
19  PRØCEDURE DIVISIØN.
20  START. READ SALES-FILE, AT END GØ TØ FINISH.
21      MØVE AC-NØ TØ ACT NØ. MULTIPLY QTY BY AMT GIVING
22      SALES-AMØUNT. MULTIPLY SALES-AMØUNT BY .03 GIVING TAX.
23      ADD SALES-AMØUNT TØ TAX GIVING TØTAL. ADD TØTAL TØ CØNTRØL-TØT.
24      WRITE EXTENDED TICKET. GØ TØ START.
25  FINISH. DISPLAY CØNTRØL-TØT. STØP RUN.
```

Figure C-3. The sales-ticket problem as it might be coded in COBOL on preprinted coding sheets.

In turn, 02 symbols on lines 09 through 11 indicate that data items named as shown exist within the record called SALES-TICKET. Each data name is followed by a PICTURE clause, which shows the computer how many characters of data exist in each field. Within the PICTURE clauses, a 9 indicates a data position, and a V tells the computer to assume the existence of a decimal point. Other symbols are also seen in use. The exact nature of these is not important to our discussion.

On line 18 an item named CØNTRØL-TØT may be seen to have the symbol 77. This indicates that this bit of data does not belong to a record or file, but instead exists apart from all other data elements.

Procedure Division

This is divided into two "paragraphs," named START and FINISH. In the first, to be seen on line 20 of Figure C-3, may be seen the command, "READ SALES-FILE, AT END GØ TØ FINISH." This instructs the computer to read a record from the named file. Finally, when no more records are available, the computer is to go to the FINISH paragraph for its remaining instructions.

Other commands in the START paragraph are in a form so similar to regular clerical instructions that they may be understood without elaborate explanation. It should be noted that all fields in the output record are filled with data. The contents of data item AC-NØ are moved to data item ACT-NØ. Other fields are filled by computations. CØNTRØL-TØT, used to accumulate all billed amounts, is increased by the amount of this billing. The output record is written, and the computer is instructed to return to START and repeat the process.

Eventually, the FINISH paragraph will be executed. Here the total of all billed sales is displayed for control purposes, and the computer is told to stop operations by the final command, "STØP RUN."

This short COBOL program and the equally abbreviated explanation are by no means complete. Several steps essential to an operative program have been omitted in the interest of clarity. However, one may observe from this the kinds of information furnished the computer by the program, and the general flow of data as they come to the machine through an input device, are manipulated and prepared for output, and are finally written through some other unit.

THE SALES-TICKET PROBLEM IN BASIC

Figure C-4 illustrates the coding for our sales-ticket problem if it were written in BASIC. The card file, called SALES, is identified in line 10 of the coding. Line 30 initializes the control variable, C, to zero.

The processing routine itself may be found in lines 40 through 90 in Figure C-4. Line 40, for example, accesses a single card, and uses the variable A to store the account number, the variable "Q" to store the quantity sold and the variable P to store the sales price. Line 50 computes the sales amount S as the product of price times quantity. The sales tax, which is equal to 3 percent of the sales price, is computed as T in line 60 of the coding. Line 70 computes the total billed amount B as the sum of the sales amount plus the tax. Line 80 adds this amount to the running control total of all sales-ticket bills calculated for the program. Finally, in line 90, the sales information, including the account number, the sales amount, the sales tax, and the total bill amount, is printed as a single line on the sales report.

Once the output for a single card has been printed, computer control is transferred back to the beginning of the processing cycle (i.e., back to instruction 40) by the "GO TO" instruction in line 100 of the code. At this stage, a new card will be accessed and the processing repeated. This looping through the program will continue until all sales records have been accessed. At the end of the card file, computer control will be transferred to line 110. Here the control total will be printed. The "END" instruction, which would be encountered next in the instruction stream, informs the computer that the processing has been completed. At this point, the computer will stop.

As compared with the preceding COBOL pro-

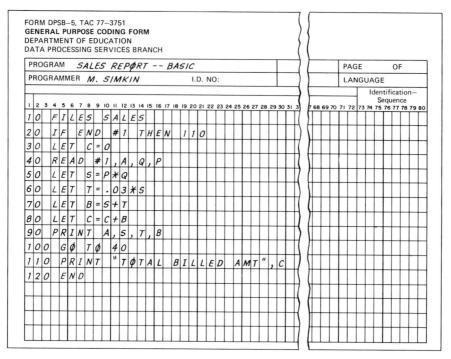

Figure C-4. The sales-ticket problem as it might be coded in BASIC on preprinted coding sheets.

gram, the BASIC program is much shorter. In particular, the COBOL program required 25 instructions of code whereas the BASIC program required only 12. Note, however, that the COBOL program uses terms and phrases that more closely resemble English usage and for this reason, the COBOL program would probably be easier for an individual untrained in computer programming to follow. Like the COBOL program, however, it is important to bear in mind that this BASIC program has been simplified for presentation. Yet additional programming instructions would actually be required to run this program on a computer.

THE SALES-TICKET PROBLEM IN FORTRAN

Figure C-5 illustrates the computer program for our sales-ticket problem if this program were written in FORTRAN. Statement numbers, which appear to the left of each instruction in the preceding BASIC program, are required only for certain instructions in FORTRAN. Where possi-

ble, therefore, these numbers have been omitted from the coding in Figure C-5. Where statement numbers do appear, FORTRAN usually requires that they appear right-justified in columns 1–5 of the program card. Column 6 of the FORTRAN program card is reserved for special use. Thus, spacing restrictions dictate that all FORTRAN instructions appear in column 7 onward.

The first FORTRAN instruction in Figure C-5 is the initialization task in which the control-total variable, CTØTAL, is set to zero. FORTRAN enables the programmer to use up to six characters to name a variable. (In contrast, BASIC allows only a single letter, or a single letter plus a single number, to name a variable.) It would have been possible for the FORTRAN programmer to name the control variable "C" as was done for the BASIC program. Because it is in the programmer's interest to be as explicit as possible when naming variables, the expression "CTØTAL" is preferable to "C" as a name for the control-total variable.

Statement 5 in the FORTRAN program is a

598

GENERAL PURPOSE CODING FORM

PROGRAM	*SALES REPØRT -- FØRTRAN*		PMS CODE	PUNCHING	GRAPHIC
PROGRAMMER	*M. SIMKIN*	I.D. NO:	DATE *10 - 15 - 78*	INSTRUCTIONS	PUNCH

```
        CTØTAL=0
   5    READ(5,10,END=40)NUMACT,NUMQTY,PRICE
  10    FØRMAT(I5,I5,F4.2)
        SLSAMT=PRICE*NUMQTY
        TAX=.03*SLSAMT
        BILAMT=SLSAMT+TAX
        CTØTAL=CTØTAL+BILAMT
        WRITE(6,20)NUMACT,SLSAMT,TAX,BILAMT
  20    FØRMAT("1",5X,I5,5X,F7.2,5X,F6.2,5X,F8.2)
        GØ TØ 5
  40    WRITE(6,50)CTØTAL
  50    FØRMAT("1",F10.2)
        STØP
        END
```

Figure C-5. The sales-ticket problem as it might be coded in FORTRAN on preprinted coding sheets.

READ instruction that accesses the information on a computer card. The FORTRAN variables initialized by this instruction are the account-number variable NUMACT, the quantity variable NUMQTY, and the price variable PRICE. The numbers in parentheses in this instruction identify the input device as the card reader (i.e., device #5) and also reference FORMAT instruction (statement number 10). The FORMAT statement describes how the account number, quantity, and price information will appear on the input card. In this example, the FORMAT instruction describes a five-digit integer field for account number (i.e., "I5" in the FORMAT instruction), a five-digit integer field for quantity ("I5" again), and a four-digit floating point (or decimal) field for price, with two digits set aside for the cents portion of the number (i.e., F4.2). Thus, for the data of the input card shown in Figure C-1, the FORMAT instruction interprets the

data numbers 12345001000200 appearing in columns 1 through 14 of the card as:

account number:	12345
quantity:	100
price:	$2.00

The FORTRAN instructions following the READ and FORMAT instructions discussed above perform the actual data processing. First, the sales amount SLSAMT is computed as the product of price times quantity. Next, the sales tax TAX is computed as 3 percent of the sales amount. Next, the billing amount BILAMT is computed as the sum of the sales amount plus the sales tax. Finally, the billing amount for the current transaction is added to the control total.

When the computer reaches this point in the processing, the information for one sales transaction has been readied for printing on the sales

599

report. The WRITE instruction performs this task. The number "6" in the WRITE instruction identifies the printer (device #6), and the number "20" in this instruction references the sequential FORMAT statement. The information to be printed includes the account number, the sales amount, the sales tax, and the billing amount, as identified by the variables listed in the right-hand portion of the WRITE instruction.

The FORMAT instruction in statement 30 describes how the output is to appear on the printed page. The integer (I) and floating-point (F) fields correspond to the output list of the WRITE instruction just above the FORMAT instruction. The interpretation of the complete FORMAT instruction is as follows:

the last card has been processed, the "END=40" portion of the READ instruction will automatically transfer computer control to the "WRITE (6,50)CTØTAL" instruction near the bottom of Figure C-5. This final WRITE instruction will print the control total. The interpretation of the WRITE instruction and the referenced FORMAT instruction is analogous to the discussion above. Note however, that 10 spaces, as compared with 7 or 8 spaces, have been reserved for the control total amount on the output page (see the "F10.2" in the FORMAT instruction). This is to allow enough spaces on the output page to accommodate a potentially large number.

The next sequential instruction is the STOP instruction. This instruction will halt execution, as

Field Description	Corresponding Variable	Meaning
"1"	none	carriage-control code: tells the printer to advance one line
5X	none	skip 5 spaces to the right (start counting from left margin)
I5	NUMACT	reserve 5 spaces for integer account number
5X	none	skip 5 spaces
F7.2	SLSAMT	reserve 7 spaces for the (decimal) sales amount. Output is: XXXX.XX
5X	none	skip 5 spaces
F8.2	BILAMT	reserve 8 spaces for the (decimal) bill amount. Output is: XXXXX.XX

The FORTRAN instructions between (and including) the READ instruction and the WRITE instruction form the basis of one complete processing cycle. The "GO TO 5" instruction transfers computer control back to the READ instruction, where a new card may be accessed and the processing cycle begun anew. This looping will continue until all cards have been read. After desired, when the processing has been completed. Note that, in contrast to BASIC, which only required an "END" instruction to complete the program, the FORTRAN program requires both a "STOP" instruction and an "END" instruction. Do not ponder over this too much—that is just the way it is.

APPENDIX D

The Binary Number System

HOW THE BINARY NUMBER SYSTEM WORKS

Although the arabic number system is used throughout the world, it is not the number system that is used by a computer. This is because a decimal system requires 10 symbols (i.e., the numbers 0, 1, 2, 3, 4, 5, 6, 7, 8, 9), whereas a computer works with only two symbols, 0 and 1, which are the basis of the binary system. The reason for this is tied to the circuitry of a computer's central processing system. The memory of the CPU uses bits that have only two settings—"on" or "off." With only two possible values for each bit in computer memory, it is logical that the computer should use a binary numbering system which only uses two symbols. Thus, the "on" bit can be used for the (binary) number "1" and the same bit, when "off," can be used to represent the (binary) number "0."

To understand how the binary number system works, it is useful to review first the mechanics of the decimal system. Consider, for example, the decimal number 253. We know to read this "two hundred fifty three" because there is a "2" in the hundredths place, a "5" in the tens place, and a "3" in the units place. So actually, the decimal number 253 is really the sum:

$$
\begin{aligned}
& 2 \times (10)^2 = 2 \times 100 = 200 \\
+ \; & 5 \times (10)^1 = 5 \times 10 \;\;= \;\; 50 \\
+ \; & 3 \times (10)^0 = 3 \times 1 \;\;\;\; = \;\;\;\; \underline{3} \\
& = \underline{\underline{253}}
\end{aligned}
$$

Another way of viewing the value 253 is by formally recognizing the "place-holding" orientation of our decimal system. The same idea as that above may be found in the schematic

number	2	5	3
power of 10	$(10)^2$	$(10)^1$	$(10)^0$

which says that the elements in our number 253 each multiplies a different power of 10, and that it is the particular position of each element in this number that determines this power. The fact that we implicitly use powers of 10 in our numbering system is why it is said that the decimal number system is "to the base 10."

The binary number system is just like the decimal number system, except that it uses powers to the base 2—that is, powers of 2. Consider the *binary* number 11011. This binary value is really:

number	1	1	0	1	1
power of 2	$(2)^4$	$(2)^3$	$(2)^2$	$(2)^1$	$(2)^0$

Using our multiplication approach developed for the previous example of the decimal number 253, we therefore have the decimal number 27, as follows:

$$
\begin{aligned}
& 1 \times (2)^4 = 1 \times 16 = 16 \\
+ \; & 1 \times (2)^3 = 1 \times \;\; 8 = \;\; 8 \\
+ \; & 0 \times (2)^2 = 0 \times \;\; 4 = \;\; 0 \\
+ \; & 1 \times (2)^1 = 1 \times \;\; 2 = \;\; 2 \\
+ \; & 1 \times (2)^0 = 1 \times \;\; 1 = \;\; \underline{1} \\
& = \underline{\underline{27}}
\end{aligned}
$$

Once you stare at this for a while, the analogy between decimal notation and binary notation is quite straightforward. It is just that the decimal system uses ascending powers of 10 (reading the number from right to left), whereas the binary number system uses ascending powers of 2. If this seems clear to you, see if you can verify that the decimal equivalent of the binary number 11111 is 31.

A computer user would have quite a chore expressing all decimal numbers in their binary equivalents before the decimal-numbered data could be fed into a computer. Fortunately, the conversion of numbers from decimal to binary is performed automatically by the computer at the time that the (decimal) data are read into the machine—for example, from a card reader. It should be kept in mind that a computer "thinks" in binary—not in decimals like the rest of us mortals. Moreover, every time a computation is performed by a computer and is printed on a piece of paper, the binary "answer" must be transformed back into decimal format for our benefit. Of course this means extra work for the computer, but the incredible speeds at which computers operate today make the burden of such extra tasks negligible.

Because data are stored in a binary form within a computer's memory, the data are also manipulated in binary arithmetic when data processing is required. This means that all additions, subtractions, multiplications, divisions, exponentiations, as well as certain other tasks, are computed using electronic circuitry functioning with binary-arithmetic logic. The mechanics of such manipulation are quite interesting (at least to some people), but need not concern us here. Sometimes, however, an audit trail is complicated enough to require the verification of certain data as they are stored in binary form within the CPU or on magnetic tape. For this reason, an understanding of binary representation is important.

When the binary-numbered contents of computer storage are to be observed, it is necessary to take a picture, or "dump," of such storage and have it printed on a page. Because there are thousands upon thousands of bits in computer memory, such dumps usually are limited to certain portions of computer storage. To save space on the printer sheet, moreover, EDP personnel have taken to using two other types of numbering systems to represent binary numbers in a more compact format. These are the *octal* and *hexadecimal* number systems. As their names imply, the octal system is a number system to the base 8, whereas the hexadecimal system is a number system to the base 16. Programmers and systems analysts who use the hexadecimal system require 16 different symbols to represent the decimal numbers 0, 1, 2, . . . 14, 15. For convenience, the letters of the alphabet are used. Thus, the symbols for these decimal numbers are 0, 1, 2, 3, 4, 5, 6, 7, 8, 9, A, B, C, D, E, and F. Figure D-1 illustrates the symbols for the first 20 decimal numbers in binary, octal, and hexadecimal.

To verify the values in the table, it is necessary to use the appropriate base when computing decimal equivalencies. Thus, the number "11" in binary is really $1x(2)^1 + 1x(2)^0 = 2 + 1 = 3$ in decimal. However, the same number "11" written in octal is really $1x(8)^1 + 1x(8)^0 = 8 + 1 = 9$ in decimal. Finally, that same number "11" in hexadecimal is really $1x(16)^1 + 1x(16)^0 = 16 + 1 = 17$ in decimal. As you can see, therefore, the number "11" is ambiguous unless we know whether the number is written in binary, octal, hexadecimal, or our familiar decimal notation.

Figure D-1

THE FIRST 20 DECIMAL NUMBERS AS THEY WOULD BE CODED IN BINARY, OCTAL, AND HEXADECIMAL NOTATION

Decimal (Base 10)	Binary (Base 2)	Octal (Base 8)	Hexadecimal (Base 16)
1	00001	1	1
2	00010	2	2
3	00011	3	3
4	00100	4	4
5	00101	5	5
6	00110	6	6
7	00111	7	7
8	01000	10	8
9	01001	11	9
10	01010	12	A
11	01011	13	B
12	01100	14	C
13	01101	15	D
14	01110	16	E
15	01111	17	F
16	10000	20	10
17	10001	21	11
18	10010	22	12
19	10011	23	13
20	10100	24	14

The reason that programmers use octal or hexadecimal notation when dumping CPU memories should be clear when examining the space-saving characteristics of these notations as compared with binary notation in Figure D-1. For example, the binary number 10100 would require 5 print positions on an output page, whereas the same number written in hexadecimal ("14" in Figure D-1) would require only two print positions. The reduction in print positions from five to two represents a 60 percent reduction in space requirements—a considerable savings when multiplied by the many thousands of bits in the CPU memory.

APPENDIX E

Processing Accounts Receivable Sales Transactions Using Punched-Card Data Processing

It is possible to implement an entire accounting information system with nothing more than punched cards and punched-card processing equipment. Figure E-1, for example, illustrates the data flow for an accounts receivable processing system. As illustrated in this figure, customer sales transactions are initially written on sales invoices, which then serve as source documents for keypunching (box A). Figure E-2 is a representative card format. A special card verifier (box B) is next utilized to check the accuracy of the keypunch work, using the original sales document to rekey the data. Errors in the sales cards are returned to the initial keypunching phase for correction. The sales-invoice documents may then be collected and placed in a sales file (e.g., a standard office filing cabinet) where they would be maintained for reference purposes.

Once the sales transactions have been keypunched and verified, they are next grouped together (i.e., "batched") and input to a card sorter for arrangement by customer account number (box C). The output from the sort step is therefore a set of sales cards sequenced in ascending numeric order according to the customer account number. For any particular accounting-period processing "run," some of the firm's credit customers are likely to have many transaction cards, whereas other credit customers may have no transactions (and thus no transaction cards) during the period.

Once the sales cards have been sorted, they are coordinated with the company's accounts receivable "master file" cards. These master file cards are also punched cards, but contain summary information about each customer's account—for example, account number, cus-

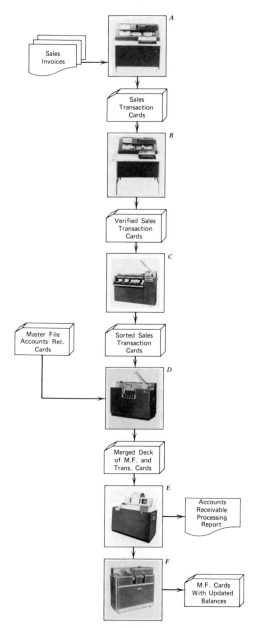

Figure E-1. Processing accounts receivable sales transactions using punched card data processing.

Account number	Invoice number	Quantity purchased	Price per unit	Date	
				.	

Figure E-2. The card format for a credit sales transaction.

tomer name and address, and balance forward (e.g., the amount due as of the last processing date). The coordination of the cards is performed with the assistance of a collator (box D), which merges the deck of master file cards with the sales cards discussed above. The output from this phase of the processing, therefore, is a single deck of punched cards, with each master file card followed by the "detail" sales card(s), if any, re-

quired to update the master file customer account balance.

The above steps prepare the way for the actual data-processing phase. This phase is performed with the assistance of an accounting machine (box E), which uses the single, merged deck of master file and sales cards to prepare two outputs. The first output is an accounts receivable processing report (Figure E-3), which lists each customer's account number, name, and old balance on one line, the sales transactions pertinent to the customer on the following lines, and the new updated balance on a final, summary line of the report. For the second output, the accounting machine is wired to a card punch machine (box F). The card punch machine punches new master file cards with updated account balances, which then serve as master file input cards for the next processing run.

ALAN COMPANY.
Accounts Receivable Processing Report

For Period Beginning   October 1, 1984
and Ending   October 31, 1984

Account Number	Name	Date	Salesman Number	Invoice Number	Balance
775221	Sneaks and Cleats				$ 350.00
		10/14	323	18977	+970.00
		10/21	323	18994	+130.00
				Balance Forward	$1,450.00
775222	Stan's Sports				$ 0.00
		10/2	339	22014	+185.50
				Balance Forward	$ 185.50

Figure E-3. An accounts receivable processing report generated by a card-processing system.

INDEX